THE SCIENCE
OF FALSE MEMORY

OXFORD PSYCHOLOGY SERIES

Editors

Mark D'Esposito   Daniel Schacter
Jon Driver   Anne Treisman
Trevor Robbins   Lawrence Weiskrantz

THE SCIENCE OF FALSE MEMORY

C. J. BRAINERD
and
V. F. REYNA

OXFORD PSYCHOLOGY SERIES
NUMBER 38

UNIVERSITY PRESS
2005

OXFORD
UNIVERSITY PRESS

Oxford University Press, Inc., publishes works that further
Oxford University's objective of excellence
in research, scholarship, and education.

Oxford   New York
Auckland   Cape Town   Dar es Salaam   Hong Kong   Karachi
Kuala Lumpur   Madrid   Melbourne   Mexico City   Nairobi
New Delhi   Shanghai   Taipei   Toronto

With offices in
Argentina   Austria   Brazil   Chile   Czech Republic   France   Greece
Guatemala   Hungary   Italy   Japan   Poland   Portugal   Singapore
South Korea   Switzerland   Thailand   Turkey   Ukraine   Vietnam

Published by Oxford University Press, Inc.
198 Madison Avenue, New York, New York 10016

www.oup.com

Oxford is a registered trademark of Oxford University Press

Library of Congress Cataloging-in-Publication Data
Brainerd, Charles J.
The science of false memory / C.J. Brainerd and V.F. Reyna.
p. cm.—(Oxford psychology series; no. 38)
Includes bibliographical references.
ISBN-13 978-0-19-515405-4
ISBN 0-19-515405-3
1. False memory syndrome. I. Reyna, Valerie F., 1955– II. Title. III. Series.
RC455.2.F35B73 2005
616.89—dc22
2004012958

9 8 7 6 5 4 3 2 1

Printed in the United States of America
on acid-free paper

For our beloved son, Bertrand Reyna-Brainerd,
and for our dear friends, Katherine W. Estes and William K. Estes

Preface

The past few years have witnessed a broad-based outpouring of research on the circumstances in which normal people are possessed of positive, confident memories of things that never happened to them. The flood of new data has stimulated comparable advances in our theoretical understanding of these false-memory phenomena, though this fact is not yet widely appreciated. The historical significance of these events within psychology is considerable. When the authoritative history of 20th-century psychology is written, we think it likely that the rise of the science of false memory during the 1990s will be seen as marking the definitive end of the century's most influential school of thought: the American learning-theory tradition. It is true that this tradition, which had been preeminent in experimental psychology and related fields since John Watson's era, underwent important transformations during the preceding 2 decades. The long-dominant associationist perspective was augmented by the growing acceptance of an alternative cognitive perspective; the study of learning evolved into the study of memory; the prototypical subject populations of research became humans rather than animals; and college courses that had formerly been entitled "the psychology of learning" were now entitled "the psychology of memory." Such changes notwithstanding, there remained a deep continuity between old and new at the level of behavior—namely, that the old emphasis upon how correct responses are learned by animals was preserved in a new emphasis upon how humans remember events that they actually experience, which has now come to be called *true memory*. There is an equally deep discontinuity between the latter emphasis and the science of false memory's focus upon falsity and error. Owing to that focus, as others before us have observed, contemporary false-memory research is more closely connected to the historical centerpieces of the psychology of perception, such as visual illusions, than it is to the historical center-pieces of the psychology of learning.

Following a decade or so of intensive experimentation, much has been learned that is not well understood outside the circles of specialists who populate the domains in which false-memory research has been concentrated. As the implications of what has been discovered extend well beyond those domains into fields that are central to human welfare, such as the law and medicine, it seems to us that this is a situation in need of rectification. Thus, our core aim in writing this book has been to document and explicate the major things, or at least most of the major things, that have been learned about false memory during this rather short span of years. A further aim has been to communicate this information more broadly than is customary in a research monograph. Bertrand Russell once remarked that a noteworthy difference between British empiricist philosophers and their continental European counterparts of the same era is that the former wrote for an audience of educated professionals from many disciplines, whereas the latter wrote solely for other philosophers. Likewise, our intention has been to write for a wider audience than our fellow memory researchers. While we trust that this book will prove to be a useful resource for them and for their students, it is essential that key research findings and theoretical ideas be comprehensible to readers in a number of fields in which the possibility of errors of commission in memory reports is a prime consideration. Cases in point include child protective services workers, clinical psychologists, defense attorneys, elementary- and secondary-school teachers, general medical practitioners, journalists, judges, nurses, police investigators, prosecutors, and psychiatrists. Indeed, it was vexing examples of false-memory phenomena from some of these spheres that first stimulated intensification of the research.

As we surveyed the published literature, it soon became clear that the ground to be covered fell naturally into four territories: essential background material, basic research on false memory, applied research on false memory, and emerging themes. The first domain forms the substance of part I. There, we sketch the historical roots of false-memory research (chapter 1) and provide an exegesis of the experimental paradigms that account for the bulk of published studies (chapter 2). It turns out that the research programs of some of the early giants of psychology anticipated the questions that motivate modern false-memory research to a quite remarkable degree, which is a story well worth telling. It also turns out that, although experimental paradigms seem extremely heterogeneous on the surface, there are some fundamental underlying commonalities that make it sensible to speak of a unified science of false memory. Part II focuses upon basic laboratory research on false memory. The hallmark of such research is that it is theory-driven, so this section begins (chapter 3) with an overview of current theoretical models of false memory. In the course of that overview, we stress predictive power—rather than ex post facto explanation of existing phenomena—as a criterion for evaluating theories' respective levels of success. More specifically, although a credible theory must always begin by delivering satisfactory explanations of existing phenomena, that is the easy part. A theory cannot be deemed to be truly successful unless its explanatory principles also achieve predictive control over false memory by forecasting new phenomena that can be confirmed in experimentation. In the next two chapters, we assess the extent to which predictive control has been achieved by examining tests of key predictions that have been made by modern opponent-processes theories, placing emphasis upon counterintuitive findings that were not anticipated by older theories. Findings on adults from the mainstream experimental literature are covered in chapter 4, and findings on children from the corresponding developmental literature are covered in chapter 5. It will be seen that although research is still in its early phases, impressive levels of predictive control have been achieved over certain phenomena, which suggests that a good deal of theoretical understanding has been acquired.

The applied science of false memory is taken up in part III, but it would be more accurate to call it the field science of false memory because the relationship between the material in part II and the material in part III is very much like that between biology and botany or between physical chemistry and geology. Also, certain lines of research that figure in part III, though they deal with topics that are unquestionably applied, are every bit as theory-driven as the research that is considered in part II, and for that reason, the theme of achieving predictive control over false-memory phenomena runs through part III as well as through part II.

There are three applied domains that have sparked extensive research because the consequences of false-memory reports in those areas can be horrendous. The first is the interviewing of victims, witnesses, and suspects in criminal investigations, situations in which false-memory reports may arise from suggestive questioning. The record shows that such reports can send investigations up blind alleys, can result in innocent persons being charged and convicted, and can even result in false confessions being obtained from innocent suspects—all of which allows the real perpetrators to go free. Such pervasive effects are rooted in the fact that statements from victims, witnesses, and suspects, including sworn testimony, are the chief source of evidence, often the only source of evidence, in criminal investigations and prosecutions. Research on the suggestive interviewing of adults is explored in chapter 6, and research on the suggestive interviewing of children, which revolves around the prosecution of crimes of sexual abuse, is explored in chapter 7.

The second domain of extensive applied research on false memory is the identification of criminal suspects by victims and witnesses. A primary impetus for research in this area is that false identifications of innocent suspects—usually, from crime-scene show-ups or later photo spreads or line-ups—is far and away the leading cause of wrongful convictions in the United States. Findings from research on false eyewitness identification of criminal suspects, which is confined almost entirely to studies of adult eyewitnesses, are examined in chapter 6. Our method of presenting these findings owes much to our conversations with J. Boylen, a leading specialist in crime scene facial reconstruction.

The last domain of applied research that we consider, in chapter 8, is psychotherapy. During the mid-1990s, some celebrated cases of therapeutically induced false memories received national and international media attention. Most of them involved the recovery by adult patients of repressed memories of ghastly childhood experiences, such as being victims of incest or forced participation in gruesome Satanic rituals. The scientific explanation of these fictive recovery experiences appears to lie in some highly suggestive therapeutic procedures that have been found, in controlled experimentation, to be capable of inducing false memories of interconnected life experiences in adults.

Throughout part III, we stress that applied questions about false memory provide exceptionally fertile ground for theory-driven research and that such research demonstrates, once again, the probity of the maxim that there is nothing so practical as a good theory. In that connection, some key manipulations that are used to test theoretical predictions in part II have also been used in the research that figures in part III and have been found to yield much the same effects.

In part IV (chapter 9), we consider what the near future of the science of false memory may hold by exploring some emerging areas of experimentation. The specific areas—mathematical models, aging effects, and cognitive neuroscience—are ones whose significance in broadening our understanding of false memory seems self-evident. Research in each of these areas is capable of resolving some major empirical questions that are not addressed in the work that is covered in parts II and III. Although false-memory research in these areas is still finding its bearings, the work that has accumulated to date is of such high quality as to inspire confidence that important new knowledge will be emerging from all three domains during the course of the next few years.

Ancient Roman teachers of rhetoric cautioned speakers about naming people in the audience who had influenced their work on the ground that those who were not mentioned would be sorely displeased. However, science is truly a communal enterprise, so that in a book such as this, the content ultimately owes more to others' work than it does to the authors'—the authors' role being to analyze the extant literature, assemble the results, and lay them before the reader. It is inevitable, therefore, that the outcome is founded squarely upon the contributions of others, and people whose experimental findings, methodological innovations, or theoretical ideas have had particularly strong influences upon the outcome deserve public acknowledgment. In our case, those people fall into two groups: our students, including postdoctoral fellows, and our fellow memory researchers. With respect to students, a time-honored function of any university-based laboratory is to train prospective scientists by involving them in ongoing programs of research. During the course of their training, prospective scientists may produce new knowledge, often in their doctoral dissertations, that substantially advances the research objectives of their supervisors. The following people deserve mention in that vein: T. Forrest, D. Karibian, B. Kiernan, J. Kingma, R. Kneer, P. Lim, A. Mojardin, T. Odegard, L. Stein, and A. Titcomb. With respect to our fellow memory researchers, the people whose work has influenced the content of this book in major ways come from three branches of the science of false memory: basic experimental research, basic developmental research, and applied research. The experimental researchers whose contributions have had substantial effects on particular sections of this book are J. C. Bartlett, G. H. Bower, H. C. Clark, F. I. M. Craik, W. K. Estes, M. Goldsmith, D. L. Hintzman, L. L. Jacoby, M. K. Johnson, P. N. Johnson-Laird, W. Kintsch, A. Koriat, W. Koutstaal, J. M. Lampinen, D. S. Lindsay, G. Mandler, K. B. McDermott, D. L. Medin, G. A. Miller, A. J. Parkin, D. G. Payne, H. L. Roediger, D. L. Schacter, J. G. Seamon, R. M. Shiffrin, E. E. Smith, M. P. Toglia, E. Tulving, M. Verfaellie, and R. Wright. Developmental researchers whose contributions have had analogous effects are B. P. Ackerman, D. F. Bjorklund, J. S. DeLoache, R. E. Holliday, M. L. Howe, L. S. Liben, T. A. Marche, P. A. Ornstein, M. E. Pipe, and M. S. Zaragoza. Last, the applied researchers whose work has had the greatest impact on this book come from the fields of forensic psychology, criminology, and psychotherapy. They are M. Bruck, S. J. Ceci, G. S. Goodman, G. H. Gudjonsson, L. Haber, R. N. Haber, S. M. Kassin, M. E. Lamb, E. F. Loftus, L. S. McGough, R. J. McNally, A. Memon, K. Pezdek, D. A. Poole, P. Simpson, A. R. Warren, and G. L. Wells. We also owe an intellectual debt to numerous philosophers and linguists, especially D. Davidson, G. Harman, J. J. Katz, S. Kripke, and J. D. McCawley. Special thanks are due to A. B. Anderson and R. E. Holliday, who read the book in manuscript form and provided a detailed list of typographical and grammatical corrections.

Our personal research program on false memory, including the preparation of this volume, has been made possible by grants from the Academic Medicine and Managed Care Forum, the American Psychology and Law Society, the Consejo Nacional de Investigacion Cientifica, the Department of Commerce, the Department of Health and Human Services, the Spencer Foundation, the National Institutes of Health, and the National Science Foundation. The support of these agencies is gratefully acknowledged.

C. J. Brainerd and V. F. Reyna

Contents

PART IV   FUTURE DIRECTIONS

PART I

BACKGROUND

1

Your Ancients

In 1992, after a series of celebrated cases of adults who recovered previously un-suspected memories of childhood sexual abuse, the False Memory Syndrome Foundation was formed by a group of professionals and families who, at the time, were affiliated with the University of Pennsylvania and Johns Hopkins University. The Foundation's initial aims were to study and document how families were being torn apart when adults suddenly declared that they had recovered repressed memories of having been abused as children, often by their parents. In 1994, following the sub-mission of an amicus brief by a committee of concerned scientists, the Supreme Court of New Jersey reversed the conviction of a preschool teacher whom a lower court had found guilty on 115 counts of child sexual abuse involving 20 children. The brief marshaled research findings from studies of children's memory that sup-ported the scientists' conclusion that the abuse allegations against the teacher may have been false-memory reports that were stimulated by suggestive interviewing procedures. Reversals of similar convictions in other states soon followed and con-tinue to the time of this writing. In 1995, a group of patients sued a Minneapolis psychiatrist, accusing the psychiatrist of therapeutic implantation of false memories of ghastly childhood experiences, including incestuous sexual abuse and forced par-ticipation in Satanic practices such as infanticide and cannibalism. The juries agreed, awarding $3.3 million in damages to one plaintiff and $2.5 million in damages to another. In 1996, the National Institute of Justice released a study of several docu-mented cases in which, following conviction, defendants were exonerated by DNA evidence. The report concluded that 90% of these wrongful convictions could be traced to a specific type of false-memory report that had been presented as evidence of guilt—namely, positive identifications of innocent suspects by eyewitnesses. In 1998, the insurance carrier for a Chicago psychiatrist and the hospital in which his multiple personality disorders clinic was housed reached an out-of-court settlement of $10.6 million with a patient who had sued the psychiatrist for malpractice. The suit alleged that the psychiatrist had implanted false memories of multiple person-alities, of childhood sexual abuse, and of participation in a transgenerational cult in the patient and in the patient's children. During the decade of the 1990s, more than 200 murder confessions were thrown out by courts in Cook County, Illinois. The predominant reason was that the confessions were judged to be based on unreliable memory reports, which had been induced through the use of a variety of suggestive interrogation methods by police investigators.

At the beginning of the 1990s, the science of human memory was already a man-sion with many rooms, far too many some would say (Tulving & Madigan, 1970). Nevertheless, widely publicized events such as those just mentioned convinced many researchers that construction should begin on a major new addition: false memory. The work was well under way by the turn of the 21st century, and it had already produced landmark changes in the vernacular that memory researchers use to com-municate with one another. Prior to that time, for instance, it would have seemed utterly redundant or, worse, affected to qualify the word *memory* with the adjec-tives "true" or "false." Although, as we shall discuss in this chapter, there was some early interest in memory falsification among a few great psychologists of the 19th and 20th centuries, "true" was understood when speaking of memory because mem-ory research was synonymous with the remembrance of actual experiences. By the end of the 1990s, however, "true memory" and "false memory" had become con-structions of necessity. Owing to a remarkable flowering of false-memory studies in a short space of years, remembrance of actual experiences was no longer the de-fault option in scientific discourse, and researchers therefore had to take care to alert each other as to which type of memory was the topic of discussion.

It is essential, at this early stage, to distinguish *false memory* from the more fa-miliar idea of *memory fallibility*. Memory, as everyone knows, is an imperfect archive of our experience. Examples are so commonplace that memory fallibility has long been enshrined in the instructions that juries receive about how to inter-pret sworn testimony. Although witnesses are admonished to tell the truth, the whole truth, and nothing but the truth, it is acknowledged that they can only testify to the best of their errant recollective powers. Even if the admonition is scrupulously fol-lowed, therefore, testimony can only be true to a reasonable degree of probability. Under the U.S. Constitution, it is the jury's prerogative to decide what truth prob-abilities to assign to testimony in reaching a verdict, a process known as *credibil-ity determination*. Also, witnesses who are discovered to have testified falsely are rarely subjected to perjury charges. The baseline assumption is that false testimony arises from memory fallibility, not deceptive intent, and consequently, the hurdles that must be overcome to warrant charging a witness with perjury are formidable.

When speaking of memory fallibility, the law, laypersons, and researchers alike are usually referring to the erosion of memory through normal forgetting; without the aid of external memory stores (notes, reminders from other people, audio or video recordings), we are able to retrieve only a tiny fraction of the content of our experience as time passes. To illustrate, at a trial being held several weeks after a baseball game at which a stabbing occurred, a witness who attended the game may not be able to remember whether one of the pitchers was left-handed, whether there were any double plays, where he parked his car, or what he had to eat or drink. However, there is another, less traditional, meaning of memory fallibility—namely, false memory. In its most general sense, *false memory* refers to circumstances in which we are possessed of positive, definite memories of events—although the degree of definiteness may vary—that did not actually happen to us, as when the defendant in the stabbing case is wrongfully convicted because our witness testifies to having seen the defendant standing behind the victim just before the stabbing, when in fact he saw them on separate occasions, or testifies to having seen the defendant with a knife in his hand when in fact he had seen a hairbrush. It is this second form of memory fallibility—errors of commission rather than omission—that is the focus of the science of false memory and of this book, though we shall see (chapters 4 and 5) that research has established that the two are related in sensible ways.

Another key feature of false memory, as it has come to be studied, is that it is an enduring characteristic of normal, rather than pathological, remembering. Although false-memory research is new as a field of systematic investigation in normal subjects, positive memories of events that did not happen have long been of interest in abnormal psychology (e.g., the phenomenon of hearing voices that accompanies certain forms of psychosis), in medicine (e.g., hallucinations that are induced by drugs or by invasive neurological procedures), and in literature. A familiar example of literary allusion to false memories, one that also illustrates the distinction between forgetting and false memory, comes from the St. Crispin's Day speech in Shakespeare's *Henry V*, which reads in part:

> He that shall live this day, and see old age,
> Will yearly on the vigil feast his neighbors,
> And say "Tomorrow is St. Crispian":
> Then will he strip his sleeve and show his scars.
> And say "These wounds I had on Crispin's day."
> Old men forget: yet all shall be forgot,
> But he'll remember with advantages
> What feats he did that day.
> *(Act V, Scene iii)*

We chose the example of remembering "with advantages," first, because it illustrates a common type of memory falsification, among those who fought on St. Crispin's Day, to which we will come later in this chapter when we consider F. C. Bartlett's (1932) work—namely, over repeated tellings, we remember "events" in ways that conform to what we believe to have been the crux of our experience (usually called a *gist memory*). We also chose this example because it illustrates yet another common type of memory falsification, but among those who quote Shakespeare's phrase, to which we will also come later—namely, illusions of familiarity and plausibility (chapters 3 and 7). Specifically, the phrase seems so familiar as a pithy observation on the human condition that it has often been misattributed to other wise commentators who could plausibly have said it, especially to Winston Churchill and Albert Einstein. Misattribution of the observation to Churchill is further encouraged by the fact that he quoted the St. Crispin's Day speech (with proper attribution to *Henry V*) in his own speeches, a form of false memory that is called *source confusion* nowadays (chapter 2).

Although the systematic study of false memory in normal subjects is a comparatively recent phenomenon, the history of psychology presents a few examples of connected programs of research on this topic. In the remainder of this chapter, we discuss what we believe to be the three most comprehensive examples: Alfred Binet's career-long interest in the suggestive forms of questioning that are commonplace in the legal arena, Jean Piaget's studies of constructive memory in children, and F. C. Bartlett's (1932) studies of repeated recall of narrative text by adults. We describe the work of these early investigators not merely for the sake of historical completeness, as appropriate as that would be in a volume such as this, but because their studies anticipated many themes that figure centrally in contemporary false-memory research. Thus, consideration of their work, including claims or results that have been disconfirmed by contemporary researchers, will pay dividends in later chapters: Binet's work is on point with respect to the research on suggestive interviewing and interrogation, which is covered in chapters 6, 7, and 8; Piaget's work is on point with respect to the research on age differences in susceptibility to false memory, which is covered in chapters 5, 7, and 9; and Bartlett's work is on point with respect to theoretical principles of memory falsification, which are discussed from chapter 3 onward.

Alfred Binet

Our image of Alfred Binet (1857–1911) is of an applied psychologist—specifically, the originator of the mental tests that are used to diagnose children's aptitude for learning in school. While it is true that one of the most familiar mental tests still bears his name (the Stanford-Binet), the reality of Binet's research is different than the image. It would be more accurate to characterize Binet, who was a lawyer by training, as the leading French experimental psychologist of the late 19th and early 20th centuries. He specialized in questions that would be recognized as cognitive psychology today, making major contributions to fundamental research topics of his day. Two examples are Binet's research on animal magnetism (Binet & Fere, 1887) and on reasoning (Binet, 1903).

The studies of animal magnetism were focused on widely used medical treatments of that era. Some decades before, Franz Mesmer had formulated a theory of disease that was based upon the hypothesis that the human body generates magnetic fields, that those fields are produced by a magnetic fluid that is concentrated within the body, and that some forms of disease are by-products of misalignment of those fields due to imbalances in the magnetic fluid. The theory began to take shape in 1773 following some attempts to treat a patient who was suffering from an unusual combination of symptoms and who had been unsuccessfully treated by many other physicians. Mesmer recalled some conversations that he had once had with a Jesuit priest, Maximillian Hell, about some surprising properties of magnets, and he decided, on a whim, to treat the patient by applying magnets to her body. The patient immediately went into convulsions, but she recovered shortly and reported that her symptoms were greatly reduced. Subsequent treatment sessions produced analogous results—convulsions followed by a reported reduction in symptoms. Mesmer was soon treating other patients with similar success. Importantly from the perspective of this volume, he carefully explained to each new patient what would happen as a result of magnetic treatment (i.e., muscle tremors, followed by relief of symptoms), a form of suggestion that is quite similar to modern misinformation experiments (chapter 6). His explanation of the success of his treatment was that the application of magnets restored imbalanced magnetic fields to their proper orientation.

By Binet's time, the application of magnets had become a common method of treating symptoms that were not amenable to standard therapies. There was an obvious alternative explanation for Mesmer's results, obvious to Binet at least: suggestion from the explanations that patients were given prior to magnetic treatment. In research with Fere, Binet debunked this treatment, and with it the theory of animal magnetism, by implementing procedures that we would call *double-blinding* today. Specifically, he showed that relief from symptoms was no more likely when patients were treated with actual magnets than when they were treated with unmagnetized objects. Readers who are familiar with treatments being advocated by contemporary proponents of so-called alternative medicine will no doubt appreciate the continuing currency of Binet's research.

Turning to Binet's (1903) work on reasoning, this research was stimulated by what historians of psychology refer to as the *imageless thought* controversy. In Binet's time, it was generally assumed that reasoning consisted of retrieving mental images (pictures that flash in the mind's eye, sounds that echo in the mind's ear) and then mentally manipulating those images to produce solutions to problems. This view was associated, for instance, with Wilhelm Wundt's structuralist school in Germany, the leading academic school of psychology of that period. Binet rejected the image-manipulation model of reasoning based upon experiments with his two daughters, who were high school students at the time. In those experiments, Binet administered familiar reasoning problems to his daughters (e.g., John is taller than Jim, and Jim is taller than Don. Who is tallest?), followed by a series of questions in which his daughters were asked to introspect on the conscious phenomenology that accompanied their reasoning. In many instances, they reported no accompanying images and vigorously denied the presence of images when directly asked, leading Binet to conclude, not surprisingly, that reasoning was imageless thought.

It was in consequence of Binet's eminence as an experimental psychologist that his work on mental testing came about. This was not work that he chose to do as part of his own research program, but rather, it was work that he was contracted to undertake in 1904 by the French Ministry of Education. At that time, Binet was director of the Sorbonne's Laboratory of Experimental Psychology and also a leading member of France's society for child study. The contract was pursuant to the conclusion of a ministerial commission that had been formed to investigate the problem of "backward children," the problem being that certain children, who were seemingly indistinguishable from other children, were unable to benefit from the Paris public-school curriculum of the day. Binet was contracted to devise procedures that would identify these slow learners so that a more appropriate curriculum could be

Figure 1-1. Alfred Binet and Jean Charcot. (*Binet photo:* Bettman/CORBIS. *Charcot photo:* Getty Images.)

developed for them. The result, in collaboration with his former student Theodore Simon, was the first modern intelligence test.

The work of Binet that chiefly concerns us, though, as exemplified in his demonstration that the effects of magnetic treatments on adult patients were due to memory suggestion, are his investigations of false-memory phenomena. This work was a career-long occupation growing out of his training as a lawyer and his early experiences in Jean Charcot's neurological clinic (Figure 1-1). Soon after receiving a law degree in 1878, he abandoned the practice of law and began studying psychology in the National Library in Paris. In 1883, following a period of intensive self-study, he was appointed as a researcher in the Neurological Clinic of Salpetriere Hospital, working under the influential psychiatrist Charcot. Charcot's clinic focused on hysteria, and he used hypnosis, a new research methodology at the time, to study it. Charcot advocated a theory in which hypnosis was viewed as a neurological phenomenon and hypnotic states were viewed as analogous to hysterical states—indeed, as induced hysterical states. Binet became a strong proponent of this theory, but he was much criticized for failing to consider the suggestive nature of hypnosis. (This criticism resurfaces periodically in psychotherapeutic applications of hypnosis, most recently in connection with the use of hypnosis in attempts to recover repressed memories of childhood sexual abuse [see chapter 8].) Binet's critics proposed that the hysterical symptoms that had been demonstrated under hypnosis were not neurological in origin, that those symptoms originated instead from the highly suggestive nature of hypnosis, and that hypnotic states were therefore psychological rather than neurological. Fortunately, as a lawyer, Binet was well aware of the power of suggestive questions and instructions. Eventually, through his own research, he concluded, as did two other famous students of Charcot, Sigmund Freud and Pierre Janet, that the critics were right.

Of course, the work that Binet reported a few years later with Fere is another example of the power of suggestive questions and instructions, as was some further research that he reported in a book that was published in 1900. The latter research was chiefly directed toward the psychology of testimony, rather than psychotherapy (e.g., see also Binet, 1911; Whipple, 1909). Those studies anticipated three important characteristics of modern false-memory research. The first is the distinction (see chapter 2) between false memories that arise from spontaneous distortion processes (which Binet called *autosuggestion*) and false memories that arise from inadvertent or deliberate misinformation (which Binet called *suggestion*). The second characteristic concerns his choice of research methodologies. His procedure for studying autosuggestion featured the technique of exposing subjects to a series of stimuli that established a strong "event flow" (e.g., stimuli of increasing magnitude) and then asking subjects to remember particular items in that series. This procedure, in its basic outlines, is the same as the modern *representational momentum* and *transitive inference* paradigms (e.g., Freyd & Jones, 1994; Freyd, Kelly, & DeKay, 1990; Piaget & Inhelder, 1973). Binet's procedure for studying suggestion, on the other hand, involved exposing subjects to some objects or events, then verbally recapping the experience for subjects in ways that mischaracterized those objects or events, and finally asking the subjects to remember the original experience. This procedure, in its basic outlines, is the same as the modern *memory misinformation* paradigm (e.g., Loftus, Miller, & Burns, 1978), which is used to study memory suggestion both in adults and children (chapters 6 and 7). A third characteristic of contemporary research that Binet anticipated was to design his research in such a way that it would have transparent implications for important applied domains in which false memories were matters of serious concern, particularly forensic psychology (chapters 6 and 7) and, to a lesser extent, psychotherapy (chapter 8).

An illustration of Binet's (1900) autosuggestibility technique is shown in Figure 1-2. His general notion of autosuggestion was that some compelling thought or idea interferes with normal memory processes, distorting subsequent recollections. The task in Figure 1-2, which he administered to one of his daughters, is an attempt to induce such a compelling thought. Five lines of demonstrably different lengths were first presented for viewing, one at a time and in order of increasing length, with the intention of creating an expectation of continuing magnitude increases. Next, a series of to-be-remembered lines was presented, each of which was the same length as the last line in the autosuggestion sequence. Following presentation of each of the to-be-remembered lines, subjects were asked to draw it (from memory) as faithfully as possible. The major result, much like the findings of contemporary studies of representational momentum, was that the drawings of the test lines were consistently too long, with each drawing being longer than the preceding line. Another of Binet's results anticipated modern disputes over whether false-memory reports represent true memory distortions or whether they are mere compliance effects (e.g., Ceci & Bruck, 1993b). Binet questioned subjects about their drawings and was told by some that they realized that their drawings were longer than the test lines. When those subjects were asked to redraw the test lines, they reproduced the true lengths

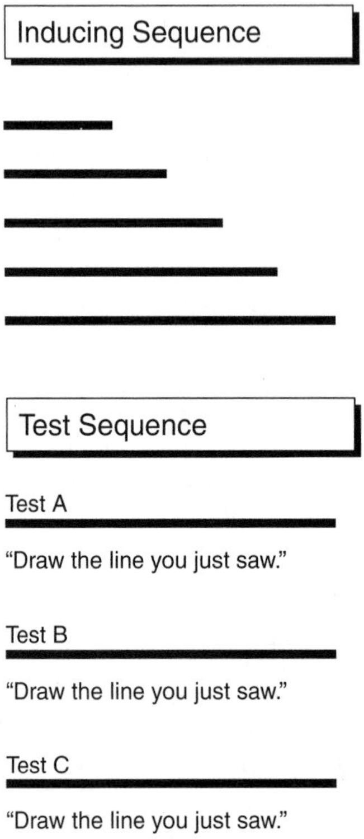

Inducing Sequence

Test Sequence

Test A

"Draw the line you just saw."

Test B

"Draw the line you just saw."

Test C

"Draw the line you just saw."

Figure 1-2. Example of an ascending magnitude sequence used by Binet (1900) to study autosuggestibility.

more accurately. Interestingly, Binet's daughter, who was quite experienced as a subject in his experiments, voiced a suspicion that each of the test lines was the same length, but she nevertheless followed the pattern of drawing each successive line longer than the preceding one.

That some subjects could not resist the influence of the initial sequence of stimuli, notwithstanding that they were quite aware of the trick, led him to conclude that factors other than their own intrusive ideas were operative. Those factors were considered to be external to the subjects' cognitive processes and were grouped under the heading of suggestion, much like modern proposals about suggestion (e.g., Loftus and Loftus, 1980; see chapters 2, 6, and 7). Those factors were thought to be capable of permanently tainting the contents of memory. Binet's best-known task for studying suggestion was modeled on lawyerly leading questions. Subjects were shown an array of familiar objects glued to a board and allowed to inspect them for 10 seconds. Some subjects were then asked to recall all of the objects. However, others received a short interview in which the experimenter questioned them about the objects. Some of these subjects, who would be called the control group today, received straightforward cued-recall questions. For instance, if one of the objects were a button, they might be asked to describe how the button was affixed to the board. The remaining subjects, who would be called the experimental group today, received questions that ranged from moderately leading (Was the button attached by a thread?) to strongly leading (What color was the thread that held the button on the board?). Subjects who recalled the objects without any interpolated questions were highly accurate, which is not surprising seeing as how the recall test was immediate and there were only a few objects. For subjects who received interpolated questions, moderately misled subjects gave more incorrect answers than control subjects, and strongly misled subjects gave more incorrect answers than moderately misled subjects. Two further results prompted Binet to conclude that these effects were actual memory falsifications. First, unlike his studies of autosuggestion, misled subjects could not readily be debriefed: They did not amend their answers to misleading questions when given the opportunity to do so. This is reminiscent of modern findings of resistance to debriefing following memory suggestion (e.g., Ceci, Crotteau-Huffman, Smith, & Loftus, 1994; see chapter 7). Second, when asked to rate their confidence in their answers, confidence ratings for incorrect answers to misleading questions were as high as confidence ratings for correct answers to control questions. This is reminiscent of modern findings of poor correlations between the accuracy of eyewitness identifications of criminal suspects and the confidence ratings of such identifications (e.g., Wells, Small, Penrod, Malpass, Fulero, & Brimacombe, 1998; see chapter 6).

On the basis of his findings, Binet (1900) offered four conclusions about false-memory reports that are still significant today. First, he concluded that the memories of younger children, older children, and adults are all susceptible to memory distortion, whether by autosuggestion or by external misinformation, but that young children are most highly susceptible. This notion of developmental decline in susceptibility to memory suggestion, though intuitively reasonable and supported by research other than Binet's, has required modification in light of recent evidence (see chapters 5 and 7). Second, Binet concluded, consistent with what lawyers and criminal investigators have long believed about leading questions, that the nature of an interviewer's language and the form of the questions that are posed can powerfully distort memory reports (see chapters 6 and 7). Third, Binet interpreted his finding of a lack of relationship between confidence and accuracy as demonstrating that once an erroneous response is given, it is incorporated into memory as a faithful representation of the original events. As we shall discuss on the following pages, this conclusion has also required revision in light of more recent data. Fourth, Binet concluded that subjects, particularly children, were more susceptible to suggestion when tested in groups than when tested individually. This last conclusion, though it has not been central in the modern false-memory literature, anticipated much classical work on group conformity in 20th-century social psychology (e.g., Asch, 1950).

Jean Piaget

Our image of Jean Piaget (1896–1980; Figure 1-3) as the leading developmental psychologist of the past century is quite accurate, unlike our image of Binet. Of course, Piaget, a child science prodigy who published his first journal article at age 10 and was well known in European zoology circles by age 15, was many things

Figure 1-3. Jean Piaget. (Getty Images.)

other than a student of psychological development. In the course of a long and hugely prolific career, he contributed important scholarly work to fields as diverse as the philosophy of science, linguistics, education, sociology, and evolutionary biology. Above all, however, he was *the* developmental psychologist of the 20th century. For two decades, from the early 1960s to the early 1980s, Piagetian theory and Piaget's research findings dominated developmental psychology worldwide, much as Freud's ideas had dominated abnormal psychology a generation before. Almost single-handedly, he shifted the focus of developmental research away from its traditional concerns with social and emotional development and toward cognitive development. A large slice of the primary developmental research literature of that era consists of articles reporting studies of age changes in children's performance on reasoning tasks that Piaget created (e.g., class inclusion, conservation, perspective taking, seriation, transitive inference) and studies of variables that accelerate or retard such performance (see Brainerd, 1983; Flavell, 1970). Although the influence of Piaget's work has waned since his death and the focus of developmental research has drifted back to social and emotional behavior, his influence nevertheless continues to be enormous. To illustrate, notwithstanding the shift back to research on social and emotional behavior, models of cognitive development continue to dominate the theoretical side of developmental psychology.

   Piaget's contributions to the scientific study of false memory were closely intertwined with his stage theory of development (e.g., Piaget, 1970b), as was most of his research during the last 3 decades of his life. This theory did not become widely known outside European circles until the 1960s, but the research upon which it was based—the studies of children's scientific and mathematical reasoning for which Piaget is canonized in undergraduate psychology textbooks—was published prior to World War II. The long obscurity of that research is attributable in large part to the fact that it was, well, odd by the standards of American psychology, which was then more concerned with animal conditioning than with higher intellectual abilities. Indeed, that research might have remained obscure had not certain political events of the 1950s, such as the so-called missile gap with the Soviet Union and the Soviet Union's launching of Sputnik, prompted substantial funding to be devoted to the investigation of children's understanding of scientific and mathematical concepts (Kessen, 1996).

Piaget's stage model was first published in 1947 in a book called *The Psychology of Intelligence*, which was based upon a series of lectures that he had given at the College de France during the German occupation in World War II. As is well known, the theory's core hypothesis is that cognitive development is morphological. More particularly, Piaget thought that the ontogenesis of intelligence consists of a sequence of qualitatively distinct stages, and he ultimately posited four major ones: the sensorimotor period (roughly, birth to age 2), the preoperational period (roughly, age 2 to 7), the concrete-operational period (roughly, age 7 to 11), and the formal-operational period (roughly, age 11 and beyond). To use a modern computer analogy, he thought that during the life span the brain successively runs four different cognitive operating systems, which he called *cognitive structures*. The two stages that are of central interest to students of cognitive development are also the two that were integral to Piaget's research on false memory—namely, the preoperational and concrete-operational periods. To continue the computer analogy, preoperational cognition is controlled by a fairly restricted operating system (say, DOS) and concrete-operational cognition is controlled by a far more powerful operating system (say, Windows) but by no means the most sophisticated one (say, Linux). The principal difference between the two operating systems is that the concrete-operational one is logical, by which Piaget meant that it executes forms of reasoning that do not violate the basic canons of logic and mathematics. Piaget's most familiar reasoning problems, such as conservation (Are initial quantitative relations between objects conserved across irrelevant visual deformations of those objects? see Figure 1-4) and class inclusion (A baseball team has four infielders, three outfielders, one pitcher, and one catcher. Are there more infielders or more baseball players?), which most children do not solve until mid-elementary school, were intended as demonstrations of this fundamental point.

During the last 3 decades of his life, Piaget turned to programs of research that were designed to apply his stage theory to classical topics of psychological experimentation, such as perception, memory, and imagery. His studies of false memory were part of this theory-application phase. That work focused on certain memory distortions that Piaget expected in children who had not yet reached the concrete-operational level. Although Bartlett is credited with proposing the concept of schema, related concepts form the basis of many theories, including Piaget's (e.g., Alba & Hasher, 1983; see chapter 3). For Piaget, the principle in question was that memory does not store a verbatim record of experience, but rather, experience is first assimilated (modern psychologists would say *encoded*) according to the constraints of the current cognitive operating system, and the products are then stored: "the schemata of the memory are borrowed from the intelligence" (Piaget & Inhelder, 1973, p. 382). This led to the prediction that preoperational children's memory for stimuli that follow the dictates of logical concepts that are not understood

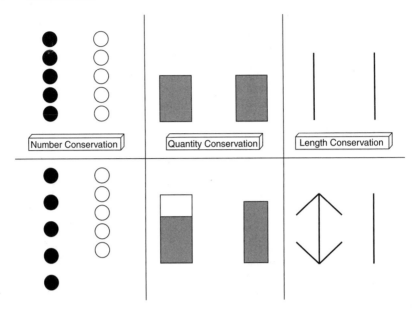

Figure 1-4. Conservation of number, quantity, and length problems. In each problem, children are first presented with a pair of objects that are both visually identical and equivalent with respect to the indicated property (*top*). One of the objects is then deformed, so that the visual identity of the pair is destroyed (*bottom*). Children are then questioned to determine whether they understand that the deformation did not destroy the objects' quantitative equivalence.

until the concrete-operational level will be distorted in the direction of the illogic of preoperations. Although multiple examples of this prediction were presented in the Piaget and Inhelder (1973) volume, the best-known one, which involves seriation, was given by Piaget in a series of lectures at Clark University, the University of Michigan, and the University of Minnesota in 1968 (Piaget, 1968).

Piaget had previously conducted extensive studies of children's understanding of seriation, using a task in which children are presented with 10 rods that differ in length by very small amounts (say, 0.5 centimeters), so that the rods' inherent ordering cannot be detected merely by glancing at them (Inhelder & Piaget, 1964). Children are then told that the rods are of slightly different lengths and are given the task of placing the rods in sequence, which, owing to the imperceptible length differences, requires an overall plan and careful pairwise comparisons to fit individual rods within the overall sequence. Piaget found that children's performance progressed through a series of levels. Young preoperational children (3- and 4-year-olds) thought that the rods were all the same length (because they looked alike) and were unable to construct even partial sequences. Older preoperational children were also unable to solve the problem, but they were able to construct partial sequences. For instance, some children were able to order pairs of rods, and other children, usually somewhat older ones, were able to order triplets or quartets of rods. Finally, younger concrete-operational children (7-year-olds) were able to construct nearly

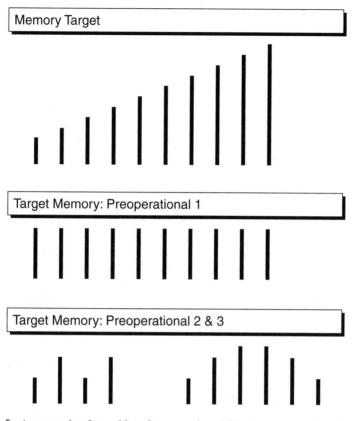

Figure 1-5. An example of a problem for measuring children's memory distortions and long-term memory improvements *(top, Memory Target)*, and examples of drawings produced by children *(bottom, Target Memory drawings)*.

perfect sequences, and older concrete-operational children rapidly constructed perfect sequences. Piaget used these earlier findings in studies of the falsification of children's memory for serial arrays.

The best known of these studies involved a three-step procedure. First, a sample of 3- to 6-year-old children were shown a picture of a seriated array of 10 rods, such as the one at the top of Figure 1-5, and were asked to study it carefully. Second, 1 week later, they were administered a memory test, followed by the aforementioned test of seriation ability. On the memory test, they were asked to draw the picture that they had seen 1 week earlier. Their subsequent performance on the seriation test was then used to classify them according to the four developmental levels noted above. Their memory drawings were also classified according to three developmental levels: (a) preoperational, (b) transitional, and (c) concrete-operational. The third level is simply an accurate drawing of the array at the top of Figure 1-5. The first level, a clearly preoperational memory, is a drawing of several rods of equal length (Figure 1-5, *middle*). The second level, memories that obvi-

Table 1-1. Results from Piaget's Studies of
Children's False Memory for Serial Arrays

	Memory test		
Seriation test	Level 1	Level 2	Level 3
Level 1	83%	7%	
Level 2		65%	35%
Level 3		27%	73%
Level 4			100%

Note. The numbers in the cells are the percentages of children at
each developmental level on the seriation tests who were classified
at each developmental level on the memory test. Data from Piaget
and Inhelder (1973).

ously are of intermediate accuracy, are partially seriated drawings (Figure 1-5, *bottom*). The third step in the study was to readminister the memory test 8 months after the second session.

Piaget made two predictions about memory falsification in this study. Because the picture that the children were shown during Session 1 represents an arrangement whose underlying logic is not grasped before the concrete-operational level, children who have not yet reached that level will be unable to assimilate the drawing correctly, and their memories of it will be distorted accordingly. Thus, during Session 2, there should be a close correspondence between the developmental classification of the drawings and the classification of children's levels of cognitive development, based upon the seriation test. Piaget's findings are shown in Table 1-1, and as can be seen, they are in close agreement with the prediction: All of the children with concrete-operational classifications produced perfect memory drawings, and 83% of the children with preoperational classifications remembered the array as being composed of rods of the same length.

Piaget's second, and more crucial prediction, is what Altemeyer, Fulton, and Burney (1968) dubbed *the long-memory improvement effect*. On the 8-month test, contrary to the commonsense prediction of forgetting-induced deterioration, the memory of children who were classified below the concrete-operational level should be *better* than on the 1-week test. The reason is that many children will have made transitions to higher levels of cognitive development, giving them a better grasp of the logical concept that is necessary (according to Piaget) for accurate memory. Piaget found this pattern in the Session 3 data. Specifically, in a subsample of children who were classified as below the concrete-operational level during Session 2, 92% of them produced *more-accurate* drawings of the seriated array at 8 months than at 1 week, and *none* produced less-accurate drawings.

Piaget reported similar confirmation of these two predictions in follow-up studies of memory for pictures that portrayed other concrete-operational concepts, such as conservation, horizontality, and double seriation (e.g., see various chapters in Piaget & Inhelder, 1973). Thus, there appeared to be broad and consistent evidence for the principle that what children remember about their experience is controlled by how their experience is assimilated by their current cognitive operating system. Nevertheless, this evidence was not accepted at face value by researchers outside Piagetian circles for methodological reasons. All of Piaget's research relied on a nonstandardized, and therefore unreplicable, procedure known as the *méthode clinique*. In this procedure, somewhat different problems and questions are posed to different subjects, depending upon their responses to earlier problems and questions. Because each subject is treated differently, the basic conditions that are required for making statistical inferences from subject samples to populations are not met, and, consequently, replication studies that implement designs that satisfy those conditions were necessary before Piaget's data could be interpreted.

Several such replications were conducted in the years immediately following Piaget's series of lectures (e.g., Altemeyer et al., 1969; Liben, 1974, 1975), and the findings of most of them were reviewed by Liben (1977). Those findings were not such as to confirm Piaget's basic principle of memory falsification. Generally speaking, most of the data showed, as Piaget's had, that a few days after inspecting pictures that portrayed some logical concept, children whose ages placed them below the concrete-operational level made memory drawings that misrepresented the concept in various ways, with younger children's drawings being more distorted than older children's. Rather than being due to assimilation of experience by preoperational cognitive structures, however, this pattern could be due to normal forgetting, which is usually more pronounced in younger children. Which interpretation is more viable depends upon children's memory drawings after delays of many months. If long-term improvement is the rule and long-term deterioration is rare, as Piaget reported, then his principle of memory distortion provides a better fit to the data than the forgetting interpretation. This was not the pattern that emerged from replication studies, however. Although it was found that memory drawings often improved after several months, it was also found that they often deteriorated and, crucially, that the rate of long-term memory improvement did not exceed the rate of long-term deterioration.

Frederic C. Bartlett

Frederic C. Bartlett (1886–1969; Figure 1-6) was Cambridge University's first professor of psychology (from 1931 to 1952) and is generally regarded as Britain's most influential experimental psychologist during the period between World War I and World War II. Latterly, he has become the most influential historical figure in the experimental psychology of false memory (chapter 4), with one of his publications, *Remembering: A Study in Experimental and Social Psychology*, being the single most highly cited reference in the mainstream experimental literature. At the time of this writing, that publication has been cited in more than 2,600 separate articles that have appeared in primary research journals.

Bartlett was trained in Ebbinghaus's (1885/1913) exact method of studying memory (so called to distinguish it from the introspective methodologies that were then predominant in European psychology) in C. S. Meyer's experimental psychology laboratory at Cambridge, where he continued conducting research for the remain-

Figure 1-6. Frederic C. Bartlett (*right*). (Getty Images.)

der of his career. Ebbinghaus's method featured learning to recall lists of nonsense syllables, followed by relearning sessions at various intervals following initial learning. Bartlett began work in Meyer's laboratory in 1913 and conducted many experiments using this paradigm. Gradually, during the course of these studies, he became dissatisfied. On the one hand, he concluded that one feature of the exact method was productive and should be preserved—namely, the measurement of objective memory responses (recall of learned material) rather than subjective ones (introspective analysis of the contents of memory). On the other hand, he concluded that another feature of the exact method—the use of nonsense syllables as memory materials—was stultifying and prevented the exact method from revealing the most important properties of human memory in everyday life. He therefore evolved a research plan in which the objectivity of the exact method would be preserved, but nonsense syllables would be replaced by materials that more closely resembled the normal contents of memory, which are rich in meaning. This work began during World War I and eventually made use of materials such as pictures of faces, pictures of familiar objects and scenes, and narratives.

Many of the results of this research program appeared in the aforementioned volume, which was published in 1932 and remains Bartlett's most enduring contribu-

Table 1-2. The War of the Ghosts

One night two young men from Egulac went down to the river to hunt seals and while they were there it became foggy and calm. Then they heard war cries, and they thought: "Maybe this is a war party." They escaped to the shore, and hid behind a log. Now canoes came up, and they heard the noise of paddles, and saw one canoe coming up to them. There were five men in the canoe, and they said:

"What do you think? We wish to take you along. We are going up the river to make war on the people."

One of the young men said," I have no arrows."

"Arrows are in the canoe," they said.

"I will not go along. I might be killed. My relatives do not know where I have gone. But you," he said, turning to the other, "may go with them."

So one of the young men went, but the other returned home.

And the warriors went on up the river to a town on the other side of Kalama. The people came down to the water and they began to fight, and many were killed. But presently the young man heard one of the warriors say, "Quick, let us go home: that Indian has been hit." Now he thought: "Oh, they are ghosts." He did not feel sick, but they said he had been shot.

So the canoes went back to Egulac and the young man went ashore to his house and made a fire. And he told everybody and said: "Behold I accompanied the ghosts, and we went to fight. Many of our fellows were killed, and many of those who attacked us were killed. They said I was hit, and I did not feel sick."

He told it all, and then he became quiet. When the sun rose he fell down. Something black came out of his mouth. His face became contorted. The people jumped up and cried.

He was dead.

Note. Story from Bartlett (1932).

tion to memory research. The book reports the results of various experiments that followed the pattern of measuring objective memory responses in connection with realistic, meaningful material. An interesting historical fact is that some of those experiments were concerned with errors in memory for faces, and although those experiments anticipated many contemporary questions about the false identification of suspects in criminal investigations (chapters 6 and 9), they are largely unknown and are rarely mentioned in the literature on eyewitness identification (cf. Wells et al., 1998). The particular results in Bartlett's book that have been of continuing interest to students of false memory were reported in chapters 5 and 7 of the volume. Those results anticipated modern findings on constructive memory and schema-based memory falsification. Also, Bartlett's interpretations of his results, like Piaget's, provided the foundation for an important modern theory of false memory. Bartlett's results were concerned with subjects' recall of a previously studied narrative, which appears in Table 1-2. The narrative, *The War of the Ghosts*, was a Native American folktale that had been translated by the anthropologist Franz Boas. Bartlett chose this material because it presented some unusual features that he thought could yield informative results, which it did. Although it was clearly a narrative, in the sense of having a plot structure in which certain events fit logically, Bartlett's subjects, Cambridge students for the most part, were unfamiliar with Native American culture, leading him to hypothesize that they might transform some of the material to fit their own cultural precepts. Further, some of the events in the narrative were not interconnected in any definite way, leading him to hypothesize that the events might be transformed so as to establish clearer connections.

Each of Bartlett's subjects read the narrative twice, at their normal reading pace. Fifteen minutes later, they were given a written recall test, in which the task was simply to write what they had read. Subsequent written recall tests were then administered after intervals of a few hours, days, weeks, months, and years. Bartlett made no attempt to standardize the intervals for these delayed tests across subjects, preferring to retest them "at intervals as opportunity offered" (p. 65). The data that he reported, both from the initial recall test and from the retests, were qualitative and anecdotal in nature, consisting of general descriptions of the content of the subjects' written productions illustrated with excerpts from specific protocols. Bartlett's key conclusion, or at least the conclusion that has most influenced false-memory researchers, was that recall of the narrative was constructive in the sense that protocols took on a specific "form" (what would be called a *gist memory* nowadays) from the first attempt and that this form was preserved on delayed tests. Some of the specific findings that were revealed in relation to this conclusion were that the productions (both the first and all subsequent ones) were more concise and tightly organized than the narrative itself; many details from the narrative were omitted; and many of the reported details were recalled in a distorted manner, including additions of unstated objects and events. All of these features were present in the very first (after 15 minutes) and the second (hours, days, weeks, or months later) protocols of the subjects. It is distortions, of course, that are of greatest interest to false-memory researchers. According to Bartlett, such responses ranged from fairly minor distortions (e.g., a detail was rephrased in language that was more familiar to the subject but was essentially unchanged) to major distortions. Major distortions included such things as normalization (e.g., changing "day" to "night," because most events in the narrative usually occur during the day, or changing "hunting seals" to "fishing," because fishing is a much more familiar activity), inference (e.g., connecting objects and events in the narrative in ways that were implied but were not stated, such as recalling that the Indian was wounded by an arrow), and addition (e.g., importing new objects and events into the protocol that did not appear in the narrative but were consistent with its form, such as the presence of a totem). Bartlett reported that although the initial form of subjects' recall was preserved even on tests that occurred after intervals of a few years, the other tendencies—omission of details and distorted recall of details—increased steadily as the delay interval lengthened. A final result, which echoes one of Binet's (1900) findings, is that subjects expressed high confidence in their false-memory reports, even ones that were confabulations. For instance, one subject confabulated the following details 6.5 years after reading the narrative: a totem, who was a family god; two characters, who were brothers; the brothers were on a pilgrimage; the pilgrimage was for reasons of filial piety; and the river flowed through a dark forest. According to Bartlett, this subject expressed greatest confidence in the details that were confabulations—specifically, the totem, filial piety, and the pilgrimage.

In view of the nonstandardized nature of this study and the fact that only qualitative descriptions of the results were given, the same questions arise as with Piaget's *méthode clinique*. Can the basic patterns be replicated? If they can, what are
the actual numbers? Uncertainty about these questions has continued until fairly recently, for two reasons. First, the necessary replications of Bartlett's (1932) research
were not undertaken for many years, owing to the fact that, through the 1960s, memory research was dominated by list-learning studies in the Ebbinghaus tradition. Second, an initial attempt by two British researchers, Gauld and Stephenson (1967), to
replicate Bartlett's findings, especially the widespread and systematic distortions in
recall, under controlled conditions failed. Bartlett did not report the memory-test instructions that he provided to his subjects in detail, and Gauld and Stephenson con-
jectured that the instructions may have led subjects to conclude that their task was
to retell the story, which would have encouraged distortions that enhanced plot coherence, rather than to faithfully recall what they had read. To test this hypothesis,
they conducted three experiments using recall instructions of varying stringency.
They found that distortions occurred only under lenient instructions that did not
stress accuracy. Two other British investigators, Wynn and Logie (1998), reported
a similar failure to find distortions of the type Bartlett reported for college students'
recall of an autobiographical episode.

More recently, however, Bergman and Roediger (1999) conducted a carefully
controlled replication that showed that the memory-distortion results that Bartlett
(1932) reported can indeed be reproduced under comparable conditions. In contrast
to other investigators, Bergman and Roediger reproduced Bartlett's original procedures with great fidelity. Thirty subjects read *The War of the Ghosts* twice (see
Table 1-2) and 20 performed written recall 15 minutes later, half under strict instructions and half under lenient instructions. All 30 subjects returned 1 week later
and performed written recall, for the first time for 10 subjects. Six months later, the
subjects were recruited again, and all who were contacted returned for a final recall
test. The recall protocols were scored using propositional analysis (Mandler & Johnson, 1977), which represents a narrative as a series of idea units called *propositions*.
Explicitly, protocols were scored for the number of correctly recalled propositions
(out of 42 propositions that are present in *The War of the Ghosts*), for the number
of minor distortions, and for the number of major distortions. The patterns of principal interest are shown in Figure 1-7, which provides the proportions of accurately
recalled propositions, of propositions recalled with minor distortions, and of propositions recalled with major distortions. As can be seen, both major and minor distortions were common, even on the immediate test, just as Bartlett originally reported. Also, responses that we would term false-memory reports were not only
common on the immediate test, they increased markedly as a proportion of overall
output as one moves from the immediate to the 1-week, and to the 6-month test, a
phenomenon that is called the *false-memory sleeper effect* and that has been the subject of a good deal of recent investigation, particularly in child witnesses (chapter
7). Note that by 6 months, propositions that are recalled with major distortions constitute the major form of output. Strictly speaking, then, as Bartlett concluded, after a few months, narrative recall consists mostly of false-memory reports. This re-

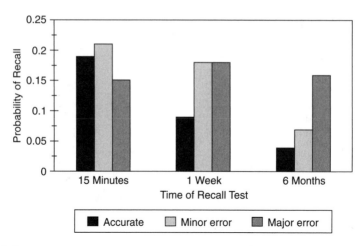

Figure 1-7. Immediate, 1-week, and 6-month recall in Bergman and Roediger's (1999) replication of Bartlett (1932).

markable pattern anticipates recent findings on the relative persistence of false versus true memories, findings that have been the focus of much theoretical controversy (chapters 4 and 5).

Synopsis

Research on false-memory phenomena was desultory throughout most of the history of psychology, but some psychologists of historical importance contributed systematic work on this topic, work that posed questions of enduring significance and that generated findings that remain influential today. Alfred Binet, Jean Piaget, and Frederic Bartlett are notable examples. Although Binet's research was conducted at the dawn of experimental psychology, it presaged modern false-memory research to an extraordinary degree. His distinction between memory falsifications that are rooted in endogenous distortion mechanisms (autosuggestion) versus memory falsifications that are rooted in exogenous misinformation (suggestion) is still fundamental and demarcates two of the major branches of current investigation. Binet's emphasis on the legal ramifications of false memories, especially with respect to the veracity of testimony following suggestive questioning, is also strikingly contemporaneous. Such implications have supplied a major stimulus for the recent intensification of false-memory research. Finally, Binet's thesis that children are more prone than adults to false-memory reports, particularly ones that arise from suggestion, echoes a core theme of current research.

Piaget's and Bartlett's respective contributions similarly anticipated key themes of current research. Piaget, like Binet, did much to popularize the notion that children's memories are inherently more susceptible to falsification than adults'. However, Piaget's research focused exclusively on false memories that he believed to be by-products of a particular type of endogenous distortion mechanism, which was associated with his stage theory of cognitive development—namely, false memories that are generated by preoperational cognitive structures, structures that distort underlying logical and mathematical relations between objects and events. Although Piaget's research relied on the nonstandardized *méthode clinique*, the key memory-distortion phenomena that he reported have been replicated by contemporary researchers under controlled conditions. His explanations of those findings are not well regarded today, but echoes of those explanations can nevertheless be found in modern theoretical ideas, such as memory schemas.

Bartlett's output of false-memory research was minuscule in comparison to Binet's and Piaget's, being confined primarily to reports in two chapters of his 1932 book. Nevertheless, that research and the theoretical ideas that motivated it are more influential today than either Binet's or Piaget's contributions. Bartlett's study of subjects' memory of the narrative *The War of the Ghosts* anticipated modern studies of false memories that arise from narrative comprehension, from exposure to familiar collections of events (so-called event schemas), and from exposure to familiar collections of objects that occupy consistent spatial positions (so-called spatial schemas). Each of these three types of false memory has been an area of vigorous research activity. In addition, Bartlett's interest in studying memory for meaningful everyday materials is well preserved in contemporary false-memory research, as is his emphasis upon the underlying organizational properties of memory, which is the linchpin of one of the first modern theories of false memory.

2

Varieties of False Memory

A Modern Taxonomy

In experimentation, psychological variables, such as false memory, are synonymous with their operational definitions. They are what we measure. Once measurements are effected, however, a quantitative theory is needed, which is usually called a *scaling model*, which specifies precisely how those measurements (the *response scale*) are related to amounts of the underlying psychological variable (the *psychological scale*). Such a model is essential if informative quantitative comparisons are to be made between a target variable (e.g., false memory) and other psychological variables (e.g., true memory, intelligence, introversion, repression) (Anderson, 1981; Krantz, Luce, & Tversky, 1971). However, most research in psychology proceeds without the aid of an explicit scaling model and simply operates under the implicit monotonicity assumption that subjects who exhibit higher scores on a measured variable (e.g., a standardized mental test) possess as much or more of the underlying psychological variable (e.g., intelligence) as subjects who exhibit lower scores (Krantz & Tversky, 1971).

False-memory research is no exception to this rule. Although the primary research literature contains a few examples of formal quantitative theories (see chapter 9), the great bulk of research has relied upon the implicit monotonicity assumption that the memories of subjects who score higher on a false-memory task are falsified as much or more than the memories of subjects who score lower. The weakness of this measurement assumption can cause serious interpretative problems in some types of false-memory research. We are getting well ahead of our story, however.

Because false memories, like other psychological variables, are what we measure, understanding what has been discovered about them requires, in the first instance, a grasp of the basic research paradigms that have been used to study false memory, along with an understanding of the characteristic data patterns (*false-memory effects*) that each has produced. That is the purpose of the present chapter. The chapter proceeds in two steps. First, we describe nine modern paradigms, in their approximate order of historical appearance in the literature, and we sketch some false-memory effects that are identified with each. These paradigms account for the great bulk of accumulated findings about false memory, and they will concern us throughout the forthcoming chapters. There are a few others that might have been included, some of which may be the reader's special favorites, but they are minor ones that have not generated large numbers of studies. Second, the chapter concludes with a short integrative analysis of the nine paradigms. Their key similarities and differences are noted, and the paradigms are arranged along a dimension of relative suggestiveness.

False-Memory Paradigms

Semantic Intrusions in List Recall

Imagine that the subjects in a memory experiment are assigned to study one of two lists, each consisting of several familiar words. The respective lists are shown in Table 2-1. Although both consist of familiar words, note that they differ in their degree of meaning relatedness. List 1 words are fairly unrelated, but List 2 words fall into three common taxonomic categories (colors, animals, and furniture). After studying their respective lists, the subjects are asked to recall them, either immediately after the last word is studied or following a short irrelevant buffer activity (e.g., counting backward) that makes it impossible to hold the last few words in short-term memory (Glanzer & Cunitz, 1966). Subjects' task is merely to recall as many of the just-studied words as they can remember, and no others, though some subjects who studied List 2 might be cued to recall the words in each category. (For instance, List 2 subjects might be told to "recall all of the colors," then "recall all of the animals," and finally "recall all of the furniture.")

This list-recall procedure has been central to memory research for decades (e.g., Bousefield, 1953; Cohen, 1963), the best-known findings being for true memory. More studied words are recalled when lists are categorized than when they are semantically unrelated, and when lists are categorized, more studied words are recalled if the individual categories are cued than if they are not. Importantly, as we

Table 2-1. Illustrative Word Lists for Semantic Intrusions in Recall

List	Words
1: unrelated	Paper, Car, Diamond, Ill, Lamp, Habit, Movie, Calculator, Baby, Swamp, Prank, Disk, Present, Emotion, Concept
2: categorized	Red, Yellow, Orange, Green, Purple, Dog, Cow, Sheep, Cat, Pig, Chair, Couch, Bed, Stool, Television

shall discuss, both findings are for adults. Neither occurs in children (Bjorklund & Thompson, 1983). This paradigm also yields a characteristic false-memory effect—namely, the recall, contrary to subjects' instructions, of some unstudied words that preserve the meaning of studied words. These false recalls are known as *semantic intrusions*. Examples for List 1 would be *jewel* or *ruby* (for *diamond*) and *sick* or *disease* (for *ill*), and examples for List 2 could be *animal* or *horse* (for the five animal words) and *furniture* or *table* (for the five furniture words). Further, semantic intrusions are usually more common for categorized lists than for unrelated lists, though the intrusion rate rarely exceeds 5% of total recall in adults (Bjorklund & Muir, 1988). The intrusion rate can be increased somewhat by certain manipulations, however. For instance, the rate is higher if recall follows a short irrelevant activity rather than occurring immediately, and it is higher if recall does not occur until a few days after the list was studied.

The rate can also be increased via a proactive interference procedure in which subjects study and recall several short lists (each composed of, say, 10 words), all of which are semantically related (Postman & Keppel, 1977). To illustrate, subjects might study and recall a series of eight lists, all of them composed of words from a single taxonomic category (e.g., women's names, cities in the United States). Recall of words from a just-studied list is poorer for later lists than for earlier ones, which is the characteristic *proactive interference effect*. In addition, the level of semantic intrusion, as a percentage of total recall, is higher on later lists, with subjects falsely recalling same-category words that they have not studied at all and same-category words that appeared on earlier lists (an error that contemporary researchers would call *source confusion*; see below). [Again, these effects are for adults. Children do not exhibit such meaning-based proactive interference (Bjorklund & Hock, 1982).]

Deese (1959) devised a procedure that yielded extraordinarily high levels of semantic intrusions for certain words, even on an immediate recall test, and hence, this particular procedure has come to figure prominently in contemporary false-memory research (e.g., Payne, Elie, Blackwell, & Neuschatz, 1996; Roediger & McDermott, 1995). Deese reported two studies. In the first, he used available norms of word association (Russell & Jenkins, 1954) to construct 36 lists of 12 words apiece. Each list was constructed by selecting the first 12 forward associates of a familiar stimulus word. (The 36 stimulus words are shown in Table 2-2.) For instance, the first 12 associates of *high* (i.e., the 12 words that people most commonly say when they are asked to pronounce the first word that comes to mind when they hear the word *high*) are *low, clouds, up, tall, tower, jump, above, building, noon, cliff, sky,* and *over.* Deese's subjects listened to each list, and immediately after hearing the 12th word, they recalled as many of the list words as they could remember. The key result for our purposes is that the stimulus word that was used to generate each list was falsely recalled by large percentages of subjects. The actual percentages that Deese reported are shown in Table 2-2. Note that all but 4 of the lists produced intrusion rates that were at least twice the 5% level that is often obtained with categorized lists. Note too that fully two thirds of the lists produced intrusion rates of 20% or more. In interpreting these data, remember that recall occurred *immediately* after listening to a very short list, so that a substantial proportion of the presented words were still echoing in the mind's ear.

Table 2-2. Stimulus Words Used to Construct Lists
of Associates for Free Recall

Stimulus Word	Percentage Intrusions of Stimulus Word
Table	18
Dark	10
Music	30
Man	32
Deep	14
Soft	40
Mountain	36
House	12
Black	28
Mutton	4
Hand	22
Short	30
Fruit	20
Butterfly	0
Smooth	26
Command	10
Chair	36
Sweet	36
Whistle	4
Cold	34
Slow	30
Wish	12
River	20
White	16
Beautiful	8
Window	30
Rough	42
Foot	36
Needle	42
Red	24
Sleep	44
Anger	34
Carpet	10
Girl	32
High	30
Sour	20

Note. Word list from Deese (1959).

The purpose of Deese's (1959) study was to explain variations in false recall of
the stimulus words. It is clear from Table 2-2 that false recall varied considerably,
from 0% for *butterfly* to 44% for *sleep*. Why? Deese proposed that variations in
backward associations from list words to stimulus words were responsible. For instance, although the word *high* causes words such as *low*, *clouds*, *up*, and so on to
come to mind with some probability (forward associations), each of these latter
words causes *high* to come to mind with some probability (backward associations).
To measure this backward-association variable, Deese presented the 36 lists to a
new sample of subjects, asking them to perform a word association test for the lists

rather than to recall them. Specifically, individual subjects were given printed pages containing 200 words, most of them drawn from the 36 target lists, and were asked to write the first word that came to mind as they read each word. Level of backward association was then computed for each of the 36 stimulus words, which was simply the mean percentage of times that each stimulus came to mind when subjects read one of the list words for that stimulus. Deese found that backward-association level was a strong predictor of false recall: The observed correlation between a stimulus word's backward-association level (as measured in the second study) and its level of false recall (as measured in the first study) was .873.

Semantic False Alarms in List Recognition

In a word-recognition experiment, subjects study lists of words, as in a recall study, but on the memory test, a series of word probes is presented, with the subjects' task being to respond "old" or "new" (or "yes" or "no"), accordingly, as they judge a probe word to have been presented or not presented on the just-studied list. The test probes may consist of individual words, some presented (usually called *targets*) and some unpresented (usually called *distractors* or *lures*), or the test probes may consist of small sets of words, a target plus one or more distractors. Subjects make old-new judgments about each probe in the former case, whereas the task is to select the target in the latter case. Correct old judgments for targets are called *hits*, and incorrect old judgments for distractors are called *false alarms*. False alarms are the false-memory responses in recognition studies.

Underwood (1965) developed a procedure for studying semantically based false memories that is a recognition analogue of the aforementioned false-recall procedure. His subjects listened to a tape-recorded list of 200 words being read at a very slow rate, 10 seconds per item, with each word being read twice during that interval. A portion of Underwood's list is shown in Table 2-3, with the words being divided into the first and second halves of the list. Underwood used a continuous-recognition method in which subjects were required to make an old-new judgment about each word as it was read, rather than listening to all 200 words and then taking a recognition test. At the beginning of the list presentation, each successive word was new, and therefore, the only appropriate response was new. Before long, however, earlier words began to repeat, so that after this point (the 12th word in the upper half of Table 2-3), each succeeding word could be either old or new. Repetitions are printed in italics in the upper part of Table 2-3.

In Underwood's (1965) experiment, principal interest attached to subjects' responses to certain distractors that appeared in the second half of the list, from position 113 onward. These words are printed in bold in the lower part of Table 2-3. As can be seen, these words were semantically related to words that the subjects had heard earlier: *top*, *night*, *smooth*, and *soft* are antonyms of *bottom*, *day*, *rough*, and *hard*, respectively. *Bread* is a semantic associate of *butter*, *sandwich*, and *crumb*; and *dog* is a semantic associate of *animal*, *cat*, and *bark*. The characteristic false-memory phenomenon in this situation is known as *semantic false recognition*, and it is concerned with the difference between the false-alarm rates for distractors that are unrelated to the meaning of previously studied words (e.g., items such as *prince*,

Table 2-3. Illustrative Items from Word Lists

Portion of List	Words
First half	Happy, Bottom, Sandwich, Couch, Boot, Citrus, Dress, Tower, Mouse, Top, Horn, *Bottom*, Stream, *Citrus*, . . . Dress, Butter, *Couch*, . . . Day, *Boot*, Crumb, . . . *Tower*, Animal, Rough, . . . Hard, *Sandwich*, Cat, . . . Snooze, Bark, *Horn*, . . . Animal, Germ, Chalk
Second half	**Top**, Prince, Friend, . . . **Bread**, Rich, Fish, . . . Sharp, Fat, **Night**, . . . Salt, **Dog**, Cloud, . . . **Smooth**, Dirty, Short, Taste, . . . Cop, Ledge, Red, **Soft**

Note. Repeated targets are in italics and semantically related distractors are in bold. Word lists from Understood (1965).

sharp, and *ledge* in the lower part of Table 2-3) and the false-alarm rates for distractors that preserve some of the meaning of previously studied words (i.e., items such as *top*, *night*, *smooth*, *soft*, *bread*, and *dog*). For every new word that appears on the list, there is naturally some baseline probability that subjects will make a false alarm, for a variety of nonmemorial reasons such as inattentiveness, guessing, and yea-saying bias. If in addition, however, there is a tendency for meaning relations to instill false memories, as we saw that they do in recall, this should show up as false-alarm rates for meaning-preserving distractors that exceed the baseline false-alarm rate for unrelated distractors.

Underwood (1965) obtained this semantic false-recognition effect for both antonyms and semantic associates of studied words. The baseline false-alarm rate for unrelated distractors was 12%. The false-alarm rate for antonyms was 20%, rising to 30% if the corresponding target had been studied three times. The false-alarm rate for semantic associates was 26%. Underwood's finding of false-alarm rates in the 20–30% range for meaning-preserving distractors is fairly typical when recognition tests of such items are administered within a few minutes of having studied the corresponding targets (e.g., Seamon, Luo, Schlegel, Greene, & Goldenberg, 2000; Tussing & Greene, 1999). However, the size of this effect can be increased considerably by using word lists on which the items are all semantically related to each other. For instance, this can be done with the Deese (1959) procedure that was described earlier in connection with false recall. Instead of studying a single list and then performing free recall, subjects might study several of these short lists and then respond to a recognition test on which some of the distractors are unrelated to any of the lists but others are the missing stimulus words that were used to generate the lists in the first place. When this procedure is followed, baseline false-alarm rates for unrelated distractors are similar to the levels that Underwood reported, but false-alarm rates for the stimulus words are in the 70–80% range (Payne et al., 1996; Roediger & McDermott, 1995).

False Memory for Semantic Inferences

As the story unfolds in a detective novel, the author presents enticing morsels of information, the clues, which readers attempt to piece together, before arriving at the last chapter, to find the solution to who done it? Because the readers' task is ef-

Table 2-4. Illustrative Sentences from the Semantic-Integration Procedure

Complexity	Sentences
Level 1	The ants were in the kitchen. **(target, untested)**
	The jelly was on the table. **(target, untested)**
	The jelly was sweet. **(distractor)**
	The ants ate the jelly. **(distractor)**
Level 2	The ants in the kitchen ate the jelly. **(target, untested)**
	The ants ate the sweet jelly. **(target, tested)**
	The sweet jelly was on the table. **(distractor)**
	The ants ate the jelly which was on the table. **(distractor)**
Level 3	The ants ate the sweet jelly which was on the table. **(target, untested)**
	The ants in the kitchen ate the jelly which was on the table. **(target, untested)**
	The ants in the kitchen ate the sweet jelly. **(distractor)**
Level 4	The ants in the kitchen ate the sweet jelly which was on the table. **(distractor)**

Note. From Bransford and Franks (1971).

fortful and deliberate, particularly if the author is clever and inserts a few red herrings, there is little chance that when the solution is found, they will mistake the answer for a "memory" of information that was presented earlier in the story. That is, it is highly unlikely that readers will think that they actually read the solution verbatim at some earlier point in the novel because they have worked so hard to find it. However, in one of the truly classic papers in the false-memory literature, Bransford and Franks (1971) reported that this is precisely what happens in certain situations in which subjects study items of information that can be integrated into a single complex idea. They produced these findings in experiments in which subjects studied sentences containing different numbers of propositions (idea units) and then responded to recognition tests on which some probes were targets and others were unpresented sentences containing the studied propositions.

Bransford and Franks's (1971) procedure is illustrated in Table 2-4. The 12 sentences in this table specify four propositions: (a) the ants are in the kitchen; (b) the jelly is sweet; (c) the jelly is on the table; and (d) the ants ate the jelly. As can be seen, the number of propositions presented in each sentence is one (Level 1), two (Level 2), three (Level 3), or four (Level 4). As can be seen, only half of the sentences are targets (i.e., were actually presented to the subjects to study), but they are sufficient to infer the Level 4 statement that "The ants in the kitchen ate the sweet jelly which was on the table." The remaining sentences are meaning-preserving distractors that were presented on recognition tests. Note that the complete complex idea (Level 4) was not presented for study. Bransford and Franks developed a series of sentence sets like those in Table 2-4, which specified a total of eight complex ideas. (Two others were "The girl who lives next door broke the large window on the porch" and "The old car pulling the trailer climbed the steep hill"). They reported two experiments, one in which the complete complex idea was not presented for any of the sentence sets and one in which it was presented for half of the sets and not presented for the other half.

Bransford and Franks's (1971) procedure consisted of four steps. First, subjects were given instructions about the experiment, which did not inform them that their

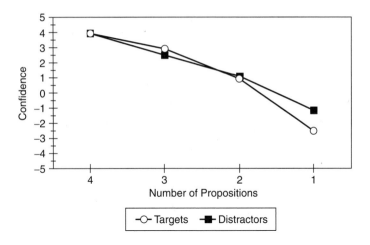

Figure 2-1. Mean confidence ratings for targets and meaning-preserving distractors in Bransford and Franks's (1971) studies of false memory for semantic inferences.

memories would be tested. Instead, they were told that they would listen to a series of sentences read by the experimenter and that their task would be to answer questions about the meaning of each sentence. (Thus, insofar as later memory for the actual sentences, the procedure is what researchers would call an *incidental memory design.*) Second, the experimenter read 24 sentences, one at a time (e.g., the 6 sentences for the complex idea in Table 2-4, plus 18 more sentences, 6 for each of three other complex ideas). After each sentence was read, the experimenter held up a card with four colors on it and asked the subject to name the colors aloud, and then the subject read an elliptical question about the meaning of the sentence (e.g., Did what?) and wrote an answer to the question on a sheet of paper. Third, following presentation of all 24 sentences, the subject was given a 4- to 5-minute break. Fourth, a surprise sentence-recognition test was administered in which the probes consisted of targets, meaning-preserving distractors, and meaning-violating distractors (sentences that presented the studied propositions in inappropriate relations to each other). As each probe was presented, subjects were asked to make an old-new judgment about it and then to rate their confidence in that judgment on a 5-point scale (1 = very low, 5 = very high).

Bransford and Franks's (1971) subjects were very good at identifying meaning-violating distractors as new: Most of these sentences were judged to be new at mean confidence levels between 4 and 5. However, the data of principal interest, which are for targets versus meaning-preserving distractors, are shown in Figure 2-1. Subjects' performance on targets and meaning-preserving distractors was scored as follows: The confidence rating for a probe was given a positive sign when the recognition judgment was old and a negative sign when it was new. If levels of false memory were low and subjects were readily able to discriminate targets from meaning-preserving distractors, the expected pattern would be that targets would be recognized as old with high (positive) confidence ratings, and distractors would be recognized as new with equally high (negative) confidence ratings. This is not the pattern in Figure 2-1, however. To begin, subjects incorrectly recognized distractors as old at very high levels, levels that were only slightly lower than correct recognition of targets as old. Further, true- and false-memory responses could not be discriminated on the basis of confidence. As can be seen in Figure 2–1, confidence ratings for targets and meaning-preserving distractors were virtually the same for sentences that contained four, three, or two propositions, though there was roughly a 50% confidence advantage for presented sentences over unpresented sentences that contained only one proposition (-1.11 versus -2.46). The major trend that is apparent in this figure is that subjects' confidence in the accuracy of their memory judgments depended upon something different than whether a sentence had actually been presented. It depended upon how many propositions a probe sentence contained: The more propositions, out of four possible propositions, the more confident subjects were in their memory judgments about the probe, *regardless of whether those judgments were accurate (true memories) or inaccurate (false memories).* Bransford and Franks's theoretical interpretation of their findings was that what subjects remembered from the sentences that they studied were not the sentences themselves but "holistic semantic structures" (1971, p. 349). That is, the propositions in the studied sentences were integrated into an overall semantic representation (which served as the basis for memory judgments), but the surface forms of those sentences were not preserved in memory (at least not after 4–5 minutes).

This research was controversial from the start, not only because true and false memories were found to be virtually indistinguishable but also because confidence in memory judgments seemed to depend upon meaning coherence rather than on actual presentation. Experiments were soon reported by other investigators that cut much of the ground from under Bransford and Franks's (1971) theoretical interpretation of their data (i.e., that what is preserved in memory is only an overall semantic representation that integrates the individual propositions). More particularly, it was shown that their conclusions about two findings that led to this interpretation— the finding that targets and meaning-preserving distractors were judged to be old at nearly equal rates and that confidence in memory judgments depended primarily on the number of propositions contained in recognition probes—were incorrect.

Bransford and Franks's conclusion about the first finding was that the exact surface form of the presented sentences was not preserved in memory. However, Reyna and Kiernan (1994) reported that a *week* after listening to a series of sentences, even children could still discriminate between targets and distractors that had the same meaning and differed only slightly in surface form (e.g., "The cage was under the table" versus "The table was above the cage"). Bransford and Franks's conclusion about the second finding was that the strong positive relation between memory confidence and the number of propositions that a probe contained was due to the storage of integrative semantic representations. However, Reitman and Bower (1973) demonstrated that this relation could be produced with meaningless materials and, therefore, was not necessarily due to semantic representations. In their experiments, the targets were meaningless letter strings, with individual strings consisting of one, two, three, or four letters. For example, suppose that subjects study strings sampled from two different quartets of letters, ABCD and WXYZ, and suppose, on analogy with Table 2-4, that the strings that they study for the first quartet are A, B, AD,

CD, BCD, and ABD, so that the overall "idea" ABCD is not presented and that for the other string the overall "idea" WXYZ is one of the presented strings. Using materials of this sort, as well as parallel materials in which studied strings were sampled from quartets of digits, Reitman and Bower found that the relation between memory confidence and the number of letters in a probe was the same as Bransford and Franks's relation between memory confidence and the number of propositions in a meaningful sentence: Confidence was highest for four-letter strings, regardless of whether they were targets (WXYZ) or distractors (e.g., ABCD); confidence was next highest for three-letter strings, regardless of whether they were targets (e.g., ABD) or distractors (e.g., ABC); and so on.

In light of subsequent experiments, therefore, neither the conclusion that the surface form of targets is lost from memory shortly after study nor the conclusion that the relation between memory confidence and number of propositions means that only holistic semantic structures are preserved appears to be correct. Importantly for present purposes, however, it should be borne in mind that these experiments do not challenge the actual findings that Bransford and Franks (1971) reported. They only raise questions about their theoretical interpretation (specifically, about the type of information that is retained in memory). Data are data, after all.

Suggestibility of Eyewitness Memory

In legal cases, the guilt or innocence of defendants often turns on incidental details that are associated with crimes (Was it 11:30 p.m. or 11:45 p.m.? Was the temperature 65 degrees or 75 degrees? Did the robber have a tattoo on the left or the right forearm? Did the suspect touch the child on the back or on the buttocks?) rather than on the meaning of events, which is obvious to all concerned (i.e., a crime was committed). As a rule, no objective record of these details exists that can be introduced as evidence (e.g., contemporaneous written notes, audio recordings, video recordings), so that the testimony of eyewitnesses is critical to juries in the determination of guilt (see chapter 6). For this reason, false memories for the details of experience are of grave concern in legal cases. This concern is heightened by a prominent characteristic of the investigative phase of such cases: The questioning of witnesses can be quite leading, and indeed, leading questions and suggestive statements are integral parts of methods of interviewing witnesses and interrogating suspects in which police receive formal training (e.g., see the techniques described in Inbau, Reid, Buckley, & Jayne, 2001; see also chapter 6). Moreover, although this is not well understood by witnesses, it is considered both legal and ethical, though unsavory, for police interviewers to attempt to secure relevant testimony by making suggestive statements to them, including statements that interviewers know to be false. As an example, here is an excerpt from a witness interview that was placed in evidence in a recent murder trial:

OFFICER: Where'd you guys eat lunch on Saturday?

WITNESS: Don't remember.

OFFICER: Really?

WITNESS: Just can't recall.

OFFICER: Well, I talked to your brother's wife, and she said that you guys ate a lunch at Burger King.

WITNESS: She said that?

OFFICER: Yeah.

WITNESS: Yup, I remember now. It was Burger King.

OFFICER: You certain of that?

WITNESS: Absolutely.

The indicated conversation with the brother's wife, which led this witness to "remember" with absolute certainty that he and his brother ate at Burger King, never occurred.

Loftus (Loftus, 1975; Loftus et al., 1978; Loftus & Palmer, 1974) developed a procedure, which has stimulated hundreds of subsequent experiments, for studying whether such suggestive lines of questioning falsify witnesses' memory for crucial details. A central hypothesis behind her research was that the inherent constraints of eyewitness situations may make the resulting memories especially vulnerable to distortion via suggestion. Crimes involve complex event sequences (e.g., the objects and actions pursuant to an assault or a robbery) that revolve around a theme (the specific crime), with most of those events being only briefly experienced and poorly attended to. Thus, although eyewitnesses' memory for certain events might be excellent (e.g., that there was a purple convertible in the parking lot), it is predictable that their memory for many details will be sketchy to nonexistent. The baseline situation in an eyewitness interview, then, is one in which people are attempting to recall complex collections of events for which they have only fragmentary memories. Further, there is considerable pressure on witnesses, much of it self-imposed, to recall as much as possible, because otherwise crimes cannot be solved and the guilty cannot be prosecuted. Given this scenario of high-stakes retrieval of sketchy memories, eyewitnesses may be prone to rely on external supports to enrich their fragmentary memories. Of particular concern, leading questions and suggestive statements may cause eyewitnesses to add suggested details to their memories that cohere with the gist of their experience, including details that are false and could result in the prosecution of innocent defendants. For instance, in an example from another murder trial, following an armed robbery of a convenience store, a teenage witness was led to "remember" that an innocent suspect with a prior robbery arrest was holding a weapon when, according to his father, they were never in a position that allowed them to see the suspect's hands.

In forensic memory research (research dealing with the reliability of memory reports that figure in legal cases), a fundamental obstacle to assessing the falsifiability of witnesses' memories is that in actual legal cases, we normally do not know the precise events that occurred and are therefore dependent upon witnesses' memory reports for a record of those events. This means that we cannot determine with certainty which of their memory reports are true and which are false, unless the reports happen to be confirmed or disconfirmed by unimpeachable physical evidence. A key feature of the methodology that Loftus developed was to eliminate this uncertainty by exposing witnesses to a precisely controlled sequence of events that had been prepared in advance by the experimenter. To ensure forensic relevance, such a sequence should be one that might be the focus of police investigation.

In Loftus's original studies, the sequence consisted of 30 color slides depicting events immediately before, during, and immediately after an automobile accident on a residential street in which a pedestrian was injured. One of the slides in the sequence contained a detail that would be highly relevant to determining the driver's degree of negligence. That slide showed the car (a red Datsun) at an intersection. The slide also showed either a stop sign (for half of the subjects) or a yield sign (for the other half of the subjects) that was obscured by the foliage of a tree—just the sort of detail that might be the topic of suggestive questioning in a police interview. The slides following the critical one showed the car turning right and hitting a pedestrian. Immediately after showing the slides, the experimenter interviewed the subject, using a standardized 20-question interview. Question 17 in the interview was the suggestive one: "Did another car pass the Datsun while it was stopped at the stop sign?" for half the subjects, or "Did another car pass the Datsun while it was stopped at the yield sign?" for the other half. (Although only a single question was suggestive in this interview, suggestions have been presented multiple times in subsequent studies [e.g., Ceci et al., 1994].) As half of the subjects had been shown a slide with a stop sign while half had been shown a slide with a yield sign, question 17 was suggestive for half of them. Following the interview, there was a 20-minute filler activity in which the subject read a story and answered questions about it. Finally, the subject was administered a yes-no recognition test in which another series of slides, some of which were old and some of which were new, was presented.

Loftus et al. (1978) employed this procedure in five experiments with 1,242 subjects. The procedure was first administered to 129 pilot subjects who produced promising evidence of memory distortion. The subjects for whom question 17 was suggestive made fewer hits for the actual critical slide (i.e., the one containing the sign that they saw) and more false alarms for the new critical slide (i.e., the one containing the suggested sign) than subjects for whom question 17 was not suggestive. Further, the hit and false-alarm rates for subjects who received suggestion were equal, which means that they could not discriminate the sign that they saw from the suggested sign. Loftus repeated this procedure with a new sample of 195 subjects and again found that subjects were unable to recognize the correct sign better than the suggested sign. Although such data seem to show that suggestive questioning distorts the contents of eyewitnesses' memory, there is another interpretation that has less serious implications for eyewitness memory—namely, social compliance. It is possible that subjects' memories of the actual sign were unimpaired, that they were aware that question 17 was suggestive, and that they simply went along with the suggestion on the memory test. To evaluate this possibility, Loftus et al. repeated the procedure with another 90 subjects. During the interview following the slide sequence, either the critical question mentioned the sign that the subject saw (for 30 subjects) or it mentioned the sign that the subject did not see (for 30 subjects) or it did not mention the sign at all. Later, after the memory test, in a procedure that resembled Binet's (1900) studies of autosuggestion, all subjects received a debriefing questionnaire, which informed them that one of the questions during the interview may have incorrectly stated the sign that they saw. Subjects were then given another opportunity to report which sign they saw. On the memory test, as in Loftus et al.'s previous experiments, subjects who received the misleading question chose the correct sign only 43% of the time, whereas subjects who were not misled chose the correct sign 67% of the time. The debriefing questionnaire did not eliminate the effects of suggestive questioning: Only 12% of the misled subjects reported that they had seen one sign but that the other sign had been suggested to them during the interview.

Loftus et al. (1978) also found that, quite sensibly, the suggestibility of memory was affected by a factor that is common to police interviews of eyewitnesses: the delay between events and interviews. In the studies just described, the memory interview with the leading question occurred immediately after subjects viewed the slide sequence. After such a short delay, vivid memories of some of the slides would still be accessible during the interview. If subjects were able to access a vivid memory of the slide with the traffic sign, in particular, they would presumably notice the misinformation in the suggestive question and therefore not accept it (performing what will be called *recollection rejection* in chapter 3). Suppose that the interview is delayed for some time, however. As time passes, subjects will be less able to access vivid memories of the slides, so their ability to recognize the misinformation in the suggestive question and avoid incorporating it into their memories ought to be correspondingly reduced. This possibility was tested by repeating the procedure with a new sample of 648 subjects. The memory interview about the slide sequence was administered immediately after the sequence for half of the subjects and just before the recognition test for half of the subjects. However, the recognition test occurred 20 minutes after the sequence for some subjects, 1 day later for some subjects, 2 days later for some subjects, and 1 week later for some subjects. The results showed, first, that when the memory interview occurred immediately after the slide sequence, performance on the critical test slides was poorer if subjects received misinformation than if they did not but that the size of the impairment was no larger on delayed tests than it was on the 20-minute test. The results showed, second, that when the memory interview occurred just before the recognition test, the performance of subjects who received misinformation became progressively worse as the interval between the slide sequence and the recognition test lengthened. These subjects' responses to critical test slides were correct roughly 40% of the time when the recognition test was administered 20 minutes after the slide sequence, but the rate dropped to roughly 18% correct when the test was administered 1 week later. In addition to being intuitively reasonable, this pattern is of considerable significance in forensic evaluation of the reliability of eyewitness memory reports because police interviews often do not occur until a few days, sometimes a few weeks or more, after the events under investigation. Delay manipulations will also figure centrally in most of the lines of false-memory research that we consider in chapters 4 through 8.

False Identification of Criminal Suspects

The incidental detail of crimes that is of the greatest interest to juries, of course, is the identity of culprits. Sometimes, identity can be firmly established with physical evidence from the crime scene, such as fingerprints, shoeprints, blood samples, or DNA derived from hair or other body parts. However, even such seemingly authoritative evidence is by no means unimpeachable. Suppose, for example, that following a bank robbery, a suspect's fingerprints are lifted from the counter in front of the window of the teller who was robbed. This appears to be compelling evidence of guilt, but following arrest, the suspect claims that he was at the window earlier in the day engaging in a routine banking activity (e.g., exchanging coins for paper currency, changing larger bills into smaller ones). Although the teller does not remember this, that does not prove that the suspect is lying. What sort of additional information would support the fingerprint evidence and challenge the suspect's explanation? The standard answer is an identification of the suspect by the teller. In most cases, police investigators use one of three methods to secure such identifications: (a) *line-ups*, in which witnesses view four to six individuals and attempt to select the culprit; (b) *show-ups*, in which witnesses view a single individual or a picture of the face of a single individual and state whether he or she is the culprit; and (c) *photo spreads*, in which witnesses view photographs of the faces of four to six individuals and attempt to select the culprit. When witnesses make positive identifications via any of these methods, they are typically asked to state their level of confidence in the identification.

On occasion, eyewitness identification is made easy by some distinctive and rather unique physical feature of the suspect, such as a peculiar tattoo (e.g., a Greek letter) in an unusual location (e.g., left forefinger), or a distinctive physical deformity (e.g., a pronounced facial scar), or by virtue of the fact that the suspect is well known to the witness (e.g., a fellow employee). More often than not, however, such aids are absent, and an eyewitness must simply remember and recognize the face of a stranger who falls within the normal range of experience. Are such identifications reliable evidence of guilt, or are they often false-memory responses? We saw in chapter 1 that as early as the turn of the 20th century, Binet (1900) raised doubts about the general reliability of witnesses' memories pursuant to findings about the distorting effects of autosuggestion and leading questions. Shortly thereafter, in the United States, Münsterberg (1908) argued that such doubts were reinforced by what was then known about the attentional and perceptual limitations of humans. Obviously, the research on the suggestibility of eyewitness memories that was sketched above also argues eloquently for caution in the interpretation of witnesses' memory reports. However, eyewitness *identifications* may be an exception; memory for everyday faces may be especially good, and witnesses may therefore be able to make highly accurate suspect identifications.

This possibility has been intensively researched during the past quarter century. Although many researchers have contributed to the body of published findings, Wells and his associates have been the most productive and influential research group throughout this period (e.g., Wells, 1978, 1984, 1985, 1988). As we mentioned earlier, a fundamental obstacle in all research that deals with the reliability of memory reports that figure in legal cases is that the exact events that occurred are unknown, and we are therefore unable to determine with certainty which memory reports are true and which are false. Eyewitness identifications are special cases of this problem inasmuch as identifications are not even necessary if culprits' identities can be firmly established by other methods. In research on eyewitness identification, this problem is solved in the same manner as in Loftus's (e.g., 1975) classic studies of eyewitness suggestibility: At the start of an experiment, witnesses are exposed to a precisely controlled sequence of events that has been prepared by the experimenter. This may take the form of a video, a live staged performance, or a slide sequence, which depicts the persons and events involved in a crime of some sort (e.g., a bicycle theft). In some instances, witnesses may participate unknowingly in a staged sequence of events in which the other participants are trained confederates. Regardless of how such information is presented to witnesses, the important point is that the identity of the culprits is known in advance, so that later identifications can be unambiguously classified as true- or false-memory responses. Some time after presentation, eyewitness identification tests are administered that follow one of the three standard formats. Regardless of the test format, there are two basic types of stimuli: culprit present or culprit absent.

Hundreds of studies have been reported that make use of this basic paradigm. As these studies have produced findings of great importance, both for understanding false memory and for determining the contributions that expert psychological testimony can make in legal cases, we shall have much more to say about them in chapter 6. For now, we note that the overriding question of just how accurate eyewitness identifications are apt to be has been explored in a recent review of selected studies (Haber & Haber, 2004). Haber and Haber asked a simple question that is critical to juries' interpretation of eyewitness identifications: *Under good conditions, just how accurate are eyewitness identifications?* They reviewed more than 500 publications, ultimately selecting 37 articles reporting a total of 48 experiments in which eyewitness identifications were made under good conditions (e.g., culprits could be clearly seen; identifications were made within a reasonable time after observation; identifications were made using line-ups or photo spreads with four or more choices). In the stimuli that are used in such identifications, as mentioned above, the culprit may be either present or absent. Data for culprit-absent identifications were reported in 27 of the experiments, while data for culprit-present identifications were reported in 40.

A summary of what Haber and Haber (2004) discovered is shown in Table 2-5. When the culprit is absent from the test stimuli, there are two possible responses: a wrong choice (false-memory response) and no choice (true-memory response). When the culprit is present in the test stimuli, however, there are three possible responses: a wrong choice (false-memory response), a correct choice (true-memory response), and no choice (a no-memory response). In criminal proceedings, it is the culprit-absent data that are of greatest interest because defendants enjoy a constitutional presumption of innocence. Therefore, if an eyewitness has identified a defendant, the defense's position will normally be that the actual culprit was not pres-

Table 2-5. Summary of Review of Research on the
Accuracy of Eyewitness Identifications

	Type of Identification	
Type of Response	Culprit Absent	Culprit Present
Wrong choice	57%	27%
Correct choice	——	51%
No choice	43%	22%

Note. From Haber and Haber (2004).

ent in the line-up, photo spread, or show-up that was used and that the identification is therefore false. Inspecting the data in Table 2-5, the defense position receives strong support from Haber and Haber's findings. When the culprit was absent, subjects falsely identified someone 57% of the time, on average. The prosecution position, on the other hand, will be that the culprit was present in the test stimuli, that the defendant is the culprit, and that the identification is therefore correct. Returning to Table 2-5, the prosecution's position is not supported. When the culprit was present, subjects correctly identified that person only 51% of the time, on average, and they falsely identified some other person 27% of the time. When one adds the further consideration that the conditions surrounding eyewitness identifications in most crimes are not as ideal as those in the experiments that Haber and Haber reviewed, such identifications become rather worrisome as evidence on which juries are asked to base convictions.

Is this worry well placed? Do false eyewitness identifications cause significant numbers of false convictions, or are there sufficient checks and balances in the legal system that convictions due to false identification are extremely rare? This question cannot be answered with certainty, because in order to do so, it would be necessary to compute the percentage of innocent defendants who are convicted on the basis of eyewitness identifications. That percentage cannot be computed because all such defendants have been judged to be guilty on the basis of available evidence and, therefore, none is innocent by legal definition. It is possible, however, to compute a related statistic—the percentage of convicted *but later exonerated* defendants for whom positive eyewitness identifications were presented at trial. Those data are troubling indeed. In 1996, several years after the introduction of DNA evidence, the National Institute of Justice released a study of 28 cases in which convicted defendants were exonerated by such evidence after serving prison terms of varying lengths (Connors, Lundregan, Miller, & McEwan, 1996). In *every* case, there was one or more positive eyewitness identifications of the defendant, with as many as five positive identifications of one defendant. Two years later, Wells et al. (1998) added 12 other cases to Connors et al.'s sample and found that there were positive identifications in 36 of the 40 cases. They and other researchers (e.g., Kassin, 1998) have concluded that false identifications lead to more wrongful convictions than all other causes combined.

False Memory for Schema-Consistent Events

During the 1970s, another line of false-memory research emerged that was focused on memory for well-defined situations from everyday life. Nominally, this research was inspired by Bartlett's (1932) earlier work on false memory for narratives. Bartlett explained the findings that we discussed in chapter 1 by postulating that the representation of experience in memory is *schematic*, a view that was also advocated by Piaget (1968). Bartlett failed, however, to provide a formal theoretical definition of the concept of memory schema and so did later researchers (see Alba & Hasher, 1983). Although we shall have more to say about this concept in chapter 3, the rough idea is that a *schema* consists of general knowledge that people possess in particular areas and that this knowledge determines the types of information that they encode and store on the basis of their experience. An illustration is provided by what Schank and Abelson (1977) called *scripts*. A script is a knowledge structure about stereotypical situations, ones that have been frequently encountered by most people (e.g., an appointment at a doctor's office). A script contains both general knowledge about the types of information that one may expect to encounter in such situations (e.g., information about diseases, medical tests, and treatments) and knowledge about specific events that will occur (e.g., signing in at the receptionist's desk, sitting in the waiting room, stepping on a scale, having a blood pressure cuff attached to one's arm).

The possibility that concerns us here is that people will have false memories about situations for which they possess memory schemas. This possibility has been investigated with a variety of schematic-memory tasks (e.g., Barclay, 1973; Bower, Black, & Turner, 1979; Graesser, Gordon, & Sawyer, 1979; Smith & Graesser, 1981). A concrete example is provided by a room-schema task that was originally developed by Brewer and Treyens (1981). There are certain types of familiar rooms that are occupied by specific types of people, who perform specific types of actions in specific sequences, and in which specific types of objects are invariably found. Examples include classrooms, teachers' offices, athletic arenas, dentists' and physicians' offices, kitchens, restaurants, and music stores. As these rooms are familiar to us, the people, actions, and objects associated with them are very well learned, and it is assumed that we have memory schemas for such rooms. The chief advantage of these room schemas is that when they are activated, we can process information about people, objects, and actions that we encounter with minimal effort and attention. Efficiency may come at a cost in memory falsification, however: After occupying a room for which a memory schema can be activated, subjects may falsely remember the presence of schema-consistent people, objects, and actions that were in fact absent. The Brewer and Treyens procedure for detecting such false memories was, first, to have subjects occupy such a room for a period of time, without knowing that they were participating in a memory experiment, and, second, to administer a surprise memory test at some later point. The offices of professors and graduate assistants constitute a type of room with which college students are especially well acquainted, and because college students were to serve as subjects, the particular room that was used was one that had been carefully arranged to look like a graduate student's office: It contained a typewriter, table, standard desk items, and a familiar apparatus used in psychological research (a Skinner box).

Some of the findings that are usually obtained with this procedure can be illustrated with two experiments by Lampinen, Copeland, and Neuschatz (2001). Lampinen et al. recruited subjects from undergraduate psychology classes, asking them to report to a particular room in the psychology building. The room was prepared to look like a graduate assistant's office. It contained 10 target objects that were typical of such an office (e.g., a stapler) and 10 target objects that were atypical for such an office (e.g., a toy car). Upon arrival at the office, the subject was greeted by a graduate student, asked to sit down, and was then left alone in the room for 1 minute (to allow time for uninterrupted inspection of the room's contents). Each subject was assigned to one of two treatment conditions, with half of the subjects being told by the graduate student that they would subsequently receive a memory test for objects in the room (*intentional condition*) and the other half not being told about the memory test (*incidental condition*). (Note that the incidental condition corresponds closely to everyday life in that we do not normally expect to have our memories tested after occupying a room.) The graduate student returned after 1 minute and informed the subject that he would be moving to another room for the memory test. It was a recognition test for the room's objects, consisting of 20 targets (10 typical, 10 atypical) and 20 distractors (10 typical, 10 atypical).

The memory test produced four key results. First, there were high levels of false memory for schema-consistent (typical) objects: The false-alarm rate for such distractors was 51%. Second, there were low levels of false memory for schema-discrepant (atypical) objects: The false-alarm rate for such distractors was only 6%. Third, although warning the subjects about the upcoming memory test enhanced true memory (the target hit rate was 67% in the intentional condition and 48% in the incidental condition), it failed to reduce false memory. Fourth and most dramatically, in the incidental condition, which is the one that parallels everyday life, subjects were unable to discriminate objects that had actually been in the room from schema-consistent objects that had not been in the room: The hit rate was 55%, while the false-alarm rate for typical distractors was 51%. Lampinen et al. (2001) repeated their experiment and included a further manipulation. As in the first experiment, half of the subjects received a recognition test immediately after occupying the office, but the recognition test for the other half was delayed for 48 hours. This manipulation yielded a fifth important datum: Levels of false memory for schema-consistent objects nearly doubled between the immediate and 48-hour tests, but false memory for schema-discrepant objects did not increase reliably.

For present purposes, the outcomes of greatest significance are that (a) subjects sometimes falsely remember schema-consistent information at remarkably high levels *immediately following* exposure to situations for which a memory schema can ostensibly be activated (note the parallel with the earlier Deese [1959] schematic word-list task); (b) it is rare for subjects to falsely remember schema-discrepant information; and (c) the passage of time markedly elevates false memory for schema-consistent information but not for schema-discrepant information. Importantly, these results are characteristic of other situations in which subjects ostensibly have schemas available because such results have been obtained using memory materials that are quite different than familiar rooms, such as narratives that revolve around familiar plots (e.g., Reyna, 2000b). Such results have even been obtained in schematized situations in which subjects have undergone physical or emotional trauma, such as visits to hospital emergency rooms for treatment of injuries (Howe, 1997).

False Memories in Reality Monitoring

Johnson and Raye (1981) proposed a memory distinction that fomented a great deal of follow-up research, much of it concerned with false memories: "People remember information from two basic sources: that derived from external sources (obtained through perceptual processes) and that generated by internal processes, such as reasoning, imagination, and thought" (p. 67). As stated, this distinction between the two realities of physical experience and mental life is about true memory—events in both spheres are palpable and therefore one can possess true memories for either type of event. Johnson and Raye used the related idea of *reality monitoring* to refer to the ability to discriminate between true memories of actual external events versus false memories of external events that in fact were not experienced but were only thought about. The latter, which are termed *reality-monitoring failures*, are an interesting variety of partly-true-and-partly-false memories. They are true in the sense that they refer to events that are within the compass of one's experience, but they are false in the sense that the origin of the events (internal rather than external) has been misidentified.

This species of false memory has long been of special interest in abnormal psychology, where it serves as a diagnostic criterion for certain types of psychoses (e.g., Mellor, 1970; Mintz & Albert, 1972). Through the work of Johnson and her associates, however, reality-monitoring failures have come to figure centrally in the study of false memory in normal subjects (e.g., Johnson, 1988; Johnson, Foley, Suengas, & Raye, 1988; Suengas & Johnson, 1988). As in all of the false-memory methodologies discussed in this chapter, except for the Loftus suggestibility paradigm and the reasoning-remembering paradigm introduced below, the procedure for measuring reality-monitoring failures consists simply of presenting subjects with some to-be-remembered material and then administering memory tests to detect false memories, in this instance false memories for material that was thought of rather than presented. The distinguishing feature of the reality-monitoring procedure lies in the nature of the to-be-remembered material. If the procedure is to deliver sensitive tests of reality-monitoring failures, that material must be such as to prompt thoughts about definite objects and events, which might then be included as distractors on recognition tests or about which subjects could be asked to make confidence ratings. A simple example would be a long list of, say, 200 words, presented one at a time to subjects, which contains the items *black*, *hot*, *mother*, *nurse*, *salt*, and *up*. Each of these items has a strong first associate that tends to come to mind when the item is read or heard. It is therefore reasonable to suppose that at least some of these strong associates (*white*, *cold*, *father*, *doctor*, *pepper*, and *down*) would echo in the mind's ear during list presentation. To measure reality-monitoring failures, one could determine whether those associates were falsely recalled or falsely recognized at high

Table 2-6. Illustrative Story and Memory Probes from Studies of
Reality-Monitoring Failures

Type of Statement	Statements
Story sentences	Nancy was walking around the house.
	Nancy washed five shirts and planned to get them dry in the dryer. **(goal)**
	She put the shirts in the dryer. **(clue)**
	She turned the dryer on. **(clue)**
	The clothes dryer was broken.
	She hung the shirts outside on the clothesline. (surprising outcome)
	She finished up the rest of her chores.
	Then she sat down and relaxed.
Memory probes	Did Nancy wash three shirts? **(false distractor)**
	Was she shopping at the mall? **(unrelated distractor)**
	Was her clothes dryer broken? **(inference)**
	If you said "yes" to the last question, did you figure it out that the clothes dryer was broken, or was it stated in the story? **(reality-monitoring probe)**

Note. From Ackerman (1992).

levels on later memory tests, or one could measure whether subjects were highly confident that those associates had been presented.

Most research on reality-monitoring failures has not relied on word lists, however. Instead, like the Loftus suggestibility paradigm and the schema-memory procedure, the focus has been on memory for complex events, such as narratives (e.g., a story about a family outing, a story about doing the laundry) or autobiographical experiences (e.g., a party, a visit to the dentist, a trip to the library). Nevertheless, these more complex materials share with the word-list example the property of being designed to stimulate certain thoughts that could be mistaken for real events on a subsequent memory test. An excellent illustration is provided by a series of experiments reported by Ackerman (1992). The to-be-remembered material was a series of short stories (seven or eight sentences in length), each of which consisted of a sequence of goal-oriented actions that produced a surprising outcome. An example of one of the stories is exhibited in the upper half of Table 2-6. Note the fifth and sixth sentences, in particular. The sixth sentence is a surprising outcome, given the content of sentences one through four, and the fifth sentence is a likely reason for that outcome. It is the fifth sentence, which is set in boldface, that is the potential false memory. Prior research on narrative comprehension (e.g., Trabasso & van den Broek, 1985) has shown that subjects' memory for narrative content is dominated by the causal relations that exist among characters, objects, and events, and that when relevant causal relations are not stated, subjects infer them. Thus, from the standpoint of reality monitoring, the idea that the dryer was broken is something that subjects would be very likely to infer and think about *if the fifth sentence is not presented as part of the story.* The third and fourth sentences in the story were clues that were intended to trigger such inferences (see Table 2-6). In Ackerman's design, subjects listened to a total of 16 stories, with the sentence stating the cause of the surprising outcome being absent in 8 stories and present in 8 stories. During story presentation, subjects were reminded four times not to confuse what they explicitly heard with what they figured out on their own.

The question of interest is whether the subjects displayed reality-monitoring failures for the absent causes. They did. After the stories had been read, the subjects responded to a recognition test containing probes like those shown at the bottom of Table 2-6. The third and fourth probes are the crucial ones. In all instances, the correct response to the third probe is yes, regardless of whether the causal statement was actually presented, and subjects gave this response with high frequency both when the cause had been stated (96%) and when it had not been (69%). Whenever this response was given, the fourth question determined whether reality monitoring was accurate. When the response was yes and the cause had been stated, subjects mistakenly attributed it to thought rather than presentation only 4% of the time. But when the response was yes and the cause had *not* been stated, subjects mistakenly attributed it to presentation rather than thought 41% of the time, notwithstanding that the stories had been presented only a few minutes before and that subjects had been repeatedly warned not to confuse what they actually heard with what they inferred.

Since the task in reality monitoring is to discriminate inferences from physical experiences, reality-monitoring failures ought to increase if manipulations are imposed that more strongly encourage causal inferences or that impair subjects' memory for the actual sentences that they hear. Consistent with such predictions, Ackerman (1992) found that reality-monitoring failures were more frequent when stories contained causal clues (like those in the third and fourth sentences of the story in Table 2-6) than when they did not, and he found that such failures were more frequent when memory tests were administered after a delay. Findings of the latter sort help us to explain reality-monitoring failures in theoretical terms. For now, however, the instructive baseline pattern is that subjects do, indeed, exhibit reliable memorial confusion of the two realities. Interestingly, though, as Ackerman's data illustrate, the confusion is not bidirectional. As long as specific to-be-remembered material that is under the experimenter's control has been presented (as opposed to, say, asking subjects to recall autobiographical experiences from the distant past), subjects exhibit a marked tendency to remember thoughts as physical experiences but not to remember physical experiences as thoughts. This asymmetry is one of several key findings in the false-memory literature that motivate the dual-process theories that are discussed in chapter 3.

False Memories from Reasoning

The next false-memory paradigm is another procedure with strong ties to Binet's (1900) early work, specifically to his studies of autosuggestion. The paradigm centers on the possibility that memory falsification can be an outgrowth of reasoning errors. That humans often reason illogically is a ubiquitous datum. In cognitive psychology, some informative lines of experimentation have established that such behavior is both routine and difficult to eradicate, even with reasoning problems that seem, on their face, to be quite elementary. Two well-known examples from Tversky and Kahneman's work are conjunction problems and *decision-framing* prob-

Table 2-7. Illustrative Conjunction and Decision-Framing Problems

Type of Problem	Statements
Conjunction	
Story	Linda is 31 years old, single, outspoken, and very bright. She majored in philosophy. As a student, she was deeply concerned with issues of discrimination and social justice, and also participated in antinuclear demonstrations.
Statements	(1) Linda is a teacher in an elementary school. (2) Linda works in a bookstore and takes yoga classes. (3) Linda is active in the feminist movement. (4) Linda is a psychiatric social worker. (5) Linda is a member of the League of Women Voters. **(6) Linda is a bank teller.** (7) Linda is an insurance salesperson. **(8) Linda is a bank teller and is active in the feminist movement.**
Decision framing	
Problem	The United States is preparing for the outbreak of an unusual Asian disease. If nothing is done, 600 people will die.
Gain frame	Choose between the following alternative treatments to combat the disease: A. If Program A is adopted, 200 people will be saved. B. If Program B is adopted, there is a one-third probability that 600 people will be saved and a two-thirds probability that no people will be saved.
Loss frame	Choose between the following alternative treatments to combat the disease: C. If Program C is adopted, 400 people will die. D. If Program D is adopted, there is a one-third probability that nobody will die and a two-thirds probability that 600 people will die.

Note. From Tversky and Kahneman (1982, 1983).

lems (Tversky & Kahneman, 1974, 1983); an illustration of each appears in Table 2-7. With conjunction problems, subjects first read some background information about a character (Linda) and are then asked to rank order a series of statements with respect to their relative probability of being true of that character. The key statements are the sixth (Linda is a bank teller) and eighth (Linda is a bank teller and is active in the feminist movement). In any rank ordering of these statements, the sixth one, logically, *must* be ranked more highly than the eighth because feminist bank tellers are a proper subset of bank tellers in the same way that red apples are a proper subset of apples (Reyna, 1991). However, subjects predominantly rank the eighth statement more highly than the sixth, because they mistakenly focus upon the fact that feminists are unlikely to be bank tellers (see Reyna, 1991; 2004).

Turning to framing problems, subjects are given two mathematically equivalent versions of a decision-making task, a medical one involving the outbreak of an Asian disease (see Table 2-7). Half of the subjects receive what is called the *gain-frame* version, in which the results of the decision are phrased as positive outcomes (lives saved), and half receive what is called the *loss-frame* version, in which the same results are phrased as negative outcomes (lives lost). With each version, subjects must choose between two treatment programs whose results, with respect to lives saved or lost, are equal. The difference between each pair of treatments is that the results of one are *certain* (Treatment A saves 200 lives; Treatment C loses 400 lives), whereas the results of the other are *risky* (Treatment B saves 600 lives with a one-third probability and no lives with a two-thirds probability; Treatment D loses no lives with a one-third probability and 600 lives with a two-thirds probability). The medical consequences of all four treatments, with respect to lives saved, are the same, so logically they should be chosen with equal frequency across large samples of subjects. They are not, however. When the decision is phrased positively, subjects are risk-averse: They overwhelmingly prefer a certain gain to an equivalent chance of a much larger gain. But when the decision is phrased negatively, subjects are risk-seeking: They overwhelmingly prefer an equivalent chance of losing nothing to a certain loss.

What are the consequences of illogical reasoning for memory? An interesting possibility is that illogical outcomes might redound to the detriment of subjects' memory for the information on which reasoning was based, distorting memory so that it coheres with the outcomes of reasoning (Reyna, 1995). If such distortions occur, they would be difficult to detect with problems such as those in Table 2-7 because the background information on which illogical reasoning is based (the Linda story, the Asian disease outbreak) is continuously present in the form of written statements. What would happen if the background information were absent during reasoning and later on?

Piaget's familiar concrete-operational tasks provide a convenient collection of well-studied mathematical and scientific problems that satisfy this requirement that the original background information be no longer available once reasoning has begun. Most of these tasks follow a three-step sequence in which (a) subjects are presented with whatever background information is necessary to solve some target problem; (b) the problem itself is posed to subjects; and finally (c) subjects provide their solutions. Reasoning-based memory distortions can be investigated by merely adding a fourth step in which subjects are administered a surprise memory test for the original background information (Brainerd & Reyna, 1990a, 1993; Chapman & Lindenberger, 1992; Reyna, 1992; Reyna & Brainerd, 1990). We have reported several experiments using this basic procedure. The subjects were children, of course, as it is children who supply illogical solutions to concrete-operational problems—asserting, for instance, that quantitative relations are controlled by objects' visual appearance (conservation and transitive inference problems), that physical forces are overridden by psychological forces (causal-reasoning problems), and that the chance that a probabilistic event will occur depends upon its frequency rather than on the ratio of target to nontarget events (probability-judgment problems).

A particularly robust form of illogical reasoning, which is present from the preschool years through early adolescence, occurs with the class-inclusion task that was introduced in chapter 1. In the simplest version of this task (Inhelder & Piaget, 1964), the background information consists of the cardinal numbers of two disjoint sets, the larger denoted A and the smaller denoted A', along with the cardinal number of a superordinate set (B) to which they obviously both belong, for example, Farmer Brown owns 10 animals (B), 8 cows (A), and 2 horses (A'). The reasoning problem is to infer the numerical relation between the larger subordinate set and the superordinate set (e.g., Does Farmer Brown own more cows or more animals?), the surprising outcome being that even though children fully understand that the larger subordinate set is a proper subset of the superordinate set (e.g., no child fails to understand that the cows are animals), they overwhelmingly rely on the relation between the two subordinate sets to solve the problem—concluding that the larger subordinate set contains more elements than its superordinate set. Notice that such reasoning could be reconciled with the original background information if the memory for that information were distorted in the same illogical direction as the reasoning. That possibility was explored in a series of experiments (Brainerd & Reyna, 1995), and we found that, indeed, children's responses to memory probes for subordinate and superordinate sets were distorted in the same direction as their reasoning.

The basic methodology involved presenting children, ranging in age from 5 to 9 years, with eight class-inclusion problems involving familiar superordinate and subordinate sets, such as musical instruments (violins and guitars), clothing (shoes and hats), and furniture (tables and chairs). Each problem was administered in the usual way (i.e., first the numerical values of all the sets were presented; then inclusion problems were posed; and finally children provided their solutions). Following children's solutions, a surprise recognition test for the cardinal numbers of the subordinate and superordinate sets was administered. For simple problems involving the sets A, A′, and B, there were two memory probes for each set, each of which was a forced-choice item with the correct number and one of the other two numbers as the alternatives. To illustrate, in the Farmer Brown problem, the memory probes would be:

B1: Does Farmer Brown own 10 animals or 8 animals?

B2: Does Farmer Brown own 10 animals or 2 animals?

A1: Does Farmer Brown own 10 cows or 8 cows?

A2: Does Farmer Brown own 8 cows or 2 cows?

A′1: Does Farmer Brown own 10 horses or 2 horses?

A′2: Does Farmer Brown own 8 horses or 2 horses?

Consider a group of children, say a sample of 5-year-olds, who overwhelmingly provide illogical solutions to this class-inclusion problem, responding "more cows" to the question of "more animals or more cows?" If such responses distort children's memories in the same direction, the expectation would be that performance would be impaired for certain memory probes *but not for others*. The probes in question are B1 and A1 because the correct memory response, that Farmer Brown owns 10 animals and 8 cows, violates the inference that there are more cows than anything else. In the top portion of Table 2-8, we provide some data from an experiment in which 60 5-year-olds responded to such memory probes (Brainerd & Reyna, 1995). Note that their performance on B1 and A1 probes (boldface entries) was quite poor, considering that the relevant numerical information had been provided roughly 1 minute earlier, but it was consistent with their solutions to class-inclusion problems. In contrast, their responses to the other four memory probes, which do not directly conflict with their reasoning about the relation between A and B, were quite accurate. For comparison, we have also provided data from 60 8-year-old children (Table

Table 2-8. Proportion of Correct Responses to Number-Memory
Probes on Class-Inclusion Problems

Age and Memory Probes	Testing Order	
	Memory Probes Last	Memory Probes First
5-year-olds		
animals: 10 or 8?	**.43**	**.38**
animals: 10 or 2?	.77	.76
cows: 10 or 8?	**.48**	**.41**
cows: 8 or 2?	.95	.91
horses: 10 or 2?	.95	.88
horses: 10 or 8?	.96	.92
8-year-olds		
animals: 10 or 8?	**.60**	**.57d**
animals: 10 or 2?	.96	.94
cows: 10 or 8?	**.62**	**.59**
cows: 8 or 2?	.94	.93
horses: 10 or 2?	.99	.96
horses: 10 or 8?	.99	.97

Note. The illustrative memory probes are for a hypothetical class-inclusion task with 10 animals: 8 cows and 2 horses. The numbers in boldface are for probes for which the incorrect choice is consistent with illogical solutions to class-inclusion problems.

Data from Brainerd and Reyna (1995).

2-8, *bottom*), who showed much lower levels of illogical reasoning and who therefore should be less prone to memory distortion. As can be seen, their responses to B1 and A1 were indeed much more accurate, though performance on the other probes was similar to the 5-year-olds'.

At the level of cognitive processes, such reasoning-based memory distortions might arise in one or both of two distinct ways. First, generating an illogical solution to a *specific* reasoning problem (e.g., for "more animals or more cows?" but not for "more musical instruments or more violins?") may distort memory for the specific background facts on that problem but not on other problems (e.g., for the fact that there are 10 animals but not for the fact that there are 10 musical instruments). Second, the processes that are responsible for illogical reasoning may produce related memory distortions without regard to whether specific problems are solved incorrectly. That is, in subject samples that are prone to illogical class-inclusion reasoning, their performance on probes for the numerical values of a superordinate set and a large subordinate set will tend to be poor, regardless of whether they solved an inclusion problem about those sets incorrectly.

Consistent with the second mechanism, research on several types of childhood reasoning problems has shown that memory distortions are usually independent of performance on particular reasoning problems (Reyna & Brainerd, 1992, 1995a). To illustrate, in the same series of experiments that produced the data in the top portion of Table 2-8, we conducted a study in which the memory probes were always administered *before* children were asked to solve the relevant class-inclusion problem. If the first mechanism is responsible for the distortions in B1 and A1 performance, then performance should be much better before children have had the opportunity to generate illogical inferences about a particular inclusion relation. As can be seen, however, responses to B1 and A1 probes were just as inaccurate when the probes were administered before class-inclusion problems as when they were administered after. This result, like the earlier finding of one-way confusion in reality monitoring, has important ramifications for theories of false memory (see chapter 3).

Autobiographical False Memory

Our concluding example of a false-memory paradigm is the least controlled and most naturalistic of the lot. The downside of low levels of experimental control and high levels of naturalism is that it is difficult to effect clean measurements of true and false memory and to execute clean experimental manipulations, which means that it is correspondingly difficult to establish cause-effect relations between specific variables and the creation of false memories. The upside is ecological validity. Because the to-be-remembered information is neither contrived nor artificial and because the procedure does not interfere with the normal ebb and flow of subjects' lives, the resulting data may dispel some nagging doubts about the reality of false memories and about the generality of inferences from laboratory results. For example, these data bear on questions such as: Are false memories commonplace with unstructured everyday experience, as opposed to collections of events that have been designed to foster false memories? If false memories are commonplace with everyday experience, do they seem to follow the same rules as other types of false memories? Upon first impression, such baseline questions may not seem interesting to most memory researchers, but they can become bones of extreme contention when false-memory research is used in important applied contexts, such as sworn testimony or psychotherapy (see chapters 6 and 8).

In autobiographical false memory, the ideal is for subjects to lead their lives in the ordinary way, without the presence of interloping experimenters, and then, at some later point, to have subjects respond to tests that measure true and false memory for the events of their lives. This ideal poses an obstacle to research, one that is also a routine dilemma in forensic analysis of the accuracy of witnesses' memory. If the experimenter does not enter the picture until sometime after the target events have been experienced, how can we know what those events were? Such knowledge is crucial to the whole research enterprise. Unless we know which events are actually part of a subject's biography, we have no basis for declaring that some memory responses are true and others are false. The events of subjects' lives could be identified with high accuracy if subjects were unobtrusively filmed during their waking hours. Most institutional review boards at universities would take a dim view of such an invasion of privacy, though producers of reality television programs would not be troubled by it. A less objectionable solution is for subjects to keep diaries; to write a few of the day's events each evening. Admittedly, errors can creep into diaries because, as we have seen, false memories about target events may form even as the events are being experienced. However, experienced diarists can minimize such accuracy slippage by, for example, making mental notes during the course of the day of particular occurrences that they intend to record in their diaries.

Conway and associates (e.g., Conway, Collins, Gathercole, & Anderson, 1996) have exploited this methodology to considerable advantage in some informative studies of autobiographical false memory. In the cited article, for example, two subjects, both of whom were memory researchers, kept diaries over a period of 5 months. They made diary entries for a total of 147 days, with the entries for each day being recorded either late in the evening or early the following morning. The subjects were instructed to make entries for both personal experiences and news events of the day. Diary entries for individual days were roughly six or seven sentences in length. In addition to recording true events and thoughts, subjects were asked to record *altered* events and thoughts and *false* events and thoughts. Altered events and thoughts were generated by the subjects themselves by modifying the surface form of a true event or thought while preserving its meaning (e.g., recording that person A took person B out to shop while person C remained at home when in fact A took C out while B remained at home, or saying that one had a dream about a TV quiz show in which onions figured prominently when in fact it was peas that figured prominently). False events and thoughts were things that could have happened on a particular day but did not (e.g., "took the kids and the dog for a walk," or "thought about how the word 'man' was used in the 1960s"). Thus, the altered events/thoughts and the false events/thoughts were generated pursuant to the constraint that they had to be consistent with the subjects' understanding of their daily experience, rather than being bizarre or otherwise atypical.

For each day's diary entry, subjects were instructed to record one true event, one true thought, and either an altered event and a false thought or a false event and an altered thought. By the end of the recording period, 5 months later, this procedure had yielded a large pool of entries of all six types. After the recording period was complete, a further 7 months elapsed. At the end of the 7-month interval, comprehensive recognition tests were administered, with the probes consisting of entries of all six types from subjects' diaries. The recognition tests were personalized for each subject because, of course, their respective diary entries were not the same. For each probe (e.g., Did you take the kids and the dog for a walk?), the subject first made a true-false judgment and then rated his confidence in that judgment. For each probe that was judged to be false, the subject indicated whether it was an altered event/thought or a false event/thought. For each probe that was judged to be true, the subject indicated whether or not its occurrence had been consciously remembered. Later, this yes-no recognition test was followed up with a less demanding forced-choice test on which each probe consisted of a true event/thought paired with an altered event/thought or a false event/thought. Here, the subjects' task was simply to select the true member of each pair.

In this design, false memories are represented by erroneous "true" judgments about altered events/thoughts and about false events/thoughts. There were four major findings. First, 7 months after their diaries had been completed, the subjects still exhibited reliable discrimination of true events/thoughts from altered events/thoughts and false events/thoughts. Of the probes classified as true during yes-no recognition, two thirds were in fact true. Second, false-memory levels, for events/thoughts that subjects were fully aware to be untrue when they recorded them, were also high at the end of this period because one third of the probes classified as true on this same test were not. Third, consistent with the aforementioned research on reality monitoring, false-memory levels were higher for thoughts than for events. Of probes that were erroneously classified as true during yes-no recognition, 57% referred to thoughts and 43% referred to feelings. Fourth, there was a dramatic difference in the phenomenology that accompanied correct versus erroneous true judgments. For correct true judgments, the subjects reported that they could consciously remember the occurrence of the relevant event or thought 59% of the time. For erroneous true judgments, on the other hand, the subjects reported that they could *not* consciously remember the occurrence of the event 78% of the time. From a theoretical point of view, this discrepancy between the phenomenologies that accompany true- and false-memory reports is pivotal datum. We postpone consideration of it for the present, however, as it will be discussed in chapter 3 in connection with dual-process theories of true memory and also in connection with opponent-processes theories of false memory.

Distinctive and Common Features

Skimming back through the nine false-memory paradigms, perhaps the most striking thing is that the differences that separate them seem deep and substantive, while the similarities that unite them, apart from the fact that they all produce false-memory responses, seem superficial and methodological. The more obvious differences include (a) the to-be-remembered material that generates false reports varies in complexity from simple word lists (recall intrusions, false recognition), through more complex narratives (false memory for inferences, reality-monitoring failures), to even more complex autobiographical situations (suggestibility of eyewitness memory, false identification of suspects, schema-consistent false memories), to mathematical and scientific problem solving; (b) some of the paradigms focus on false memories for emotionally charged events with legal consequences (suggestibility of eyewitness memory, false identification of suspects), while the rest focus on more prosaic false memories; (c) some of the paradigms focus on false memories that might be thought of as preexistent (intrusions in recall, false recognition, schema-consistent false memories), while the rest implement procedures that generate the false memories that are measured; and (d) some paradigms make subjects aware from the start that they are participating in a memory experiment and that the central task is therefore to preserve an accurate record of the to-be-remembered material (recall intrusions, false recognition, false memory for inferences, reality monitoring), whereas subjects are unaware of this in other paradigms.

As we said, the similarities among the paradigms seem superficial and methodological. Two that are immediately apparent are that subjects are always exposed to some target material whose content is usually known to the experimenter, though the exact content varies dramatically, and that memory is always tested via recognition or recall, so that false-memory reports are either intrusions or false alarms. If one looks below the surface, however, there is an underlying thread that weaves all of the paradigms together. The modal false-memory situation, as defined by these paradigms, is one in which *false reports are consistent with the gist of participants'* *experience*. For example, the gist of List 2 in Table 2-1 is that the words come from three familiar categories, and the intrusions that occur when subjects recall this list come from those same categories; one of the gists of the list at the top of Table 2-3 is that words with familiar antonyms were presented, and subjects make false alarms to those antonyms on recognition tests; the gist of the sentences in Table 2-4 is that this is a story about ants eating jelly that has been left on the kitchen table, and subjects make false alarms to distractor sentences that preserve this gist; in the illustration of eyewitness suggestibility that we considered, the gist of the slide show is a car accident, and subjects are susceptible to suggestions about details that are relevant to car accidents (traffic signs); the gist of a culprit's face is that he or she is of a certain gender, age, and race, and falsely identified suspects overwhelmingly share those features with culprits; the gist of a schema-memory task is that a familiar situation is experienced, and subjects exhibit false memory for people, objects, and events that are normally part of that situation; the gist of the sentences in Table 2-6 is that this is a story about washing clothes, and subjects display false memories for events that they would be apt to think about in connection with washing clothes; the gist of class-inclusion reasoning is a numerical relation between two sets, and subjects falsely remember numerical values that fit with that relation [as understood]; and in autobiographical memory experiments, false items are deliberately selected so as to be consistent with the gist of the diarists' daily experiences. In all of these instances, although falsely remembered information was not experienced as part of the target material, it seemed familiar to subjects because it preserves their understanding of the meaning of their experience. This basal feature of the most frequently studied false-memory paradigms—that the target material specifies connected meanings (gists) and that falsely remembered information will seem familiar because it coheres with those meanings—provides the chief ground for hope that false-memory research need not be disjoint and chaotic and that, on the contrary, it may be possible to explain the most common examples of false memory with a single set of theoretical principles.

Two qualifications of the gist-consistency property of false-memory paradigms is in order. First, although the experienced material in these paradigms specifies connected meanings that are preserved in falsely remembered information, they vary considerably in just how thoroughly those meanings are specified for subjects. At the low end are word-list experiments, in which a target meaning may be conveyed by only a single presented word, and reasoning experiments, in which a target meaning may be conveyed by only a single erroneous conclusion. At an intermediate level are semantic inference and reality-monitoring experiments, in which a target meaning is usually specified by a few statements, and false-identification experiments, in which a target meaning (e.g., "Hispanic male") is specified by some brief observations and perhaps a later suggestive statement. At the high end are studies of eyewitness suggestibility, schema-consistent events, and autobiographical memory in which a target meaning is repeatedly cued by numerous events in familiar everyday situations. The second qualification is that although the standard research procedures focus on false memories of gist-preserving events, this should not be interpreted as demonstrating that false memories must be consistent with the gist of experience. On the contrary, it is clear that some people form convincing false mem-

Table 2-9. Continuum of Suggestibility in False-Memory Paradigms

Suggestibility	Description
Level 1	Subjects falsely recognize or recall items that are consistent with salient meanings that are present in to-be-remembered material and that therefore seem familiar (examples: semantic intrusion, semantic false recognition, false identification of criminal suspects).
Level 2	Subjects falsely recognize or recall items that not only seem familiar because they are consistent with salient meanings that are present in to-be-remembered material but that are better examples of that meaning than the to-be-remembered material (examples: false memory for semantic inferences, false memory for stimulus words in Deese [1959] lists).
Level 3	Subjects falsely recognize or recall items that not only seem familiar because they are consistent with salient meanings that are present in to-be-remembered material but that have been previously experienced in similar contexts. (example: Schema-consistent false memories).
Level 4	Subjects falsely recognize or recall items that not only seem familiar because they are consistent with salient meanings that are present in to-be-remembered material but that are also in better agreement with subsequent events (example: false memories following illogical reasoning).
Level 5	Subjects falsely recognize or recall items that not only seem familiar because they are consistent with salient meanings that are present in to-be-remembered material but that came to mind while the material was being presented (example: reality-monitoring failures).
Level 6	Subjects falsely recognize or recall items that not only seem familiar because they are consistent with salient meanings that are present in to-be-remembered material but that have been explicitly suggested to them as part of the presented material (examples: suggestibility of eyewitness memory).
Level 7	Subjects falsely recognize or recall items that not only seem familiar because they are consistent with salient meanings that are present in to-be-remembered material but that have been explicitly suggested to them in a coercive manner (example: suggestibility of eyewitness memory with forced confabulation).

ories that are not consistent with the meaning of their experience, that others form convincing false memories that are not consistent with the meaning of anyone's experience, and that still others form convincing false memories that violate the laws of nature as we understand them. The first type of false memory is illustrated by memories of Satanic ritual abuse (e.g., Leavitt & Labott, 1998; Paley, 1997), the second by memories of alien abductions (e.g., Gottlib, 1997; Takhar, 1995), and the third by memories of previous lives (e.g., Stevenson, 2000). Quite obviously, these latter false memories are not the garden variety, but as we shall see in chapter 8, they can be brought under the same explanatory umbrella as the phenomena considered in this chapter.

There is a final thread running through false-memory paradigms that both unites and separates them—namely, the property of *relative suggestibility*. In the literature, it has become routine to speak of some forms of false memory as arising spontaneously and to speak of others as being by-products of deliberate suggestion. However, Reyna and Lloyd (1997) pointed out that it is more accurate to speak of a continuum of relative suggestibility, along which false-memory paradigms can be ordered. Seven levels of relative suggestibility are described in Table 2-9 and illustrated with corresponding paradigms (see Reyna & Lloyd, 1997, for additional details). At all levels, the information that is being falsely reported, though it was not experienced as part of the to-be-remembered material, will seem familiar to subjects because it shares the material's salient gists. At the first two levels, such meaning resemblance is the only apparent basis for false-memory responses. At the third level, there is no suggestion in the current context, but there is historical suggestion inasmuch as falsely remembered items have been previously experienced in similar circumstances. At the fourth level, a weak and indirect form of suggestion is present in the current context in the form of events occurring after presentation of the to-be-remembered material that are consistent with falsely remembered items. At the fifth level, suggestion is stronger and more direct because falsely remembered items came to mind as inferences or associations when the to-be-remembered material was presented. At the sixth level, suggestion is stronger still and even more direct because falsely remembered information is deliberately presented to subjects as postevent misinformation. The seventh level is a variant on the sixth. Here, subjects are required to express their acceptance of postevent misinformation as being true information that was part of the to-be-remembered material. In addition to representing the highest level of suggestion in Table 2-9, this procedure, which is usually called *forced confabulation* (Kassin & Kiechel, 1996; Zaragoza & Mitchell, 1996; Zaragoza, Payment, Ackil, Drivdahl, & Beck, 2001), has important applications in legal cases in which defendants have falsely confessed to crimes during the course of police interrogations (Brainerd, Reyna, & Poole, 2000; Reyna, 1998; Reyna, Holliday, & Marche, 2002; see chapter 6).

Synopsis

For the most part, two types of responses have been used to detect the presence of false memories: intrusions of meaning-preserving information on recall tests and false alarms to meaning-preserving distractors on recognition tests. These responses have been measured in a wide assortment of experimental paradigms, some of which have become staple research procedures. Two of those paradigms—semantic intrusions in recall of word lists and semantic false alarms in recognition of word lists—implement standard Ebbinghaus-type verbal-learning procedures. With those procedures, false-memory responses can be induced at high levels when subjects read or listen to word lists that repeatedly cue certain familiar meanings.

Although the other major instances of false-memory paradigms rely on these same behavioral indexes, they do not use verbal-learning procedures to set the stage for false memories. Instead, all of them use procedures that expose subjects to familiar collections of events or objects that are interconnected by meaning relations that are well known to subjects, with false memories being by-products of such preexperimental knowledge. In certain of these paradigms, events and objects are abstractly presented by requiring subjects to read or listen to prose statements. Three of the paradigms—false memory for semantic inferences, false memory in reality monitoring, and false memory from reasoning—make use of this procedure. In other paradigms, events and objects are concretely presented, by having subjects participate in sequences of events, by having subjects observe live or filmed sequences of events, or by having subjects inspect drawings or photos depicting sequences of events. Such procedures are used in four other major paradigms: suggestibility of eyewitness memory, false identification of criminal suspects, false memory for schema-consistent events, and autobiographical false memory. In addition, some of the paradigms, most notably suggestibility of eyewitness memory and false identification of criminal suspects, incorporate deliberate misinformation that is intended to distort subjects' memory for actual objects and events. All of these paradigms have been found to produce characteristic types of false-memory responses under controlled conditions.

Other key differences between the major false-memory paradigms are that the target material to which subjects are exposed differs greatly in cognitive complexity from one paradigm to another, that the emotional content of false memories varies from one paradigm to another, that some paradigms focus on spontaneous false memories while others focus on implanted ones, and that some paradigms disguise the fact that the objective is to measure false-memory reports while others do not. Despite such differences, there are underlying commonalities that make it possible to think of these paradigms as tapping analogous memory mechanisms. The most fundamental commonality is that the false-memory responses that are characteristic of each paradigm consist of errors that are congruent with the gist of the subjects' experience, as specified in the target materials to which they were exposed—notwithstanding that those materials might be anything from word lists to eating dinner at a restaurant. Another important commonality is that all of the paradigms incorporate features that could be interpreted as suggestive, at least broadly defined. Such suggestion may vary from weak and indirect to strong and explicit, but regardless of such variability, all of the paradigms seek to nudge memory reports away from actual experience and toward specific errors of commission.

PART II

THE BASIC SCIENCE OF FALSE MEMORY

3

Theoretical Explanations of False Memory

In researching any phenomenon, science has three broad objectives: describe it, explain it, and make new predictions about it. The previous chapter was given over to the job of describing false-memory effects, and this task will continue to occupy us throughout the remainder of this volume. The task of making predictions about false memory must be postponed for the present as we lack the necessary machinery for forecasting new findings. In science, explanation is the engine of prediction, so it will first be necessary to examine some theoretical principles that are currently used to account for effects such as those that were considered in chapter 2. That is the aim of the present chapter.

Our exploration of theoretical principles proceeds in three steps. First, we consider three early explanations of false memory: constructivism, a more detailed version of constructivism that is known as schema theory, and the source-monitoring framework. We refer to them as "early explanations" because each had appeared in the literature well before the current surge in false-memory research. As a result, these theories were not designed to explain the broad range of false-memory effects that have accrued in the literature, but in the tradition of cumulative scientific knowledge, each contains important features that have influenced more recent theories. Second, we discuss the dual-process tradition in memory research. Although theories in the dual-process vein were originally formulated as explanations of true memory, they incorporate a key principle—the notion of dissociated retrieval operations— that is central to contemporary accounts of false memory. Third, we consider what, at present, is the modal approach to explaining false memories: opponent-processes theories. In situations that generate false-memory reports, like those reviewed in chapter 2, these theories posit that dissociated memory mechanisms are operating, with some elevating such reports and others suppressing them—thus, the "opponent" in opponent processes.

Early Explanations

The first of our three early theories, *constructivism*, is associated with the studies of false memory for semantic inferences that were conducted by Bransford and Franks (1971) and other psycholinguists (e.g., Kintsch, 1974), as well as with Bartlett's (1932) classic work on false memory for ambiguous narratives, and consequently, it was intended to explain errors in memory for complex narrative material. The second theory, *schema theory*, evolved from constructivism and from research on schema-consistent memory (e.g., Brewer & Treyens, 1981; Lampinen et al., 2001), and it therefore centers on erroneous memories of people, objects, and events that are normally experienced as part of familiar everyday situations, such as attending a baseball game or dining at a restaurant. The third theory, the *source-monitoring framework*, emerged during the course of studies of reality monitoring (e.g., Johnson et al., 1988) and was therefore designed to account for those partly-true-and-partly-false memories in which the remembered event was actually experienced in, for example, dreams or thoughts about events (in contrast to false semantic inferences or false memories of schema-consistent events). According to source-monitoring theory, the origins of such experiences are often incorrectly remembered by relying on cues that are generally but not invariably reliable discriminators of real versus mental experiences. We will discuss these three early theories separately.

Constructivism

The core precept of constructivism is that people remember what they understand to be the *meaning* of their experience, not their experience per se (Bransford, Barclay, & Franks, 1972; Paris & Carter, 1973; Reyna, 1996). If people remember what they understand, it is not in the least surprising that they remember false information that preserves the gist of their experience. However, to say that people remember what they understand requires a detailed set of assumptions about memory that is capable of delivering this state of affairs, and once such assumptions are spelled out, they are subject to experimental confirmation or disconfirmation. The relevant assumptions, as noted in chapter 2, are that events are interpreted once they have been experienced, that these interpretations are integrated into semantic structures (what Bartlett [1932] would have called *schemas*), and that the actual content of experience (usually called its *surface form*) is then quickly jettisoned from memory. Thus, shortly after events are experienced, within just a few minutes according to Bransford and Franks's (1971) interpretation of their data, a person's only remaining memories are based upon an integrated representation of the meaning of events.

These assumptions were later fine-tuned by other investigators to incorporate additional ideas that would make them more plausible. One example is the inclusion of the familiar distinction between short- and long-term memory. According to that refinement, short-term memory is a *veridical* (i.e., verbatim) storage system and long-term memory is an *interpretative* (i.e., semantic) storage system. It is assumed that the exact surface form of experience is encoded into the short-term store and the meaning of that information is then extracted using semantic concepts from long-term memory. The extracted meaning is then stored in long-term memory, and finally, the contents of the short-term store are erased, so that the stored meanings are all that survive.

Beyond the experiments on semantic inferences that first inspired constructivism, this theory has often been used to explain memory errors in two of the other paradigms in chapter 2: the suggestibility of eyewitness memory (e.g., Loftus, 1995) and false memories from reasoning (e.g., Liben, 1977). As we mentioned, though, soon after the appearance of constructivist assumptions, data that challenged them were reported. In that connection, it is important to be clear about precisely what aspects of these assumptions were and were not disconfirmed. That people store memories of the meaning of their experience and later recollect the events of their lives in ways that are congruent with stored meanings was never in serious doubt. Although Reitman and Bower (1972) and others found that such memories were not *required* to produce high levels of false memory and high confidence in false memories (because the same findings could be generated by meaningless materials), it would be a misinterpretation to conclude that meaning-based remembering is perforce not a prominent characteristic of memory performance. Nothing could be further from the truth. One of the most enduring findings of memory research is that manipulations that encourage people to extract meaning from target materials are among the most powerful of all influences on performance (Craik & Lockhart, 1972; Craik & Tulving, 1975). Thus, constructivism's emphasis on the importance of the meaning content of experience is highly consistent with what we know about memory performance.

The key point that was disconfirmed by the experimental data is the notion that meaning content is all, or just about all, that there is to memory performance, that the surface content of material vanishes from storage once its meaning has been stored and that surface content does not contribute to performance thereafter. Against this notion, it was found that surface features of experience can be retained in memory for periods that far exceed the few minutes allowed by constructivism, even when those features consist of incidental perceptual details that are of no conceivable use in meaning comprehension (e.g., Hintzman, Block, & Inskeep, 1973; Kolers, 1976). Three experiments reported by Hintzman et al., in which the presentation modality of target material provided the incidental surface details, generated singularly clear demonstrations of this result. In each experiment, the subjects studied eight word lists, which were composed of 18 words apiece. Within each list, half of the words were presented in one form or modality, and half were presented in another form or modality, with the specific manipulations being visual versus auditory (Experiment 1), uppercase versus lowercase letters (Experiment 2), and male versus female voice (Experiment 3). Subjects were told that they were participating in a memory experiment in which their task would be to recall as many words as possible from each list after they had studied it. Being able to remember the presentation form or modality of each word would be of no obvious help, and indeed,

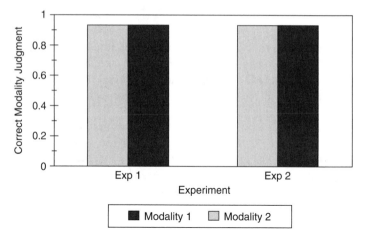

Figure 3-1. Proportion of recalled words in Hintzman, Block, and Inskeep's (1973) experiments for which subjects were later able to identify the words' presentation modalities. These data are from Hintzman and co-workers' first two experiments.

it would be natural for subjects to regard such information as dead weight that ought to be ignored rather than preserved. Following presentation of each list, subjects were given 3 minutes to write as many words from that list as possible. Following the written recall of the last list, a surprise modality test was administered in which subjects were asked to identify test words that had been presented on the study lists and then to identify the presentation modality of each. By the time the modality test was administered, more than a half-hour had elapsed since the first list was studied. Nevertheless, as can be seen in Figure 3-1, subjects' memory for this irrelevant, incidental surface detail was excellent, nearly perfect in fact.

As with Reitman and Bower's (1972) data, it is essential to avoid overinterpretation of findings such as those in Figure 3-1. Such findings should not, in particular, be interpreted as demonstrating that memory for surface content is just as robust as memory for meaning content. Such a conclusion violates the data of any number of experiments, especially experiments dealing with memory for sentences and narratives (e.g., Gernsbacher, 1985; Kintsch, Welsch, Schmalhofer, & Zimny, 1990; Murphy & Shapiro, 1994). Those experiments have consistently shown that, as time passes, memory for the surface features of experience become inaccessible more rapidly than does memory for its meaning. The appropriate conclusion about data such as those in Figure 3-1 is twofold. On the one hand, memories of *specific* surface information may remain accessible for long intervals: a few days (Kintsch et al., 1990), a week (Reyna & Kiernan, 1995), several weeks (Brainerd & Mojardin, 1998), or even years (Kolers, 1976). On the other hand, such memories are more labile than memory for meaning content, so that over time there is a progressive shift away from reliance on memory for surface information toward reliance on memory for meaning (Kintsch et al., 1990). Because, as we saw in chapter 2, false-memory responses can occur immediately after target events are experienced, this places an important constraint on theories of false memory, which we shall call the *coexistence constraint*. The data show that true and false memories of the same material can coexist; that people will exhibit false memory for gist-consistent information (e.g., drinking a Coke at a baseball game), *notwithstanding* that true memories that contradict the false information (e.g., the taste, smell, and color of the 7-Up that was actually consumed) are also accessible. Successful theories must be capable of explaining this seemingly paradoxical result.

Schema Theory

Basic Principles

Schema theory evolved from the constructivist tradition and may be viewed as a specific implementation of constructivist thinking about memory. Thus, although the assumptions of schema theory (e.g., Brewer & Treyens, 1981; Minsky, 1975; Schank & Abelson, 1977) are more detailed and formal than those of constructivism, they are quite in the same spirit, including that of Bartlett's (1932) original work. Four key principles are used in explaining false memories: selection, abstraction, interpretation, and integration. We summarize each under its own heading before discussing the limitations of schema theory.

Selection   This principle stipulates that of the people, objects, and events that are components of a target experience, only some will be encoded into memory and preserved in the eventual memory representation. Memory encoding can therefore be thought of as a sieve: Some items fall through and the rest do not. Not surprisingly, the items that fall through (are encoded) depend upon the availability of a relevant memory schema, such as a script or a frame. If the target experience (e.g., visiting the office of a professor) fits with an existing schema and if that schema is activated at the time of the experience, the schema will determine which items of information are encoded. The key assumption (e.g., Brown & Smiley, 1977) is that the items that are most central to the schema (e.g., the desk and books in a professor's office) will receive privileged attention and will therefore be most likely to be preserved in the eventual memory representation. A further refinement, which was proposed by Schank & Abelson (1977), deals with memory schemas for familiar situations, which are frequently activated in the course of everyday life, such as eating at a restaurant. When people participate in a specific instance of one of these familiar situations, some of the events will be highly typical of that situation (e.g., a menu or a waiter) and others will be less typical, though still schema-consistent (e.g., an espresso machine or a tea samovar). People are thought to be able to remember the schema-consistent information at a later time, sometimes falsely interpolating it into their memory for an episode when it was not explicitly experienced. It is assumed that the details of highly typical events will not be fully encoded and will be rapidly forgotten, so although it is easy to "remember" the presence of such events on later tests (e.g., I read a menu), it is difficult to remember their exact features (e.g., I can't recall what the menu looked like). Additional details not present in generic schemas could be remembered or added as tags to the schema. Some theorists have claimed that events that violated schemas would also be privileged in memory (e.g., a fast-food restaurant with cloth napkins), leading to the unfortunately unclear prediction that both schema-consistent and -inconsistent items would be remembered better, presumably relative to the elusive schema-neutral details. In general, however, the loss of detail in memory over time—that memory was schematic rather than detailed—was a pivotal finding explained by selective encoding, selective retrieval, and selective forgetting, which are governed by schematic knowledge about typical events.

Abstraction   For items that are selected for encoding, this principle specifies that there will be lawful fluctuations in the level of detail about them that is preserved in memory. More particularly, the level of preserved detail is assumed to depend upon the degree to which an item is prototypical of an activated schema. The more prototypical an item is, the more likely it is to be subjected, once it has been encoded, to a form of processing known as abstraction, which strips its memory representation of any distinctive features (e.g., by paring away the color, size, and height of a professor's desk from its memory representation). Note the similarity between this principle and constructivism's assumption that the surface form of experience is erased from memory once its meaning has been extracted.

Interpretation   While abstraction reduces the information in an item's memory representation, interpretation enriches it. The interpretation principle incorporates the effects of processes such as elaboration and inference, which generate schema-consistent information that goes beyond actual experience. When a memory schema is activated, generated information includes concrete details for items that are only indirectly experienced or items that were not experienced but are typical of that schema. As an example of the first type of enrichment, suppose that a student takes a make-up examination in a professor's office, and that while the student is reading and answering questions, the professor answers a telephone call out of the student's sight. Even though the telephone was not observed, the student may later "remember" seeing the professor speaking into a standard desk telephone. As an example of the second type of enrichment, the student may later remember seeing a bookshelf lined with scholarly volumes, when this particular office contained no books or bookshelves. When it comes to accounting for false memories, the interpretation principle is the most important feature of schema theory because it is the putative source of spurious memories for schema-consistent information.

Integration   The last principle, like the earlier abstraction idea, is a clear illustration of schema theory's roots in constructivism. Integration refers to the post-storage consolidation of memory representations that fit with an activated schema. If a memory schema has been activated, it is assumed that once memory representations of the target experience have been formed (in accordance with the first three principles), they undergo a final assimilation process that integrates them into a single, coherent, long-term memory structure. Thus, the memories that we retain of people, objects, and events from situations in which memory schemas were activated do not exist in isolation but, rather, are all part of a unitary, consolidated representation. This is a crucial notion from the perspective of false memory because it implies that true memories of actual experience and false memories that were generated in accordance with the interpretation principle are stored together in the same memory representation. In the false-memory literature, this is known as a *one-process hypothesis* because it assumes that on memory tests, true- and false-memory responses ultimately derive from a mutual source—namely, a common representational basis. Although the terms *unitary* and *one-process* are used, they do not mean that only one factor or element or process of memory is involved, only that all of these are linked together, as opposed to being independent. This, in turn, leads to characteristic empirical predictions about statistical dependencies and experimental associations between true and false memories, which are used to test one-process explanations.

Limitations: Scope, True-False Memory Dissociation, and Developmental Variability

Schema theory has three chief limitations as an account of false memory. The first is scope. The theory's assumptions are intended to apply to target material for which memory schemas are available and to the memories that result when such schemas are activated. There are important circumstances that produce characteristic false memories that do not meet these specifications. Of the nine paradigms in chapter 2, memory schemas might reasonably be assumed to predominate in four of them (false memory for semantic inferences, suggestibility of eyewitness memory, false identification of suspects, and false memory for schema-consistent events) but not in the remainder. With respect to the semantic intrusion and semantic false-alarm procedures, for instance, their characteristic forms of false memory arise from target material that seems decidedly nonschematic (word lists). It could be argued in connection with semantic intrusions in recall that categorized word lists activate schemas such as "a bunch of color names," "a bunch of animal names," "a bunch of furniture names," and so forth. This is a stretch, however, and it is tantamount to assuming that whenever false memories result from exposure to words that are related in some way, there must be a memory schema for that relationship, which smacks of circular reasoning. Further, this argument would not apply to semantic false alarms in recognition because in most experiments, this form of false memory is produced by word lists that have been carefully constructed so that individual items are unrelated to each other. Also, schema theory would not seem to be applicable to false memories from reasoning because such memories arise from inferences that violate logic and that therefore would not be generated via the interpretation process that produces schema-consistent false memories. Insofar as autobiographical false memories are concerned, there might be memory schemas that correspond to some of these false memories, but surely not to others.

Schema theory also does not seem to provide a satisfactory explanation of reality-monitoring errors. It is true that the materials that have most often been used to investigate such errors have been connected narratives about situations for which memory schemas might be available (e.g., the story about washing clothes in Table 2-6). This is not a necessary precondition for reality-monitoring errors, though, as they can easily be produced by materials that would not activate memory schemas.

To illustrate, suppose that subjects study a long list of sentences of the following general form:

Nuj is hot.
Faw is tall.
Mep is black.
Lix is north.
Zad is happy.

Thus, each sentence on the list has a nonsense noun and a meaningful adjective that has a strong semantic associate (cold, short, white, south, sad, and so on). By virtue of the first property, there are no corresponding memory schemas for these sentences to activate. By virtue of the second property, specific unpresented words will come to mind as the sentences are studied. If a recognition test is administered on which some probes are presented adjectives (e.g., hot, tall), others are associates of presented adjectives (e.g., white, south), and others are unrelated unpresented adjectives (e.g., tired, fast), subjects will display the usual semantically consistent reality-monitoring errors (i.e., false-alarm rates will be higher for the second group of words than for the third).

The other two limitations of schema theory are in the nature of findings that seem to cast doubt upon the theory's basic perspective on false memory, the first being concerned with the relation between true and false memory and the other being concerned with developmental variability in false memory. Regarding the relation between true and false memory, schema theory, like constructivism, predicts some degree of dependency between true and false memory. If it is assumed, as schema theory (and constructivism) assumes, that true and false memories of a target experience are generated by the same integrated memory structure, it is apparent that on memory tests, responses that reflect true and false memory ought to be positively associated with each other, both within individual subjects and between experimental conditions. That is, subjects who are better able to form such integrated representations will necessarily exhibit higher levels of both true and false memory (positive correlations), and experimental conditions that make it easier to form these representations will necessarily yield higher levels of both (experimental associations). Although these are straightforward expectations of schema theory, each has often been disconfirmed in research. According to literature reviews on this point (Reyna & Brainerd, 1995a; Reyna & Lloyd, 1997), the standard patterns in the literature are that (a) true- and false-memory responses (e.g., hits and semantic false alarms on recognition tests) are uncorrelated; (b) several manipulations affect one type of response without affecting the other (single dissociations); and (c) still other manipulations actually have opposite effects on the two types of responses (double dissociations).

The Reyna and Kiernan (1994) study that was mentioned in chapter 2 is an example of research that produced all three of these patterns. Their subjects studied a series of short, three-sentence vignettes that should activate well-established spatial and linear-ordering schemas, and then the subjects responded to a recognition test on which the probes were studied sentences (e.g., The coffee is hotter than the tea; the tea is hotter than the cocoa), unpresented meaning-consistent sentences (e.g.,

The coffee is hotter than the cocoa), and unpresented meaning-violating sentences (e.g., The cocoa is hotter than the coffee). Subjects' tendency to correctly recognize presented sentences was uncorrelated with their tendency to falsely recognize unpresented meaning-consistent sentences (Pattern a). False-recognition levels for meaning-consistent sentences were higher for spatial vignettes than for linear-ordering vignettes, but correct-recognition rates for presented sentences were not affected by the spatial-linear manipulation (Pattern b). Age differences between subjects drove true- and false-memory performance in opposite directions (Pattern c): Older subjects had higher hit rates and lower false-alarm rates than did younger subjects.

The other finding that runs counter to schema theory concerns developmental trends. According to schema theory, a memory schema is a by-product of repeated experience with the corresponding situation, and thus, it takes time to develop. (Alba and Hasher [1983] provide an account of the mechanisms whereby memory schemas might be formed on the basis of repeated experience.) Generally speaking, therefore, a memory schema for a given situation (going to the movies, eating at a restaurant) is more apt to be available to adults than to children, and when it is available to both, it will be stronger and more likely to be activated in adults because they have more extensive experience with the target situation (Liben & Posnansky, 1977). Therefore, if false-memory responses are by-products of the activation of memory schemas, the overriding developmental trend, from the preschool years to early adulthood, should be a steady increase in such responses.

Age variability in false memory has been a topic of intense research in recent years, owing to concerns about false reports in legal cases involving child witnesses (see chapter 7), and the most common pattern of age variability is not what schema theory expects. In most instances, younger children have been found to be more vulnerable to false memories than have older children or adults. For example, this result has been obtained in many developmental studies of the eyewitness suggestibility paradigm (e.g., Bruck & Ceci, 1997; Ceci & Bruck, 1995). Likewise, it has been obtained in studies of false memory for semantic inferences (e.g., Reyna & Kiernan, 1994), false identification of suspects (e.g., Kassin, 2001), false memory for schema-consistent events (e.g., Pipe, Gee, Wilson, & Egerton, 1999; Poole & White, 1991), reality-monitoring errors (e.g., Ackerman, 1992, 1994), and false memory from illogical reasoning (e.g., Brainerd & Reyna, 1995). In studies of intrusions or false alarms following exposure to word lists, the predominant age trend has been the same—lower intrusion rates (e.g., Bjorklund & Muir, 1988) and lower false-alarm rates (e.g., Brainerd, Reyna, & Kneer, 1995) with increasing age. Similar developmental improvements are seen using the misinformation paradigm in which children are deliberately misled (e.g., Reyna, Holliday, & Marche, 2002). As our later discussion makes clear, however, memory development is not unidimensional (Reyna et al., in press).

The Source-Monitoring Framework

The source-monitoring framework (Johnson, Hashtroudi, & Lindsay, 1993) interprets false memories on analogy to reality-monitoring errors, using the more general concept of source-monitoring errors as its core explanatory mechanism. False memories are viewed as failures to accurately monitor the origin of the information that produces the memories. At bottom, false memories are seen as incorrect attributions about sources of information or as confusions about sources, and thus, all false memories have the partly-true-and-partly-false quality of reality-monitoring errors. The probity of this characterization outside the reality-monitoring sphere is most readily seen in the eyewitness suggestibility paradigm, which can be regarded as a variation on the reality-monitoring procedure in which falsely reported events have actually been experienced (rather than merely thought about). Recall that in eyewitness suggestibility, after subjects observe a series of events that might figure in a police investigation, further events are suggested to them during a simulated investigative interview (e.g., Did the car pass a stop sign or a yield sign?). On later memory tests, suggested events are falsely reported at substantial levels, and they are assigned confidence ratings that approximate those for true events. According to the source-monitoring framework, these false reports are source confusions (e.g., Lindsay & Johnson, 1989a). Subjects were in fact exposed to the events in question during the interview, and when they falsely report those events on a later test, they may simply be confused about where the memories came from (interview suggestion versus original experience). More specifically, the subjects may be confounding memories from a verbal source with memories from a visual source.

It is possible to conceptualize some other false-memory paradigms in much the same fashion. In false identification of suspects, for example, false identifications may be pursuant to suggestions that were given to witnesses after they observed culprits, and hence, witnesses may again be confounding a verbal source with a visual source. In other paradigms, subjects may be confusing internal with external sources, precisely as in the reality-monitoring paradigm, because the falsely reported information came to mind during the course of the target experience. This is a clear possibility with schema-consistent false memories inasmuch as the items that are part of memory schemas for familiar situations may come to mind without being encoded (e.g., one might think about eating a hot dog at a baseball game without actually doing so). Thinking about unpresented items is also a clear possibility with some of the examples of semantic intrusions and false alarms in list memory that were given in chapter 2: An unpresented animal name might intrude during free recall because it came to mind while studying several other animal names, or a strong semantic associate (e.g., white) might be falsely recognized because it came to mind when the subject studied the corresponding word (black).

Although the notion of source-monitoring errors can thus be extended to various types of false-memory responses, it cannot be extended to all. In many forms of false memory, falsely-remembered information has not been presented as a suggestion (which would set the stage for confusion between two external sources), and it cannot plausibly be assumed that falsely-remembered information would have come to mind during the course of the target experience (which would set the stage for confusion between internal and external sources). With respect to the former qualification, eyewitnesses exhibit the same false-memory effect (identifying innocent suspects whose general features overlap with culprits'), even when they have not received postevent suggestions. With respect to the latter qualification, in false memories from reasoning, it cannot reasonably be supposed that subjects would

THEORETICAL EXPLANATIONS OF FALSE MEMORY   69

spontaneously think of background information that is the opposite of information that they have just been given (e.g., 8 animals and 10 cows rather than 10 animals and 8 cows). The source-monitoring framework handles these latter situations by positing that subjects adopt a familiarity criterion rather than a source-monitoring criterion on memory tests (if it's familiar, I must have experienced it *externally*). Explicitly, subjects allow their recall or recognition performance to be guided by whether information is familiar to them in the present context, rather than by whether it was actually experienced. This is neither an illogical nor inappropriate approach to memory tests, of course, because items that were experienced will be familiar, but it will result in false recall and false recognition of items that preserve the gist of experience because the meanings of such items will necessarily be familiar. If adoption of a familiarity criterion rather than a source-monitoring criterion produces false-memory responses, it follows that instructing subjects to use source information on memory tests ought to reduce such responses (Lindsay & Johnson, 1989a; Zaragoza & Koshmide, 1989), as should instructions simply to emphasize accuracy rather than quantity in responding (Koriat & Goldsmith, 1996).

In sum, there are two senses in which false memories could be characterized as source-monitoring errors: failures to discriminate the sources of memories when a source criterion is being used on a memory test and failures to adopt a source criterion in the first place. The memory processes that are responsible for source monitoring are pivotal because without them, the source-monitoring framework would simply be a description of a useful cognitive skill. Importantly, the posited memory processes differ from constructivism and schema theory in that memory traces of the component events in a target experience are not assumed to be integrated into a single memory structure but, rather, are assumed to retain their individual identities. When making a source decision about an individual item on a memory test (e.g., Should I recall/recognize "white" or not?), information that is stored in many such traces is retrieved and processed by a *judgment operation*. The source of a particular memory is not stored as a specific feature that is directly accessed on memory tests. Instead, a source judgment is "the product of a decision process that involves evaluating the characteristics of memories" (Zaragoza, Lane, Ackil, & Chambers, 1997, p. 406). Source-monitoring decisions are therefore based upon the processing and interpretation via the judgment operation of multiple features that are stored in memory traces. When a source-monitoring error occurs, it may be because the memory traces that are retrieved in connection with the falsely reported item share many features with items that were actually experienced, or because subjects fail to retrieve memory traces that contain sufficient information to accurately specify the item's source. The general notion of a judgment operation that processes and interprets multiple features of stored memories also figures centrally in Schacter's constructive memory framework (Schacter, Norman, & Koutstaal, 1998; see below).

The judgment operation that processes retrieved memory traces is affected by two principal variables: (a) whether a memory test specifically encourages subjects to retrieve information that is pertinent to making source judgments (or whether, instead, it allows them to resort to more lax familiarity retrieval), and (b) whether retrieved memory traces contain the types of information that accurately identify the source. These two variables, in turn, are influenced by numerous contextual factors, such as the cognitive operations that were performed during the course of the target experience, whether retrieved memory traces provoke vivid imagery, subjects' background knowledge about the types of information that specify the source, subjects' reporting biases, the length of the delay between the target experience and the memory tests, whether retrieved memory traces provoke emotions, and the types of metamemorial assumptions that subjects make (Johnson et al., 1993).

An exegesis of evidence bearing on this theoretical explanation of false memory appears in prior articles by one of this book's authors (Reyna, 2000a; Reyna & Lloyd, 1997). It turns out that there are both theoretical and empirical challenges to the explanation. On the theoretical side, there is a problem of potential incompleteness arising from the fact that not all false memories are source errors per se, either in the sense of failure to discriminate between different external sources or in the sense of failure to discriminate between external and internal sources (Schacter, Israel, & Racine, 1999). Many false memories can be conceptualized as pure familiarity errors, not source discrimination errors, as when an eyewitness falsely identifies a mug shot of a Hispanic male or a subject in a semantic-inference experiment falsely accepts an unpresented sentence that coheres with the meanings of presented sentences because, in both instances, the falsely recognized item seems familiar on the basis of information that was stored during the target experience. Consequently, although the source-monitoring framework provides a characterization of the memory processes that are responsible for erroneous source decisions, a similar characterization of the memory processes that are responsible for familiarity errors is demanded for completeness. This matter is taken up in the next section.

On the empirical side, there are some findings about false memory that seem to run counter to the assumptions of the source-monitoring framework (Reyna, 2000a; Reyna & Lloyd, 1997). We discuss two in depth by way of illustration, followed by more cursory treatment of an additional four findings. The first concerns the aforementioned findings of statistical independence and experimental dissociation between true- and false-memory responses. The source-monitoring framework, like constructivism and schema theory, is a one-memory explanation of false memory, for example, in that all of the stored information that is retrieved to make source decisions is funneled through a single judgment operation, which is then responsible for true and false recall/recognition. Generally speaking, the more memory support that is in storage for an item, regardless of whether that item is true or false, and the more memory support that can be retrieved for an item, regardless of whether that item is true or false, the more likely is the judgment operation to classify it as having been part of the target experience. Again, like constructivism and schema theory, this leads to predictions of positive correlations between true- and false-memory responses and of positive experimental associations between them. But as we discussed in connection with schema theory, standard results in the literature are a lack of positive correlation between true- and false-memory responses, manipulations that singly dissociate the two types of responses, and manipulations that doubly dissociate them. More detailed illustrations of these results will be presented in chapter 4.

The other illustrative finding deals with the types of experimental conditions that should, in theory, make it easier for subjects to arrive at accurate source judgments about nonexperienced false-but-gist-consistent items. As the key property that differentiates such items from true ones is that they were not part of the target experience, the memory information that is most diagnostic in making accurate source judgments about them are surface cues that accompanied the experience (e.g., presentation modality, physical features of the experimental room, physical characteristics of the experimenter, or any extraneous contextual cues, for example, sights and sounds, that were present). If correct source judgments are to be made about nonexperienced false-but-gist-consistent items, it is crucial that on memory tests, these items do not provoke the retrieval of memories of such surface information, *which would make it seem as though those items were part of the target experience.* Because the relevant surface information was encoded in connection with true items but not false ones, the baseline tendency to retrieve it on memory tests will naturally be higher for true items, but beyond this, the accuracy of source judgments should be increased by manipulations that suppress the tendency of false items to access such information. The types of manipulations that ought to have this effect are specified by the well-known *encoding variability principle* (Tulving & Thomson, 1971), according to which the level of the match between information that was encoded during a target experience and information that is present in retrieval cues determines whether that information will be accessed—the stronger the match, the more likely that the encoded information will be accessed. In general, then, reducing the amount of overlap between surface cues that were present during the target experience and surface cues that are present on memory tests (e.g., administering the target experience and the memory test in different modalities, arranging for the target experience and the memory test to occur in different rooms) will reduce the tendency of false items to access memories of such information, thereby reducing the incidence of false-memory responses. However, studies in which the level of the match between surface features of target experiences and memory tests has been manipulated have failed to confirm this prediction. The opposite pattern has been obtained: In experiments in which the target materials consisted of such things as word lists, picture lists, sentences, narratives, and autobiographical events, manipulations that decreased the surface resemblance between target experiences and memory tests were often found to *increase* false-memory responses (e.g., Bernstein, Whittlesea, & Loftus, 2002; Brainerd et al., 1995; Brainerd & Mojardin, 1998; Chandler & Gargano, 1995; Dodhia & Metcalfe, 1999; Gallo, McDermott, Percer, & Roediger, 2001; Hunt & McDaniel, 1993; Israel & Schacter, 1997; Schacter et al., 1999; see chapter 4 for further details).

In-depth analyses of evidence bearing on this theoretical explanation of false memory yield the following results, some of which figure in chapters 4 and 5 (Reyna, 2000a; Reyna & Lloyd, 1997). In particular, Reyna also summarized important examples of nonsupportive evidence concerning (a) mere-memory testing, (b) false-memory persistence, (c) repeated cuing, and (d) contradiction. With respect to the first category of effects, mere-memory testing, it has been found that simply administering a memory test that contains unpresented material as well as presented material to subjects can increase false memory for the former on subsequent memory tests. Reyna pointed out that the source-monitoring framework explains this inflation of false memory by assuming that on the later tests, subjects confuse the source of the unpresented material with that of the presented material (i.e., they assume that unpresented material was part of the original presented material when, in fact, it only appeared on the memory test). She observed that under this explanation, false memory ought to be higher for *any* type of unpresented material that appeared on an earlier test but that, in fact, it has usually been found that it is only higher when unpresented material is closely related to presented material (e.g., the two share meaning). With respect to the second category of effects, false-memory persistence, the source-monitoring framework expects that false-memory responses will be less consistent over time than true-memory responses because the source information on which judgments are based is obviously more reliable and stable for true-memory responses than for false-memory responses. However, Reyna noted that most studies have found the opposite pattern for false events that preserve the meaning of true events (e.g., for words such as ANIMAL when words such as DOG, COW, and HORSE were presented).

Turning to the remaining categories of nonsupportive evidence that were discussed by Reyna (2000a) and Reyna and Lloyd (1997), repeated cuing refers to situations in which subjects are repeatedly encouraged to draw inferences that are later measured as false memories. For instance, in the story in Table 2-6, which encourages the the inference that the central character's clothes dryer is broken, suppose that instead of reading one story, subjects read three stories that imply this same inference. How should this affect their tendency to falsely remember that inference as having actually been presented in the story (the reality-monitoring probe at the bottom of Table 2-6)? According to the source-monitoring framework, false memory for the inference should decrease because memories of the relevant cognitive operations are generated each time the inference is cued, providing more memory information that the judgment operation can use for accurate reality monitoring. In fact, however, as Reyna pointed out, repeated cuing increases rather than decreases false-memory responses. Finally, concerning contradiction effects, contradiction is a variant of repeated cuing in which subjects are presented with different versions of the same events that imply contradictory inferences. For instance, imagine that subjects are exposed to two versions of the story in Table 2-6: For half of the subjects, both stories imply that the cloths dryer is broken, whereas for the other half, one story implies that the cloths dryer is broken and the other implies that it is working. The source-monitoring framework expects that source discrimination should be better, and therefore the tendency to falsely remember the statement that the cloths dryer was broken should be lower when the stories are inconsistent, because the memories on which source discriminations are based will necessarily be more distinctive. In contrast, Reyna discussed research which not only revealed higher levels of false memory for inferences that were inconsistently implied but also showed that false memory was higher in conditions in which subjects showed *better* source discrimination than in conditions in which they showed poorer source discrimination.

Dual-Process Theories of True Memory

The opponent-processes view of false memory, which is considered in the final section of this chapter, evolved from a perspective on true memory that became prominent during the last decade of the 20th century. Specifically, this perspective, the *dual-process approach*, promulgates some theoretical distinctions that also figure in the opponent-processes view of false memory. Hence, although the material in this section deals with explanations of true-memory responses, it is an essential prologue to contemporary explanations of false-memory responses.

Although the popularity of the dual-process approach is a relatively recent phenomenon (Clark & Gronlund, 1996), its core distinctions can be traced to empirical observations that were made decades ago by Strong (1913). Strong's research program focused on the role of memory in consumer product choice—explicitly, on people's ability to recognize information that had been previously presented as part of product advertisements. However, the experiments that yielded the observations that are of chief interest to us were standard word-recognition studies in which subjects read a word list and, following a mental arithmetic task, responded to a recognition test composed of presented and unpresented words. An interesting feature of the study phase of Strong's experiments is that his subjects were instructed to read words at a rapid pace, focusing on the meaning of each and not paying attention to relations between them (a feature to which we will be referring as a deep-processing instruction in chapter 4). After studying a list, subjects responded to the test and also introspected on the mental experiences that were provoked by words that were recognized as having been on the study list. Upon review of his subjects' introspective reports, Strong concluded that word recognition was accompanied by two distinct varieties of mental experience, the first vague and global and the second clear and specific:

> Recognitions are made: 1. When the word was recognized by itself without any other associations of any sort coming to mind. For example, "tarry [a list word]—I know it was there" (A) [a subject in the experiment], or "period [another list word]—I know it was in the list" (D) [another subject]. . . . Many words with such introspections were wrong, they had not been seen in the exposure lists. . . . 2. Recognitions were made when at sight of the word in the second [test] list an association with it came to consciousness. The association was then recognized as having been met with before— very often directly connected with the exposure list—and then the word was identified as having been in the exposure list. Generally speaking, as soon as the association came to mind the subject was sure of the recognition. (Strong, 1913, p. 368)

In the dual-process approach to true memory, Strong's first form of recognition is usually called *familiarity* and his second form is usually called *recollection*. Contemporary dual-process theories revolve around this distinction between remembering that is accompanied by vague, global feelings that an item must have been part of a target experience versus remembering that is accompanied by the vivid reinstatement of specific events that occurred when the item appeared during a target experience. There are two classes of such theories: *recognition* theories and *recall* theories. We consider examples of recognition theories first, followed by examples of recall theories.

Dual-Process Theories of Recognition

Dual-process theories have been far more prevalent in the study of recognition than in the study of recall. One reason for this imbalance is that in some early articles on recognition, such as an important article by Mandler (1980), it was proposed that recall always involves the recollective form of remembering and that recall data can therefore be treated as pure measures of recollection. Because dual-process distinctions have now become entrenched in recognition research, there are multiple theories of this sort in the recognition literature, many of which have been reviewed by Yonelinas (2002). Below, we outline the most influential of these theories and sketch key experimental findings that have been taken to support dual-process distinctions.

The classical account of recognition performance was provided in signal-detection theory (Green & Swets, 1966; Macmillan & Creelman, 1991), according to which target hits are due to a single retrieval process called familiarity, which accesses a continuous memory-strength scale. To make recognition decisions, subjects were assumed to set a subjective strength criterion and then to accept (as old) any probe whose strength fell above that criterion. Further, the memory strengths of presented targets and unpresented distractors were assumed to form Gaussian distributions, with the mean of target distributions being higher on average than the mean of distractor distributions (because targets are presented and distractors are not). Dual-process theories are the major alternative to this one-process familiarity conception, with the three major examples being theories that were developed by Atkinson and associates (Atkinson & Juola, 1973, 1974; Atkinson & Wescourt, 1975; Juola, Fischler, Wood, & Atkinson, 1971), by Mandler and associates (Mandler, 1980; Graf & Mandler, 1984; Graf, Squire, & Mandler, 1984), and by Jacoby (1991, 1996). Each of these theories was formulated for standard word-recognition experiments in which subjects study a list and then respond to a yes-no test on which some words are previously presented targets and the rest are unpresented distractors. These experiments are *not* false-memory designs because the test lists do not include distractors that preserve salient features of targets (and provoke high false-alarm rates), and hence, the theories were only intended to account for a form of true memory (hits to targets).

The Atkinson Theory

Atkinson and associates proposed that when words are presented for study, they activate nodes in a lexical store that contains entries for individual words (called *p* codes), but they are also stored as a list structure in a separate event-knowledge archive (called *c* codes). On a recognition test, performance is said to be governed by two processes, a faster familiarity operation, which was assumed to be well described by signal-detection theory, and a slower list-search operation, which was not. First, subjects evaluate the global familiarity of test probes using two subjective criteria, a high one (definitely a target) and a low one (definitely a distractor). They accept (as old) or reject (as new) each probe, accordingly, as the familiarity evidence that accumulates from memory exceeds the high criterion or falls below the low criterion. However, familiarity evaluation may deliver an indeterminate value that falls between the two criteria, so that a recognition decision cannot be made. When this happens, the slower back-up operation, recollection, is engaged. It searches the event store to determine if the probe in question can be found in the list structure. The probe is accepted if it is found. If it is not found, memory evidence is inconclusive, and the subject must respond by guessing or resorting to some form of response bias.

The Mandler Theory

Mandler and associates preserved the idea of two retrieval processes, a faster one that evaluates a probe's global familiarity and a slower, item-specific recollection operation, as well as the idea that the two processes are based upon different forms of learning that occur when a target is studied. However, the posited forms of learning are different, as is the posited relation between the two processes.

Concerning Mandler's distinctions about learning, one form, which serves as the basis for familiarity, is perceptual and involves *intra*-item integration of a target's perceptual features. The other form, which serves as the basis for recollection, is conceptual and involves *inter*-item elaborations that relate a target to the study context or to other targets on the list (e.g., noting that the targets *dog*, *cow*, and *horse* are all animals). Thus, global-familiarity evaluation involves assessing a probe's level of perceptual integration in memory, while item-specific recollection involves retrieving elaborations that were generated during study. However, Mandler's assumptions about the on-line relation between recollection and familiarity are perhaps the most important contribution of his theory. In the Atkinson theory, recollection is conditional on familiarity in that the recollection operation is not engaged unless the familiarity evaluation is inconclusive. In contrast, Mandler proposed that although familiarity evaluation is faster than recollection, "the two separate processes occur conjointly; recognition involves the additive effects of familiarity and retrieval [recollection]" (1980, p. 253). Mandler captures this key assumption in the equation

$$p(H) = F + R - RF \qquad (1)$$

where $p(H)$ is the probability of a hit, F is the probability that a hit is due to familiarity evaluation, and R is the probability that a hit is due to recollection. As the two processes are assumed to function independently, Mandler's version of the recollection-familiarity distinction predicts single and double dissociations between the processes.

The Jacoby Theory

Jacoby preserved Atkinson and associates' notion of a faster familiarity operation and a slower recollection operation, and he also preserved Mandler's assumption that the two function independently during recognition. However, he made important conceptual and methodological additions to these core ideas. Conceptually, although recollection is again assumed to involve retrieval of study-phase contextual cues and elaborations, Jacoby proposed that familiarity evaluation involves an assessment of the fluency with which a probe is processed on a recognition test. This is a noteworthy refinement because processing fluency can be grounded in factors other than whether a probe appeared on the study list. For instance, although the appearance of a word on a study list increases later processing fluency, processing will be more fluent (easier, faster) for distractors that are common words (e.g., *football*, *bathtub*) than for distractors that are uncommon words (e.g., *lachrymose*, *derivative*). Also on the conceptual side, the Jacoby theory stresses that familiarity is an automatic process that is not amenable to conscious control, whereas recollection is an effortful process that is under conscious control.

The second contribution of the Jacoby theory is methodological. Equation 1 specifies that recollection and familiarity make independent contributions to hit rates, which leads to predictions of dissociations between them. Such predictions are untestable, however, unless independent estimates of recollection and familiarity can be extracted from the data of individual experiments. By itself, Equation 1 is inadequate for this purpose because it contains two unknown quantities, R and F, and only one known quantity that can be estimated from data, $p(H)$. Algebraically, at least one more equation containing the same two unknown quantities (and no new ones) but a different known quantity is needed to obtain independent estimates of recollection and familiarity. Jacoby (1991) solved this problem with an experimental procedure called the *process-dissociation paradigm*. Subjects first study a list of words, with individual items being presented in two distinct ways. For example, subjects might read a column of printed words, half of which are reproduced normally and half of which are reproduced as anagrams that must be unscrambled before the words can be read. Subjects then respond to a normal test list, but they do so under two different sets of instructions. Those who respond under *inclusion* instructions are told to accept all targets that appeared on the study list and to reject all distractors. However, subjects who respond under *exclusion* instructions are told to accept only targets that were printed normally and to reject both distractors and anagram targets (or, alternatively, to accept only anagram targets and reject all other probes).

When data for both instructional conditions are available, recollection and familiarity can be separately estimated using the equation for false alarms for to-be-excluded targets in the exclusion condition plus the equation for hits to the same targets in the inclusion condition. The latter equation is

$$p_I(H) = F + R - RF \tag{2}$$

which is the same as Mandler's (1980) expression. The equation for false alarms for to-be-excluded targets in the exclusion condition is

$$p_E(FA) = (1 - R)F \tag{3}$$

which specifies that such targets will be mistakenly accepted only if the familiarity value is high enough to indicate that the probe is a target but its specific presentation on the study list cannot be recollected. Estimates of recollection and familiarity are then obtained by solving these equations for the two unknown quantities:

$$R = p_I(H) - p_E(FA) \tag{4}$$

and

$$F = p_E(FA) \div (1 - R) \tag{5}$$

Evidence: Dissociations Between Recollection and Familiarity.   Experimental dissociations between recollection and familiarity have been thought to provide especially compelling support for the hypothesis that two distinct retrieval processes are operating in recognition. Considerable evidence of single dissociations has accumulated from experiments that have relied upon Jacoby's (1991) process-dissociation methodology. Remember, here, that single dissociations refer to situations in which some manipulation affects one variable—in this instance, R or F—without affecting another variable. Manipulations have been reported in several experiments to which R reacted but F did not. The most extensive results are for a study-phase manipulation: full versus divided attention. Subjects who study word lists under full attention simply read the words as they appear on a computer screen. Subjects who study word lists under divided attention read the words as they appear on a computer screen, but they simultaneously monitor a stream of unrelated auditory material (e.g., digit strings). A consistent finding has been that R values are larger in full-attention conditions than in divided-attention conditions, but that F values are equivalent (Jacoby, 1991, 1996). Other illustrative manipulations that produce the same single dissociation are semantic versus nonsemantic study instructions (Yonelinas, Regehr, & Jacoby, 1995) and studying words that are frequent in the lexicon versus those that are infrequent (Yonelinas et al., 1995).

Converging evidence of recollection-familiarity dissociations has been reported using a different methodology, which was originally devised by Tulving (1985). This procedure, which is reminiscent of Strong's (1913) research, requires that subjects make introspective reports, called *remember* judgments and *know* judgments, about subjective experiences that accompany the acceptance of recognition probes. Subjects study a word list and then respond to the usual yes-no probes. However, they are asked to provide follow-up information about *accepted* probes. In particular, they are told to make a remember judgment for an accepted probe if it provoked mental reinstatement of specific experiences that accompanied its presentation during the study phase, and they are told to make a know judgment if it failed to provoke such mental reinstatement but they were nevertheless sure that it was on the study list. Detailed instructions for making remember and know judgments, which are derived from an article by Rajaram (1996), are shown in Table 3-1. Note the parallels between the mental experiences that are described in these instructions and the introspective reports of Strong's (1913) subjects.

In this second methodology, the proportion of accepted targets that is classified as remember provides the estimate of recollection and the proportion of accepted targets that is classified as know provides the estimate of familiarity. Remember/know experiments, like process-dissociation experiments, have yielded extensive evidence of experimental dissociations in which recollection is affected but familiarity is not (for a review, see Gardiner & Java, 1991). Among the manipulations that produce this pattern are semantic versus nonsemantic study instructions and instructions to rehearse versus not to rehearse words as they are studied. Importantly, studying words under full versus divided attention (e.g., Gardiner & Parkin, 1990) and studying frequent versus infrequent words (e.g., Gardiner & Java, 1990) produce the same dissociative pattern in remember/know experiments as in process-dissociation experiments. In addition, remember/know experiments have identified

Table 3-1. Instructions for Making Remember and Know Judgments
About Recognition Probes

Judgment	Instructions
Remember	If your recognition of the item is accompanied by a conscious recollection of its prior occurrence in the study list, then write R. "Remember" is the ability to become consciously aware of some aspect or aspects of what happened or what was experienced at the time the word was presented (e.g., aspects of the physical appearance of the word, or something that happened in the room, or what you were thinking or doing at the time). In other words, the "remembered" word should bring back to mind a particular association, image, or something more personal from the time of study or something about its appearance or position (e.g., what came before or after that word).
Know	"Know" responses should be made when you recognize that the word was in the study list, but you cannot consciously recollect anything about its actual occurrence, or what happened, or what was experienced at the time of its occurrence. In other words, write K (for know) when you are certain of recognizing the words but these words fail to evoke any specific recollection from the study list.

Note. From Rajaram (1996).

manipulations that produce double dissociations between recollection and familiarity (i.e., both processes are affected but in opposite ways). Two manipulations that yield this latter type of dissociation are studying meaningful words versus nonsense words (e.g., Gardiner & Java, 1990) and chronological age (elderly adults produce fewer remember judgments but more know judgments than do young adults [e.g., Gardiner & Java, 1991]).

It might seem remarkable, at first glance, that such dissimilar ways of estimating recollection and familiarity, one based upon a mathematical model of retrieval and the other based upon introspective reports of remembering phenomenology, would yield similar patterns of dissociation. However, independent results from other experiments suggest that despite their methodological differences, the two procedures probably measure similar things. In those experiments, levels of recollection and familiarity for the same study lists were estimated using both the process-dissociation procedure and remember/know judgments (Jacoby, Debner, & Hay, 2001; Yonelinas, Kroll, Dobbins, Lazzara, & Knight, 1998). Surprisingly, the two sets of estimates have been in close agreement.

Dual-Process Theories of Recall

The use of dual-process distinctions has been less common in studies of recall, and as mentioned, it has been proposed by some that recall necessarily involves recollective retrieval, largely because subjects must generate specific items for output on their own. Lately, however, dual-process treatments of particular recall tasks have begun to appear (for a review, see Bellezza, 2003). There have been two types of dual-process treatments of recall, which we consider below. One is for recall tasks that resemble recognition in that output items are only partially generated by subjects. The other is for pure recall tasks in which output items must be entirely generated by subjects.

Recognition-Like Recall

Stem completion and *fragment completion* are recall tests that provide a part of each target as a cue, and subjects must fill in the rest of it. Subjects study a word list and then they respond to probes consisting of letter strings in which the first few letters of targets have been omitted (stem completion) or to probes consisting of letter strings in which blanks and letters are interspersed (fragment completion). To illustrate, suppose that the word *locked* appeared on the study list. On a stem-completion test, the probe for this target might be __*ked*. On a fragment completion test, the probe for this same target might be __*o__ked*. Note that although *locked* was studied, the stem and the fragment could also be completed with other common words that were not studied (e.g., *docked, hocked, rocked, socked*).

Jacoby, Toth, and Yonelinas (1993) proposed that the recollection-familiarity account of recognition can be extended to these particular recall tasks. Experimentally, such an extension is made rather seamless by the fact that it is easy to use the process-dissociation procedure with stem and fragment completion. Stems and fragments can be completed with words that were not studied, and consequently, the two types of tests can be performed under inclusion or exclusion instructions that parallel those for recognition. After studying a word list, inclusion subjects are told to complete stems and fragments with the first word that comes to mind that will fit (i.e., if *locked* is a target, *locked, rocked*, and *socked* are equally acceptable completions of __*ked* and __*o__ked*). The term $p_I(H)$ in Equation 2 then becomes the probability of completing stems or fragments with the *studied* word. Exclusion subjects are told to complete stems and fragments only with words that were *not* studied (i.e., *rocked* and *socked* are acceptable completions but *locked* is not). The term $p_E(H)$ in Equation 3 therefore becomes the probability of incorrectly completing stems or fragments with studied rather than unstudied words.

Several experiments have been reported using the process-dissociation procedure to estimate R and F for stem and fragment completion. These experiments, like recognition studies, have identified several manipulations that produce single dissociations between recollection and familiarity, thereby suggesting that separate retrieval processes are operating in recall as well as in recognition. For instance, the full- versus divided-attention manipulation produces the same dissociative pattern as in recognition (i.e., R reacts but F does not; see Jacoby, 1996; Jacoby et al., 1993). Other manipulations that yield the same pattern as in recognition include the presentation rate of the study list (Curran and Hintzman, 1995; Hay & Jacoby, 1996) and the amount of time that subjects are given to respond to test probes (Hay & Jacoby, 1996).

Pure Recall

By *pure recall*, we mean tasks on which each output item is fully controlled by the subject. The most common tasks of this sort are free recall, associative recall, and cued recall. In *free recall*, subjects study a list of unrelated (or, sometimes, related) words and then simply speak or write as many of them as they can remember, in any order. In *associative recall*, subjects study a series of unique cue-target pairs (e.g., *paper-speaker*, *photograph-cement*, *trumpet-hydrogen*) and then attempt to speak or write each target when its corresponding cue is presented as a prompt (e.g., *paper-?*, *photograph-?*, *trumpet-?*). In *cued recall*, subjects study a list composed of subsets of related words (e.g., the example in Table 2-1 of a list of five color names, five animal names, and five furniture names) and then attempt to recall as many items as possible in each subset when its label is presented as a retrieval cue (e.g., "recall all the color names that you can remember," "recall all the animal names that you can remember," "recall all the furniture names that you can re-member"). With tasks such as these, subjects lack even partial information about the to-be-recalled items, and it is therefore difficult to fathom how a retrieval operation such as familiarity, which evaluates global familiarity but does not generate item-specific information, could produce successful performance by itself. Consequently, a different sort of dual-process theory, one in which both operations can meet the more complex demands of pure recall, seems to be in order.

A few years back, such a theory was formulated to explain a puzzling collection of phenomena in free recall: cognitive triage effects. Cognitive triage effects are concerned with relations between a target's recall *difficulty*, which is measured by the errors that subjects make on recall tests, and a target's recall *order*, which is merely the position in which it is recalled during a free-recall test. The common-sense view is that output order ought to be a monotonic function of a target's difficulty; the easier the item, the sooner it should come to mind and be recalled. How-ever, evidence against this prediction was obtained in the 1960s in some experiments by Battig (1965; Battig, Allen, & Jensen, 1965). Battig's subjects studied a word list, responded to a free-recall test, studied the list again, and responded to a sec-ond free-recall test. The prediction was then tested by computing the mean output positions of words that were recalled on Test 2 for two different types of words: easy (items that had also been recalled on Test 1) and hard (items that had not been recalled on Test 1). The result, which proved to be a typical one in such experi-ments, is shown in Figure 3-2, from which it is apparent that easier words are not recalled first but that, on the contrary, harder words are recalled first. Many years later, we replicated Battig's finding, but we also investigated the relation between recall order and target difficulty when the latter was treated as a continuous vari-able rather than as two categories (Brainerd, Reyna, Howe, & Kevershan, 1990, 1991). To do that, our experiments were criterion designs: Individual subjects stud-ied and recalled a list however many times was necessary for their recall to be er-rorless. Then, we plotted the order in which words were recalled on the final (er-rorless) recall test as a function of their overall difficulty on all prior tests, using total previous errors or the total number of trials that were required to produce er-rorless recall as difficulty measures. The pattern that emerged from these experi-ments is shown in Figure 3-3, which is based on data reported by Brainerd, Reyna, Harnishfeger, and Howe (1993), where it can be seen that the recall order–recall difficulty relation was U-shaped: The hardest words were output at the beginning and end of a free-recall test, and the easiest words were output in the middle.

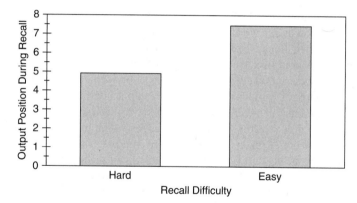

Figure 3-2. Mean output position of words on Test 2 of a free-recall experiment as a function of word difficulty. Easy words were those recalled on Test 1, while hard words were recalled only on Test 2. The plotted data are from Brainerd, Reyna, Harnishfeger, and Howe (1993).

We shall see in chapter 4 that U-shaped curves relating false memory to various experimental manipulations have become central to theoretical interpretation because such curves are diagnostic of opponent processes. For the present, however, our concern lies with the explanation of the patterns in Figures 3-2 and 3-3, which rely on a distinction between direct access to verbatim traces of targets' presentation on study trials versus reconstructive processing of their meaning (Reyna & Brainerd, 1995a). The first of these retrieval operations, *direct access*, is thought to be the more accurate of the two (i.e., to be more likely to produce output of a studied word) and to predominate at the start of a free-recall test. When verbatim traces

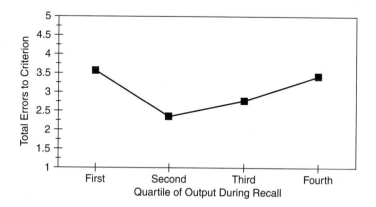

Figure 3-3. Relation among the output positions of words on criterion (errorless) tests of a free-recall experiment as a function of the words' overall difficulty on prior tests. Output position is the quartile (first, second, third, fourth) of a criterion free-recall test in which a word was recalled, and its difficulty was rated according to the total number of errors that it produced on previous trials. The plotted data are from Brainerd et al. (1993).

of target presentations are accessed, subjects can recall words by merely reading, surface information as it echoes in the mind's ear or flashes in the mind's eye, just as actors recite their lines when they are whispered by a prompter or seen on cue cards. Because readout of surface information from consciousness is all that is involved, direct access produces recall that is fast, confident, and virtually errorless. However, this form of retrieval is sensitive to output interference, which accumulates during the course of recall, so that the number of targets that can be recalled in this fashion is maximized by retrieving weaker verbatim traces (more interference-sensitive) before stronger ones (less interference-sensitive). While direct access is under way at the start of recall, then, the recall difficulty–recall order relation will be harder to easier. The second retrieval operation, *reconstruction*, which is less sensitive to accumulating interference, becomes more prominent as free recall proceeds. This operation, which is slower and less accurate, *regenerates* targets by processing gist traces of the meaning content of studied lists. Because meaning content is not unique to individual targets, reconstructive retrieval will sometimes generate candidate items that were not on the list (e.g., if *blue* were on the list, reconstruction might generate *blue*, *red*, *color*, and *sad* as candidates). For this reason, subjects must submit candidate items to further metacognitive processing to decide whether they are confident enough that items were studied to be willing to output them. A large amount of work on the production of category exemplars suggests that gist traces of meaning content, unlike verbatim traces of presentation events, are accessed in a stronger-to-weaker order (e.g., Battig & Montague, 1969). Thus, the overall pattern in Figure 3-2 follows from the hypothesis that more targets are recalled via the direct-access operation (traces accessed in harder-to-easier order) than via the reconstruction operation, and the pattern in Figure 3-3 follows from the hypothesis that direct access (weaker-to-stronger access) predominates at the start, but reconstruction (stronger-to-weaker access) predominates subsequently.

Recent experimentation on this dual-process model has produced evidence of experimental dissociations between measures of direct access and reconstruction, suggesting that separate retrieval processes are indeed operating in pure recall as well as in recognition-like recall (e.g., Barnhardt, Choi, Gerkens, Corbisier, Smith, 2004; Brainerd, Wright, Reyna, and Payne, 2002). To illustrate, a series of experiments reported by Brainerd et al., (2002) yielded both single and double dissociations. Concerning single dissociations, providing category labels as retrieval cues, after subjects had studied a list composed of words from a few familiar categories, increased reconstruction without affecting direct access, while interfering with subjects' normal mode of reading words during the study phase decreased direct access without affecting reconstruction. Concerning double dissociations, having subjects study lists in which the words induced vivid mental imagery simultaneously increased direct access and reduced reconstruction.

Dual-Process Explanations of False Memory

We conclude this chapter by considering examples of contemporary theories that explain false-memory phenomena by extending dual-process distinctions to false recognition and false recall. We begin with *fuzzy-trace theory*, an account of false memory that uses some expanded dual-process ideas to explain all of the standard phenomena in chapter 2. Although this theory has other key properties, the core idea is that false-memory responses are affected by memory mechanisms that operate in opposition to each other. This idea stands in contrast to the assumption in dual-process theories of true memory that recollection and familiarity reinforce each other to support recognition of targets and that direct access and reconstruction reinforce each other to support recall of targets. After considering this opponent-processes model, we then consider two other theories that have been developed to account for false-memory data that are produced by the Deese-Roediger-McDermott (DRM) word-list procedure (Deese, 1959; Roediger & McDermott, 2000; see Table 2-2).

Opponent Processes in False Memory: Fuzzy-Trace Theory

Fuzzy-trace theory first evolved as a model of reasoning and decision making, rather than as an explanation of false memory (Brainerd & Reyna, 2001a, 2002a; Reyna, 1995; Reyna & Brainerd, 1995a). This theory was originally motivated by two considerations. The first was how semantic effects in psycholinguistics relate to memory processes (e.g., Reyna, 1981). The second was an accumulation of counterintuitive findings on a question whose answer had long seemed self-evident to researchers: How is memory development related to the development of specific reasoning abilities, such as Piaget's familiar logical-reasoning problems? Up until the mid-1980s, there were two conventional answers to this latter question. The initial one had been given by Piaget himself (1970a; see also Elkind, 1967; Smedslund, 1969), and it also could be found in the information-processing models of cognition that were influential in that era (e.g., Bryant & Trabasso, 1971; Trabasso, 1977). This answer, the *necessity hypothesis*, stipulates that retention of veridical representations of problem information (e.g., the numerical values of sets in class-inclusion or probability-judgment problems) until the appropriate reasoning operations can be executed is a necessary-but-not-sufficient condition for valid reasoning—hence, "necessity" hypothesis. The subsequent answer was given in the constructivism of Bransford and Franks (1971) and in some of Piaget's later work (Piaget, 1968; Piaget & Inhelder, 1973). As we saw earlier, constructivism posits that memory representations of problem information are not veridical in any authentic sense but, rather, are altered (constructed) by the same reasoning operations that are used in problem solving.

Unless necessity and constructivism are qualified by ad hoc assumptions, both predict strong positive relations between children's ability to solve specific reasoning problems and their ability to remember the specific background facts that authorize those solutions, albeit for different reasons. Even with post hoc assumptions, both predict significant positive relations (Reyna, 1996b; Reyna & Kiernan, 1994, 1995). To evaluate this prediction, several experiments were conducted in the late 1980s in which the relations between children's solutions of standard reasoning problems, such as class inclusion, conservation, probability judgment, and transitive inference, and their ability to recognize or recall the background facts on these same problems were assessed (e.g., Brainerd & Kingma, 1985; Brainerd & Reyna,

1988). With few exceptions, the results ran counter to prediction. For instance, across several studies of children's performance on transitive-inference problems, the ability to remember the premises upon which transitive inferences are based (e.g., John is taller than Jim; Jim is taller than Don; Don is taller than Sam) and the ability to make the relevant inferences (e.g., Jim is taller than Sam) were statistically independent. Children who could remember the premises were no better and no worse at making transitive inferences than children who could not remember them (Chapman & Lindenberger, 1992; Rabinowitz, Grant, Howe, & Walsh, 1994; Reyna & Brainerd, 1990). These results for transitive inference were not aberrations because other reasoning problems produced similar memory-reasoning independence, in adults as well as in children (Hastie & Park, 1986; Reyna & Brainerd, 1991).

In the course of these experiments, a theoretical account of memory-reasoning relations, fuzzy-trace theory, evolved that emphasized dissociated storage and retrieval operations, with certain operations supporting reasoning itself and others supporting memory for presented information that is determinative in reasoning (Brainerd & Reyna, 1990a; Reyna & Brainerd, 1990). As studies of false memory began to multiply in the mid-1990s, the assumptions that had been used to explain memory-reasoning relations were refined and applied to false-memory phenomena (e.g., Brainerd & Gordon, 1994; Reyna, 1992, 1995; Reyna & Kiernan, 1994). The nature of that explanation occupies the remainder of this subsection.

Currently, fuzzy-trace theory relies on five principles to effect explanations: (a) parallel storage of verbatim and gist traces; (b) dissociated retrieval of verbatim and gist traces; (c) opponent judgments about false-memory items; (d) different time courses of verbatim and gist memory; and (e) developmental variability. The theory also makes new predictions about false memory, some of them counterintuitive, on the basis of these principles (Ceci & Bruck, 1998; Seamon, Luo, Schwartz, Jones, Lee, & Jones, 2002; Seamon, Schlegel, Hiester, Landau, & Blumenthal, 2002), but this matter will be taken up in chapter 4. For now, we confine our attention to summarizing the five principles.

Parallel Storage of Verbatim and Gist Traces

Evidence from a variety of sources, some of which was discussed in connection with constructivism and schema theory, points to the conclusion that subjects deposit and preserve separate verbatim and gist traces of targets. *Verbatim traces* are integrated representations of a target's surface content and other item-specific information. *Gist traces* are representations of semantic, relational, and elaborative information. Because verbatim and gist traces contain information that originates in the same targets, it is natural to suppose that the storage of these different representations would be serially dependent—specifically, that verbatim traces would be deposited first (e.g., in short-term memory) and that their gist would then be extracted and stored. We saw earlier that just such a serial relationship between verbatim and gist storage was postulated in constructivism, and it has been a longstanding assumption in psycholinguistics (Reyna & Brainerd, 1992).

More recent experimental findings have rendered this model untenable, however. Among other things, it has been found that subjects begin to process and store the meaning content of targets within 30–50 milliseconds after target onset (e.g., Abrams & Greenwald, 2000, 2002; Buchanan, Brown, & Westbury, 1999; Draine & Greenwald, 1998; Seamon, Luo, & Gallo, 1998), which is far too brief an interval to fully process targets' surface forms and store verbatim traces, prior to initiating semantic processing (see chapter 4 for details). Moreover, evidence of a series of effects has accumulated in the memory literature, which are now seen as consequences of this rapid parallel initiation of meaning processing. One example is the word-superiority effect (Ankrum & Palmer, 1989). In the word-superiority effect, familiar words are presented at very short exposure durations (e.g., less than 100 milliseconds), and following each exposure, subjects are given either a probe *word* to identify (e.g., Was the word *table*?) or a probe *letter* to identify (e.g., Did the word contain the letter *b*?). The key finding that is indicative of fast parallel meaning processing is that whole words produce above-chance performance at *shorter* exposure durations than do their constituent letters (see also Reyna & Brainerd, 1992).

To accommodate such data, fuzzy-trace theory assumes that verbatim and gist traces are stored in parallel. With respect to verbatim traces, we have previously seen (in connection with the source-monitoring framework, for instance) that there are other theories that postulate that subjects retain representations of surface features of targets and of accompanying contextual cues. A hallmark of fuzzy-trace theory's notion of verbatim traces, however, is integration. Although other theories posit the storage of individual surface features that may subsequently be retrieved together, fuzzy-trace theory assumes that verbatim traces are integrated representations of multiple surface features, so that the retrieval of such traces on memory tests induces vivid mental reinstatement of experiences that accompanied targets' earlier presentations. Forgetting of verbatim traces creates *dis*integration of features (Reyna, 1998; Reyna & Titcomb, 1997). This seems to be the only obvious way to account for the aforementioned fact that increasing the similarity between surface features of target materials and surface features of memory tests can reduce the incidence of false-memory responses.

Turning to gist traces, these representations are episodic interpretations of concepts (meanings, relations, patterns) that subjects access, or elaborations that they generate, as they encode targets' surface form. More explicitly, the initial encoding of targets' surface features is assumed to initiate a corresponding mechanism of meaning access and elaboration, with these different storage mechanisms running in parallel as encoding continues. Wallace and associates (Wallace, Stewart, & Malone, 1995; Wallace, Stewart, Shaffer, & Barry, 1998) have developed a detailed model of parallel surface and semantic processing for word targets, though such models have yet to be developed for more complex materials. For present purposes, however, the major consideration is that with materials like those that figure in false-memory paradigms, the processing and storage of the gist of experience goes on simultaneously with the processing and storage of verbatim memories, and for that reason, subjects may retain considerable information about a target's meaning even if they fail to completely process its surface form or even be aware that a target was presented (because it was exposed for only a few milliseconds). Another important consideration is that because targets participate in multiple meanings, subjects can store multiple gist traces on the basis of a single target. An interesting by-product, which is significant in false memory, is that gist traces of targets may vary in their degree of specificity with respect to a target. For instance, suppose that the words *Hereford, collie, tiger,* and *python* appear on some study list. These words would likely cause subjects to access the concepts "cow," "dog," "cat," and "snake," which are meanings that are specific to each word. However, subjects might also access concepts such as "farm animal" and "jungle animal," which are less specific, or simply "animal," which applies to all of them. The latter concepts are sometimes called *integrative* or *connected meanings* because they unite many targets. Collections of gist traces that vary in their degree of specificity with respect to targets are called *fuzzy-to-verbatim continua* in fuzzy-trace theory.

Dissociated Retrieval of Verbatim and Gist Traces

If subjects store dissociated verbatim and gist traces of individual targets, there will be latitude in the types of representations that may be accessed on memory tests, and therefore, the types of representations that are accessed will depend heavily upon the retrieval cues that are provided. Here, two findings have been reported that have important ramifications for false memory. As long as verbatim traces are still accessible, (a) target probes are better retrieval cues for verbatim than for gist traces on recognition tests; and (b) both hits (on recognition tests) and target recall (on recall tests) are based predominantly upon the retrieval of verbatim rather than gist traces (Reyna, Holliday, & Marche, 2002; Reyna & Titcomb, 1997). Two parallel findings also have important ramifications for false memory. Regardless of whether verbatim traces are still accessible, (c) semantically related distractors are better retrieval cues for gist than for verbatim traces on recognition tests; and (d) both semantic false alarms (on recognition tests) and intrusions (on recall tests) are based predominantly upon the retrieval of gist rather than verbatim traces (Reyna, 1995, 1998; Reyna & Kiernan, 1994, 1995). The findings in question, which were noted earlier in the discussions of constructivism and schema theory, reveal impressive levels of statistical independence and experimental dissociation between true recognition/recall of presented material and false recognition/recall of information that preserves its meaning. The key results, however, show that true-false statistical independence and experimental dissociation can be transformed into dependency and association by instructing subjects to rely on the meaning of presented material and to ignore its surface form when responding to memory tests (Reyna & Kiernan, 1994, 1995). These results are key because they demonstrate that actively manipulating the tendency to use meaning representations of presented material (gist) versus memory for surface form produces theoretically predicted relations.

Although the notion of retrieval dissociation seems to be required by specific experimental findings, this principle, in combination with that of parallel storage of verbatim and gist traces, is used to explain a paradox about false memory that was mentioned earlier: the *coexistence constraint* (i.e., that subjects may provide true- and false-memory reports about the same event). Upon first impression, the inconsistency in subjects reporting with equal confidence that they read the word *collie* and the word *poodle* on a list, when only *collie* was presented, or reporting with equal confidence that they read the statement "the plane is above the tree" and the statement "the tree is below the plane" in a narrative, when only the first statement appeared, seems dramatic. According to fuzzy-trace theory's first two principles, the explanation of the coexistence constraint is actually quite simple: Memory is of two minds—minds that are not well integrated with each other, neither when memories of experience are first stored nor when they are subsequently retrieved (Reyna & Brainerd, 1995a; Reyna & Titcomb, 1997).

Opposing Judgments About False-Memory Items

Fuzzy-trace theory assumes that in true recognition/recall, retrieval of verbatim traces induces a vivid form of remembering in which subjects consciously reexperience targets' occurrence in specific contexts; targets echo in the mind's ear or flash in the mind's eye. This, of course, is the first of the two phenomenologies described by Strong (1913), which is traditionally called *recollection* in dual-process theories. Verbatim retrieval supports mental comparisons between retrieved memories and recognition probes in which memories and probes are perceived to exactly match, and it supports the simple readout of targets in recall. The former is called *identity judgment*, while the latter is called *direct access*. Because verbatim retrieval is assumed to predominate with targets, identity judgment and direct access are the principal bases for true-memory responses when memory is tested promptly. However, targets may fail to provoke verbatim retrieval and may instead provoke gist retrieval, which usually induces the more global and inchoate form of remembering that is called *familiarity* in dual-process theories. Gist retrieval supports mental comparisons between retrieved memories and recognition probes in which probes' meanings are perceived to overlap with meanings that were processed during target experiences, and it supports meaning-based regeneration of targets in recall. The former is called *similarity judgment* when it produces probe acceptance, and the latter is called *reconstruction* when it results in target recall. Note that verbatim and gist retrieval are *convergent* processes in true memory because identity and similarity judgments both support recognition of targets, and direct access and reconstruction both support recall of targets.

With false memory, however, verbatim and gist retrieval are assumed to be opponent processes, with gist retrieval supporting false-memory responses and verbatim retrieval suppressing them. We know that gist retrieval is assumed to predominate with false-but-gist-consistent items, so that such items will usually induce global feelings of meaning overlap with target experiences, which result in semantic false alarms and semantic intrusions. Gist processing that results in false alarms is again called *similarity judgment*, and gist retrieval that results in intrusions is again called *reconstruction*. Verbatim retrieval, on the other hand, works against false memory in two ways, one general and the other specific. At a general level, because verbatim processing does not support false-memory responses, such responses will necessarily decrease as the overall level of verbatim retrieval on memory tests increases. That is, *as a statistical matter*, without considering what happens at the level of individual items, the rate of false-memory responses will drop to the extent that verbatim processing crowds out gist processing, so that manipulations that enhance the general accessibility of verbatim traces on memory tests will, on average, reduce the incidence of false-memory responses (Reyna & Kiernan, 1995). The other, more specific way in which verbatim retrieval works against false-memory responses takes advantage of the vivid mental states that are provoked by verbatim traces. False-but-gist-consistent items may sometimes produce the retrieval of verbatim traces of presentations of related targets (e.g., presentation of the recognition probe "ate a hot dog at the baseball game" may prompt retrieval of verbatim traces of eating a hamburger, or reconstructing "drank a Coke" while recalling events from a baseball game may prompt retrieval of verbatim traces of drinking a 7-Up). Simultaneous processing of two related items, one of which is *known* to have been experienced (because verbatim retrieval brings to mind realistic features of target presentations) and the other of which is similar in meaning but different in surface form, can generate mismatches at the level of verbatim detail (e.g., Reyna, 1996b). On the one hand, hot dogs and hamburgers have similar meanings, inasmuch as both are common foods that are routinely eaten at baseball games, so that hot dogs will seem familiar in this retrieval context. Likewise, Coke and 7-Up have similar meanings, inasmuch as both are common beverages that are routinely drunk at baseball games, so that Coke will also seem familiar in this retrieval context. But on the other hand, hot dogs mismatch hamburgers in salient ways and Coke mismatches 7-Up in salient ways. The two sandwiches look, taste, and smell different, and so do Coke and 7-Up. Such verbatim mismatches provide reliable, principled bases for correctly rejecting *specific* distractor probes in recognition and for suppressing *specific* intrusions in recall because they supply a compelling explanation of how events that were not experienced could nevertheless seem familiar: "I ate something at the game, but it wasn't a hot dog because I distinctly remember eating a hamburger, and I had a soda at the game, but it wasn't a Coke because I distinctly remember drinking 7-Up." We will refer to this ability to weed out specific intrusions and false alarms from memory reports by relying on the vivid mental states that are induced by verbatim retrieval as *recollection rejection.*

Recollection rejection can suppress specific intrusions and false alarms in either of two ways, and in the following discussion, we will use this term interchangeably to refer to both. One method is the procedure that was just described: Particular candidate items (hot dog, Coke) are edited out of memory reports because verbatim traces of the corresponding true items (hamburger, 7-Up) are accessed, generating verbatim mismatches that neutralize the familiarity of false-but-gist-consistent items. In everyday life, all of us, even young children, have vast experience with this false-memory suppression procedure (I remember playing on the swings today but not on the slide because there was no shade over by the slide; No, mom, he definitely hit me first). A reasonable extrapolation from people's extensive acquaintance with the fact that plausible candidates for true experiences often provoke verbatim mismatches with actual experiences is that one ought to be cautious about "remembering" things that are not accompanied by vivid recollective phenomenology. If this rule were applied on memory tests, it would dictate that recognition and recall should be suppressed for all items that fail to provoke such phenomenology. This second, more strategic variety of recollection rejection has sometimes been referred to as a *strong remembering criterion* and has recently been investigated under the rubric of the *distinctiveness heuristic* (see below).

The two forms of recollection rejection have their respective advantages and disadvantages. An advantage of the first form is that it has a high level of specificity: It suppresses only false items, for which verbatim traces will not be accessible, while allowing true items for which only gist traces are accessible to be remembered. A disadvantage is that it has a low level of sensitivity: It will allow false items to be remembered for which verbatim traces of the corresponding true items cannot be retrieved, a problem that becomes increasingly acute as time passes. In contrast, an advantage of the second form of recollection rejection is that it has a high level of sensitivity: In principle, it is capable of preventing all false items from being remembered, again because verbatim traces will not be accessible for such items. A disadvantage is that its level of specificity is low: It prevents true items from being recalled whenever their verbatim traces are no longer accessible, which is also a problem that becomes increasingly acute as time passes. In sum, although recollection rejection can be exploited to suppress specific intrusions and false alarms, it is an imperfect mechanism, which may not weed out all errors and may weed out correct responses as well.

Moreover, there is a further imperfection in the processes of false-memory rejection that is concerned with the phenomenologies that accompany gist retrieval. Fuzzy-trace theory assumes that targets predominantly prompt verbatim retrieval and recollective phenomenology, whereas false-but-gist-consistent items predominantly prompt gist retrieval and familiarity phenomenology. This assumption is consistent with the results of numerous studies using Tulving's remember/know methodology (recall, too, the Conway et al. [1996] results in chapter 2). Subjects judge the phenomenology that accompanies hits to be "remember" 70–80% of the time, and they judge the phenomenology that accompanies false alarms to be "know" 70–80% of the time (for a review, see Donaldson, 1996). However, fuzzy-trace theory posits that there are some special circumstances in which gist retrieval induces illusory, vivid recollective phenomenology that simulates the true recollective phenomenology that is induced by verbatim retrieval (e.g., the prior presentation of a false-but-gist-consistent item echoes in the mind's ear or flashes in the mind's eye). This is the phenomenon of *phantom recollection* (Brainerd, Wright, Reyna, & Mojardin, 2001; Reyna & Brainerd, 1995a; Reyna & Lloyd, 1997). Phantom recollection is assumed to occur when (a) certain familiar meanings have been repeatedly cued by target experiences; and (b) false-but-gist-consistent items are especially good examples of those meanings. Known cases include the Deese (1959) stimulus words in Table 2-2, which are excellent examples of meanings that are cued by all of the words on their corresponding lists, and narratives in which familiar but unstated events are repeatedly implied (e.g., Reyna, 2000b). An important feature of phantom recollection is that it foils both forms of recollection rejection because the accompanying phenomenology simulates that of verbatim traces.

Different Time Courses of Verbatim and Gist Memory

According to the principle of dissociated verbatim and gist retrieval, the types of representations that are retrieved depend strongly upon the retrieval cues that are supplied on memory tests, with verbatim access being favored when the surface content of retrieval cues matches that of targets and gist access being favored when retrieval cues match targets in meaning content but not in surface form. Beyond this, which representations are retrieved also depends upon their relative accessibility in memory (Reyna, 1995, 1998; Reyna & Titcomb, 1997). This consideration is crucial when it comes to verbatim and gist memory because so many findings (e.g., Kintsch et al., 1990; Koriat, Levy-Sadot, Edry, & de Marcas, 2003; Murphy & Shapiro, 1994) converge on the conclusion that over time, the accessibility of verbatim traces declines more rapidly than that of gist traces. The obvious implication is that the tendency for true recognition/recall to be based predominantly upon verbatim retrieval will depend upon how much time has passed since the target experience. As time goes by, there will be a shift toward reliance upon the same memorial basis that supports false memory (gist retrieval). This, in turn, means that the high levels of statistical independence and experimental dissociation that are initially observed between true- and false-memory responses ought to be replaced by dependency and association as time goes by, an outcome that has been reported by several investigators (e.g., Brainerd & Reyna, 1996; Brainerd et al., 1995; Lim, 1993; Marx & Henderson, 1996; Reyna & Kiernan, 1994, 1995). Two other obvious implications are (a) false-memory responses, even though they refer to events that were not experienced, will be fairly stable over time because the accessibility of gist memories declines slowly; and (b) subjects' ability to avoid false recognition/recall via verbatim mismatches will decline markedly with time because the verbatim traces that yield such mismatches are rapidly becoming inaccessible (Reyna & Titcomb, 1997).

Developmental Variability

Fuzzy-trace theory posits developmental changes in both verbatim and gist storage, in subjects' ability to access such traces on memory tests, and in long-term retention. Relevant experimental evidence comes from developmental studies whose designs provide separate estimates of the strengths of verbatim memory and gist memory. The standard patterns in such studies are that estimates of verbatim memory and gist memory both improve between early childhood and young adulthood, although the precise amounts of improvement vary from study to study, and that these age improvements are independent of each other. These patterns are illustrated by two results from developmental studies of free recall. First, recall of individual targets (a measure of verbatim memory) and the clustering together of meaning-sharing items during recall (a measure of gist memory) both increase during the preschool to young adult years (Bjorklund & Muir, 1988). Second, between early childhood and early adolescence, the age range during which most of the improvement in both measures occurs, subjects' levels of performance on the two measures are statistically independent and experimentally dissociated (e.g., DeMarie-Dreblow, 1991).

Parallel developmental data are available from studies that dealt with verbatim and gist forgetting (for reviews, see Brainerd, 1997; Reyna, 1996a). The relevant studies included forgetting intervals of varying lengths, and subjects ranged in age from younger elementary-schoolers to aged adults. In many studies, subjects were trained to a perfect-performance criterion during study sessions, so that verbatim and gist memories were both at ceiling, and then verbatim memory and gist memory were separately measured after retention intervals of various lengths. The life-span pattern that emerged was that verbatim and gist retention both improved during early childhood, that they also improved between later childhood and early adolescence, and that verbatim retention declined while gist retention remained relatively constant between young and late adulthood. Several studies in the aging literature provide further evidence on the last point (e.g., Schacter, Koutstaal, Johnson, Gross, & Angell, 1997; Tun, Wingfield, Rosen, & Blanchard, 1998).

The traditional view of developmental variability in false memory, as noted earlier in connection with schema theory, is that susceptibility to false-memory reports decreases between early childhood and young adulthood and then increases again late in life (e.g., Bruck & Ceci, 1997; Ceci & Bruck, 1993b, 1995). Fuzzy-trace theory's assumption, in contrast, is that there are not monolithic developmental trends in false memory. If verbatim and gist abilities both contribute to false memory, albeit in opposite ways, and if verbatim and gist abilities both vary with age, it follows that age differences in measured levels of false memory will necessarily be highly task-dependent (Reyna, 1995). In particular, it is easy to see that such age differences will turn on whether a false-memory task poses greater obstacles to verbatim memory than to gist memory, or whether conversely, it poses greater obstacles to gist memory than to verbatim memory. Suppose that the former is the case, that a false-memory task is hard from a verbatim point of view but easy from a gist point of view. To illustrate, the targets might consist of statements with similar surface forms, which makes it difficult to store distinctive verbatim traces, and simple meanings that are familiar to young children, which makes it easy to store gist traces that support false-memory responses (e.g., John is taller than Jim; Jim is taller than Sam; Sam is taller than Stan; Stan is taller than Fred; Fred is taller than Frank; Frank is taller than Ron; Ron is taller than Rob). Here, the relevant gist memory (a linear ordering with respect to height) ought to be easy to store, but the verbatim side of the information is confusing. If this task were administered to elementary-schoolers, one would expect developmental decreases in the false recognition/recall of statements such as "Stan is taller than Ron" and "Jim is taller than Frank" because developmental improvements in verbatim memory will contribute more to performance than will developmental improvements in gist memory. In contrast, suppose that the task is easy from a verbatim point of view (e.g., a narrative consisting of a series of highly distinctive sentences) but hard from a gist point of view (e.g., the narrative revolves around a mature theme that is unfamiliar to most young children). Here, one would expect the opposite developmental trend, increasing levels of false memory, because age improvements in gist memory (resulting from increased acquaintance with the theme) will be more pronounced in this task than will age improvements in verbatim memory (e.g., Reyna & Kiernan, 1994; Reyna, Mills, Estrada, & Brainerd, in press).

Activation/Monitoring Theory and the Distinctiveness Heuristic

We have just seen that fuzzy-trace theory posits dissociated memory mechanisms that act in concert to support true-memory responses, but that act in opposition with respect to false-memory responses. In the present section, we consider two further theories in which dissociated memory mechanisms are posited. Both theories were developed to explain performance on the Deese-Roediger-McDermott (DRM) word-list task.

Since the 1990s, the DRM task has been the most frequently studied of all false-memory paradigms, probably producing more published experimentation than all other paradigms except for eyewitness identification. There are excellent reasons for researchers' reliance on this procedure. First, it is simple and easy to use. Subjects merely study a short word list (or lists) and perform free recall or respond to a series of recognition probes. Second, the materials, the false-memory items as well as the lists themselves, are highly standardized. Unlike, say, the uncontrolled experiences that figure in studies of autobiographical false memory or the everyday situations that are used in studies of schema-consistent false memories or the crime scenarios that are used in studies of eyewitness suggestibility and false identification, detailed normative information is available for words (e.g., Battig & Montague, 1969; McEvoy, Nelson, & Komatsu, 1999; Paivio, Yuille, & Madigan, 1968), which allows DRM materials to be precisely localized on several key dimensions of difficulty and content (e.g., associativity, concreteness, frequency, imageability, meaningfulness), providing researchers with a handy catalog of quantitative variables that may influence false memory. Third, the DRM task produces exceptionally robust false-memory effects, without the need for deception or other extraordinary interventions (Reyna & Lloyd, 1997). Indeed, even when memory tests include warnings about the possibility of falsely remembering the stimulus words, such warnings have little effect (McDermott & Roediger, 1998). Fourth and most important, because the DRM task is a laboratory procedure, it is possible to achieve high levels of experimental control over manipulations and outcomes. This minimizes the chances that findings are due to uncontrolled factors (always a key consideration in false-memory research), making it easier to draw cause-effect conclusions about factors that are responsible for false memory.

Because the DRM procedure has been so pivotal in recent research, it is especially important to account for this particular memory illusion, and two theories have been developed for that purpose: *activation/monitoring theory* (McDermott & Watson, 2001; Roediger & McDermott, 2000; Roediger, Watson, McDermott, & Gallo, 2001) and the *distinctiveness heuristic* (Dodson & Schacter, 2002b; Schacter et al., 1999). The first theory's key explanatory concepts are *memory activation*, which occurs principally when DRM lists are studied but can also occur on memory tests, and *memory-source monitoring*, which occurs primarily on memory tests but can also occur when DRM lists are studied. Concerning activation, a familiar way of thinking about how semantic information is represented in long-term memory is as a network of interconnected nodes (Anderson & Pirolli, 1984; Collins & Loftus, 1975). The nodes are assumed to be occupied by concepts or propositions (e.g., "dog"), and there are assumed to be semantic connections between nodes. The semantic "distance" between nodes is determined by just how similar the concepts are in meaning (e.g., the distance between the "dog" and "cat" nodes is less than the distance between the "dog" and "fish" nodes). When a word is heard, read, or thought about (e.g., *collie*), it activates certain nodes in the semantic network (e.g., the "dog" and "pet" nodes), from which activation spreads through the network, with proximal nodes (e.g., "cat" and "sheep") receiving considerable activation, and distal nodes (e.g., "fruit" and "metal") receiving little activation. According to activation/monitoring theory, other salient properties of a word, particularly its lexical properties and its associations to other words, can also be thought of as being represented in networks of nodes and interconnections through which activation spreads when a word is encountered. The distance between nodes, and therefore the amount of activation that spreads from one node to another, is again determined by how similar the two nodes are with respect to the property that the network captures. When a word list is studied, then, it activates the nodes that correspond to its salient semantic, associative, lexical, and other properties. In addition to semantic, associative, and lexical properties, the activation concept encompasses other integrative memory representations, particularly the memory schemas of schema theory (Roediger, Watson, et al., 2001).

The peculiar feature of DRM lists is that even though the stimulus words are not presented, the manner in which the lists are constructed guarantees that their corresponding nodes in semantic and associative networks will receive large amounts of activation, larger in fact than the amounts that are received by the nodes for list words. This can be seen by considering the stimulus word *doctor* and its generating list: *nurse, sick, lawyer, medicine, health, hospital, dentist, physician, ill, patient, office, stethoscope, surgeon, clinic, cure*. All of these words, except for *lawyer* and *office*, have medical meaning as their most obvious semantic property, and "doctor" is the most prototypical of all of these medical concepts. Therefore, in a semantic network, the node that corresponds to the "doctor" concept will be close to the nodes that correspond to the other words and will therefore receive considerable activation whenever these other nodes are activated. In addition, *doctor* is a high backward associate of some of the list words—*nurse, dentist, physician, patient, stethoscope*, and *clinic*—so that it is apt to come to mind while listening to this list. Thus, by the time the entire list has been presented, each list word will have been heard and its meaning content will have been activated, but *doctor*'s meaning will have been repeatedly activated and it may have been "heard" one or more times. This, then, is the first process that is responsible for false recognition/ recall, as well as true recognition/recall, of stimulus words: The greater the activation of a stimulus word's or a list word's component features that is produced by a DRM list, the greater the tendency to falsely recognize or recall it.

The second process, *memory-source monitoring*, works in the opposite direction, suppressing both true and false recognition/recall, and is derived from the judgment operation of the source-monitoring framework. On memory tests, the tendency to recognize or recall words varies directly with their level of activation during list presentation. Because the words on DRM lists are closely related in meaning, activation will be high for list words, stimulus words, and even for other semantically related words (e.g., *disease*). Thus, although basing recall and recognition purely on meaning activation will yield a large number of items that are consistent with list meanings, accuracy will be impaired because some of these will be false. Roediger, Watson, et al. (2001) proposed that the latter problem can be dealt with to some degree by monitoring the sources of memories for individual words, particularly by monitoring salient differences for stimulus words versus list words. As emphasized in the source-monitoring framework, all forms of memory retrieval are not equal when it comes to deciding whether or not an item was actually presented. Some types of retrieval, such as the retrieval of visual and auditory features that accompany a word's presentation or the activation of other contextual cues that were unique to the presentation of a specific word, are highly diagnostic of actual presentation. In general, in other theories, these are the sorts of features that are associated with recollective retrieval (dual-process model of recognition) or direct-access retrieval (dual-process model of recall). However, other properties, such as words' meaning content or what was heard in the mind's ear, are not diagnostic of actual presentation. By monitoring the types of properties that words provoke and, specifically, discriminating diagnostic types of properties from nondiagnostic types, recall/recognition of unpresented words will be suppressed, but so will recall/recognition of list words that do not provoke diagnostic properties. Although true recall/recognition will also be suppressed, relative to what it would be if only meaning were relied upon, monitoring is nevertheless an adaptive procedure because it redounds to the overall accuracy of performance, as opposed to the quantity of performance (Koriat et al., 1999). Specifically, the claim is that, because list words are more likely to produce forms of activation that are diagnostic of actual presentation, activation monitoring will suppress recall/recognition of list words less than it will suppress recall/recognition of false-but-gist-consistent words, delivering a net gain in accuracy.

The other model of the DRM task, the *distinctiveness heuristic* of Schacter and associates (Dodson & Schacter, 2002b; Schacter et al., 1999) is focused on a particular metacognitive suppression operation and does not contain any competing proposals about the memory representations that generate intrusions and false alarms. (However, proposals about the latter were made in earlier articles by Schacter and associates [e.g., Schacter, Norman, & Koutstaal, 1998]. Those proposals were called the *constructive memory framework*.) This distinctiveness heuristic resembles memory monitoring in the broad sense that it is also a method of dealing with the problem that reliance upon semantic activation will produce recognition/recall performance that is high in quantity but low in accuracy. More specifically, the distinctiveness heuristic is rooted in certain presuppositions about the nature of the memory representations that are created during the presentation of DRM lists, presuppositions that were described above in connection with the negative form of recollection rejection. Study-phase variables that promote the storage of vivid memories of the surface features of list words (e.g., presenting a picture of the object that is named by each word or presenting each word several times), will create an *expectation* of phenomenological vividness in subjects when they respond to memory tests. Subjects will anticipate that words that were actually studied, as opposed to words that merely produce high meaning activation, will provoke the retrieval of memories that contain vivid perceptual content because they know that vivid memories of those words were stored. The distinctiveness heuristic then consists of using this expectation strategically to guide performance on memory tests by requiring that recognition/recall be restricted to items that provoke the retrieval of vivid memories of list-presentation experiences. Note that, like the monitoring operation in activation/monitoring theory and the negative form of recollection rejection in fuzzy-trace theory, the distinctiveness heuristic suppresses recall/recognition of true as well as false items. Also like the activation/monitoring operation and recollection rejection, the distinctiveness heuristic ought to redound to the overall accuracy of performance because false-but-gist-consistent words will be less apt to provoke such retrieval than will list words. Unlike the monitoring operation, however, the distinctiveness heuristic is not a process that operates primarily on memory tests. First and foremost, it is a metacognitive belief that is created earlier, during the course of target experiences, and is only later implemented, with some probability, if memory tests are administered.

Because activation/monitoring theory and the distinctiveness heuristic were developed as explanations of the DRM illusion, that is where research on both has been concentrated to date (e.g., Thapar & McDermott, 2001; Watson et al., 2001). However, both theories may eventually prove to be applicable to many other standard false-memory paradigms. The reason is that the potential purview of their respective explanatory processes extends beyond DRM lists. Concerning the activation process, the notion of spreading activation, by itself, has been previously applied to a large number of memory and reasoning tasks (see Anderson, 1983). If one adds to this the notions of activation in associative networks, lexical networks, and memory schemas, this process is potentially applicable to true and false memory for all types of material. Concerning the monitoring process, we have already seen in connection with the source-monitoring framework's judgment operation that this concept's scope of application is far broader than memory for semantically related word lists. We saw, more explicitly, that Johnson and Raye's (1981) original concept of reality monitoring can be applied without substantial modification to eyewitness suggestibility, schema-consistent false memory, and, in principle, to any other paradigm in which falsely remembered information is actually presented in some way. We saw, further, that by extending reality monitoring to include the more generic idea of source monitoring, the concept becomes applicable to further paradigms. There remain some paradigms that cannot easily be brought under the source-monitoring umbrella, but the notion of monitoring the nature of memory activation is broader still and seems to extend to all of the procedures in chapter 2. Finally, concerning the distinctiveness heuristic, there might be ways to induce later expectations of memorial vividness for the target material in many of the false-memory paradigms in chapter 2. This would mean that subjects could adopt this expectation to guide memory performance in these same paradigms.

Synopsis

Looking back on this chapter and setting aside the details of individual explanatory proposals, it can be seen that the two groups of theories that we reviewed adopt fundamentally different perspectives on how best to approach the problem of accounting for false memories. One perspective, which was explicated in the early theories, stresses commonalities between the processes that are responsible for true and false memories, in effect treating false memories as limiting cases or variants of true memories. This perspective has the considerable advantage of parsimony. It has the further advantage of plausibility because it makes robust false-memory effects seem more comprehensible and less surprising by positing that, at the level of the processes that control them, true and false memories are quite similar. According to constructivism, the same semantic code is used to make both true- and false-memory responses, the reason being that this is the only information about experience that is preserved in memory because information about its surface form is jettisoned as soon as its meaning content has been stored. According to schema theory, when subjects experience a familiar situation whose components are already represented in a well-established memory structure (memory schema), that structure generates both true- and false-memory responses about the experience. According to the source-monitoring framework, false memories are to be treated on analogy to reality-monitoring errors, which means that false memories are incorrect attributions about sources of information or confusions about sources and therefore have the partly-true-and-partly-false quality of reality-monitoring errors. The advantages of parsimony and plausibility that these one-process theories confer notwithstanding, they have difficulty handling key results, such as statistical independence and experimental dissociation, that have been observed between true and false memories for the same material, as well as some other counterintuitive findings, which will be featured in chapters 4 and 5.

The other perspective, which is implemented in opponent-processes theories, has grown out of recent dual-process approaches to true memory, which distinguish between the operations of recollection and familiarity in true recognition and between the operations of direct access and reconstruction in true recall. This second approach to false memory stresses differences as well as similarities between the processes that are responsible for true and false memories. Specifically, dissociated mechanisms are posited that either (a) act in concert to support true memories while acting in opposition to support or suppress false memories (fuzzy-trace theory), or (b) act in concert to support both true and false memories under some conditions while acting in concert to suppress both true and false memories under other conditions (activation/monitoring theory and the distinctiveness heuristic). Although this alternative perspective appears to be more assumptively complex than the first (requiring more than one process), it is rendered plausible by 2 decades of research on dual-process theories of true memory, research that points to dissociated mechanisms that support recognition and recall of target events. Because additional assumptions must be grafted onto one-process theories to accommodate these results, they are not necessarily less complex than opponent-processes theories. More important, however, this perspective provides an elegant explanation of findings of statistical independence and experimental dissociation, and as we shall see in the next two chapters, it predicts a number of counterintuitive findings.

4

Controlling False Memories
with Opponent Processes

1—Laboratory Research
with Adults

Up to this point, it has been necessary to temporize in the matter of prediction, but sufficient ground has now been laid to enable us to take up this topic in the present chapter, in chapter 5, and throughout the remainder of this volume. By "prediction," we simply mean the ability to forecast new empirical effects on the basis of current theoretical ideas about false memory. It is not commonly appreciated that in science, predictive power, not explanation, is the gold standard for judging a theory's effectiveness. Experience has shown that it is normally possible to formulate several competing explanations of the same set of phenomena. For instance, we know of no examples of important psychological phenomena (which is to say phenomena that have been topics of extensive investigation) for which multiple explanations, often involving very different assumptions, have not been put forward. Although such theoretical profligacy, as it applies to memory research, will already be apparent from chapter 3, it must be understood that it is not a circumstance that is unique to psychology. Literally dozens of explanations of the same basic phenomena are extant in some of the most advanced branches of science, with quantum physics being a prominent case in point (e.g., Gribben, 1995). This situation is a consequence of what theories are, epistemologically speaking. They are *models* of reality—that is, of the target phenomena—not reality itself, and it is always possible, in principle, to model the same reality in different ways, often remarkably disparate ways, and nonetheless account for the facts equally well. This is a troubling and uncomfortable fact, but it is something with which science must live.

Such ideas have an odor of solipsism about them. Working scientists are notoriously impatient with such counsels of despair, and although they understand that solipsism is logically impeccable, they are apt to regard it as frivolous and slightly degenerate. To avoid this trap, it is necessary to have an acceptable criterion whereby some theories can be identified as being more successful than others, even when they all cover the known facts. One familiar and trustworthy criterion is Ockam's Razor: Given that two (or more) theories account for the same set of phenomena, the best one is the most assumptively parsimonious one—the theory that covers the facts with the fewest assumptions. The problem with parsimony is that it has been a rule of good theoretical conduct for so long that today it rarely discriminates between competing explanations. An experienced theorist would not knowingly propose a new model that is less frugal than extant theories, which brings us to a second familiar criterion: plausibility.

Plausibility is concerned with how sensible one's assumptions seem to be. Some theories make assumptions that strike one as quite reasonable (intuitive, feasible, and so on) ideas about how the world works, and it seems natural to regard such theories as inherently superior to those that vex our common sense. Although this criterion is routinely applied in evaluating theories, most often during the gestation phase before theories reach print, it is fallible. Two of its better-known limitations are historical relativity and demonstrated instances of failure. The first limitation says that common sense is educable; it evolves over time, as human knowledge expands, and consequently, assumptions that seem intuitive to one generation (that the earth is flat, that women are incapable of higher mathematical reasoning) seem absurd to another. Plausibility is therefore revealed as a subjective yardstick that yields different measurements for people with different knowledge levels. Its other limitation is that the history of science is replete with examples in which theories that made intuitively troubling assumptions proved to be far more successful, in the end, than theories that meshed nicely with received wisdom. Again, one need look no further than quantum physics, where wildly counterintuitive theories, such as the so-called Copenhagen interpretation and quantum electrodynamics, have long since triumphed over their more sensible competitors (Gribben, 1995). These theories are so strange that the late Richard Feynman was forced to conclude that "no one understands quantum mechanics."

A third, less subjective, criterion for what constitutes a successful theory, one that allows reasonable assumptions and far-fetched ones to compete on the same footing, is predictive power. Given that two (or more) theories are able to explain the same set of phenomena, the most successful theory is the one that does the best job of predicting new and interesting findings. That predicted effects ought to be new is self-evident because, otherwise, we are not being told anything that is not already known. But what is an "interesting" prediction? The answer involves putting plausibility back in the picture, but in a different way. When predicting new effects, as opposed to explaining old ones, implausibility is a prized commodity: The most interesting predictions are ones that violate expectations. Hence, in the prediction business, one seeks rather than avoids phenomena that are counterintuitive, from either the perspective of common sense or of older, widely accepted theories of memory. If a theory is capable of generating at least a few predictions of this sort, there are grounds for supposing that it is leading us in new directions. Of course, new directions are not necessarily correct directions that yield deeper understanding of the target phenomena. That is where experimental verification comes in. Only confirmed predictions count as successes and redound to a theory's credit. A successful theory must consistently forecast effects that are verified experimentally. In short, a good theory is one that makes confirmed predictions, but it is especially successful if some of those predictions happen to be counterintuitive.

In the present chapter, we explore several false-memory effects that fall out as predictions from the opponent-processes ideas that were discussed in the last chapter. If opponent-processes distinctions provide the correct take on false memory, then, armed with those distinctions, we should be able to exercise considerable control over false memories by predicting the sorts of variables that will increase or decrease them. The variables and predicted effects that we consider emanate from laboratory studies of false memory in adults, studies that make use of materials such as word lists, picture lists, or sentence lists, that present those materials under controlled conditions, and that measure false memory under controlled conditions. In later chapters, some of these predicted effects will be extrapolated to more naturalistic false-memory situations, such as forensic interviews, sworn testimony, and psychotherapy, and further effects that are characteristic of naturalistic situations will be considered. Such extrapolations must be postponed, however, until it has been firmly established that false memories can be made to vary systematically under controlled conditions; otherwise, there is nothing reliable from which to extrapolate.

The predicted effects that are discussed below are a mixture of the sensible and the surprising. As surprising effects are especially instructive, more emphasis will be placed upon them. Also, we shall adopt the convenient organizing tactic of grouping predictions and effects according to three successive stages of remembering: (a) *storage*, which includes encoding (the translation of experience into symbolic representations), and post-storage consolidation of memory traces; (b) *retrieval*, which refers to any form of access to previously stored traces, but usually refers to the supervised access that occurs on recognition or recall tests, and which also refers to any modifications of memory traces that are produced by such access (e.g., redintegration of weak traces [strengthening the bonds that hold them together]; Horowitz & Prytulak, 1969); and (c) *forgetting*, which refers to declines in either the quality of stored traces or their accessibility that occur in the dead spaces between consecutive memory tests. Thanks to the long and rich influence of information-processing conceptions of cognition (e.g., Atkinson & Shiffrin, 1968), this modal model of memory is well known to anyone who has taken an introductory psychology course, making it a useful common language in which to present and organize any body of memory research.

In this and subsequent chapters, we shall rely on the opponent-processes concepts of fuzzy-trace theory, rather than those of activation/monitoring theory or the distinctiveness heuristic, as a means of generating theoretical predictions about false memory. This is necessary because, as mentioned in chapter 3, the explanatory scope of the latter theories is not yet clear. Fuzzy-trace theory's assumptions have been formulated in such a way that they encompass the various experimental and naturalistic false-memory situations that we shall encounter in this volume, and its predictions about those situations are therefore easy to derive. In contrast, the other two theories are aimed at accounting for DRM false memories, and although it is possible to extend them to other types of false memories, the fact that such work is still in progress makes it more difficult to derive unambiguous predictions about other types of false memories.

Storing Memories

In this section, we consider five dimensions of experience that are present as memories are first being stored and that turn out to influence the levels of false memory that subjects display later, when they are responding to memory tests. These dimensions are *duration* (the length of time that target events are experienced), *repetition* (how many times target events or their meanings are experienced), *deep* and *shallow processing* (concentrating on the meaning content of experience or its surface form), *distinctiveness* (the perceptual salience of target events), and *consolidation activity* (concentrating on deleting or preserving particular aspects of experience). A much larger group of variables might be examined under the heading of storage variables, but opponent-processes ideas make straightforward predictions about these five, which means that these variables show how such ideas may be used to construct a coherent account of the relation between storage and subsequent false memories.

A slight detour is necessary before taking up predictions about these dimensions of experience, however. Some of the predictions about them turn on prior findings about relations between how the brain represents the surface form of experience, which we called *verbatim traces* in chapter 3, and how the brain represents the meaning of experience, which we called *gist traces*, when those representations are first being stored and as they are being consolidated immediately after storage. Two findings, in particular, about these on-line relations between verbatim and gist storage are central to opponent-processes predictions: the advanced storage of gist traces and the preferential consolidation of gist traces. We explicate each finding before proceeding to the main business of this section.

On-Line Relations Between Verbatim and Gist Memory

Advanced Storage of Gist Traces

The initial finding that underlies predictions about storage variables is that subjects appear to deposit meaning information about target events (the basis of gist traces) well before they have completed processing the events' surface forms (the basis of verbatim traces), which means that the memorial mechanism for generating false-memory reports tends to become available in the brain earlier than the memorial mechanism for suppressing such reports. A series of experimental paradigms that measure memory for the surface and meaning content of events following rapid exposure (below 100 milliseconds) has produced several specific examples of this general outcome. The illustration that we present is one of the more compelling in that subjects demonstrate memory for some of the meaning content of words even though, owing to extremely rapid exposure, they are unaware that words were even presented. This is the phenomenon of *unconscious semantic priming.*

Unconscious semantic priming is investigated in experiments dealing with what was once called subliminal perception. Suppose that a print of a typical adventure movie is screened for an audience. Suppose, further, that several frames of the print contain words such as *action, thrill, danger,* and *fun* in such enormous letters that they occupy the entire frame. Because each frame is projected for only a small fraction of a second, members of the audience are unaware of the presence of these words. They are only aware of the normal flow of pictures, dialogue, and music. The question is whether the theatergoers are nevertheless influenced by the subliminal words. Of particular interest to movie producers: Does the theater audience experience the film as more adventuresome and exciting than do control audiences (who view prints that do not contain these words)? In a laboratory analogue of the film example, which is called *masked priming,* subjects who have observed briefly flashed words respond to two types of memory tests: *direct* tests, which are intended to measure whether they were aware of the presence of those words, and *indirect* tests, which are intended to measure whether salient features of the words' meanings were stored (regardless of whether subjects were aware of the words). Performance on the two types of tests is compared to determine whether there is evidence of subliminal semantic activation when the words were flashed (e.g., Marcel, 1983). The empirical pattern that is said to support subliminal semantic activation, which is called *indirect-without-direct,* is one in which performance on indirect tests is successful (suggesting that semantic content was processed as words were flashed) but performance on direct tests is unsuccessful (suggesting that there was no conscious awareness that words were being "read").

A concrete example of how subliminal semantic activation has been demonstrated comes from some influential masked-priming experiments by Draine and Greenwald (1998), which will be described with the aid of Figure 4-1. In these experiments, the indirect tests measured whether the emotional content of emotion-laden words (e.g., *abuse, cheer, filth, love*) or the gender content of common names (e.g., *Fred, Jane, Larry, Sally*) was processed when such words were briefly flashed, and the direct tests measured whether the surface form (letter strings) of the words was processed. Both types of test are shown in Figure 4-1, which illustrates tests involving gender. In the indirect task at the top, subjects received many trials of the sort shown on the left and right. On each trial, they judged whether the gender of a target word (*Jane* in the figure) was male or female. Normally, this would be trivially easy to do with such familiar names, but the targets were exposed for an interval that is barely long enough to identify the words (183 milliseconds) and subjects were required to make gender judgments within 250 milliseconds of the onset of each target (i.e., only 67 milliseconds of additional time for responding was supplied beyond the 183 milliseconds that targets were exposed). To make accurate judgments, therefore, subjects had to identify the gender of each target very quickly. Under such severe time pressure, it is helpful if appropriate meaning information has already been partially activated; that is, subjects' judgments will be more accurate if the relevant gender has been "primed," so that it does not have to be acti-

Indirect Memory Task

	Matching Trial	Mismatching Trial
Forward Mask	KQHYTPEQFPBYL	KQHYTPEQFPBYL
Prime	SALLY	FRED
Backward Mask	ZBLYPZMVKTHLC	ZBLYPZMVKTHLC
Target	JANE	JANE
Judgment	MALE OR FEMALE?	MALE OR FEMALE?

Direct Memory Task

	Word Trial	Nonsense Trial
Forward Mask	KQHYTPEQFPBYL	KQHYTPEQFPBYL
Prime	EVIL	GXGX
Backward Mask	ZBLYPZMVKTHLC	ZBLYPZMVKTHLC
Target	JANE	JANE
Judgment	WORD OR LETTERS?	WORD OR LETTERS?

Figure 4-1. Experimental design based on Draine and Greenwald (1998) for demonstrating that salient features of words' meanings are processed and stored before subjects have fully processed words' surface forms (because subjects are not consciously aware that words have been presented).

vated from scratch when targets are exposed. That was the function of a prior prime word (*Sally* in the figure). In Draine and Greenwald's experiments, these prime words were flashed for either 17, 30, or 50 milliseconds. As can be seen, the presentation of each prime word was preceded and followed by a string of consonants (called a *forward mask* and a *backward mask*, respectively), which were also briefly flashed so that any influences of the prime word on gender judgments would have to come from memory rather than from visual afterimages. The finding that indicates successful indirect performance is that gender judgments are more accurate when the genders of the prime and target words match (Figure 4-1, *left*) than when they do not (Figure 4-1, *right*). There was no evidence of subliminal semantic activation at 17 milliseconds, but as illustrated in Figure 4-2, there was clear evidence of it at 33 and 55 milliseconds. Specifically, at these presentation rates, there were reliable differences in accuracy on matching versus mismatching trials, measured in units of d' (a standard index of subjects' ability to make memory discriminations between different types of test items).

Draine and Greenwald's (1998) direct test, which is shown at the bottom of Figure 4-1, measured subjects' ability to make judgments about the surface form of primes—specifically, to say whether each briefly flashed prime was a word or was

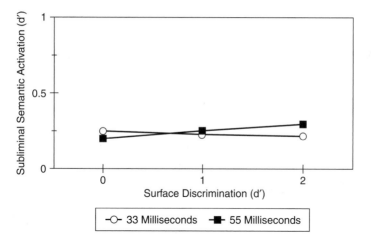

Figure 4-2. Evidence of subliminal semantic activation and the indirect-without-direct pattern in the experiments of Draine and Greenwald (1998).

a nonsense-letter sequence. The trials of the direct test were the same as those of the indirect test, except for two changes. First, the letter string that was flashed between the forward and backward masks was either a familiar word (*evil* on the left side of the figure) or a nonsense string of the same length (GXGX on the right side of the figure). Second, when the target word (*Jane*) was presented for a word-nonsense judgment, subjects were asked to decide whether the letter string that was previously flashed as a prime had been a word or a nonsense string. Subjects' ability to make this surface discrimination was measured in the same units as the accuracy of their gender judgments about targets (d' units). In Figure 4-2, the accuracy of gender judgments is plotted against the accuracy of surface discrimination, with above-zero values of either indicating that the ability was present. The first finding to consider is that under these experimental conditions, surface and semantic accuracy were unrelated to each other. As can be seen, there were only very weak relations between the two variables, and the relations were not consistent: Semantic accuracy decreased very slightly as surface accuracy increased in the 33-millisecond condition, but semantic accuracy increased very slightly as surface accuracy increased in the 55-millisecond condition. This lack of relationship suggests that the initial storage of semantic information is independent of the initial storage of surface information, which supports one of the opponent-processes principles that we introduced in chapter 3—namely, that verbatim and gist traces of experience are stored in a parallel, dissociated manner. The second finding to consider is that the indirect-without-direct pattern was present: Subjects were able to make gender judgments when they were unable to make surface discriminations. This pattern is confirmed by evidence that semantic performance was above zero when surface performance was not. That evidence can be found in Figure 4-2 in the far left points, which plot the level of semantic accuracy *when surface accuracy is zero*. Note that both points are well above zero. Therefore, on this showing, information about the meaning content of primes becomes available in memory before information about their surface form.

For the sake of completeness, it must be noted that the literature on subliminal semantic activation is not without controversy. On the contrary, it is a literature of vigorous dispute over experimental methodology—specifically, over which paradigms provide the most convincing demonstrations that items that produce carryover to semantic judgment tasks (and whose meaning content must therefore have been stored) were not consciously perceived. For instance, there are important variants of the masked-priming procedure that we have not considered here, which some investigators regard as superior indicators of unconscious semantic priming. As Merikle and Reingold (1998) pointed out, however, the indirect-without-direct pattern has been obtained using multiple methodologies, so that "there is now a growing consensus that perception in the absence of the subjective experience of perceiving is a genuine phenomenon" (p. 304). For our purposes, however, a much weaker conclusion suffices to make predictions about how certain storage variables affect subsequent false-memory reports. If subjects are not consciously aware that an item was presented, then, obviously they did not fully process its surface form to the point that the item was consciously identified and a verbatim trace was stored, which could be used to override false-but-gist-consistent memory reports (e.g., No, I didn't see *collie*. I saw *poodle*). However, if subjects process and store meaning content ("dog") even when they are not consciously aware that an item was presented, the stage is set for false-memory reports that are consistent with that meaning. From the perspective of opponent-processes distinctions, an ideal situation for fomenting such reports is one in which subjects are able to process much of the meaning content of experience without being able to process its surface content fully, so that they are unaware of the exact nature of their experiences.

Preferential Consolidation of Gist Traces

We move now from situations in which target events are only briefly experienced to more common circumstances in which experience is leisurely, so that there is ample time to process both surface and semantic content. In the seconds and minutes that follow a target event, a process that memory researchers call *consolidation* takes place. The existence of this process is predicated upon a number of findings showing that the period during which memories are stored extends well beyond the interval during which target events are actually being experienced (e.g., Crowder, 1976). There appears to be a postexperience interval during which memory traces are somehow being solidified, so that the information that they contain will be more likely to influence later performance on memory tests than if such consolidation did not occur. There are various experimental demonstrations of this phenomenon, but anterograde amnesia is a classic and persuasive one. People sometimes receive minor brain injuries that cause them to lose consciousness for a few seconds or minutes—for instance, concussions that occur during participation in contact sports, such as football, hockey, or rugby. A common occurrence in those situations is an inability to remember some or all of the events that immediately preceded the loss of consciousness, notwithstanding that people were aware of those

Table 4-1. Examples of Target Sentences and Memory Probes

Item	Content
Target sentences	The cocoa is hotter than the tea. The tea is hotter than the coffee. The cocoa is sweet.
Memory probes	
Targets	The cocoa is hotter than the tea. (TPO: true premise/old words)
	The tea is hotter than the coffee. (TPO: true premise/old words)
	The cocoa is sweet. (TPO: true premise/old words)
Meaning preserving	The tea is cooler than the cocoa. (TPN: true premise/new word)
	The cocoa is hotter than the coffee. (TIO: true inference/old words)
	The coffee is cooler than the cocoa. (TIN: true inference/new word)
Meaning violating	The tea is hotter than the cocoa. (FPO: false premise/old words)
	The cocoa is cooler than the tea. (FPN: false premise/new word)
	The coffee is hotter than the cocoa. (FIO: false inference/old words)
	The cocoa is cooler than the coffee. (FIN: false inference/new word)

Note. From Reyna and Kiernan (1994).

events when they occurred and presumably processed them fully (i.e., payed attention to them adequately). Evidently, there is a subsequent process that determines whether memory traces of fully processed events survive.

If there is a consolidation mechanism that determines which traces survive beyond the first few seconds and minutes, that mechanism might favor traces containing certain types of information over traces containing other types of information. Here, there is considerable evidence, some of which was encountered in our discussion of false memory for semantic inferences (chapter 2), that consolidation has a decided preference for gist traces over verbatim traces. The procedures that were used in the previously described (chapter 3) sentence-recognition experiments of Reyna and Kiernan (1994) provide a clear illustration of this preference. Examples of their targets and memory probes are displayed in Table 4-1. As can be seen, subjects first listened to a sequence of three sentences that established a familiar magnitude relation (temperature) between three familiar objects (coffee, tea, cocoa). Immediately after the third sentence was read, the subjects responded to a series of recognition probes, like those in Table 4-1, under instructions to accept only sentences that were exactly the same as sentences that they had heard and to reject all other sentences. Because the test sequence began immediately after the last target sentence, all of the probes were presented and answered within 20–30 seconds of target presentation. Thus, there was no time for forgetting, in the usual sense, and differences in probe performance are chiefly a measure of differences in the consolidation of memories for different aspects of the information in the target sentences.

Findings that are illustrative of preferential gist consolidation are shown in Figure 4-3. As our concern lies with differences in verbatim and gist consolidation, acceptance rates for targets are not of central interest because they could be based upon memory for sentences' exact surface form, or memory for their meaning, or both. With distractors, however, it is possible to tease apart memory for the two

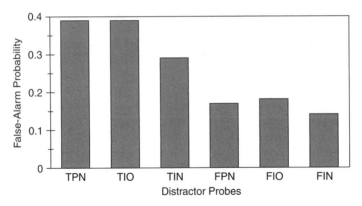

Figure 4-3. Evidence of preferential consolidation of gist traces in the experiments of Reyna and Kiernan (1994). TPN = true premise/new word, TIO = true inference/old words, TIN = true inference/new word, FPN = false premise/new word, FIO = false inference/old words, and FIN = false inference/new word.

types of information. The first three distractor probes in Table 4-1 preserve the meaning of the target sentences but not their surface form (because none was presented), while the remaining distractors preserve neither the meaning nor the surface form of targets. Further, the surface content (words) contained in each meaning-preserving distractor matches that of one of the meaning-violating distractors (TPN maps with FPN, TIO maps with FIO, and TIN maps with FIN). So, a comparison of the (false) acceptance rates for the members of each pair is a measure of the consolidation of gist traces with surface content controlled. It can be seen that acceptance rates were much higher, .21 higher on average, for meaning-preserving than for meaning-violating distractors, indicating consolidation of gist traces. On the other hand, it is possible to obtain a parallel measure of the consolidation of verbatim traces, with meaning content controlled, by comparing pairs of distractors that do not differ in meaning content but differ in whether they contain new words. It can be seen in Table 4-1 that there are two pairs of distractors that are equivalent in meaning content, one of which contains a new word and the other of which contains only old words (TIO maps with TIN and FIO maps with FIN). Inspection of the relevant pairs in Figure 4-3 reveals that although there are interpair differences in acceptance rates, which favor probes containing only old words, those differences are much smaller (.07 on average) than the corresponding differences for meaning-preserving versus meaning-violating distractors. Thus, although it seems that verbatim and gist traces were both being consolidated immediately after sentence presentation, gist consolidation was much more pronounced inasmuch as subjects were considerably more adept at discriminating old meanings from new ones than they were at discriminating old words from new ones.

Duration of Events

If observed levels of false memory are driven in opposite directions by the retrieval of verbatim traces versus gist traces, as envisioned in opponent-processes analysis, experiences that lead to the storage of gist traces in the *absence* of verbatim traces are guaranteed to produce false memory for gist-consistent events. This is an unambiguous prediction of the opponent-processes approach. A straightforward way to test it, in light of positive evidence of subliminal semantic activation, is to present target events very rapidly—so rapidly that complete processing of surface content is precluded, but not so rapidly that semantic processing is precluded (not at, say, 17 milliseconds [Draine & Greenwald, 1998]). Experiments have been reported that implemented this approach, using both false alarms and intrusions as measures of false memory. These experiments have involved word-list tasks like those exhibited earlier in Tables 2-1, 2-2, and 2-3. In the specific experiments that we shall summarize, the DRM task that was introduced in chapter 2 provided the target materials. Remember that in DRM studies, subjects' basic task is to listen to (or read) a short list of words (e.g., *low, clouds, up, tall, tower, jump, above, building, noon, cliff, sky, over*), all of which are forward associates of an unpresented stimulus word (*high*), and then perform free recall or respond to a series of recognition probes. In the typical study, several such lists are presented, with recall or recognition tests being administered for each of them. The finding of interest is that intrusion rates and false-alarm rates for unpresented stimulus words are quite high, often approaching the corresponding levels of true recall and true recognition.

Two early attempts to detect false memory for gist-consistent events following rapid exposure of DRM lists were reported by Seamon, Luo, and Gallo (1998) and by Buchanan, Brown, and Westbury (1999). Seamon et al. reported two experiments in which eight DRM lists were presented to subjects at a rate of 20 milliseconds per word, under conditions of full or divided attention. (Subjects in the divided-attention condition were given a sequence of seven random digits to hold in memory while DRM lists were presented.) Following presentation of all of the lists, subjects responded to a standard recognition task consisting of target probes, meaning-preserving distractors (the unpresented stimulus words), and unrelated distractors. In Buchanan et al.'s experiment, on the other hand, DRM lists were presented at a 72-millisecond rate, with each list being presented either three or six times. Subjects responded to a recognition test following presentation of each DRM list (rather than after all lists had been presented). It was found that false-alarm rates for unpresented stimulus words were quite high following rapid presentation of DRM lists: .65 on average in the full-attention conditions of Seamon et al. and .99 on average in Buchanan et al. Both of these values represent sizable false-memory effects, rather than the high levels of guessing that are sometimes produced by presentations that are too rapid to identify individual targets, because the false-alarm rates for unrelated distractors were much lower (.31 on average in the full-attention condition of Seamon et al. and .42 in Buchanan et al.).

McDermott and Watson (2001) reported an analogous demonstration of false recall of unpresented stimulus words following the rapid presentation of DRM lists. In their experiment, one group of subjects studied 36 DRM lists, using the same fast exposure duration (20 milliseconds) as Seamon et al. (1998). The instructions that the subjects read included the warning, "The words will be presented *very quickly*." Following the presentation of each list, subjects were given a 45-second written free-recall test (i.e., they were told to write as many words as they could remember from the just-presented list). The results showed that, on average, the unpresented stimulus word was recalled following 14% of the lists, which is remarkable evidence of meaning processing considering that none of the presented words could be "seen."

Consistent with opponent-processes predictions, therefore, false memory for meaning-preserving items can be demonstrated under conditions in which verbatim traces presumably are not stored because targets' surface forms cannot be identified. However, two further predictions follow. The first deals with the effect of repeated rapid presentations of the same target events. Although some meaning content is processed when presentation is so brief that targets cannot be identified, such meaning processing is necessarily far from complete. Hence, repeated rapid presentation should allow for more complete meaning processing, leading to higher levels of false memory, but without the storage of the verbatim traces that would lower levels of false memory (because presentation is still too rapid for targets to be identified). The other prediction concerns the effect on false memory of gradually lengthening the duration of presentation. A clear but counterintuitive prediction of the opponent-processes approach is that the effect will not be a simple one in which false-memory levels merely increase or decrease as duration lengthens. Instead, as long as the shortest presentation duration in such a sequence is a very rapid one of the type that produces subliminal semantic activation, an inverted-U relation is predicted, such that false-memory levels increase with initial increases in duration but eventually decrease with further increases in duration.

The finding of advanced storage of gist traces is the basis for this inverted-U prediction. At very short presentation durations (e.g., 20 milliseconds), there will be partial storage of gist traces coupled with no storage of verbatim traces. As duration lengthens from this baseline, the fact that meaning processing is more rapid than surface processing means that memorial support for reporting false memories (gist traces) will accumulate more rapidly than memorial support for suppressing them (verbatim traces). During this part of the lengthening sequence, therefore, false-memory levels will increase as presentation duration increases. At some point in the sequence, however, a duration will be attained that is long enough for meaning processing to be completed but is still too short for surface processing to be completed. During the remaining part of the sequence, therefore, memorial support for making false-memory reports will remain constant while memorial support for suppressing them will increase, resulting in net declines in levels of false memory.

Both of the just-mentioned predictions have been confirmed. With respect to the relation between false memory and repetition at very fast presentation rates, Seamon, Luo, Schwartz, Jones, Lee, and Jones (2002) verified the predicted relation in two experiments, both using the DRM procedure. In one experiment, nine DRM lists were presented to subjects at a 20-millisecond rate. Each list was presented once, 5 times, or 10 times at that rate. After all of the lists had been presented, subjects responded to a recognition test in which probes for stimulus words for presented lists (1, 5, or 10 presentations) were intermixed with targets from those lists and stimulus words from unpresented lists. The same procedure was followed in a second experiment, except that the nine DRM lists were presented 1, 5, or 25 times. Levels of false memory (false alarms to stimulus words) are plotted as a function of the number of times that a DRM list was presented in Figure 4-4. The first point

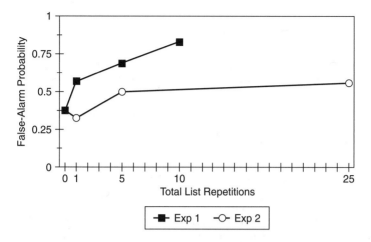

Figure 4-4. The relation between false memory and number of list repetitions when presentation rate is slow enough to permit some semantic processing but too fast to permit conscious identification of target events. The plotted data are for 20-millisecond presentations of DRM lists in two experiments reported by Seamon, Luo, Schwartz, Jones, Lee, and Jones (2002).

in each plot, the "0 presentations" point on the far left, is the false-alarm rate for stimulus words from DRM lists that were *not* presented, while the remaining points are for stimulus words from DRM lists that were presented different numbers of times. As can be seen, the trend in both experiments was for levels of false memory to increase as the number of list presentations increased.

With respect to the remaining prediction about the duration of target events, the relation between levels of false memory and variations in presentation rate has been investigated in several experiments, some using false recognition (Arndt & Hirshman, 1998; Seamon et al., 1998) and some using false recall (Gallo, 2000; McDermott & Watson, 2001; Roediger, Robinson, & Balota, 2001; Toglia & Neuschatz, 1996). In some of these studies, false-memory levels have only been found to increase or decrease as a function of presentation duration. For instance, Roediger et al. presented DRM lists at rates of 20, 80, 160, and 320 milliseconds per target and found that the proportion of lists that produced false recall of the stimulus word increased from .10 to .25 to .31 to .33. In contrast, Gallo (2000) found that the proportion of DRM lists that produced false recall *decreased* from .47 to .40 to .26 as presentation duration increased from 500 to 1000 to 3000 milliseconds. Although these studies failed to detect the predicted inverted-U relation, note that they have a design limitation: The range of presentation durations was restricted in both cases and may not have been broad enough to reveal an inverted-U relation. According to the opponent-processes approach, this relation will only be revealed in sequences for which (a) initial durations are so fleeting that they only allow for partial processing of meaning, and (b) later durations include ones for which meaning processing is complete but surface processing is still increasing. Thus, the contrasting results of Roediger et al. and Gallo may be due to the

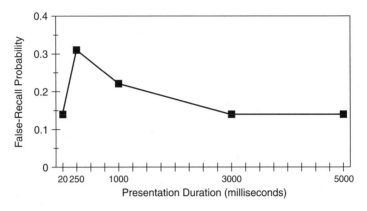

Figure 4-5. The relation between false memory and presentation duration. The plotted data are for intrusions of stimulus words on free-recall tests following presentation of DRM lists in an experiment reported by McDermott and Watson (2001).

fact that a 20- to 320-millisecond sequence satisfies only Condition a, whereas a 500- to 3000-millisecond sequence satisfies only Condition b.

This problem was eliminated in an experiment by McDermott and Watson (2001) that included a much broader range of presentation rates. In this experiment, 36 DRM lists were presented, with subjects performing 45 seconds of written free recall following the presentation of each. For different groups of subjects, the lists were presented at rates of 20, 250, 1000, 3000, and 5000 milliseconds per item. The mean level of intrusion of unpresented stimulus words at each presentation rate is plotted in Figure 4-5. As can be seen, the predicted pattern of initial increases in duration producing higher levels of false memory and later increases producing lower levels of false memory emerged quite clearly.

Although we have seen in this section that false memory is lawfully related to the duration of target experiences, it might be thought that laboratory experiments in which presentation rate is varied from intervals of several milliseconds up to intervals of several seconds would have no relevance to everyday forms of false memory. Such a criticism would not be well placed, however. To see why, one need only consider eyewitness testimony in criminal cases in which events that determine the guilt or innocence of defendants have been only briefly observed by witnesses. For instance, consider eyewitnesses to a drive-by shooting who saw the culprit's face for only a fraction of a second through the window of a speeding car (e.g., *State of Arizona v. Sagarnaga*, 2001). Or, consider an eyewitness to a bank robbery who saw the culprit's face for only a fraction of a second as he ran out of a bank (e.g., *State of Arizona v. Mejia*, 2002). In these situations, and others in which testimony focuses on very briefly experienced events, data such as those considered above raise obvious questions about the possibility that testimony could be infected by false memories arising from the fact that salient meaning content (e.g., gender and race) was stored but not verbatim traces of the exact details of the experience.

Repetition of Events

We have already encountered repetition in connection with the speed of presentation of target events. As we now consider it, however, repetition refers to multiple presentations of events when individual presentations are of sufficient duration to allow ample time for both the meaning content and the surface form of experience to be processed. We treat this as a distinct form of repetition because the duration of individual presentations has exceeded 2 seconds in the great preponderance of experiments in which repetition has been studied (usually with words, pictures, or sentences serving as the target material).

Repetition in this more leisurely sense is one of the oldest manipulations in the scientific study of memory, the first systematic data on it having been reported by Ebbinghaus (1885/1913). Ebbinghaus investigated the relation between true-memory performance and the number of presentations of a list—typically a list of nonsense syllables—using savings in relearning as his performance measure. In a relearning experiment, subjects study a list at time T1, and then, at some later time T2, the list is re-presented as many times as is necessary for subjects to learn it to a criterion of errorless recall. The performance measure—savings—is the reduction in the number of repetitions that is required to relearn a previously studied list at T2, relative to the number of repetitions that is required to learn a new list to the same criterion. Ebbinghaus found that the savings measurement at T2 was proportional to the number of list repetitions at T1. Thus, by way of illustration, if T2 is a week after T1, the reduction in the number of repetitions that is required to relearn a list will be greater if the list had been presented five times in the first presentation than if it had been presented once. Since Ebbinghaus, many experiments have shown that levels of performance on measures of true memory improve as a consequence of repetition in a negatively accelerated fashion (i.e., initial repetitions produce more improvement than do subsequent ones).

There are two basic varieties of repetition in false-memory research, both of which are important in their way and about which opponent-processes distinctions make some counterintuitive predictions. The first is what we shall call *verbatim repetition*. As its name suggests, this form of repetition consists of multiple presentations (at leisurely presentation rates) of the same events in the same way. The other variety is what we shall call *gist repetition*. Because different events can have the same or very similar meaning, it is possible to repeat aspects of their meaning content without repeating the events themselves. To illustrate, consider the following word list: *green, Mary, soccer, Chicago, horse, oak, kidney, diamond, July, Buick*. If this were the target list in a memory experiment, verbatim repetition would involve multiple presentations of these same 10 words, perhaps in different orders. But, gist repetition would involve presenting these 10 words, followed by 10 new words with similar meanings (say, *blue, Alice, baseball, Denver, cow, elm, liver, ruby, September, Ford*), followed by 10 more new words with similar meanings (say, *orange, Kathy, hockey, Cleveland, sheep, pine, stomach, sapphire, February, Plymouth*), and so on. From the standpoint of false-memory research, the fundamental difference between the two forms of repetition is that both surface form *and* meaning recur in verbatim repetition, but only meaning recurs in gist repetition. When it comes to predicting repetition effects, this fact entails that the different consolidation rates for verbatim and gist traces are central to predictions about verbatim repetition (because surface form and meaning are both repeated), but not to predictions about gist repetition.

In everyday life, verbatim and gist repetition are confounded in that recurrences of familiar events (driving an automobile, attending a baseball game, eating at your favorite restaurant) are normally mixtures of verbatim and gist repetition. To understand how each type of repetition affects false memory, however, they must be separated experimentally, with the effects of variations in one being assessed while the other is held constant. Evidence of this sort is summarized in the two subsections that follow.

Verbatim Repetition

We noted in chapter 3 that one-process theories are constrained to forecast that variables that have marked effects on true memory will have similar effects on false memory. Repetition is a case in point. In Underwood's (1965) original research on semantic false recognition, for instance, it was proposed that verbatim repetition of targets would increase false alarms to their synonyms and antonyms because hits and false alarms to meaning-preserving distractors are supported by a shared memory-strength variable. At the time, this proposal seemed quite plausible to researchers (see Hall & Kolzoff, 1970), if for no other reason than the obvious fact that true and false memories are both by-products of experiencing the same target events. However, opponent-processes distinctions yield the more surprising proposal that verbatim repetition ought to drive levels of true and false memory in opposite directions, a possibility that follows from apparent differences in the consolidation rates for true and false memories.

Suppose that subjects are exposed to a series of target events that satisfy the baseline criterion that exposure shall be sufficiently unhurried so that surface and meaning content can be fully processed. We know from the earlier discussion of consolidation that this does not guarantee that verbatim and gist traces of targets will both be preserved and that, indeed, consolidation favors the latter over the former. Because consolidation is imperfect, subsequent repetitions of these targets will strengthen both verbatim and gist memories. But because gist memories are stronger than verbatim memories after initial exposure, owing to differential consolidation, subsequent presentations will benefit verbatim memory more than gist memory. In other words, across a few verbatim repetitions, net increases in verbatim memory ought to be greater than net increases in gist memory. As verbatim traces are the memorial basis for suppressing false recognition and false recall, both forms of error ought to decrease as repetitions increase.

Repetition-induced decreases in false memory have been obtained for a variety of meaning-preserving distractors. For example, we have reported several experiments in which false recognition of associates, synonyms, antonyms, same-category exemplars, and category labels of target words was measured when the target words had been presented once versus multiple times (Brainerd & Reyna, 1996; Brainerd,

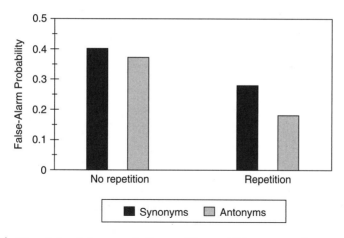

Figure 4-6. The relation between verbatim repetition and false memory for synonyms and antonyms. The plotted data are from Experiments 1 and 2 of Brainerd, Reyna, and Mojardin (1999).

Reyna, & Kneer, 1995; Brainerd, Reyna, & Mojardin, 1999). Although procedural details varied from experiment to experiment, the shared features of interest were that subjects studied a target list on which some items were presented only once, while others were repeated various numbers of times (depending upon the experiment). Subjects then responded to a standard recognition test on which the probes were targets, semantically related distractors (i.e., synonyms, antonyms, or category labels), and unrelated distractors. In most experiments, semantic false-recognition effects were significantly smaller for distractors whose corresponding targets had been presented more than once. Some illustrative data from Brainerd et al. (1999) are shown in Figure 4-6, where it can be seen that repetition produced a reduction of roughly .10 in the probability of false alarms to synonyms and antonyms of targets. Repetition-induced reductions have also been reported for false recognition and false recall of stimulus words for DRM lists. Concerning false recognition, Benjamin (2001) discovered that when DRM lists were presented at a rate of 3 seconds per target, the false-alarm probability for stimulus words was approximately .25 higher following a single presentation than following three presentations. Schacter, Verfaellie, Anes, and Racine (1998) found similar reductions in false alarms to stimulus words across a series of five presentations of a set of DRM lists. Concerning false recall, Brainerd, Payne, Wright, and Reyna (2003) found that stimulus words intruded in 43% of free-recall protocols following one presentation of a set of DRM lists but in only 18% of free-recall protocols following three presentations.

Seamon, Luo, Schwartz, Jones, Lee, and Jones (2002) refined opponent-processes predictions about verbatim repetition by pointing out that overall, the expected relation between repetition and false memory must be an inverted U. That this ought to be the overall relation becomes trivially obvious when one considers that zero presentations of target events counts as a "repetition"—specifically, as the lowest possible number of repetitions. Levels of false memory for meaning-preserving dis-

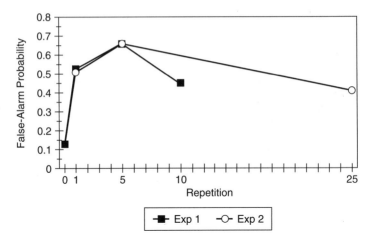

Figure 4-7. Inverted-U relation between repetition of DRM lists and false alarms to unpresented stimulus words. The plotted data are from Experiments 1 and 2 of Seamon, Luo, Schwartz, Jones, Lee, and Jones (2002).

tractors must increase as one moves from zero presentations to one presentation. Beyond this, however, one must allow for the possibility that there could be further increases as a consequence of additional repetitions if, for some reason, meaning processing was not complete following a single presentation. To investigate this proposal, Seamon, Luo, Schwartz, et al. presented nine DRM lists to their subjects at a rate of 2 seconds per item. In one experiment, three lists were presented once, three lists were presented 5 times, and three lists were presented 10 times. In a second experiment, three lists were presented once, three lists were presented 5 times, and three lists were presented 25 times. The lists were followed by a recognition test composed of target probes, the unpresented stimulus words for the nine lists, and the stimulus words for nine other DRM lists that had not been presented (zero repetitions). The pattern that emerged in each experiment is shown in Figure 4-7. As Seamon, Luo, Schwartz, et al. had anticipated, the overall relation between repetition and false recognition of stimulus words was an inverted U. In both experiments, false recognition increased as the number of list presentations increased from zero to five, but it declined thereafter.

Gist Repetition

Upon first impression, it appears that the opponent-processes approach should predict that levels of false memory will increase if targets themselves are not repeated but their meanings are. This prediction seems to follow because the memorial basis for false recognition and false recall (gist traces) is being strengthened but the memorial basis for suppressing them is not. There is a complication with respect to this notion, however. Although verbatim traces of *individual* targets are not being strengthened by gist repetition, additional verbatim traces that can be used to suppress false-memory reports are accumulating on each repetition. To see the nature of this complication, consider the above example of a 10-word list that begins with *green* and ends with *Buick*. Suppose that following presentation of this list, there is a .2 probability of consolidating an accessible verbatim trace of *green* that will suppress the unpresented color name *purple* on a subsequent recognition test. If there is one verbatim repetition of the list, the probability that an accessible verbatim trace of *green* will be available to suppress false recognition of *purple* is $.2 + .2(1 - .2)$ or .36. But if there is one gist repetition and the same probabilities apply, there will be a .2 probability that an accessible verbatim trace of *green* is available (from the presentation of the first list) and a .2 probability that an accessible verbatim trace of *blue* is available (from presentation of the *blue . . . Ford* list), for a total probability of .4 that a verbatim trace of *some* color name will be available to suppress false recognition of *purple*.

The way out of this quandary is to realize that the probabilities of consolidating verbatim traces across repetitions are not the same for the two types of repetition; instead, they are higher for verbatim repetition. The reason, which has been established in many studies of the phenomenon of *processing fluency* (e.g., Whittlesea, Jacoby, & Girard, 1990; Whittlesea & Williams, 2000), is that the ease with which a target's surface or semantic features are processed and retained in memory does not remain constant over a series of repetitions. According to research on processing fluency, it is easier to process a feature if it has been previously presented than if it has not. During a series of gist repetitions, targets' meaning content is repeated but their surface form is not. Therefore, it becomes progressively easier to process and retain meaning content but not to process and retain surface content, which should result in net increases in false memory—at least up to the point at which meaning processing is complete.

Data showing that, indeed, false memory increases over a sequence of gist repetitions have been reported for both false recognition and false recall. Dewhurst (2001) and the authors of this book (Brainerd & Reyna, 1998b) have detected this pattern in false recognition. In Dewhurst's experiments, subjects viewed a single long list (156 words). Some of the presented words were exemplars of 12 familiar taxonomic categories, such as colors, musical instruments, cities, and professions. For each category that was embedded in the list, a total of one, four, or eight *different* exemplar words were presented. Later, subjects responded to a recognition test on which the false-memory items were unpresented exemplars from these same categories. As the number of presented exemplars increased from one to four to eight, the false-recognition probability for embedded-category distractors increased from .16 to .34 to .36. Our data were similar. Our subjects also viewed a single long list (96 words) in which 12 familiar categories were embedded. One exemplar was presented for half of the categories, and three exemplars were presented for the other half of the categories. The false-memory items on the subsequent recognition test were the names of the 12 categories. The false-recognition probability for these category names increased from .19 to .27 as the number of presented exemplars increased from one to three.

Robinson and Roediger (1997) reported some experiments in which false recognition and false recall of DRM stimulus words increased systematically as a function of the number of target words in each DRM list. Twenty lists were presented

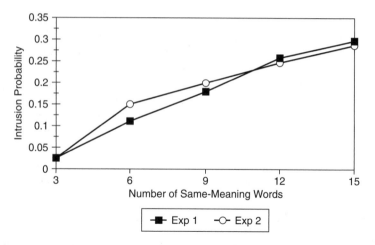

Figure 4-8. Relation between the number of same-meaning words in DRM lists and intrusions of unpresented stimulus words in free recall. The plotted data are from Robinson and Roediger (1997).

to each subject, with individual lists consisting of 3, 6, 9, 12, or 15 words. After presentation of each list, subjects performed 30 seconds of irrelevant buffer activity (arithmetic problems), which was followed by a 90-second free-recall test. After all 20 lists had been presented and recalled, subjects responded to a recognition test on which the false-memory items were the unpresented stimulus words for these lists. The overall pattern for recall is shown in Figure 4-8, and the overall pattern for recognition is shown in Figure 4-9. It is clear in both instances that gist repetition (i.e., adding new words that recapitulate meanings) dramatically elevated measured levels of false memory.

Deep and Shallow Processing

In the opponent-processes approach, verbatim traces of target events suppress false memories by neutralizing the familiarity of false-but-gist-consistent events. A seemingly reasonable extrapolation from this principle is that storage variables that improve the accuracy of true memory ought to reduce false recognition and false recall. However, opponent-processes distinctions lead to the more subtle expectation that this relation will not hold in general and that, instead, whether the relation holds in a particular experiment ought to depend upon the memorial basis for increases in the accuracy of true memory. Remember that verbatim memory and gist memory reinforce each other when it comes to true memory; improvements in one or the other or both will increase hit rates and correct recall. The situation is different for false memory. Storage variables will (a) increase false-alarm rates and intrusion rates if gist memory is strengthened more than verbatim memory, (b) decrease false-alarm rates and intrusion rates if verbatim memory is strengthened more than gist memory, and (c) have no effect on false-alarm rates and intrusion rates if verbatim and gist memory are strengthened by comparable amounts. This leads to the sur-

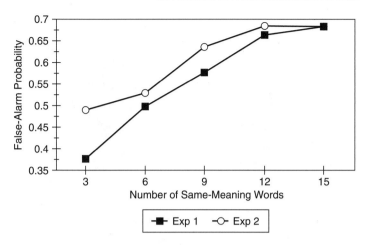

Figure 4-9. Relation between the number of same-meaning words in DRM lists and false alarms to unpresented stimulus words on recognition tests. The plotted data are from Robinson and Roediger (1997).

prising prediction that even variables that produce dramatic improvements in true memory may also increase false memory. The types of variables for which this pattern is expected are ones whose principal effect is to strengthen subjects' memory for the meaning content of experience.

This pattern is expected, for instance, for one of the most frequently studied storage manipulations of the past 3 decades: *deep-processing instructions.* Craik and Lockhart (1972) referred to the sort of processing that we have been calling surface and semantic as "shallow" and "deep," respectively, and they stressed the role of the latter in true memory. They stressed, more especially, that subjects are more likely to recall or recognize targets if storage-phase processing is deep rather than shallow, and hence, factors that increase deep processing should enhance true memory. Although many manipulations could have this effect, one with high face validity is simply requesting of subjects, prior to the presentation of the target material, that they focus on the meaning of events. In addition, Craik and Lockhart viewed this instructional approach as being of special theoretical significance. They thought that deep processing required that subjects adopt an active, elaborative approach to remembering target material, which presumably could be ensured by telling or requiring them to extract meaning. This line of thinking prompted many studies in which the effects of different study-phase orienting instructions were compared. In a typical design, one group of subjects (deep processing) would be oriented toward some aspect of the meaning of the target materials, and a second group of subjects (shallow processing) would be oriented toward some aspect of the surface form of these materials. To illustrate, consider again the list *green . . . Buick.* Subjects in a deep-processing condition might be asked to rate the pleasantness of each word on a 1–5 scale, or to think of another word with the same meaning, or to think of a phrase in which the word fits. Subjects in a shallow-processing condition might be asked to count the number of vowels in each word, or to count the number of

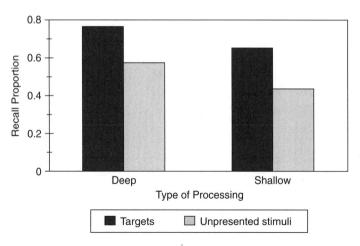

Figure 4-10. Elevation of true and false recall of unpresented DRM stimulus words by deep encoding instructions. The plotted data are from Toglia, Neuschatz, and Goodwin (1999).

consonants in each word, or to identify the second letter in each word. Many studies (e.g., Bower & Karlin, 1974; Craik & Tulving, 1975) have shown that deep-processing instructions produce substantial improvements in true recall and recognition, relative to shallow-processing conditions. These improvements have been reported for materials as varied as word lists, pictures, and narratives.

Although it is conceivable that deep-processing instructions could also enhance the processing of targets' surface forms (e.g., by compelling subjects to pay close attention to individual targets), the obvious interpretation is that regardless of what its other effects may be, its overwhelming effect is to enhance the processing of meaning. Therefore, this is a candidate for a variable that could have the counter-intuitive effect of simultaneously making memory more and less accurate by elevating true recall/recognition and also elevating false recall/recognition. Evidence has accumulated that deep-processing instructions do, in fact, have this paradoxical effect (e.g., Rhodes & Anastasi, 2000; Thapar & McDermott, 2001; Toglia, Neuschatz, & Goodwin, 1999). Toglia et al. reported such an experiment, using the DRM procedure. Subjects listened to six DRM lists, with deep-processing subjects rating the pleasantness of each word on a 5-point scale and shallow-processing subjects judging whether each word contained the letter *a*. As can be seen in Figure 4-10, where the proportions of true and false recall have been plotted for this experiment, deep processing had the familiar effect of increasing true recall, but it also increased intrusions of unpresented stimulus words by about the same amount. Thapar and McDermott extended Toglia et al.'s research in two noteworthy respects: They measured the effects of deep-processing instructions on false recognition and false recall, and they measured such effects on delayed and immediate memory tests. In their experiments, subjects studied eight DRM lists under either deep-processing instructions (rating the pleasantness of each word) or shallow-processing instructions (counting the number of vowels in each word or identifying the color of the ink in which each word was presented). The subjects in one experiment performed

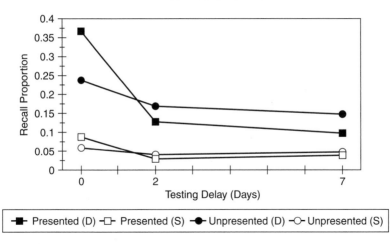

Figure 4-11. Elevation of true and false recall of unpresented DRM stimulus words by deep-encoding instructions over a 7-day interval. The plotted data are from Thapar and McDermott (2001). Presented (D) = targets from deeply processed lists; presented (S) = targets from shallowly processed lists; unpresented (D) = stimulus words for deeply processed lists; and unpresented (S) = stimulus words for shallowly processed lists.

free recall immediately following list presentation or 2 days later or 7 days later. The subjects in another experiment responded to a recognition test on which the false-memory items were unpresented stimulus words immediately after list presentation or 2 days later or 7 days later. As in Toglia et al.'s experiment, deep processing elevated false as well as true recall, and these effects were still present 7 days later (see Figure 4-11). In addition, deep processing elevated false as well as true recognition, and these effects also were still present 7 days later (see Figure 4-12).

There are more subtle means of encouraging subjects to process the meaning content of targets, however, without encouraging or discouraging the processing of surface content. One such method is to block together during presentation targets with similar meanings. To illustrate, reconsider the experiments of Dewhurst (2001) and Brainerd and Reyna (1998b), in which a single long word list was presented with several taxonomic categories being exemplified within the list. Remember that some categories were exemplified four or eight times in Dewhurst's experiment and some categories were exemplified three times in Brainerd and Reyna's experiment. In both experiments, the overall ordering of presented words was random. Suppose, however, that the words for the multiply exemplified categories had been presented together, in a sequence, within the list (e.g., if color were exemplified by four words, the words *green*, *blue*, *orange*, and *yellow* would be presented in sequence somewhere within the list). Presumably, such blocking would ensure that subjects noticed that multiple color names were presented and would orient them toward processing that meaning, but it would not be expected to affect the processing of these words' surface forms because individual words are still being presented in the same way as before. Thus, the opponent-processes prediction would be that this simple

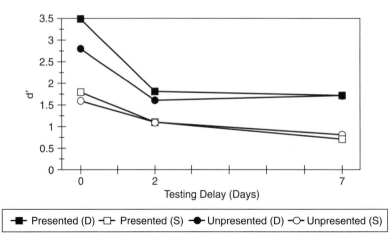

Figure 4-12. Elevation of true and false recognition of unpresented DRM stimulus words by deep-encoding instructions over a 7-day interval. The plotted data are from Thapar and McDermott (2001). Presented (D) = targets from deeply processed lists; presented (S) = targets from shallowly processed lists; unpresented (D) = stimulus words for deeply processed lists; and unpresented (S) = stimulus words for shallowly processed lists.

technique of ordering target events so that those with similar meanings appear in close proximity should elevate false memory.

This prediction has been verified in several DRM experiments. The earliest one was reported by McDermott (1996). Her subjects were presented with a single list of 45 words, composed of three DRM lists of 15 words apiece. The 45 words were presented in random order for half the subjects, but the words were grouped by DRM list for the other half of the subjects (e.g., referring back to the stimulus words in Table 2-2, the 15 associates of *sweet* were presented first, followed by the 15 associates of *chair*, followed by the 15 associates of *short*). List presentation was followed by a free-recall test. The list was then presented four more times, with each subsequent presentation also being followed by a free-recall test. The subjects returned to the laboratory 2 days later for a final free-recall test. On all of these tests, intrusions of unpresented stimulus words were higher (.15 higher, on average) following blocked presentation than following random presentation (see Figure 4-13). The same pattern was obtained in later experiments by Toglia et al. (1999) and Brainerd et al. (2003). Toglia et al.'s subjects were presented with a single 60-word list, composed of five DRM sublists in either blocked or random order. The subjects performed free recall immediately after list presentation or 1 week later or 3 weeks later. Across these tests, the proportion of unpresented stimulus words that intruded during free recall was .15 higher following blocked presentation than following random presentation. Brainerd et al.'s subjects were presented with a single 90-word list, composed of six DRM sublists in either blocked or random order. Following list presentation, they performed three free-recall tests, with 2 minutes of buffer activity (arithmetic problems) interpolated between each pair of tests. Across the three tests, the proportion of unpresented stimulus words that intruded during

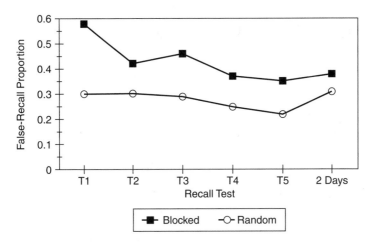

Figure 4-13. Elevation of false recall by blocked presentation of DRM lists. The plotted data are from McDermott (1996).

free recall was .16 higher following blocked presentation than following random presentation.

In line with opponent-processes analysis, these studies establish that focusing attention on the meaning content of experience elevates subsequent levels of false memory. Some further studies by Seamon, Lee, Toner, Wheeler, Goodkind, and Birch (2002) showed that it is possible to identify precise connections between semantic processing and false memory, such that a specific variety of false memory is elevated following a focused form of semantic processing. We saw in chapters 2 and 3 that Deese (1959), Johnson and Raye (1981), and Underwood (1965) all thought that events are falsely remembered because aspects of our experience cause us to think of those events. In the specific case of word lists, Underwood proposed that studying a list will induce mental pronunciation of words that are frequently associated with list items (implicit associative responses), which will increase the tendency to falsely recall and falsely recognize mentally pronounced items. Although mental pronunciations cannot be measured with current technology, Seamon, Lee, et al. did the next best thing. They first informed their subjects about the phenomenon of mental pronunciation. Then, the subjects read a total of eight DRM lists, which were presented on a computer screen. Half of the subjects were instructed to think aloud as they read, stating any word or thought that came to mind, even if it seemed to have nothing to do with the words on the screen. Because (as we saw in chapter 2) such lists revolve around a single stimulus word, this think-aloud procedure allows one to determine (a) whether stimulus words spontaneously come to mind as their corresponding lists are read (as Deese [1959] assumed), and (b) whether such events elevate false memory for the stimulus words. Seamon, Lee, et al. found evidence in support of both propositions. Concerning item a, when a leisurely presentation rate was used (5 seconds per word), presentation of a given DRM list produced verbalization of its stimulus word approximately 28% of the time. Concerning item b, when a free-recall test was administered for the presented lists, the probability of falsely recalling a stimulus word was .20 when the word had not been verbalized during list presentation, but the probability nearly doubled (to .39) when the word had been verbalized during list presentation.

Event Distinctiveness

If semantic processing of target events elevates false memories by making the meaning of experience more salient, opponent-processes concepts would surely expect the reverse pattern for the salience of surface content—that making the surface form of experience more distinctive ought to lower false memory. The question is how best to evaluate this possibility experimentally. To anyone who has taken an introductory psychology course, the classic von Restorff effect will undoubtedly be the first approach that comes to mind. Consider the following two word lists:

List 1	List 2
Green	Green
Brown	Brown
Chicago	Purple
Grey	Grey
Yellow	Yellow
White	White
Orange	Orange
Pink	Pink
Blue	Blue
Tan	Tan

Whereas all the words in List 2 are color names, List 1 contains a single word, the name of a familiar city, that breaks the mold. If a free-recall test is administered following list presentation, this particular word is much more likely to be recalled than any of the other words (e.g., Howe, Courage, Vernescu, & Hunt, 2000; Hunt & Lamb, 2001). This is the *von Restorff effect,* and the customary explanation is that the isolated word is distinctive, that it stands out against the background of the other words. The problem is that it is not clear *why* it stands out. Of particular concern from the perspective of false memory, it may be that the contrasting meaning (big city) stands out against the background of color meaning. Consequently, even though *Chicago* is more likely to be recalled than any of the color words, it does not follow that false memory for other city names will be suppressed unless the meaning contrast leads to enhanced processing of surface information.

Such ambiguities can be avoided by attempting to increase the distinctiveness of targets' surface content via more surgical manipulations, which are specifically designed to promote the processing of surface content without promoting the processing of meaning content. Here, the opponent-processes prediction is clear: Such manipulations should improve true recall and true recognition by strengthening verbatim traces, and because those improvements are verbatim-based, there should be correlated reductions in false memory. Seamon, Goodkind, Dumey, Dick, Aufseeser, Strickland, Woulfin, and Fung (2003) evaluated this prediction using a variant on deep versus shallow processing. Seamon et al. reasoned that verbatim memory would

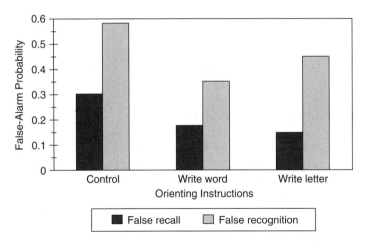

Figure 4-14. Suppression of false recall and false recognition via surface-encoding instructions. The plotted data are from Seamon, Goodkind, Dumey, Dick, Aufseeser, Strickland, Woulfin, and Fung (2003).

be strengthened by surface-processing instructions and that this would produce correlated reductions in false recall and false recognition. They reported two experiments in which their subjects studied six DRM lists, with some subjects simply listening to the words being read (control condition) and others performing one of two types of surface processing. One type (*write-word* condition) consisted of subjects simply writing each target word as they heard it, while the other (*write-letter* condition) involved subjects writing the second letter of each word as they heard it. In one experiment, subjects performed 3 minutes of written free recall following presentation of all six lists. Intrusions of unpresented stimulus words provided the measure of false memory. This was followed by four more trials of list presentation and free recall. In a second experiment, the procedure was the same, except that each presentation of the six lists was followed by a recognition test, with false recognition of unpresented stimulus words providing the measure of false memory. The general patterns that emerged are shown in Figure 4-14. Consistent with the view that selective strengthening of verbatim traces via shallow processing reduces false memory for gist-consistent information, false recall and false recognition of unpresented stimulus words were considerably lower in the write-word and write-letter conditions than in the control condition.

A second line of attack on increasing the distinctiveness of surface information is to present target events that, for one reason or another, are known to attract surface-processing attention. This approach has been used in experiments by Reyna and Kiernan (1995), Schacter and associates (e.g., Israel & Schacter, 1997; Schacter et al., 1999), Seamon, Luo, Schlegel, Greene, and Goldenberg (2000), and the authors of this book (Brainerd & Reyna, 1993). Following a review of the literature on memory for metaphors, Reyna and Kiernan concluded that comprehension of a metaphor requires especially careful processing of the surface form of metaphorical statements (exact wording mattered for interpretation), which would be expected to result in the storage of robust verbatim traces of such statements. If so, false memory for statements that preserve the meaning of metaphors ought to be exceptionally low. Reyna and Kiernan evaluated this prediction using much the same procedures as in their earlier studies of false memory for sentences (Reyna & Kiernan, 1994), the only modification being that the target events were three-sentence vignettes that ended in metaphorical statements (e.g., The woman was shopping in the grocery store; the woman saw the lost boy near the door; *the woman was an aspirin, kneeling by the lost boy*) rather than three-sentence vignettes that specified spatial or magnitude relations. The false-memory items, then, were sentences that preserved the meaning of the metaphorical statements (e.g., The woman was medicine, kneeling by the lost boy; The woman made him feel better, kneeling by the lost boy). Across the various conditions of their experiments, false-alarm rates for such unpresented statements were indeed very low (.08 overall), as predicted. These false-alarm rates were so low that a false-memory effect was not observed in most immediate testing conditions (i.e., distractors that preserved the meaning of metaphors failed to produce higher false-alarm rates than distractors that did not preserve meaning). After a delay, false memories of metaphors increased, but not to the levels observed for literal sentences.

The procedures of Schacter and associates (Israel & Schacter, 1997; Schacter et al., 1999), Seamon et al. (2000), and Brainerd and Reyna (1993) are grounded in the extensive literature on memory for pictures versus printed words (e.g., Humphreys & Yuille, 1973; Paivio, 1971). In a traditional type of design, subjects are exposed to a list of concrete nouns (e.g., *baby, book, car, chair, fish, football, lamp, snake, star, tree*), which they are told to remember for a later memory test. Because these words refer to familiar objects, subjects can be exposed to them in two ways: as the indicated series of printed letter strings or as a series of pictures (or line drawings) that depict the various objects. When this is done, recall and recognition are superior following pictorial presentation. On its face, the picture-word manipulation is a variation in surface content, specifically a variation in the perceptual formatting of the same sequence of words. Because the same meanings are being presented, a plausible explanation of the picture-word effect is that pictures yield more robust verbatim traces than do letter strings. If so, pictorial presentation should suppress false memory for gist-consistent events. This pattern has been observed by Schacter and associates for the stimulus words of DRM lists, by Seamon et al. for unpresented category exemplars, and by the authors for unpresented sentences.

In the two initial experiments of Schacter and associates, Israel and Schacter (1997) introduced a design in which subjects listened to 14 DRM lists, with oral presentation of each list being accompanied by either of two types of visual support. In the first condition (word), the printed form of each list word was displayed on a computer screen as it was being read aloud. In the second condition (picture), a line drawing of the corresponding object was displayed on the computer screen as each word was being read aloud. List presentation was followed by a recognition test on which the unpresented stimulus word for each list and one other semantically related distractor were the false-memory items. If it is true that pictures

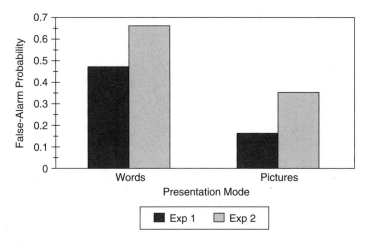

Figure 4-15. Suppression of false recognition following pictorial presentation of DRM lists. The plotted data are from Israel and Schacter (1997).

produce stronger verbatim traces than printed words, levels of false memory should have been lower in the second condition. They were. Average false-alarm rates for the two types of semantically related distractors are shown in Figure 4-15, where it can be seen that the reduction following pictorial presentation relative to word presentation was quite dramatic. Similar reductions have been observed in later experiments (Schacter et al., 1999), and reductions have also been observed using other presentation methods that selectively strengthen verbatim traces. For example, Dodson and Schacter (2001) reasoned that reductions in false memory should also be observed if a condition in which subjects pronounced each word aloud as they heard it were compared to a condition in which subjects only listened to words. The results confirmed their prediction. Seamon et al.'s (2000) subjects were presented with six lists consisting of nine targets apiece, with each list being composed entirely of exemplars of a single taxonomic category (e.g., animals, fruit, insects). However, the targets were presented as a series of line drawings (Snodgrass & Vanderwart, 1980), rather than as a list of spoken or printed words. This was followed by a recognition test, with unpresented exemplars from the same categories serving as false-memory items. On this test, the probability of adults making false alarms to meaning-preserving distractors was very low (.08 on average). In a later experiment, Seamon et al. presented these categorized lists as printed words rather than as pictures, and the false-alarm rate for unpresented distractors more than tripled (to .29 on average). Finally, Brainerd and Reyna (1993) presented the three-sentence vignettes of Reyna and Kiernan (1994) in two ways: as oral statements (which is how Reyna and Kiernan had presented them) and as pictures (line drawings). This was followed by recognition tests on which subjects were instructed to identify presented targets and distractors that were consistent with the meaning of presented targets. Relative to oral presentation, pictorial presentation increased subjects' ability to identify targets but decreased their ability to identify meaning-preserving distractors.

Schacter et al. (1999) pointed out that these procedures for ensuring the storage of more robust traces might suppress false memories in either or both of two ways. First, suppression might occur at the item level. That is, subjects might avoid recalling or recognizing false-but-gist-consistent items (e.g., *poodle*) because they vividly remember the presentation of the corresponding items (e.g., No, I didn't hear *poodle* because I distinctly remember hearing *collie.*). Second, suppression might also occur at the metacognitive level by creating what Schacter et al. termed a *distinctiveness heuristic* (see chapter 3). According to Schacter et al., the experience of having been exposed to events that produce especially vivid verbatim traces (e.g., pictures) may create an expectation in subjects' minds that true items on memory tests will provoke vivid mental phenomenology (the "remember" phenomenology discussed in chapter 3). If this expectation is applied when subjects are responding to memory tests, it will cause them to avoid recalling or recognizing items whose prior presentation is not vividly recollected. Because false-but-gist-consistent items are not presented, recall and recognition of such items ought to be suppressed because unpresented items should not provoke vivid phenomenology on memory tests, or at least not at nearly the levels that true items provoke it. Available research suggests that storage manipulations that enhance verbatim traces suppress false memories via both the item-level route and the metacognitive route (Brainerd, Reyna, Wright, & Mojardin, 2003). Indeed, the fact that such manipulations make two suppression paths available may be the reason that those manipulations have been so successful.

Last, there are two other presentation manipulations that should, on their face, affect verbatim traces, in one case strengthening them and in the other case weakening them, which have also been found to affect false memory in ways that are consistent with an opponent-processes framework. The first manipulation involves presenting target events as spoken words versus printed words. This method of presentation should lead to stronger verbatim traces of printed words than of spoken words and, therefore, lower levels of false memory. The reason can be found in the literature on memory processes in reading. In numerous studies (e.g., Pollatsek, Lesch, Morris, & Rayner, 1992), it has been observed that reading words also activates their corresponding phonological codes (e.g., reading *collie* causes "collie" to echo in the mind's ear), but the reverse is not usually true (e.g., hearing *collie* does not typically cause the letter string c-o-l-l-i-e to flash in the mind's eye). The obvious inference is that following visual presentation, subjects will be much more likely to have stored *both* visual and auditory verbatim traces than following auditory presentation. Consistent with this inference, levels of false recall and false recognition of gist-consistent information have been found to be lower following visual than following auditory presentation (e.g., Gallo et al., 2001; Smith & Hunt, 1998).

The second method of presentation, the one that should weaken verbatim traces and, hence, inflate false memory, has been mentioned earlier in other contexts: divided attention. It follows from the earlier discussion of subliminal semantic activation that as long as the presentation rate is rather leisurely (e.g., >2 seconds), presenting events under conditions of divided attention (e.g., reading a list of target words while simultaneously monitoring a sequence of orally presented digits) ought to interfere much more with the storage of verbatim traces than with the storage of gist traces, leading to net increases in false recall and false recognition. In line with this prediction, Seamon et al. (1998, Experiment 2) found that false-recognition levels for DRM stimulus words were 30% higher following divided-attention presentation than following full-attention presentation.

Consolidation Activity

A final storage variable that provides a particularly compelling illustration of the difference between the older one-process view of false memory and the opponent-processes view is a variable that focuses on the consolidation interval following exposure to target events. In the earlier discussion of consolidation, we saw that even when the surface form and meaning content of a target are fully processed during exposure, this does not guarantee that the corresponding verbatim and gist traces will survive the postexposure consolidation period. It should therefore be possible to improve or impair a trace's chances of survival by interpolating various manipulations in the interval between exposure and test. Perhaps the most obvious one, which was first studied by Bjork (1970), is merely to instruct subjects either to remember the events that they have just experienced or to forget them. Intuitively, the former instruction should increase consolidation of whatever was stored during target exposure, whereas the latter instruction should decrease consolidation. Empirically, it has been found in many studies (e.g., Basden, Basden, & Gargano, 1993; Cloitre, Cancienne, Brodsky, Dulit, & Perry, 1996) that true recall and true recognition are better on memory tests that follow a "remember" instruction than on memory tests that follow a "forget" instruction.

But what about false memory for meaning-preserving events? Surprisingly, an opponent-processes analysis forecasts that remember-forget instructions ought to affect true memory without affecting false memory. The explanation for true-memory effects, according to this analysis, is that verbatim and gist traces reinforce each other when it comes to recalling or recognizing target events. Presumably, a "forget" instruction impairs consolidation of both verbatim and gist traces, relative to a "remember" instruction, for the simple reason that the instructions are not specific as to what should or should not be preserved. So, the effect is to encourage across-the-board elimination or retention of both verbatim and gist traces, and for that reason, true-memory effects are assured. False-memory effects are not assured because verbatim and gist traces are assumed to have opposite effects on false memory. A reduction in the consolidation of verbatim traces from a "forget" instruction will increase false recall and false recognition, but a reduction in the consolidation of gist traces will decrease false recall and false recognition.

What do the data show? Available findings agree with the counterintuitive prediction from opponent processes. The first set of published data was reported by Kimball and Bjork (2002). Subjects receiving forget or remember instructions were exposed to two DRM lists, one after the other. Following the first list, half of the subjects were told to forget it, and half were told to remember it for a later memory test. The second list was then presented, and this was followed by free-recall tests on which subjects in both instructional conditions were told to write as many words as they could remember from *both* List 1 and List 2. The usual true-memory effect was detected: Fewer List 1 targets were recalled following a forget instruction than following a remember instruction. However, levels of false recall (intrusions of unpresented stimulus words) were the same for the two types of instructions.

This pattern has been replicated by Seamon, Luo, Shulman, Toner, and Calgar (2002), using somewhat different procedures. In their experiment, 8 DRM lists were presented to half of the subjects (in two blocks of 4 lists each), and 12 DRM lists were presented to the other half of the subjects (in two blocks of 6 lists each). Following the first block of lists, half of the subjects in each group were told that an error had been made in presenting the first block of lists and that those lists should be forgotten, while the remaining subjects were told to remember those lists. The second block of lists was then presented to all subjects, which was followed by a free-recall test in which subjects were instructed to write as many words as they could remember from *both* blocks of lists. In this design, the effects of remember and forget instructions could be measured by two comparisons: (a) the Block 1 intrusion rates for subjects given each type of instruction, and (b) the Block 1 versus Block 2 intrusion rates for subjects given a forget instruction following Block 1. Both comparisons showed that false recall of unpresented stimulus words was not affected by such instructions.

Retrieving Memories

Assume that some target material, such as a narrative or a word list, has been experienced in a sufficiently leisurely fashion that there is ample time for the processing of targets' surface form and meaning content to be completed, that verbatim and gist traces have been stored in memory, and that traces of both types have survived consolidation. Assume, too, that memory tests are administered soon enough thereafter that there is little opportunity for forgetting, so that both types of traces will still be accessible. With these provisos in mind, we now consider variables that would be predicted, on the basis of opponent-processes distinctions, to influence the types of traces that are retrieved on memory tests. The general expectations, naturally, are that retrieval variables that increase subjects' tendency to access verbatim traces (relative to some baseline) ought to lower measured levels of false memory by increasing the incidence of recollection rejection and that retrieval variables that increase subjects' tendency to access gist traces ought to increase measured levels of false memory. Although there are several variables that might have such effects, we confine our attention to three that have produced clear and consistent evidence: *retrieval duration* (how much time passes before a response occurs on recognition or recall tests), *verbatim cuing* (presentation of test cues that should slant retrieval toward verbatim access), and *retrieval instructions* (presentation of test instructions that should slant retrieval toward verbatim access or gist access).

Retrieval Duration

In the earlier section on storage variables, we explored the effects of event duration. Retrieval duration is an analogous variable that is characteristic of memory tests, rather than of target exposure. Obviously, the amount of time that subjects must wait before they respond to an individual recognition probe or the amount of time that subjects are allowed to freely recall prior events can easily be varied experimentally. What predictions do opponent-processes ideas make about how such variations affect false-memory responses? The answer, interestingly, is that opposite predictions are made about false recognition and false recall. We discuss recognition first, followed by recall.

Recognition

We mentioned in the previous discussion of event duration that, overall, an inverted-U relation is expected between the false recognition of meaning-preserving distractors and event duration. The same type of relation is predicted between false recognition and retrieval time, for two reasons. First, we saw in chapter 3 that dual-process accounts of recognition specify that familiarity is a faster form of retrieval than recollection—for some reason, the memories that support feelings of global familiarity about a probe (gist traces in the case of meaning-preserving distractors) are accessed more rapidly than are the memories that support item-specific recollection (Atkinson & Juola, 1973, 1974; Mandler, 1980). We also saw that, according to the opponent-processes perspective on false memory, familiarity retrieval supports semantic false recognition, while recollective retrieval suppresses it. Suppose that subjects are allowed various amounts of time to respond to a recognition probe. Suppose, more explicitly, that on analogy to the previously discussed studies of event duration, retrieval duration varies from some value that is so fleeting that there is insufficient time for any information to be accessed in memory (e.g., 100 milliseconds) up to some value that is sufficiently long that all of the relevant information about a probe can be accessed (e.g., 3 seconds). If familiarity retrieval is faster than recollective retrieval, then as duration increases from its initial brief value, most of the memory information that accumulates at first will support familiarity, from which it follows that initial increases in retrieval duration will produce increases in false alarms to meaning-preserving distractors. However, as retrieval duration is further lengthened, memory information that supports recollection will also begin to accumulate, and eventually, a point will be reached beyond which the bulk of the information that accumulates from memory will support recollection, from which it follows that false alarms to meaning-preserving distractors will decline after that point.

The other reason for expecting an inverted-U relation was also mentioned in chapter 3. According to opponent-processes distinctions, meaning-preserving distractors are usually better retrieval cues for gist traces than for verbatim traces. If *davenport* is presented as a target and *sofa* is presented as a recognition probe, it is obvious that the two are very similar in meaning content but wildly different in surface form. Therefore, by the principle of encoding variability (Tulving & Thomson, 1971), it will be easier for *sofa* to access gist traces of *davenport*'s meaning than to access verbatim traces of its actual presentation (Brainerd, Reyna, & Kneer, 1995). It follows that if both types of traces are available in memory, it ought to take more time, on average, for meaning-preserving distractors to access verbatim traces of their corresponding targets than to access gist traces. Therefore, initial increases in retrieval duration ought to favor gist access (and increases in semantic false recognition), and subsequent increases ought to favor verbatim access (and decreases in semantic false recognition).

How are experimental tests of the predicted inverted-U relation to be conducted? Questions about how retrieval duration affects recognition performance have been studied with a procedure known as the *response-signal paradigm*, which was developed by Dosher (1984a, 1984b; Dosher & Rosedale, 1991). In this paradigm, the recognition test takes place with subjects looking at a computer screen. Probes (targets, meaning-preserving distractors, unrelated distractors) are flashed on the screen. The retrieval time for individual probes is manipulated by varying the length of time that the probe appears on the screen (e.g., 100–3000 milliseconds). To prevent subjects from taking uncontrolled additional amounts of time to access memory information, they are required to make their response within a very brief interval after each probe disappears from the screen. After a probe disappears, a signal (usually a tone) is given almost immediately thereafter (e.g., 300 milliseconds later), and subjects must respond immediately. Whenever a subject delays response for more than 100 milliseconds following the signal, that response is discarded from the data analysis. In two of Dosher's experiments (1984b; Dosher & Rosedale, 1991), the target materials were pairs of familiar words. Some of these pairs were semantically related (e.g., *chance-opportunity*), and others were not (e.g., *open-vegetable*). Later, a recognition test was administered in which the probes were also word pairs. Some pairs were targets, of course. Distractors consisted of both related pairs (e.g., *pursue-follow*) and unrelated pairs (e.g., *hire-suppress*). The meaning-preserving distractors were a subset of the latter group of distractors, consisting of unrelated pairs (e.g., *joy-shell*) in which one of the two words had been studied as part of a pair of semantically related targets (e.g., *sorrow-joy*). These false-memory items exhibited the predicted inverted-U relation: False alarms increased as retrieval time was lengthened from 100 to 300 milliseconds, but false alarms decreased as retrieval time was lengthened from 300 to 3500 milliseconds.

A follow-up literature is available on the response-signal paradigm, which has revealed inverted-U relations between retrieval duration and false-alarm rates for distractors that preserve features of targets (Gronlund & Ratcliff, 1989; Hintzman & Curran, 1994; Rotello & Heit, 1999, 2000; Rotello, Macmillan, & Van Tassel, 2000). An early example is provided by two experiments that Gronlund and Ratcliff reported. These experiments made use of target materials and recognition probes of the following general sort:

Targets	Probes
Month-River	Month-River (*AB*)
Baby-Star	Telephone-Pump (*XY*)
Paper	Paper (*C*)
Cake-Ball	Cake-Star (*AB′*)
Store-Bird	Baby-Trash (*AX*)
Lamp	Mind-Ball (*XB*)
Tree	Bottle (*Z*)

As can be seen, both target materials and recognition probes were mixtures of word pairs and single words. However, note the three test probes *cake-star, baby-trash,*

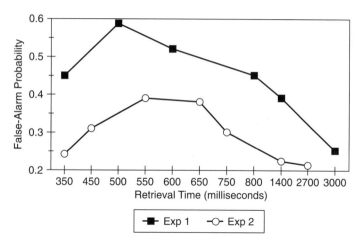

Figure 4-16. Inverted-U relation between retrieval duration and false recognition of related distractors in two experiments reported by Gronlund and Ratcliff (1989).

and *mind-ball.* These are false-memory items in that the first pair consists of two words that were presented in different target pairs (called *AB′* probes by Gronlund and Ratcliff); the second pair consists of an initial word that was presented followed by a word that was not presented (called *AX* probes by Gronlund and Ratcliff), and the third pair consists of an initial unpresented word followed by a presented word (denoted *XB* probes by Gronlund and Ratcliff). Retrieval durations in the 300- to 3500-millisecond range were used. In one experiment, the subjects were told that following the signal to respond, they should accept targets (*AB* and *C* probes) and pairs of words that had been presented but not together (*AB′* probes), which means that the false-memory probes were the *AX* and *XB* pairs. In the second experiment, the subjects were told to accept only targets (*AB* and *C* probes), so that *AB′*, *AX*, and *XB* pairs were all false-memory probes. The key data for these two experiments— the false-alarm probabilities at each retrieval duration—are displayed in Figure 4-16. In both experiments, as predicted, initial increases in retrieval duration (from 350 to 500 milliseconds in Experiment 1 and from 350 to 550 milliseconds in Experiment 2) produced increases in false-alarm probabilities. However, subsequent increases (beyond 500 milliseconds in Experiment 1 and beyond 650 milliseconds in Experiment 2) produced declines in false-alarm probabilities.

Hintzman and Curran (1994, Experiment 2) reported a study that provides further data on the inverted-U relation using different materials. Their target materials and recognition probes consisted of individual words. Some of the targets were plural nouns (e.g., *frogs, paintings*), while others were singular nouns (e.g., *computer, street*). Some of these targets were presented once, and others were presented twice. On the recognition test, the false-memory probes were singular versions of plural targets (e.g., *painting*) and plural versions of singular targets (e.g., *streets*). Retrieval durations were in the 350- to 2200-millisecond range. The relation between duration and false-alarm probability is plotted separately in Figure 4-17 for

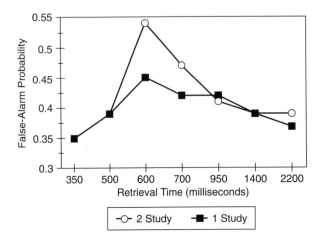

Figure 4-17. Inverted-U relation between retrieval duration and false recognition of related distractors whose corresponding targets had been studied once or twice in an experiment reported by Hintzman and Curran (1994).

distractors whose corresponding targets were presented once or twice. In both instances, the false-alarm probability initially increased as retrieval duration lengthened from 350 milliseconds to 600 milliseconds. Beyond 600 milliseconds, further increases in retrieval duration reduced the false-alarm rate.

Recall

We saw in chapter 3 that when subjects freely recall a series of prior events, two retrieval processes are thought to be operative: direct access of the verbatim traces of individual events and reconstruction of events via gist processing. The two retrieval processes are assumed to be independent, like familiarity and recollection in recognition, and they are assumed to differ temporally, also like familiarity and recollection in recognition. Unlike recognition, however, the retrieval process that suppresses false recall (direct access) is assumed to dominate the early phases of recall, whereas the process that supports false recall (reconstruction) is assumed to make increased contributions as recall unfolds. The straightforward prediction about retrieval duration, then, is that false events will take longer to be recalled than true events.

When subjects are freely recalling prior events, this prediction can be evaluated by determining whether false events tend to appear later in subjects' output sequences than true events appear. To do so, however, requires a technique called *Vincentized analysis*, which takes account of the fact that different subjects will recall different numbers of true and false events during a given interval of time. For example, imagine that we repeat the Brewer and Treyens (1981) and Lampinen, Copeland, and Neuschatz (2001) room-schema experiments that were summarized in chapter 2. Instead of responding to recognition probes for office objects, however, suppose that the subjects are administered a free-recall test on which they are given 2 minutes to write the names of as many of the objects that they saw in the office as they can remember. Two of the subjects produce the following written protocols, where true objects are in regular type and false objects are in bold type:

Subject A: Desk, Books, Computer, Chairs, Bookshelf, Wastebasket, Tablet, Calculator, Coffee Cup, Pencils, **Stapler**, **Telephone**

Subject B: Wastebasket, Pencils, Chalkboard, Eraser, Desk, Calculator, Coffee Pot, Filing Cabinet, Coffee Cup, Tablet, **Telephone**, **Stapler**, Computer, Chairs, **Pens**, Books

Subject A recalled 10 true objects and 2 false ones, and Subject B recalled 13 true objects and 3 false ones. If these two subjects' protocols are not equated for the difference in numbers of items recalled, the average output positions of the false items will be later for Subject B (the mean position of the intrusions is [11 + 12 + 15] ÷ 3 = 12.67) than for Subject A (the mean position of the intrusions is [11 + 12] ÷ 2 = 11.5). This result misrepresents the obvious fact that, relatively speaking, intrusions occur later in Subject A's protocol (in the last and next-to-last positions) than in Subject B's protocol (in the next-to-last, fourth-to-last, and fifth-to-last positions), which is being obscured by the fact that Subject B recalled four more objects than did Subject A. Vincentized analysis eliminates this problem by first splitting the individual protocols into equal segments of output (e.g., thirds, fourths, fifths) and then analyzing true and false recall by output segment. To illustrate, because Subject A recalled 12 words and Subject B recalled 16 words, the two protocols can be equated by splitting them into quartiles (Quartile 1 = words 1–3 for Subject A and words 1–4 for Subject B, Quartile 2 = words 4–6 for Subject A and words 5–8 for Subject B, and so on). Once the data are arranged in this manner, the confounding influence of between-subject differences in total output can be eliminated by analyzing true and false recall *by quartile*. Now, mean output positions are calculated by recording the quartile in which items appear and then computing the mean quartile in which true and false items are recalled. With this procedure, the mean quartiles for true and false recall are 2.2 and 4, respectively, for Subject A and 2.31 and 3.3, respectively, for Subject B. Note that these Vincentized results accurately represent the fact that Subject A's intrusions occurred later, relatively speaking, than did Subject B's. In addition, note that the results for both of these hypothetical subjects illustrate opponent-processes predictions: Mean quartiles for false recall are later than mean quartiles for true recall.

Following recall of DRM lists, Vincentized analysis has been used to measure the output positions of falsely recalled stimulus words, and the results have been in line with opponent-processes predictions. The earliest results were reported by Roediger and McDermott (1995), with follow-up data being reported by Payne et al. (1996); Brainerd, Payne, Wright, and Reyna (2003); and others. In Roediger and McDermott's initial experiment, the subjects studied a total of 6 DRM lists and attempted to recall the words on each list immediately after it was presented. Vincentized quintiles were used to plot the output positions of intrusions. As can be seen in Figure 4-18, the relation between recall duration and semantic intrusions was as expected: The intrusion rate was near-floor during the first and second quintiles; it increased to above 10% during the third and fourth quintiles; and it jumped dramatically (to above 60%) during the last quintile. The same qualitative pattern was detected by Payne et al. and Brainerd et al. In the former experiment, the subjects recalled 8 DRM lists, while the subjects recalled 18 DRM lists in the latter ex-

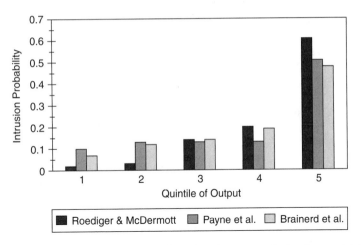

Figure 4-18. Output position of semantic intrusions (unpresented stimulus words) in free recall of individual DRM lists. Data from Brainerd, Payne, Wright, and Reyna (2003); Payne, Elie, Blackwell, and Neuschatz (1996); and Roediger and McDermott (1995).

periment. The relation between recall duration and semantic intrusions for these experiments is also shown in Figure 4-18, where it is quite apparent that the probability of falsely recalling unpresented stimulus words was low at the start of recall but very high at the end. In all three of the data sets in this figure, the modal position in which false recall occurred was the final quintile, and the mean quintiles of false recall for the three data sets were 4.4 (Roediger & McDermott), 3.8 (Payne et al.), and 4.1 (Brainerd et al.). As the midpoint of Vincentized quintiles is 2.5, it was not until well into the second half of recall, on average, that semantic intrusions appeared.

There is another technique for studying the relation between recall duration and semantic intrusions that is used when subjects have extensive amounts of time to recall target events that are so numerous that there is no chance that more than a fraction of them can be remembered. This is often the state of affairs in the everyday life situations in which false recall is worrisome, such as police interviews or psychotherapy. For instance, when police investigators interview crime witnesses, they may ask them to recall everything that they can remember, no matter how seemingly trivial, during the hours immediately preceding a target crime, during the crime itself, and during the hours immediately following the crime. A common method of gathering such investigative information is to ask witnesses to write narrative reports of their experiences, taking whatever time is necessary to recall as much as possible. Obviously, it is important to know whether the relation in Figure 4-18 also holds in circumstances in which both retrieval duration and the amount of target information are much greater than when subjects recall small numbers of targets.

In the laboratory, these more-extended recall situations are emulated using experimental designs in which subjects are exposed to large numbers of target events (e.g., a slide presentation of 60–100 pictures of familiar objects and events), and they are allowed lengthy retrieval periods (e.g., 10 minutes) in which to recall them. Although no subject will be able to recall all of the target material, all subjects' protocols will contain a fairly large number of responses, some of which will be semantic intrusions (e.g., recalling "Thanksgiving" when one of the slides depicted a Christmas celebration). With such protocols, it is possible to study the relation between retrieval duration and the appearance of semantic intrusions by selecting the minimum number of items that any subject recalls (e.g., 20) and plotting the probability of intrusions as a function of output positions. Because even the minimum number of items recalled is a fairly large number and retrieval duration is lengthy, all subjects' protocols will presumably involve a mixture of direct access and reconstruction, with reconstruction contributing more to later recall than to earlier recall. Note that the earlier problem of different subjects recalling different numbers of items does not crop up with this method because the number of items that is being analyzed is the same for all subjects (i.e., the minimum recall number).

Several experiments that fit this description have been reported (e.g., Erdelyi, Finks, & Feigin-Pfau, 1989; Roediger & Payne, 1985; Roediger, Srinivas, & Waddill, 1989), and like the aforementioned DRM studies, the data are congruent with opponent-processes predictions about how retrieval duration affects false recall. Indeed, one can say that when subjects perform extended intervals of free recall for large amounts of previously presented information, the tendency of semantic intrusions to appear later in such intervals is a well-established finding (Brainerd et al., 1993). Data from an experiment by Erdelyi et al. (1989) will be used to illustrate this conclusion.

Erdelyi et al.'s subjects read 70 common words as the words appeared on a computer screen. Later, the subjects were given a sheet of paper containing 50 blank spaces in which to write words from the presented list. They were allowed 12 minutes to write as many words as could be recalled. When the subjects' protocols were examined, it was discovered that all of them had filled in at least 25 of the blanks with words. Erdelyi et al. identified all recall errors that occurred anywhere in these first 25 positions, and then they plotted the error probability as a function of recall position. Their particular method of analysis involved looking at consecutive triads of recall, with each triad overlapping with the last position of the previous triad (e.g., Triad 1 = positions 1–3, Triad 2 = positions 3–5, Triad 3 = positions 5–7, and so on). The recall-error probability was then plotted as a function of each triad. The overall pattern, which is shown in Figure 4-19, is precisely what opponent-processes distinctions would expect. Note three features of this pattern, in particular. First, the likelihood of recall errors is very low at the beginning and during the first half of output, less than 10% before the midpoint is reached. Second, after the midpoint is reached, the error probability starts to climb steadily. Third, the error probability has become very high by the end of recall, with output positions 24–25 containing one or more errors for more than 80% of the subjects.

Verbatim Cuing

We have just seen that the opponent-processes approach makes contrasting predictions about how retrieval duration affects false recognition and false recall—an inverted-U relation is expected for false alarms and a monotonic-increasing relation is expected for intrusions—and that data favoring both predictions have been reported. What about the cuing of memories of the exact surface form of target events?

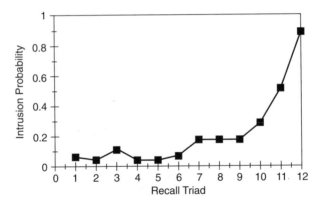

Figure 4-19. The cumulative probability of the occurrence of at least one semantic intrusion as a function of the number of words recalled. Data from Erdelyi, Finks, and Feigin-Pfau (1989).

Assuming that verbatim and gist traces are both accessible, the opponent-processes approach expects that such cuing will tend to reduce false recall and false recognition by increasing subjects' inclination to process the verbatim memories rather than the gist memories. As in the above discussion of inverted-U relations for retrieval duration, the encoding variability principle (Tulving & Thomson, 1971) is part of the basis for this prediction. Although opponent-processes distinctions expect that increased verbatim processing will suppress semantic false memories, that cuing surface information should increase verbatim processing follows from the idea that the types of memory representations that subjects access depends upon the level of match between the contents of retrieval cues and the contents of representations (i.e., encoding variability).

We introduced an early recognition procedure for investigating this prediction, which was called *target priming* (Brainerd, Reyna, & Kneer, 1995; Brainerd et al., 1999). The procedure implemented the notion that meaning-preserving distractors (e.g., *table*) are normally better retrieval cues for the semantic content of their corresponding targets (e.g., *couch*) than for verbatim traces of actual target presentations. If so, it might be possible to make it easier for such distractors to retrieve verbatim traces by priming those traces (i.e., making them highly accessible) before distractor probes are presented. In the 1995 article, we proposed that this might be accomplished by testing distractors' corresponding targets just prior to testing distractors that preserve aspects of targets' meaning. If it is true that targets are superior retrieval cues for verbatim traces, a large proportion of these target probes should produce verbatim access, and when verbatim traces are accessed, they ought to remain in a state of high activation for at least a short time thereafter. If meaning-preserving distractors are administered within that time window (whatever it may be), they should produce lower false-alarm rates, relative to control conditions in which target verbatim primes do not precede distractors. We reported some experiments that made use of this procedure for distractors that preserved different aspects of the meaning content of targets—distractors that were antonyms, associates, synonyms, and same-category exemplars of targets.

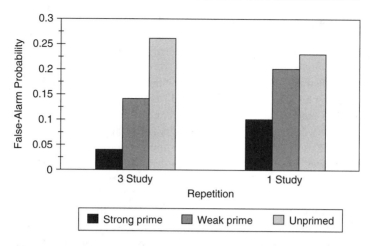

Figure 4-20. False-alarm probability for meaning-preserving distractors (synonyms, associates, same-category exemplars) for distractors that received verbatim priming and for distractors that did not receive verbatim priming. For primed items, the verbatim prime was administered either immediately before the distractor was tested (strong prime) or was administered four positions earlier (weak prime). Data from Brainerd, Reyna, and Kneer (1995).

The hypothesis that administering target probes before meaning-preserving distractor probes could lower false-alarm rates is another example of a surprising prediction. Reyna and Lloyd (1997) pointed out that classical one-process accounts of false memory expect the opposite result because the presentation of target probes would necessarily activate the same memory information that is responsible for false recognition of meaning-preserving distractors. The data of our experiments did not agree. Rather, testing target probes before testing their related distractors reduced false-alarm rates to the latter. Some illustrative data from these experiments are shown in Figure 4-20. These data are a compilation of results from various experiments in which the subjects studied word lists and then responded to recognition tests on which meaning-preserving distractors were associates (e.g., *blue* when *sky* was a target), same-category exemplars (e.g., *sheep* when *horse* was a target), or synonyms (e.g., *gown* when *dress* was a target). Two further manipulations were included that, according to opponent-processes distinctions, ought to enhance the tendency of verbatim priming to reduce semantic false recognition: verbatim repetition and the spacing between target primes and distractor probes. Concerning repetition, we saw in the above section on storage variables that repeated presentation of targets should strengthen verbatim traces more than gist traces, which means that a target probe will be more likely to produce verbatim retrieval if it is presented multiple times than if it is presented only once. Therefore, in our experiments, some targets were presented three times, whereas others were presented once. Concerning spacing, if retrieval of verbatim traces places them in a state of high accessibility for a short time, whether accessibility is still high when distractors are administered will depend upon how long it has been since retrieval occurred. This can be controlled by varying the spacing between the presentation of target probes and of related distractors. Therefore, in our experiments, some targets were tested immediately before their related distractors, but for other related distractors, three other recognition probes intervened. An illustration of the spaced testing procedure would be **horse**, *telephone, carton, ground*, **sheep**, in which *horse* is the target and *sheep* is the related distractor (see also Reyna, 1996b, and Reyna & Kiernan, 1995, for additional examples of effects of enhanced verbatim accessibility, but with more complex verbal materials, such as sentences and stories.).

In Figure 4-20, data are reported for two types of meaning-preserving distractors—namely, distractors that received verbatim priming (e.g., *sheep*, which was preceded by the target *horse*) and control distractors that did not receive verbatim priming (e.g., *table*, which was not preceded by the target *couch*). The overall pattern is consistent with opponent-processes predictions in that false-alarm rates are consistently lower for distractors that received target priming. Note, too, that this pattern varies predictably as a function of verbatim repetition and spacing. When priming involved targets that had been repeatedly presented (and whose verbatim traces should therefore be quite strong), the result was larger reductions in false-alarm rates than when targets had been presented only once. With respect to spacing, when target primes were administered immediately before related distractors (strong primes), reductions in false-alarm rates were more dramatic than when target primes were administered four positions earlier (weak primes).

We turn now to another verbatim-cuing manipulation, which also generates surprising predictions about semantic false recognition: *match/mismatch* of surface cues during study and test. When target materials are presented, they are accompanied by certain surface cues. For instance, suppose that the target materials consist of narratives that subjects read while looking at a computer screen, such as the short vignette in Table 4-1. The narratives are presented in letters of a certain size, color, and font, and the sentences that comprise the narrative are presented in a certain position on the screen. For instance, subjects might see the following sentences, in green type, presented one after the other:

The cocoa is hotter than the tea.
The tea is hotter than the coffee.
The cocoa is sweet.

Thus, subjects see sentences printed in 10-point boldface green Arial font, centered on the computer screen. These are all surface cues that are incidental to the actual words and sentences, but according to opponent-processes assumptions, they are the type of information that should be stored in verbatim traces. Following the presentation of one or more vignettes of this sort, suppose that subjects receive a recognition test on which the recognition probes are sentences that might have appeared in the narrative. As usual, the task is to accept targets and to reject meaning-preserving distractors and meaning-violating distractors, with the difference between the false-alarm rates for the two types of distractors being the measure of false memory. If we so choose, we can vary the extent to which the recognition probes that are presented to subjects contain the same surface cues as the earlier target materials. At one extreme, the surface content of the probes may exactly match that of the target materials with respect to details such as size, color, font, and position:

The cocoa is hotter than the tea.
The tea is hotter than the coffee.
The cocoa is sweet.

Or, the surface content of the probes might mismatch that of the target materials in size, color, font, and position:

The cocoa is hotter than the tea.
The tea is hotter than the coffee.
The cocoa is sweet.

One could make the surface mismatch even more pronounced by presenting recognition probes orally rather that visually.

Match/mismatch manipulations of this general sort have figured in many studies of true memory, the standard result being that performance is better when test cues match study cues than when they mismatch (e.g., Jacoby, 1996). What about false memory? The most obvious prediction, which is made by one-process theories of false memory, such as the source-monitoring framework (e.g., Johnson et al., 1993), and also by classical theories of recognition memory (see Tulving, 1981), is that items like the three meaning-preserving distractors above will be more apt to be falsely accepted under matching conditions than under mismatching conditions. The ostensible reason, which appears self-evident when one compares the target sentences above to the two methods of presenting the distractors, is that the distractors look so much like targets with the first method that subjects should be less able to discriminate them from targets than when the second method is used. Although it is certainly true that high levels of target/distractor surface resemblance may create confusion and elevate false-memory levels, opponent-processes ideas suggest the opposite possibility, that high levels of surface match could lower false-memory levels. By the principle of encoding variability, recognition probes that match the surface content of targets ought to be better retrieval cues for verbatim traces than probes that mismatch targets, and verbatim traces suppress rather than support false alarms to meaning-preserving distractors.

This leads to two predictions about surface match/mismatch, one negative and the other positive. The negative prediction is that it ought to be surprisingly difficult to confirm the seemingly self-evident notion of higher false-memory levels for matching than for mismatching probes; experiments that have attempted to evaluate this notion have sometimes failed to do so. Reyna and Lloyd (1997) reviewed such studies in the course of evaluating one-process theories of false memory and concluded that, indeed, the pattern in the literature was inconsistent. The positive prediction is that, under appropriate conditions, it should be possible to show that matching probes produce lower levels of false memory than do mismatching probes. This result, too, has been reported. One example is provided by the previously discussed studies of target priming of meaning-preserving distractors (Brainerd, Reyna, & Kneer, 1995). In one of these experiments, we investigated how match/mismatch would affect the power of target priming to reduce false alarms using a voice manipulation. Target words were first presented orally in a single voice, and the target primes that preceded distractors on recognition tests were either pronounced in

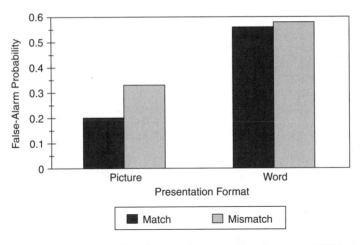

Figure 4-21. False-alarm probability for meaning-preserving distractors (DRM stimulus words) when the format of recognition probes (picture or word) matches or mismatches the format of target materials. Data from Israel and Schacter (1997).

the same voice as before (match) or in a new voice (mismatch). Target priming produced larger reductions in false alarms under matching conditions than under mismatching conditions, consistent with the hypothesis that matching makes verbatim traces more readily accessible.

Another example of this pattern is provided by the picture-word studies of Schacter and associates (Israel & Schacter, 1997; Schacter et al., 1999). Remember that in these studies, orally presented DRM lists were accompanied by one of two types of parallel visual lists: line drawings of the individual targets (picture condition) or the printed form of each target (word condition). On subsequent recognition tests, there was a match/mismatch manipulation. Lists that had been presented in the picture format might be tested in either the picture (match) or word (mismatch) format, and lists that had been presented in the word format might be tested in either format. The results from Israel and Schacter's two experiments are exhibited in Figure 4-21, where it can be seen that both the negative and positive predictions of opponent processes received support. On the negative side, there was no evidence of higher levels of false memory when presentation and test formats matched in either the word or the picture condition. On the positive side, in the picture condition, the false-alarm probability was much lower when presentation and test formats matched than when they did not.

Up to this point in our treatment of verbatim cuing, we have focused on verbatim cuing on recognition tests. Our reason for doing so is that the content of retrieval cues is easy to control on recognition tests because those cues are presented by the experimenter as part of recognition probes, and subjects must respond to each probe before moving on to the next. In sharp contrast, when subjects are in the midst of freely recalling objects or events from a pool of previously experienced items, it is difficult to control the retrieval cues that are being used as each item is recalled. Nevertheless, it is possible to impose some global constraints that ought to slant retrieval toward verbatim access and to determine whether those constraints have the predicted effect of lowering the rate of semantic intrusions. An obvious manipulation of this sort on which data are available is a procedure known as *part-list cuing* (e.g., Rundus, 1973; Slamecka, 1968). In this procedure, subjects respond to a standard free-recall test for previously experienced material ("recall all the items that you can remember"), save for one modification. A few of those items (say, four to six) are presented on the test as reminders and do not have to be recalled. The target material typically consists of a list of visually presented words or pictures with subjects performing written or oral recall while looking at visual representations of a few list members (e.g., words or pictures printed on a sheet of paper)—hence, part-list cuing. From the opponent-processes perspective, this is a verbatim-cuing manipulation because the exact surface form of some of the targets is represented, which would be expected to encourage the retrieval of verbatim traces and to suppress semantic intrusions.

Although virtually all studies of part-list cuing have focused on true recall (for a review, see Nickerson, 1984), Kimball and Bjork (2002) investigated its effects on false recall in the DRM paradigm, and the predicted suppression effect was detected. In Kimball and Bjork's design, subjects studied a total of 12 DRM lists and performed written free recall following the presentation of each list. Part-list cuing was manipulated by presenting different types of symbols at the top of each test sheet. For instance, suppose that a group of subjects had just studied the "high" list (the first 15 forward associates of the word *high*). The test sheet that was given to each subject contained a column of eight symbols, but the symbols in the column were different for different test sheets. In all, there were five distinct types of test sheets:

Control	Strong 4	Weak 4	Strong 8	Weak 8
########	Low	Over	Low	Building
########	Clouds	Airplane	Clouds	Noon
########	Up	Dive	Up	Cliff
########	Tall	Elevate	Tall	Sky
########	########	########	Tower	Over
########	########	########	Jump	Airplane
########	########	########	Above	Dive
########	########	########	Building	Elevate

Thus, only nonword cues (pound signs) were presented during some tests, while either four or eight word cues were presented during other tests. For the four types of tests on which word cues were presented, the cues were either the strongest or weakest associates of the unpresented stimulus word. Here, remember that DRM lists are composed of the first several associates of the stimulus word. Thus, *low* and *clouds* are the 1st and 2d associates of *high* (i.e., the two responses that subjects most often give to *high* on free-association tests), whereas *dive* and *elevate* are the 14th and 15th associates.

Kimball and Bjork (2002) found that intrusions of DRM stimulus words were reduced by part-list cuing, as expected. On uncued control tests, subjects falsely recalled stimulus words on 54% of the tests. When target words were presented, however, the false-recall rate dropped to 44%. A related expectation is that larger numbers of word cues ought to produce more suppression than smaller numbers. This effect, too, was observed. The false-recall rate was 47% when recall occurred in the presence of four target words and 40% when it occurred in the presence of eight target words. Finally, the highest associates on DRM lists are usually words that are more familiar and more easily remembered than the lowest associates, which suggests that verbatim traces of high associates are apt to be stronger and more readily retrievable than verbatim traces of low associates. Thus, although all forms of part-list cuing should suppress false recall by promoting verbatim processing, high associates should be particularly effective. Consistent with this reasoning, the mean false-recall rate was lower on Strong 4 and Strong 8 tests (37%) than on Weak 4 and Weak 8 tests (50%).

Retrieval Instructions

According to opponent-processes analysis, memory is of two minds when it comes to false-but-meaning-preserving events. Specifically, it is thought to be a normal feature of memory performance that some events of this sort will be erroneously reported (because subjects process gist memories) while others will be correctly suppressed (because subjects are able to access verbatim traces that neutralize the events' familiarity). If so, it is natural to wonder whether it is possible to nudge performance in one direction or the other, but particularly in the direction of fewer false alarms and intrusions, merely by instructing subjects to beware of relying on meaning familiarity or by stressing verbatim processing or both (Reyna & Kiernan, 1994; 1995). Of course, it may be that the opponent retrieval processes operate so automatically that there is little room for any deliberate adjustments in response to instructions. However, there have been some successful demonstrations that both false recall and false recognition can be influenced by instructions that encourage subjects to exert deliberate control over the types of memorial evidence upon which their performance is based.

The oldest and most influential program of research on this topic is that of Koriat, Goldsmith, and their associates, which revolves around a procedure known as *optional report* (e.g., Koriat & Goldsmith, 1994, 1996; Koriat, Goldsmith, & Pansky, 1999; Koriat, Goldsmith, Schneider, & Nakash-Dura, 2001). Koriat and Goldsmith (1994) theorized that although there are many items of information in memory that bear on whether an event was actually experienced, some items are more diagnostic than others. For instance, if a subject were asked what she did last Saturday evening, remembering "attended a baseball game" is a highly diagnostic item of information because it rules out all manner of events that do not happen at baseball games (e.g., seeing a slap shot, dancing the waltz, hearing an announcer exclaim, "Touchdown!"). Koriat and Goldsmith theorized, further, that it might be possible to induce subjects to shift their memory performance toward reliance on more highly diagnostic information merely by providing them with the option of not reporting some of the memories that come to mind during the course of a memory test. The underlying assumption is that subjects are capable of *metacognitive monitoring*, a mechanism whereby they introspect upon the properties of their retrieved memories, and that on the basis of the results of those introspections, they adjust their performance to emphasize properties that figure in the instructions that they receive. On an optional-report test, the more specific assumption is that subjects will weed out retrieved memories whose properties make them seem potentially unreliable.

The original methodology for evaluating these ideas required subjects to respond to one of two types of memory tests, which varied dramatically in the latitude that subjects were permitted for weeding out memories that they deemed to be unreliable. Specifically, some subjects were administered optional-report tests on which they could abstain from responding to *any* of the items, and other subjects were administered *forced-report* tests on which they were required to respond to *all* of the items (even if the responses were pure guesses). In Koriat and Goldsmith's (1994) initial experiment with this methodology, autobiographical memory for general knowledge was tested using facts for which it could reasonably be expected that college-student subjects would know some and not know others (e.g., Who composed the Moonlight Sonata? What is the chemical process that is responsible for the formation of glucose?). Half of the subjects were administered cued-recall tests (e.g., _____ composed the Moonlight Sonata) and half were administered multiple-choice recognition tests (e.g., Which of the following composed the Moonlight Sonata: (a) Bach; (b) Beethoven; (c) Schumann; (d) Brahms; (e) Tchaikovsky?). On both recall and recognition tests, half of the subjects responded under optional-report instructions and half responded under forced-report instructions. Of course, optional-report tests will necessarily reduce output somewhat, relative to forced-choice tests. But where are those reductions localized? The obvious opponent-processes prediction is that optional-report tests ought to decrease false-memory responses more than true-memory responses by decreasing reliance upon gist processing. Remember from chapter 3 that under opponent-processes assumptions, the proportion of memory responses that are due to gist processing is much greater for false than for true reports, from which it follows that optional-report tests will decrease the former more than the latter.

The findings of Koriat and Goldsmith's (1994) initial experiment are summarized in Figure 4-22. It is apparent from these patterns that the data fell out as anticipated. Optional reporting of general-knowledge facts produced no reduction in true memory, relative to forced reporting, on recall tests and only a slight reduction on recognition tests (which was not statistically reliable). Concerning false reports, on the other hand, it can be seen that optional reporting produced substantial reductions, with the reduction being larger for recall than for recognition (29% versus 10%). The data in Figure 4-22 seem to represent the correct state of affairs for memory tests that vary in the extent to which subjects are permitted to avoid reporting memories that they deem to be unreliable because Koriat and Goldsmith obtained analogous patterns in other experiments using other types of materials (e.g., word lists).

Importantly, other investigators have also obtained such patterns. An example is a free- versus forced-report experiment that was conducted by Payne et al. (1996). The target materials were DRM lists, and the memory tests involved written recall. First, six DRM lists were visually presented to subjects, with individual words be-

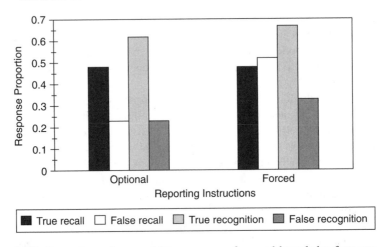

Figure 4-22. Proportions of true and false memory of general-knowledge facts reported on recall or recognition tests under either optional- or forced-report instructions. Data from Koriat and Goldsmith (1994).

ing presented at a 4-second rate. The subjects then responded to three free-recall tests for the presented lists, with a pause for instructions interleaved between consecutive tests. Each test lasted for 7 minutes. Subjects in the free-recall condition were simply told to write words that they had seen during the presentation phase. Subjects in the forced-recall condition were given the further instruction that they must write at least 60 words by the end of the 7-minute interval. As expected, the reductions in recall under free versus forced conditions were considerably greater for the false recall of unpresented stimulus words (20%, averaged over the three tests) than for true recall of list words (10%, averaged over the three tests).

Patterns that are consistent with opponent-processes assumptions have been obtained for two other instructional procedures, called *conjoint recognition* and *conjoint recall*, which were developed in our laboratory to measure the contributions of opponent processes to false-memory reports. The key point of difference between these procedures and those that we have just discussed lies in the level of specificity that the instructions provide to subjects about the nature of false memories. In optional reporting, the instructions are not explicit about the types of information that are likely to be falsely reported. In conjoint recognition or conjoint recall, however, subjects are given detailed instructions as to the types of items that are likely to be erroneously recalled or recognized. As in most false-memory experiments, subjects are first exposed to some target materials, which may be just about anything—word or picture or sentence lists, written or spoken narratives, videos of everyday events or crimes, or even live staged events. Next, some subjects respond to a standard recall or recognition test, which is called a V (for "verbatim") test because the normal instruction on memory tests is to recognize or recall only items that were actually presented. As part of these standard instructions, however, the subjects are also told about the types of items that are apt to be falsely recalled or recognized on the basis of the target materials. For instance, if the target material consists of a narrative or a video about an armed robbery at a convenience store, subjects would be warned that people are apt to falsely report objects and events that are typical of such crimes (e.g., weapons, faces hidden by masks, threatening utterances). Other subjects receive nonstandard memory instructions. Some receive G (for "gist") memory instructions, in which they are told to recognize or recall only items that were *not* presented as part of the target material but that are consistent with the gist of that material (e.g., that the robber in an armed-robbery story was holding a pistol). Other subjects receive V+G (for "verbatim plus gist") memory instructions, in which they are told to recognize and recall two types of items: those that were actually presented and unpresented items that are consistent with the gist of the target material.

The interesting comparison, which is analogous to optional versus forced reporting, is that between performance in the V and V+G conditions. Naturally, the more relaxed V+G instructions should result in larger numbers of items being recalled and recognized than the more conservative V instructions. The underlying memory difference between the two conditions, according to an opponent-processes analysis, should be the same as in optional versus forced reporting—namely, that reliance on gist processing as a basis for recall or recognition should be greater under V+G instructions than under V instructions. Therefore, by the same reasoning as above, V+G instructions should increase the recall and recognition of unpresented-but-meaning-preserving items more than the recall and recognition of presented items. This pattern has been detected in experiments in which conjoint-recognition or conjoint-recall procedures were used (e.g., Brainerd & Reyna, 1998b; Brainerd et al., 1999; Brainerd, Payne, Wright, & Reyna, 2003).

In an initial series of experiments (Brainerd & Reyna, 1998b), we restricted comparisons to these two conditions (the G condition was not included). In some experiments, the target materials were word lists whose members belonged to a few familiar taxonomic categories (e.g., furniture, clothing, cities), and in other experiments the target materials were DRM lists. The memory tests always involved recognition. Relative to V instructions, it was found that the number of acceptances of meaning-preserving distractors tripled under V+G instructions when the target materials were categorized lists and that the number of acceptances nearly doubled when the target materials were DRM lists. For targets, on the other hand, there were only slight increases in acceptance rates with both types of materials, and the increases were not reliable when the data were corrected for differences in guessing rates. The pattern for recall is similar. For instance, Brainerd, Payne, Wright, and Reyna (2003) reported an experiment in which subjects responded to free-recall tests for DRM lists under V, G, or V+G instructions. A total of 18 DRM lists were presented, with subjects performing free recall following each. After the last word on a list had been presented, there was a 1-minute interval, during which subjects read a sheet containing V, G, or V+G instructions. Then, they were given 1.5 minutes to perform written recall in accordance with the instructions. Relative to V instructions, V+G instructions increased true recall slightly, from 45% to 51%. However, there was a dramatic increase in the false recall of unpresented stimulus words, from 52% to 78%.

On the whole, therefore, instructions to shift performance away from outputting potential false memories (optional versus forced reporting) or to shift performance toward reporting such memories (conjoint recognition and conjoint recall) have produced findings that are consistent with opponent-processes assumptions. It should be added, however, that successful demonstrations of instructional effects should not be misinterpreted as also establishing that retrieval instructions are capable of entirely eliminating false-memory effects. On the contrary, it is known that such effects persist under instructions that, relative to baseline tests, are very explicit about the types of information that subjects are prone to falsely report (e.g., Reyna & Kiernan, 1994). Studies of this sort have been reported in connection with the DRM illusion, for instance, appearing in an article by McDermott and Roediger (1998). In their experiments, McDermott and Roediger attempted to eliminate false recognition of unpresented stimulus words by adding extremely detailed warnings to the standard instructions. Depending upon the experiment, their subjects studied either 12 or 20 DRM lists and then responded to a recognition test consisting of targets, distractors that were unpresented stimulus words, and distractors that were unrelated to presented lists. Subjects received the usual instructions to recognize only presented items and to avoid recognizing unpresented ones, but the instructions were enriched to include particularized warnings about the nature of the DRM illusion. Subjects were told that people mistakenly remember unpresented stimulus words that link together presented words; they were given examples of DRM lists and the lists' stimulus words; and they were told to especially avoid falsely recognizing stimulus words. Across three experiments, the DRM illusion was reduced somewhat by such instructions, but levels of false recognition remained high, ranging from a low of 38% to a high of 64%. However, as in other experiments (and in line with opponent-processes predictions), the effects of these explicit warnings on true recognition were slight in comparison to the effects on false recognition.

Forgetting Memories

We now take up the final topic of this chapter, which is how false-memory reports are influenced by forgetting intervals. In memory experiments, the length of time that qualifies as a legitimate forgetting interval depends upon the purposes of the research. A few seconds is ample in studies of short-term memory, whereas an hour may be the minimum interval in other types of experiments. In studies of false memory, the minimum interval is usually even more substantial, ranging from a day or two (e.g., McDermott, 1996; Payne et al., 1996) to a few weeks (e.g., Brainerd & Mojardin, 1998; Toglia et al., 1999) to even a few years (e.g., Pipe et al., 1999). The principal desideratum in making predictions about how memory performance varies over such intervals is the relative forgetting rates of stored representations of different aspects of experience. Here, a key finding, which was mentioned in chapter 3, is that memories of the exact surface form of events seem to become inaccessible far more rapidly than memories of their meaning. This finding, together with opponent-processes assumptions, generates a highly counterintuitive series of predictions, to which we will refer collectively as *false-persistence effects*.

To see why the predictions in question are counterintuitive, we first need to ask what common sense would expect about the relation between false-memory reports and the passage of time. The key consideration for common sense is that such reports refer to events that were never experienced, whereas true-memory reports refer to actual experiences. Therefore, common sense would say that the former lack the genuine memorial support that the latter enjoy. On this line of reasoning, false-memory reports ought to be highly unstable over time, and even though the stability of true-memory reports is far from perfect, it should greatly exceed that of false-memory reports. Interestingly, these two assumptions, that false-memory reports are highly unstable and that the stability of true-memory reports greatly exceeds that of false-memory reports, are enshrined in the law, where they form what is known as the *consistency principle* of testimony. In court proceedings, it is the job of juries and judges to weigh the evidence in a case and decide which items of proffered evidence are credible, which is why judges and juries are called triers of fact. In the case of witnesses who are testifying about their memories of the same target events, different witnesses sometimes give different accounts of crucial features of the events, so that triers of fact must decide which version to accept. This is where the aforementioned consistency principle comes into play. Studies by Fisher and Cutler (1992) and others have found that the criterion that is most commonly applied in such circumstances is the consistency of memory reports over time. Specifically, it is assumed that events that have been inconsistently reported are less likely to be true than events that have been consistently reported. Information on consistency is often available to triers of fact, particularly in criminal cases, because witnesses have been questioned multiple times about target events (e.g., during police investigative interviews) before they testify at trial.

Contrary to these commonsense expectations, opponent-processes distinctions lead to the predictions that false-memory reports can be quite stable over time, and that under certain conditions, they can be *more* stable than true-memory reports. A third prediction, which is concerned with the relative levels of true and false memory rather than their consistency, is that under certain conditions, the incidence of false-memory reports can increase over time, even as the incidence of true-memory reports for the same events is declining. These predictions, which are the false-persistence effects to which we referred earlier, fall out of three points: (a) initial false-memory reports are rooted in gist memory; (b) initial true-memory reports are slanted toward verbatim memory; and (c) over time, verbatim memories become inaccessible more rapidly than do gist memories. Obviously, the first false-persistence effect follows from points a and c. The second follows from all three points. If the same, stable memorial content supports initial and subsequent false-memory reports while the initial (verbatim) basis for true-memory reports becomes rapidly inaccessible, false reports will be more stable over time in situations in which they are overwhelmingly gist-based (rather than due to guessing or prevarication) and in which initial true-memory reports are overwhelmingly verbatim-based.

The third false-persistence effect follows from points a and c. Remember that, according to opponent-processes analysis, retrieval of verbatim traces suppresses false-memory reports by neutralizing the familiarity of false-but-meaning-consistent events. However, verbatim retrieval is more likely to occur on initial memory tests than on delayed tests. Therefore, if an experimental procedure can be devised in which verbatim retrieval is highly likely to occur on initial memory tests (so that verbatim suppression of false memories is the rule), the expectation is that the incidence of false-memory reports will increase substantially on delayed tests.

Persistence of False Memories

The first false-persistence effect was originally investigated in a series of experiments that were conducted in our laboratory (Brainerd, Reyna, & Brandse, 1995). If false-memory reports are ephemeral, they ought to be highly variable from one memory test to another, as the consistency principle of testimony envisions. The critical datum, therefore, is the level of false-memory continuity over time, which can be assessed by simply computing correlations between individual false-memory reports on initial and delayed memory tests. If such reports are ephemeral, the fact that some false event A is erroneously reported on an initial test will not increase the chances that it is reported on a delayed test, and conversely, the fact that some other false event B is correctly rejected on an initial test will not increase the chances that it is also correctly rejected on a delayed test. In our experiments, we evaluated this possibility using a design in which subjects first studied fairly lengthy word lists and then responded to a recognition test containing targets, semantically related distractors (the names of categories whose exemplars had been presented as targets), and unrelated distractors. One week later, the same recognition test was reprised. The measure of false-memory persistence was the relation between the *unconditional* probability of a false alarm to a related distractor on the delayed test, $P(FA_D)$, and the *conditional* probability of a delayed false alarm given an initial false alarm to that same distractor, $P(FA_D|FA_I)$. False memories are not persistent if $P(FA_D) = P(FA_D|FA_I)$, but they are persistent if $P(FA_D) < P(FA_D|FA_I)$. The latter finding was obtained. For category names, $P(FA_D) = .48$ and $P(FA_D|FA_I) = .92$. Thus, false alarms to meaning-preserving distractors were not only persistent across a 1-week forgetting interval, they were highly persistent. Considering that the maximum value of $P(FA_D|FA_I)$ is 1, the value of .92 means that all but 8% of the distractors that were recognized on the delayed test had been recognized 1 week earlier. Subsequent experiments, using other target materials and longer forgetting intervals, have produced similar evidence of false-memory persistence (e.g., Blair, Lenton, & Hastie, 2002; Marx & Henderson, 1996). For example, using narrative materials, Brainerd and Mojardin (1998) found strong positive correlations between false alarms to meaning-preserving sentences on immediate tests and on 1-month delayed tests.

Greater Persistence of False Than True Memories

The second false-persistence effect, that the survival of false memories over time can sometimes be superior to the survival of true memories, has typically been studied with a two-session independent-groups design. During the first session, all subjects are exposed to the same set of target materials. Next, the individual subjects are randomly assigned to two or more memory-testing conditions. One condition involves an immediate test, which is conducted during the first session. As a rule, the subjects who are assigned to this condition do not participate further in the experiment after responding to the immediate test. The remaining subjects are assigned to one or more delayed-testing conditions, with the shortest delay usually being on the order of 1 day. The subjects who are assigned to these conditions do not receive memory tests during the first session, a procedure that is followed in order to avoid confounding the effects of forgetting intervals with the effects of prior memory testing. During the first session, these subjects' participation is usually terminated after they have been exposed to the target materials. They are instructed to return to the laboratory after a specified interval for a second session, during which their memories will be tested. The memory tests that are administered during these delayed sessions are identical to the tests that were administered to subjects who were assigned to the immediate condition. The true- and false-memory performance of subjects receiving delayed tests is then compared to that of subjects receiving immediate tests, and the amount of decline between the immediate and delayed sessions is computed for both types of performance.

An early experiment that implemented this basic design and produced the predicted pattern was reported by Payne et al. (1996). The target materials were DRM lists. During the first session, a series of DRM lists was presented to each subject. Following the presentation of each list, the subject either performed 2 minutes of written free recall (for that list) or solved mathematics problems for 2 minutes. After all of the lists had been presented, subjects who were assigned to the immediate-testing condition were administered a recognition test containing the usual types of probes (targets, unpresented stimulus words, and unrelated distractors). Subjects who were assigned to the delayed-testing condition were dismissed and told to return 1 day later, at which time they were administered the same recognition tests. Concerning true memory, the hit rates for targets on the immediate test were .73 (recalled lists) and .62 (unrecalled lists), with the corresponding hit rates on the 1-day tests being .64 and .47, respectively. Thus, the average decline in true-memory performance was .12. Concerning false memory, the false-alarm rates for unpresented stimulus words on the immediate test were .70 for both recalled and unrecalled lists, with the corresponding false-alarm rates on the delayed test being .71 (recalled lists) and .62 (unrecalled lists). Thus, the average decline in false alarms (.04) was only one third of the decline for hits.

A more complete picture of variations in true and false memory over extended forgetting intervals has been provided in subsequent DRM experiments. For instance, Seamon, Luo, Kopecky, Price, Rothschild, Fung, and Schwartz (2002) and Toglia et al. (1999) have compared forgetting rates for true and false memories across intervals of a few weeks. Toglia et al.'s subjects were exposed to a total of five DRM lists, which were embedded in a single list of 60 words. The items comprising each list were presented together in consecutive positions for half of the subjects (blocked condition), whereas the items were presented in random order for the other half of the subjects (random condition). As we mentioned earlier, blocking is a procedure that is expected to strengthen gist memories (and therefore false-memory reports) because similar meanings are repeatedly cued by adjacent targets. After listening to the list, each subject in each of the two presentation conditions was assigned to one of three testing conditions: immediate recall, 1-week delayed

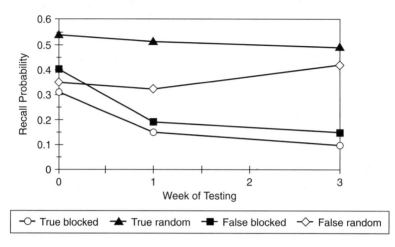

Figure 4-23. Probability of true recall of DRM-list targets and unpresented stimulus words immediately after presentation, 1 week after presentation, and 3 weeks after presentation. Data from Toglia, Neuschatz, and Goodwin (1999).

recall, and 3-week delayed recall. The memory test for each condition consisted of performing 5 minutes of written free recall. Variations in true and false recall over the 3-week interval are plotted in Figure 4-23, where dramatic differences in forgetting rates for true and false memories are evident. For true memory, there are sharp declines in the recall of target words between the immediate test and the 1-week test, followed by further small declines between the 1-week and 3-week tests. For false memory, in marked contrast, the recall of unpresented stimulus words did not decline reliably between the immediate and 1-week tests or between the 1-week and 3-week tests, and in fact, the overall probability of false recall at 3 weeks (.46) was virtually the same as on the immediate test (.45). As can be seen, this stability was due to the fact that although false memory decreased over time in one condition (blocked), it actually increased in the other. See below for more on these sleeper effects.

In a more recent experiment, Seamon, Luo, Kopecky, et al. (2002) obtained similar findings across one retention interval and different findings across another retention interval. Specifically, after listening to eight DRM lists presented in blocked format, subjects performed immediate free recall or 2-week delayed free recall or 2-month delayed free recall. When performance on the immediate and 2-week tests were compared, the pattern was the same as in Toglia et al.'s experiment. The probability of true recall declined markedly (from .17 to .07) but the probability of false recall remained constant. When performance on the 2-week and 2-month tests were compared, however, the decline in false recall (from .27 to .12) was larger than the decline in true recall. Combining these findings with those of Toglia et al., the suggestion is that with DRM lists, the verbatim traces that support true memory and suppression of false memory become rapidly inaccessible during the first few days following exposure, whereas the gist traces that support false memory remain relatively stable for at least 3 weeks but begin to become inaccessible thereafter.

This same pattern of more rapid declines in correct recognition and correct recall than in false recognition and false recall across forgetting intervals has been confirmed with other materials as well. For instance, this pattern has been detected with complex verbal materials, such as narratives and naturalistic scenes. Studies reported by Kintsch et al. (1990), Lampinen et al. (2001), Lim (1993), and Neuschatz, Lampinen, Preston, Hawkins, and Toglia (2002) are all cases in point. Taking the Kintsch et al. study as an illustration, these authors investigated true and false memory for a series of stories that had been previously developed by Zimny (1987). Each story was 150–200 words in length and was scripted such that the events revolved around a central plot (e.g., Nick goes to the movies). Subjects were exposed to 18 stories, with each subject then being assigned to one of four testing conditions: immediate, 40-minute delay, 2-day delay, and 4-day delay. A recognition test was administered to the subjects in each group. The probes were (a) target sentences that had been presented in a story (e.g., Nick looked at the newspaper), (b) unpresented sentences that were paraphrases of targets (e.g., Nick studied the newspaper), (c) unpresented inferences that connected the meaning of different presented sentences (e.g., Nick wanted to see a film), and (d) unpresented sentences that were unrelated to the story (e.g., Nick went swimming). Type b and c sentences, of course, were the meaning-preserving distractors. Once acceptance rates for targets and meaning-preserving distractors were corrected for the fact that acceptances of unrelated materials tended to increase as time passed, the predicted pattern of steeper declines in true memory than in false memory was detected. Indeed, as in the Toglia et al. (1999) and Seamon, Luo, Kopecky, et al. (2002) data for DRM stimulus words, the was *no* decline in levels of false memory for some of the meaning-preserving distractors (the inferences) between the immediate tests and the 4-day delayed tests.

False-Memory Sleeper Effects

The last false-memory persistence effect is the most counterintuitive of the three—that false memory can sometimes display sleeper effects, with erroneous reports of false-but-meaning-preserving events increasing as time passes while correct reports of actual events are declining. This effect is only possible under the assumption that verbatim and gist traces have opposite effects on false-memory reports, and it is therefore a highly diagnostic result with respect to that assumption. If verbatim and gist traces of experience become inaccessible at different rates, the baseline relation between the forgetting of true and false memories ought to be the one that we have just considered (i.e., the former decline more than the latter). However, if verbatim memories trump gist memories, causing subjects to suppress recognition or recall of false-but-meaning-preserving events, there is a theoretical scenario in which the recognition or recall of such events could increase over forgetting intervals, while the recognition or recall of true events is declining sharply. For this scenario to operate, two conditions would have to be met. First, the forgetting interval would have to be short enough so that there would be little or no decline in gist memory but there would be a substantial decline in verbatim memory. In the absence of other data, the studies of DRM lists and narratives that we have just mentioned suggest that forgetting intervals of a few days might satisfy this first criterion. Second, ver-

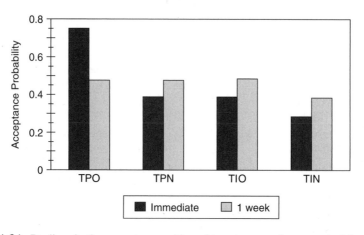

Figure 4-24. Declines in the correct recognition of targets versus increases in false recognition of meaning-preserving distractors over a 1-week forgetting interval. Data from Reyna and Kiernan (1994).

batim traces of targets must be readily accessible by false-memory items on immediate memory tests, so that the level of verbatim suppression of false recognition or false recall is high. If this second condition is met, then the steep forgetting function for verbatim memories, coupled with the relative stability of gist memories, might combine to produce sleeper effects for false memory.

There are multiple experimental approaches that could be taken to ensure that this second condition is met. Perhaps the most obvious is to present only a small amount of target information and administer memory tests immediately thereafter. If the amount of information were small enough, verbatim traces of all of it could presumably be held in short-term memory during testing, causing high rates of verbatim suppression of false-memory reports. A few days later, however, those verbatim traces would be mostly inaccessible, yielding substantial increases in false-memory reports.

This type of design was used in one of the experiments reported in Reyna and Kiernan's (1994) research. In that experiment, the presentation of each three-sentence vignette (e.g., Table 4-1, *top*) was followed immediately by recognition probes for target sentences, meaning-preserving distractor sentences, and meaning-violating distractor sentences (Table 4-1, *bottom*). Recognition probes for these same sentences were readministered 1 week later. The mean levels of true recognition of targets and false recognition of meaning-preserving distractors are plotted in Figure 4-24. It is apparent that across the 1-week forgetting interval, false-memory performance increased substantially while true-memory performance declined substantially. This pattern of delayed increases in false memory for meaning-preserving sentences, coupled with declines in true memory for targets, has been reported in other studies that have used these same procedures (Kiernan, 1993; Lim, 1993).

A second approach to ensuring high levels of verbatim suppression on immediate tests is to present the target materials multiple times, which should create strong verbatim traces (see the earlier discussion of verbatim repetition). This approach was taken in a recent DRM experiment in our laboratory (Brainerd, Payne et al., 2003). Six DRM lists were presented to subjects, with three lists being presented once and three being presented three times. Half of the subjects performed written free recall immediately after all of the lists were presented, and the other half of the subjects did not perform written free recall until a week later. The assumption is that verbatim suppression of false recall should be high for immediate recall of lists that were presented three times and that these particular lists might therefore display sleeper effects. They did. The probability of false recall increased from .17 on the immediate test to .22 on the delayed test.

A third and final approach to ensuring high levels of verbatim suppression on immediate tests is provided by the target-priming manipulation that we discussed in the earlier section on verbatim-retrieval cuing. In the original studies of this manipulation (Brainerd, Reyna, & Kneer, 1995), some of the target materials had been presented three times. Hence, when meaning-preserving distractors for those particular materials were preceded by target primes on immediate recognition tests, the rate of verbatim suppression of false alarms should have been high. In some of those experiments, both immediate and 1-week delayed tests were administered. If the line of reasoning that we have been following is correct, the rate of verbatim suppression should have dropped dramatically over the 1-week forgetting interval, while the accessibility of gist memories should have remained high. Consistent with such reasoning, we found increases in levels of semantic false recognition for distractors that were primed by targets that had been presented three times. In one experiment, for instance, the false-alarm rate for such distractors (the names of familiar categories of which targets were exemplars) was .02, and the hit rate for the corresponding targets was .93 on immediate recognition tests. On 1-week delayed tests, the false-alarm rate for such distractors rose to .28, but the hit rate for the corresponding targets dropped to .61.

Synopsis

The bottom line of this chapter could hardly be less complicated. The study of false memory under controlled laboratory conditions has yielded impressive levels of experimental control over the recognition and recall of false-but-meaning-preserving events. Experimental control has been achieved pursuant to theoretical predictions, the predictions in question being ones that follow from opponent-processes distinctions about false memory. This would be less of an accomplishment if the relevant theoretical distinctions were complex. However, as we saw in chapter 3, those distinctions are relatively straightforward by the standards of contemporary theories of memory, the core idea being merely that the human brain stores and retrieves dissociated representations of experience that reinforce each other when it comes to true-memory reports but oppose each other when it comes to false ones.

An especially impressive aspect of the level of experimental control that has been achieved is that such control is, so to speak, front to back. More explicitly, we have seen that opponent-processes concepts lead to predictions about the initial encoding and storage of memories, about their subsequent retrieval, and about their eventual loss through forgetting, predictions that therefore permit experimental control of false memories across all of the traditional stages of information processing. During encoding and storage, the key bases for prediction are the notion that much of the meaning content of events can be extracted without fully processing their surface forms, plus the notion that gist traces of meaning content are more apt to survive consolidation than are verbatim traces of surface form. This allows false recognition and false recall to be controlled with variables such as the presentation duration of target materials (duration is related to levels of false reporting by inverted-U functions), the repetition of target materials (verbatim repetition is related to levels of false reporting by inverted-U functions, and gist repetition is related to levels of false reporting by monotonic-increasing functions), encoding instructions (deep-processing instructions increase false reporting, and shallow-processing instructions decrease it), distinctiveness (target materials whose surface forms are particularly distinctive decrease false reporting), and consolidation activity (instructions to forget presented material have more substantial effects on true reporting than on false reporting).

Later, during retrieval of previously stored memories, the key bases for prediction are that target events are better retrieval cues for verbatim traces than are false-but-meaning-consistent events and that different amounts of time may be required to retrieve verbatim and gist traces. This allows false recognition and false recall to be controlled via memory-test manipulations, such as retrieval duration (false recognition is related to retrieval duration by inverted-U functions, and false recall is related to retrieval duration by monotonic-increasing functions), verbatim cuing (manipulations that help false-but-meaning-preserving events access verbatim traces rather than gist traces decrease false reporting), and retrieval instructions (instructions that warn subjects about the nature of semantic false memory decrease false reporting).

Finally, across forgetting intervals, the key basis for prediction is the notion that verbatim traces become inaccessible more rapidly than do gist traces. This allows three different false-persistence effects to be detected under selected experimental conditions: high rates of consistency between false reports on immediate and delayed tests; lower levels of decline in false than in true reports between immediate and delayed tests; and increases in false reports, coupled with decreases in true reports, between immediate and delayed tests. These findings of variability across memory interviews pose problems in important real-world contexts. The consistency principle in law, for example, is called into question by these results.

5

Controlling False Memories with Opponent Processes

2—Developmental Research with Children and Adolescents

For some years, children have received special attention in false-memory research. We saw in chapter 1 that childhood false memories figured centrally in the work of two of the field's historical giants, Binet and Piaget. It will be remembered that Binet concluded that young children were highly susceptible to the intrusive thoughts that he believed were the basis of autosuggestion, whereas Piaget concluded that children's memories are distorted for certain types of stimuli (e.g., serial arrays) whose underlying organizational principles are beyond their current levels of logical development and that, surprisingly, those distortions dissipate with time (as logical development proceeds). In the modern era, the prominence of child subjects in false-memory research has been rooted in legal rather than scientific considerations. We shall have much more to say on this topic in chapter 7, but a few prefatory remarks are essential here to appreciate why children should be singled out for intensive investigation.

The law, especially the criminal law, incorporates certain procedural safeguards—defendants' rights—whose motivation is to protect against conviction of the innocent. Examples include the right to confront accusers, the right to vigorously cross-examine and impeach witnesses, the right to challenge the competency of witnesses, the right to avoid self-incrimination, and the prohibition against hearsay testimony. Generally speaking, these strictures are intended to avoid exposing triers of fact to evidence that is unreliable, tainted, or false. Some strictures are by no means absolute, however, and they may be waived in special circumstances in which it is deemed that justice is best served by such waivers. As is commonly known, for instance, the hearsay prohibition may be waived in cases of deathbed testimony. Following the commission of crimes, before defendants stand trial, it sometimes hap-

pens that the only witnesses with firsthand knowledge of the events die without providing evidence under oath. It may be, however, that deceased witnesses gave statements about the target events to relatives, friends, police investigators, or others.
Those statements may not be critical if there is ample physical evidence pointing to
the guilt or innocence of particular suspects, but when they are essential, the deathbed
exemption to hearsay testimony may be invoked, and persons to whom dead witnesses made pertinent statements may be allowed to testify as to their content.

This brings us back to children. Certain defendants' rights combine to make it
difficult for children to testify as witnesses in criminal proceedings. Child witnesses
may be challenged during pretrial voir dire as being incompetent to provide reliable
evidence; child witnesses who previously gave accurate statements about events to
adults may forget those events prior to trial; child witnesses may be too frightened
to testify when they are confronted by defendants at trial; or child witnesses may
become confused under vigorous cross-examination and therefore give inaccurate
and inconsistent testimony. Although these possibilities need not be worrisome when
other sources of trustworthy evidence are available, there are certain crimes for
which children's testimony may supply the only probative information as to guilt
or innocence. Those are crimes in which the sole parties to the events are child victims and adult perpetrators, and the criminal acts are not such as to generate a stable physical record. Sexual abuse of children by adults is the most pervasive example. As a rule, the only firsthand witnesses to such a crime are a child victim and
an adult perpetrator (who enjoys constitutional protection against self-incrimination), and some specific criminal acts (e.g., touching, fondling, sexual statements
and requests) leave no physical residue that could be detected, for instance, via medical examination. Further, even when sexual abuse involves genital penetration, no
physical evidence of the crime may remain if there is a delay of more than several
hours in reporting it. Owing to these special circumstances, it is quite difficult to
prosecute child sexual abuse cases without the testimony of child victims.

To deal with this problem, during the 1970s and 1980s, new trial procedures
evolved in sexual abuse cases that made it progressively easier to secure testimony
from child witnesses. For example, it became more difficult to challenge the competency of children purely on the basis of their age, and it became more common
to grant hearsay exemptions for adult witnesses to whom children had made abuse
allegations. The new procedures led to a number of convictions of defendants who
could not even have been prosecuted under traditional procedures. However, some
of those convictions troubled the consciences of researchers who specialize in the
study of memory development. The chief reason for their concern was that the new
procedures placed the burden of proof squarely on children's memories, when there
were scientific grounds for supposing that children's memories might not be sufficiently reliable to stand as the sole evidentiary basis for conviction, from which it
follows that the procedures may elevate the incidence of wrongful conviction. Thus,
researchers were concerned about children's errors of commission (false memory
reports) which result in wrongful convictions, in addition to errors of omission (true
events that are not reported). That those concerns were well placed seemed evident
from the fact that in some cases, perhaps the most conspicuous example being the
McMartin Preschool trial in California (*State of California v. Buckey*, 1990), pros-

ecutions of defendants were being allowed to proceed notwithstanding that the statements of potential child witnesses contained detailed descriptions of features of putative crimes that were disproved by physical evidence.

During the late 1980s and early 1990s, researchers communicated their concerns in a number of journal articles and presentations at scientific conferences, the single most influential collection of contributions being the proceedings of a conference on children's memory and the law that was sponsored by Cornell University (Doris, 1991). Beyond such formal scientific documents, many researchers provided expert scientific evidence, often in the form of amicus curiae briefs, in sexual abuse trials and in appeals of previous convictions of defendants. The latter activity resulted in reversals of some high-profile convictions. Surely the best known was the conviction of Kelly Michaels in the Wee Care Nursery School case (*State of New Jersey v. Michaels*, 1988). In the Michaels appeal, a large group of child memory researchers, called the Committee of Concerned Scientists, submitted an amicus brief that summarized a considerable amount of research bearing on the reliability of children's memory reports, with special emphasis on errors of commission. The opinion written by the New Jersey Supreme Court in reversing Michaels's conviction emphasized that the evidence of child witnesses may have been tainted by false-memory reports, and it also stressed the need to consider expert scientific evidence bearing on the possibility of such taint in future trials (Bruck & Ceci, 1995; Rosenthal, 1995; *State of New Jersey v. Michaels*, 1994). Subsequent court opinions in other cases advanced similar conclusions. This prompted a response from researchers, to whom it was apparent that the new responsibility of advising the courts in connection with the reliability of children's testimony would require a much more extensive scientific literature on children's false memories. The result, since the early 1990s, has been the emergence of children as subjects of intensive investigation.

Against the legal backdrop of contemporary studies of children's false-memory reports, it is more than usually important to determine whether it is possible to achieve predictive control over such reports. Our approach to answering this question is the same as in chapter 4—namely, we will evaluate opponent-processes predictions about variables that ought to affect levels of false memory. The discussion will follow much the same organizational structure as in chapter 4, beginning with memory storage, continuing with memory retrieval, and ending with forgetting. There will be an important new consideration, however: age variability in opponent processes. In chapter 4, we had the luxury of ignoring this issue. Because that chapter was confined to studies of adults, the question of the immaturity of memory processes did not arise. With children, however, it is not possible to make confident predictions using opponent-processes distinctions without making assumptions about ontogenetic trends in those processes. It will be the business of the first section below to spell out the assumptions that are supported by available research. We will then move on to the topic of predictive control of the storage, retrieval, and forgetting stages of information processing. As this latter discussion unfolds, it will be seen that age changes in verbatim memory and gist memory introduce an important new consideration into predictive control: *developmental interactions*. It will be seen, more particularly, that when a memory task is sensitive to underlying age variability, a manipulation that is known to have specific effects on the levels of false memory that are exhibited by adults or adolescents may have larger, smaller, or even opposite effects on the corresponding levels of false memory in children.

Developmental Trends in Opponent Processes

During the course of the historical discussion in chapter 1, we mentioned, in connection with Binet's work, the hoary hypothesis that younger children's memory reports are more habitually infected with false memories than those of older children or adults. However, we also remarked that the developmental situation is more complicated than this hypothesis envisions. It is now time to consider the nature of those complications.

According to opponent-processes distinctions, recognition or recall of false-but-meaning-preserving events is supported by gist memories of the meaning of experience, but such responses can often be suppressed by retrieving verbatim memories of actual experiences. Thus, expressed levels of false memory for particular events that are observed in children will depend jointly upon (a) whether children can store, retrieve, and preserve the gist memories that support those false memories, and (b) whether they can store, retrieve, and preserve the verbatim memories that suppress them. Obviously, there is one pattern of age variability that would provide unambiguous support for the standard view that levels of false memory are inversely related to chronological age: If memory for the surface form of experience improves massively between early childhood and young adulthood but memory for its meaning content improves but little, the outcome would be universal developmental declines in false memory (pursuant to the increasing ability of verbatim traces of actual events to neutralize the familiarity of false-but-meaning-preserving events). This is not the pattern that has been revealed in developmental research, however. Instead, it seems that both verbatim and gist memory improve considerably with age, though the nature of the improvements in gist memory require some explanation if their implications for false memory are to be understood. Given that there are substantial improvements in both verbatim and gist memory, whether, in a particular study, levels of expressed false memory are found to increase with age, decrease with age, or remain constant is critically dependent upon the memory tasks that are administered, and more especially, developmental changes in expressed false memory depend upon the mix of processes that are tapped by particular tasks. But more on this later. It is first necessary to summarize what is known about age variability in verbatim and gist memory.

Verbatim Memory

The picture for verbatim memory is straightforward. For the types of materials that have traditionally been the centerpieces of false-memory research (see chapter 2), memory for their exact surface form exhibits age improvements between early childhood and young adulthood, with initial improvements, during the preschool and early elementary-school years, being more pronounced than subsequent improvements (for reviews, see Brainerd, 1997; Brainerd & Reyna, 1998a, 2001a; Reyna,

1996; Reyna & Brainerd, 1995a). This finding is present in any number of studies in which the task was to use memory for the surface form of events to discriminate between new and previously presented stimuli whose visual or auditory features are similar, such as sentences that differ in a single word (e.g., Kiernan, 1993; Paris & Mahoney, 1974; Reyna & Kiernan, 1994; Weismer, 1985). In most of these studies, the materials were meaningful items (e.g., familiar words, sentences describing familiar events, pictures of familiar events), so that developmental changes in verbatim memory might to some extent have been due to the fact that children were also processing meaning. However, evidence of pure age improvements in verbatim memory is also available from studies in which the task was to use memory for the surface form of events to discriminate between new and previously presented *nonsense* materials whose visual or auditory features are similar, such as nonsense shapes (e.g., Posner & Keele, 1968) or nonsense syllables.

The bulk of the relevant findings are from studies in which the target materials were nonsense words. For instance, Brainerd, Stein, & Reyna (1998) administered a long list of words to 7- and 11-year-old children using the continuous recognition procedure that Underwood (1965) employed in his classic investigation of semantic false recognition. That is, children listened to each word as it was read and decided whether or not they had previously heard it. Many of the list words were nonsense targets such as CEXIB, TIVIG, and ZUTEB. Sometimes these nonsense targets appeared *twice* on the list, in earlier and later positions, whereas at other times, nonsense targets were replaced by rhyming distractors (e.g., LEXIB, MIVIG, KUTEB). In one condition of this experiment, children were instructed to identify these rhyming distractors, which requires that they be able to access a trace of the phonetic structure of an earlier target (e.g., CEXIB) and compare it to the encoded phonetic structure of a recognition probe (e.g., LEXIB) in order to determine that the latter is similar to but different from the former. Because targets had been presented only a few seconds before, performance was quite good at both age levels. Nevertheless, there was a significant age increase in accuracy, from 84% for the 7-year-olds to 91% for the 11-year-olds.

Much larger improvements in the accuracy of verbatim memory were obtained in other studies that we conducted (e.g., Brainerd & Reyna, 2001b; Brainerd, Reyna, & Brandse, 1995; Reyna & Kiernan, 1994, 1995). In one of them, the subjects were 5- and 11-year-olds. They listened to the same list as in the Brainerd et al. (1998) experiment, but there were two procedural changes. First, the study-test method was used, rather than continuous recognition. The children listened to the entire list, and then, following a short buffer activity, they responded to a test list composed of nonsense targets, distractors that rhymed with nonsense targets, and unrelated nonsense distractors. As before, the task was to identify distractors that rhymed with previously presented nonsense words. The other procedural change occurred during presentation of the study list, where some nonsense targets were read once and others were read three times (which should yield stronger verbatim traces). The results are shown in Figure 5-1, where proportions of accepted rhymes, which have been corrected for erroneous acceptances of the corresponding targets, are shown for both age levels and both levels of target repetition. There are two features of interest. First, when nonsense targets were presented only once (weaker verbatim traces),

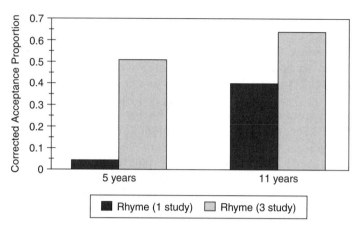

Figure 5-1. Development of verbatim memory illustrated by age changes in the ability to discriminate nonsense rhymes (e.g., LEXIB, MIVIG) from previously presented nonsense targets (e.g., CEXIB, TIVIG). Data from Brainerd and Reyna (2001b).

younger children exhibited virtually no ability to discriminate targets from unpresented rhymes, and the amount of developmental improvement in this ability was dramatic. Second, when nonsense targets had been presented three times (stronger verbatim traces), there was still a clear age improvement in this verbatim-memory skill, but the improvement was only one third as great (.14) because younger children performed much better following three target presentations (51% accuracy) than following one presentation (4% accuracy). This second finding is an example of a continuing theme of this chapter—namely, developmental interactions. A manipulation (repetition, in this case) that strengthens a particular process (verbatim memory, in this case) is apt to have larger effects at age levels at which the process is less highly developed.

Gist Memory

Developmental improvements in verbatim memory imply an improving ability to suppress false-memory reports by using memory for the exact surface form of experience to neutralize the familiarity of false-but-meaning-preserving events. The problem is that this age trend does not translate into straightforward predictions about children's false memories because memory for the meaning content of experience, the reason that false-but-meaning-preserving events seem familiar in the first place, also varies with age and in a complex fashion. The complexity of age variability stems from the fact that even young children have little difficulty storing some types of gist memories (e.g., Hall & Halperin, 1972), whereas the ability to store others undergoes protracted periods of development. As an example of an early facility with meaning content, even human infants extract from their experience simple forms of meaning, such as membership in perceptual categories, numerosity, and cause-effect relations (Haith & Benson, 1998; Mandler, 1998). Likewise, preschoolers readily classify pictures of horses, cows, and sheep as animals; pictures of shirts, pants, and coats as clothing; pictures of hamburgers, hot dogs, and pizza as food. Further, when 3- and 4-year-olds are read pairs of familiar words that are associatively related (e.g., *fork, spoon*) or categorically related (e.g., *cookie, lollipop*), the meaning overlap affects their memories because it is easier for them to recall such pairs than to recall pairs of semantically unrelated words (Goldberg, Perlmutter, & Myers, 1974; Perlmutter & Myers, 1979). At the level of individual objects and events, therefore, it is well established that young children are often able to store some of the same familiar meanings as adolescents or adults. It is equally well established, however, that there are forms of meaning extraction that lag far behind in young children.

Connecting the Gist

An example that has fundamental implications for false memory, a rather surprising one in view of its seeming simplicity, is a capability to which we have referred elsewhere as *connecting the gist* (Reyna & Lloyd, 1997). It refers to the extraction of meaning relations *between* events when subjects encounter a series of superficially distinct events that share some familiar meaning. Historically, children's connecting-the-gist limitations were first systematically articulated with a family of elementary memory tasks known as discrimination-shift problems (e.g., Kuenne, 1946). A much-studied example of such a task, which involves two phases, is shown in Figure 5-2. During Phase 1, children memorize the classifications of the four objects at the top of Figure 5-2, the correct classifications being that the black rectangle and the black circle have been arbitrarily designated as "winners" (+ = winner) and the white rectangle and the white circle have been arbitrarily designated as "losers" (− = loser). In order to learn these classifications, the objects may be presented one at a time, and children may be asked to guess the classification of each as it is presented. Children are then informed of the correct classification following each of their responses and may also be given a reward for each correct response. Note that beyond the classifications of the individual objects, there is an underlying gist: Color determines winners and losers. Even 2- and 3-year-olds rapidly memorize the object classifications, usually committing fewer than 10 errors before making a criterion run of several consecutive perfect responses. The question is: Do they also connect the color gist across individual winners and losers? Apparently not.

Failure to connect this simple gist is revealed during Phase 2. After children make a criterion run, the experimenter unexpectedly changes the classifications of the objects. The child's task is to memorize the new classifications until another criterion run can be made. To diagnose gist connection, the experimenter changes the object classifications in either of two ways, one that preserves the gist of Phase 1 and one that does not. The gist-preserving reclassification, which is known as a *reversal shift*, is shown in the center of Figure 5-2: Color still determines winners and losers, but previous winners are now losers and previous losers are now winners. The gist-violating reclassification, which is known as a *nonreversal shift*, is shown at the bottom of Figure 5-2: Color no longer determines winners and losers; shape does. If subjects connected the color gist during Phase 1, the reversal reclassification ought to be easier to learn than the nonreversal reclassification. That pattern is routinely exhibited by adults and adolescents, who often commit only a single error before

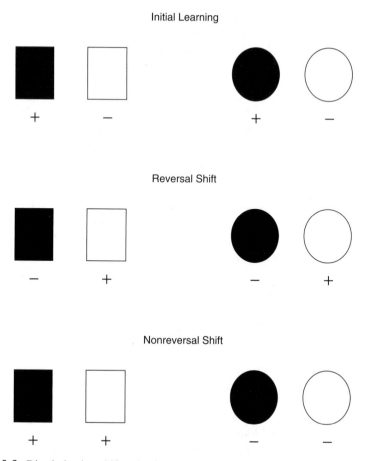

Figure 5-2. Discrimination-shift tasks that reveal children's limitations in connecting the gist between superficially distinct objects that share familiar meanings. Children first memorize the classifications of the objects at the top (+ = winner; − = loser). Then, they memorize either a reclassification of the objects that preserves the gist of the original classification (reversal shift) or a reclassification that violates the gist of the original classification (nonreversal shift).

making a second criterion run (e.g., Esposito, 1975). However, if subjects only memorized the object classifications during Phase 1 *without connecting the gist between the objects*, the reversal reclassification ought to be *harder* to learn than the nonreversal reclassification. Four new classifications must be memorized with the reversal shift but only two must be memorized with the nonreversal shift. As Kendler and Kendler (1962) pointed out in a landmark review, across tasks involving different types of relations between objects (e.g., color, shape, size, numerosity, position), young children typically find nonreversal shifts to be easier than reversal shifts (e.g., Kendler, Kendler, & Wells, 1960). They also pointed out that, across various versions of this paradigm, the adult pattern of fewer errors on the reversal reclassification is not clearly evident until after age 7.

Later, Tighe and Tighe provided direct evidence that young children fail to connect the gist using a procedure called *subproblem analysis,* in which reclassification errors during Phase 2 are separately analyzed for each of the four objects in the (easier) nonreversal reclassification. If young children only memorize individual object classifications during Phase 1 without connecting the gist, they will necessarily make more errors on the white rectangle and the black circle (whose classifications have changed) than on the black rectangle and the white circle (whose classifications have been preserved). This between-object difference in Phase 2 errors has been consistently observed at age levels at which nonreversal reclassification is easier than is reversal reclassification (e.g., Cole, 1976; Kulig & Tighe, 1976; Tighe, Tighe, & Schechter, 1975). In adults and adolescents, however, the four objects produce comparable error rates, as would be expected if subjects connected the color gist during Phase 1.

However, as is obvious from the paradigms that were reviewed in chapter 2, discrimination-shift problems are not the sorts of tasks that have been used to study false memory. Classic examples of children's connecting-the-gist limitations that are more apropos to false memory can be found in free-recall experiments in which the individual targets on word or picture lists belong to a few common categories (e.g., some targets are women's names, some targets are names of furniture, some targets are names of clothing, some targets are names of colors). When adults are exposed to such materials, they store the meanings of individual targets as they are presented, but they also form higher-order meaning relations between targets that share salient meaning—in effect, they understand that the target materials fall into a few semantic groups. We know that adults do this because they exhibit characteristic performance effects that depend upon the formation of connected meanings. Two well-known examples are *category clustering* and *proactive interference,* both of which are measured in free recall. Concerning category clustering, when adults freely recall lists of the aforementioned sort, they output words in a highly organized fashion. Essentially, their recall can be characterized as a burst of words from one category (e.g., *table, sofa, bed, bookcase*), followed by a burst of words from another category (e.g., *orange, mauve, pink, ivory*), and so on. Adults who display higher levels of such output organization also display higher levels of true recall (e.g., Bjorklund & Muir, 1988). Concerning proactive interference, suppose that adults study and recall a series of short lists that share salient meaning. For instance, suppose that the following lists are studied and recalled, one after the other:

List 1	*List 2*	*List 3*	*List 4*
Mary	Sue	Ann	Jane
Judy	Carol	Barbara	Kathy
Linda	Joan	Nancy	Betty
Jean	Karen	Pat	Joyce
Diane	Sharon	Sally	Alice
Lynn	Sandy	Allen	Helen
Ruth	Margaret	Janet	Pam
Carolyn	Gail	Jill	June
Joann	Marie	Bonnie	Debbie
Donna	Janice	Louise	Elaine

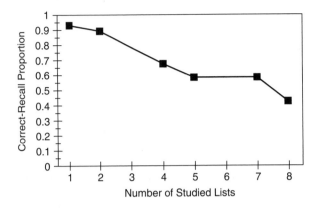

Figure 5-3. Proactive interference in the recall of successive lists whose members are exemplars of the same taxonomic category. Data extrapolated from Postman and Keppel (1977).

As each successive list is studied and recalled, the number of targets that appear in subjects' free-recall protocols declines (e.g., Greenberg & Underwood, 1950), and subjects exhibit intrusions from previously studied lists, which resemble the source-monitoring errors that were discussed in chapter 2. An illustration of just how sharp are the declines in recall over a series of lists is shown in Figure 5-3, which presents data from an experiment by Postman and Keppel (1977) in which adults studied and recalled a total of eight lists like those shown above. As can be seen, recall accuracy is cut in half between the first and eighth list.

Children, unlike adults, fail to exhibit these diagnostic signs of the formation of meaning connections between familiar words. Developmental research on the first diagnostic sign—category clustering—is extensive, and available studies indicate that such clustering does not appear spontaneously in free-recall protocols until early adolescence (e.g., Bjorklund & Jacobs, 1985; DeMarie-Dreblow, 1991). Moreover, once clustering appears, further time must still pass before clustering predicts recall accuracy (e.g., Bjorklund, Miller, Coyle, Slawinski, 1997; Miller & Seier, 1994). With respect to the second diagnostic sign, available developmental data show, similarly, that category-based proactive interference does not appear spontaneously before early adolescence and that it does not reach adult levels until some years later (e.g., Bjorklund & Hock, 1982).

Other ubiquitous instances of children's failure to connect the gist across target events occur in the comprehension of simple narratives that are composed of only short declarative sentences consisting of familiar words. Relative to older children and adults, many findings point to the conclusion that young children have difficulty storing the meaning of simple declarative sentences (which involves connecting meaning across separate words) and that they also have difficulty storing the meanings that follow from two or more such sentences (which involves connecting meaning across separate sentences). Developmental data on comprehension of the meaning of simple narratives like those in Table 2-6 and Table 4-1 serve to illustrate these points. With the materials in the latter table, for instance, Reyna and Kiernan (1994), Kiernan (1993), Forrest (2002), and Brainerd and Reyna (1993) have all reported demonstrations of childhood improvements in storing sentence meanings and meanings that bind multiple sentences. Remember that with these materials, subjects first listen to three-sentence narratives that specify familiar spatial or magnitude relations between everyday objects (Table 4-1, *top*) and they then listen to test probes, some of which are presented sentences (TPO), some of which are meaning-preserving unpresented sentences (TPN, TIO, and TIN), and some of which are meaning-violating unpresented sentences (FPO, FPN, FIO, and FIN). In the aforementioned studies, testing conditions were included that measured the extent to which children could extract the meanings specified by the narratives, *without regard to whether they could remember the exact surface form of the sentences.* In those conditions, children in the elementary-school age range were instructed to listen to each narrative, to try to understand its meaning, but not to worry about remembering the exact wording of the sentences. Prior to testing, the children were presented with demonstration narratives and demonstration probes, and they were not permitted to continue into the testing phase of the experiment unless they performed flawlessly on these warm-up tasks. During the test phase, children listened to a series of three-sentence narratives like the one at the top of Table 4-1. Immediately following each narrative, they responded to a series of sentence probes like those in the remainder of the table, under instructions to accept all sentences that were *true* on the basis of the narrative (ignoring whether the sentences had actually been presented) and to reject all sentences that were *false*. Thus, the sentence probes measured memory for meaning, not memory for the actual sentences. That the probes were administered immediately after each narrative is a crucial feature of the procedure because it rules out forgetting as a possible source of developmental differences in memory for meaning. If such differences are observed, the fact that there has been no opportunity for forgetting implies that the differences are principally due to age variability in storing the meaning content of the narratives.

Although the sentences in these narratives are composed of familiar words whose meanings are well understood by preschoolers, the consistent finding has been that performance on immediate tests of meaning recognition improves substantially during the elementary-school years. To illustrate this trend, we present data in Figure 5-4 from a developmental study that Reyna and Kiernan (1994) reported. The aforementioned tests were administered to a sample of 6-year-olds and a sample of 9-year-olds. The resulting levels of meaning-recognition accuracy are plotted separately for the two age levels and are also plotted separately for presented sentences (TPO) and for unpresented meaning-preserving sentences (TPN, TIO, and TIN). In order to provide a clear picture of developmental trends in meaning storage, the performance levels in Figure 5-4 have been corrected for erroneous acceptances of false sentences. (Remember that for each of the four meaning-preserving sentences, there is a matching meaning-violating sentence [FPO, FPN, FIO, FIN]. Hence, the true level of meaning-recognition accuracy for, say, presented sentences is not merely the acceptance rate for TPO, but it is that acceptance rate minus the acceptance rate for FPO.) It can be seen that the results point to large improvements in meaning storage for these simple sentences between the ages of 6 and 9. The three unpresented sentences that preserve meaning are of special interest because verbatim memory could not contribute to the acceptance of these items. For these particular probes, there was an average age improvement of one third in the accuracy of meaning recognition. Moreover, the improvement in children's ability to recognize the mean-

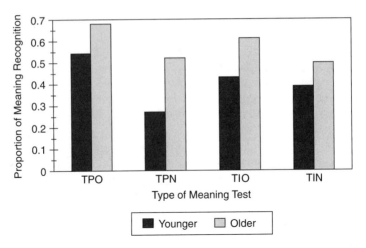

Figure 5-4. Developmental improvements in children's ability to store the meaning of simple declarative sentences and to connect meanings across sentences. Data from Reyna and Kiernan (1994).

ing content of individual sentences, which involves connecting meaning across the individual words of a sentence, displayed greater improvement (48%) than the ability to recognize meanings that bind two sentences, which involves connecting meaning across the individual words of the sentences and also connecting meaning across different sentences (27%).

Unfamiliar Gists

Thus, regardless of whether the target materials are lists of familiar words with familiar meanings or whether the materials are sentences composed of such words, it would seem that there are major improvements between early childhood and adolescence in the tendency to form interconnected meanings on the basis of such items. Of course, it should be added that there is another, simpler variety of meaning extraction that will necessarily increase with age during this same period—namely, extraction of the meaning of *individual* items when those items are not extremely familiar ones whose meanings are part of the everyday experience of young children. To illustrate, at the level of individual words, the average preschooler knows that *red* denotes a color, that *couch* denotes an article of furniture, and that *pants* denotes an article of clothing. However, the average preschooler is unaware that the words *crimson*, *chesterfield*, and *britches*, respectively, have the same meanings. The developmental literature supplies a wealth of examples of the same phenomenon—developmental improvements in the storage of item-level meanings—for materials that are used in most of the major false-memory paradigms that were reviewed in chapter 2. As one such example, consider tasks that involve schematic memories, such as event schemas, spatial schemas, and social schemas (e.g., gender concepts). There are certain schematic situations, especially ones that involve everyday events and spatial relations, that are highly familiar to young children and for which they would therefore be expected to possess memory schemas. Cases in point would be "eating meals with the family," "getting ready to go to school in the morning," "shopping for groceries," and "playing at the park." Even young children are well aware that certain events are characteristic of those situations, and they would therefore be apt to extract the relevant meaning if exposed to such events (e.g., Sally went down the slide, climbed on the monkey bars, pushed her friend on the swings, and sat on the teeter-totter). On the other hand, there are many schematic situations that, though familiar to adults, fall outside the scope of young children's experience, and for which they would not possess the memory schemas that would allow meaning to be extracted from instantiating events. The office schemas that were mentioned in chapter 2 (Brewer & Treyens, 1981; Lampinen et al., 2001) are cases in point, though young children would be expected to possess schemas for other familiar rooms (e.g., kitchen, bedroom). Perhaps the most ubiquitous examples of memory schemas that have been extensively studied in adults but that young children would not possess are ones that involve social conventions, such as gender concepts and ethnic concepts (e.g., see Alba & Hasher, 1983; Reyna et al., in press).

What is currently known about developmental trends in gist extraction supports two generalizations that are central to predictive control of children's false-memory responses. On the one hand, children from the youngest age levels that have been studied in false-memory research are able to extract some of the salient meaning content from familiar words, pictures, objects, and events. On the other hand, less salient meaning content may not be extracted from familiar items, and there is a wide assortment of items for which young children will not extract even salient meanings (because the items fall outside of their everyday experience). In this latter connection, until fairly advanced ages, children fail to connect salient meanings that they have extracted from individual items across multiple items that share those meanings.

Developmental Variability in False Memory

What are the implications of the foregoing age trends in verbatim and gist memory for false-memory responses? The most straightforward implication is that depending upon the gist memories that support a particular type of false-memory response and the age levels that are being compared, the incidence of that response may be found to increase, decrease, or remain invariant with age (see also Koriat et al., 2001). For instance, suppose that we are dealing with false-memory responses that are supported by gist memories of individual items whose meanings are well understood by young children (e.g., the names of familiar objects, such as *water, table, sun*, and *snake*, or pictures of familiar objects). Developmental improvements in meaning storage will be negligible, relative to developmental improvements in verbatim memory, and such responses should therefore decline with age because improvements in verbatim suppression will swamp improvements in gist support. Suppose, in contrast, that we are dealing with false-memory responses that either (a) are supported by gist memories of individual items whose meanings are unfamiliar to young children (e.g., words such as *buzzard, juggler*, and *hyena*, or narratives that involve unfamiliar concepts, such as adult emotional relationships), or (b) are supported by gist memories that are formed by connecting meaning across items whose individual meanings are understood (e.g., simple declarative sentences). Here, both of the mechanisms that are pertinent to age variability in false-memory responses—the gist mechanism that supports them and the verbatim mechanism that suppresses them—may be expected to undergo substantial developmental improvement. It follows that whether false-memory responses increase or decrease with age (or remain unchanged) must turn on the *relative* amounts of improvement in the supportive and suppressive mechanisms but, less obviously, developmental trends will also turn on the mix of those mechanisms that is tapped by particular memory tasks. On the latter point, imagine that a certain false-memory task minimizes the demands on children's verbatim memories by making it easy to access information about the surface form of experience on memory tests (e.g., by providing continuously available external representations of target events [Brainerd & Reyna, 1995]). With such a hypothetical task, the contributions of underlying improvements in verbatim memory will be minimized, so that age variability in performance will be chiefly due to underlying improvements in gist memory, which should yield developmental increases in false-memory responses (Ceci & Bruck, 1998; Reyna & Brainerd, 1998). Alternatively, imagine that some other false-memory task minimizes the demands on children's gist memories by making it easy for them to access the meaning content of experience on memory tests (e.g., by stating relevant meanings to children as events are experienced and issuing meaning reminders as memory tests are administered). With such a task, the contributions of underlying improvements in gist memory will be minimized, leaving improvements in verbatim memory as primarily responsible for age variability in performance, which should translate into developmental decreases in false-memory responses (e.g., Brainerd & Reyna, 1998a; Holliday, Reyna, & Hayes, 2001; Reyna et al., 2002).

These abstract possibilities are borne out by extant developmental studies of false memory. Because opponent-processes distinctions have appeared so recently, the great bulk of that literature consists of studies whose designs do not take such distinctions into account and, indeed, were motivated purely by empirical considerations. Owing to this lack of guiding theoretical principles, although the literature contains several studies concerned with children's false memories following presentation of word lists, beginning with early work by Bach and Underwood (1971), Cramer (1972), and Felzen and Anisfeld (1971) that followed up Underwood's (1965) classic research, plus several studies concerned with children's false memories following presentation of simple narratives, beginning with early work by Paris and associates (Paris & Carter, 1973; Paris & Mahoney, 1974) that followed up Bransford and Franks's equally classic research, plus some studies of children's false memories following visual presentation of narratives (e.g., Ackil & Zaragoza, 1995; Ceci, Ross, & Toglia, 1987; Pezdek & Roe, 1995; Poole & Lindsay, 1995), design factors vary haphazardly from study to study that, according to opponent-processes distinctions, ought to affect either supportive processes, suppressive processes, or both. Consequently, the overriding expectation would be that reported age changes in false memory would also vary haphazardly from study to study, even when the same age levels are being compared and children are exposed to analogous target materials.

Reyna and Kiernan (1994) have already noted that this pattern of inconsistent age trends holds across early developmental studies of false memory for narrative statements. Specifically, they observed that such a pattern holds across studies reported by Brown, Smiley, Day, Townsend, and Lawton (1977), Paris and associates (1973, 1974), Prawat and Cancelli (1976), and Weismer (1985). Inconsistent age trends can also be identified in more recent developmental studies of false memory for narrative statements (e.g., Ackerman, 1992, 1994). Reyna and Kiernan (1994) argued that such inconsistencies are more apparent than real and that they can be reconciled by applying opponent-processes analysis. Consistent with that argument, they found that the tendency to recognize unpresented meaning-preserving sentences could be made to increase or decrease with age via theory-driven manipulations that selectively influence verbatim or gist memories. More on that in the sequel, however.

We mentioned that other segments of the developmental literature on false memory display the same pattern of inconsistent age trends across studies. In the largest segment of that literature—developmental studies of false memory for word lists—this pattern was evident in the earliest experiments. With children in the elementary-school range, Bach and Underwood (1971) found that false recognition of semantic associates of presented words increased with age; Cramer (1972) reported that false recognition of associates decreased with age; and Felzen and Anisfeld (1971) reported that false recognition of associates was age invariant. Consistent with Reyna and Kiernan's (1994) explanation of conflicting age trends in false memory for sentences, comparisons of the designs of some word-recognition studies suggest that conflicting age trends can be explained by design factors that selectively influence verbatim memory or gist memory (Brainerd & Reyna, 1998a). This can be illustrated with a subset of studies, which are concerned with false recognition of familiar words that preserve the category membership of other familiar words that were previously studied. Here, we briefly compare some developmental studies reported by Hall and Halperin (1972) and the authors of this book (e.g., Brainerd & Reyna, 1996; Brainerd, Reyna, & Brandse, 1995; Brainerd, Reyna, & Kneer, 1995) to studies reported by Seamon and his associates (Seamon et al., 2000).

In all of these studies, children listened to fairly long word lists on which some of the items were exemplars of familiar taxonomic categories (e.g., *dog*, *red*). On recognition tests, the meaning-preserving distractors were either unpresented exemplars of the same categories (e.g., *cat*, *green*) or unpresented labels of the exemplified categories (e.g., *animal*, *color*). In Hall and Halperin's (1972) experiments, it was found that false recognition of such distractors decreased with age during the preschool years, and in our experiments, it was found that false recognition of such distractors decreased with age during the elementary-school years. Such findings are in conformity with the traditional hypothesis about developmental changes in false memory. In contrast, Seamon et al.'s data showed that false recognition of unpresented members of categories that had been exemplified on the study list did not vary even slightly between the ages of 6 and 20. However, with the aid of opponent-processes distinctions, a close comparison of the methodologies of these studies reveals the likely reason for the contrasting findings. Familiar words that are exemplars of everyday categories are instances of materials for which even young children will be able to extract item-level meanings that support false recognition.

Thus, age variability in the memorial basis of false recognition will be minimal, which means that at any rate, developmental *increases* in the false recognition of same-category exemplars would not be expected. (Note that, importantly, this was borne out in all of the studies.) This leaves age improvements in children's ability to access verbatim memories of presented exemplars as the chief basis for developmental changes in false recognition. Normally, that would mean developmental decreases in false recognition, which is the result that was obtained by Hall and Halperin and the authors of this book. But if procedures are adopted that make it easy for subjects of all ages to access such verbatim memories, underlying age improvements in verbatim access would not express themselves (much like recessive genes whose phenotypes are not expressed in the presence of dominant genes), and developmental decreases would not be detected. In Seamon et al.'s procedure, study lists were not presented simply as spoken words but, rather, were presented as pictures of category exemplars, which were named as they were presented. As we know from research that was discussed in chapter 4 (e.g., Israel & Schacter, 1997; Schacter et al., 1999), pictures seem to instill robust verbatim traces that are readily accessible on recognition tests. This would make it difficult for underlying age differences in verbatim access to express themselves, which in turn would make it difficult to detect developmental declines in false recognition.

In light of the traditional hypothesis that false-memory reports simply decline with age, it is crucial to add, before passing on to other matters, that developmental researchers have been able to produce consistent evidence of age *increases* in such reports in circumstances in which opponent-processes distinctions unambiguously forecast such increases. The most obvious circumstance of this sort would have two characteristics: The relevant gist memories improve considerably with age (so that memory support for false recognition and false recall is growing), and the memory tests that are administered make it difficult for subjects of all ages to use verbatim traces of experience to suppress false recognition and false recall (so that underlying age differences in verbatim-suppression abilities cannot express themselves). A procedure that satisfies these criteria is one in which (a) false memory for unpresented items that *connect the meaning* of multiple targets is measured; and (b) memory tests are delayed long enough so that verbatim traces will be mostly inaccessible.

One illustration of such a procedure is delayed memory tests for distractors that preserve the meaning of narratives. Brainerd and Mojardin (1998) and Mojardin (1997) reported some experiments of this sort, using the Reyna and Kiernan (1994) materials, and Liben and Posnansky (1977) reported analogous experiments using similar narrative materials. In both instances, false recognition of meaning-preserving distractor sentences increased with age. For instance, Brainerd and Mojardin modified Reyna and Kiernan's original procedure by merely delaying memory tests until after all of the three-sentence narratives had been read, whereas Reyna and Kiernan's memory tests had been administered following each narrative. When pilot testing was conducted with adults, the subjects stated that the modified procedure made it hard for them to remember the exact wording of narrative sentences, from which it seemed reasonable to suppose that the procedure would make it difficult for developmental differences in verbatim retrieval to express themselves. Con-

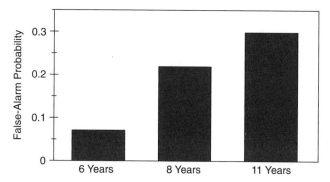

Figure 5-5. Developmental increases in false memory for narrative statements when verbatim retrieval is made difficult for all age levels. The plotted data are corrected false-alarm rates for meaning-preserving distractor sentences (false-alarm rates for meaning-violating distractors have been subtracted from false-alarm rates for meaning-preserving distractors). Data from Brainerd and Mojardin (1998).

sistent with this supposition, the procedure yielded dramatic increases in false recognition of meaning-preserving distractors for subjects between the ages of 6 and 11. Pooled data from the various conditions of this experiment are displayed in Figure 5-5, where the false-alarm probabilities for such distractors range from .07 in 6-year-olds to .30 in 11-year-olds.

The production of consistent age increases in false memory is not confined to complex tasks such as narrative comprehension, however. The same result has been produced with false recall and false recognition of word lists composed of items whose meanings are familiar to young children. Here, the finding that has been exploited to produce age increases in false memory is young children's limited ability to connect meaning across items that share meaning, even though that meaning is a familiar one. The DRM task, which has figured so centrally in adult experimentation, is a handy tool for capitalizing on this finding to produce age increases in false recall and false recognition. It will be remembered from earlier discussions that DRM lists are composed of familiar words (e.g., *nurse, hospital, sick*) and that the missing stimulus words (e.g., *doctor*) are also familiar. The distinctive feature of these lists, which presumably contributes to the illusion that the missing stimulus words were presented, is that all of the words share salient meaning (e.g., "medicine"). This fact is readily apparent to adults, of course, but according to what we know about memory development, it will not be apparent to young children, implying that the high rates at which adults falsely recall and falsely recognize unpresented stimulus words will not be obtained in children. Of late, this prediction has been evaluated in several developmental studies, with subject samples spanning the kindergarten to mid–high school age ranges (Brainerd, Holliday, & Reyna, 2004; Forrest, 2002; Price, Metzger, Williams, Phelps, & Phelps, 2001). As expected on the basis of children's known limitations in forming connected meanings between items, false recall and false recognition of unpresented stimulus words have been

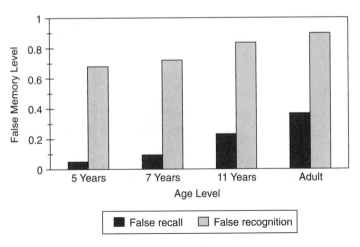

Figure 5-6. Developmental increases in false memory for DRM stimulus words. The plotted data are pooled findings from Brainerd et al. (2004), Brainerd, Reyna, and Forrest (2002), and Forrest (2002).

found to increase between early childhood and young adulthood. Developmental trends in false recall and false recognition are illustrated in Figure 5-6, which displays composite data from multiple studies. Note that this particular variety of false memory develops very gradually and that there are increases during early adolescence as well as during childhood (for a review of both published and unpublished studies in this area, see Reyna et al., in press).

Storing Memories

We turn now to the question of predictive control of children's false-memory reports. From here on, we follow the presentation format of chapter 4, taking up storage variables that should affect false-memory reports in the present section, followed by retrieval variables in the next section, followed by forgetting in the section after that. In the course of all three sections, it will be evident that opponent-processes distinctions allow us to control children's false memories, even as they allow us to do likewise with adults' false memories. However, two differences will become apparent between theory-driven research on children and corresponding research on adults. First, there is far less of it. Some of the key variables that figured in chapter 4 have either not been manipulated in studies of children's false memories, or if they have, the accumulated findings are less extensive. Second, when theoretically specified variables are manipulated, they are not necessarily expected to have the unqualified effects that they have in adults. Instead, owing to ontogenetic changes in opponent processes, the variables' effects may interact with age (i.e., a manipulation may have larger, smaller, or opposite effects in younger versus older children). Despite this added complication, predictive control remains possible because the nature of those interactions can be forecast in advance, using the developmental and task considerations that were reviewed in the preceding section.

In chapter 4, the discussion of storage variables that affect false recall and false recognition began with an examination of on-line relations between verbatim and gist storage, with special emphasis on the finding of advanced gist storage in adults. The pertinent research made use of masked-priming procedures, which yielded a key finding—subliminal semantic activation—which is a variant of the familiar semantic-priming effect. Some of the meaning content of a word can be stored when presentation rates are so fast that subjects are not even aware that it was presented. Unfortunately, there is no parallel developmental literature that provides clear guidance as to age trends in subliminal semantic activation. It is true that developmental studies of semantic priming have been reported, particularly in the literature on children's reading (e.g., Siegel, 1993; Sprenger-Charolles, 1991), as have developmental studies of speeded word recognition (e.g., Case, Kurland, & Goldberg, 1982). However, the presentation rates in such studies are much slower than those that have been used in adult research, so that the data do not tell us anything definite about comparative rates of storage of representations that support versus suppress false-memory responses. Further, even if extremely rapid presentation speeds had been used, the performance demands of the tasks that have been employed to demonstrate subliminal semantic activation in adults (see Figure 4-1) are far beyond the abilities of preschoolers and young elementary-schoolers.

Despite the lack of a developmental database on masked priming, some of the developmental findings that we have already mentioned are sufficient for understanding how the phenomenon of advanced storage of gist must vary with age. Although preschoolers can extract the salient meanings of familiar words, pictures, and objects, they cannot extract other, less salient meanings, and further, the tendency to connect salient meanings across familiar stimuli develops slowly throughout childhood. Even salient meanings that are stored by preschoolers will surely be stored more rapidly by older children and adults. The obvious implication is that advanced storage of gist will emerge with age, paralleling (and perhaps contributing to) developmental improvements in the extraction and connection of meaning. For the types of materials that have been administered in studies of false memory, the expectation therefore is that manipulations whose adult effects hinge on the advanced storage of gist will have reduced effects in children.

Unfortunately, the key manipulation of this sort that was considered in chapter 4—presentation duration—has not been investigated in children. However, the nature of age variability in its effects can be predicted. Remember that, in adults, inverted-U relations (i.e., false memories increase with initial increases in duration but decline with subsequent increases in duration) are predicted and have been confirmed (McDermott & Watson, 2001; Seamon et al., 2002c). Because such inverted-U relations depend upon meaning processing being completed more rapidly than surface processing, they ought to emerge with development, and one would not expect to find them in young children. To the extent that meaning storage is slow and inefficient in children, the clear prediction is that, below a certain age level, the types of materials that have yielded inverted-U relations in adults will yield simple monotonic relations in children (i.e., false-memory responses will merely increase as presentation duration lengthens). Thus, the anticipated developmental interaction between presentation duration and false memory is that, in children, the relation between presentation duration and false recognition or false recall will resemble the left side of Figure 4-7 but not the right side.

Beyond presentation duration, we examined four other storage variables (repetition of events, deep versus shallow processing, distinctiveness, and consolidation activity) in chapter 4. Whereas predictions about duration turned on the notion of advanced gist storage, predictions about these other four variables turned on the fact that postexposure consolidation favors gist memories over verbatim memories. How should the effects of these variables be constrained by age? The answer follows from two basic considerations. First, in the earlier discussion of adult consolidation, it was assumed that with the materials that are used in false-memory research, a single leisurely presentation of an item is typically sufficient for subjects to complete their processing of its surface form and meaning content. Such an assumption is not warranted for children. As the ability to extract the meaning content of individual items and the ability to connect meaning across items both improve massively between the preschool years and young adulthood, children's meaning processing is not normally complete following a single leisurely presentation. Second, when the target materials consist of familiar items from which children are able to extract salient meaning, gist consolidation is favored over verbatim consolidation in children as well as in adults. The Reyna and Kiernan (1994) experiments that were used to illustrate preferential gist consolidation in chapter 4 can be used to illustrate this second point (other data illustrating preferential gist consolidation in children can be found in Paris & Carter [1973] and Paris & Mahoney [1974]).

Reyna and Kiernan reported some developmental comparisons of gist and verbatim consolidation in 6- and 9-year-olds, which are summarized in Figure 5-6 and which follow the same format as the earlier figure that depicted preferential gist consolidation (Figure 4-3). Note, first, that at both age levels, gist consolidation occurred because the false-alarm rate for each meaning-preserving distractor (TPN, TIO, TIN) was much higher than the false-alarm rate for its corresponding meaning-violating distractor (FPN, FIO, FIN), and that, second, verbatim consolidation also occurred because the false-alarm rate for distractors that did not differ in meaning content (TIO versus TIN and FIO versus FIN) was higher if the distractors contained only old words. Note, next, that as before, gist consolidation exceeds verbatim consolidation because the discrepancy between false-alarm rates for distractors with different meaning but the same words (e.g., TPN versus FPN) was greater than the discrepancy for distractors with the same meaning but different words (e.g., FIO versus FIN). Most important of all, however, note that both gist and verbatim consolidation improved with age but verbatim consolidation improved more. Developmentally, therefore, one can expect that gist and verbatim consolidation will both increase with age, which means enhanced survival of both false-memory supportive and false-memory suppressive mechanisms, and one can expect that, in particular tasks, improvements in one type of consolidation may exceed improvements in the other, leading to corresponding increases or decreases in false-memory reports.

We now use these developmental findings to generate predictions about children's false-memory reports ought to react to storage manipulations. Of the five storage variables that we considered in chapter 4, only three have been investigated in developmental studies of false memory: repetition of events, deep versus shallow processing, and distinctiveness of events. We have already remarked on the lack of evidence with respect to the duration of events, though as we also remarked, developmental predictions about this variable do not seem controversial. The other variable that has not been investigated is directed forgetting instructions. A few developmental studies have been reported in which the effects of such instructions on *true* memory were explored (Gaultney, Kipp, Weinstein, & McNeill, 1999; Hasselhorn & Richter, 2002; Kress & Hasselhorn, 2000; Lehman, McKinley-Pace, Leonard, Thompson, & Johns, 2001; Wilson & Kipp, 1998). As yet, however, Kimball and Bjork's (2002) and Seamon et al.'s (in press) idea of extrapolating directed forgetting to false memory has not been implemented in developmental studies. Hence, the discussion of storage variables will be confined to repetition, deep versus shallow processing, and distinctiveness.

Repetition of Events

As we already know, there are two basic forms of repetition in false-memory research: verbatim (recapitulating the same events in the same way) and gist (reprising the meaning of events without recapitulating the events themselves). As we also know, in adults, opponent-processes analysis predicts that the two varieties of repetition will have opposite effects on false-memory reports (e.g., Reyna & Lloyd, 1997). Verbatim repetition, it is thought, should strengthen both verbatim and gist memories, but over a series of repetitions, the net effect on the former will be greater owing to the inherently lower rate of verbatim consolidation, which leads to the overall prediction of an inverted-U relation between repetition and both false recall and false recognition. Because gist repetition repeatedly cues the same meanings, it should generate increasingly strong gist memories that are more apt to be processed on memory tests because although the pool of verbatim memories is being increased too, the latter memories are less likely to survive consolidation, which leads to net increases in false recall and false recognition.

How should these ideas be affected by what is known about memory development? The answer is that both manipulations should interact with age in a specific way—namely, verbatim repetition should have reduced effects and gist repetition should have increased effects in children. We postpone predictions about gist repetition until we have considered verbatim repetition. If meaning processing is normally incomplete following a single presentation, verbatim repetition will have more pronounced effects on children's gist memories than on adults' because initial repetitions will not only strengthen previously stored gist memories (as in adults), but they will increase the chances that those memories are stored in the first place. Further, the fact that the gap between verbatim and gist consolidation rates is larger in young children (see Figure 5-4) means that the tendency of verbatim retrieval to close this gap will be lessened in children. All of this implies that the adult finding that a few verbatim repetitions lower false-memory reports (except for special materials such as DRM lists) will be less evident in children. It is even possible that the finding would be reversed in some instances, with a few verbatim repetitions leading to *increased* false-memory reports.

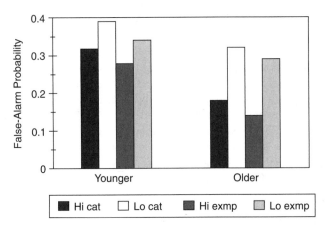

Figure 5-7. Developmental increases in the tendency of verbatim repetition of category exemplars to suppress the false recognition of category labels and other category exemplars. *Hi cat* = unpresented labels of categories (e.g., *animal*) for which one exemplar (e.g., *dog*) had been presented three times; *Lo cat* = unpresented labels of categories for which one exemplar had been presented once; *Hi exmp* = unpresented exemplars of categories (e.g., *cat*) for which one other exemplar (e.g., *dog*) had been presented three times; *Lo exmp* = unpresented exemplars of categories for which one other exemplar had been presented once. Data from Brainerd and Reyna (1996).

Although verbatim repetition has not been investigated in a large number of developmental studies, extant data are quite consistent with the notion that verbatim repetition is less likely to reduce false-memory reports in children. Direct developmental comparisons of younger and older children's false memories for word lists were made in a series of experiments conducted in our laboratory (Brainerd & Reyna, 1996; Brainerd, Reyna, and Kneer, 1995). Across the various experiments, children listened to word lists and then responded to recognition tests on which the false-memory items were antonyms of list words, associates of list words, synonyms of list words, new members of categories that had been exemplified on the list, and the names of categories that had been exemplified on the list. Depending upon the experiment, the subjects ranged in age from 5 years old to 16 years old. Verbatim repetition was manipulated by presenting the individual words that would later be replaced by semantically related distractors from one to three times. The consistent outcome was that the tendency of a few verbatim repetitions to reduce semantic false recognition increased during childhood.

To illustrate, Figure 5-7 contains data from Experiment 1 of Brainerd and Reyna (1996). In that experiment, 40 kindergartners and 40 third-graders listened to a tape recording of 100 familiar concrete nouns (e.g., *clock, arrow, baby, pipe, cat, rose, steel, table*) and then responded to a recognition test on which the semantically related distractors were either category exemplars (e.g., *steel* was replaced by *iron*) or category labels (e.g., *cat* was replaced by *animal*). For these distractors, the corresponding target words had been presented either once or twice on the study list. As can be seen in Figure 5-7, false-alarm rates were lower when distractors' corresponding targets had been presented three times than when they had been presented once, but the suppressive effect was larger for third-graders than for kindergartners. Other investigators have noted the same developmental pattern with different procedures. For instance, Pezdek and her associates have reported several studies of false memory for scripted events—such as grocery shopping, preparing a meal in the kitchen, and shopping at the mall—which are so familiar that children would be expected to possess memory schemas for those events (Pezdek, Finger, & Hodge, 1997; Pezdek & Hodge, 1999; Pezdek & Roe, 1995, 1997). Repetition was varied in one of them (Pezdek & Roe, 1995). In that study, children of two age levels—4 years old and 10 years old—were exposed either to a slide sequence depicting events that are typical of putting away groceries in the kitchen and baking a cake or to a slide sequence depicting events that are typical of construction work on a house. In each sequence, certain key events were presented once (e.g., taking a spoon out of a drawer, picking up a hammer), while other key events were presented twice (e.g., taking a plate out of a cupboard, picking up a brick). On a later recognition test, some of the once-presented events were replaced by related unpresented ones (e.g., spoon became fork), and some of the twice-presented events were also replaced by related unpresented ones (e.g., brick became rock). Overall, these unpresented events were accepted more often when the corresponding target events had been presented only once than when they had been presented twice (70% versus 59%). However, as in the word-list data in Figure 5-7, the difference between the two types of distractors was greater for 10-year-olds than for 4-year-olds (19% versus 3%).

Developmental studies have also been reported in which the suppressive effect of a few verbatim repetitions has reversed itself and increased children's false-memory reports. From what has already been said, the types of situations that would be apt to produce such a result are ones in which young children's extraction of the meaning content that supports such reports is sketchy following a single presentation. Here, the earlier example of false memory for simple narrative sentences is a promising candidate because even if young children understand the meanings of all of the words, they will have difficulty connecting them so as to understand the meaning of the individual sentences. Mojardin (1997) administered the Reyna and Kiernan (1994) materials to children of three age levels: 6, 9, and 11 years old. Moreover, the testing procedure that was previously described in connection with the Brainerd and Mojardin (1998) experiments, which made it difficult for children of all ages to access verbatim traces of target sentences, was used. This procedure should greatly reduce the tendency of repetition to enhance the accessibility of verbatim traces, leaving its tendency to improve gist memory as its principal effect, an effect that should increase with age. In Mojardin's study, half of the children at each age level listened to all of Reyna and Kiernan's three-sentence vignettes once before responding to a recognition test, and the other half listened to the same vignettes three times before responding to the same test. When the false-alarm rates of the two conditions were compared, it was found that the false-alarm rates for certain distractors were roughly 15% higher following three presentations than following one. Moreover, as would be expected on theoretical grounds, this effect decreased with age: Repetition increased the false-alarm rates of 6-year-olds by roughly 25%, but it increased the false-alarm rates of 11-year-olds by less than 10%.

So far, we have postponed discussion of gist repetition because the developmental predictions and their theoretical rationale are different than the predictions and rationale for verbatim repetition. Given that the ability to extract and connect meaning improves with age, gist repetitions will ordinarily strengthen young children's gist memories more than older children's and adults' because young children will preserve less meaning content from an initial presentation. The implication for developmental variability is that although gist repetition should elevate false-memory reports at all age levels, the effect ought to be more marked in children (assuming that the relevant meaning content is not so abstruse as to be understood only by adults). Some studies by Ceci, Crotteau-Huffman, Smith, and Loftus (1994) and Roberts and Blades (1995) provide evidence that bears directly on this possibility.

In Ceci et al.'s research, 122 children in the 3- to 6-year-old range were interviewed about two major scripted events that they were known to have recently experienced (e.g., a trip to Disneyland) and about two other events that they were known never to have experienced (e.g., a trip to the hospital to treat an injury). During each interview, the gist of each of the four events was stated, and children were asked to think about it hard and to try to figure out whether it had happened to them. These gist repetitions occurred over a 10-day period, with individual children being asked to think hard about the scripted events on 7–10 occasions. The false-memory measure during each interview was whether or not children assented to having experienced false events. Ten weeks after the think-hard interviews, children were administered final memory tests in which they were asked to provide free narratives about the two events that had happened to them and the two events that had not. The false-memory data from the original interview sessions are shown in Figure 5-8, where the probability of erroneously assenting to events that had not been experienced is plotted. This probability is plotted separately for preschoolers (3- and 4-year-olds) and young elementary-schoolers (5- and 6-year-olds) for 1, 3, 5, and 7 repetitions. Note that, as expected, gist repetition elevated the false-memory reports of preschoolers more than it elevated those of young elementary-schoolers. However, the elementary-schoolers' false-memory reports were elevated too (overall, they assented to nonexperienced events 32% of the time). Further, the cumulative effect of gist repetitions was to narrow the gap between the two age levels, so that the difference between them by the end of the experiment was no longer statistically significant.

As a further illustration, Roberts and Blades (2000) exposed preschool children and older elementary-schoolers (10-year-olds) to a live staged story called "children's hospital." In the story, a nurse treated the injuries of a baby doll. Two days later, half of the children at each age level viewed a video in which the basic event structure of the story was repeated (a character reprised the nurse's actions in a different context, using a mannequin rather than a baby doll), while the other half of the children viewed a very different video (a story about baking cakes). One week later, the children were interviewed about the live staged events and the events in the video. The false-memory measure was children's tendency to falsely recall events that happened during the video as having happened during the live story. In this design, the effect of gist repetition was measured by comparing levels of false recall

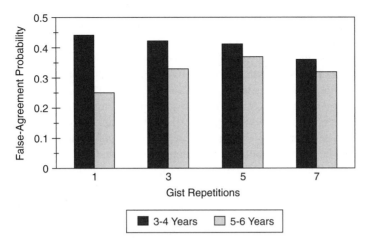

Figure 5-8. Effects of gist repetition on the tendency of 3-year-old to 6-year-old children to falsely believe that they had participated in a major life event, such as being taken to the hospital to be treated for an injury. Data extrapolated from Ceci, Crotteau-Huffman, Smith, and Loftus (1994).

for children who viewed the video whose content was similar to the live story to the levels of false recall for children who viewed the baking-cakes video. It was confirmed that gist repetition tended to falsify children's memories because children who viewed the similar video recalled more false events while giving a free narrative of the live story and while responding to direct questions about the live story. Importantly, however, although gist repetition increased false recall at both age levels, many more false details were reported by the preschoolers than by the elementary-schoolers.

Deep Versus Shallow Processing

As we know from chapter 4, deep- versus shallow-processing instructions have been investigated in literally hundreds of studies of true memory in adults, and they have also been investigated in a few false-memory studies. In children, there is a much more modest literature concerned with the effects of these encoding instructions, and as is the case with adults, virtually all studies have focused on true memory (Arlin, 1986; Evans, 1980; Lorsbach & Mueller, 1979; Perlmutter, Schork, & Lewis, 1982; Puff, Tyrrell, Heibeck, & VanSlyke, 1984; Weiss, Robinson, & Hastie, 1977). Generally speaking, those studies have revealed that the advantages for true recall/ recognition that accrue from deep-processing instructions are smaller in children than in adults and that, during childhood, the magnitude of such effects increases with age. These patterns are, of course, predictable from the developmental trends in meaning processing that we have discussed: Instructions to focus processing on the meaning content of targets are bound to be less effective with subjects whose semantic abilities are more limited.

In addition to the few developmental studies of true memory, a single developmental study of the effects of deep-processing instructions on false memory was published more than 3 decades ago by Cramer (1972). The pattern that would be expected on theoretical grounds is that such instructions should elevate false-memory reports in children as they do in adults (because they focus attention on storing the types of memories that support such reports and direct attention away from storing the types of memories that suppress them) but that the elevation should be less than in adults. This is precisely what Cramer found. It will be recalled that, in adult studies, the most common types of deep-processing instructions involve asking subjects to rate studied words on some semantic dimension, such as pleasantness, or asking subjects to think of other words as they study target words (e.g., synonyms). Cramer used the latter instruction in a false-recognition design in which the semantically related distractors that were administered on recognition tests were synonyms of targets. In her design, first- and fifth-grade children listened to a list of familiar words. Some of the children were given deep-processing instructions (think of other words that mean the same thing as each word you hear), and others were not. After the list had been presented, children responded to a recognition test on which some of the words were replaced by synonyms. The think-of-other-words instruction increased false alarms to synonyms, relative to control instructions, in first-graders (20% versus 15%), but it did not increase false alarms reliably in fifth-graders. Thus, although considerable additional research would be required to draw confident conclusions about age trends in the false-memory effects of deep versus shallow processing, at least the results of this single study are in accordance with theoretical expectations.

Event Distinctiveness

In contrast to deep versus shallow processing, much more evidence is available on the question of how children's false-memory reports react to manipulations that make target events more distinctive. We saw in chapter 4 that two types of manipulations have been used to increase distinctiveness in adults: (a) encoding tasks that require subjects to pay attention to the surface structure of events, such as writing words while listening to them (e.g., Seamon et al., 2003), and (b) presenting events that are known to attract surface-processing attention, such as pictures (e.g., Israel & Schacter, 1997; Schacter et al., 1999) or metaphorical statements (e.g., Reyna & Kiernan, 1995). The first class of manipulations has not been systematically investigated in studies of children's false memories, but the second has. In particular, the effects of both pictorial events and metaphorical events have been investigated.

Taking pictures first, the presentation of verbal materials in visual format has long been a common feature of children's books, the assumption being that it will be easier for children to read and remember text if words' meanings are backed up with concrete depictions. This is also one of the classic manipulations in memory-development research (for reviews, see Paivio, 1970; Reese, 1970; Rohwer, 1970). With recall memory, the general finding has been that when children are exposed to verbal events (e.g., listening to narratives or to word lists), their performance is poorer on tests such as free and associative recall than when verbal events are accompanied by pictures. Moreover, this picture superiority effect increases between early childhood and young adulthood (Brainerd & Howe, 1982; Rohwer, Kee, & Guy, 1975). Both the picture superiority effect in recall and developmental improvements in the effect are found in learning-disabled children as well as in normal children (Howe, Brainerd, & Kingma, 1985; Howe, O'Sullivan, Brainerd, & Kingma, 1989).

The pattern for recognition is different. When lists of unrelated words are presented either as spoken lists or as spoken lists in which each word is accompanied by a picture of the named object or event, there is also a picture superiority effect, but there is only limited evidence of developmental improvement. The reason for the latter finding is not profound, however: The effect of pictorial presentation is so powerful on recognition tests that performance is often elevated to near-ceiling levels in both younger and older children, so that there is simply no room to detect age changes (Corsini, Jacobus, & Leonard, 1979; Merriman, Azmita, & Perlmutter, 1988; Morrison, Haith, & Kagan, 1980). The key point, however, is that because pictures improve children's true-memory performance, as they do adults', and because pictorial presentation is a surface-distinctiveness manipulation, rather than a meaning manipulation, pictorial presentation would be expected to suppress semantic false alarms and intrusions in children.

In developmental research, the effects of pictorial presentation on false recognition and false recall have been studied with both narrative materials and word lists. Regarding false memory for narratives, some of the earliest developmental studies compared children's true and false recognition following narratives that had been presented with or without accompanying pictures. Two examples are the experiments of Paris and Mahoney (1974) and of Weismer (1985), both of which presented short narratives to younger and older elementary-schoolers, followed by recognition tests that measured hits to target sentences and false alarms to meaning-preserving distractors. The effects of pictorial presentation on children's hits and false alarms are shown in Figure 5-9, with Paris and Mahoney's results appearing in Panel a and Weismer's results appearing in Panel b. It can be seen in Panel a that, as expected by opponent-processes distinctions, pictorial presentation drove children's hits and false alarms in opposite directions. Children were more likely to correctly accept presented sentences and less likely to falsely accept meaning-preserving distractors when narratives were accompanied by pictures. Further, the tendency of pictures to suppress false recognition was more pronounced in younger than in older children. It can be seen in Panel b that in Weismer's experiment, the overall pattern was the same in that pictorial presentation again drove children's hit rates up and their false-alarm rates down. The only notable difference between Weismer's findings and Paris and Mahoney's was that in Weismer's experiment, pictures suppressed false recognition by equal amounts in younger and older children.

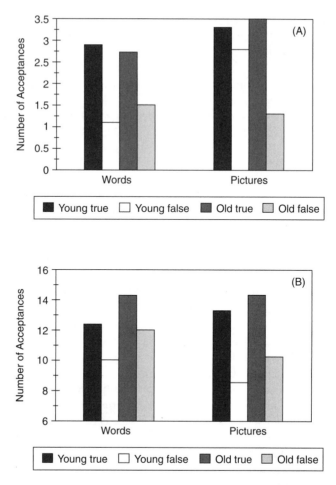

Figure 5-9. Effects of pictorial presentation of narratives on children's true and false recognition of narrative sentences. Data in Panel A are extrapolated from Paris and Mahoney (1974), and data in Panel B are extrapolated from Weismer (1985).

More recently, Kiernan (1993) and the present writers (Brainerd & Reyna, 1993) administered the Reyna and Kiernan (1994) narratives to younger and older children, using a presentation manipulation that was similar to Paris and Mahoney's (1974) and Weismer's (1985). Although Kiernan did not report her data in such a way that the effects of pictures on targets versus distractors could be separated, we did. We conducted three experiments in which preschoolers and second-graders were read the Reyna-Kiernan narratives with or without supporting pictures. In Figure 5-10, the average levels of acceptance of target sentences and meaning-preserving distractor sentences are displayed by age level and presentation condition. Generally speaking, the results parallel those of Paris and Mahoney (1974), despite the fact that the narratives, the supporting pictures, and the memory probes were dif-

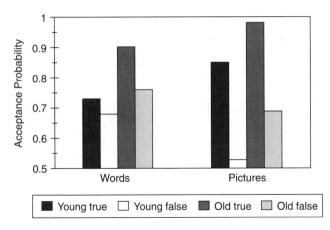

Figure 5-10. Effects of pictorial presentation of narratives on children's recognition of target sentences and meaning-preserving distractor sentences. Data from Brainerd and Reyna (1993).

ferent in our experiments. As can be seen, pictorial presentation again increased acceptances of targets and decreased acceptances of meaning-preserving distractors, as would be expected on theoretical grounds, and pictures suppressed acceptance of unpresented sentences more in younger children than it did in older ones.

Turning from narratives to word lists, it will be remembered from chapter 4 that the picture-word manipulation has been investigated in several DRM experiments with adults. Recently, Ghetti, Qin, and Goodman (2002) reported an analogous study with children of two age levels, kindergartners and second-graders. Children at both age levels listened to a total of 10 DRM lists. The lists were simply read to half of the children at each age level, while pictures of the named objects accompanied list presentation for the other half of the children. Following the presentation of each list, the children performed free recall. After the tenth list had been presented and recalled, the children responded to a typical DRM recognition test composed of target words, unpresented stimulus words (the false-memory items), and unrelated words. Ghetti et al.'s findings, which are not unlike those for narrative false memories, are summarized in Figure 5-11 for recall (Panel a) and recognition (Panel b). With respect to recall, it can be seen that pictures again had opposite effects on true and false memory. Pictures suppressed intrusions of unpresented stimulus words in both kindergartners (lowering the intrusion rate from 32% to 18%) and second-graders (lowering the intrusion rate from 25% to 13%), whereas pictures increased recall of presented words in second-graders (increasing correct recall from 61% to 70%) and did not have a reliable effect on true recall in kindergartners. (Remember that it has been found in prior studies that the tendency of pictorial presentation to enhance true recall increases with age.) With respect to recognition, it can be seen that pictures also had opposite effects on true and false recognition. Pictures suppressed the recognition of unpresented stimulus words in both kindergartners

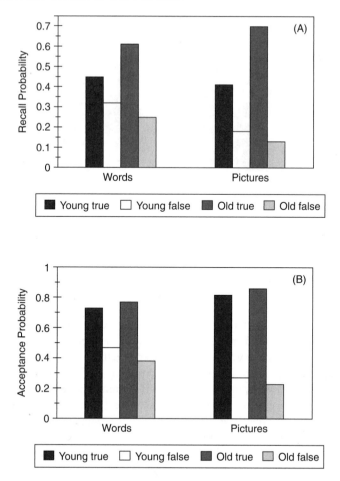

Figure 5-11. Effects of pictorial presentation on children's true and false recall (Panel A) and true and false recognition (Panel B) of unpresented stimulus words from DRM lists. Data extrapolated from Ghetti, Qin, and Goodman (2002).

(lowering the false-alarm rate from 47% to 27%) and second-graders (lowering the false-alarm rate from 38% to 23%), and pictures increased the recognition of presented words in kindergartners (increasing the hit rate from 73% to 82%) and second-graders (increasing the hit rate from 77% to 86%).

Finally, Reyna and Kiernan (1995) studied the influence of metaphorical statements on children's false recognition of distractor sentences that preserved the meaning of those metaphors. It will be remembered from chapter 4 that because metaphorical sentences involve odd combinations of words (e.g., The woman was an aspirin, kneeling by the lost boy), such sentences attract more surface processing than equivalent literal sentences, so that subjects can figure out what they mean. Reyna and Kiernan administered the three-sentence metaphorical vignettes that were described in chapter 4 to samples of 6- and 9-year-olds. After each vignette, the children re-

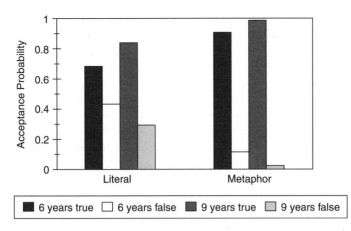

Figure 5-12. Children's hit rates for metaphorical and literal sentences and children's false-alarm rates for sentences that preserve the gist of metaphorical and literal sentences. Data from Reyna and Kiernan (1994, 1995).

sponded to a recognition test on which the probes were target sentences, unpresented sentences that preserved the meaning of metaphorical statements (e.g., The woman was medicine, kneeling by the lost boy), and unpresented sentences that violated the meaning of target sentences. The results, which are shown in Figure 5-12, were quite dramatic, even more striking than those for pictorial presentation. In Figure 5-12, hit rates for metaphorical targets and their meaning-preserving distractors are separately plotted for 6- and 9-year-olds, and for purposes of determining the effects of metaphor presentation on both true and false memory, hit and false-alarm rates for literal targets and their meaning-preserving distractors are also plotted for both age levels. The first point to note is that the developmental patterns for metaphorical materials are much the same as for literal materials—specifically, younger children's hit rates were lower and their false-alarm rates were higher than were older children's. However, the key data are the strong and opposing effects of metaphorical content on true and false memory. Concerning true memory, there was a notable inflation in the hit rates of both 6- and 9-year-olds, with older children's performance being near-ceiling (98%). This pattern is consistent with the notion that, as with adults, metaphorical sentences yield better memory for their surface form than literal sentences do. Concerning false memory, metaphorical statements produced an even larger deflation in the false-alarm rates of both age levels, with the deflation being larger for 6- than for 9-year-olds. This pattern is consistent with the opponent-processes hypothesis that improvements in verbatim memory tend to suppress false recognition and that verbatim-memory prosthetics (metaphorical statements, in this instance) are therefore more helpful to subjects whose baseline verbatim skills are poorer (6-year-olds, in this instance).

In the discussion of distinctiveness manipulations in chapter 4, we mentioned two further variables on which adult data are available: presenting target events as spoken words versus printed words (with the latter yielding stronger verbatim traces because subjects process words' phonology as well as their orthography during visual presentation) and presenting target events under conditions of full versus divided attention (with the former producing stronger verbatim traces). Neither of these variables has yet figured in false-memory research with children by reason of children's performance limitations. Obviously, the first manipulation makes no sense at all for children who have not learned to read, or who have not been reading long. Although, with such subjects, false-memory levels would again be expected to be lower for printed than for spoken materials, it would be for the utterly uninteresting reason that meaning content would not be extracted from printed materials. Concerning the divided-attention manipulation, the ability of preschoolers and younger elementary-schoolers to pay attention during memory experiments is limited to begin with, so much so that experimental sessions exceeding 15–20 minutes are rarely used with such subjects. The types of divided-attention manipulations that are routinely implemented with adults, which involve monitoring a secondary stream of information while processing a primary stream, are beyond young children's capabilities and would simply drive performance to near-floor levels on all memory measures.

Retrieving Memories

In our earlier discussion of how retrieval variables influence adults' false memories, readers were asked to assume that (a) target material had been experienced in a sufficiently leisurely fashion that its surface and meaning content were fully processed; (b) verbatim and gist traces had therefore been stored in memory; (c) traces of both types had survived consolidation; and (d) memory tests were administered punctually (so that both types of traces were still accessible). It goes without saying that such assumptions are problematic with children. No matter how leisurely the presentation rate or how rapidly we contrive to administer memory tests, it is hardly prudent to assume, with most false-memory tasks, that the children will necessarily have access to the memories that support erroneous responses and the memories that suppress them. Nevertheless, the basal opponent-processes expectation continues to be that retrieval variables that enhance children's tendency to access verbatim traces of events will lower false recall and false recognition, while variables that enhance children's tendency to access gist traces will have the opposite effect. As was the case with storage variables, however, it is also expected that the effects of retrieval variables will be qualified by developmental interactions: The ability of retrieval variables to promote either verbatim or gist access will necessarily turn on the extent to which such information is available in storage. Owing to the fact that, as a general matter, both types of representations will become more available with development, some tasks will compensate more for verbatim deficits than for gist deficits, whereas other tasks will compensate more for gist deficits than for verbatim deficits. Consequently, whether a developmental interaction is forecast for a retrieval variable, as well as the type of interaction that is forecast, depends upon whether a given memory task provides transparent prosthetic support for children's verbatim limitations, their gist limitations, or both.

With this proviso in mind, we turn to variables that would be predicted, on the basis of opponent-processes distinctions, to influence children's false-memory reports by affecting the types of representations that they retrieve on memory tests. The general expectations, naturally, continue to be that variables that increase verbatim access (relative to some baseline) ought to lower measured levels of false memory and that variables that increase gist access ought to have the opposite effect. In our discussion of retrieval in chapter 4, we considered three groups of variables that bear on these predictions, which have been investigated in adults: *retrieval duration* (manipulations of the time that is allowed for subjects to respond to recognition or recall tests), *verbatim cuing* (presentation of test cues that should slant retrieval toward verbatim access), and *retrieval instructions* (presentation of test instructions that should slant retrieval toward verbatim or gist access). Of these variables, the effects of retrieval duration on children's false memories have not been systematically investigated. In light of children's attention limitations, as well as their tendency to fatigue rapidly when performing demanding tasks, the standard procedure is to administer very leisurely memory tests, often permitting retrieval duration to be self-paced (i.e., children are permitted whatever amount of time they require to respond). The other two groups of variables have been investigated in children, though the respective literatures are more modest than the corresponding ones for adults. In addition, another type of retrieval variable, *repeated memory testing*, has been extensively studied in children because it has forensic ramifications. We sketch the developmental findings for verbatim cuing, retrieval instructions, and repeated testing below.

Verbatim Cuing

The opponent-processes approach anticipates that verbatim cuing will reduce false recall and false recognition by increasing children's access to memories of the surface form of experience, which will tend to neutralize the familiarity of false-but-gist-consistent events (Reyna & Brainerd, 1998; Reyna & Lloyd, 1997). But, developmental interactions are also anticipated because verbatim traces will customarily be less accessible at younger age levels. Such interactions have been detected in developmental studies of two of the three verbatim-cuing manipulations that we considered in chapter 4: target priming and match/mismatch of surface cues during study and test.

With respect to target priming, Brainerd, Reyna, and Kneer (1995) reported developmental data on this manipulation, using subjects in the 5- to 16-year-old range. Our target-priming procedure for children had three principal features. First, children listened to a long list (60 items) of familiar words, which was presented at an unhurried pace (3 seconds per word). Second, following a 5-minute attention-consuming buffer activity (a spatial search task), children responded to a standard yes-no recognition test on which some of the target words were replaced by semantically related distractors such as synonyms (e.g., *couch*, if *sofa* were a target), antonyms (e.g., *long*, if *short* were a target), same-category exemplars (e.g., *collie*, if *poodle* were a target), category labels (e.g., *jewel*, if *diamond* were a target), and so forth. Third, some of these distractors were preceded by their corresponding tar-

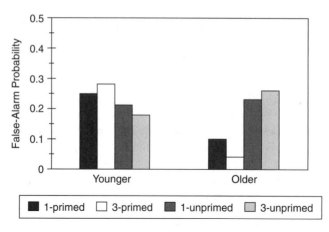

Figure 5-13. Effects of target priming on semantic false recognition in younger children (5 years) and older children (8 years). Data from Brainerd, Reyna, and Kneer (1995).

gets (e.g., *sofa* was tested shortly before *couch, diamond* was tested shortly before *jewel*), and others were not (e.g., *short* and *poodle* did not appear on the test lists). We saw that in adults, target priming lowers semantic false recognition (e.g., false-alarm rates are lower for *couch* and *jewel* than for *long* and *collie*), sometimes to below false-recognition levels for unrelated distractors (Brainerd et al., 1999). In children, however, opponent-processes distinctions predict that such effects should vary with age. On the one hand, as long as the words are very familiar ones, even young children will extract meanings such as "furniture" and "dog," which support semantic false recognition. Thus, although age increases in gist memory will be present, they will not be dramatic, as they would be if the words were unfamiliar or if it were necessary for children to connect meaning across several words. On the other hand, even with familiar words, there will be substantial age increases in the availability of verbatim traces on any task that involves a large number of target events. Consequently, the test materials are ones that ought to provide better support for verbatim retrieval than for gist retrieval, leading to the prediction that the suppressive effect of the target-priming manipulation will wax with age.

This was the pattern that Brainerd, Reyna, and Kneer (1995) detected. In two of the studies in our series of experiments, the effects of target priming were compared in 5-year-olds and 8-year-olds. An additional feature of these experiments was that some of the distractors' related targets were presented once and others were presented three times. A summary of the results, which have been pooled across the various types of semantically related distractors that were administered, is shown in Figure 5-13. A marked developmental interaction is evident. The qualitative pattern for older children was the same as the pattern for adults in chapter 4: Target-primed distractors produced lower false-alarm rates than unprimed distractors, and the suppressive effect of priming was greater when targets had been presented three times (stronger verbatim traces). For younger children, however, the pattern was different: Target priming produced no diminution of semantic false recognition, either for once-presented or thrice-presented targets, and on the contrary, it slightly elevated false-alarm rates. It appears, then, that 5-year-olds' verbatim traces of the target words are so labile that, following the 5-minute buffer activity, not enough representations of this sort are sufficiently accessible for target priming to have any suppressive effect at all.

Brainerd and Reyna (1993) also studied the effects of target priming on children's recognition of unpresented but meaning-preserving sentences, using Reyna and Kiernan's (1994, 1995) narrative-memory procedure. Children from two age levels (6 and 9 years old) listened to several of these narratives and responded to a recognition test immediately following each pair of narratives. The recognition test consisted of four probes for each narrative: a target (TPO), a true inference (TIO), a false paraphrase of the tested target (FPO), and a false inference (FIO). The order in which these probes were administered was manipulated so that targets were sometimes tested immediately before true inferences and sometimes were tested after true inferences. At both age levels, the acceptance rate for true inferences was lower when they were primed by targets than when they were not. The suppression was present in the younger children, whereas it was absent in Brainerd, Reyna, and Kneer's (1995) younger children. This is presumably due to the better support that the narrative-memory procedure provides for verbatim memory. Remember here that in Brainerd et al.'s procedure, children listened to 60 words and then performed 5 minutes of spatial search before responding to recognition probes. However, in Brainerd and Reyna's procedure, children listened to only six sentences, which required less than 20 seconds, and then responded to recognition probes immediately after that. Moreover, the number of recognition probes that were administered (8) was small in comparison to the number administered by Brainerd et al. (60), which further reduced the elapsed time between target presentation and the administration of any given recognition probe.

Match/mismatch of surface cues during study and test is another verbatim-cuing manipulation that has been found to suppress false-memory reports in adults. Developmental data on this manipulation have been reported by Brainerd, Reyna, and Kneer (1995) and Brainerd and Mojardin (1998). Brainerd et al. obtained findings on a presentation-modality variable that is similar in spirit to those that were discussed in chapter 4. They conducted a target-priming experiment with 5-year-olds that used the design just described, except for one modification: Study lists and test lists were read to children in the same voice. In the experiments that are summarized in Figure 5-13, the items on study and test lists had not been presented in matching voices, and target priming failed to suppress false recognition in 5-year-olds. When presentation and test voices matched, however, it was found that 5-year-olds' false recognition of same-category exemplars and semantic associates were both suppressed by verbatim priming. Their conclusion was that even very young children retained sufficient verbatim information in memory for priming to be effective when the accessibility of that information was enhanced (by matching voices).

Brainerd and Mojardin (1998), on the other hand, studied false recognition of some of the sentence distractors that had been administered in Reyna and Kiernan's (1994) narrative-memory procedure. Children of three age levels (6, 8, and 11 years old) listened to several of the Reyna-Kiernan narratives and then responded to sentence-recognition tests that contained four types of probes (see Table 4-1): targets (TPO: The cocoa is hotter than the tea), true paraphrases of targets that contained new words (TPN: The tea is cooler than the cocoa), false paraphrases of targets that contained only old words (FPO: The tea is hotter than the cocoa), and false paraphrases of targets that contained new words (FPN: The cocoa is cooler than the tea). They then compared children's false-alarm rates for the last two types of distractors, arguing that FPO items ought to be better retrieval cues for verbatim traces of presented sentences because they contained only words that would have actually been stored as part of those sentences' surface representations. Consistent with this conjecture, false-alarm rates at the two older age levels (subjects with better verbatim memories) were lower for FPO distractors than for FPN distractors (49% versus 55% in 8-year-olds and 32% versus 39% in 11-year-olds).

A third retrieval manipulation that we shall classify, for convenience, under the heading of verbatim cuing has been rather extensively discussed in connection with children's false-memory reports during investigative interviews (Ceci & Bruck, 1995; Poole & Lamb, 1998). These discussions revolve around the finding that when children respond to free-recall tests about the events of their lives, which are usually called *free narratives* or *open-ended questions* in the literature on investigative interviewing, they give fewer erroneous answers than when they respond to recognition tests, which are usually called *direct questions* in that literature (Pipe et al., 1999; Pipe & Wilson, 1994; Salmon & Pipe, 2000). Such erroneous answers are of special significance because they may lead to innocent people being treated as suspects in crimes and sometimes even to innocent people being charged with and convicted of crimes (see chapters 6 and 7).

One of the earliest demonstrations, under controlled conditions, of the effects of recall versus recognition in the investigative interviewing of children was reported by Poole and White (1991). Children of three age levels (4, 6, and 8 years old) observed a staged sequence of events involving a man and a woman. The man was searching for a lost pen, questioned the woman about it, and, eventually, a playful struggle took place between the two characters. After observing the events, the children performed a task (drawing a picture of a stuffed animal), and then they received a surprise memory test about the events that they had witnessed. First, they were asked to recall features like those that would be the focus of a forensic interview if the woman character had reported the playful struggle as an assault, such as the man's physical appearance during the staged events. This was followed by recognition questions for forensically relevant features (e.g., Did the man hurt the woman?). The incidence of erroneous (and incriminating) answers was much higher on the latter questions, especially among the youngest children.

Earlier in this chapter, we summarized some findings that illustrate the same pattern in a more traditional false-memory paradigm when we considered findings from developmental studies of the DRM procedure (e.g., Ghetti et al., 2002; Price et al., 2001). In Figure 5-6, we plotted findings from several studies that were conducted in our laboratory. Another glance at that figure will reveal both of the results that have been featured in studies of child forensic interviewing: Intrusions of unpresented stimulus words were much lower than false alarms to those words, and the gap between the intrusion and false-alarm rates was greater in younger children than in older children or adults.

From the opponent-processes perspective, such findings are quite predictable, for two reasons. First, when it comes to false reports of meaning-preserving events, a free-recall test slants retrieval more toward verbatim memory than a recognition test does. A standard recall instruction such as "tell me all you can remember about what happened" does not cue the meaning content of experience but, rather, directs attention toward actual events. In contrast, the presentation of semantically related distractors on a recognition test (e.g., *doctor* following presentation of the corresponding DRM list) cues the meaning content of the experience without cuing any *specific* verbatim trace (because the distractor was not experienced and therefore could not have generated that verbatim trace). Second, in view of the memory limitations of young children that we have discussed, their performance should be particularly sensitive to this difference between recognition and recall. On a recognition test, young children's verbatim limitations, in particular, mean that when a distractor directly cues the meaning content of their experience, it will be more difficult for them to neutralize the familiarity of the distractor by accessing verbatim traces of actual events.

Retrieval Instructions

Available data on how children's false-memory reports react to retrieval instructions recapitulate three themes that have been present in virtually all sections of the present chapter. That is, the types of retrieval instructions that were discussed in chapter 4 have also been studied in children; the extant data are much thinner for children; and those data reveal developmental interactions. As with adults' false memories, the question of interest is whether it is possible to prod memory performance in the direction of fewer false alarms and intrusions by stressing the importance of verbatim processing, or the pitfalls of gist processing, or both. Although we saw that it is possible to accomplish this, within limits, when the subjects are adults, the memory limitations of children will make it a more difficult proposition, especially with preschoolers and younger elementary-schoolers. Nevertheless, successes have been reported, both with Koriat and Goldsmith's (1994, 1996) procedure of encouraging rememberers to exert deliberate control over the types of memorial evidence upon which they rely and with our conjoint-recognition methodology.

With respect to the Koriat-Goldsmith procedure, Koriat et al. (2001) reported three experiments in which children of two age levels (8 and 11 years old) responded to recognition and recall tests under forced-report and optional-report instructions. It should be remembered that when this procedure is implemented with adults, optional-report instructions have little effect on true memory, relative to forced-report instructions, regardless of whether memory tests involve recall or recognition, but optional-report instructions reduce false-memory reports, with the effect being noticeably larger for recall than for recognition. In their experiments with children, Koriat et al. exposed their subjects first to a 5-minute slide show depicting events at a picnic and then administered memory tests for the slide show. They found that optional-report instructions reduced both intrusions and false alarms at both age levels. There were developmental interactions, however. For the recognition tests, optional reporting reduced false alarms more for older children than for younger children. For the recall tests, optional reporting reduced intrusions more for younger children than for older children. Unlike adults, however, the reductions in false memory that were produced by optional reporting came at the cost of parallel reductions in true memory at both age levels, though the reductions in false memory were greater than those in true memory (yielding a net accuracy advantage for optional reporting). There were also developmental interactions in the effects of optional reporting on children's true-memory reports: Younger children's performance was impaired more on recognition tests, whereas older children's performance was impaired more on recall tests.

Turning to the other instructional procedure, conjoint-recognition experiments with children of different ages have been reported by Brainerd et al. (1998) and by Brainerd, Holliday, and Reyna (2004). In the first article, Brainerd et al. reported an experiment using a continuous-recognition procedure that resembled Underwood's (1965) original false-recognition study with adults. Children were read a long list of words on which each succeeding word had either been previously read (targets) or had not been previously read (distractors). In addition, some of the distractors were related to previously read words, whereas others were not. The former were the false-memory items. The children's task was to accept or reject each succeeding word as it was read. However, they made accept-reject decisions under two of the three conjoint-recognition instructions: verbatim (accept only targets) and gist (accept only related distractors). As is the case with adults, these instructions produced dramatic differences in the rates at which children accepted targets versus related distractors, suggesting that instructions affected the types of memories that were being processed. Under verbatim instructions, the overall acceptance rates for targets and related distractors were .78 and .08, respectively, whereas the corresponding values under gist instructions were .05 and .50, respectively.

The other study by Brainerd et al. (2004) provides more comprehensive information because children responded to recognition tests under all three types of conjoint-recognition instructions. We will summarize findings from one of the experiments in this article to illustrate the general patterns that were obtained. DRM lists were presented to subjects of three ages (7, 11, and 14 years old), who then responded to a recognition test composed of target probes and the usual three types of distractor probes (unpresented stimulus words, other semantically related words, and unrelated words). Children responded to this test under verbatim (V), gist (G), or verbatim-plus-gist (V+G) instructions. Some key findings are shown in Table 5-1, which displays the acceptance probabilities for targets and related distractors in each instructional condition. To begin, it appears that, like adults, children are able to use these retrieval instructions to control the types of memories that they process on recognition tests. Pooling across the three age levels, the probability of accepting targets was .73 in the conditions in which they were supposed to be ac-

Table 5-1. Effects of Retrieval Instructions
on True and False Recognition in Children
of Three Age Levels

	Age (years)		
Condition/item	7	11	14
Verbatim			
Targets	.70	.71	.80
Related distractors	.22	.17	.17
Gist			
Targets	.45	.45	.24
Related distractors	.31	.55	.68
Verbatim + Gist			
Targets	.68	.72	.77
Related distractors	.38	.42	.63

Note. The numbers are the probabilities of accepting targets
and semantically related distractors in each of the conditions
of this experiment. Data from Brainerd, Holliday, and Reyna
(2004).

cepted (V and V+G) but was only .38 in the condition in which they were supposed to be rejected (G), and the probability of accepting the two types of meaning-preserving distractors was .50 in the conditions in which they were supposed to
be accepted (G and V+G) but it was only .19 in the condition in which they were
supposed to be rejected (V). Beyond this overall pattern, however, there were marked
developmental interactions in children's ability to use these retrieval instructions.
With respect to true memory, the oldest subjects were much better at suppressing
acceptance of targets in the G condition than were younger subjects. The acceptance
rate for targets dropped by an average of .79 (in the V and V+G conditions) to an
average of .24 (in the G condition) in 14-year-olds, whereas the corresponding drop
for 7- and 11-year-olds was much smaller (from .70 to .45). With respect to false
memory, the youngest subjects were much poorer at increasing acceptance rates for
meaning-preserving distractors in the G and V+G conditions than were the older
children. The 7-year-olds' distractor-acceptance rate increased from an average of
.22 (in the V condition) to an average of .35 (in the other two conditions), while
the corresponding increase for the two older age levels was three times as great
(from .17 to .57).

Both of these developmental interactions in the ability to use retrieval instructions to determine which probes are accepted and which are rejected make excellent opponent-processes sense. Concerning the developmental interaction for target
probes, verbatim memory is obviously the key to rejecting a target under gist in-

structions that is then accepted under verbatim instructions. If a target probe's acceptance in the V condition is based upon retrieval of verbatim traces of its presentation, rather than gist traces, the vivid recollective phenomenology that is induced by verbatim traces will also support rejection in the G condition (because subjects will know that such an item could not possibly be an unpresented distractor). Because we know, from earlier discussions, that verbatim retrieval improves with age, it follows that the ability to accept a target under verbatim instructions but to reject that same probe under gist instructions should also improve with age. Concerning the developmental interaction for false memory, opponent-processes analysis posits that gist memory is the key to simultaneously accepting a meaning-preserving distractor under G and V+G instructions and rejecting it under V instructions. Because gist memories induce nonspecific feelings of meaning familiarity, an item that provokes such a phenomenology is more likely to be a meaning-preserving distractor than a target, which means that it should be rejected in the V condition while being accepted in the other two conditions. However, the DRM task is one in which the characteristic gist memories involve connecting meaning across multiple words, an ability that is known to develop gradually during childhood (e.g., Bjorklund & Hock, 1982; Bjorklund & Jacobs, 1985). If those are the gist memories that support simultaneous acceptance (in the G and V+G conditions) and rejection (in the V condition) of meaning-preserving distractors, younger children will be less capable of such simultaneous acceptance and rejection than will older children.

Repeated Testing

The last retrieval variable that we shall consider, though rarely investigated in adult false-memory research, has been extensively studied in developmental research pursuant to concerns about the effects of repeated testing in criminal investigations. When children are witnesses to crimes or are victims of crimes, they are typically interviewed about the details of their experiences on multiple occasions by a variety of people (e.g., parents, teachers, siblings, classmates, police officers, child protective services workers, prosecutors, defense attorneys). For instance, one legal scholar estimated that the average child witness is interviewed up to 12 times during the course of a criminal investigation (Whitcomb, 1992). The reasons for such large numbers of interviews are many and varied. Parents and teachers may question children repeatedly in order to be sure of the details of their reports before notifying law enforcement; police and child protective services investigators will normally want to hear a child's report firsthand rather than in the form of hearsay from parents or teachers; police and child protective services investigators may wish to conduct multiple interviews of a child merely to allow more than one opportunity for all of the relevant facts to be recovered; new facts may surface during the course of an investigation that necessitate that a child be reinterviewed to establish whether she is aware of those facts; siblings and classmates will be inquisitive as to why a child is participating in a criminal investigation; prosecutors will want to check the details that children have reported to investigators before going to trial; and defense attorneys may need to interview child witnesses in order to provide adequate representation for their clients. Within our legal system, all of these reasons are legitimate grounds for repeated questioning of children. However, given the consequent reality of multiple interviews, it is natural to wonder whether children's memory reports are helped, harmed, or unaffected by repeated testing.

Some guidance with respect to this question can be found in the classic literature on repeated memory testing in adults. That literature deals with true rather than false memory, however. In the standard design (e.g., Carrier & Pashler, 1992; Cull, 2000; Kuo & Hirshman, 1996; Runquist, 1983), subjects first study a list of target items. Then, they are assigned to one of two testing conditions: (a) immediate test plus delayed test, or (b) delayed test only. ("Immediate" and "delayed" are relative terms. The time between them may be only a few minutes, or it may be hours or days.) Finally, performance on the delayed test is analyzed as a function of whether subjects received a prior memory test. Although there has been considerable debate about possible methodological confounds (e.g., Runquist, 1983), the resulting literature has produced two findings of general interest. The first is the *true-memory inoculation* effect, which states that recall and recognition of targets on delayed tests are better if subjects have received a prior test for those items. The other is the *test-specificity* effect, which states that the amount of true-memory inoculation increases as the level of surface match between the immediate and delayed tests increases. (See earlier discussions of match/mismatch of surface cues between study and test.) Some investigators have interpreted the true-memory inoculation effect as a by-product of verbatim preservation (e.g., Warren & Lane, 1995). That is, because, as we have seen, initial memory tests for targets tend to cue the retrieval of verbatim traces, such tests may help to inoculate labile verbatim traces against subsequent forgetting, thereby making them more accessible on delayed tests. The test-specificity effect, on the other hand, has usually been interpreted as a standard encoding-variability result, much like the findings for study-test match/mismatch that were discussed earlier in this chapter and in chapter 4.

What about the effect of repeated testing on children's false memory? Several early studies of child interviewing in quasi-forensic contexts administered immediate and delayed recall tests and analyzed the delayed data for both true-memory inoculation and false-memory creation as a function of whether a prior test had been administered (e.g., Baker-Ward, Hess, & Flannagan, 1990; Dent & Stephenson, 1979). Such studies were reviewed by Poole and White (1995), and these authors concluded that repeated testing had yielded true-memory inoculation without false-memory creation: "[L]aboratory simulations of eyewitness testimony offer strong corroborating evidence that multiple testing sessions preserve memories over time. . . . We are aware of no studies in which multiple interviews with nonsuggestive questions were associated with increases in the amount of inaccurate information recalled by children" (p. 34). In a subsequent article, we argued that such null results were not easy to interpret, and that they could not be accepted as proof that repeated testing does not increase children's false-memory reports (Brainerd & Reyna, 1996). We mentioned two general problems. First, null results are inherently difficult to interpret because the logic of experimental design requires that a null hypothesis of "no effect" be rejected before an inference can be made. This logic is predicated on the fact that numerous uncontrolled factors can produce null re-

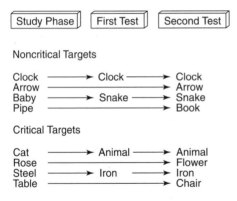

Figure 5-14. Design of Brainerd and Reyna's (1996) repeated-testing experiment.

sults, so that such results fail to demonstrate that an experimental manipulation (repeated testing, in this instance) does not affect performance. Second, certain design limitations of early experiments (e.g., small numbers of subjects, small numbers of items on memory tests) suggested that they may not have had adequate power to detect any memory-falsifying effects of repeated testing.

We therefore conducted two further experiments that eliminated these design limitations and found that, indeed, repeated testing elevated children's false-memory responses and that the amount of elevation interacted with age. The design of the first experiment is shown in Figure 5-14. A total of 80 children participated, half of them 5-year-olds and half of them 8-year-olds. First, each child listened to a list of 100 familiar concrete nouns like those shown on the left of Figure 5-14. The items labeled "noncritical targets" would later be presented as probes on immediate and delayed tests, whereas the items labeled "critical targets" would be replaced by false-memory items (semantically related distractors) on immediate and delayed tests. There was a repetition manipulation: Half of the words were presented once, and half were presented three times. After the list had been presented, each child responded to an immediate recognition test. As usual, some of the probes were targets (*clock*); some were false-memory items; and some were unrelated distractors. The false-memory items were either the names of categories to which targets belonged (*animal*), or they were new exemplars from the same category as targets (*iron*). The children returned to the laboratory 1 week later to receive a second recognition test, which was twice as long as the immediate test (Figure 5-14, *right*). Half of the probes on the delayed test were simply the ones that had been tested 1 week earlier. These were the repeatedly tested items. The other half of the probes were previously untested ones and consisted of targets (*arrow*), false-memory items (*flower, chair*), and unrelated distractors. The effects of repeated testing on true and false memory were then determined by computing the delayed acceptance rates for targets and false-memory items as a function of whether they had been tested 1 week earlier.

Those comparisons produced five key findings, which can all be seen in Figure 5-15. First, as in all prior studies, true-memory performance (acceptance of targets)

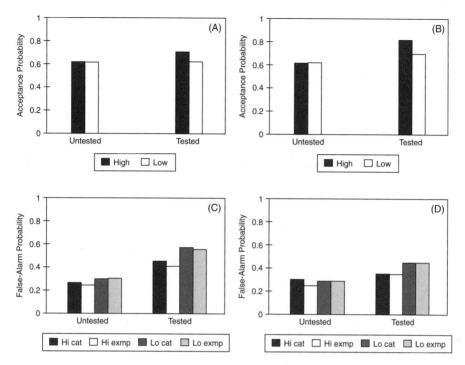

Figure 5-15. Repeated testing effects for true memory (Panels A and B) and false memory (Panels C and D) for 5-year-olds (Panels A and C) and 8-year-olds (Panels B and D). *High* and *low* refer to targets that were presented once or three times and to semantically related distractors whose corresponding targets were presented once or three times. *Hi cat* = unpresented labels of categories for which one exemplar had been presented three times; *Lo cat* = unpresented labels of categories for which one exemplar had been presented once; *Hi exmp* = unpresented exemplars of categories (e.g., *cat*) for which one other exemplar (e.g., *dog*) had been presented three times; *Lo exmp* = unpresented exemplars of categories for which one other exemplar had been presented once. Based upon Brainerd and Reyna (1996).

was higher on the delayed test for items that had been previously tested than for items that had not. The relevant data are shown in Panels a and b. Second, contrary to earlier studies, prior testing increased false-memory responses on the delayed test (i.e., false-alarm rates were higher for category names and same-category exemplars that had been previously tested). The relevant data are shown in Panels c and d. Third, the true-memory inoculation effect of prior testing was *smaller* than the false-memory creation effect, and it interacted with repetition: True-memory inoculation only occurred for targets that had been presented three times 1 week earlier. Fourth, the false-memory creation effect of prior testing interacted in the opposite way with repetition: Although false-memory creation occurred for distractors whose corresponding targets had been presented either once or three times, it was larger for distractors whose corresponding targets had only been presented once. Fifth, both true-memory inoculation and false-memory inoculation interacted with age, but in opposite ways. True-memory inoculation was more marked in older children, and false-memory creation was more marked in younger children. Note that these interactions are quite sensible in that both are consistent with the notion that older children's verbatim-memory abilities are superior to younger children's. That is, older children's correct recognition of targets is more likely to benefit from a recognition test because they are more likely to have verbatim traces available to be inoculated, and older children's false recognition of meaning-preserving distractors is less likely to be increased by a recognition test because they are more likely to have verbatim traces available to suppress false recognition.

Brainerd and Reyna (1996) also reported a second experiment that was the same as the first, except for the timing of the two memory tests. In this study, children listened to the word list during an initial session, returned 1 week later to receive the first recognition test, and then returned 2 weeks later to receive the second recognition test. The effects of prior testing on true and false memory were then determined by comparing the hit and false-alarm rates on the 2-week test for items that had been tested versus not tested at 1 week. This design modification was motivated by the hypothesis that if the effects of a prior memory test depend upon the accessibility of verbatim traces, those effects should be very different if the first test is administered 1 week after target presentation (when verbatim accessibility is compromised). Explicitly, opponent-processes distinctions would expect that the true-memory inoculation effect would be much reduced (because there is less verbatim memory left to preserve) and that the false-memory creation effect would be increased (because there is less verbatim memory left to suppress the effect). Both findings were obtained. The true-memory inoculation effect was only about half as large as in the first experiment, while the false-memory creation effect was nearly twice as large. Both effects exhibited the same developmental interactions as in the first experiment: True-memory inoculation was slightly greater in the older children, while false-memory creation was much greater in the younger children.

Before passing on to other matters, it should be noted that these basic patterns for repeated testing have been replicated in other experiments conducted in our laboratory. For instance, in the experiments by Brainerd and Mojardin (1998) and Mojardin (1997) that were mentioned earlier, subjects received immediate memory tests, 1-week delayed tests, and 1-month delayed tests for narrative sentences. In one of the experiments, the subjects were children from three age levels (6, 8, and 11 years old). It was possible to detect repeated-testing effects in this experiment because (a) the 1-week test consisted of the items from the immediate test plus previously untested items; and (b) the 1-month test consisted of the items from the first two tests plus previously untested items. On the 1-week test, there was a true-memory inoculation effect: The average hit rate was 81% for previously tested target sentences and 75% for previously untested sentences. There was also a false-memory creation effect: The average false-alarm rate was 63% for previously tested distractor sentences and 52% for previously untested distractors. On the 1-month test, there was no longer any evidence of true-memory inoculation, but there was still a false-memory creation effect: The average false-alarm rate was 58% for distractors that had been tested either immediately or at 1 week and 50% for previously untested distractors.

Forgetting Memories

Up to this point, we have seen that in developmental studies of false memory, research on storage and retrieval variables differs from corresponding adult research in at least two ways: There is less of it, and it is less often guided by theoretical hypotheses that forecast particular empirical outcomes. Although the second limitation makes the developmental literature more haphazard than the adult literature, we have seen that the lack of theoretical grounding can be mitigated, to some extent, through the retrospective reorganization of developmental studies around opponent-processes principles. Such reorganization is possible because some of the storage and retrieval variables that have been studied in adults (and whose theoretical interpretations are therefore well specified) have also been investigated in children. However, the other limitation of the developmental literature, the sheer lack of data on some manipulations of high theoretical interest (e.g., presentation duration, directed-forgetting instructions), cannot be overcome by any amount of retrospective interpretation. Fortunately, this limitation does not apply to the last group of variables that we considered in connection with adult false memory: forgetting variables. The role of forgetting in false memory has been extensively investigated in children.

In fact, the developmental literature on forgetting and false memory is more extensive than its adult counterpart. Moreover, forgetting became a consideration in adult false-memory research as a result of findings that had been obtained in developmental studies (Blair, Lenton, & Hastie, 2002). Forgetting has been a central issue in developmental work for the same reason that repeated testing has been: forensic relevance. When children are witnesses to crimes or are victims of crimes, there may be protracted intervals between the time that the target events are experienced and the time when those memory reports are given as evidence in legal proceedings. In the United States, for common felonies such as robbery, assault, and drug possession or sales, an interval of several months is the *minimum* delay between the commission of a crime and the trial of a suspect, and delays of 1 or 2 years are not uncommon. Delays of the latter sort, or even longer ones, are the rule in capital cases. Further, there are often substantial delays between the commission of a crime and the time when a child witness is first interviewed by police investigators. For instance, we have reviewed several cases in which investigative interviews were delayed for days or weeks because child witnesses were emotionally distraught or physically injured, because their parents declined to make them available, or because police officers' workloads were too heavy for interviews to be conducted promptly. Another routine cause of interview delays is the discovery of new evidence during the course of an investigation. The evidence that initially accumulates may not point to a particular child as a witness or a victim. Then, at some later stage, new evidence points to that child, and the child will then be interviewed about what he or she remembers. Given that delays in securing memory reports from child witnesses are inherent in legal proceedings, it is important to know what basic research can show about the accuracy of delayed reports. Indeed, this is crucial scientific information for triers of fact, who must decide what level of credibility to assign to different sources of evidence.

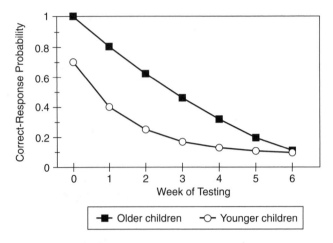

Figure 5-16. Typical forgetting functions for true memory for older and younger children. Based upon findings reviewed in Brainerd (1997).

That the frequency of children's true-memory reports will decline over delays is well understood from numerous developmental studies of forgetting functions for recall and recognition of target events (for a review, see Brainerd, 1997). Idealized forgetting functions that convey the standard developmental patterns are exhibited in Figure 5-16. These functions are for a hypothetical study in which younger and older elementary-schoolers are exposed to some target material and then respond to recall tests either immediately (time of testing = 0) or after delays of 1–6 weeks. Three features of the functions are of interest. First, true recall declines as a function of delay at both age levels, and it declines in a negatively accelerated fashion (i.e., the absolute reduction in correct-response probability is greater following initial delays than following later delays). Second, the average rate of decline is greater for younger children than for older ones. In the illustrative functions, the average rate of decline between consecutive testing points is .2 for older children and .33 for younger children. Third, although older children's performance is at first superior to younger children's (older children will initially remember almost anything better than younger children), forgetting tends to erase this difference (Reyna, 1995). In the illustrative functions, there is a 30% difference between the two age levels on the immediate test but only a 2% difference after 6 weeks. Thus, forgetting produces a characteristic developmental interaction in true-memory performance such that age differences in performance are more likely to occur after short delays than after long ones.

What about the effects of delay on false-memory reports? In that connection, opponent-processes distinctions make the same three false-persistence predictions about children as they make about adults (see chapter 4). First, contrary to commonsense expectations, children's false-memory reports should exhibit significant stability over forgetting intervals. Second, under certain conditions, children's false-memory reports can be more stable than their true-memory reports. Third, under certain conditions, there can be sleeper effects, such that the incidence of false-memory reports increases over time, while the incidence of true-memory reports for the same events usually decreases. These false-persistence effects fall out of the same principles that generated the predictions for adults—namely, that initial false-memory reports are rooted in gist memories, that initial true-memory reports are slanted toward verbatim memories, and that verbatim memories become inaccessible more rapidly than do gist memories. With children, however, there is a fourth principle with which we must reckon: developmental variability in the processes that support true memories and suppress false memories. Thus, the three false-persistence effects may exhibit developmental interactions depending upon the types of events that were experienced, the types of memory tests that are administered, and the supports that each provide for children's verbatim and gist limitations.

Persistence of False Memories

The earliest studies that supplied developmental evidence on the first false-persistence effect appeared in the article by Brainerd, Reyna, and Brandse (1995) that was considered in chapter 4 and in an article by Poole (1995) that followed up the Poole and White (1991) study. It will be recalled that the Brainerd et al. experiments focused on a transparent prediction of the consistency principle of testimony: If false memories are ephemeral, they ought to be highly unstable over time, so that the fact that some false event A is erroneously reported (or not reported) on an initial test should not increase the chances that it will be reported (or not reported) on a subsequent test. This prediction is easily tested by computing correlations between individual false-memory reports on initial and delayed memory tests, with zero correlations or very small correlations demonstrating high instability. In the Brainerd et al. experiments, these correlations took the form of conditional probabilities, with the crucial measures being the statistic $P(FA_D|FA_I)$, the conditional probability of making a false alarm to a meaning-preserving distractor on a delayed test *given a false alarm to that distractor on an immediate test*, and the statistic $P(FA_D)$, the unconditional probability of a false alarm to that distractor on the delayed test. If false-memory responses are unstable, then $P(FA_D|FA_I) = P(FA_D)$ should be the observed relation. Brainerd et al. found, in an experiment with children from two age levels (5 and 8 years old), that this prediction was violated, and false alarms to meaning-preserving distractors (the names of categories whose exemplars had been presented as targets) were very stable over a 1-week delay between initial and subsequent tests. For the younger children, $P(FA_D|FA_I) = .91$ and $P(FA_D) = .49$, and for the older children, $P(FA_D|FA_I) = .93$ and $P(FA_D) = .48$.

Turning to Poole's (1995) findings, it will be recalled that Poole and White (1991) exposed 4-, 6-, and 8-year-olds to an ambiguous sequence of events involving a male and a female character, which could conceivably generate false-memory reports of an assault. The children's memories were tested, using a combination of recall and recognition, immediately after the events and again 1 week later. Using the combined data of all of the children to enhance statistical power, Poole computed two measures of the stability of false-memory reports: a within-session measure and a between-session measure. Concerning the first measure, some questions on the immediate test queried the same information twice (e.g., the man's appearance). For such repeated questions, Poole computed the conditional probability of a false-memory report on the second query given a false-memory report on the first. Like Brainerd, Reyna, and Brandse (1995), she found that this conditional probability (.76) was quite high and was much higher than the unconditional probability of a false-memory report on the second query. Concerning the other measure of stability, Poole computed the conditional probability of a false-memory report about specific items of information on the 1-week test given a false-memory report about those same items on the immediate test. Once again, she found that this conditional probability (.80) was quite high and was much higher than the unconditional probability of a false-memory report on the 1-week test.

The pattern of good false-memory stability across intervals of a few minutes to a week has been replicated and extended in later developmental studies. For instance, Newcombe and Siegal (1997), Salmon and Pipe (1997, 2000), and Sussman (2001) have all reported experiments concerned with children's false-memory reports for everyday experiences over intervals that ranged from 1 week to 1 year. There was evidence of stability across all of these intervals. Brainerd and Reyna (1996) reported an experiment that used materials and procedures that were very similar to Brainerd, Reyna, and Brandse's (1995), except for the fact that the interval between exposure to the target material and the second memory test was 2 weeks rather than 1 week. Children's false alarms to meaning-preserving distractors were also found to be stable over this longer interval. Finally, in the Brainerd and Mojardin (1998) experiment that was described earlier, it will be remembered that recognition tests for narrative statements were administered immediately after presentation, 1 week later, and 1 month later, and it will also be remembered that some of the statements were tested on all three occasions. To assess the stability of false memories, correlations were computed for these distractors between (a) false alarms on the immediate test and false alarms on the 1-week test, (b) false alarms on the immediate test and false alarms on the 1-month test, and (c) false alarms on the 1-week test and false alarms on the 1-month test. Substantial correlations were obtained in each instance.

Thus, there is an important convergence between the data on the stability of adults' false memories (chapter 4) and the data on the stability of children's false memories: Evidence of stability over substantial forgetting intervals has been obtained in children as well as in adults. Therefore, notwithstanding that the processes that support and suppress false memories undergo considerable development between early childhood and young adulthood, those processes are not so immature in young children that their responses are utterly inconsistent from one memory test to the next.

Greater Persistence of False Than True Memories

We saw in chapter 4 that the second false-persistence effect, which is concerned with the relative stability of true and false memories, has been studied in adults using a multiple-session design with independent groups of subjects. That is, one group of subjects receives an immediate memory test for the target material, and other groups of subjects receive only delayed memory tests (e.g., after 1 day, 1 week, and

1 month). The relative persistence of true and false memories is then indexed by determining the changes in performance on the measures of each type of memory between immediate and delayed tests. From a methodological point of view, this between-group procedure is the cleanest technique for assessing the relative persistence of true and false memories. However, it has an important practical limitation in developmental research—namely, it requires large numbers of subjects because individual subjects receive only one memory test (immediate or delayed). This is not usually a serious obstacle in adult research because such work normally relies upon large pools of undergraduate subjects, which are maintained by academic departments in the universities where the research is conducted. Developmental research, on the other hand, usually relies on much smaller subject populations, which are recruited from preschools and elementary schools. Consequently, it is more practical, in some cases essential, to adopt repeated-testing designs.

Two types of repeated-testing designs have been used in developmental studies, both of which were described earlier in connection with other research questions: (a) intra-item correlations of performance on immediate and delayed tests, and (b) inter-item comparisons of performance on items that are only tested immediately versus items that are only tested after a delay. The first type of design, which consists of simply administering the same memory test on two occasions and then correlating immediate and delayed performance on the same items, was just described in connection with the stability of children's false memories. To assess the relative stability of true and false memories, one simply computes the same immediate/delayed correlations for recognition (or recall) of presented items versus recognition (or recall) of unpresented items and compares the relative magnitudes of the correlations. The preponderance of developmental studies have implemented this first design, and many of those studies were reviewed by Brainerd and Poole (1997), who concluded that, like adult studies, most developmental studies had shown that children's false memories were just as stable as their true memories and that, under some conditions, children's false memories were more stable than their true memories.

The earliest studies that produced this pattern were reported in the aforementioned articles by Brainerd, Reyna, and Brandse (1995) and Poole (1995). Brainerd et al. obtained two key results. First, on recognition tests for previously presented word lists, the immediate/delayed correlation in 5-year-olds was higher for meaning-preserving distractors (category labels) than it was for the corresponding targets (.91 versus .68). Second, the same immediate/delayed correlation in 8-year-olds was higher for meaning-preserving distractors than it was for targets (.93 versus .77). Similarly, on recall tests for previously experienced staged events, Poole found that the correlation between immediate and 1-week delayed performance was higher for intrusions of incorrect details than for recall of correct details (.80 versus .71). Finally, in the previously mentioned Brainerd and Mojardin (1998) studies of sentence recognition, correlational comparisons of this sort were undertaken for immediate versus 1-week tests, immediate versus 1-month tests, and 1-week versus 1-month tests. These more extensive findings are displayed in Figure 5-17, with Panel a containing the 6-year-old data, Panel b containing the 8-year-old data, and Panel c containing the 11-year-old data. The general pattern to note involves a comparison of the bars on the left side of each graph to the bars on the right side. It can

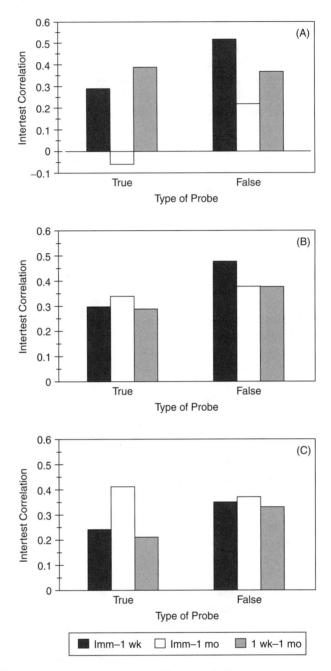

Figure 5-17. Intertest correlations between hits to particular target sentences and false alarms to particular distractor sentences on immediate versus 1-week tests (Imm–1 wk), immediate versus 1-month tests (Imm–1 mo), and 1-week versus 1-month tests (1 wk–1 mo) for items that appeared on all three tests. Intertest correlations are displayed separately for 6-year-olds (Panel A), 8-year-olds (Panel B), and 11-year-olds (Panel C). Data from Brainerd and Mojardin (1998).

be seen that the height of the bars on the left side, which represent intertest correlations for target sentences, is generally less than or equal to the height of the bars on the right side, which represent intertest correlations for distractor sentences.

The second method of determining the relative stability of true and false memories, making inter-item comparisons of performance for items that only appeared on some earlier test versus items that only appear on some later test, was also used by Brainerd and Mojardin (1998) and in a study by Forrest (2002). The latter experiment is particularly interesting because it parallels some of the adult experiments that were summarized in chapter 4—specifically, the Payne et al. (1996), Seamon, Luo, Kopecky, et al. (2002), and Toglia et al. (1999) experiments. In those adult experiments, it will be remembered, DRM lists were presented, and recognition or recall tests were administered immediately and following delays that ranged from 1 day to 2 months. In Forrest's experiment, children of two age levels (6 and 11 years old) listened to a series of DRM lists. Following each list, they either attempted to recall it, or they performed an irrelevant activity (solving arithmetic problems). Finally, the children responded to a recognition test containing the usual four types of probes (targets, unpresented stimulus words, other semantically related distractors, and unrelated distractors). However, only half of the presented DRM lists were tested on this immediate recognition test. One week later, the children returned to the laboratory and responded to a second recognition test. All of the previously tested items appeared on the delayed test, and in addition, items for the previously untested DRM lists appeared on the delayed test. Forrest also included data from a previously published adult experiment in which the subjects had been tested under similar conditions. Findings for the relative stability of true and false memories at all three age levels (Panels a, b, and c) are shown in Figure 5-18, where acceptance rates on the immediate and delayed tests (for items that were tested for the first time on that test) are plotted for targets and the two types of false-memory items (unpresented stimulus words and other related distractors). Three results are apparent, from which conclusions about the relative stability of true and false memory fall out. First, at all three age levels, acceptance rates for targets declined considerably between the immediate and 1-week tests, regardless of whether or not DRM lists were followed by a recall test. Second, at all three age levels, false-alarm rates for related distractors did not decline between immediate and delayed tests, regardless of whether or not DRM lists were followed by a recall test. Therefore, the pattern of greater stability for false than for true memories held for related distractors at all age levels and in all conditions. Third, false-alarm rates for unpresented stimulus words declined by about the same amount as target hit rates in adults, but false-alarm rates for unpresented stimulus words declined little or not at all (depending upon the condition) in 6- and 11-year-olds. Hence, the pattern of greater stability for false than for true memories held consistently with children for unpresented stimulus words, but it did not hold for the adult data.

False-Memory Sleeper Effects

Of the three types of forgetting phenomena that we are considering in this section, false-memory sleeper effects have generated the greatest interest among develop-

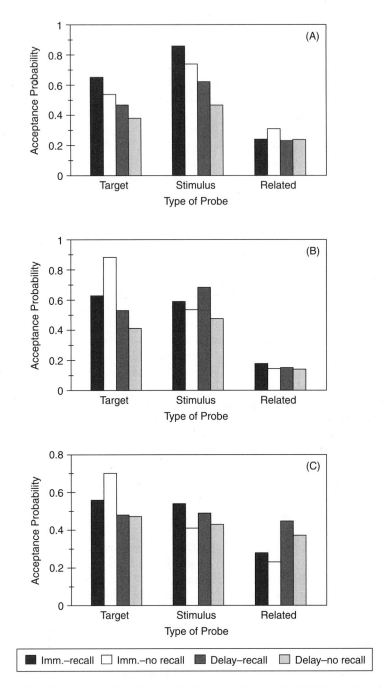

Figure 5-18. Relative stability of true and false recognition in the DRM paradigm for adults (Panel A), 11-year-olds (Panel B), and 6-year-olds (Panel C). Imm.–recall = immediate recognition tests for DRM lists that were previously recalled; Imm.–no recall = immediate recognition tests for DRM lists that were not previously recalled; Delay–recall = 1-week-delayed recognition tests for DRM lists that were previously recalled; and Delay–no recall = 1-week-delayed recognition tests for DRM lists that were not previously recalled. Data from Forrest (2002).

mental researchers. Some of the earliest developmental studies of the relation between forgetting and false memory were concerned with this possibility (e.g., Poole
& White, 1991, 1993; Reyna & Kiernan, 1994), and data on potential false-memory sleeper effects continue to be a feature of such studies (e.g., Jones & Pipe, 2002).
Forensic relevance is again responsible because sleeper effects are of particular concern with child victims and child witnesses. As mentioned, field conditions in criminal investigations sometimes create delays of days or weeks between the commission of a crime and initial interviews of child victims and witnesses, and there are
invariably delays of months or even years between the commission of a crime and
sworn testimony. We already know that owing to forgetting functions for true memory (e.g., Figure 5-16), errors of omission for actual events will increase across such
delays (making it more difficult to obtain valid evidence that leads to convictions
of guilty defendants), and such increases will typically be greater for younger than
for older children. Could children's errors of commission—recall or recognition of
false-but-meaning-preserving events—also increase across such delays? If so, as
time passes, child victims and witnesses will be more likely to provide invalid evidence that could lead to the conviction of innocent defendants. As it happens, this
is a more worrisome possibility than the increased difficulty of obtaining valid evidence because the law regards conviction of the innocent as a more serious error
than failure to convict the guilty (Ceci & Friedman, 2000)—hence, the strong interest among developmental investigators in possible false-memory sleeper effects
(Reyna, 1998).

We saw in chapter 4 that opponent-processes distinctions provide a theoretical
basis for expecting sleeper effects under certain conditions. There, we noted that if
verbatim and gist traces of experience become inaccessible at different rates and if
verbatim memories trump gist memories when both are accessible (causing recognition or recall of false-but-meaning-preserving events to be suppressed), one can
imagine scenarios in which false recall or false recognition would increase over forgetting intervals that produce declines in true recall or true recognition. An obvious
scenario is one in which, first, the forgetting interval produces large declines in verbatim memory but small declines in gist memory and, second, verbatim traces of
targets are readily accessible by false-memory items on early memory tests (so that
verbatim suppression of false recall or false recognition is commonplace). It should
be added that because verbatim-forgetting rates apparently decline with age (see
earlier discussion), one would expect that, other things being equal, false-memory
sleeper effects would be more likely to occur in younger than in older children and
would be more pronounced in younger children when they occur in both younger
and older children. However, the nature of developmental interactions will also depend upon the initial levels of false recall and false recognition. When those levels
are comparable for younger and older children, underlying developmental differences in verbatim-forgetting rates lead to the prediction that sleeper effects will be
more marked in younger children. We have seen, though, that initial levels of false
recall and false recognition are often much higher in younger than in older children,
which normally means that memories of the exact surface form of experience are
less accessible in younger children. In such circumstances, the potential for increases
over time is greater in older children because the potential for verbatim forgetting

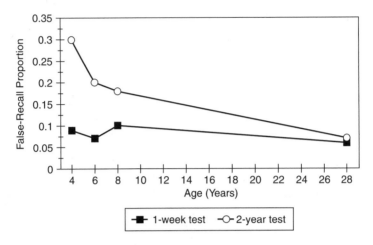

Figure 5-19. False-memory sleeper effects at four age levels on free-recall tests over a 2-year delay. Data from Poole and White (1993).

is greater, and consequently, there may be no developmental interaction or sleeper effects may be more pronounced in older children. Consistent with this line of reasoning, the literature contains examples of both developmental decreases in sleeper effects when initial false-memory levels are comparable across age levels and developmental increases when they are not.

First, it should be mentioned in passing that developmental evidence of false-memory sleeper effects has already been presented in Figure 5-18. Over the 1-week delay in Forrest's (2002) experiment, while target hit rates were declining, false-alarm rates for other semantically related distractors sometimes increased, but such increases only occurred in the youngest subjects (see Panel c). However, the earliest systematic evidence was reported in some articles that we have previously encountered—namely, those by Poole and White (1991) and by Reyna and Kiernan (1994). As the methodologies of both studies have already been described, we shall not reprise them here. We simply remind readers that in each instance, children received both immediate memory tests and 1-week delayed tests, with the children being 4, 6, and 8 years old in Poole and White's research and 6 and 9 years old in Reyna and Kiernan's research.

The patterns in Poole and White's (1991) data were false-memory sleeper effects that decreased with age. Poole and White (1993) administered 2-year follow-up memory tests to all of the subjects from their original 1991 study who could be located. Then, they computed the total proportion of inaccurate information that their subjects produced on free-recall tests administered after 1 week and 2 years. The results are displayed in Figure 5-19. There are four points of interest. First, initial levels of false recall were quite low (8% on average) and were comparable for different age levels. This is consistent with the tendency of free-recall tests to produce fewer false-memory reports than cued-recall or recognition tests (see earlier discussions), but importantly, it also sets the stage for developmental declines in sleeper effects because initial levels of false recall were not markedly higher for younger subjects. Second, there was clear evidence of a sleeper effect inasmuch as levels of false recall generally increased during the 2-year delay (while, during the same interval, true recall declined dramatically). Third, the sleeper effect exhibited a distinct developmental interaction. It was present among all three groups of children, but it was absent in adults. Fourth, this developmental interaction was also evident when only the data of the children were considered. Specifically, after the 2-year delay, 4-year-olds' and 6-year-olds' false recall were three times higher than after 1 week, while 8-year-olds' false recall was only twice as high. Thus, in this particular study, the pattern of developmental variability in the sleeper effect conformed closely to theoretical expectations based upon the notion that verbatim suppression of false memories declines more rapidly over time than gist support does and that this differential is greater in younger children, other things being equal.

The patterns in Reyna and Kiernan's (1994) article were sleeper effects that increased with age. These authors reported some developmental data in which 6- and 9-year-olds responded to both immediate and 1-week delayed tests for recognition probes like those in Table 4-1. As our concern lies with sleeper effects, we consider only the findings for true recognition (TPO probes) and false recognition of meaning-preserving distractors (TPN, TIO, and TIN probes). Immediate and delayed hit and false-alarm rates are shown in Figure 5-20 for younger (Panel a) and older (Panel b) children. Obviously, sleeper effects occurred at both age levels as there were across-the-board increases in false-alarm rates for all meaning-preserving distractors. Although sleeper effects were substantial at both age levels, they were more pronounced among the older children: The average delayed increase in false-alarm rates was .24 for 6-year-olds and .51 for 9-year-olds. Notice in this connection that the initial false-alarm rates were much lower—indeed, only about half as great—for 9-year-olds than for 6-year-olds. Thus, there was far less room for increases among the younger children. Further, from the perspective of opponent processes, the much higher initial false-alarm rates for 6-year-olds presumably means that their verbatim memories were initially much poorer than 9-year-olds'. This, in turn, means that the gap between verbatim and gist forgetting rates would have been wider in the older children, and it is this gap that is the ostensible basis for sleeper effects.

Data that are consistent with this interpretation appear in an article by Seamon et al. (2000), which was discussed in chapter 4. A key feature of Seamon et al.'s experiments is that when the target materials (categorized word lists) were originally presented, they were accompanied by pictures of the named objects. Pictorial presentation, it will be remembered, is thought to produce especially robust verbatim traces that render the suppression of false recognition or false recall far easier than it would otherwise be (Israel & Schacter, 1997; Kiernan, 1993). This should reduce developmental differences in the initial accessibility of verbatim traces by compensating for younger children's verbatim-memory limitations, which should in turn have two effects on performance: (a) Developmental differences in false recognition and false recall on immediate memory tests will be reduced because younger children's suppression ability has been selectively enhanced; and (b) developmental decreases in false-memory sleeper effects will be more likely to show up because initial developmental differences in verbatim accessibility have been reduced.

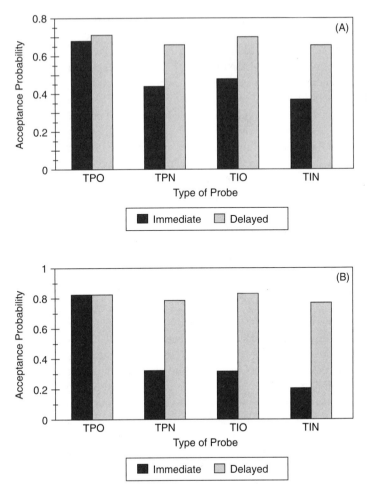

Figure 5-20. False-memory sleeper effects at two age levels (Panel A = 6-year-olds, Panel B = 9-year-olds) for false recognition of three types of meaning-preserving distractor sentences (TPN, TIO, TIN) over a 1-week delay. Data from Reyna and Kiernan (1994).

Seamon et al. reported a developmental study in which both of these effects were observed. The subjects were 7-year-olds, 11-year-olds, and 22-year-olds (college students). Following the procedure that was outlined in chapter 4, subjects from all three age levels listened to a series of categorized word lists that were accompanied by pictures of the named objects. Some subjects then responded to an immediate recognition test, whereas others returned to the laboratory 3 days later for a recognition test. The false-memory items on both tests were missing exemplars from categories that had appeared on the presented lists. The two findings of principal interest can be seen in Figure 5-21, where the false-alarm rates for missing exemplars on the immediate and delayed tests are plotted for each age level. First, note that the false-alarm rates on the immediate test were low (in the neighborhood of .1) for

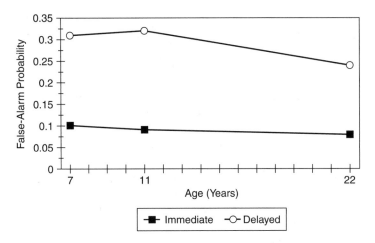

Figure 5-21. False-memory sleeper effects at three age levels for false recognition of missing exemplars from categorized word lists over a 3-day delay. Data from Seamon et al. (2000).

all groups and did not vary with age, which is consistent with the notion that pictorial presentation makes verbatim suppression easier, especially for subjects whose baseline ability to access verbatim traces is poorer. Second, note that although there were false-memory sleeper effects at all three age levels, the immediate-to-delayed increase in false recognition was greater in children than in adults. Thus, combining the recall data of Poole and White (1993) with Seamon et al.'s recognition data and the findings of some other developmental studies that included delayed tests (e.g., Brainerd & Reyna, 1996), it appears that developmental decreases in sleeper effects can be obtained when baseline developmental differences in initial accessibility of verbatim traces are equalized.

Since the 1990s, the major source of new developmental findings on false-memory sleeper effects has been an important series of investigations by Pipe, Salmon, and their associates (e.g., Gee & Pipe, 1999; Jones & Pipe, 2002; Pipe & Wilson, 1994; Pipe et al., 1999; Salmon & Pipe, 1997, 2000). As an example of those findings, we consider the Pipe et al. article, which also incorporated data from the 1999 Gee and Pipe article and the 1994 Pipe and Wilson article. Pipe et al. reported two studies, one of them being a 2-year follow-up of a study that was reported in the Pipe and Wilson article and the other being a 1-year follow-up of a study that was reported in the Gee and Pipe article. In both articles, 6- and 9-year-old children had originally participated in a staged interaction with a magician, and interviews about events that occurred during the interaction had been conducted 10 days later and 10 weeks later, using both a free-recall test and a series of cued-recall questions. Pipe et al. then repeated the interview 2 years later for only the younger children tested by Pipe and Wilson, and they repeated the interview 1 year later for both the younger and older children tested by Gee and Pipe. As the latter data provide a more powerful test of sleeper effects, we confine our attention to the 1-year retest of Gee and Pipe's children.

To begin, there were substantial developmental differences in true recall in the original Gee and Pipe study. On the first test (after 10 days), 6-year-olds recalled only about 7% of the target events, whereas 9-year-olds recalled 20%. The near-floor level of performance in 6-year-olds meant that their true recall could not decline significantly as time passed. However, 9-year-olds showed the usual declines over time. Turning to false recall, there was no evidence of sleeper effects on free-recall tests over the 1-year delay. For cued-recall tests, however, there were clear sleeper effects at both age levels. In absolute terms, the total increase in false recall over the three testing sessions was quite large. The average number of errors on cued-recall tests was 1.5 at 10 days, 3.6 at 10 weeks, and 5.7 at 1 year. Another interesting finding concerns the accuracy of information that was recalled for the first time after a long delay (1 year, in this case). According to opponent-processes distinctions, such information is more likely to be false than information that has been previously reported because earlier reports are more likely than later ones to have been based upon direct access of verbatim traces (and therefore to be true). Consistent with this prediction, 30% of the information that children remembered for the first time on 1-year free-recall tests was false, and 62% of the information that children remembered for the first time on 1-year cued-recall tests was false. This pattern of information that children recall for the first time on delayed tests containing a large proportion of false reports has been obtained in other studies in which free- or cued-recall tests have been administered after long delays (e.g., Peterson, Moores, & White, 2001; Reyna & Titcomb, 1997; Salmon & Pipe, 2000).

The developmental literature contains other examples of studies in which children's recall or recognition of false-but-meaning-preserving events increased following a forgetting interval (e.g., Brainerd & Reyna, 1996; Brainerd, Reyna, & Kneer, 1995; Koriat et al., 2001), as well as some examples of studies in which false recall (but not false recognition) failed to increase following a forgetting interval (e.g., Quas, Goodman, Bidrose, Pipe, Craw, & Ablin, 1999). However, the preceding studies suffice to establish that false-memory sleeper effects have been observed in developmental studies with both recall and recognition tests, consistent with opponent-processes predictions. Also consistent with opponent-processes predictions, our survey of these studies indicates that sleeper effects have been more commonly detected with recognition tests than with recall tests. (Here, the relevant theoretical principle is that recognition probes for false-but-meaning-preserving events are better retrieval cues for the gist of experience than are recall tests, particularly free-recall tests.) Finally, predicted developmental decreases have been detected under theoretically specified conditions (i.e., conditions in which developmental differences in the accessibility of verbatim traces on initial memory tests are not wildly different).

Synopsis

A fundamental consideration when studying any aspect of children's memories is that major developmental changes, by way of brain maturation and learning, are still on the horizon, and those changes will shape the manner in which memory eventually works. It is therefore natural to suppose that predictive control of children's false memories will be more elusive than predictive control of adults' false memories. The research that we have examined in this chapter demonstrates that this need not be the case. Opponent-processes distinctions make straightforward predictions about how storage, retrieval, and forgetting variables affect children's false-memory reports, and such predictions have been confirmed in various developmental studies. There is, however, a factor that must be weighed in achieving predictive control of children's false memories that does not figure in the predictive control of adults' false memories—namely, that the memory mechanisms that support intrusions and false alarms and the memory mechanisms that suppress such erroneous responses are still evolving. Predictive control therefore requires unusually close attention to the characteristics of the tasks that are used to measure children's false memories. Inevitably, extraction of, access to, and preservation of the meaning content of events will be easier with some tasks than with others, and as these abilities are developing, variables that support them are apt to increase younger children's false-memory reports more than older children's, adolescents', or adults'. Conversely, variables that interfere with such abilities are apt to decrease false-memory reports more at older age levels. It is also inevitable that some tasks will make it more difficult than others to store, retrieve, and preserve the surface form of events, and as these abilities are also developing, it follows that variables that support them will produce more marked reductions in the false-memory reports of younger children than in those of older children, adolescents, and young adults. (Again, conversely, variables that interfere with such abilities will produce larger increases at older age levels.)

In short, the key difference between the predictive control of children's and adults' false memories is the overriding expectation of developmental interactions. Depending upon the degree of support that a particular memory task provides for mechanisms that generate and suppress false-memory reports, a storage, retrieval, or forgetting variable that, according to opponent-processes analysis, ought to increase (or decrease) such errors may have larger or smaller effects in children, and it may even have opposite effects in children and adults. As long as developmental interactions are taken into account, however, predictive control of false memories is just as possible in children as it is in adults. In that connection, it is important to bear in mind that such interactions are not merely noise that must be tolerated in developmental research. Rather, as we have seen throughout this chapter, developmental interactions can be predicted on the basis of (a) known developmental trends in mechanisms that support and suppress particular false memories, and (b) whether a particular memory task makes it easier or harder for those mechanisms to express themselves. Concerning point b, a general rule for predicting developmental interactions is that tasks that make it easier for supportive or suppressive mechanisms to express themselves will have larger effects at younger age levels (because immature mechanisms are more in need of buttressing), whereas tasks that make it harder for such mechanisms to express themselves will have larger effects at older age levels (because mature mechanisms provide more latitude for interference).

Although we have emphasized the predictive control of children's false memories, it must not be overlooked that the theoretical questions that have driven false-memory research with adults have not figured as prominently in developmental research. Instead, the chief impetus for developmental work has been an assortment of applied concerns pursuant to increased reliance on children's testimony in the prosecution of crimes in which children are victims or witnesses. With certain types of crimes, most conspicuously child abuse, defendants' traditional rights to challenge, confront, and impeach witnesses have been reduced in order to secure children's testimony. Although such modifications have been motivated by the desire to convict criminals who otherwise could not be prosecuted, their net effect is to increase the reliance that triers of fact must place on children's memory reports in rendering verdicts. If children's baseline tendency is to make errors of commission at substantially higher rates than adults, or if children are more susceptible to factors that increase such errors in adults, the unintended result could be increased conviction rates for innocent defendants and, consequently, failure to apprehend real perpetrators. During the 1990s, leading child memory researchers filed amicus curiae briefs in support of appeals of previously convicted defendants, briefs that provided scientific support for the thesis that children's testimony in the focal cases may have been infected with false-memory reports.

Data on age changes in verbatim and gist memory provide the foundation for the predictive control of children's false memories. The relevant findings point to considerable improvement in both verbatim and gist memory, from which it follows that whether observed levels of false memory are found to increase with age, decrease with age, or remain constant will necessarily depend upon the mix of processes that are tapped by the tasks used to measure false memory. Known developmental patterns for verbatim memory are straightforward in that, for the traditional target materials of false-memory research, memory for their surface form improves between early childhood and young adulthood, with improvements during the preschool and early elementary-school years being greater than improvements during later childhood and adolescence. From the perspective of opponent processes, this means that in a developmental study, the core expectation is that older subjects will be better than younger subjects at verbatim suppression of intrusions and false alarms.

Developmental patterns for gist memory are more complicated, so that a correspondingly simple expectation with respect to age differences is not possible. Levels of false memory are often measured via items for which even young children readily store the relevant meaning content from the original target materials (e.g., antonyms, associates, and synonyms of familiar words or events from familiar schematic situations). In fact, these are the most common types of items in developmental studies of false memories because researchers have wished to ensure that child subjects comprehend the meaning of target materials. Age variability in storing the gist memories that support intrusions and false alarms will be minimal in such circumstances. On the other hand, levels of false memory are sometimes measured via items whose meanings cannot be stored by young children (e.g., synonyms of unfamiliar words or events from unfamiliar situations) or by items for which false-memory responses depend upon spontaneously connecting the meanings of several familiar targets (an ability that develops slowly during childhood). Age variability in storing the gist memories that support intrusions and false alarms will be maximal in such circumstances. These complex developmental trends imply that, depending upon the gist memories that support a particular type of intrusion or false alarm and depending upon the age levels that are being compared, the incidence of these errors may increase, decrease, or remain invariant with age, predictions that have been confirmed in recent studies.

With respect to storage variables that opponent-processes distinctions predict will influence expressed levels of false memory, the developmental literature is more sparse than corresponding work with adults. A particularly important omission is that paradigms that can provide unambiguous evidence of the advanced storage of gist memories have not been used in developmental research. However, three of the key storage variables for which opponent-processes predictions have been tested in adults—repetition of events, deep versus shallow processing, and distinctiveness of events—have also been investigated in developmental work. In each instance, the opponent-processes prediction is that the direction of the variable's effects should be the same in children and adults, but there should be developmental interactions such that those effects are more or less pronounced at younger age levels. Predictions of this sort have been confirmed for all three variables. Developmental interactions for repetition are especially interesting in that the effects of verbatim repetition have been found to increase with age, while the effects of gist repetition have been found to decrease with age.

With respect to retrieval variables, opponent-processes predictions in developmental studies are more complex than in adult studies because it cannot reasonably be assumed with children that a single leisurely presentation of a target will suffice to fully process its meaning content, that gist traces that support intrusions or false alarms will therefore be stored in memory after such a presentation, or that if memory tests are administered immediately, verbatim and gist traces will both be accessible. Despite the limitations that make such assumptions untenable with children, the opponent-processes expectation continues to be that variables that should enhance access to verbatim traces of events will lower intrusions and false alarms, and variables that should enhance access to gist traces will have the opposite effect. In addition, developmental interactions are again expected because the ability of retrieval variables to enhance either verbatim or gist access will necessarily be constrained by age differences in the extent to which such information is available in storage. As was the case for developmental studies of storage variables, only a subset of the retrieval variables that have been investigated in adult false-memory research have been systematically studied in developmental research. The two that have been studied developmentally are verbatim cuing and retrieval instructions. In addition, a third retrieval variable—repeated testing—has been investigated with children owing to concerns about whether repeated interviews of child witnesses tend to falsify the contents of their memories.

Qualitatively, opponent-processes predictions about verbatim cuing and retrieval instructions are the same for children as for adults. Verbatim cuing should reduce false-memory reports (by increasing verbatim access when false-memory items are administered); verbatim-retrieval instructions should also decrease false-memory reports (by directing retrieval away from gist processing); and gist-retrieval instructions should increase false-memory reports (by directing retrieval toward gist processing). All of these predictions have been confirmed in multiple developmental studies, and they have been confirmed for different manipulations of each retrieval variable (e.g., verbatim cuing has been manipulated via target priming on memory tests and via match/mismatch of study and test cues). Predicted developmental interactions have also been confirmed for each of the three retrieval variables. With respect to repeated testing, administration of prior memory tests has been found to inoculate true memories against forgetting (as measured by performance on later tests), but it has also been found to create false memories (as measured by performance on later tests). These repeated-testing effects have also been found to interact with age, such that true-memory inoculation is more marked in older children and false-memory creation is more marked in younger children.

The impact of forgetting variables on false-memory reports has been more extensively investigated in the developmental literature than in the adult literature owing to concerns about whether delays elevate children's errors of commission during forensic interviews and sworn testimony. The three false-persistence predictions that have been confirmed in adults (persistence of false-memory reports, greater persistence of false- than true-memory reports, and false-memory sleeper effects) have also been confirmed in children, and developmental interactions have been identified. Indeed, the original research on each of these predictions was conducted with children rather than with adults. With respect to the first prediction, good levels of false-memory persistence have been observed from early childhood through young adulthood. With respect to the second prediction, under theoretically specified conditions, levels of false-memory persistence that equal or exceed corresponding levels of true-memory persistence have been reported with subject samples from the preschool to the young adult range. With respect to the third prediction, false-memory sleeper effects have been confirmed for younger children, older children, and adolescents in designs that have incorporated forgetting intervals that ranged from a few days to 2 years. Moreover, age declines in sleeper effects have been detected under experimental conditions that, according to opponent-processes distinctions, ought to yield such interactions.

PART III

THE APPLIED SCIENCE
OF FALSE MEMORY

6

False Memory in Criminal Investigation

1—Adult Interviewing and Eyewitness Identification

Of the various catalysts that led to the intensification of false-memory research during the 1990s, perhaps the most important one, in retrospect, was the widespread awareness that errors of commission can cause serious problems in two applied domains: criminal investigation and psychotherapy (e.g., see Loftus, 1997). During the course of criminal investigations, witnesses or victims who report events that did not happen during the commission of crimes, or who report people or objects that were not present, can steer investigations in wrong directions, can cause other evidence to be misinterpreted, can cause innocent people to be treated as suspects, and can even lead to the prosecution and conviction of innocent people. Tragically, in the zeal to establish evidence of guilt, the truly guilty can go free and opportunities to gather additional incriminating evidence can be lost. The effects of erroneous reports on criminal investigations can be so pervasive that state and federal statutes incorporate provisions for charging with felonies witnesses who knowingly make such reports.[1] In psychotherapy, patients who present for treatment supply exten-

---

1. It is not widely understood that people who supply voluntary statements to police investigators are liable to prosecution for any errors of commission that they make. Although statutes normally specify that these errors must be made knowingly to qualify as criminal acts, the protection that such wording affords for innocent false-memory reports is limited, the reason being that "knowingly" is a judgment call that is made by investigators and prosecutors rather than by witnesses. It is not usually possible, of course, for anyone other than witnesses themselves to know with certainty that specific erroneous responses are due to deceitful intent, as opposed to other factors. Consequently, judgment calls about knowing deception are typically based upon circumstantial evidence (e.g., the reports of other witnesses, possible motivations to deceive, whether false reports are about material or incidental facts, or a desire on the part of investigators to "send a message" to other witnesses). Such decisions are therefore not error-free.

219

sive life histories, and therapists attempt to isolate events that have caused patients' presenting symptoms and to develop treatment plans to deal with the sequelae of those events. If, during the course of therapy, patients make false-memory reports regarding life events that therapists believe to be causes of maladjustment (e.g., reports of having had abusive parents or grandparents), the consequence may be therapy that fails to address the causes of their presenting symptoms. If the falsely reported events include crimes that counselors or therapists are legally obligated to report, the result may be criminal investigations, perhaps including prosecution and conviction, of innocent people.

In the next two chapters, we survey false-memory research that bears upon aspects of criminal investigation. Psychotherapy is taken up in chapter 8. In the present chapter and the one that follows it, we examine false-memory research as it relates to criminal investigations that involve adult witnesses (chapter 6) or child witnesses (chapter 7).

With adult witnesses, there are two areas of criminal investigation to which false-memory phenomena are most especially pertinent, both of which have been extensively studied: (a) witness interviews, including interrogation of suspects, and (b) eyewitness identification of suspects, usually via photo spreads, one-person show-ups, or multiperson line-ups. That false-memory reports occur with some frequency in both domains is evident from statistics on the reasons for false conviction. Periodically, government agencies or individual researchers publish reviews of cases in which defendants who were probably innocent were charged or convicted (Cassell, 1999; Gross, 1996; Harmon, 2001; Liebman, 2002). In some instances, convicted defendants were certainly innocent because they were later exonerated on the basis of unimpeachable evidence (e.g., DNA tests or evidence confirming that they were elsewhere when crimes occurred). Such reviews have determined that false information elicited during police interviews and false identifications of suspects by eyewitnesses are leading reasons for false conviction. For instance, Bedau and Radelet (1987) reviewed 350 cases in which defendants were charged, often with murder, who were probably or possibly innocent of those charges. They concluded that a particular type of false-memory report—false confession—was responsible for implicating defendants in 14% of the cases and that false identifications were responsible for implicating defendants in 55% of the cases.

False-memory phenomena in adult witness interviews and in eyewitness identification of suspects form the substance of the present chapter. The chapter is divided into two major sections, the first being devoted to police interviews of victims, witnesses, and suspects (which we shall call *witness interviews* for the sake of brevity) and the second being devoted to eyewitness identification of suspects. The first section begins with examples of police interviews of victims, witnesses, and suspects in a typical case. It continues with an overview of the centrality of police interviews in criminal investigation and the dilemmas that are posed by this fact, and it ends with a discussion of the suggestive properties of such interviews as they are found in police interviewing protocols, such as the widely used Reid technique (e.g., Inbau et al., 2001). Next, we summarize research that has been generated by the particular research paradigm from chapter 2 that is most directly apropos to false-memory reports in witness interviews: eyewitness memory suggestion. An opponent-processes analysis of how memory suggestion provokes false-memory reports is provided, and experimental findings on manipulations that are expected on theoretical grounds to enhance the effects of suggestion are summarized. The précis of experimental findings is again organized according to storage, retrieval, and forgetting variables. The first section concludes with a discussion of one of the most troubling by-products of memory suggestion: false confession by criminal suspects. Documented examples of false confession from recent legal cases are presented, and a taxonomy that has been used to guide recent scientific studies of false confession is considered. Key findings from such studies are reviewed, including studies in which false confessions have been induced under controlled laboratory conditions.

The second section begins with an overview of the basic methods that are used to secure eyewitness identifications in the field, accompanied by recent statistics on the reliability of such identifications. It continues with a taxonomy of 24 factors—some of which are storage factors, some of which are retrieval factors, some of which are forgetting factors, and some of which are enduring characteristics of witnesses—whose effects on the reliability of eyewitness identifications have been established in experiments. These factors are currently being employed by expert witnesses to conduct forensic evaluations of the identification procedures that are used in individual criminal prosecutions. The section concludes with two sets of research-based guidelines for eyewitness identifications, one promulgated by a leading scientific society (American Psychology and Law Society) and the other by the U.S. Department of Justice, both of which are intended to reduce the incidence of false-memory responses in eyewitness identification.

Suggestibility of Eyewitness Memory Reports

Interviews of Victims, Witnesses, and Suspects in Criminal Investigation

The pivotal role that is played by witness interviews and suspect interrogations is not commonly understood. These activities are often the linchpin of criminal investigation. They are regarded as indispensable by police and prosecutors because the bulk of reported crimes do not generate ancillary physical evidence that implicates specific suspects or that, in court, will provide clear and convincing proof of defendants' guilt. By way of illustration, we consider the case of Ms. W, a woman who was robbed while walking at night on a city street.[2]

---

2. At the request of defense attorneys and prosecutors, we have, over the years, reviewed the details of many cases in which witness interviews and eyewitness identifications figured prominently in the determination of guilt. Throughout this chapter and the next, we illustrate key points with examples from some of those cases. As is common practice, references to these cases are anonymous.

The Case of Ms. W

On the evening in question, a patrol car containing two police officers was dispatched to respond to a 911 call reporting a robbery. Upon their arrival, the officers were met by two individuals, Ms. W and a man who stated that he had made the 911 call at her request. The police then interviewed Ms. W about the events that had prompted the request, which led to the following statements. She had been walking alone when a man approached her and said that he knew her from college. After a brief conversation, the man glanced around, as if to determine whether any other pedestrians were watching, whereupon he grabbed Ms. W's arm and pushed her in the direction of a nearby alley. While doing so, he stated in a threatening voice that she was being robbed and that she would be raped if she resisted. Ms. W complied, and after reaching the alley, the man demanded her purse, which she promptly surrendered. Rather than leaving immediately, however, the man fondled her breasts and buttocks and kissed her forcefully, after which he ran away in the direction from which they had come. Ms. W then left the alley and observed the robber running down the street, passing pedestrians as he ran. She stopped the nearest pedestrian and requested assistance. The pedestrian immediately placed a 911 call on his cell telephone and remained with Ms. W until the patrol car arrived.

After interviewing Ms. W, the officers conducted a detailed examination of the crime scene. Although multiple felonies had been reported during Ms. W's interview, they failed to recover a single item of physical evidence from the scene that bore on any of them. Likewise, a team of forensic investigators who arrived shortly thereafter failed to recover any relevant physical evidence. Of course, verbal threats leave no physical traces, barring an audio or video recording, and sexual fondling rarely does (a point that will resurface in chapter 7 in connection with child sexual abuse). The level of physical force that the robber had exerted was insufficient to leave bruises or cuts on the victim, to leave tissue samples of the robber on the victim, or to leave tissue samples of the victim on the robber. Finally, the purse was never recovered, so that the presence of the robber's fingerprints or tissue samples on the purse could not be determined.

The only evidence that could be gathered came from interviews of the victim and witnesses who were pedestrians on the same street at the time of the robbery. During police interviews of the victim, descriptions of the suspect were provided that included some reasonably unique features (e.g., a missing front tooth, bushy black eyebrows, and a coat with a bizarre club insignia). During police interviews of other witnesses, all of these individuals were reluctant to make statements and most were distinctly uncooperative. When asked to give a free narrative of what they had seen and heard, none provided any information that confirmed the victim's statements, and most provided no pertinent information at all. However, during the course of these interviews, the police supplied the witnesses with detailed accounts of the specific events that had been described by the victim and of the specific features of the suspect that she had mentioned. The police also proposed to these other witnesses that they may have seen and heard some of these things, exhorting them to think back and try to remember, and they told certain witnesses that they must have seen or heard some of these things because their vantage points were especially good. In response to such questioning, some witnesses said that they now remembered seeing a man with the indicated features on the street that night; some said that they now remembered seeing a man with those features speaking to the victim; and some said that they now remembered seeing a running man whose coat bore an insignia resembling the one described by the victim. However, none of the witnesses remembered seeing a man with the indicated features push the victim into the alley; none remembered hearing him make threatening statements to the victim; and none remembered seeing him with the victim's purse.

Further interviews of people living in the area produced the name of a man with a missing front tooth and bushy eyebrows who was of the approximate height and build as the robber in the victim's description. A check of police computer records revealed that someone with that name had recently been interviewed in connection with another theft but had not been arrested. However, when the victim and some of the eyewitnesses were shown the suspect's photograph, which was obtained from his driver's license records, none was able to identify him. Police officers were then dispatched to locate the suspect and interview him to determine whether he had an alibi for the night and time in question.

During the interview, the suspect was repeatedly warned that he would be arrested and charged immediately if he could not provide an alibi for the previous evening. Actually, the officers had no intention of arresting him, regardless of what he said, as the evidence was insufficient to charge anyone with the crimes. Rather, they assumed that if the suspect were the perpetrator, he could be frightened into providing a false alibi, which could be disconfirmed through investigation. This, the officers knew, would accomplish two objectives. First, the suspect could be charged with intentionally making false statements to a police officer during a criminal investigation, which was a felony in their jurisdiction. This would allow the suspect to be charged with the original crimes as well. Even if the evidence ultimately proved inadequate for conviction on the original crimes, a conviction on the first charge was virtually certain. Second, a disconfirmed alibi could then be exploited as evidence of guilt in later interrogations of the suspect. Although the suspect initially was unable to recall his whereabouts, he eventually stated that he had been bowling on the night and time in question, and he provided the name of the bowling alley. More than 20 people who were at the bowling alley that evening were identified by the police via a check of credit card receipts. Interviews of six of these people revealed that none had seen the suspect or anyone else possessing any of the unique features in the victim's description. Despite the lack of a verifiable alibi, despite the fact that the suspect had apparently lied about having an alibi, and despite the fact that the suspect possessed features that matched the victim's description, the evidence was still insufficient for prosecution.

It was decided to attempt to secure an admission of guilt from the suspect via a formal interrogation. Police officers arrived at the suspect's residence at 11p.m., as he was preparing for bed, informed him that he was being arrested for robbery, and transported him to a local police station, where he was officially charged with robbery. The suspect was then placed in a small interrogation room with a single police interviewer. After warning the suspect that he was in grave trouble and that it would be better for him if he cooperated fully, the interviewer read the suspect his Miranda rights and asked him if he would waive those rights and respond to questioning, which he agreed to do. A 4-hour interrogation then ensued.

During the initial stages of the interrogation, the interviewer stated that he was sympathetic with the suspect's plight, that he understood that people are sometimes forced to steal because they are in desperate need of money, and that there is nothing immoral about theft in such circumstances, though the law regards it as a crime. The interviewer also stated that although he was very sympathetic with the suspect's plight and probably would have acted similarly himself, he had to arrest the suspect because the police had conclusive proof that the suspect had lied about his alibi. Subsequently, the interviewer repeatedly accused the suspect of having committed the robbery and repeatedly described specific acts that the suspect should state that he had committed (e.g., saying "give me your purse or I'll rape you" to Ms. W, pushing Ms. W from the street to the alley, waving his fist in Ms. W's face, fondling Ms. W, kissing Ms. W). The interviewer falsely stated to the suspect on several occasions that he knew that the suspect had committed these acts because the suspect had been observed by several witnesses. The interviewer also falsely stated to the suspect that these same witnesses had positively identified him from his driver's license photograph, and he threatened the suspect with more serious charges— sexual assault, in particular—if he did not admit to everything that Ms. W had reported. The interviewer stated that prosecutors would be more lenient with the suspect if he would admit to everything and that he would recommend to prosecutors that the suspect not be charged with sexual assault. The suspect was warned in the latter connection that imprisoned sexual offenders are liable to be beaten by other prisoners.

Near the end of the interrogation, the suspect admitted to having robbed the woman and to having fondled her. He elaborated on the threatening statements that he had made to Ms. W, though none of these elaborations were statements that Ms. W had remembered, and he elaborated on the ways in which he fondled Ms. W, though none of these latter elaborations corresponded to the acts that Ms. W remembered. Following these admissions, the interviewer prepared a written confession statement, which the suspect signed, and the interrogation was terminated. Immediately thereafter, on the basis of his signed statement, the suspect was charged with additional felonies, including sexual assault.

Prior to trial, as is common practice, the prosecuting attorneys interviewed their major witnesses concerning the events about which they would be asked to testify at trial. During Ms. W's interview, she stated that she did not remember that the suspect had fondled her sexually. When supplied with a written narrative of the statement that she had given on the night of the robbery, she continued to deny any acts of sexual fondling. She indicated that although the robber had most probably come in contact with her breasts during the course of the struggle, he had not fondled her in any way and had not kissed her either. By way of explanation of the inconsistency between the written narrative and her current recollections, Ms. W stated that she probably embellished the events because she was so angry about losing her purse, which contained irreplaceable photographs of her deceased brother. Nevertheless, the sexual assault charge was not dropped because the defendant's signed statement admitted to this charge and contained spontaneous elaborations of specific acts of fondling.

At trial, the suspect was convicted of all charges, including sexual assault. In post-trial interviews of jurors, his admissions of guilt during the interrogation were cited as the key basis for conviction on each charge. Ms. W had asserted during her trial testimony that she did not remember the suspect making most of the threatening statements that he described during his interrogation and that she did not remember him fondling her sexually. When asked by the prosecuting attorney whether she might simply have forgotten the fondling acts, Ms. W asserted that if she had been assaulted in such a manner, it was inconceivable that she would have forgotten it. This assertion notwithstanding, the jury convicted the suspect of sexual assault as well as robbery. When questioned on this point during post-trial interviews, the jurors stated that the admissions in the suspect's signed confession were more credible evidence than the victim's denials because the trauma of a potential rape, as well as the social opprobrium that sometimes attaches to rape, may have caused Ms. W to repress her memories of being sexually assaulted.

The case of Ms. W well illustrates some of the enduring dilemmas that are posed by reliance on police interviews in the prosecution of crimes, or perhaps we should say in the prosecution of reports of crimes (remember, here, that there was no physical evidence that Ms. W was even carrying a purse that evening). This case illustrates three dilemmas, in particular, upon which we will comment: (a) Criminal interviews provide the prosecution's key evidence, (b) criminal interviews can be unsavory; and (c) criminal interviews can be rife with memory suggestions.

Police Interviews Provide the Prosecution's Key Evidence

In the case of Ms. W, the memory reports that were provided during the interviews of the victim, witnesses, and suspect, rather than physical evidence, were the primary data that were used to verify the occurrence of crimes, to identify the suspect, and to prosecute the suspect. In fact, there would have been no case otherwise. The memory reports of the victim and the witnesses, together with the memory reports in the suspect's interviews and confession statement, were the only evidence. This is not an unusual circumstance in criminal investigation. Some studies have shown that physical evidence is gathered and subjected to forensic analysis in a remarkably small percentage of criminal investigations in the United States (e.g., Horvath & Meesig, 1996, 1998). For example, Horvath and Meesig (1996) reviewed empirical studies of the criminal investigation process, with special emphasis upon the collection and processing of physical evidence. They found that physical evidence was collected in *less than 10%* of their sample of cases, and that when collected, it was only subjected to forensic analysis in approximately half of the cases. They also found that, surprisingly, police investigators regard physical evidence as having little intrinsic value and that they rely upon it chiefly as an adjunct to the interviews that they conduct—specifically, as a device for stimulating statements of guilt from suspects, with such statements then being presented to triers of fact as the chief evidence of guilt.

Police Interviews Can Be Unsavory

Following the police interviews of Ms. W, the interviews of the other witnesses were manipulative. Those interviews failed to provide any pertinent information during the witnesses' initial narratives of what they remembered. Police interviewers did not accept these memory reports, however, and instead, they supplied the witnesses with detailed accounts of what the victim had reported and asked whether the witnesses remembered any of these events. They also advised witnesses that they could or must have seen or heard these events. The police interviews of the suspect were also manipulative, but in addition, those interviews were deceitful from start to finish. The principal objective of the first interview was entrapment, to entice the subject to lie to the interviewer so that he could be charged with at least one felony for which conviction was highly probable; he could also be charged with the felonies that Ms. W had reported; and his lies could be used to threaten him during later interviews.

The second interview was intentionally conducted late at night, when the suspect would be fatigued and therefore less able to stand up under a prolonged interrogation. During that interview, the suspect was inveigled to waive his Miranda rights by insinuating that things would go easier for him if he cooperated fully. Once the interview began, he was repeatedly accused of committing robbery and sexual assault, although he had previously denied having done so. The interviewer lied to the suspect about being sympathetic to his plight and about desiring to have him treated leniently. The interviewer also lied to the suspect on multiple occasions about the nature and strength of the evidence against him: Neither the victim nor the witnesses had identified the suspect, and considering that the bowling alley had been crowded on the evening in question, the suspect's alibi had not been conclusively disproved. The interviewer described specific physical acts that he "knew" the suspect had committed, described specific threatening statements that he "knew" the suspect had made to the victim, and demanded that the suspect agree that he had committed those acts and made those statements. The suspect was threatened with more serious consequences if he did *not* agree when, in fact, such consequences could only follow if he *did* agree. The suspect was led to believe that he could avoid being charged with sexual assault if he agreed with the interviewer's statements, when the actual intent was to obtain evidence that would support such a charge. Finally, the suspect was allowed to confess to confabulated threatening statements and to confabulated acts of sexual fondling (statements and acts that the victim had not described and that she presumably would have remembered).

The aforementioned features of police interviews are deeply disturbing by the standards of normal social intercourse, and they would be considered downright unethical by the standards of professional interactions. Nonetheless, the rights to entice interviewees to give false evidence, to lie about facts to interviewees, to intimidate interviewees, to make false promises to interviewees, to feign certain knowledge of the commission of specific acts by interviewees, to demand agreement from interviewees that they committed criminal acts, to conduct interviews under conditions of sleep or food deprivation, and to use other reprehensible tactics that fall short of physical violence have been consistently upheld by the courts as legitimate investigative procedures. Why? The law's presumption is that criminal interviews do not qualify as either polite social intercourse or as professional interactions. Rather, their sole intent is to secure evidence that will convict the guilty, and they must therefore be judged in that light. Witnesses, even victims, may be reticent about providing such evidence, often because they simply do not want to become involved. Witnesses may be downright uncooperative or hostile, often because they do not want to implicate a friend or relative. Thus, it may be necessary to trick witnesses into providing evidence. Further, the law's presumption is that guilty suspects will not admit their crimes and instead will be intentionally deceitful, dissembling about their motives and actions so as to make them appear innocuous (see Reyna, Holliday, & Marche, 2002 for a relevant case study). Given that innocent people are known to be untruthful about committing even minor social transgressions (e.g., uttering a racial epithet), it would be absurd not to expect high levels of deceit from guilty suspects. Therefore, the courts have reasoned, police interviewers must be allowed to use tactics to overcome deception that would be considered unethical or immoral in everyday life. After all, guilty suspects do not abide by everyday moral strictures when they commit crimes, and they have therefore violated the social covenant whereby innocent people have the right to expect fair usage. Finally, we should remind ourselves that prosecution of the bulk of crimes depends upon evidence that is produced during police interviews. Hence, the removal of duplicitous, manipulative, and untruthful techniques from interviewing would unquestionably hamper the prosecution of guilty suspects.

Police Interviews Can Be Suggestive

From the perspective of false-memory research, a crucial aspect of the police interviews in the case of Ms. W. is that they were rife with memory suggestions about the central allegations. Readers may have noticed that the *only* evidence pertaining to those allegations that was not produced pursuant to memory suggestion was gathered during the initial interview of the victim. With respect to the other witnesses, at first none of them reported seeing or hearing anything that confirmed the details of the victim's account, and none reported anything that implicated the eventual police suspect. Such evidence was only obtained when interviewers reprised the victim's allegations and asked witnesses to try to remember whether they saw or heard any of those things. These requests included suggestions to some witnesses that they *could* have seen or heard certain things and suggestions to other witnesses that they *must* have seen or heard certain things. Whether the witnesses' subsequent responses were true memories whose retrieval had been stimulated by suggestion, false memories that had been implanted by suggestion, social compliance without retrieval of relevant memories, or some combination of these possibilities remains uncertain because there was no independent physical evidence that confirmed the allegations in the case.

With respect to the suspect, stronger forms of memory suggestion were used. Initially, the suspect denied any involvement and continued to maintain his innocence at the start of the second interview. None of the physical acts or threatening statements that had been described by Ms. W were ever described by the suspect. Instead, they were suggested to him by the police interviewer, and the suspect was exhorted to agree with them. To encourage agreement, the interviewer falsely stated that he knew that the suspect had committed these acts because the suspect had been observed by witnesses. To further encourage agreement, the interviewer threatened the suspect with more serious charges and promised leniency in exchange for agreement. In the end, the suspect agreed with all of Ms. W's allegations. As with the suggestive interviews of witnesses, whether those responses were true memories whose retrieval had been stimulated by suggestion, false memories that were implanted by suggestion, social compliance without retrieval of relevant memories, or some combination of these possibilities is unknown owing to the lack of independent evidence.

As the case of Ms. W illustrates, memory suggestions are routine features of criminal investigative interviews. In Table 6-1, 14 of the most common examples of suggestive interviewing practices are displayed. This list is not exhaustive, but we have encountered all of these practices in criminal cases on which we have been asked to consult. It can be seen that the practices vary in strength. The first three items are not overtly coercive, but they are suggestive for two reasons. First, pertinent information is provided by interviewers rather than by interviewees; and second, when confronted with such questions, there is a nonzero probability that interviewees who cannot remember information will respond as though they do, rather than stating that they do not remember (e.g., Lamb & Faucher, 2001; Sternberg, Lamb, Esplin, Orbach, & Mitchell, 2001). (Note that "don't remember" is not a stated option in these questions.) Items 4 and 5 are more suggestive, though still not overtly coercive. With respect to item 4, the clear implication of repeating questions that have already been clearly answered is that the interviewer does not accept the answers (Ceci & Bruck, 1995). With respect to item 5, witnesses are being exposed to actual physical evidence that they may not have previously encountered, which can make that evidence seem (falsely) familiar when they are subsequently questioned about it. Items 6–13 are all overtly coercive, with 10–13 being more coercive than 6–9 because punishment, reward, false evidence, and stereotypes have been added to demands that interviewees accept or reject pertinent information. Finally, item 14 is a situational variable that tends to increase the frequency and strength of memory suggestions: Obviously, interviewers who are aware of the key allegations and evidence are in a better position to make such information the object of suggestive questioning than interviewers who are not (Ceci, Leichtman, & White, 1995).

The entering wedge for memory research is the acknowledgment that practices such as those in Table 6-1 are facts of life in criminal investigation. The courts have ruled that such suggestive methods are acceptable investigative procedures and that the evidence that is produced by them may be introduced in court. Such evidence will therefore continue to be used to charge and prosecute suspects. Consequently, those methods are proper topics of scientific scrutiny. With respect to the relation-

Table 6-1. Some Examples of Suggestive Features of Criminal-Investigation Interviews

Procedure	Description
1. Yes-no	Interviewees are asked to agree/disagree with pertinent items of information. (Did the robber have bushy eyebrows?)
2. Multiple choice	Interviewees are asked to choose between alternative items of information. (Did the robber grab her right arm or her left arm?)
3. Fill-in	Interviewees are asked to fill in a pertinent item of information. (Which arm did the robber grab?)
4. Question repetition	Questions are asked again and again, even though they have been clearly answered.
5. Evidence familiarization	Witnesses are exposed to evidence (e.g., pictures of victims or suspects or details of the crime scene) about which they will later be asked to testify.
6. Noncoercive challenges	Once questions have been asked and answered, the answers are rejected, and interviewees are asked to consider whether other answers are correct. (Are you sure that the man you saw didn't have bushy eyebrows?)
7. Enforced agreement	Interviewers demand that interviewees accede to pertinent items of information that interviewers assert to be true. (You saw the robber shake his fist in her face, didn't you?)
8. Enforced disagreement	Once questions have been asked and answered, the answers are rejected, and interviewees are told that their answers are false. (You say that you didn't see his face. But, you know you did, didn't you? You were only 3 feet away.)
9. Punishment	Interviewees are punished (e.g., kept awake, deprived of food) or threatened with punishment (e.g., being charged as an accomplice in the crime under investigation, being charged with making false statements to a police investigator) for failure to provide pertinent items of information (e.g., confirming a victim's description of a suspect).
10. Negative or positive reinforcement	Interviewees are rewarded (e.g., with sleep, with food) or promised future rewards (e.g., not being charged as an accomplice, not being charged with making false statements to a police investigator) for providing pertinent items of information (e.g., confirming a victim's description of a suspect).
11. Lying about evidence	Interviewees are told that pertinent items of information have already been established as facts by other evidence (e.g., that the robber had bushy eyebrows, that he grabbed the woman's arm, that he shook his fist in the woman's face).
12. Appeals to external authority	Interviewees are told that based upon considerations of logic, fact, or common sense, pertinent items of information must be true (e.g., We both know that the street is very brightly lit at night. So, anyone that was standing nearby *must* have seen what this guy was wearing.)
13. Stereotype induction	Interviewees are provided with true or false information about suspects that is consistent with the crimes that are under investigation (e.g., witnesses are told that a suspect in a robbery investigation has a prior history of arrest for petty theft).
14. Confirmation bias	Witnesses are interviewed by investigators who are aware of the detailed facts of the case and who have interviewed victims and other witnesses; interrogation is aimed at confirming investigators' theories of events.

ship between such research and the law, the proper role of science is to assist the courts in determining the reliability of evidence—specifically, the accuracy of memory reports—that is generated by suggestive interviewing methods. Normally, this is accomplished by presenting experimental findings as expert testimony during the course of pre-trial proceedings and at trial. Then, triers of fact may weigh findings about the tendency of suggestive methods to falsify the contents of memory against the probity of evidence that has been obtained via investigative interviews to meet their constitutional obligation to determine the relative credibility of different sources of evidence. We now turn to research that is designed to generate such findings.

Research on Memory Suggestion

The present section proceeds in three steps. First, we describe the experimental paradigm that has been used to study memory suggestion, which was first introduced in chapter 2. Second, we present an opponent-processes analysis of memory performance in this paradigm. Third, we summarize some major patterns of findings from studies of this paradigm, with emphasis on findings that are predicted by opponent-processes distinctions and that are pertinent to investigative interviews.

The Misinformation Paradigm

We introduced eyewitness memory-suggestion research in chapter 2 and noted some of the early findings of Loftus and her associates (Loftus, 1975; Loftus et al., 1978; Loftus & Palmer, 1974). In recent years, the standard experimental procedure for studying eyewitness-suggestion effects has come to be called the *misinformation paradigm* (e.g., Belli, 1989; Holliday, Reyna, & Hayes, 2002; Loftus & Hoffman, 1989; Tversky & Tuchin, 1989). This procedure is best thought of as a false-memory variant of a hoary verbal-learning procedure—retroactive interference—wherein memory for a studied list is impaired by exposure to an interpolated list (e.g., Bower & Mann, 1992; Howe, 2002; Melton & Irwin, 1940). The basic methodology is illustrated by the following example:

List 1	List 2	Cued Recall
Bag-Tire	Republic-Hound	Bag-?
Glad-Splint	Chess-Element	Glad-?
Rock-Computer	Missile-Snort	Rock-?
Street-Dogma	Elastic-Flood	Street-?
Hose-Nail	Ache-Measure	Hose-?
Rest-Pin	Tempt-Under	Rest-?
Block-Sleigh	Saliva-Lens	Block-?
Photo-Lamb	Kettle-Dough	Photo-?
Greed-East	Cause-English	Greed-?
Iodine-Reptile	Passkey-Whole	Iodine-?

First, all subjects are exposed to the list of unrelated word pairs on the left, with the instruction that they should try to remember them so that they can recall the right member of each pair (the target) when the left member (the cue) is presented as a retrieval prompt. Next, treatment subjects are exposed to the second list of unrelated word pairs in the center, whereas control subjects are not. Finally, all subjects respond to the recall test on the right. The standard result is that true recall of List 1 items is poorer in treatment subjects than in controls; exposure to the interpolated list impairs memory for the original targets. Now, imagine that some of the pairs in the interpolated list are replaced by pairs consisting of an old cue word from List 1 paired with a new target word, a technique known as *AB/AC transfer*. For instance, suppose that *chess-element* is replaced by *glad-element* and that *kettle-dough* is replaced by *photo-dough*. On the cued-recall test, subjects are carefully instructed to recall only List 1 targets, so that responding "element" to *glad* or "dough" to *photo* is a false-memory response.

Based upon the discussion of eyewitness suggestion in chapter 2, it is easy to see that the misinformation paradigm is a variant of AB/AC transfer. The paradigm has three features, however, that distinguish it from AB/AC transfer in classic verbal-learning experiments. First, the initial target events are not word lists; instead, they are meaningful real-life experiences that simulate situations that might be the focus of police interviews. For instance, subjects might be shown a slide sequence depicting events associated with an automobile accident (chapter 2), or they might view a video of a bicycle theft (Bjorklund, Cassel, Bjorklund, Brown, Park, Ernst, & Owen, 2000), or they might observe a sequence of live events that result in property damage (Ceci et al., 1994), or they might participate in a sequence of live events, such as a medical examination for an injury (Ornstein, Manning, & Pelphrey, 1999). Second, the misinformation phase (List 2 in AB/AC transfer) differs from the target-exposure phase with respect to both presentation modality and informational content. As the intent of the misinformation paradigm is to isolate the effects of suggestive interviewing practices, the misinformation phase is typically a structured interview or narrative of some sort. For example, subjects may be informed that the misinformation phase is a review of what they remember about the events that they have just witnessed and that such a review will aid their retention (e.g., Titcomb, 1996). The misinformation procedure then consists of general questions that refer back to events from the exposure phase. For all subjects, most of the questions are neutral retrieval cues (e.g., from the Loftus [1975] car-accident sequence in chapter 2: Do you remember the color of the Datsun?). For treatment subjects, a few questions contain false-memory suggestions (e.g., from the Loftus [1975] car-accident sequence in chapter 2: Do you remember if another car passed the Datsun while it was stopped at the stop sign?). The third difference between the misinformation paradigm and classic AB/AC transfer experiments is that the memory tests during the final phase typically involve recognition rather than recall. Multiple-choice tests composed of a target and a distractor (Was there a stop sign or a yield sign at the corner?) predominated in early misinformation experiments (e.g., Loftus, 1975), while yes-no recognition tests for individual targets (Was there a yield sign at the corner?) and distractors (Was there a stop sign at the corner?) have become common in more recent experiments (e.g., Belli, 1989; Tversky & Tuchin, 1989).

If we take as our baseline design the experiments in which the interview phase immediately follows the exposure phase and the test phase immediately follows the interview phase, misinformation studies have produced three enduring findings with

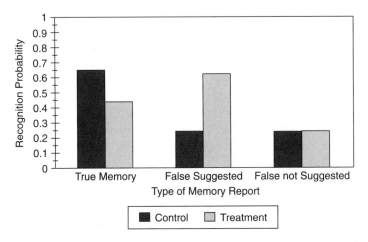

Figure 6-1. Effects of suggestive interview questions on true recognition of target events and false recognition of distractor events. Based upon Tversky and Tuchin (1989).

adult subjects: (a) false-memory elevation, (b) true-memory suppression, and (c) type of memory × misinformation interactions. Explicitly, false alarms and intrusions occur at higher rates when the falsely remembered items have been provided as brief one-time misinformation; hits and correct recall occur at lower rates when correctly remembered items have been objects of brief one-time misinformation; and misinformation usually produces more false-memory creation than true-memory suppression. All three findings can be seen in Figure 6-1, which is based upon some experiments by Tversky and Tuchin (1989).

Tversky and Tuchin's (1989) subjects viewed a 78-slide sequence that depicted events associated with an office theft of $20 and a hand calculator by a repairman who had been summoned to the office to fix a chair. The misinformation phase consisted of a written narrative that ostensibly referred back to some of the events that had just been witnessed. The narrative, which was read to the subjects by the experimenter, described the action in the slide sequence and mentioned the locations of several objects in the office (e.g., magazines, cans of soft drinks). Most of the statements in the narrative mentioned actual target objects and events (e.g., a statement that a copy of *Vogue* was sitting on a table), but one of them provided to treatment subjects an erroneous suggestion about one of the objects (e.g., a statement that a soda sitting on a desk was a can of 7-Up when, in fact, it was a can of Coke). The memory test consisted of 32 recognition probes, some of which were target probes and some of which were distractor probes. Crucially, one of the target probes and one of the distractor probes referred to the object about which a false suggestion had been provided to treatment subjects (e.g., target = there was a Coke can on the desk; distractor = there was a 7-Up can on the desk). The graph in Figure 6-1 shows the effects of this one-time suggestion on correct recognition of targets (*left*), on false recognition of distractors that had been objects of suggestion (*center*), and on false recognition of distractors that had not been mentioned in the narrative (*right*). It can be seen that false suggestions suppressed correct recognition of targets and increased false recognition of the corresponding distractors. It can also be seen that the latter effect was much larger: Suggestion caused the hit rate to drop by 22%, but it caused the false-alarm rate to increase by 38%. A fourth characteristic finding of misinformation experiments is also apparent in Figure 6-1— namely, that the level of false recognition of misinformed distractors (62%) is much higher than the levels of semantic false recognition that are usually observed in false-memory experiments that do not provide misinformation (e.g., see Figure 4-6).

Opponent-Processes Analysis of the Misinformation Paradigm

In a series of papers, we have described how the opponent-processes analysis of false memory can be extended to the misinformation paradigm, without the need of any new assumptions (Brainerd & Reyna, 1998a, 2001a; Reyna, 1995; Reyna & Brainerd, 1995a; Reyna & Titcomb, 1997), and how such an extension handles the four findings that we have just mentioned. The description of opponent-processes theory in chapter 3 revolved around five core ideas: (a) Subjects store dissociated verbatim and gist representations of experience, and they store them in parallel; (b) verbatim and gist traces are accessed via dissociated retrieval operations on memory tests; (c) retrieval of verbatim and gist traces support opposing judgments about false-memory items; (d) over time, verbatim and gist traces of experience become inaccessible at different rates; and (e) between early childhood and young adulthood, there are developmental improvements in storage and retrieval of both verbatim and gist traces. To encompass memory-falsification effects in the misinformation paradigm, it is only necessary to apply these assumptions to the misinformation phase as well as to the exposure phase and then to note the consequences for memory performance.

Because misinformation-phase material refers back to the exposure phase, this material has two distinct aspects: It provides cues that cause subjects to access memories that were stored during the exposure phase, and it is also a source of additional verbatim and gist traces, which are stored during the misinformation phase itself, traces that can be accessed on subsequent memory tests. Consider the retrieval aspect of misinformation first. When questions or statements about earlier target events (e.g., Coke can) are posed, the retrieval situation is much the same as on a memory test; subjects may access verbatim (Coke can) or gist traces (soft drink) from the exposure phase, with verbatim access predominating if the misinformation phase occurs shortly after exposure. This, in turn, will strengthen both types of representations (see the discussion of memory-testing effects in chapter 4). When questions or statements present misinformation (e.g., 7-Up can), the retrieval situation is still much the same as on a memory test; subjects may access verbatim or gist traces from the exposure phase, with gist access predominating. Beyond strengthening both types of representations, note that verbatim and gist retrieval support different subjective reactions to misinformation: Gist retrieval supports misinformation acceptance (7-Up is a soft drink), but verbatim retrieval supports the non-identity and recollection-suppression processes that were described in chapter 3 (a 7-Up can is demonstrably not a Coke can).

Now, consider the storage aspect of misinformation. On the one hand, posing questions or statements about targets will generate additional verbatim and gist traces that support true-memory responses on later memory tests. On the other hand, misinformation (a) will generate additional verbatim traces (e.g., 7-Up can) that support false-memory responses (7-up can) and impair true responses (Coke can) on later memory tests, and (b) will generate additional gist traces that support both.

This opponent-processes analysis of misinformation readily explains the key experimental findings that were mentioned above (e.g., Reyna & Brainerd, 1998). Concerning false-memory elevation, misinforming questions and statements provide additional verbatim and gist traces that support false-memory responses for the misinformed objects or events. Concerning true-memory suppression, misinforming questions and statements provide additional verbatim traces that conflict with true-memory responses for target objects or events. Concerning type of memory × misinformation interactions, false-memory elevation will normally exceed true-memory suppression because the additional verbatim traces and gist traces that are generated by misinformation *both* support false-memory responses, whereas only the additional verbatim traces interfere with true-memory responses. Finally, the explanation for the fourth finding (higher levels of false memory in misinformation studies than in standard semantic false-memory studies) is that (a) verbatim traces that support false-memory responses are available in the former studies but not the latter, and (b) the gist traces that support false-memory responses are stronger in the former studies than in the latter (because of gist activation in the misinformation phase).

Although opponent-processes distinctions can explain the fourth finding, they also predict that this finding will not be obtained under certain conditions. Here, recall that the presentation of misinformation may trigger the retrieval of verbatim traces of the corresponding target events, resulting in positive, principled rejections of the misinformation (e.g., No, I couldn't have seen a 7-Up can because I distinctly remember seeing a Coke can). If, for some reason, such principled rejections occur at high rates during the misinformation phase, levels of false memory for misinformed items might be quite low on subsequent memory tests. It is even possible, if these rejection rates are especially high, for false-memory levels to be *lower* for misinformed items than for items that are not misinformed (e.g., Cassel & Bjorklund, 1995; Cassel, Roebers, & Bjorklund, 1996).

Experimental Findings

We now sketch some core results that have accumulated from research on the misinformation paradigm, which are highly pertinent to the interviewing of witnesses. The literature on this paradigm is vast, consisting of hundreds of articles that have appeared during the course of 3 decades. Therefore, providing a comprehensive catalog of the empirical effects would be a daunting task for writers, and the result would be mind-numbing for readers. Such a catalog would not, in any case, fit with our objective in this volume, which is to shed some theoretical light on false memory—to show how existing false-memory phenomena can be explained and new phenomena predicted—rather than to recite data. Consequently, as in chapters 4 and 5, our emphasis will be on findings that bear on theoretical explanations (especially, opponent-processes explanations) of false alarms and intrusions that are congruent with erroneous suggestions. In chapter 5, we mentioned that enforcing such discipline in the interests of achieving even limited theoretical understanding is more than usually important owing to the legal context in which developmental research on false memory has been conducted. Obviously, the same dictum applies to research on the misinformation paradigm.

Our discussion of research will therefore recapitulate the earlier plan of evaluating opponent-processes predictions about variables that ought to affect false memory—in this case, false memories that reflect erroneous suggestions that occur during the misinformation phase of misinformation experiments. The discussion will also follow much the same organizational structure, beginning with memory storage, continuing with memory retrieval, and ending with forgetting. It will be remembered that the treatment of developmental research in chapter 5 added a further complexity to the basic considerations that were set forth in chapter 4, that complexity being an underlying age variability in opponent processes. Likewise, research on the misinformation paradigm adds a further complexity, which was previewed above. In chapters 4 and 5, opponent-processes predictions focused on variables that are operative during the exposure phase of an experiment (storage variables), during the test phase (retrieval variables), or during the interval between the phases (forgetting variables). The new complexity is that storage variables can affect traces that are stored during the misinformation phase as well as during the exposure phase; retrieval variables can affect traces that are accessed during the misinformation phase as well as on memory tests; and forgetting variables can operate during the interval between exposure and misinformation and during the interval between misinformation and memory tests. This new complexity, in turn, leads to new opponent-processes predictions about false alarms and intrusions (Reyna, 1998; Reyna & Titcomb, 1997).

Storing Memories   In chapters 4 and 5, the basal opponent-processes predictions were (a) false-memory reports decrease as a function of manipulations that strengthen memory for the exact surface content of experience, relative to memory for its meaning content, and (b) false-memory reports increase as a function of manipulations that have the opposite effect. With the misinformation paradigm, however, both types of manipulations can operate during the misinformation phase as well as during the exposure phase. The predicted effects of such manipulations therefore turn on which verbatim and gist traces are being strengthened: traces that are stored during the exposure phase or traces that are stored during the misinformation phase?

First, consider manipulations whose predominant effect is to strengthen memory for the surface content of experience (e.g., verbatim repetition, increasing target-presentation duration, surface-processing instructions, perceptual distinctiveness, "remember" consolidation instructions). If such manipulations are executed during the exposure phase of a misinformation study, their effect would be the same as before—namely, to strengthen verbatim memory for *target* events—which should reduce false-memory responses. But if such manipulations are executed during the misinformation phase, their effect is both to strengthen verbatim memory for *mis-*

information events (i.e., erroneous memory suggestions, such as 7-Up can) *and* to strengthen verbatim memory for target events (i.e., correct memory suggestions, such as *Vogue* magazine). The first effect will elevate false-memory reports for events for which misinformation was presented because subjects' responses will more often be based upon the retrieval of verbatim traces of the misinformation events. For the same reason, manipulations that strengthen verbatim memory for misinformation events will decrease true-memory reports for the corresponding target events. On the other hand, the second effect (strengthening verbatim memory for correct memory suggestions) will have the same influences on memory performance as strengthening verbatim memory for original target events (i.e., true-memory reports of target events will increase while false-memory reports of competing distractor events will decrease).

With respect to the exposure phase, a number of verbatim-strengthening manipulations have been investigated, and they have generally had the expected effect of decreasing false memory for misinformation events. Prominent examples are target repetition (e.g., Mojardin, 1999), presentation duration (e.g., Belli et al., 1992; Toglia, Payne, & Anastasi, 1991), visual versus verbal presentation (e.g., Bowman & Zaragoza, 1989; Toglia et al., 1991), central versus peripheral targets (e.g., Belli et al., 1992; Cassel & Bjorklund, 1995), and determining whether target events can or cannot be recalled prior to misinformation (Belli, 1989, 1993; Loftus et al., 1978). The repetition, duration, and modality manipulations (and their effects) are familiar from earlier chapters and will only be briefly discussed here.

Concerning *repetition*, Mojardin (1999) reported a misinformation experiment in which some targets were presented once, some targets were presented twice, and both types of targets were subjected to later misinformation. Unlike most misinformation experiments, Mojardin's post-misinformation memory tests measured both correct recognition of targets and false recognition of misinformation. It was found that (a) misinformation lowered correct recognition of twice-presented targets less than it lowered correct acceptance of once-presented targets, and (b) misinformation increased false recognition of distractors more if the corresponding targets had been presented only once. Concerning *duration*, Belli et al. (1992) reported some misinformation experiments in which the target event was a series of slides depicting a mother and child arguing about a jar of spilled pennies. There were four types of critical objects in the slides that were subjected to subsequent misinformation: appliances (blender, coffee maker, toaster), clothing (dress, pants, shirt), playground equipment (monkey bars, slide, swings), and reading material (book, comics, magazine). Depending upon the experiment, the slides were shown at a 3- or 5-second rate, with the latter generally producing lower rates of false memory on recognition tests. Concerning *modality*, similar to the previously discussed work of Schacter and associates (Israel & Schacter, 1997; Schacter et al., 1999), the opponent-processes prediction would be that the memory-falsifying consequences of misinformation would be lessened if target events were presented visually rather than verbally. Clear findings on this prediction are not currently available, however, owing to the fact that the procedure in virtually all experiments has been visual presentation followed by verbal misinformation, for the excellent reason that the objective is to emulate police interviews of witnesses. To test this prediction, the ideal experiment would be a target modality × misinformation modality factorial design involving visual versus verbal presentation of targets *and* misinformation. We have been unable to locate full factorial designs of this sort in the literature. However, some investigators have presented targets and misinformation in the same modality, that is, targets and misinformation have *both* been presented visually or verbally (e.g., Bowman & Zaragoza, 1989; Toglia et al., 1991). Opponent-processes distinctions make no clear predictions in this situation because, on the one hand, visual targets ought to be *more* resistant to misinformation, but on the other hand, visual misinformation ought to be more suggestive (by creating stronger verbatim traces of misinformation than those created by verbal misinformation). However, clear predictions *are* possible if there is a substantial delay between target presentation and misinformation, and we shall consider relevant findings below in the section on forgetting.

The other two presentation-phase manipulations that we mentioned—central versus peripheral targets and determining whether targets can be recalled prior to the presentation of misinformation—have not been previously considered and therefore require some explanation. The logic of these manipulations is as follows. Concerning central versus peripheral targets, some objects and events are obviously more central to a story than others. For instance, in the original Loftus (1975) accident story, the make and color of the car (red Datsun) are central, whereas the types and positions of trees along the road are not. Consequently, various investigators have remarked (e.g., Belli et al., 1992; Bruck, Ceci, Francoeur, & Barr, 1995; Cassel & Bjorklund, 1995) that subjects are more likely to attend to central events than to peripheral ones. If so, the result should be stronger verbatim traces of central targets than of peripheral ones and greater resistance to misinformation. With respect to recall, we have noted in earlier chapters that recall tests usually produce lower levels of false-memory reports than do recognition tests, the ostensible reason being that recall enforces greater reliance on verbatim memory. If subjects are able to recall a certain target following the presentation phase, it therefore follows that there is a good chance that they have an accessible verbatim trace in storage. This, in turn should increase resistance to subsequent misinformation by increasing the chances that subjects will be able to perform recollection rejection (No, I couldn't have seen a 7-Up can because I definitely remember seeing a Coke can).

A demonstration of the effects of central versus peripheral targets was reported by Cassel and Bjorklund (1995). These authors developed a short video that depicts a teenage boy arguing with a younger girl in a public park. Ultimately, the boy takes the girl's bicycle away from her and leaves the park. To identify central versus peripheral information, the video was first shown to a sample of psychology faculty and graduate students, who rated the information in the video with respect to four levels of centrality to the story. The video was then shown to samples of experimental subjects. After a 15-minute interpolated activity, the subjects received an interview that was designed to simulate an initial investigative interview by a police officer. The interview consisted of a period of free recall (Tell me everything you can about the video), followed by cued-recall items (Tell me what the girl was wearing). One week later, the subjects were interviewed again. This interview consisted of a series of prepared *leading* questions, some of which provided misinformation (e.g., The bicycle frame was painted red, wasn't it?). This interview was repeated approximately 3 weeks later. Although we shall return to this study below, in the section on forgetting, two results are of interest here. First, during the initial interview, information that the expert raters had classified as most central to the story was recalled much better than information that the raters had classified as least central, suggesting that verbatim traces were more likely to be accessible in the former case. Second, during the second and third interviews, when leading questions were presented, subjects were less likely to accept a false leading question when it referred to events that had been classified as most central than when it referred to events that had been classified as least central.

An equally clear demonstration of the effects of target recall was presented by Belli (1993). Subjects were shown slide sequences that had been developed as part of earlier misinformation experiments. Later, verbal misinformation (a narrative) was presented, and a memory test (forced-choice recognition) was administered. However, a recall test for information in the slide sequence was also administered to gauge memory for target objects and events. When responses on the memory test were analyzed so as to compare performance on probes for which subjects were able to recall the corresponding targets versus probes for which subjects were unable to recall the corresponding targets, a strong negative relation was observed between recall and susceptibility to misinformation. As opponent-processes distinctions would predict, targets that could be recalled were far less susceptible to misinformation than targets that could not be. Other relevant data on the relation between target recall and susceptibility to misinformation can be found in an article by Loftus et al. (1978).

So far, the discussion of storage factors that influence misinformation effects has been confined to factors that operate during target presentation. As we have seen, the results have been such as to confirm the opponent-processes hypothesis that factors that ought to strengthen verbatim traces of targets will reduce misinformation effects. However, storage factors that strengthen verbatim traces of *misinformation* can operate during the misinformation phase, and the opponent-processes prediction is that such factors ought to enhance misinformation effects by increasing the chances that subjects will be able to access such traces (rather than verbatim traces of targets) on post-misinformation memory tests. Here, pertinent findings have been reported in an important series of experiments by Zaragoza and associates (Ackil & Zaragoza, 1998; Mitchell & Zaragoza, 1996; Zaragoza & Mitchell, 1996; Zaragoza et al., 2001).

An obvious manipulation, for which predictions are straightforward, is misinformation repetition: Other things being equal, repeating a memory suggestion (e.g., Remember the 7-Up can on the desk?) is more likely to result in verbatim traces of misinformation that are accessible when memory tests are administered, lowering correct recognition of misinformed targets and increasing false recognition of misinformation. This manipulation was studied by Mitchell and Zaragoza (1996) and by Zaragoza and Mitchell (1996). In the latter study, subjects first viewed a 5-minute police training film that depicted the burglary of a home and a subsequent police car chase. After viewing the film, the subjects responded to a questionnaire that presented misinformation about objects and events that were not in the video but were consistent with the gist of a robbery story (e.g., the thief wore gloves, the thief had

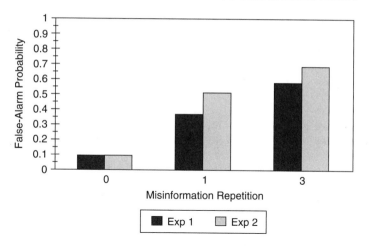

Figure 6-2. Effects of repeated memory suggestions on false memory for misinformation. Based upon two experiments reported by Zaragoza and Mitchell (1996).

a gun). Across the items on the questionnaire, there were three levels of repetition for each of the absent objects or events: zero, one, and three. Ten minutes after responding to the questionnaire, the subjects responded to a recognition test on which each probe presented a specific item of information (e.g., the thief wore gloves) and requested subjects to answer two questions (Do you remember the item from the video? Do you remember the item from the questionnaire?). Responses to the first question—specifically, instances in which subjects answered that items that had only been suggested in the questionnaire had appeared in the video—were used to measure false memory for misinformation. The overall results for the two experiments reported by Zaragoza and Mitchell are shown in Figure 6-2. Note two important outcomes. First, even a single suggestion produced a considerable jump in falsely reporting that the corresponding object or event had appeared in the video (relative to the no-suggestion control). Second, three suggestions produced a further jump (relative to a single suggestion).

Another manipulation studied by Zaragoza and associates, which should also strengthen verbatim traces of misinformation relative to verbatim traces of targets, is especially interesting because it resembles police interrogation techniques that prompt false confessions in criminal suspects (e.g., Kassin, 1997). The manipulation in question is called *forced confabulation*. The general design of forced-confabulation experiments is the same as other misinformation designs (e.g., target presentation, then misinformation, then memory tests), the only major difference being the manner in which the misinformation is delivered to subjects. In two experiments that Zaragoza et al. (2001) reported, the subjects first viewed an 8-minute excerpt from an action movie, which depicted dangerous events that are apt to cause bodily injury, such as a fight among some of the characters and an encounter with a venomous snake. Immediately thereafter, the subjects responded to 12 forced-choice questions, 8 of which were true and 4 of which were false. The latter questions suggested false events as being part of an event in the film clip (e.g., that one

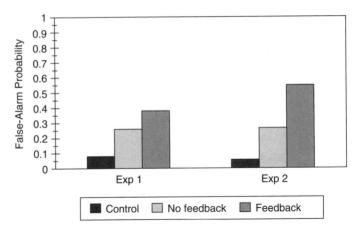

Figure 6-3. Effects of forced confabulation of physical details to support memory suggestions. Control subjects did not confabulate; no-feedback subjects confabulated, but their confabulations were not confirmed; and feedback subjects were told that their confabulations were correct. Based upon two experiments reported by Zaragoza, Payment, Ackil, Drivdahl, and Beck (2001).

of the characters had fallen off a chair, which had happened, and cut himself, which had not happened). Control subjects simply responded yes or no to such questions, but treatment subjects were required to confabulate physical details of the false event to support the memory suggestions (e.g., to state where the character had cut himself). The experimenter also provided confirming feedback for half of those confabulations (e.g., Yes, he was cut on the knee). One week later, the subjects responded to a memory-recognition test that included probes for target events, suggested false events, and confabulated supporting details. The key question is whether the treatment subjects developed false memories for the details that they had been previously required to confabulate. The relevant results, which are summarized in Figure 6-3, could not be clearer: Treatment subjects were much more likely than control subjects to falsely recognize confabulated details, and confirming feedback from the experimenter enhanced such memory falsification. Note that simply forcing subjects to confabulate, even though they neither remember nor believe the confabulation, has a large effect on *subsequent* false recognition, producing more than a threefold increase in false recognition. Note too that the effect of confirming subjects' confabulations, a procedure that is often followed in police interrogations of suspects, produces an equally large further increase in false recognition.

Summing up, the picture for storage factors is congruent with the types of opponent-processes predictions that have been discussed in earlier chapters. On the one hand, storage factors that ought to enhance the accessibility of verbatim traces of targets, relative to verbatim traces of misinformation, should reduce misinformation effects. They do. On the other hand, storage factors that ought to enhance the accessibility of verbatim traces of misinformation, relative to verbatim traces of targets, should increase misinformation effects. They do. In the latter connection, it is interesting to observe that misinformation that is provided by subjects themselves (confabulation) yields false-memory reports, just like misinformation that is provided by the experimenter. This is an instructive datum because common sense would suggest that information that is provided by the experimenter would be regarded as more authoritative by subjects and that they might therefore be unaffected by misinformation that they generate on their own.

Retrieving Memories   Historically, the study of how retrieval factors contribute to the effects of memory suggestion has been an especially vigorous topic of research. The high level of interest in retrieval factors can be traced to an early debate over whether or not memory suggestions alter the original stored representations of targets (e.g., Belli, 1989; Loftus & Hoffman, 1989; McCloskey & Zaragoza, 1985). Although this debate has receded in prominence since the advent of opponent-processes models of suggestion (e.g., Reyna, 1995; Reyna & Titcomb, 1997), it left behind a rich legacy of experimental findings that bear on the predictions of such models. Indeed, it was a retrieval manipulation, the *standard versus modified test manipulation*, that generated the most heated of all controversies about misinformation, a controversy over whether the memory-falsifying consequences of suggestion are real or chimerical. We consider this controversy first and then examine the effects of some other manipulations that ought to influence whether subjects retrieve verbatim traces of targets, verbatim traces of misinformation, or gist traces on memory tests.

Recall that in early misinformation experiments, such as Loftus (1975) and Loftus and Palmer (1974), false memory was measured by multiple-choice probes that pitted original target events against corresponding misinformation (e.g., stop sign versus yield sign). The fact that misinformation increased errors on such standard tests had been interpreted as showing that memory for the original information had been destroyed (e.g., overwritten) by misinformation (Loftus & Loftus, 1980). However, McCloskey and Zaragoza (1985) pointed out that such an interpretation was far from ineluctable. They remarked that because the alternative to the target item is the misinformation item in the standard test, the fact that misinformation increases the tendency to choose the latter item might simply reflect a retrieval bias (toward misinformation) rather than destruction or alteration of original target memories. To decide the issue, McCloskey and Zaragoza proposed that a modified test was needed in which the alternative choice was a distractor from the same general category of things as the target but that had not been presented as misinformation (e.g., stop sign versus railroad sign). They reported data from misinformation experiments in which subjects' performance on standard and modified tests was compared following misinformation. They found that, on the one hand, standard tests yielded misinformation effects, which was merely a replication of prior experiments, but that, on the other hand, there was no evidence of misinformation effects on modified tests. They concluded that the increases in recognition errors that are produced by misinformation are a matter of retrieval bias rather than actual memory distortion.

Opponent-processes distinctions reveal that McCloskey and Zaragoza's (1985) conclusion does not necessarily follow. The failure of misinformation to increase errors is merely a null result, and null results are not amenable to straightforward interpretation. Further, the earlier opponent-processes account of misinformation leads to differential predictions about standard and modified tests. According to this account, two features are present in these tests that support false-memory responses, with standard tests possessing both features and modified tests possessing only one. Remember here that misinformation strengthens memory for the gist of experience (e.g., traffic sign, soft drink) and adds verbatim traces of false items (e.g., yield sign, 7-Up can). On standard tests, both choices match strengthened gist; one matches verbatim traces of targets; and one matches verbatim traces of misinformation. On modified tests, both choices match strengthened gist; one matches verbatim traces of targets; and neither matches verbatim traces of misinformation. Therefore, when it comes to representations that support false-memory responses, standard tests cue retrieval of both gist traces and verbatim traces of misinformation, but modified tests only cue retrieval of the former. Thus, the obvious opponent-processes prediction is that both types of tests will yield misinformation effects (when the performances of control and treatment subjects are compared), but misinformation effects will be larger on standard tests. This pattern, rather than McCloskey and Zaragoza's (1985) null finding, has been obtained in several subsequent experiments (e.g., Belli et al., 1992; Ceci, Ross, & Toglia, 1987; Chandler, 1989, 1991).

Forgetting Memories

The basal design of a misinformation experiment is:

$$\text{Target Presentation} \xrightarrow{\quad A \quad} \text{Misinformation} \xrightarrow{\quad B \quad} \text{Memory Tests}$$

The two arrows are time intervals during which forgetting may occur if sufficient time passes. Obviously, the length of either interval could vary considerably in criminal investigation and could be manipulated systematically in experimentation. Importantly, opponent-processes distinctions make contrasting predictions about how the memory-falsifying properties of suggestion should vary as a function of the lengths of these intervals. Consider Interval A first. The key consideration here is the differential accessibility rule from chapter 3. If verbatim traces of targets become rapidly inaccessible as time passes, relative to the gist of experience, lengthening Interval A ought to reduce subjects' ability to retrieve those traces and perform recollection rejection when memory suggestions are presented during the misinformation phase. The effects of those suggestions should therefore be enhanced, which ought to increase the spread between the rates of memory error in control versus misinformation subjects (Reyna, 1995). Next, consider Interval B. Again, owing to the differential accessibility rule, the chief consequence of lengthening this interval will be to decrease the accessibility of verbatim traces, relative to gist traces. Now, however, both verbatim traces of targets *and* verbatim traces of misinformation are undergoing increased forgetting. Consequently, according to opponent-processes assumptions, this manipulation, by itself, would be expected to enhance the power of memory suggestion: Although decreased accessibility of verbatim traces of targets would tend to increase the power of memory suggestion, de-

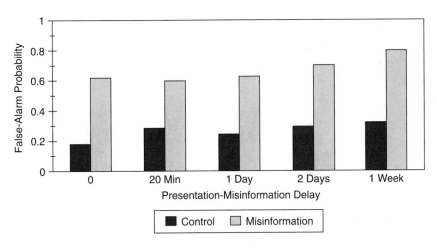

Figure 6-4. Effects on memory suggestion of lengthening the interval between target presentation and misinformation. Extrapolated from Loftus et al. (1978).

creased accessibility of verbatim traces of misinformation would tend to decrease the power of memory suggestion.

Ideally, these opponent-processes predictions should be evaluated in A × B misinformation experiments in which two or more levels of Interval A are factorially combined with two or more levels of Interval B. In early experiments, all three steps in the basal misinformation design were executed during a single experimental session, usually within a few minutes of each other (e.g., Loftus, 1975; Loftus & Palmer, 1974). Subsequently, however, experiments have been reported in which two or more levels of Interval A have been used, and other experiments have been reported in which two or more levels of Interval B have been used. Unfortunately, we have been unable to locate systematic factorial experiments in the adult literature in which both intervals have been varied in the same experiment. We therefore restrict attention to two examples of experiments in which Interval A was manipulated (Loftus et al., 1978; Belli et al., 1992) and two examples of experiments in which Interval B was manipulated (Zaragoza & Mitchell, 1996; Zaragoza et al., 2001).

An early experiment by Loftus et al. (1978) provided some preliminary data on the effects of lengthening the presentation-to-misinformation interval. These authors replicated the basic elements of Loftus's (1975) original methodology (i.e., presentation of the slide show about the pedestrian accident, followed by the questionnaire containing misinformation, followed by the standard recognition test). However, Loftus et al.'s subjects each participated in one of five delay conditions: (a) no delay, (b) 20-minute delay, (c) 1-day delay, (d) 2-day delay, and (e) 1-week delay. The results with respect to the hypothesis that the spread between the error rates of control versus misinformed subjects ought to increase with delay were mixed. The false-alarm probabilities of the two conditions are plotted as a function of presentation-to-misinformation delay in Figure 6-4. It is apparent that there was no consistent pattern of increasing separation between the conditions with increasing delay. Although the false-alarm rate was always considerably higher in the misin-

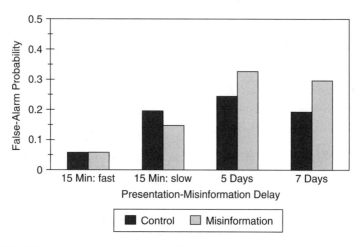

Figure 6-5. Effects on memory suggestion of lengthening the interval between target presentation and misinformation. Based upon four experiments reported by Belli, Windschitl, McCarthy, and Winfrey (1992).

formation condition (i.e., there was a robust misinformation effect), the control-versus-misinformation spread in the no-delay condition was virtually the same as in the 1-week delay condition. On the other hand, two other features of the data were supportive of the hypothesis. First, note that between the 1-day and 1-week delays, there was a clear increase in the control-versus-misinformation spread. Second, if false alarms in the no-delay and 20-minute delay conditions are pooled, on the ground that presentation and misinformation occur in the same session in these conditions but in different sessions in the other conditions, there is again a clear increase in the control-versus-misinformation spread with increasing delay (from .37 to .48).

Although Loftus et al.'s (1978) results were mixed, subsequent experiments have provided more consistent support for the notion that misinformation effects increase as the presentation-to-misinformation interval is lengthened (Titcomb & Reyna, 1995). A case in point can be found in a series of experiments by Belli et al. (1992). These authors reported four misinformation experiments using the procedure that was described above. In two of the experiments, the narrative that contained misinformation was administered during the same session as the slide show about a mother and child arguing over a jar of spilled pennies. In both of those experiments, the memory tests were administered 15 minutes after the slide show, the difference being that the slides had been presented at a slower rate in one of the experiments. In the other two experiments, misinformation was delayed until a subsequent session, which occurred either 5 days or 7 days after the slide show. Modified tests were administered 10 minutes after narrative presentation in all experiments. The results are shown in Figure 6-5, where the probability of false alarms on modified tests has been plotted for control and misinformation subjects as a function of delay. There is clear support for the hypothesis that the control-versus-misinformation spread increases when memory suggestions are delayed. On the one hand, there was no misinformation effect in either of the experiments in which misinformation was administered in the same session as target presentation. On the other hand, misinformed

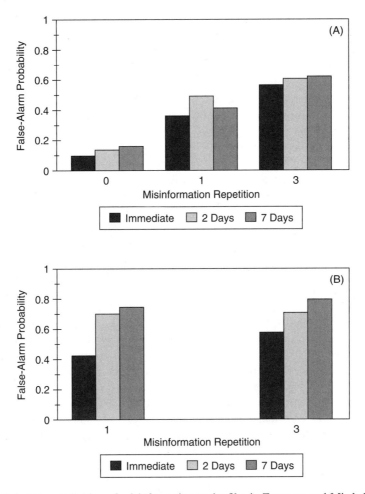

Figure 6-6. False attribution of misinformation to the film in Zaragoza and Mitchell's (1996) experiments, with false alarms plotted as a function of misinformation repetition and the misinformation-to-memory-test interval. Panel A is based upon Zaragoza and Mitchell's first experiment, while Panel B is based upon their second experiment.

subjects exhibited higher false-alarm rates than control subjects in both of the experiments in which misinformation occurred a few days after target presentation.

Turning to findings on Interval B (the misinformation-to-memory test interval), recall that the opponent-processes prediction is that lengthening this interval should not have the simple directional effect that lengthening Interval A has because verbatim traces of both targets and misinformation are becoming inaccessible, relative to memory for the gist of events. Here, the previously discussed misinformation-repetition studies of Zaragoza and Mitchell (1996) provide illustrative evidence. In these experiments, misinformation was always presented during the same session as the police training film depicting a burglary. However, the memory tests were either administered immediately thereafter or were delayed for 2 days or 7 days. The results are shown in Figure 6-6, where the false-alarm probability (attributing misinformation events to the film) for each of the repetition conditions is plotted as a function of the misinformation-to-memory test interval. The results for Zaragoza and Mitchell's first experiment are shown in Figure 6-6a, while those for their second experiment are shown in Figure 6-6b. (In the latter experiment, Zaragoza and Mitchell did not report the performance for zero misinformation items, so that only data for one and three repetitions are plotted.) It is apparent at a glance that there was no tendency for the spread between the false-alarm rates for items receiving different repetitions of misinformation to increase as the misinformation-to-memory test interval was increased. The dominant pattern in these experiments, as the differential-forgetting rule would predict, was simply for false-alarm rates for all types of items to increase as this interval was lengthened, but not for false-alarm rates to increase differentially as a function of misinformation.

In brief, available data indicate that imposing delays in Loftus's (1975) basic target-presentation-to-misinformation-to-memory-tests design influences the power of suggestion to falsify the contents of subjects' memories. However, the data also indicate that those influences depend upon where delays are imposed. Inspection of Figures 6-4, 6-5, and 6-6 reveals a consistent tendency for false-alarm rates to drift upward as time goes by, which is what one would forecast on the ground that verbatim traces of the surface content of experience are becoming inaccessible more rapidly than are the gist traces of its meaning. (This is similar to the delay effects that were discussed in chapters 4 and 5, although we saw there that if delay is manipulated through a sufficiently broad range of values, opponent-processes distinctions predict an inverted-U relation with false-alarm and intrusion rates.) The question to which principal interest attaches, however, is whether the upward drift is greater when subjects receive misinformation than when they do not, so that the control-versus-misinformation spread increases over time. So far, the answer seems to be yes when the presentation-to-misinformation interval is lengthened but not when the misinformation-to-memory-test interval is lengthened.

Extreme Memory Suggestion Effects: False Confession

Now, we turn to a phenomenon that represents the outer extremity of the pernicious consequences of memory suggestion in criminal cases. As previously discussed, experimental studies of the misinformation paradigm indicate that postevent memory suggestions can impair the contents of witnesses' memory reports in two basic ways: by lowering their ability to recognize or recall actual events and by elevating their tendency to recognize or recall misinformation as though it were actual experience. Suppose, however, that a witness is a suspect in a criminal investigation. In this special circumstance, suggestions that foment false-memory reports may create false confessions, if those reports refer to self-incriminating events. Although false-memory reports by witnesses may cause innocent people to be charged and convicted, the probability that self-incriminating false-memory reports will have such consequences is much higher because triers of fact regard confessions as particularly probative evidence of guilt (Kassin, 1997). Indeed, this latter fact is responsible for the strong emphasis that police interviewing practices place on obtaining confessions (Inbau et al., 2001).

Our consideration of false-confession research is in two parts. In the first sub-section, we sketch two criminal cases that illustrate key points that are at issue in false-confession evidence. In the second subsection, we summarize information from the scientific literature on false confession. It might be thought that suspects, as op-posed to witnesses, would be utterly resistant to self-incriminating memory sug-gestions because, after all, there are conspicuous negative consequences for accepting them. We shall see that, remarkably, this is not the case.

The Case of Mr. K

In this case, the defendant was an engineer who was employed by a defense con-tractor and was the father of 9- and 11-year-old sons. On a Monday morning, one of Mr. K's neighbors, Mrs. L, telephoned the local police station with a sexual abuse complaint involving her 9-year-old son. The substance of the complaint was that Mr. K had sexually fondled the child on the previous evening, while the child was visiting Mr. K's home at the invitation of his sons. Mrs. L's son reported that he, Mr. K's sons, and Mr. K were lounging on a couch bed that evening, watching videos. Her son further reported that Mr. K fell asleep early in the evening and that he himself fell asleep later on, though he thought that Mr. K's sons remained awake throughout the evening. Eventually, the report continued, Mrs. L's son awoke from a bad dream to discover that Mr. K was fondling his penis. The boy stated that he yelled, "Get your paws off my weenie," in a loud voice, whereupon Mr. K with-drew his hand and went to his bedroom. According to Mrs. L's son, he and the other boys then went to sleep on the couch bed.

Police investigators were dispatched to Mrs. L's son's school to interview him about his complaint. After the boy confirmed the statements that he had made to his mother, the investigators removed Mr. K's sons from their classes and inter-viewed them about the events of the previous evening. Both boys confirmed that Mrs. L's son had slept at their home on the previous evening, but neither could remember seeing or hearing any of the events associated with the alleged fondling. The investigators then proceeded to Mr. K's house to interview his wife, who also reported no knowledge of the events complained of by Mrs. L's son. They did learn, however, that Mr. K was a heavy drinker, who was in a state of moderate intoxication during most evenings, who had been encouraged to seek medical treat-ment for his drinking problem, and who had been drinking on the previous evening. A call was then placed to Mr. K's office, requesting that he stop at the police sta-tion for an interview on his way home from work. He complied and was inter-viewed that evening by the same investigators. He vigorously denied the fondling allegation, calling the complaint nauseating and morally repugnant, and stated that the boy had probably had a bad dream. Before closing the case for lack of evi-dence, the investigators initiated an overnight check to determine if Mr. K had a police record. Upon arrival at the police station the next morning, the investiga-tors discovered that the check had revealed a single item: Four years earlier, when Mr. K was serving as den master of a Cub Scout troop, the parents of one boy had reported to the police that Mr. K had fondled the boy's buttocks. The inves-tigators concluded that Mr. K was a possible pedophile who should be interviewed further.

At 9 p.m. that evening, the investigators arrived at Mr. K's home and asked him to accompany them to the police station for a "routine interview" to "clear up a few loose ends." Mr. K had evidently been drinking. He smelled strongly of alcohol, and his voice and demeanor were quite different than during his previous interview. At the police station, the investigators placed Mr. K in a sparsely furnished interrogation room, asked him to read a sheet of paper containing a Miranda warning, asked him if he understood the warning, and then informed him that things would be far better for him if he waived his rights and agreed to be interviewed. Mr. K agreed to be interviewed. He was then subjected to a high-pressure interrogation, using techniques like those described in the earlier case of Ms. W. Initially, Mr. K was accused of being a secret pedophile who had molested boys when he was a Cub Scout den master. He vigorously denied such accusations, and he vigorously denied the further suggestion that he had molested Mrs. L's son. The investigators then switched to questioning Mr. K about his drinking, suggesting that he was often so intoxicated that his memory was hazy the next morning. After Mr. K had agreed to this, it was further suggested that he had been quite drunk on Sunday evening, and to stimulate agreement, the investigators stated that they had been told this by his wife. After Mr. K agreed to having been intoxicated, the interviewers suggested that he had molested the boy unknowingly while in this state. When Mr. K denied that this was even conceivable, he was bombarded with statements such as:

"You're lying. You can't possibly know that."

"Come on. Your memory's so foggy you can't even remember what movie you were watching, can you?"

"When you were that drunk, how can you rule that out?"

"No one could possibly know what they did if they were that loaded."

"You already said you can't remember most of Sunday night. So, how can you ask us to believe you remember that so well?"

In response to these repeated and seemingly unassailable challenges to his denials, Mr. K eventually made the following statements:

"Well, I suppose I can't be 100% sure that it didn't happen."

"I was so blotto that maybe I can't rule it out completely, but I sure don't think anything like that could happen."

"Yeah, the boy hadn't been drinking and I had been, so I suppose his memory of Sunday night would have to be clearer than mine."

Once such statements had been obtained, the interview was terminated, and Mr. K was charged with having molested Mrs. L's son. At trial, the prosecutor stated during his opening argument to the jury that they would hear Mr. K confess to child molestation in his own words. Later, an audiotape of Mr. K's second interview was played for the jury during the testimony of one of his interrogators. The prosecuting attorney drew attention to each of the preceding statements, representing them as a confession that confirmed the testimony of Mrs. L's son. The crucial point for readers of this book is that most of you, particularly after reading prior chapters, would not regard such statements as constituting a confession of guilt. Rather, you would probably say that Mr. K's agreement with the initial questions in a suggestive line of interrogation had placed him in a logic trap in which he was unable to deny with certainty that he had molested the boy. Nevertheless, the fact that he did not categorically deny the allegation in response to multiple questions is self-incriminating and, indeed, can be represented to triers of fact as a confession of guilt. The jury in Mr. K's case saw it in exactly this light. They convicted him, and during post-trial interviews, they cited his failure to thoroughly and consistently deny the charge against him as a confession that sought to minimize personal responsibility for his actions.

The Case of Mr. E

At 2 a.m. on a Sunday morning, Mr. E, a moderately retarded man with an infant son, placed a 911 call, requesting emergency assistance for his son, who had stopped breathing. Upon arrival at Mr. E's home, paramedics made unsuccessful attempts to resuscitate the infant, and he was pronounced dead. The paramedics noted a bruise on the back of the infant's skull. Two police officers arrived shortly thereafter, one of whom had been Mr. E's coach when he played Little League baseball as a child. The officers interviewed Mr. E, who provided the following information.

Mr. E, his wife, and their infant had been attending a family reunion a few miles from their home on Saturday. Mr. E was very tired because he had not slept on the previous two evenings, the reason being a change from the day shift to the night shift at his place of employment. At 8 p.m., he asked his wife if they might return home so that he could sleep. When they arrived home, Mrs. E stated that she wished to return to the reunion, and asked if Mr. E would be willing to sleep on a couch next to their infant's crib. After Mr. E agreed, she placed the infant in the crib and left for the reunion. Mr. E immediately went to sleep, but he was awakened at 11 p.m. by the infant, who was crying loudly. He picked up the infant, intending to walk with him and soothe him until he went sleep again. However, Mr. E was still very drowsy, and he tripped, the infant falling from his arms and striking the back of his head on the sharp edge of a coffee table. The baby whimpered after striking his head, but did not cry loudly, and soon fell asleep. Mr. E returned to the couch and fell asleep again. Shortly before 2 a.m., he was awakened by a loud noise and decided to check his son. He was shocked to discover that the infant was not breathing and that the baby's skin had begun to turn blue. He then placed the 911 call.

Throughout this interview, which terminated at 4:30 a.m., Mr. E was distraught and weeping over the death of his son. At 6 a.m., an autopsy was performed on the infant. The medical examiner who conducted the autopsy reported to the police officers that the skull below the bruise was broken and that the infant had died from collateral brain damage. It was decided to interrogate Mr. E, who had now been sleep-deprived for 3 days, to determine if he had murdered his son. To charge a suspect with murder, it is normally necessary to produce evidence of method, motive, and opportunity. Although the first and last items were obviously present, there was nothing to suggest a motive. The police officers hypothesized that Mr. E might have been violently angry with his wife for returning to the reunion, rather than taking charge of child care so that Mr. E could sleep, and that Mr. E intentionally battered the infant to punish his wife.

The second interview, which was conducted at the local police station by the officer who had been Mr. E's Little League coach, began with questions on this point. As in the case of Mr. K, Mr. E's second interview began with a request that he read the Miranda warning, followed by statements from the police officer to the effect that he would be treated more leniently if he agreed to be interviewed, which he did. At the start of the interview, Mr. E repeatedly denied that he had been even moderately upset at anyone when he returned home. The officer then dropped this line of questioning, moved on to a series of more innocuous questions about Mr. and Mrs. E's respective jobs, but eventually returned to the topic: "Everyone knows you were dead tired last night. You'd been working hard for your family and hadn't slept since Wednesday. Everyone, you and me both, are grouchy when they're that wiped out."

Mr. E replied: "Well, yeah."

The officer then dropped this line of questioning again and returned to innocuous questions for a few minutes. He then returned to the topic, and the following series of questions and answers ensued:

"And you said a while ago that you were pretty grouchy when you got home last night."

"Yeah."

"Pretty mad at her for dumping you with the baby."

"Grouchy, but not really mad."

This line of questioning was then dropped again while the officer recounted some gruesome details of the infant's skull and brain injuries. Mr. E became agitated by these details, and tears formed, which were followed by this sequence of questions and answers:

"And it was her damned fault that this happened, wasn't it?"

"Yeah."

"She should've stayed home instead of leaving her baby with someone who could hardly stand up any more."

"Yeah."

"And you had every right to be furious with her, didn't you?"

"Sure did."

"And you were really ticked off at her when she walked out that door."

"I guess."

"You were such a nice guy about it. Most other guys would have socked her one."

"Probably."

"You were mad enough to sock her but just too nice to do it."

"Yeah."

Now that motive was established, the questioning moved along to other lines, particularly to requests that Mr. E retell the details of how he accidentally dropped the infant. When the story reached the point at which Mr. E tripped and the infant struck his head, the officer said:

> "I thought that might be true this morning, but I absolutely know it isn't now. They did an autopsy on your baby. Cut his poor little head completely open to see what went down. Doctors can find that out just by looking at the brain. The doctor said "no way" to the coffee table. The force that produced that baby's injuries was huge. The doctor said it was at least equal to falling off a four-story building."

These were lies. The medical examiner had simply described the nature of the injuries and the cause of death. When Mr. E reaffirmed that the events happened exactly as he reported, the officer stated:

> "Now I know you're lying, not just not remembering right, because I told you what you're saying is a medical impossibility. If the prosecutor thinks you're lying, he'll throw the book at you. That means the death penalty. And remember that God knows you're lying too. You may get away with lying to me, but you know you'll have to answer to him by and by."

Mr. E began sobbing after this statement, which was followed by this exchange:

> "I want to help you so the prosecutor doesn't throw the book at you and ask for the death penalty, but you gotta tell me the truth about how you hurt him."
>
> [*No response. Continued sobbing.*]
>
> "I know what you must have done to him. You were so ticked at her when the baby woke up that you grabbed him and threw him on the floor. Really slammed him a good one."
>
> "I guess so."
>
> "And you did more than that, didn't you? Because, remember, it's gotta be like a four-story fall."
>
> [*No response. Continued sobbing.*]
>
> "I think you grabbed that little guy by the leg and blasted his head on the floor. Swung him like a sledge hammer."
>
> "Swung him."

"And more than that. You were so ticked off that you didn't just put him back in the crib. You threw him at the crib and he banged his head a good one on the wall, which is why we found blood stains there." [No blood stains were found.]

"Yeah, banged his head."

The interview was terminated a short while later; Mr. E was charged with first-degree murder, and then he was transported to a jail cell. As he was taken to his cell, he complained to the attendant that the interviewer had put words into his mouth and that he had not harmed his son, which the attendant duly reported. Nevertheless, based upon his confession of motive and specific acts of injury, Mr. E was tried for the first-degree murder of his son. During opening arguments, the prosecuting attorney told the jury that they would hear Mr. E confess to savage acts of brutality to his infant son. Later, as part of the prosecution's case, an audiotape of Mr. E's second interview was played for the jury. When the medical examiner who conducted the autopsy testified, he opined that Mr. E's confessed acts of brutality were not consistent with the damage to the infant's skull. He opined, more specifically, that the skull break was consistent with impact from a sharp surface but not with impact from a flat surface, such as a floor or wall. A forensic pathologist whom the defense retained as an expert witness agreed that the skull break would most probably have been caused by a sharp rather than a flat surface.

The jury members, in their verdict, refused to convict Mr. E of first-degree murder, but they also refused to acquit him. Instead, they convicted him of manslaughter and negligence. In post-trial interviews, the jurors stated that they could not return a first-degree murder conviction because the testimony of the medical experts showed that the specific acts to which Mr. E had confessed could not have caused the injuries, because the tape recording of the second interview revealed that Mr. E's admissions to these acts were coerced, and because other evidence presented by the defense also demonstrated that Mr. E's admissions were coerced. On the other hand, the jurors stated that they could not fully exonerate Mr. E because the fact that he had confessed to such savagery left no doubt in their minds that the infant's death was not accidental and that he had done something to the baby. As substantiation for this latter opinion, they made reference to Mr. E's admissions that he had been violently angry with his wife for leaving him alone to care for the infant, notwithstanding their conclusion that he had been subjected to coercion.

The Scientific Study of False Confession

The phenomenon of suspects who make false self-incriminating statements is well established in the literatures of psychology and criminology. Münsterberg (1908) documented some early examples. More recently, Gudjonsson (1992); Parloff (1993); Radelet, Bedeau, and Putnam (1993); Ofshe and Watters (1994); and others have provided examples of modern cases, with particular emphasis on the use of confession evidence in capital crimes. However, if the study of false confessions is to move from anecdote to scientific analysis and if the role of false memory in false confession is to be understood, it is first essential to formulate a taxonomy of the basic varieties of false confession, much like we did for false-memory phenomena in chapter 3. That work has been undertaken by Kassin and his associates (e.g., Kassin, 1997; Kassin & Sukel, 1997; Kassin & Wrightsman, 1981, 1985).

Kassin and Wrightsman (1985) surveyed documented cases of false confession that were available in the early 1980s, as well as historical anecdotes about the phenomenon. They concluded that meaningful distinctions could be drawn among three types of false confession: *voluntary, coerced-compliant,* and *coerced-internalized.* The last two types are pursuant to memory suggestion and are therefore of greatest interest to us, whereas the first is not. During the intervening years, this taxonomy has become widely accepted by researchers. Below, we explicate the three components of the taxonomy. As it happens, the second and third types of false confessions differentiate between suggestion effects that do and do not result in false memories of self-incriminating events. Consequently, we explore these two components of the taxonomy in greater detail.

Voluntary   False confessions of this ilk are ones that, to the best of our knowledge, were not elicited by suggestive interviewing tactics. In fact, voluntary false confessions may occur *prior* to an interview by police investigators—even prior to the police being notified that a crime has been committed. For instance, suspects may make self-incriminating statements to relatives or friends, who then report those statements to law enforcement personnel. Alternatively, suspects may place telephone calls to the police for the purpose of confessing to crimes, or they may mail written statements of confession to the police. Highly publicized crimes involving prominent people—such as movie actors, television personalities, sports figures, or politicians—are notorious for stimulating voluntary false confessions. In one of the most famous kidnapping cases in the United States—the abduction and murder of the infant son of Charles Lindbergh—more than 200 people voluntarily confessed (Note, 1953). Mental illness, including delusional states, is routinely cited as a reason for voluntary false confessions (Kassin, 1997). Sane individuals who make such confessions sometimes state that they simply craved attention (Wrightsman & Kassin, 1993). Others state that they wished to impress their friends or that they falsely incriminated themselves to cover up other acts that they regarded as more serious (Radelet et al., 1992). Finally, Gudjonsson (1992) found that juvenile suspects, in particular, are prone to altruistic false confessions in which they incriminate themselves to protect friends or relatives. Regardless of the precise reasons behind a voluntary false confession, memory suggestion is not an issue, though false memories may often be present in delusional false confessors.

Coerced-Compliant   False confessions of this type are ones that (a) are elicited by suggestive interviewing tactics but that (b) are not founded upon false memories of criminal acts. In such cases, suspects make self-incriminating statements during the course of police interviews and often sign written confession statements. However, such suspects have no memory of the crimes and do not believe that they committed the acts that are described in their statements. Research has shown that coerced-compliant confessions typically occur for one or more of the following five reasons.

The first is deprivation of primary biological needs. The suspect may be interrogated in a state of sleep deprivation (e.g., Mr. E), or food may be withheld from the suspect, or the suspect may not be permitted to urinate or defecate as the need arises (perhaps to the point of causing involuntary bladder or bowel releases). Under such conditions, suspects may confess merely to relieve the pain and discomfort of continuing deprivation. Second, the suspect may be interviewed during a state of alcohol or drug intoxication (e.g., Mr. K). Intoxicated suspects may falsely confess because they are unable to judge the consequences of their actions. Third, false self-incriminating statements may be stimulated by threats of punishment. That is, suspects may decide to agree with interviewers' suggestions because they are told that disagreement will lead to even more serious consequences. In the case of Mr. E, for example, recall that he was told that prosecutors would throw the book at him if he did not admit to injuring his son. Fourth, false self-incriminating statements may be stimulated by the opposite proposal: promises of leniency. That is, suspects may accept interviewers' suggestions because they are told that they will be released if they do so or that they will only be charged with minor offenses. Fifth, a permissible police interviewing tactic is to lie to suspects about the strength of the evidence against them. To illustrate, interviewers may state that suspects' fingerprints or DNA were found at the crime scene, that suspects have been positively identified by witnesses, or that suspects have failed infallible polygraph tests. The false medical evidence that was given to Mr. E is a classic example of this tactic. When confronted by false evidence that seems unimpeachable, suspects may falsely confess because they believe that this is their only chance to secure more lenient treatment or because they judge that this evidence is more trustworthy than their own memories.

Coerced-compliant confessions are staples of movie and television plots, and there are many documented instances of such confessions in the scientific literature (e.g., Gudjonsson & MacKeith, 1990). A rich trove of recent examples that was uncovered by three *Chicago Tribune* reporters provides evidence of the potential scope of this phenomenon (Armstrong, Milles, & Possley, 2001). These reporters conducted a review of court records of murder cases dating back to 1991. Their review was prompted by the fact that in Cook County, Illinois, where the city of Chicago is located, police procedures strongly emphasize securing confessions from suspects, and by the additional fact that murder cases were regularly brought to trial in which there was neither physical evidence nor eyewitness identifications—only confession statements. Armstrong et al. identified 247 murder cases in which police interviewers had obtained self-incriminating statements from defendants, and in which the statements were either thrown out by judges as being transparently false or tainted or the statements had failed to produce convictions because juries interpreted them in a similar light. As examples of transparent falsity, the 247 cases included confessions from suspects who were in jail when the target crimes occurred, confessions that were refuted by DNA evidence, and confessions that were refuted by other physical evidence. In the latter connection, a suspect confessed to shooting at point-blank range a victim who was known to have been shot from across the street; another suspect confessed to shooting from across the street a victim who was known to have been shot at point-blank range; and another suspect confessed to stabbing a victim to death when there were no knife wounds on the victim's body. All of these statements are unambiguous examples of coerced-compliant confessions because, in each instance, the suspect recanted and stated that he had made self-incriminating statements for one or more of the reasons cited above. Many of the confessions reviewed by Armstrong et al. were obtained from mildly or moderately retarded individuals or from juveniles.

One of the most dramatic examples discussed was that of Mr. Sang Kim. Before being released, Kim spent more than 3 years in jail awaiting trial for murdering a fetus. He was charged with inflicting blunt trauma to the abdomen of his pregnant girlfriend, kicking and pushing her with such force that she went into premature labor and delivered an infant who died shortly after birth. Kim signed a confession statement after a marathon interrogation lasting more than 30 hours. He subsequently stated that during the interrogation, he was repeatedly lied to about the nature of the evidence that would be brought against him and was threatened with more severe punishment if he did not confess. Kim stated that he was also told that he could go home immediately if he confessed but that otherwise he could expect a 40–50-year jail term. Eventually, he signed a seven-and-a-half-page statement that had been handwritten by the prosecuting attorney. Curiously, the body of the statement contained no mention of the death of the infant, but the first page of the statement indicated that the charge was "battery and death" of "Elizabeth Xiong and child." Kim, who maintained his innocence throughout and retracted this statement shortly after signing it, stated that the phrases "and death" and "and child" were inserted after he signed the statement. However, Kim was jailed and told that the prosecutor would seek the death penalty. He was only freed when his former girlfriend stated that she had lied and that Kim had not assaulted her. Interestingly, the autopsy that had been conducted at the time of Kim's arrest revealed no evidence of traumatic injuries that could have led to either premature labor or to the infant's death, consistent with Kim's version of events.

It should not be thought that false confessions in the coerced-compliant vein are unique to criminal investigations in Chicago. There are many contemporary examples from other jurisdictions. A prominent one is the 1989 "Central Park jogger" case in New York City. The victim was an investment banker who, according to the indictments in the case, had been gang raped and beaten by a group of Hispanic and African-American youths. The defendants were convicted on the basis of confession statements that were obtained during police interrogations, despite the fact that DNA tests of semen samples taken from the victim did not match any of the defendants. Their convictions were appealed, and during the course of the appeal process, evidence that exonerated the youths was produced in the form of a confession by a man who had recently been convicted of rape and murder. This individual stated that he alone had beaten and raped the victim. He also provided DNA samples that, when tested, matched the DNA in the semen samples from the victim (Ryan, 1989). At the opposite end of the country, the Michael Crowe case is a further prominent example of a false coerced-compliant confession. In this case, a 14-year-old confessed during a police interrogation to murdering his sister, but the confession was ruled inadmissible when DNA evidence implicated another person in the murder (Sauer, 2002).

Coerced-Internalized   The last variety of false confession is the most intriguing of all, and it is the one that makes the most intimate contact with research on false memory. Here, suspects make self-incriminating statements that are disproved by other evidence, but they remember the events in these statements as actual occurrences. In the case of Mr. E, for example, this defendant underwent a lengthy pretrial forensic interview that included a series of memory tests administered by a memory researcher. During the course of the interview, Mr. E was questioned as to his memory for the injurious acts that had been suggested by his police interviewer, which Mr. E had admitted to having committed. It will be remembered that Mr. E later recanted and that the medical evidence was inconsistent with the acts to which he had confessed. Mr. E stated in response to the researcher's questioning that although he was sure that he could not have done such terrible things, some of the events seemed quite real to him, both at the time of the police interrogation and at the time of the forensic interview. This was particularly true of the alleged motive for the crime: being very angry toward his wife for leaving him alone with the infant when he was in a state of sleep deprivation. He further stated that at the time of the interrogation, he thought that the police interviewer's knowledge of events must be far more accurate than his own memory and that, even now, he would be inclined to believe that some of the acts of brutality happened if it were not for the fact that he knew himself to be incapable of such savagery. The case of Mr. E also illustrates that the boundary between coerced-compliant confessions and coerced-internalized ones can become blurred. Although Mr. E recanted his confession and staunchly maintained his innocence subsequently, which is a determinative feature of a coerced-compliant confession, he also reported false memories of events that were suggested to him by the police interviewer.

Another documented instance of coerced-internalized false confession occurred in a case that received national media attention during the early 1990s. Paul Ingram was a police officer in Olympia, the state capital of Washington. He was accused of raping his daughter, of being a secret practitioner of Satanic rituals, and of having murdered babies as part of Satanic practices. Ingram was interrogated more than 20 times, was hypnotized, and was supplied with vivid details of horrific crimes. The minister of his church implored him to confess, and a psychologist counseled him that sexual abusers usually repress all memory of their crimes. Ultimately, Ingram began to remember having committed such crimes. His recollections included vivid details, some of which had been provided to him and some of which had not. Ingram eventually entered a guilty plea to the charges against him and received a 20-year sentence. However, when a sociologist, Robert Ofshe, was retained by the state to review the case, he concluded that it was an instance of coerced-internalized false confession growing out of memory suggestion. As a proof of his thesis, Ofshe first formulated a fictitious crime. He then interviewed Ingram, suggesting that this was another crime that he had committed. (Note that although knowingly implanting a false memory of a crime would be unethical under normal conditions, it would not be in this instance because the demonstration, if successful, might be used to reverse Ingram's conviction.) Ingram denied committing the fictitious crime during the initial interview. One day later, however, during another interview, he confessed to the crime and confabulated details to support his confession.

In coerced-internalized confessions, then, otherwise normal suspects remember false events as having happened, much as subjects in misinformation experiments falsely recognize or recall memory suggestions. Historically, it seemed astonishing, even unbelievable, to criminologists that suspects would make false confessions because their memories told them that events that did not happen were true (Kassin, 1997). With the benefit of research on memory suggestion, however, this possibility seems neither surprising nor inexplicable. We know from such research that brief, one-time suggestions can elevate false-alarm and intrusion rates, even to the point where false-memory responses are accompanied by illusory vivid mental phenomenology (e.g., Heaps & Nash, 2001), and that they can also lower true-memory reports. If these memory-falsification effects are responsible for coerced-compliant confessions, one would predict that documented instances of such confessions should reveal consistent evidence of memory suggestion, perhaps from sources other than police interviewers (e.g., friends, therapists, religious advisors). Consistent with this hypothesis, Kassin concluded that two factors were typically present in confirmed cases of coerced-compliant confession: (a) strong memory suggestion in the form of false evidence that seems inherently more reliable than memory (e.g., rigged polygraph results; false fingerprint, DNA, or blood results; false statements allegedly made by accomplices; false eyewitness identifications), and (b) suspects who are particularly vulnerable to memory falsification (e.g., retarded persons, such as Mr. E; children or juveniles; intoxicated people; fatigued people; people who are especially trusting of others).

With respect to the second factor identified by Kassin (1997), Gudjonsson (1984) developed an instrument to measure individual differences in susceptibility to memory suggestions about events of forensic significance, one that has been extensively used in false-confession research. The instrument, which is shown in Table 6-2, consists of three parts. First, subjects read or listen to the narrative at the top, which relates events surrounding a mugging and theft that occurred while the central character was on a vacation in Spain. Second, subjects respond to the 20 questions in the middle of Table 6-2. Note that 15 of these questions suggest false information that did not appear in the narrative. These questions are designed to measure initial susceptibility to memory suggestion, with each subject receiving a score between 0 (lowest susceptibility) and 15 (highest susceptibility). Third, the subjects respond to the 20 questions at the bottom of Table 6-2. Note that this second series of questions is the same as the first. The second series is administered under the cover story that people often remember events more accurately when they are allowed further opportunities to answer the same questions. Actually, the second series is intended to measure susceptibility to repeated memory suggestion. Subjects receive a *shift score*, which is simply the proportion of the items to which different answers are given on the first and second administrations. Research with this instrument has established that individuals with poor verbatim memories, low self-esteem, high anxiety levels, and low self-assertiveness—traits that would be expected to elevate susceptibility to memory suggestion—receive higher suggestibility scores. Another pertinent datum, which is reminiscent of the case of Mr. E, is that individuals who are sleep-deprived—a common characteristic of police interrogations, which are often conducted late at night—also show elevated suggestibility on the Gudjonsson instrument.

Although documented examples of coerced-internalized false confessions are compelling as existence proofs, their scientific value is limited because they do not establish cause-effect connections between the conditions that are hypothesized to

Table 6-2. The Interrogative Suggestibility Scale

Component	Material
Narrative	Anna Thomson / of South / Croydon / was on holiday / in Spain / when she was held up / outside her hotel / and robbed of her handbag / which contained $50 worth / of travelers cheques / and her passport. / She screamed for help / and attempted to put up a fight / by kicking one of the assailants / in the shins. / A police car shortly arrived / and the woman was taken to the nearest police station / where she was interviewed by Detective / Sergeant / Delgado. / The woman reported that she had been attacked by three men / one of whom she described as oriental looking. / The men were said to be slim / and in their early 20s. / The police officer was touched by the woman's story / and advised her to contact the British Embassy. / Six days later / the police recovered the lady's handbag / but the contents were never found. / Three men were subsequently charged / two of whom were convicted / and given prison sentences. / Only one / had had previous convictions / for similar offenses. / The lady returned to Britain / with her husband / Simon / and two friends / but remained frightened of being out on her own. /
Questions	Did the woman have a husband called Simon? Did the woman have one or two children? Did the woman's glasses break in the struggle? Was the woman's name Anna Wilkinson? Was the woman interviewed by a detective sergeant? Were the assailants black or white? Was the woman taken to the central police station? Did the woman's handbag get damaged in the struggle? Was the woman on holiday in Spain? Were the assailants convicted 6 weeks after their arrest? Did the woman's husband support her during the police interview? Did the woman hit one of the assailants with her fist or handbag? Was the woman from South Croydon? Did one of the assailants shout at the woman? Were the assailants tall or short? Did the woman's screams frighten the assailants? Was the police officer's name Delgado? Did the police give the woman a lift back to her hotel? Were the assailants armed with knives or guns? Did the woman's clothes get torn in the struggle?
Shift	Did the woman have a husband called Simon? Did the woman have one or two children? Did the woman's glasses break in the struggle? Was the woman's name Anna Wilkinson? Was the woman interviewed by a detective sergeant? Were the assailants black or white? Was the woman taken to the central police station? Did the woman's handbag get damaged in the struggle? Was the woman on holiday in Spain? Were the assailants convicted 6 weeks after their arrest? Did the woman's husband support her during the police interview? Did the woman hit one of the assailants with her fist or handbag? Was the woman from South Croydon? Did one of the assailants shout at the woman? Were the assailants tall or short? Did the woman's screams frighten the assailants? Was the police officer's name Delgado? Did the police give the woman a lift back to her hotel? Were the assailants armed with knives or guns? Did the woman's clothes get torn in the struggle?

Note. From Gudjonsson (1984).

foment such confessions and the occurrence of confessions. The question therefore arises: Can such confessions be produced experimentally, under controlled conditions that leave no doubt as to cause-effect connections? The answer is yes, and the most important work on this topic is again that of Kassin and his associates.

An especially probative experiment was reported by Kassin and Kiechel (1996). These authors manipulated two variables that are believed to be common to coerced-internalized confessions—subjects' susceptibility to memory suggestion and the presentation of credible false evidence of guilt—in a 2 × 2 factorial design. Pairs of subjects, an actual naive subject and a confederate of the experimenter, performed a data-entry task in which the confederate read a sheet of data aloud to the actual subject, who was instructed to type the data into a computer file. The instructions strongly stated that the subject should not press the ALT key next to the space bar because that would cause the computer to crash and the data file to be lost. By design, the computer crashed 1 minute after data entry had begun. During an interview after the computer crash, the experimenter accused the naive subject of pressing the ALT key, much as a police interviewer would do when interrogating a suspect. The two factors, susceptibility to suggestion and suggestion in the form of false evidence, were manipulated as follows. Concerning susceptibility, half of the subjects had been forced to enter the data at a rapid pace, while the other half entered the data at a leisurely pace, the sensible assumption being that the former subjects would be more likely to accept the experimenter's suggestion that they had pressed the ALT key. Concerning the false evidence, during the interview the confederate announced that she had seen the subject press the ALT key for half of the subjects but not for the other half of the subjects.

During the interview, the experimenter prepared a written confession statement for all of the subjects and exhorted them to sign it, which is another standard interrogation tactic. Following the interview, each subject left the laboratory and proceeded to an anteroom, where he was met by another confederate. The second confederate struck up a conversation with the subject, saying that she had overheard loud voices and asked what had happened. Following this staged conversation, the subject was asked by the experimenter to return to the laboratory. He was then asked to provide a description of how he had hit the ALT key.

The results revealed remarkably high levels of false confession in response to suggestion under conditions that combined credible false evidence with increased susceptibility to suggestion, conditions that are common in police interrogations, coupled with high levels of false memory for self-incriminating behaviors. With respect to the former result, 100% of the subjects in the high-susceptibility-plus-false-evidence condition signed the written statement of guilt. In addition, 65% of these subjects showed that they believed in their guilt by admitting during the conversations with the second confederate (who did *not* press them to admit guilt) that they had caused the computer to crash. Third and perhaps most interesting from the perspective of the role of false memory in false confession, when they returned to the laboratory, 35% of the subjects who showed that they believed in their guilt reported detailed recollections of how they had caused the computer to crash: "Yes, here, I hit it with the side of my hand right after you called out the letter 'A'" (Kassin & Kiechel, 1996, p. 127).

Afterword on the Legal Significance of False-Confession Research

The scientific study of false confession and of the role of false memory in such self-incrimination are of enduring importance in the legal sphere, for three general reasons. In the first place, as we saw in the cases of Mr. K and Mr. E, so much attention in police interrogation centers on obtaining confessions that research-based doubts as to the reliability of such evidence are not a matter of uncertainties about incidental evidence that falls on the margins of criminal law. Confession evidence is so central to prosecution that doubts about its reliability go to the heart of criminal prosecutions. This can be true even in cases in which confessions seem coerced or otherwise suspicious on their face, which was a disturbing conclusion of Armstrong et al.'s (2001) investigation of Cook County murder cases.

The second reason is that post-trial interview studies of jurors have shown that in reaching verdicts, jurors assign high weight to confession evidence—indeed, weights that greatly exceed the actual reliability of such evidence. From the jury's perspective, a confession is far more significant than other types of evidence (Kassin, 1997). Further, mock jury research has demonstrated that the presentation of confession evidence raises conviction rates more than other standard sources of evidence, such as eyewitness identifications and testimony as to bad character (Kassin & Sukel, 1997). In short, the default option for most jurors seems to be that confessions are almost uniquely demonstrative of guilt (Kassin, 1997), and for that reason, it is of great importance for jurors to appreciate that this view is not consistent with research findings.

The third reason is that mock jury research has also established that the influence of confession evidence is so strong that once it is introduced, its influence cannot be entirely discarded by jurors. This research suggests, moreover, that jurors fail to disregard the influence of confession evidence even when they believe that a confession has been coerced, and even when they *say* that they have disregarded it. This is *not* because jurors are unable to identify confessions as being coerced statements: Studies conducted by Kassin and Wrightsman (1980, 1981, 1985) established that mock jury subjects were able to determine with considerable accuracy several conditions that produce coerced confessions and to classify self-incriminating statements obtained under those conditions as being untrustworthy. Nevertheless, other studies have established that confession evidence increases conviction rates *even when mock jurors identify confessions as being coerced and therefore untrustworthy*.

To illustrate, Kassin and Sukel (1997) reported an experiment involving three conditions in which the subjects read slightly different versions of a murder trial transcript: (a) a condition in which the transcript presented a confession that was obtained in a low-pressure interview; (b) a condition in which the transcript presented the same evidence as in the first condition, except that the confession was obtained in a highly coercive interrogation; and (c) a control condition in which the transcript presented the same evidence as in the first two conditions, except that no confession was included. The behavior of the subjects in Condition b is of primary interest. These subjects correctly concluded that the confession was involuntary, and most of them stated that the confession had therefore not influenced their verdict. When Condition b was compared to the control condition, however, the coerced confession had a marked effect. The conviction rate rose from 10% in the control condition to 62% in the coerced-confession condition. By now, readers will have noticed that the case of Mr. E illustrates jurors' inability to ignore coerced confessions, even when reliable physical evidence demonstrates that a defendant's self-incriminating statements are false. Remember that although medical evidence showed that the infant's injuries could not have resulted from the acts to which Mr. E confessed, the jury reasoned that the fact that Mr. E had confessed to such acts meant that the death was not accidental, notwithstanding that his statements had been coerced.

False Memory in Eyewitness Identification of Criminal Suspects

We turn now to the second area of forensic science to which false-memory research has made landmark contributions: eyewitness identification. False identification of criminal suspects is the single most extensively investigated topic in the literature on false memory, consisting of hundreds of individual experiments going back many decades. For instance, we saw in chapter 1 that Bartlett (1932) conducted studies of false identification, though this is not the work for which he is remembered today. Some excellent literature reviews are available that explicate how specific experimental manipulations influence the accuracy of eyewitness identifications (Christianson, 1992; Sporer, Penrod, Read, & Cutler, 1995; Wells & Lindsay, 1980; Wells & Turtle, 1986).

As we mentioned in chapter 2, eyewitness identifications are central to the prosecution of some of the most serious types of crimes (e.g., armed robbery, drug sales, rape, shootings), and without confessions, such cases often cannot be prosecuted without positive identification of suspects by victims or other witnesses. These are brute facts of criminal law. However, as we also mentioned in chapter 2, the scientific study of witnesses' verbatim memory for suspects' appearance has raised serious questions about the reliability of eyewitness identifications. Recall in this connection that Haber and Haber's (2004) literature review revealed that *even under favorable conditions*, high false-alarm rates are the rule. More explicitly, averaging across more than forty experiments, Haber and Haber found that subjects falsely identified an innocent suspect 57% of the time when the actual culprit was absent from recognition tests and that they falsely identified an innocent suspect 27% of the time when the actual culprit was present in recognition tests (see Table 2-5). (Remember from chapter 2 that familiar people are exceptions. When culprits are well known to witnesses, baseline error rates are near-zero and factors that substantially elevate error rates in the identification of strangers [see below] have little effect.) Although both statistics are worrisome from the perspective of the integrity of legal evidence, the first is especially troubling when it comes to the potential for false conviction in cases in which eyewitness identifications are not buttressed by physical evidence of defendants' guilt (e.g., fingerprints, blood samples, tissue samples).

Why is the incidence of false identification of innocent suspects so high? Opponent-processes distinctions provide a straightforward answer. To begin, recognizing the face of a suspect who was observed at a crime scene is a quintessentially verbatim-memory task: It is that person and absolutely no other, no matter how similar in appearance, who should be liable to investigation and prosecution.

However, we know that the sorts of memory representations that support such responses become rapidly inaccessible after a culprit is observed. We also know that stable gist memories that can lead to false identification are stored at the same time. Just about anyone who is observed at a crime scene will fall into some very familiar categories of physical appearance that most of us experience multiple times during the course of any day (e.g., tall, young, thin, male, Hispanic), which means that the gist traces of such categories will be stored when a suspect is observed. Later, those representations will support semantic false alarms on recognition tests, leading to the identification of innocent people when they are recognizable as belonging to the same categories (because their appearance cues the retrieval of those gist representations). As time passes, those representations may be the only memorial support that witnesses can access, so that any suspect that matches most or all of the categories is quite likely to be identified. Interestingly, note that opponent processes predict, consistent with Haber and Haber's (2004) findings, that this problem should be more acute with culprit-absent tests than with culprit-present tests. If verbatim traces of a culprit's face or other physical features are still accessible, culprit-present tests provide the best possible retrieval cues for those representations, whereas culprit-absent tests provide better retrieval cues for gist memories of the appearance categories to which the culprit belongs.

Beyond the overriding things that opponent processes have to say about the susceptibility of eyewitness identification to semantic false memory, there are many specific features of eyewitnesses' identifications, as they occur in field investigations, that increase or decrease such susceptibility. We explore this issue in the first section below by considering three general circumstances in which eyewitness identifications are obtained in field investigations. In the next section, we provide a taxonomy of specific factors that researchers currently believe influence the accuracy of eyewitness identifications. In the final section, we discuss research-based guidelines for eyewitness identification that have recently been promulgated by the American Psychology and Law Society and by the U.S. Department of Justice.

Identification Situations: Mug Books, Crime Scene Show-ups, and Line-ups

Although there are other circumstances in which eyewitness identifications are obtained, the three most common situations are (a) when preliminary investigation of a crime has failed to unearth any likely suspects, (b) when police have access to both suspects and witnesses at the crime scene, and (c) when police have active suspects and witnesses but they are no longer at the crime scene.

In situations of the first type, a report of a crime is received (e.g., a store clerk reports being robbed), but investigation of the crime scene and interviews of witnesses fail to point to anyone who could reasonably be regarded as a suspect. Police may then resort to techniques in which witnesses are shown photographs of people who have been previously arrested for crimes like the one under investigation, on the hypothesis that such people have a high probability of being the culprit. Most often, this is done with *mug books*, which usually consist of photographs of people who have been arrested on various changes, including a subset of people who have been arrested for the target crime. Nowadays, mug shots of people who have been arrested are maintained in computer image files, which makes it quite easy to generate a large collection of pictures for witness viewing that contain pictures of people who have been arrested locally for crimes like the target crime. In addition, if there is reason to consider some of those people as being more likely suspects than others (e.g., because they have recently been arrested), it is easy to include their pictures more than once in a mug book to ensure that they receive proper attention from witnesses. Because there are no active suspects, the investigation may be unable to proceed further if witnesses fail to make positive identifications from mug books or at least recognize one or more faces as being familiar. Consequently, witnesses may be given instructions that inform them of the importance of their task—such as statements to the effect that the continuation of the investigation hinges upon whether they are able to identify any of the mug shots.

Turning to the second circumstance in which identifications are commonly obtained, it sometimes happens that police are able to detain a suspect at a crime scene shortly after the crime is reported. For instance, this is a routine feature of crimes that occur in the course of sting operations in which undercover officers masquerade as parties to crimes (e.g., they purchase drugs, purchase stolen property, pay bribes, or participate in robberies). Once a crime has been committed, the undercover officers signal other officers to arrest the culprits, and they then make suspect identifications for the arresting officers. More commonly, however, police arrive at a crime scene and then are able to detain someone whom they regard as a probable suspect. For instance, after arriving at the scene of an armed robbery of a convenience store, a sweep of the premises may reveal someone hiding in a storeroom, or after arriving at the scene of a domestic assault, a sweep of the premises may reveal someone attempting to escape through a window. In such situations, witnesses will normally be asked whether they can identify that particular suspect and no others. More than one method may be used, however. Witnesses may simply be brought into the presence of the suspect and asked to perform an identification. If witnesses fear for their safety or if investigators wish to conceal witnesses' identity from suspects for other reasons (e.g., the witnesses are police officers who are working undercover), conditions may be arranged so that witnesses can view the suspect without being seen by the suspect. For example, witnesses may sit in a darkened automobile while the suspect is placed in the glare of the headlamps, or witnesses may stand inside a darkened room, looking out a window while investigators shine a light on the suspect's face. As the equipment in police vehicles often includes Polaroid cameras, investigators may simply photograph a suspect's face and ask witnesses to identify the suspect from the photograph. Regardless of the method that is used, the general procedure of asking witnesses whether they can identify a single person or photographs of a single person as the culprit is called a *show-up*.

In the third circumstance in which identifications are commonly obtained, witnesses are no longer at the crime scene when they are asked to perform identifications. Typically, the crime occurred some hours, days, or weeks earlier, but investigation at the crime scene either failed to identify a probable suspect, or if it did, police were unable to detain the suspect. Therefore, witnesses must perform identifications at some later time. If the suspect has not yet been located, pictures must be used, which may be such things as driver's license photographs or photographs obtained from the suspect's friends or relatives. The show-up method may again be used, with witnesses being asked whether they can identify the person in the picture as the culprit. Or, a suspect's picture may be incorporated in a photo spread of multiple pictures, with witnesses being asked whether they can identify any of the people as the culprit. If a driver's license photograph is used, a photo spread can be constructed by sampling pictures of other licensed drivers. If other types of photographs are used, most law enforcement agencies have software that will generate appropriate photo spreads. Such software first receives input information about a suspect's age, gender, ethnicity, build, and other features of general appearance, and it generates photographs from its database that match the suspect on those features. If the suspect has been located and detained, on the other hand, pictures may still be used, but there is now the option of asking witnesses to perform live identifications of the suspect, with or without concealment of their own identities. The latter may consist of a one-person show-up, or witnesses may view *line-ups* consisting of other persons in addition to the suspect.

All of the aforementioned situations contain features that, in light of research on false memory, could lead to false identifications. Considering the discussion of false memory as a result of suggestion in the first half of the chapter, for example, the feature that immediately comes to mind is the presence of powerful elements of suggestion. At a general level, it will be apparent to witnesses that they are viewing people whom the police regard as likely suspects, which will encourage them to believe that they should be able to select someone as the culprit. Of course, the fact that the people who are being viewed are suspects is utterly transparent in the case of crime-scene show-ups: Those people have been found at the scene, often as a consequence of information provided by the witnesses themselves, and they may be handcuffed or under physical restraint at the time they are viewed. Although photo spreads and line-ups are normally administered after a crime has occurred and at some other location, it is still clear to witnesses that some of the people they are viewing are suspects. In what universe, any witness would reason, would police investigators go to the trouble and expense of preparing photo spreads and line-ups that are composed entirely of innocent people and then interview witnesses about them? Nothing is to be gained, from an investigative point of view. Even in the first of the preceding situations, in which witnesses are being used as preliminary investigative tools because police lack suspects, the natural tendency will be to assume that the culprit is somewhere among the pictures in the mug books. Witnesses know, as a matter of experience, that mug books include pictures of people who have been arrested for crimes like the target crime, and they may indeed be told this when they view mug books.

Experimental findings on memory suggestion indicate that the belief that the person (show-ups) or persons (mug books, photo spreads, and line-ups) being viewed are suspects could produce false identifications in two general ways. The first, which was discussed in connection with confession evidence, is social compliance without memory falsification. That is, witnesses may simply comply with the operative social constraints and select someone, notwithstanding that they have no positive memory of the person as the culprit. Obviously, this is particularly tempting in the case of crime scene show-ups. The second way is through falsification of the contents of memory itself. Exposing witnesses to photographs of people, or to the people themselves, in a situation that portrays them as likely culprits could lead witnesses to erroneously remember innocent people as culprits, particularly when they resemble actual culprits in age, ethnicity, gender, height, and build. We know that suggestion can sometimes falsify memory to the point that subjects (witnesses, in this instance) have vivid but illusory recollections of things that they did not experience, as when they confabulate concrete details to support false memories (e.g., Kassin & Kiechel, 1996). However, suggestion could also cause witnesses to lower their standard of memorial support for identifying people as culprits. Here, two points from earlier chapters are pertinent. We know that subjects may recognize or recall an event because they have a clear verbatim memory of its occurrence, which is often called *recollection* or *remember phenomenology*, but they may also recognize or recall an item because it conforms closely to the gist of their experience, which is often called *familiarity* or *know phenomenology*. In addition, we know from the metamemorial judgment research that was mentioned in chapter 3 (e.g., Koriat & Goldsmith, 1994, 1996) that subjects can shift their subjective memory criteria in one direction or the other, depending upon instructions and other contextual factors. To avoid labeling innocent people as culprits, the appropriate criterion in eyewitness identification is one that demands clear verbatim memories of culprits. However, one of the established effects of suggestion is to cause subjects to adopt less-stringent criteria of memorability (Belli, 1989; Titcomb & Reyna, 1995).

At bottom, the high average error rates reported by Haber and Haber (2004) may be rooted in the fundamental suggestive factor that witnesses believe that they are viewing likely suspects. Beyond this property, there are other features of the three identification situations that would be expected to elevate error rates. For example, consider the first situation, in which witnesses review mug books to help police isolate potential suspects. Here, the knowledge that police lack suspects and that it may not be possible for them to arrest the culprit unless witnesses can help increases the pressure to make an identification. Like suggestion, such pressure encourages subjects to shift their subjective criteria of memorability in the direction of gist consistency. With respect to show-ups, whether they occur at a crime scene or later via the presentation of a single photograph or suspect, such identifications have the undesirable property that, if an innocent person is being viewed, his appearance will provide better retrieval cues for the gist of witnesses' experience ("young, thin, Hispanic, male") than for verbatim traces of the culprit's appearance, and as we know, the stage will be set for false recognition if witnesses cannot access verbatim traces and perform recollection rejection of gist-consistent distractors. In this respect, photo spreads and line-ups are superior methods because (a) they provide good verbatim retrieval cues as well as good gist retrieval cues *when the culprit is present*; and (b) when the culprit is absent, most or all of the options will be consistent with the gist of witnesses' experience, which makes it difficult to identify one of them with much higher subjective confidence than the others. A final factor that is bound to increase error rates is delay. When a suspect cannot be identified at the crime scene, it may take considerable time for an investigation to turn up suspects for photo spreads or line-ups, and it may take even more time for police to give up the search for suspects and resort to mug books. Of course, the opponent-processes concept of differential accessibility predicts that such delays will cause false-identification rates to drift upward, a prediction that is consistent with much research on the relation between delay and false-memory reports.

A Taxonomy of Factors That Affect Identification Accuracy

Thanks to the extensive literature on errors in eyewitness identification, it is possible to isolate several variables that have been consistently tied to such errors. For legal reasons, it is important to have a systematic taxonomy of those variables. The fact that eyewitness identifications are error prone is appreciated by judges and trial attorneys, though they may not realize just how high the baseline error rate is. This fact is not well understood by juries, however, and on the contrary, people who serve on juries are apt to regard eyewitness identifications as quite reliable (Haber & Haber, 2004). Consequently, memory researchers are routinely asked to perform forensic analyses of the identification procedures that were adopted in particular cases and to provide expert scientific evidence at trial. Such testimony will normally revolve around any specific factors that are present in a case that research has shown will increase identification errors (though it may also include background about the overall reliability of eyewitness identifications). If such testimony is to enhance the accuracy of verdicts, it must focus on factors whose effects have been firmly established and eschew factors whose effects are not yet understood. Therefore, it is particularly important to have an agreed-upon taxonomy of factors that increase eyewitness identification errors.

Such a taxonomy has been presented by Kassin (2001). Most researchers who provide expert testimony will be aware of some factors whose effects have been firmly established but be unaware of others. To isolate all of those factors, Kassin conducted an opinion survey of psychologists with forensic experience. This procedure accords with the so-called Frye standard for the admission of scientific opinions in U.S. courts (*Frye v. United States*, 1923), according to which opinions are admissible if they are based upon evidence or theories that are accepted by a majority of researchers in the relevant scientific community.

Kassin created a subject sample that was composed of individuals who had published research on eyewitness identification within the preceding 10 years and who were members of scientific societies that are concerned with such research (e.g., American Psychology and Law Society, Society for Applied Research on Memory and Cognition). A questionnaire was then mailed to those researchers. This instrument contained questions about 30 factors that might influence the rate of false identifications by eyewitnesses. All factors were ones that had been discussed in the literature, and some data were extant on each. The researchers were asked to respond to each factor in five ways: (a) to rate its reliability (i.e., the extent to which it has been clearly tied to identification errors); (b) to state whether the factor was sufficiently reliable that it could be presented in courtroom testimony; (c) to state whether they personally would be willing to present testimony on the factor; (d) to state whether their opinion was based upon published, peer-reviewed research; and

(e) to state the extent to which jurors already are aware that the factor influences the accuracy of eyewitness identifications. Although each of these questions provides important information about current practice in forensic psychological testimony, answers to the first question are of greatest scientific interest because they isolate the particular factors that meet the legal standard of acceptance by a majority of the relevant scientific community. Of the 30 factors, 24 were identified as being reliably associated with identification errors. Those factors are exhibited and defined in Table 6-3.

In Table 6-3, we have once again used the organizational device of mapping factors with the global stages of information processing with which they are associated: storage, retrieval, and forgetting. Certain factors can operate both when witnesses experience the events of a crime and when they respond to identification tests, and those particular factors therefore appear under both the storage and retrieval headings. At the bottom of the table, a new organizational category appears: witness factors. The study of individual differences is a time-honored topic in forensic psychology, no less than in other areas of applied psychology. An especially common individual differences variable that might affect identification accuracy—age—has been studied, and the factors at the bottom of the table represent the results of that research. In the discussion that follows, we consider the four categories in Table 6-3 from the perspective of the opponent-processes approach to false memory, showing how that approach predicts the effects of each factor.

Storage

For the most part, these factors, according to opponent-processes distinctions, would selectively impair verbatim memory for the surface details of crimes, including the appearance of suspects. From research discussed in this and earlier chapters, we know that storing verbatim traces poses greater difficulties than storing gist traces of salient meanings and that verbatim traces are less apt to survive the consolidation process. Four of the storage factors in Table 6-3—exposure time, weapon focus, stress, and intoxication—closely parallel some of the verbatim-interference variables that were examined in previous chapters. Concerning witnesses' exposure time during a crime, the parallel between this real-world factor and the event-duration manipulation of chapters 4 and 5 is self-evident. Thus, the theoretical expectation would be that decreased exposure time will increase false identifications of suspects for the same reason that shorter event durations (at least those in the range of conscious awareness) increase false alarms on other types of recognition tasks (i.e., witnesses are less apt to have accessible verbatim traces that can be used to suppress acceptance of false-but-gist-consistent distractors). Concerning the other three factors, false identification rates increase when weapons are present during crimes, when witnesses are in states of high stress, and when witnesses are intoxicated.

The first of these factors, weapon focus, can be thought of as analogous to the earlier distinctiveness manipulation (though an element of emotional arousal figures in weapon focus that is not part of traditional distinctiveness variables). During a crime, a weapon is a far more salient, attention-capturing feature of the crime than most other features, including the culprit's appearance (e.g., Pickel, 1999). Hence,

Table 6-3. Factors That Influence the Accuracy of Eyewitness Identifications of Suspects

Factor	Explanation
Storage	
Attitudes	The information that eyewitnesses preserve in memory is affected by their attitudes.
Color perception	Memory for colors viewed under conditions of monochromatic light is highly inaccurate.
Cross-race bias	Memory for same-race faces is more accurate than memory for different-race faces.
Exposure time	Identification errors increase as the amount of time that witnesses observe suspects during crimes decreases.
Intoxication	Intoxication increases identification errors.
Mugshot bias	Prior exposure to mug shots of innocent suspects increases the chances of later false identification.
Postevent information	Eyewitness identification reflects later information as well as what was experienced at the crime scene.
Stress	High levels of stress increase identification errors.
Weapon focus	The presence of weapons during crimes increases identification errors.
Retrieval	
Accuracy confidence	Eyewitnesses' confidence in the accuracy of their identifications is not a good predictor of actual accuracy.
Confidence malleability	Eyewitnesses' confidence in the accuracy of their identifications is influenced by factors other than accuracy.
Hypnosis	Hypnosis increases eyewitnesses' susceptibility to suggestion.
Instructions	Identification instructions affect eyewitnesses' ability to make an identification.
Intoxication	Intoxication increases identification errors.
Line-up fairness	In line-ups and photo spreads, false-identification rates increase when distractors do not resemble suspects.
Presentation format	Simultaneous photo spreads and line-ups produce more identification errors than do successive ones.
Questions	Identification accuracy is affected by the wording of interview questions.
Show-ups	False-identification rates are higher for one-person show-ups than for line-ups or photo spreads.
Stress	High levels of stress increase errors.
Transference	False-identification rates are higher for innocent suspects whom eyewitnesses have seen in other contexts.
Unmatched foils	In line-ups and photo spreads, false-identification rates are higher when distractors do not match eyewitnesses' descriptions of culprits.
Forgetting	
Forgetting curve	The rate of memory loss for the events of a crime is greatest immediately after the event and then levels off.
Recovered memories	Error rates are higher for identifications based upon recovered memories than for identifications based upon events that have been continuously remembered.
Witnesses	
Child accuracy	Identification errors are more common in children than in adults.
Child suggestibility	Children are more prone to identification errors induced by interviewer suggestions, peer pressure, and other social influences.
Elderly accuracy	Identification errors are more common in elderly adults than in young or middle-aged adults.

Note. Based upon Kassin (2001).

more processing time will normally be devoted to the weapon, resulting in rich verbatim traces of that object (e.g., the color, size, shape, and make of a gun) but also resulting in correspondingly impoverished verbatim traces of culprit-identifying information. The stress factor may be thought of as analogous to consolidation manipulations that selectively interfere with the preservation of verbatim traces, such as directed-forgetting instructions. Witnesses who are in states of high stress, a routine circumstance during violent crimes, may have the same opportunity to experience events as other witnesses. However, stress, like directed-forgetting instructions, generates a variety of thoughts and emotions that would be expected to impair the consolidation of verbatim traces of those experiences. It is well known, of course, that intoxication impairs memory storage (e.g., Yuille & Tollestrup, 1990). This is especially true of the storage of surface details (e.g., the thickness and orientation of a culprit's eyebrows), as opposed to meaning content (e.g., the fact that the culprit is Asian), because intoxication reduces attentiveness. However, intoxication is a factor that also affects consolidation because intoxicated witnesses are not apt to initiate the sorts of effortful post-storage strategies that help preserve verbatim traces.

Two of the other storage factors in Table 6-3—postevent information and mugshot bias—are variations on the misinformation manipulations that were considered in the first half of this chapter. In fact, they are specialized forms of misinformation, which affect suspect identification. Postevent information refers to the fact that when a substantial period of time elapses between the occurrence of a crime and suspect identifications, there are opportunities for witnesses to be exposed to additional information that points to specific suspects but that is not part of their original experience. Examples include conversations with other witnesses, media reports of the crime, and conversations with investigators. Such postevent information increases the tendency to identify innocent suspects (e.g., Shaw, 1996; Wells, 1993). Mugshot bias is a form of misinformation that is specific to criminal investigation. As mentioned earlier, witnesses may be asked to examine mug books in the hope of providing police with investigative leads. Later, when an investigation has turned up a suspect, these same witnesses may be asked to view a show-up, photo spread, or line-up. If the suspect is innocent, witnesses are more likely to falsely identify her if the suspect's picture was viewed in mug books (Memon, Hope, Bartlett, & Bull, 2002). Clearly, mugshot bias is a real-world analogue of misinformation studies in which the misinformation material is pictorial (e.g., Bowman & Zaragoza, 1989; Toglia et al., 1991).

The remaining storage factors are cross-race bias, color perception, and attitudes. Although none of these factors closely parallels storage variables from earlier chapters, it is apparent that each should influence the quality of witnesses' memory for the surface content of experience. This is obvious in the case of color perception: Witnesses cannot have accurate verbatim memories of the color of culprits' hair, eyes, skin, jewelry, lip gloss, nail polish, clothing, and so forth if lighting conditions at the crime scene distort the wavelengths of the light that impinges upon their retinas. In contrast, except for extreme darkness, lighting conditions do not impair witnesses' ability to store accurate gist memories of age, gender, race, build, and so forth, the net result, according to opponent-processes predictions, being an elevation in false-identification rates.

In the case of cross-race bias, eyewitnesses make fewer false identifications of suspects who belong to their own racial category than of those who belong to other racial categories. This is presumably a verbatim storage effect that is rooted in the tendency to selectively process surface features that distinguish individual members of a racial category. To illustrate, an African-American witness who interacts mostly with other African Americans and rarely with Asian Americans, will have vast experience at processing the facial details that distinguish one African-American face from another (and at ignoring the details that do not) but will lack experience at doing likewise with Asian-American faces. Consequently, an African American will be more likely to store memories of facial details that discriminate culprits from innocent suspects when culprits and innocent suspects are African American than when they are Asian American.

The final factor—attitudes—is a real-world example of some points that arose in the discussion of schema-consistent false memories in chapters 2 and 3. Recall that one of the basic postulates of schema theory is that storage is selective in the sense that people are most likely to store information that fits well with an existing schema. Attitudes toward people of a certain age, gender, race, or national origin are examples of memory schemas, some of whose predicted effects are to falsify eyewitnesses' memories by causing them to store gist features of culprits that they expect to be present (but are not) and to fail to store other gist features that they do not expect to be present (but are).

Retrieval

The retrieval factors in Table 6-3 refer to variables that may be present at the time that eyewitnesses perform suspect identifications. As a group, these factors would be expected to interfere more with eyewitnesses' ability to access verbatim traces than with their ability to access gist traces, leading to net increases in the false recognition of innocent suspects. In addition, however, some would be expected to cause eyewitnesses to shift their subjective criteria of memorability away from verbatim match toward gist consistency, and some would even be expected to impair eyewitnesses' comprehension of instructions.

Two of these factors—stress and intoxication—are also storage factors. Concerning stress, although this factor is normally more problematical at storage, while a crime is in progress, high stress levels can also be present during identifications. For example, witnesses may be fearful that they will be harmed by suspects if their own identities are discovered, or witnesses who are believed by the police to be accomplices may have been threatened with prosecution if they fail to identify other suspects. Regardless of the causes of witness stress, either stress or intoxication will interfere with witnesses' ability to focus on the memorial task at hand, which should particularly impair access to interference-sensitive verbatim traces.

The other 10 retrieval factors do not overlap with storage. Two of them—accuracy confidence and confidence malleability—are concerned with an important additional feature of suspect identifications, which goes beyond mere acceptance or rejection of recognition probes. We have previously seen—for instance, in Bransford and Franks's (1971) classic studies of false memory for semantic inferences—

that the subjects in recognition experiments are sometimes asked to rate their subjective confidence in their responses. In criminal cases, investigators and juries naturally wish to know just how certain witnesses are that suspects are culprits. Therefore, requests for confidence ratings, often on a 0–100 scale, are standard concomitants of eyewitness identifications. Such requests may occur immediately after a suspect has been identified, though sometimes they are delayed until some later point in an investigation, and such requests may be repeatedly made of witnesses (e.g., during initial identifications, during subsequent interviews with police or prosecutors, during trial testimony). The heavy use of confidence ratings reflects the commonsense belief that identifications that are made with high confidence are most likely to be correct. However, opponent-processes distinctions raise doubts about the validity of this belief because, as we saw with Bransford and Franks's research, false-memory responses that fit well with the gist of experience can produce high confidence ratings. Because confidence ratings are common in eyewitness identifications, the relation between identification accuracy and confidence is one of the most extensively investigated issues in the eyewitness-memory literature (e.g., Fleet, Brigham, & Bothwell, 1987; Kassin, 1985; Sporer, 1992, 1993; Wells & Lindsay, 1985). The general finding has been that the data are more consistent with theoretical predictions than with common sense: Accuracy and confidence are not highly correlated, and it is therefore inadvisable for juries to give strong weight to confidence ratings. A related finding, which likewise violates common sense but is quite understandable if confidence ratings reflect consistency with the gist of experience, is that confidence ratings can be altered by factors other than the accuracy of a suspect identification. For example, confidence ratings can be affected by such things as the method that is used to produce the ratings (Fleet et al., 1987) or by feedback about the accuracy of prior identifications (Wells & Bradfield, 1998). Perhaps the most surprising illustration of confidence malleability, however, which in itself is demonstrative of the limited reliability of confidence ratings, is that confidence ratings associated with a particular suspect identification tend to increase as time passes, *even though the memories on which accurate identifications are based are degrading.* For example, a common experience in criminal prosecutions that involve eyewitness identifications is that witnesses' stated confidence levels at trial are substantially higher than the levels that were stated months earlier during original suspect identifications.

Of the remaining eight retrieval factors, four are concerned with the composition of the recognition stimuli that are presented to eyewitnesses: presentation format, show-ups, line-up fairness, and unmatched foils. *Presentation format* refers to a variable that is already familiar from the earlier discussion of misinformation experiments: yes-no recognition tests (called *successive* tests in the eyewitness literature) versus forced-choice tests (called *simultaneous* tests in the eyewitness literature). In standard recognition experiments, comparisons of performance on these tests suggest that of the two forms of memorial support for accepting a recognition probe—exact verbatim match and gist consistency—subjects rely more on the relative gist consistency of the choices in forced-choice than in yes-no recognition (Aggleton & Shaw, 1996; Bastin & Van der Linden, 2003). Consequently, opponent-processes analysis predicts that false-identification rates will be higher with simultaneous tests than with successive tests (because, with the former, witnesses will tend to select alternatives that are *most consistent* with the gist of their experience of culprits rather than selecting alternatives that exactly match culprits). This is the usual finding in the eyewitness literature (Lindsay, Lea, Nosworthy, Fulford, Hector, LeVan, & Seabrook, 1991; Lindsay & Wells, 1985).

The second stimulus-composition variable refers to a special type of yes-no test that has been mentioned before: the one-person show-up. From a theoretical standpoint, the inherently suggestive features of show-ups (e.g., the fact that they often occur at crime scenes, the implication that the police are so certain that they have the culprit that they deem it unnecessary to provide alternative choices) imply that, relative to line-ups or photo spreads, show-ups encourage witnesses to shift their subjective criteria of memorability away from exact verbatim matching toward gist consistency, thereby increasing the false-identification rate. Consistent with this prediction, studies have typically found that false-identification rates are higher for show-ups than for line-ups or photo spreads, with some studies producing false-identification rates in excess of 75% (see Wells et al., 1998).

The last two stimulus-composition variables—line-up fairness and unmatched foils—both refer to the nature of the distractor probes that are administered with line-ups and photo spreads (using either the successive or simultaneous method of presentation). The principle of *line-up fairness* specifies that distractors should be chosen in such a way that the "target" (the police suspect) should not stand out as being dramatically different from the distractors. Suspects will stand out, for instance, if distractors fail to match them in age, build, height, race, and other salient features of appearance. Assuming that a suspect's appearance is consistent with the gist of eyewitnesses' experience of the culprit, the theoretical prediction is that error rates will be elevated for such tests because an innocent suspect will seem much more familiar than any of the distractors. This prediction has been confirmed in so many experiments (e.g., Lindsay, Smith, & Pryke, 1999; Wells, Rydell, & Seelau, 1993) that U.S. Justice Department guidelines caution police investigators about avoiding tests of this sort (Technical Working Group for Eyewitness Evidence, 1999).

The other distractor-content factor—*unmatched foils*—is a special case of line-up fairness. As a rule, eyewitnesses are able to provide descriptions of the general categories of people into which culprits fall, and they may also be able to provide descriptions of unusual features (e.g., scars, tattoos, physical disabilities). When such eyewitnesses are administered line-ups or photo spreads, an obvious way to ensure fairness is to select distractors based upon those descriptions because, by definition, all choices will then be consistent with the gist of their experience. This, in turn, should prod eyewitnesses to base identifications on exact verbatim matches because gist consistency does not readily discriminate among the choices. Again, the data are consistent with theoretical reasoning: Lower false-identification rates have been observed when descriptions of suspects have been used to select distractors than when distractors have been chosen at random (e.g., Hosch & Bothwell, 1990).

The next three retrieval factors—questions, instructions, and hypnosis—are variations on a theme, the theme being the details of how eyewitnesses are questioned during the course of identification tests. The first factor is concerned with the specific questions that are asked of eyewitnesses as identification stimuli are presented. It is clear from the earlier discussion of misinformation research that questions that are suggestive, that allude to the guilt of the suspect in a show-up, or that point to a particular choice in a line-up or photo spread would be expected to elevate false-identification rates when the suggested persons are innocent. Likewise, questions that encourage witnesses to adopt memory criteria that are less stringent than verbatim matches or that pressure witnesses to make identifications despite uncertainty (e.g., in order to provide investigative leads) would be expected to elevate false-identification rates. In line with such hypotheses, the accuracy of eyewitness identifications has been consistently tied to the content of the questions that are asked during identifications (Wells et al., 1998).

Concerning instructions, this factor differs from the question factor in its proximity to identification responses. Specifically, the instructions are the overall explanation that witnesses receive *prior* to performing an identification task, whereas the question factor refers to the individual interrogatories that prompt acceptance or rejection responses from witnesses. With this proviso, instructions that are suggestive (e.g., that either state that the police are confident they have the culprit or that fail to counteract such an impression on the part of witnesses), that encourage suspects to adopt criteria that are weaker than verbatim match, or that authorize identifications when eyewitnesses are uncertain of their choices should elevate the false identification of innocent suspects. Empirically, identification instructions have been found to have just such consequences (Kohnken & Malpass, 1988; Malpass & Devine, 1981).

Finally, when witnesses state that they are unable to recall details of culprits' appearance or are unable to identify culprits, it has sometimes been thought that their memories could be refreshed by hypnosis (Newman & Thompson, 2001). Consistent with this belief, witnesses typically recall more details if they are placed in a hypnotic state, and they are more apt to identify suspects following hypnotic refreshment. However, it does not necessarily follow that the exhumed memory reports are true. Studies of memory performance under hypnosis show that retrieval processes change in fundamental ways (e.g., Ran, Shapiro, Fan, & Posner, 2002), one of which is a shift away from the vivid recollection of surface details. Such studies have also shown that hypnotized subjects are more susceptible to suggestion (e.g., Yapko, 1994; see chapter 8) and that hypnotized subjects exhibit higher levels of both spontaneous false-memory reports and false reports that are consistent with memory suggestions (e.g., Tarrance, Matheson, Mallard, & Schnarr, 2000). Although the latter effects occur when subjects are hypnotized, the effects persist during post-hypnotic performance (e.g., Scoboria, Mazzoni, Kirsch, & Milling, 2002; see chapter 8). For these reasons, eyewitness identifications that are performed during hypnosis or following hypnotic memory refreshment are at increased risk of yielding false identifications of innocent suspects.

The last retrieval factor—*transference*—is another variable that is concerned with the composition of the stimuli, the distractors in particular, that are administered on identification tests. On theoretical grounds, one would predict that if the distractors that are presented in line-ups or photo spreads consist of faces of strangers whom witnesses have previously seen in contexts other than the target crimes, witnesses would be more likely to make false identifications because the faces are familiar. This effect has been observed in experimentation (e.g., Ross, Ceci, Dunning, & Toglia, 1994). The earlier example of mugshot bias is evidently a special instance of transference. Additionally, however, as a practical investigative technique, police may include people in line-ups or photo spreads who were in the vicinity of a crime and who lack alibis. Although police investigators correctly regard such people as being more likely to be culprits than randomly chosen individuals, witnesses will naturally be more likely to have seen those people, *although they may be innocent*. If so, thanks to the transference principle, witnesses will be more likely to identify those innocent people as culprits.

Forgetting

Only two forgetting factors appear in Table 6-3: the *forgetting curve* and *recovered memories*. The former refers to the implications for eyewitness identification of the hoary fact that memory loss over time is negatively accelerated, with the hypothetical curves in Figure 6-7 being illustrative. The chief forensic ramification of negative acceleration is that because forgetting (in this case, of culprits' appearance) is greatest in the stretch of time that immediately follows target events, a high premium should be placed on securing identifications as soon as possible after crimes are reported. A few hours can make a great difference in accuracy at the start, though it will make little difference several days later. This fact can stimulate various investigative choices in the field that will redound to the ultimate accuracy of identifications. For instance, personnel availability often confronts investigators with a choice between securing statements from other people in the vicinity of a crime who were not eyewitnesses or administering timely identification tests to eyewitnesses. From the perspective of obtaining accurate identifications, the forgetting curve says that the latter choice is preferable. Similarly, if a likely suspect (e.g., one who closely matches descriptions provided by eyewitnesses) is in custody at the crime scene, an immediate show-up is more likely to produce an accurate identification than the same show-up conducted on the following day, and an immediate line-up (e.g., containing the suspect plus other people in the vicinity who are of similar appearance) is more likely to produce accurate responses than the same line-up conducted on the following day. On the other hand, the forgetting curve says that analogous choices need not be made if there has already been a delay of several days. If the crime occurred, say, a week ago, the accuracy gain that results from administering identification tests today versus tomorrow is minuscule.

Although the forgetting curve generates such investigative rules of thumb, it does not account for the fine-grained details of how the accuracy of eyewitness identifications fluctuates over time. By itself, the curve merely tells us that witnesses lose access to features of culprits' appearance more rapidly at first than later, but it is silent about variations in the rate of loss for different aspects of suspects' appearance. If raw memory loss is the sole consideration, the obvious prediction from the forgetting curve is that the chief effect of delay will be to increase errors of omission (i.e., reluctance to identify anyone) because memory is becoming progressively more hazy. This is not the overriding effect of delay, however. Instead, consistent

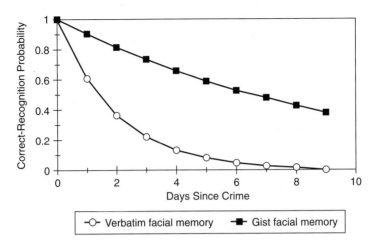

Figure 6-7. Hypothetical forgetting curves for verbatim and gist memories.

with discussions in chapters 4 and 5 concerning how delay affects semantic false recognition, the chief effect is to increase a specific type of commission error—explicitly, false identification of suspects who share salient categories of physical appearance with culprits. To explain this pattern, the forgetting curve must be enriched with opponent-processes concepts, so that a distinction can be drawn between forgetting rates for verbatim traces of crucial incidental features of suspects' appearance and for gist traces of salient categories of physical appearance (e.g., age, gender, height, race).

Returning to Figure 6-7, two hypothetical forgetting curves are displayed, one for the first type of memory loss and one for the second. Inspection of the two curves readily explains why delay increases false identification of suspects who share salient categories of culprits' appearance. In the first hours and days following a crime, the spread between witnesses' abilities to access the two types of memories rapidly widens, with verbatim access dropping to near-floor after several days while gist access remains at high levels. Thus, when an eyewitness is confronted with an identification test after a few days, innocent suspects who share salient categories of appearance with culprits will seem familiar (which supports false identification), but verbatim traces of incidental features that differentiate culprits from such suspects are no longer readily accessible (which makes it difficult to perform recollection rejection on such suspects). Of course, we should remind ourselves here of a point that figured in earlier discussions of the relation between delay and false memory: The basal relation posited by opponent processes is U-shaped. That is, although the false identification of suspects who preserve the gist of culprits' appearance will increase in the short run, as the spread between verbatim and gist accessibility widens, eventually it will decline, as gist accessibility continues to deteriorate after verbatim accessibility has already reached floor.

The other forgetting factor—*recovered memories*—does not refer to the so-called recovery of repressed memories of traumatic experiences (e.g., sexual abuse), a topic that will be explored in chapter 8. Rather, it denotes situations in which, at first, eyewitnesses lack memory for the verbatim details of culprits' appearance, but later on, such details are exhumed; positive identifications of suspects are then made; and the suspects are charged on the basis of those identifications. Although claims of such recovered memories most often occur over spans of a few days or weeks following a crime, there are incidents on record in which defendants were prosecuted for capital crimes on the basis of memories that were recovered years and even decades following crimes. An illustration is provided by the case of Mr. Z, a Taiwanese immigrant who was tried for first-degree murder 3 decades after the commission of the crime.

Mr. Z arrived in the United States as a teenager. He resided in a West Coast city, rooming with another Taiwanese immigrant, Mr. H. Late one afternoon, a third Taiwanese immigrant, the foreman of a small factory, was shot to death in the factory parking lot. The shooting was observed by two factory employees who were on their lunch break, a 19-year-old man and a 26-year-old woman. According to their account, a car pulled up beside the foreman in the parking lot, and a young Asian male jumped out of the passenger side, yelling loudly in an Oriental language, pulled a gun from his jacket pocket, pointed it at the foreman's head, and shot him three times at point-blank range. Both witnesses were able to supply detailed descriptions of the murderer—so detailed that when police investigators interviewed three of the foreman's friends about possible enemies, they all named Mr. H as a known enemy whose appearance tallied with the witnesses' descriptions. Neither witness was able to provide a detailed description of the driver of the car, who, under that state's laws, would be guilty of first-degree murder if he had driven the car to aid Mr. H's designs. The male witness stated that the driver was a "young Asian guy," and the female witness simply said that he was a young man. In the archived police reports of the witnesses' interviews, the male witness's statements about the driver consisted of two sentences, with the phrase "young Asian guy" appearing in one of them, and the female witness's statements about the driver consisted of a single sentence in which the phrase "young man" appeared. Based upon the interviews of the foreman's friends, a warrant was issued for the arrest of Mr. H, and a warrant was also issued for the arrest of Mr. Z as the driver of the car. Photographs of the two men were circulated throughout the city, published in local newspapers, and shown on local television stations. The two men's names and descriptions were also broadcast on local radio stations. This material was supplied to the two witnesses by the police, but they were not asked to make identifications because neither suspect was in custody. Both witnesses saw multiple television stories about the crime in which the suspects' photographs were displayed, read multiple newspaper accounts of the crime in which the suspects' photographs appeared, and heard multiple radio accounts of the crime in which the suspects' names and descriptions were provided.

On the afternoon following the murder, an informant told police investigators that Mr. H was drinking in the back room of a social club and was bragging loudly about executing the foreman for running an extortion racket that preyed upon Taiwanese immigrants. When the police arrived at the social club, Mr. H began shooting at them through a window. The police returned his fire, and Mr. H was killed in the ensuing gun battle. Mr. Z, however, had fled the city upon learning that a warrant had been issued for his arrest. He was hidden by his brother, who lived in another state, until arrangements could be made for his return to Taiwan. Mr. Z returned to Taiwan, using the passport of a deceased relative. He was subsequently convicted of first-degree murder in absentia. After 5 years had passed, he returned to the United States under a different name. He took up residence in a midwestern city, became a high school teacher, married, and eventually had two children.

Thirty years after the murder, when Mr. Z's children were grown and settled in their careers and Mr. Z was retired from teaching, he and his wife decided that the time had come to clear himself of the murder conviction. They contacted Mr. Z's brother, who had become an attorney, and he in turn contacted the police in the West Coast city. Mr. Z was soon taken into custody. During the course of a police interview that was attended by his defense counsel, Mr. Z stated repeatedly that he had not been the driver of the car, but he had fled because he assumed that he would be convicted, regardless of his innocence, because he was Mr. H's best friend. The next step was to determine whether the two witnesses, both of whom were still living, could identify Mr. Z. Both were shown photographs of Mr. Z from thirty years before, the same photographs that had been widely broadcast and published in stories about the murder and that had been provided to the witnesses in the days following the murder. Although the witnesses had been unable to remember details of the driver's appearance when they were interviewed at the crime scene, both of them now identified the photographs as the person whom they had seen driving the car, and both of them rated their confidence as "90–100% sure." On that basis, Mr. Z was charged with first-degree murder and was jailed without bail pending trial.

During the 18 months that Mr. Z was imprisoned awaiting trial, his attorney asked a memory researcher to review the facts of the case and to prepare a report, based upon available research, that isolated factors that might have caused these witnesses to falsely identify Mr. Z's photographs as those of the driver. The report was introduced at trial as part of the defense's case. After hearing the report, the judge became so concerned about the potential unreliability of the identifications that she dismissed the jury and directed the two attorneys to negotiate a plea bargain with Mr. Z, the key elements of which were that the murder charge would be dropped; he would plead guilty to unlawful flight to avoid prosecution; and he would receive a sentence consisting of the time he had already served awaiting trial.

In situations such as this, false-memory research suggests that recovered memories of details of culprits' appearance might not be true memories that were stored in the course of a crime but might be (a) false memories that were stored on the basis of postevent information, (b) false memories that were stored on the basis of pre-event information, or (c) false memories that are by-products of reconstructive remembering. Concerning item a, during the hours, days, and weeks following a crime, witnesses may be exposed to sources of postevent information about the crime, including information that they did not experience. In the earlier discussion of storage factors, it was noted that eyewitness identifications are influenced by such postevent information, and the accuracy of identifications can therefore be compromised when the information is false, with mugshot bias being a special case of such taint. In the case of Mr. Z, postevent information is obviously the central concern owing to the large amount of identifying information to which the witnesses were subsequently exposed. However, postevent information is also a worrisome possibility in any case in which witnesses recover memories of culprits' appearance (or of other crucial details) following media coverage or after being provided with postevent information by the police. Concerning item b, in the previous discussion of transference, it was noted that research has shown that witnesses may import the appearance of someone whom they have recently seen (e.g., another person who was encountered in the vicinity of a crime) into culprit identifications, resulting in false identifications of such people. Logically, this is a potential source of recovered memories of a suspect's appearance. Finally, concerning item c, we know from earlier discussions of forgetting and false memories that surface details that are reported on an initial memory test (e.g., a witness interview at the crime scene) are more accurate than details that are reported for the first time on a delayed memory test. The opponent-processes explanation of this datum is that details of the latter sort are more apt to have been generated via gist processing than are details that are reported on an immediate memory test. Evidently, recovered memories of culprits' appearance are special cases of this situation—hence, the third concern about their accuracy.

That recovered memories are susceptible to these sources of falsification must not be misinterpreted as implying that recovered memories are automatically inaccurate. On the contrary, we have all had the experience of being unable to remember a true piece of information at Time 1, which later came to mind at Time 2. *Reminiscence* is the technical name for this phenomenon. With respect to eyewitness memory, factors may operate during initial interviews that interfere with witnesses' ability to remember pertinent details, details that may be recovered later when the interfering factors are no longer operating. The most obvious examples of such factors are fear and stress. Crimes such as assault, murder, rape, and robbery are dangerous ones that place witnesses in states of high stress and make them fearful of personal injury, conditions that are apt to still be present and to impair memory during initial crime-scene interviews. Such conditions are less apt to be present during later interviews that are conducted in safe environments, which may result in reminiscence of details.

Supportive findings have been reported. For example, Bornstein, Liebel, and Scarberry (1998) exposed a group of subjects to events that had the propensity to induce stress—specifically, to a violent, emotionally arousing film. Following the film, the subjects made three separate attempts to recall its contents. More true information was reported on Test 2 than Test 1, and more true information was reported on Test 3 than on Test 2. There was also an increase across tests in the amount of false information that was reported, but it was minuscule in comparison to the increase in true information, so that recovered memories were predominantly true ones. The bottom line is that although recovered memories are more likely to be false than are initial memory reports, recovered memories can be true as well as false, and there are circumstances in which they can be overwhelmingly true.

Witnesses

The last factor is concerned with two special categories of eyewitnesses: children and the aged. There is a good deal of experimental evidence to the effect that the baseline rate of false identification of suspects is higher when witnesses are children (Ceci et al., 1987; McGough, 1993) or aged adults (Memon & Bartlett, 2002; Memon et al., 2002; Searcy, Bartlett, Memon, & Swanson, 2001) than when witnesses are young or middle-aged adults. With both of these witness categories, the opponent-processes explanation of higher false-identification rates is age-related impairments of verbatim memory, relative to gist memory. Regarding children, we saw in chapter 5 that, relative to adolescents and young adults, children exhibit poorer memory for the surface details of experience, and they therefore exhibit higher levels of false memory for gist-consistent events, as long as the target experiences are ones whose meaning content is well understood. Identification of culprits is evidently just such a situation inasmuch as the categories of physical appearance that lead to false identifications (age, gender, height, race) are ones with which even young children are acquainted. Turning to aging, there is no question, of course, that elderly subjects will be highly familiar with these same categories of physical appearance. Further, although this topic will be explored in greater detail in chapter 9, studies of aging deficits in memory have shown that, as a general rule, declines in memory for the gist of experience are less pronounced than declines in memory for surface details (e.g., Bastin & Van der Linden, 2003; Java, 1996; Maylor, 1995). If elderly witnesses are able to access the gist of culprits' appearance but are less able than younger adults to access incidental details of culprits' appearance, it follows that they are at increased risk of making false identifications.

Beyond children's elevated baseline levels of false identification, the third witness factor specifies that they are also more susceptible to the sources of memory suggestion that have been found to increase adults' false-identification rates (e.g., mugshot bias, postevent information, transference). As children's memory suggestibility is the subject of the next chapter, we shall postpone further comment on this factor.

Research-Based Field Guidelines

It is not difficult to see, given the direction of the discussion so far, that eyewitness identification evidence confronts the criminal justice system with a three-pronged dilemma. First, eyewitness identifications sometimes provide the only evidence of a culprit's guilt. However, second, laboratory and field studies have demonstrated that, even under favorable conditions, such identifications are not highly accurate. Roughly speaking, the chance of an error under favorable conditions is 50–50, regardless of whether the culprit is present or absent from a line-up or photo spread. Third, laboratory and field studies have also pinpointed several factors that increase false-identification rates.

Responses to this dilemma have varied from country to country. In Great Britain, the response has been to prohibit convictions that are based solely on eyewitness identifications of defendants. Although such identifications may still be placed in evidence at trial, current British law does not permit defendants to be convicted unless identifications are buttressed by other, more reliable, forms of evidence. Practically speaking, this means that some very serious crimes simply cannot be prosecuted. In the United States, responses have been somewhat different. One response has been the routine inclusion in trials of expert scientific evidence on the reliability of eyewitness identifications, typically as part of the defense's case. The general objective is to counteract the commonsense assumption that confident identifications are highly accurate by educating the triers of fact about research findings. Another, more important, response has been to encourage police investigators to adopt field procedures that, based upon the same research, will reduce the chances of false identifications. Returning to Table 6-3, it is clear that many of the factors that elevate false-identification rates are out of the control of investigators in the field. For instance, all three of the witness factors are beyond investigative control, as are all of the storage factors that are inherent properties of crimes themselves. Other than the witness category, however, there are some factors in each of the other categories whose influence can be minimized by appropriate investigative procedures, with an obvious example being to administer prompt identification tests to minimize the effects of the forgetting curve.

To stimulate the implementation of such research-based procedures, the leading professional organization of forensic psychologists, the American Psychology and Law Society (APLS), commissioned a group of six prominent researchers to prepare a review of the scientific literature on eyewitness identification and to generate a series of procedural rules for administering line-ups and photo spreads (the implicit assumption being that show-ups should not be used in view of their high false-identification rates). In 1998, that review was published (Wells et al., 1998), along with an important addendum by a seventh researcher (Kassin, 1998). Shortly thereafter, the U.S. Department of Justice published a manual for the treatment of eyewitness evidence by law enforcement personnel that incorporated some of the same scientific findings (Technical Working Group for Eyewitness Evidence, 1999). This manual had its origins in a committee of 34 people formed by the then–attorney general, Janet Reno, to develop improved protocols for handling eyewitness evidence. Three members of the APLS reviewing team (Fulero, Malpass, and Wells) were also members of the Department of Justice committee, thereby ensuring some degree of continuity in the recommendations of the respective groups. The recommendations that emerged are an exceptional illustration of how experimentation on false-memory reports can be of practical assistance in circumstances in which it is crucial to minimize such errors. We conclude this section with sketches of the APLS and Department of Justice recommendations.

APLS Guidelines

Wells et al. (1998) began their article by noting a point that we have previously mentioned—namely, that in established cases of wrongful conviction, false eyewitness identifications are by far the leading cause of such convictions. The literature review itself revolved around variables such as those in Table 6-3, leading to four rules whose implementation should reduce false identifications and also reduce inflated confidence in false identifications. The authors concluded that there was especially strong research favoring these particular rules and that each could be implemented by introducing simple controls into standard police investigative procedures. As will be seen, each rule minimizes more than one of the reliability factors in Table 6-3, so that together they ought to achieve significant reductions in eye-witness identification errors.

Rule 1: Who Conducts Identifications?   It is standard practice in criminal cases for eyewitness identification tests to be administered by the same police officers who are investigating the case. At first glance, this procedure seems only natural because those officers will be well acquainted with the details of the case, includ-ing the identity of the principal suspects, and, in most instances, will already have established rapport with the witnesses. However, Wells et al.'s first recommenda-tion was that eyewitness identifications should not be administered by officers who are aware of the identity of suspects.

As we have seen, eyewitness identifications are influenced by a variety of postevent information that was not experienced at the crime scene, with informa-tion that points to a particular suspect being especially problematic. We have also seen that identifications are influenced by the instructions that witnesses receive, with error rates being inflated by instructions that encourage witnesses to make iden-tifications; by the questions that witnesses are asked, with error rates being inflated by questions that are suggestive or that encourage adoption of less-stringent mem-ory criteria; and by the construction of line-ups and photo spreads, with error rates being inflated by unfair tests that make innocent suspects stand out from other al-ternatives. In addition, we know that witnesses' confidence in their identifications is malleable (e.g., if witnesses are told that they have identified the police suspect [Wells & Bradfield, 1998] or if they are told that another witness has identified the same suspect [Luus & Wells, 1994]). Rule 1 is designed to reduce the contaminat-ing influence of all of these factors.

By reason of their detailed knowledge of a case, investigating officers are in the unique position of being able to introduce all of these sources of taint into eyewit-ness identifications, either intentionally or unwittingly. Concerning postevent in-formation, for example, we saw in the case of Mr. Z that the investigating officers were able to provide the two witnesses with an assortment of information that pointed to Mr. Z. Moreover, at the time that identification tests are administered, investi-gating officers who know that their suspect is present and who that suspect is, will be more likely to provide instructions that encourage witnesses to make identifica-tions, will be able to ask suggestive questions that direct witnesses toward their sus-pect, will be able to construct line-ups and photo spreads in which the suspect stands out from the other alternatives, and will be able to provide witnesses with infor-mation that inflates confidence in their identifications. Adoption of Rule 1 greatly reduces concerns about the influence of these factors because test administrators lack the essential information that is required to point witnesses to particular suspects.

Those concerns are not entirely eliminated, however. To illustrate, witnesses might receive contaminating postevent information in advance of identification tests, as in the case of Mr. Z. Similarly, even non–investigating officers who are blind to the identity of suspects are aware that the suspect is present in line-ups and photo spreads, and for that reason, they may provide witnesses with instructions that encourage them to make identifications, and they may provide witnesses who make identifications with information that inflates confidence in those identifications. However, the latter possibilities can be controlled to a considerable degree via Rules 2, 3, and 4.

Rule 2: What Are the Identification Instructions?   In principle, the problem of instructions that encourage subjects to weaken their subjective criteria of memorability and to make identifications when their memories are unable to provide verbatim matches can be controlled by formulating standardized instructions that must be used on all identification tests. Wells et al. (1998) recommended that identification instructions incorporate three features: (a) Witnesses should be told that the culprit may not be present in a line-up or photo spread; (b) because the culprit may not be present, witnesses should also be told that they are under no obligation to make an identification; and (c) witnesses should also be told that the person administering the test does not know the identity of the suspect, even if he or she *does* know the suspect's identity. It is obvious that the net effect of the first two features should be to discourage witnesses from using lax memory criteria and to encourage them to rely instead on verbatim matches. The net effect of the third feature is to reduce the influence of any postevent information, suggestive questions, or confidence-inflating information that may be provided by test administrators. Although it would be better for accuracy if none of these factors were present, their influences can be mitigated to some degree if witnesses do not believe that test administrators are in a position to provide information that is pertinent to the identity of culprits. A long research tradition in the social psychology of persuasion establishes that subjects are more likely to base their judgments on information that is provided by other people when those people are believed to possess relevant knowledge, an effect that is known as *source credibility* (e.g., Jones, Sinclair, & Courneya, 2003; McComas & Trumbo, 2003).

Rule 3: How Are Line-ups and Photo Spreads Constructed?   Wells et al.'s third rule is designed to address the problems of line-up fairness and unmatched foils. According to this rule, line-ups and photo spreads should be constructed so that suspects do not stand out from the other alternatives (e.g., the suspect is not the only tall person; the suspect is not the only Asian American) and so that choices other than suspects do not differ in major ways from witnesses' descriptions of culprits. Although these two construction principles are easy to state, they can be quite difficult to implement in practice. When an identification test involves a suspect plus several alternative choices (say, 4–6), it may be difficult for a single administrator to ensure that all of the alternatives match the suspect in all major categories of physical appearance or that they match all of the key features in witnesses' descriptions. With line-ups, this difficulty can be addressed by having multiple people review the line-up before it is administered, which is usually called a *mock witness* procedure. In this procedure, individuals who are not witnesses to index crimes are asked to select culprits from line-ups, the idea being that line-ups that produce the police suspect as the predominant choice of uninformed "witnesses" are clearly unfair (e.g., Malpass, 1981; Malpass & Devine, 1983; Wells, Leippe, & Ostrom,

1979). With photo spreads, on the other hand, the procedure is less cumbersome and more mechanical. Law enforcement agencies maintain large databases of photographs to be used in constructing photo spreads (e.g., mug shots from prior arrests, driver's license photographs). Computer programs are now available that will accept the photograph of a police suspect as input and then generate photographs from the database that match the suspect's photograph in major categories of physical appearance and that can therefore be used in constructing a photo spread. Some of these programs will also accept witnesses' descriptions of culprits' appearance as input.

Rule 4: How Should Confidence Be Assessed?   The next rule is intended to improve the reliability of witnesses' ratings of their confidence in their responses. Little can be done about the low baseline correlation between the accuracy of identifications and witnesses' confidence in those identifications. This is another brute fact of forensic life, to which a possible response would be simply not to request confidence ratings following identifications. However, requesting confidence ratings is standard practice, and the results are routinely presented in court. These circumstances, together with the fact that jurors tend to assume that accuracy and confidence are strongly correlated, means that thought must be given to the known malleability of confidence. More explicitly, because it has been demonstrated that postidentification confidence can be inflated by various sources of postidentification information—such as, in addition to factors we have already mentioned, something as trivial as witnesses thinking about how to answer questions about their identifications (Wells, Ferguson, & Lindsay, 1981), the intent of Rule 4 is to eliminate as much potentially contaminating postidentification information as possible. It simply states that if a confidence rating is to be obtained, it should be requested immediately following an identification response, without time for the witness to reflect extensively upon the response or for the administrator to provide postidentification feedback or elaboration.

Rule 5: How Shall Identification Evidence Be Preserved?   The four rules that we have just considered were advocated by Wells et al. (1998) as being both well grounded in extant research and as ones that are not difficult to incorporate into current police procedures. In a commentary on Wells et al.'s recommendations, Kassin (1998) proposed a fifth rule: The administration of line-ups and photo spreads should be preserved on videotape, so that those records can then be introduced at trial as the actual identification evidence (rather than witnesses reprising their earlier identifications during testimony). Kassin noted that, like Wells et al.'s recommendations, this fifth rule would not be difficult to incorporate into current police procedures because most police stations have videotaping facilities to record witness interviews and suspect interrogations, and those tapes are later introduced as trial evidence. It would only be necessary to also use those facilities to conduct identification tests. This would accomplish several objectives, all of which should redound to the reliability of the evidence that is presented to juries. The most obvious one is that it overcomes limitations in the ability of witnesses and test administrators to remember exactly what was said and done during the course of an identification session when they testify about those details months or years later. Beyond this, it allows juries and forensic experts to review videotapes for the presence of factors that are known to increase witnesses' false-identification rates and to inflate witnesses' confidence in their identifications. For instance, juries and forensic experts will be able to determine whether suggestive questions were asked, whether hints as to the identity of police suspects were provided, whether instructions encouraged witnesses to make identifications even if they did not clearly recall the culprit's appearance, and whether postidentification information was provided prior to obtaining confidence ratings. In addition, the speech of witnesses during an identification test, along with other aspects of their demeanor, will help to determine if they were intoxicated.

Department of Justice Guidelines

The specific recommendations promulgated by the Department of Justice (Technical Working Group for Eyewitness Evidence, 1999) go beyond eyewitness identification tests to encompass mug-book procedures as well. The mug-book recommendations fall into four categories, two of which are based upon findings from false-memory research: (a) procedures for constructing mug books, and (b) instructions for viewing mug books. In category a, all recommendations are intended to adhere to the principle that mug books should be as nonsuggestive as possible, so as to increase the chances that witnesses will provide *reliable* leads in cases in which preliminary investigation has failed to turn up suspects. (*Nonsuggestive* simply means that mug books should not be constructed so as to favor the selection of certain photographs *independent of the contents of witnesses' memories*.) Specific recommendations that are intended to reduce suggestiveness are to group photographs according to format (e.g., color versus black-and-white), to select photographs of people who are uniform with respect to major categories of physical appearance, and to include only one photograph of each individual. Obviously, based upon research that we have already considered, each of these constraints should reduce the probability that photographs of innocent individuals will be selected because they stand out, relative to other photographs.

In category b, all recommendations are intended to adhere to the principle that viewing instructions should help witnesses to identify actual culprits. Specific recommendations are to instruct the witness that mug books are only collections of photographs (rather than depictions of criminals), that actual culprits may not be present in mug books, that investigation will continue regardless of whether identifications are made, and that witnesses should think back to the events of the crime and to their frame of mind at the time. It is clear that the first three instructions should combine to discourage witnesses from making identifications based upon weak memories or on no memory information. The last instruction may be thought of as an application of the encoding-variability principle (Tulving & Thomson, 1971), which we discussed in chapter 3. Thinking about the events of the crime or about one's frame of mind may reinstate some of the surface cues that were present at the time, thereby facilitating retrieval of verbatim traces of other surface information (such as culprits' appearance).

Turning to identification tests proper, the Department of Justice guidelines provide separate recommendations for line-ups and photo spreads, which differ in certain nuances. For both types of tests, there are separate series of recommendations about construction of the stimuli that witnesses view and about the viewing instructions that they receive. Regarding construction, the objective of all recommendations about line-ups and photo spreads is to implement the principle that a fair set of stimuli will help witnesses to provide an accurate identification or nonidentification. (*Fair* has essentially the same meaning as *nonsuggestive*.) With respect to line-ups, test administrators are advised to include only one suspect per line-up, to include nonsuspects in each line-up who match witnesses' descriptions of the culprit (or to include nonsuspects who match the major categories of a suspect's appearance if good descriptions are not available), to position suspects randomly, to avoid reusing nonsuspects if witnesses view multiple line-ups, not to select nonsuspects who are so similar to suspects that witnesses will have difficulty discriminating between them, to create uniformity between nonsuspects and suspects with respect to unusual features (e.g., scars, tattoos) by adding those features to nonsuspects or by subtracting them from suspects, and to include a minimum of four nonsuspects. Available research data indicate that all of these recommendations ought to reduce the incidence of false identification of innocent suspects and that, in addition, the fifth recommendation ought to reduce the incidence of false rejection of actual culprits.

With respect to photo spreads, the first six recommendations are reiterated, and the seventh is changed to a minimum of five nonsuspects (additional nonsuspect photographs are easier to obtain than additional nonsuspects for live line-ups), and two recommendations are added: to ensure that no information concerning previous arrests is visible on photographs and to have one or more people view a photo spread before it is administered to ensure that certain choices do not stand out from the others. Obviously, photographs of innocent suspects that contain arrest information are highly suggestive, as are photographs that stand out from the other choices.

Finally, Department of Justice instructional guidelines for both line-ups and photo spreads are predicated on the principle that the content of the instructions that witnesses receive can help them to base identifications or nonidentifications on their memories of crimes rather than on information that was not experienced as part of index crimes. For *both* line-ups and photo spreads, before witnesses view stimulus sets, administrators are advised to inform them that it is just as important to clear innocent suspects as to implicate guilty ones, that photographs of culprits may differ from their appearance during crimes because features such as head and facial hair may have changed, that culprits' photographs (or culprits themselves) may not be present, that the investigation of crimes will continue regardless of whether identifications are made, and that the procedure requires that witnesses supply confidence ratings following identifications or nonidentifications. Based upon the experimental findings that we have considered, these elements should discourage witnesses from adopting weak memory criteria or relying on extraneous information.

With respect to the last element, the obvious intent of forewarning witnesses about confidence ratings is to provide further encouragement for adopting stringent memory criteria. Although this may indeed be the effect of such an instruction, some data in the eyewitness-memory literature suggest that it may have the opposite effect. Presumably, forewarning witnesses about confidence ratings will cause them to think about their levels of confidence as they view individual stimuli (the assumption being that low levels of perceived confidence will discourage identification). However, findings reported in a study of confidence malleability by Wells et al. (1981) suggest that forewarning could also have the undesirable effect of inflating confidence ratings. Wells et al. asked some subjects to merely think about how they would answer subsequent questions about the accuracy of their identifications, whereas other subjects did not receive this instruction. Subjects who received the "think" instruction exhibited higher confidence in their responses than subjects who did not receive the instruction. Beyond this datum, the previously mentioned finding that confidence tends to drift upward over time, as witnesses reflect upon their identifications, also raises the possibility that the forewarning instruction could inflate confidence ratings.

Synopsis

Witness interviewing and eyewitness identification of culprits are remarkable examples of successful translations of laboratory research on false memory to applied domains in which it is crucial to minimize false-memory reports. Interviews of victims, witnesses, and suspects, and identifications of culprits by victims and witnesses are linchpins of police investigation and prosecution. The criminal justice system leans so heavily upon both procedures that victims and witnesses who report events that did not happen or who wrongly identify individuals as culprits can cause the system to go completely astray. Innocent people can be subjected to the annoyance of police investigation, to the humiliation of being charged with felonies, to the frightening experience of standing trial, and even to the trauma of being convicted and, in the case of capital crimes, of being sentenced to death. It is of the first importance, then, to exploit the findings of false-memory research to minimize the frequency of such miscarriages of justice, not only to avoid subjecting innocent people to the anguish of criminal proceedings but also to foster confidence among the citizenry that the best available research is being put to work to enhance the reliability of the criminal justice system.

Regarding witness interviews, the degree to which such interviews are central to the process of criminal investigation is not widely appreciated. More often than not, entire investigations and subsequent prosecutions revolve around information that is obtained in interviews of witnesses and suspects, with records of those interviews—in the form of written narratives, videotapes, or audiotapes—being introduced as evidence at trial. Not infrequently, this is a matter of necessity because, with many crimes, there is no probative physical evidence, so that there is no case beyond the memory reports of victims, witnesses, and suspects. However, reliance on such evidence can also be due to failures to gather probative physical evidence that was available at the crime scene or to a downright preference for memory reports from interviews over physical evidence. Regardless of the reasons, two facts converge to raise concerns about strong reliance on memory reports that are obtained in investigative interviews as evidence in criminal proceedings. First, there is a rich experimental literature, dating back more than 3 decades and consisting of hundreds of studies, that is focused on the tendency of suggestive questioning to foment false recognition and false recall in connection with previously observed events. That suggestive questioning has such effects is firmly established, with even brief, one-time suggestions being known to produce reliable elevations in false-memory responses. Further, a number of factors have been isolated that increase the tendency of suggestive questioning to falsify memory reports, such as limited exposure to the target events, inaccessibility of verbatim memories of target events, whether target events are central versus peripheral to a crime, whether there are substantial delays between exposure to target events and suggestive questions, whether suggestions are repeated, and whether suggestions are accompanied by coercion. Generally speaking, the known effects of such factors are predicted by opponent-processes distinctions.

Second, standard police interviewing protocols, especially protocols for interviewing suspects, incorporate a number of suggestive features whose effects have been studied in the experimental literature. In addition, these suggestive features are present at much stronger levels than would be ethically permissible in experimentation. For instance, memory suggestions may be accompanied by threats of punishment if interviewees do not accede to the suggestions or by promises of reward if they do. Or, interviewees may be deprived of sleep or food prior to being suggestively questioned, or they may be intoxicated at the time.

Concerns about strong reliance on interview evidence are reinforced by documented instances of erroneous prosecution and conviction pursuant to false information that was provided during the course of suggestive interviews. Perhaps the most troubling examples come from documented instances of false confession by police suspects who were subjected to intensely suggestive questioning, often under physical conditions that are known to heighten susceptibility to suggestion. A further point about criminal prosecution that is not generally understood is that certain forms of evidence can be represented to triers of fact as confessions that are quite different than the layperson's conception of confession. To illustrate, a defendant's failure to vigorously deny an incriminating version of events that was suggested during questioning can be represented as a confession, as can a defendant's acceptance of an incriminating version of events as being plausible while simultaneously denying that he remembers things in that way. Research on false confession has shown that innocent people may falsely confess to crimes even though they were not subjected to suggestive questioning, so-called voluntary false confessions. Of greater interest from the perspective of false-memory research, innocent people may also confess to crimes during the course of suggestive interviews. People who falsely confess to crimes pursuant to suggestive questioning may be fully aware that they did not commit the proposed acts, so-called coerced-compliant confessions, or suggestive questioning may induce false memories of having committed some or all of the acts, so-called coerced-internalized confessions. Research has shown that coerced-compliant confessions are more likely to occur when interviewees have been deprived of basic biological needs, when interviewees are intoxicated, when suggestive questions are accompanied by threats of punishment or promises of leniency, and when interviewers lie to interviewees about the strength of corroborating evidence against them. More than 200 possible examples of coerced-compliant confessions were identified in a review of murder prosecutions in Chicago, Illinois, during the 1990s. Coerced-internalized confessions, on the other hand, are instances of false memory because suspects make self-incriminating statements that are disproved by other evidence, but they nevertheless remember the stated events as actual occurrences, with the case of Paul Ingram being a well-known example. The reality of coerced-internalized confessions has been established under controlled laboratory conditions in normal subjects, and some of the factors that increase the incidence of such confessions have been identified. Importantly, these factors are ones whose effects are predicted by opponent-processes distinctions and are also ones that are often present in criminal cases.

The experimental literature on eyewitness identification, which includes the generation of investigative leads via mug books as well as actual suspect-identification tests, is even more extensive than that on suggestive interviewing, and it provides an excellent scientific resource for devising field identification techniques. The need to put such techniques on a firm scientific footing is acute because the baseline level of identification accuracy, both when police suspects are culprits and when they are not, is roughly 50–50 under favorable conditions. The need is also acute because research has shown that triers of fact hold two mistaken beliefs about eyewitness identification that influence the weight that they assign to such evidence—namely, that identifications tend to be quite accurate and that there is a strong correlation between the accuracy of identifications and witnesses' expressed confidence in their identifications.

Controlled studies of eyewitness identification have isolated several variables that influence identification accuracy and whose effects are predicted by opponent-processes concepts. As in earlier discussions of false-memory research, most of these variables fall into three categories: (a) storage factors (attitudes, color perception, cross-race bias, exposure time, intoxication, mugshot bias, postevent information, stress, weapon focus); (b) retrieval factors (the accuracy-confidence relation, confidence malleability, hypnosis, instructions, line-up fairness, presentation format, questions, show-ups, stress, transference, unmatched foils); and (c) forgetting factors (the forgetting curve, recovered memories). In addition, there are three variables that refer to the reliability of special categories of witnesses: The baseline accuracy of children's identifications is lower than adults'; children's identifications are more susceptible to the influence of postevent suggestions; and the baseline accuracy of elderly adults' identifications is lower than younger adults'.

To assist law enforcement personnel, guidelines have been developed for eyewitness identification that are designed to minimize the influence of many of these factors. One set of guidelines has been promulgated by the APLS, based upon a detailed review of the scientific literature. Those guidelines, which are concerned with line-ups and photo spreads, stress five safeguards that are in the nature of general rules of procedure: test administrators should not be investigative officers who are aware of suspects' identities; test instructions should inform witnesses that culprits may not be present, they are under no obligation to make identifications, and the test administrator does not know the identity of the suspect; the choices in line-ups and photo spreads should be constructed in such a way that suspects do not stand out from the other alternatives and so that the other choices do not differ in major ways from witnesses' descriptions of culprits; confidence ratings should be requested immediately after identification responses; and the entire identification process should be preserved on videotape so that a verbatim record can be placed in evidence at trial. The other set of guidelines has been promulgated by the U.S. Department of Justice, and it consists of recommendations for mug books, line-ups, and photo spreads that are somewhat more specific than the APLS guidelines. The guidelines for mug books are intended to reduce the inherent suggestiveness of this investigative tool, and they include separate recommendations about how to construct mug books and how to instruct witnesses who are about to view mug books. The guidelines for line-ups and photo spreads also include separate recommendations about how to construct stimulus sets and about how to instruct witnesses. The construction recommendations are predicated on the principle that a fair stimulus set provides more accurate identifications and nonidentifications, whereas the instructional recommendations are predicated on the principle that proper instructions can help witnesses to base identifications and nonidentifications on actual memories of crimes (rather than on extraneous information).

7

False Memory in Criminal Investigation

2—Child Interviewing and Testimony

It sometimes happens that scientific theories or data become embroiled in public controversies. During the 1920s and 1930s, for instance, Einstein's theory of relativity was the focus of widespread attacks within Germany for its alleged heterodoxy with respect to conservative political positions of the day and its alleged sympathy with communist views. During the same period, relativity theory was criticized, outside as well as inside Germany, for promulgating cosmological models that conflicted with Christian dogma about the genesis of the universe. Of all of the examples of scientific work ensnared in the toils of public dispute, however, evolution by natural selection is surely the most enduring.

When Darwin published *Origin of Species* in November 1859, the book met with instant acclaim, with the first printing selling out within a few days. The volume was held in such high esteem by British academicians that within a month of its publication, Lord Palmerston proposed that a knighthood should be conferred upon Darwin. Palmerston's proposal had to be scuttled when a prominent official of the Church of England, Bishop Samuel Wilberforce, intervened with Queen Victoria, contending that Darwin's book espoused a heretical view of human creation. This was the first official sign of what has become a century and a half of controversy. There followed vigorous public debates over the principle of natural selection, one of the earliest and best known of which occurred at Oxford University on June 30, 1860, during the meetings of the British Association for the Advancement of Science (see Hull, 1973; Irvine, 1955). Following a paper by an American professor, William Draper, a 4-hour debate ensued between Bishop Wilberforce and two leading British naturalists of the day, Thomas Huxley and Joseph Hooker. The discourse was heated and veered off into unscholarly territory, with Wilberforce making ad hominem attacks upon supporters of natural selection and Hooker accusing Wilber-force of being utterly ignorant of natural science and of not having bothered to read *Origin of Species.*

Although the scientific evidence then and now makes an overwhelming case for evolution by natural selection, public controversies have continued. In 1925, the case of *Tennessee v. John Scopes* involved the prosecution of a high school biology instructor for teachings that violated Tennessee House Bill 185, which specified that "it shall be unlawful for any teacher in any of the Universities, Normals and all other public schools of the State which are supported in whole or in part by the public school funds of the State, to teach any theory that denies the story of the Divine Creation of man as taught in the Bible, and to teach instead that man has descended from a lower order of animals." In more recent years, advocates of "creation science" first attempted unsuccessfully to have natural selection removed from biology textbooks on the ground that it was an unproved theory, and then attempted, with greater success, to have references to religious doctrines about evolution included in biology textbooks.

The lesson that has been learned from these and many other public quarrels over scientific work is that in the public arena, the artifacts of science are not judged by dispassionate standards of evidence. Instead, they are subjected to specious argumentation, misinterpretation, outright distortion, and even attempts to gag scientific discourse through legislation and litigation. On the latter point, it is worth noting that legislative gagging did not end with the *Scopes* trial nor has it been restricted to the principle of natural selection. In July 1999, for example, the U.S. Congress passed a formal resolution condemning a peer-reviewed scientific article that had failed to find strong statistical relations between adult psychological maladjustment and childhood experiences of sexual abuse, notwithstanding that the article had based its conclusions upon a review of 59 published studies (Rind, Tromovitch, & Bauserman, 1998). During the course of public disputes, the actual details of scientific work become distorted; differences between researchers are magnified; and points of fundamental agreement between researchers recede into the background.

The research that we shall consider in the present chapter—studies of false memory in child interviewing and testimony—is another instance of scientific work that has become enmeshed in public controversy. In that respect, it is the most contentious of all of the topics that are covered in this volume, though there is little disagreement among scientists as to the general nature of research findings. The controversy is legal and social rather than scientific. Although it was not always so (e.g., see Binet, 1900; Stern, 1910; Varendock, 1911), since the 1990s, research in this domain has been closely connected to an area of the law that quite understandably evokes high emotion: child sexual abuse crimes. In fact, many experiments in the literature have been explicitly motivated by a desire to answer questions that arise in the investigation and prosecution of such crimes (e.g., Bottoms, Goodman, Schwartz-Kenney, & Thomas, 2002; Goodman & Aman, 1990; Howe, Courage, & Peterson, 1995; Pipe & Goodman, 1991; Saywitz, Nicholas, Goodman, & Moan, 1991). For that reason, much of the extant research on false memory in child interviewing and testimony has been shaped by the investigation and prosecution of sexual abuse crimes.

It is therefore necessary to begin with a precis of the recent history of how the law handles child sexual abuse allegations in the United States. After that preliminary discussion, we take up the main topic of this chapter: research on the suggestibility of children's memory reports. The chapter concludes by considering a major way in which the results of such research have benefited the investigation and prosecution of sexual abuse crimes—namely, the development of best-practice protocols for conducting forensic interviews of child victims and witnesses.

A Little History: Child Sexual Abuse and the Law

Nowadays, the criminal codes of most countries classify sexual contacts between adults and under-age persons, whether consensual or not, as felonies. Although the definitions of "sexual contacts" and "under age" vary somewhat, genital touching and genital penetration of body cavities of children by individuals who are legally classified as adults are universally regarded as felonious. Historically, legal attitudes were sometimes different. In ancient Greece, for instance, sexual contacts between adults and children were not regarded as crimes; behavior which seems repugnant to us today, such as man–boy sexual contact, although not overtly sanctioned in ancient Greece, was considered acceptable. Although the Bible enjoins against incest and other forms of child-adult sexual contact, Kessen (1965) documented that there was little concern in Western European or U.S. law for this or any other issue of child welfare before the 17th century, the chief reason being that a majority of children failed to survive beyond the fifth year of life. Also, it is good to remind ourselves that prior to that time, infanticide was a common and accepted practice in many "civilized" countries (Zigler & Hall, 1991). Eventually, as medical advances reduced infant and child mortality rates, child welfare began to figure prominently in the law. The child labor statutes of the 19th century, which restricted hours and working conditions for children, are familiar cases in point. Child sexual abuse statutes in the United States can be traced to the child welfare movement, which began in the early 20th century (Kessen, 1965). Although that movement initially focused on physical abuse and neglect, sexual abuse eventually surfaced as a focal issue.

The Social Security Act, which was passed during the first term of President Franklin Roosevelt, included provisions for child welfare. However, it was not until the 1960s that state laws criminalizing child abuse and neglect became universal. The initial impetus for such laws were highly publicized concerns about physical abuse, which were expressed by pediatric researchers (e.g., Kempe, Silver, Silverman, Droegemueller, & Silver, 1962). By 1970, all states had passed statutes mandating physician reporting of suspected physical abuse. The Child Abuse Prevention and Treatment Act, which Congress passed in 1974, incorporated sexual and emotional abuse as forms of child abuse. During the ensuing years, mandatory reporting statutes were broadened to encompass professionals other than physicians, such as psychologists, social workers, and teachers. Also, the subsequent establishment of a federal office for gathering and reporting statistics on child abuse, the National Center on Child Abuse and Neglect, made data on the incidence of abuse more widely available. Data emanating from this and other sources seemed to show

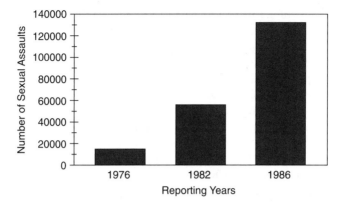

Figure 7-1. Reported cases of child sexual assault in the United States from 1976 to 1986. Data from American Association for Protecting Children (1985, 1987).

that child sexual abuse, in particular, was on the rise during the 1970s and 1980s and was therefore in urgent need of legal attention. For instance, Figure 7-1 shows an alarming increase in reported cases of child sexual assault in the decade from 1976 to 1986 (American Association for Protecting Children, 1985, 1987). Similarly, Poole and Lamb (1998) summarized statistics from the National Center on Child Abuse and Neglect, which showed that the number of investigative referrals increased from 10 reports per 1,000 children in 1976 to 43 reports per 1,000 children in 1993. As yet another example, Poole and Lamb also noted that the *proportion* of abuse and neglect reports that involved sexual abuse doubled during the 1980s.

In response, prosecutions of adults for child sexual abuse accelerated dramatically during the same interval. According to U.S. Justice Department statistics, whereas the number of adults who were arrested for sexual offenses in 1976 was roughly 150,000, the number had risen to approximately a quarter million by 1991. At the same time, however, researchers who study child sexual abuse cautioned that the statistical evidence of increases in such crimes might be illusory (e.g., Ceci & Bruck, 1995). For example, the broadening of legal definitions of sexual abuse and of the categories of professionals who are legally obligated to report suspected abuse are obvious contaminants that would elevate reported levels of abuse, even if the actual incidence of abuse remained constant or declined somewhat. Further, certain research findings seemed to conflict with the statistical evidence of apparent increases in child sexual abuse. A telling illustration is self-reports of childhood sexual victimization by younger adults who were children during the period in which sexual abuse was allegedly rising and by older adults who were children prior to that period. If sexual abuse actually rose dramatically during the indicated period, then, of course, self-reports of victimization should be higher in the former group. Ceci and Bruck (1995) noted that self-reports of victimization are equivalent for the two age groups.

From the standpoint of false-memory research, a crucial aspect of child sexual abuse, relative to physical abuse and neglect, is that such crimes leave few detectable physical traces. Children who are subjected to physical abuse will accumulate a range of injuries (bumps, bruises, fractures, and so on) that are medically inconsistent with accidental injury—the so-called battered-child syndrome (Kempe et al., 1962). Likewise, children who are neglected will exhibit visible signs, such as being unwashed, poorly clothed, or malnourished, and they may be left alone by their caretakers for extended periods (a fact that can be observed and reported by other adults). Such external signs are typically absent in child sexual abuse (McGough, 1993). As we noted in chapter 5, the sexual victimization of children most often occurs in private, with only a single adult and a single child being present, and many of the adult acts that the law defines as child sexual abuse cannot, by definition, leave evidence on children's bodies or clothing that could be detected later by medical or forensic examinations. Here, the standard examples are sexualized touching of a child's genitals or anus, verbal statements containing sexual content, showing pornographic pictures or videos to children, and reading pornographic stories to children. Even acts of sexual abuse that involve penetration of the vagina or rectum may fail to leave any reliable evidence. Vaginal and rectal tissue may heal and may not be noticeably damaged by penetration. Moreover, when tissue damage is present, this is not in itself reliable evidence of sexual penetration because these injuries can occur in other ways. As a rule, damage to vaginal or rectal tissue is only a reliable indicator of sexual penetration when it is accompanied by bodily fluids, tissue, or hair from the perpetrator. However, as we also noted in chapter 6, even when evidence of the latter sort is deposited, it may no longer be detectable if there are delays of more than a few hours in reporting the crime.

During the 1980s, two major changes occurred in the procedures for investigating and prosecuting child sexual abuse crimes, which were designed to deal with this "evidence problem" but which have stimulated much controversy ever since. The first involved the questioning methods that are used to gather memory reports from potential abuse victims, and the second, which was briefly considered in chapter 5, involved changes in the law's procedures for handling child witnesses. We describe these two changes separately below and then comment on some larger legal issues that motivate the study of the suggestibility of child witnesses.

Use of Suggestive Questions in Forensic Interviews of Children

As Ceci and Friedman (2000) documented, attitudes toward what constitutes appropriate questioning during child forensic interviews underwent substantial revision during the 1980s. As mentioned, the only witnesses to such child sexual abuse crimes are typically a single child victim and a single adult perpetrator, and the crimes do not usually leave any reliable physical evidence. Consequently, children's memory reports are necessarily the principal source of evidence that crimes have occurred. This circumstance would not pose acute reliability concerns if victims of sexual abuse were primarily adolescents or older elementary-schoolers. In fact, however, young children—preschoolers and children in the first few elementary grades—are the predominant reported victims of such crimes (Poole & Lamb, 1998). When young children are asked to provide narratives of their experiences under nonsuggestive free-recall conditions, their responses are apt to be quite sketchy (e.g., Howe, 1991), and sometimes, the only information that they are able to provide in response to open-ended questions is their names and ages. Thus, when young children volunteer information to their parents or guardians that is indicative of abuse and they are later questioned about such disclosures by official investigators, a common result is no information that will support prosecution if children are simply asked to provide a narrative of events (e.g., Tell me what Mr. Smith did to you at his house yesterday). In contrast to young children's lack of volubility in response to free-recall questions, they will often provide detailed information about specific acts of abuse in response to other types of questions, especially questions that are leading (Did Mr. Smith touch your privates yesterday?), questions that are suggestive (Mr. Smith touched your privates, didn't he?), or questions that are repeated when abuse-confirming responses are not initially forthcoming.

That young children often fail to provide reports of sexual abuse to investigators without such prompting led some authorities to argue for the benefits of including leading, suggestive, and repetitive questioning in child forensic interviews (e.g., Goodman & Clarke-Stewart, 1991; Lyon, 1995; Myers, 1995). Although questioning of this sort will yield answers that lead to criminal prosecutions at much higher rates than open-ended requests for narratives, two considerations raise concerns about the potential inaccuracy of those answers. The first will have already occurred to readers on the basis of chapter 6: Suggestive questioning about crimes has been found to induce false-memory reports in adult witnesses, even when the adults are suspects who are strongly motivated to avoid guilt-confirming responses. The second consideration is that it has been believed since Binet's (1900) ground-breaking research that children's memories, especially young children's, are highly susceptible to distortion from suggestive questioning. Upon first impression, these two points would seem to cut the ground from under the use of suggestive questioning in child forensic interviews. Not so. Proponents of suggestive questioning have argued that these two considerations are not probative when it comes to the narrow issue of children who are interviewed about traumatic events *that involve their own bodies*. It has been argued, more explicitly, that whereas children's memory reports might be readily falsified by suggestive questions that pertain to events that they have *witnessed*, their memory reports are resistant to falsification when the target memories are of traumatic events that they *directly experienced* (Ceci & Friedman, 2000).

Some early studies of children's ability to remember direct experiences of sexualized events seemed to confirm this proposal. One of the most influential was conducted by Saywitz et al. (1991). The subjects were girls who had received a pediatric examination, which involved genital and anal touches for half of the children. Following their examinations, the other half of the children, who had not received genital or anal touches, were asked direct questions about such touches. Only 1 child (out of 35) who was asked a direct question about genital touching falsely agreed that she had been touched, and only 2 children (out of 36) who were asked a direct question about anal touching falsely agreed that they had been touched. As a further illustration of such findings, Rudy and Goodman (1991) reported an experiment in which pairs of 4- and 7-year-olds played with a strange adult in a trailer.

One child watched while the adult dressed up the other child in a clown costume and took photographs of her. The children were questioned about the trailer experience 10–12 days later. The interview included suggestive questions of the sort that figure in child abuse investigations, such as, "Did he put anything in your mouth?" and "How many times did he spank you?" In response to such questions, 4-year-olds gave very few false answers (less than 10%) and 7-year-olds gave none.

Upon first impression, studies such as these seem to validate the proposal that children's memories are highly resistant to suggestions about sexualized experiences involving their own bodies, but researchers do not generally regard the studies' findings as determinative. There are two limitations. First and most obviously, the key data are *null findings*, failures to reject the null hypothesis of no treatment effect. One of the canons of experimental design and scientific inference is that nothing positive can be concluded (e.g., that children's memories are resistant to suggestion about personal sexual experiences) on the basis of null findings (e.g., a specific suggestive question failed to produce false-memory reports). Null results can be consequences of a myriad of unsuspected noise factors, and it is always possible that positive results will emerge when those factors are identified and controlled. Second, as Ceci and Friedman (2000) have shown, the forms of memory suggestion that were used in these null-results studies were brief and weak—usually, only a single yes-no question about a given false event. In actual field interviews in cases of suspected sexual abuse, much more highly suggestive interview procedures may be used. According to Ceci and Bruck's (1995) examination of illustrative court cases, those procedures may include (a) repeating a previously answered question several times within an interview, (b) selective reinforcement of desired responses (e.g., Yes, that's the right answer. You're doing great now), (c) stereotyping of suspects (e.g., Mr. Smith is a pretty bad guy), (d) peer pressure to agree with allegations of abuse (e.g., Your friend Sally was here today, and she told me that Mr. Smith touched her privates, too); and (e) guided imagery (e.g., Try to see in your head what Mr. Smith did to you. Just get a clear picture of what he did when he was touching you). We have already seen in chapter 6 that such procedures are capable of producing false-memory reports in adult witnesses, victims, and suspects. It follows that there is reason for concern that they will have analogous effects on children, even when the target events involve personal bodily experiences. This concern has spawned intense and continuing interest in the study of suggestion in children's memory.

That this concern may be well placed can be illustrated by court records from various sexual abuse prosecutions in which child plaintiffs were interviewed using highly suggestive procedures. A case in point is provided by the most famous child sexual abuse prosecution of the 20th century, the McMartin Preschool case (*State of California v. Buckey*, 1990). This case began on August 12, 1983, when Judy Johnson, the mother of a 2-year-old boy in Manhattan Beach, California, called police to report that her son had been sexually molested at the McMartin Preschool by Raymond Buckey. The call was made following a medical examination of the child for anal itching. Johnson reported to police that she had noticed a spot of blood on her son's anus following a day at school. On August 30, 1983, her son was interviewed at the police station, and he gave answers confirming that Buckey had

September 8, 1983

Dear Parent:

This Department is conducting a criminal investigation involving child molestation (288 P.C.). Ray Buckey, an employee of Virginia McMartin's Pre-School, was arrested September 7, 1983 by this Department.

The following procedure is obviously an unpleasant one, but to protect the rights of your children as well as the rights of the accused, this inquiry is necessary for a complete investigation.

Records indicate that your child has been or is currently a student at the pre-school. We are asking your assistance in this continuing investigation. Please question your child to see if he or she has been a witness to any crime or if he or she has been a victim. Our investigation indicates that possible criminal acts include: oral sex, fondling of genitals, buttock or chest area, and sodomy, possibly committed under the pretense of "taking the child's temperature." Also photos may have been taken of children without their clothing. Any information from your child regarding having ever observed Ray Buckey to leave a classroom alone with a child during any nap period, or if they have ever observed Ray Buckey tie up a child, is important.

Please complete the enclosed information form and return it to this Department in the enclosed stamped return envelope as soon as possible. We will contact you if circumstances dictate same.

We ask you to please keep this investigation strictly confidential because of the nature of the charges and the highly emotional effect it could have on our community. Please do not discuss this investigation with anyone outside your immediate family. Do not contact or discuss the investigation with Raymond Buckey, any member of the accused defendant's family, or employees connected with the McMartin Pre-School.

THERE IS NO EVIDENCE TO INDICATED [SIC] THAT THE MANAGEMENT OF VIRGINIA MCMARTIN'S PRE-SCHOOL HAD ANY KNOWLEDGE OF THIS SITUATION AND NO· DETRIMENTAL INFORMATION CONCERNING THE OPERATION OF THE SCHOOL HAS BEEN DISCOVERED DURING THIS INVESTIGATION. ALSO, NO OTHER EMPLOYEE IN THE SCHOOL IS UNDER INVESTIGATION FOR ANY CRIMINAL ACT.

Your prompt attention to this matter and reply no later than September 16, 1983 will be appreciated.

HARRY L. KUHLMEYER, JR.
Chief of Police
JOHN WEHNER, Captain

Figure 7-2. Letter to the parents of McMartin Preschool children.

sexually abused him. Buckey was arrested a week later, and a letter was soon sent to the parents of McMartin Preschool children informing them of the arrest and requesting relevant information. A reproduction of that letter appears in Figure 7-2. Note the highly suggestive material in the third paragraph, which elucidates specific sexual acts that were suspected to have occurred. The district attorney's office retained a consultant from the Children's Institute International to interview any other children who, as a result of this letter, were suspected of having been abused. By March 1984, following interviews by institute staff, more than 350 children had been diagnosed as victims of sexual abuse at the McMartin Preschool. On the basis of the children's statements and institute diagnoses, the founder of the school and six teachers were charged with more than 100 counts of child sexual abuse.

In January 1986, following 2 years of preliminary hearings, the charges against four of the teachers were dropped. The trial of the remaining two defendants, Raymond Buckey and Virginia McMartin Buckey, on 65 counts of child sexual abuse, began in July 1987. Two and a half years later, in January 1990, the jury returned a verdict that acquitted Ms. Buckey on all counts, that acquitted Mr. Buckey on 52 counts, and that failed to reach a verdict on 13 of the counts against Mr. Buckey. In post-trial interviews, some jurors stated that they had concluded, on the basis of the evidence, that some of the children had in fact been abused. However, they stated that it was impossible to convict the defendants on any of the counts because the interviews during which the children were questioned about sexual abuse, which the jurors had been shown on videotape, were highly suggestive. Two excerpts from those interviews are shown in Figure 7-3. Note the repeated use of three of the five procedures mentioned by Ceci and Bruck (1995)—namely, question repetition, selective reinforcement of desired responses, and peer pressure. Later that year, Mr. Buckey was retried on 8 of the 13 counts. Again, the jury failed to reach a verdict on any of the counts, but 7 of 12 voted to acquit Mr. Buckey on all counts. Following this outcome, prosecuting attorneys declined to seek a third trial. By that time, the cost of the legal proceedings had reached an estimated $15 million.

Legal Procedures for Handling Child Witnesses

The other category of changes involved special pre-trial and trial procedures in child sexual abuse prosecutions, procedures that are designed to allow child victims to provide their evidence in a nonthreatening, supportive atmosphere. Ironically, as McGough (1993) documented in a review of the historical circumstances surrounding these changes, they were largely stimulated by the public furor over the treatment of child witnesses in the case that we have just discussed, *State of California v. Buckey* (1990). During the course of what evolved into a 7-year investigation and prosecution, some of the media coverage focused on the seemingly outrageous ways in which some of the child plaintiffs were treated. The parents of these children, as well as the public at large, were understandably distressed by the grueling ordeals to which some children were subjected, ordeals that were utterly insensitive to the fragility of young children. According to one report, for instance, during the pre-trial phase of the prosecution, a child plaintiff was subjected to cross-examination by defense attorneys over a period of *17 days* in a manner that, in addition to being fatiguing, was intimidating and embarrassing (Rust, 1986). Although some legal scholars had previously called for modifications in criminal trial procedures that would be more accommodating to child witnesses and victims, McGough (1993) concluded that it was public outrage over the law's apparent insensitivity to the McMartin Preschool children that was the crucial factor that stimulated legal reforms. In the wake of public complaints following media depictions of the treatment of these children, members of the California State Assembly made speeches

Interview #1 (an 8-year-old boy)

Interviewer: Mr. Monkey is a little bit chicken, and he can't remember any of the naked games, but we think that you can, 'cause we know a naked game that you were around for, 'cause the other kids told us, and it's called Naked Movie Star. Do you remember that game, Mr. Alligator, or is your memory too bad?

Boy: Um, I don't remember that game.

Interviewer: Oh, Mr. Alligator.

Boy: Umm, well, it's umm, a little song that me and [a friend] heard of.

Interviewer: Oh.

Boy: Well, I heard out loud someone signing, "Naked Movie Star, Naked Movie Star."

Interviewer: You know that, Mr. Alligator? That means you're smart, 'cause that's the same song the other kids knew and that's how we really know you're smarter than you look. So you better not play dumb, Mr. Alligator.

Boy: Well, I didn't really hear a whole lot. I just heard someone yell it from out in the— Someone yelled it.

Interviewer: Maybe. Mr. Alligator, you peeked in the window one day and saw them playing it, and maybe you could remember and help us.

Boy: Well, no. I haven't seen anyone playing Naked Movie Star. I've only heard the song.

Interviewer: What good are you? You must be dumb.

Boy: Well I don't know really, umm, remember seeing anyone play that, 'cause I wasn't there, when—when people are playing it.

Interviewer: You weren't? You weren't? That's why we're hoping maybe you saw, see, a lot of these puppets weren't there, but they got to see what happened.

Boy: Well, I saw a lot of fighting.

Interviewer: I bet you can help us a lot, though, 'cause, like, Naked Movie Star is a simple game, because we know about that game, 'cause we just have had twenty kids told [sic] us about that game. Just this morning, a little girl came in and played it for us and sang it just like that. Do you think if I asked you a question, you could put your thinking cap on and you might remember, Mr. Alligator?

Boy: Maybe.

Interviewer: You could nod your head yes or no. Can you remember who took the pictures for the naked-movie-star game? That would be a great thing to feed into the secret machine [the video camera], and then it would be all gone, just like all the other kids did. You can just nod whether you remember or not, see how good your memory is.

Figure 7-3. Sample transcript of child interviews excerpted from videotapes that were introduced as evidence in *State of California v. Buckey* (1990).

(continued)

Interviewer: You do? Well, that's remarkable. I wonder if you could hold a pointer in your mouth, and then you wouldn't have to say a word and [boy] wouldn't have to say a word. And you could just point.

Boy: [Places pretend camera on adult male nude doll using alligator puppet] Sometimes he did.

Interviewer: Can I pat you on the head for that? Look what a big help you can be. You're going to help all these little children, because you're so smart—OK, did they ever pose in funny poses for the pictures?

Boy: Well, it wasn't a real camera. We just played—

Interviewer: Mr. Alligator, I'm going to—going to ask you something here. Now, we already found out from the other kids that it was a real camera, so you don't have to pretend, OK? Is that a deal?

Boy: Yes, it was a play camera that we played with.

Interviewer: Oh, and it went flash?

Boy: Well, it didn't exactly go flash.

Interviewer: It didn't exactly go flash. Went click? Did little pictures go zip, come out of it?

Boy: I don't remember that.

Interviewer: Oh, you don't remember that. Well, you're doing pretty good, Mr. Alligator. I got to shake your hand.

Interview #2 (6-year-old girl)

Interviewer: Maybe you could show me with this, with this doll [puts hand on two dolls, one naked, one dressed] how the kids danced for the Naked Movie Star.

Girl: They didn't really dance. It was just, like, a song.

Interviewer: Well, what did they do when they sang the song?

Girl: [Nods her head]

Interviewer: I heard that, I heard from several different kids that they took their clothes off. I think that [first classmate] told me that, I know that [second classmate] told me that, I know that [third classmate] told me. [Fourth classmate] and [fifth classmate] all told me that. That's kind of a hard secret, it's kind of a yucky secret to talk of—but, maybe, we could see if we could find—

Girl: Not that I remember.

Interviewer: This is my favorite puppet right here. [Picks up a bird puppet] You wanna be this

Figure 7-3. *Continued.*

300

and point on the, on the doll over here, on either one of these dolls, where, where the kids were touched? Could you do that?

Girl: I don't know.

Interviewer: I know that the kids were touched. Let's see if we can figure that out.

Girl: I don't know.

Interviewer: You don't know where they were touched?

Girl: Uh-uh. [Shakes her head]

Interviewer: Well, some of the kids told me that they were touched sometimes. They said that it was, it kinda, sometimes it kinda hurt. And some [of] the times, it felt pretty good. Do you remember that touching game that went on?

Girl: No.

Interviewer: Ok. Let me see if we can try something else and—

Girl: Wheeee! [Spins the puppet above her head]

Interviewer: Come on, bird, get down here and help us out here.

Girl: No.

Interviewer: Bird is having a hard time talking. I don't wanna hear any more no's. No no, Detective dog, we're gonna figure this out.

Figure 7-3. *Continued.*

advocating legislation to reform trial procedures for children, and the U.S. Congress, in multiple bills, appropriated more than $100 million for states to use in developing innovative reforms.

In the end, the reforms that were most widely adopted, examples of which were briefly mentioned in chapter 5, fell into three categories: (a) lowering traditional barriers to introducing evidence that consists of unsworn, out-of-court statements (hearsay); (b) simplifying and condensing the involvement of children in the pretrial investigative process; and (c) making the courtroom environment in which children supply testimony less forbidding and potentially traumatic. Concerning the last category, modifications to make the courtroom more child-friendly have proved to be uncontroversial, for the most part. They have included such changes as allowing children to provide testimony in a conversational format while seated at a table with the judge, the prosecuting attorney, and the defense attorney, rather than requiring that children be isolated in a witness box. Child-sized chairs may be supplied, and children may be allowed to draw pictures or use dolls to illustrate their statements. However, one of the modifications in category c has provoked considerable controversy: allowing children to provide testimony out of the sight of the defendants whom they are accusing. This may be accomplished by placing a screen in front of children, which obscures their view of everyone in the courtroom save the judge and the attorney who is posing questions, or by taking children's testimony in a separate room and transmitting it to the courtroom via closed-circuit television, or even by recording children's testimony in advance on videotape and then playing the tape for the jury during the trial.

Research findings showing that children can be intimidated and confused by the presence of adults who have harmed them or of whom they are otherwise afraid would seem to provide a sound empirical footing for such innovations. However, they appear to conflict with the Sixth Amendment to the U.S. Constitution, which enjoins that a criminal defendant has the right "to be confronted by the witnesses against him," a statement that the Supreme Court has long interpreted to mean the right to make eye contact with witnesses. By the beginning of the 1990s, however, the Supreme Court had reversed this interpretation in two cases that involved the shielding of child witnesses from defendants (*Coy v. State of Iowa*, 1988; *State of Maryland v. Craig*, 1990), ruling that such procedures were not unconstitutional. Nevertheless, although shielding procedures obviously reduce the chances of trauma from the experience of testifying, they remain controversial owing to a lack of clear experimental evidence that shielding does not reduce the accuracy of children's statements.

Turning to category a above, in chapter 5 we aired some of the issues surrounding this group of modifications. To reprise, the only witnesses to most child sexual abuse crimes are a child victim and an adult perpetrator (who has the constitutional right to not give self-incriminating evidence). As a rule, children who report such abuse make their initial reports to parents, other children, or teachers. (In the United States, teachers are currently the most frequent sources of initial reports of child sexual abuse to law enforcement agencies [Poole & Lamb, 1998].) However, the instability of children's memories means that detailed, specific reports that are made shortly after events may fade to vague, generic statements, or to no information at all, by the time of trial or even by the time that the first official investigative interview is conducted. If first-person testimony is required for conviction, such cases cannot be prosecuted, but that, after all, is a technicality. The crimes occurred; the children were sexually abused. Two specific reforms have been the most common responses to this problem. The first is to reduce so-called competency rules, which are legal requirements for special showings that young children are able to provide reliable evidence in court. Typically, such showings must demonstrate that children understand the difference between truth and falsity and that they understand their constitutional obligations as witnesses to provide a complete and accurate account of events. The second response is to allow broader latitude for testimony from adults to whom children make initial allegations of abuse.

Both of these reforms have been contentious because in addition to making it possible to prosecute more child sex offenders, there are grounds for supposing that they may increase the rate of false conviction by increasing the incidence of unreliable testimony. Regarding competency, children who report sexual abuse may include descriptions of accompanying events that are utterly fanciful or impossible. For example, the original child complainant in the McMartin Preschool case stated to his mother that Raymond Buckey had sodomized him while his head was in a toilet, that Buckey had driven him to a carwash and locked him in the trunk of his car, and that teachers at the preschool had cut up rabbits. Common sense suggests that although such bizarre "memories" might possibly be true, they should give one pause about a child's appreciation of the distinction between fantasy and reality, a determinative consideration if testimony is to be accurate. Such information would normally be introduced as evidence during pre-trial competency hearings, and the court may rule that children whose abuse allegations are infected with imaginary statements are not qualified to testify. If competency challenges are not permitted, however, children whose original allegations were laced with outlandish content may be permitted to testify and may be regarded as credible witnesses by juries.

Regarding the other response—relaxing hearsay restrictions—a key concern here is that the adults to whom initial reports are made are not trained child-forensic interviewers, and consequently, the information that they secure from children may not be reliable. In particular, untrained adults are apt to use multiple suggestive questioning methods when interviewing children about something as worrisome as reports of abuse, thereby perhaps producing statements that contain inaccurate information and permanently tainting children's memories of events. Further, statements alluding to abuse may not have been initially made by children themselves but, instead, may have first been generated via suggestive questioning by adults who suspect abuse for other reasons. Again, the McMartin Preschool case is illustrative. Consider, for a moment, the likely reaction of parents who received the letter in Figure 7-2. When confronted with the fact that Buckey had already been arrested for child molestation, it is difficult to imagine that most parents would not frantically and repeatedly interrogate their children about sexual acts like those listed in the third paragraph. In fact, most of the allegations of abuse that were obtained from these other children first surfaced in response to parental questioning or questioning by Child Institute International staff (which the jury judged to be unacceptably suggestive). Thus, although permitting hearsay testimony by untrained adults makes it easier to prosecute actual perpetrators, it also increases the chances of introducing unreliable evidence that has been elicited by unduly suggestive questioning. In rare circumstances (e.g., *State of Arizona v. Sweeney*, 2001), however, the latter possibility can be minimized when adult hearsay witnesses have memorialized their interviews on audio- or videotape, thereby allowing juries to make independent assessments of suggestiveness.

Last, the reforms in category b above were designed to eliminate the problem of children, like those in the McMartin Preschool case, being subjected to protracted bouts of repeated interviewing and cross-examination during the pre-trial phase of a prosecution. McGough (1993) pointed out that in a criminal investigation in which a victim makes accusations against a defendant, the victim will be interviewed a minimum of three times—by the police, by prosecutors, and by defense attorneys—but that when a case involves accusations by children, a much larger number of interviews (typically, 10 or more with sexual abuse allegations [Ceci & Bruck, 1995]) is often conducted. Repeated interviewing is prompted by the fact that children's initial interviews are apt to be incomplete or inconsistent, necessitating further clarifying questions once the interviews have been reviewed by police or attorneys. To deal with this problem, policies have been implemented in many jurisdictions that use a team approach to child interviewing, which allows multiple people to contribute to a single interview, obviating the need for these people to conduct separate interviews. The basic procedure involves a one-on-one conversation between a suspected child abuse victim and a professional who is specially trained in child-forensic interviewing, normally a social worker or police officer. The interview is conducted in a child-friendly room that has been specifically constructed for this purpose and that is equipped with video- or audiotaping capability. While the interview is being conducted, it can be seen and heard by other concerned parties (e.g., prosecutors, police investigators, parents), either through one-way glass or via closed-circuit television. These people can also communicate with the interviewer (e.g., via a small microphone in the interviewer's ear or via telephone), which allows them to put their own questions to the child by passing along queries to the interviewer as they arise and allows them to prompt the interviewer to clear up any inconsistencies or confusions in the child's responses. When the people to whom children have made initial reports (e.g., parents, teachers) are part of the team, they can remind interviewers of the exact statements that children made so that interviewers can frame appropriate questions. The tape recording of an interview can then be made available to other people who might otherwise need to conduct separate interviews, such as defense attorneys or child protective services staff. Ultimately, the tape recording can be placed in evidence at trial, so the jury can determine whether the questioning was unduly suggestive.

The reforms described in the preceding paragraph have generally been viewed with favor, both by child welfare advocates who are concerned with children's exposure to potentially traumatic experiences and by legal scholars who are concerned with the possible creation of unreliable testimony. From a child welfare perspective, minimizing pre-trial contact with the criminal investigation process will obviously reduce children's re-exposure to distressing facts associated with sexual molestation. It will also reduce their exposure to the threatening, adversarial tactics of criminal investigations. From the perspective of reliable testimony, the opportunity for suggestive lines of questioning increases as the number of child interviews increases. Even if suggestive techniques are not used, the mere fact that questions that were posed in one interview are then repeated in subsequent interviews may cause children to assume that questions were answered incorrectly and to conclude that they must now provide responses that they were unable to provide before (Ceci & Bruck, 1995). Further, repeated interviewing encourages reconstructive remembering of events that cannot be clearly recollected, which, as we know from prior chapters, is a source of false-memory reports.

Afterword on the Legal Significance of Children's Memory Suggestibility

As we have seen, the recent history of research on memory suggestibility in children has been driven by child sexual abuse crimes and, more particularly, by the desire to increase the law's ability to prosecute such crimes. It is essential not to lose sight of the fact that sexual abuse is by no means the sole motivation for such research, and hence, relevance to sexual abuse is not the sole criterion by which such research should be evaluated. Indeed, sexual abuse is not even the most important legal motivation for child suggestibility studies, a point that has often been ignored in discussions of this work. The potential for heightened susceptibility to suggestion is a material consideration in *any* legal proceeding that involves child victims, witnesses, or culprits. In that context, sexual abuse prosecutions comprise only a small fraction of the legal proceedings in which evidence is provided by children. Even if attention is restricted to prosecutions for abuse and neglect, sexual abuse remains a small segment of such cases—less than 20% according to fairly recent data (Poole & Lamb, 1998). Thus, the question of the baseline susceptibility of children's memories to suggestive interviewing and the question of which variables raise or lower such susceptibility have legal ramifications that extend far beyond sexual abuse.

In what other types of proceedings do children's memory reports provide evidence upon which legal decisions are based? Far and away the most common ones are custody evaluations that accompany the dissolution of marriages and juvenile court hearings in which the defendants are under age (McGough, 1993). In the former instance, children make memory reports (usually not under oath) of everyday experiences involving their parents or caretakers, which bear on the court's decisions about how to award their custody, and in the latter instance, children testify under oath about crimes that they have witnessed. In both of these circumstances, children provide their evidence in private hearings before a judge. Such hearings, in addition to being closed to the public, are not reported by the media. Although these are the most common legal proceedings involving child witnesses, each day, assaults, robberies, shootings, and other crimes are observed by children and, occasionally, a child is the only witness. Children are often the sole witnesses of domestic violence crimes, for example, and there are multiple defendants in capital cases who have been convicted and are awaiting execution on the basis of children's testimony (e.g., Cornell Death Penalty Project, 2002). Finally, although our focus throughout this section has been on children who are victims or witnesses of crimes, the issue of memory suggestion is transparently relevant to children who are suspects in criminal investigations. Juvenile court defendants can be subjected to highly suggestive police interviews, including the coercive tactics that were discussed in chapter 6. Given that such interviews are able to generate false-memory reports from adult suspects, they may be expected to do likewise with child suspects. It should be added that child defendants are not confined to private hearings in juvenile courts. A distressing trend, at least to us, in recent U.S. jurisprudence is to require increasing numbers of under-age defendants to stand trial as adults, especially in high-profile crimes of violence. (Recall here that in Armstrong et al.'s [2001] investigation of Cook County capital cases, many questionable confessions had been obtained from juveniles, some as young as age 8.) When the law treats child suspects as adults, the full brunt of coercive investigative tactics may be anticipated as a matter of course.

Two conclusions follow that are cornerstones of modern research on the suggestibility of children's memories. First, as already mentioned, the relevance of scientific findings on this topic is far broader than sexual abuse prosecutions. The applicability of such findings even extends to civil justice because children can be key witnesses in litigation against adults, teachers, caretakers, or physicians. Second, the question of whether children's memories are resistant to suggestion for traumatic experiences that involve their own bodies, which has been so fundamental in applying suggestibility research to sexual abuse prosecution, is not as central to the law as it would seem from the perspective of sexual abuse, simply because this is not the predominant type of case in which children are sources of evidence. The question of the comparative suggestibility of observed events versus personally experienced ones evaporates in any case in which child witnesses are third-party observers of events, and this is the most common role in which children provide input to legal proceedings. Consequently, although studies of the suggestibility of personal bodily experiences provide probative scientific information in certain types of prosecutions, it would be a mistake to argue that the methodological focus of child suggestibility research should therefore be different than that of the adult research that was considered in chapter 6. On the contrary, the types of studies that, statistically speaking, are of the broadest relevance to legal proceedings involving child as well as adult witnesses are ones that are concerned with the suggestibility of memories of observed events.

Developmental Studies of Memory Suggestibility

Throughout this volume we have accentuated the goal of gaining predictive control over false memories, using theoretical principles, preferably rather straightforward ones, to forecast the occurrence of these surprising phenomena and to anticipate the types of variables that will increase or decrease their pervasiveness. As we mentioned in chapter 4, once a theoretical account has been formulated that meets the first-cut criteria of adequacy and parsimony, passing the further tests of prediction plus experimental confirmation determines whether real understanding has been achieved. Given the heated public discussions of child suggestibility, predictive control of this particular form of false memory is an urgent social need, not just a scientific goal, because valid theoretical principles can be put to work to accomplish a number of objectives that redound to the accuracy of prosecutions that involve child witnesses (Brainerd et al., 2000). For instance, before a defendant is investigated or before charges are filed, they can be used to advise police investigators and prosecutors as to the likely reliability of statements that were provided by child witnesses under specific conditions. At trial, these principles can also be used to assist triers of fact in their (constitutionally mandated) task of deciding what level of credibility to assign to different forms of evidence (e.g., children's statements versus physical evidence). Most important, however, theoretical principles can be used proactively to reduce the chances that false evidence is put on the record. Specifically, they can be used to create model child-interviewing protocols that investigators can then implement to maximize the yield of true-memory reports, while minimizing the incidence of false-memory reports (see the concluding section of this chapter), and they can be used throughout the investigative and prosecutorial phases of criminal cases to guide decisions that may affect the accuracy of information that is obtained from children.

This brings us back to the opponent-processes account of false memory. In chapter 6, the discussion of research on adult memory suggestibility was preceded by an opponent-processes analysis of the experimental procedure that is used in such research: Loftus's (1975) misinformation paradigm. The key outcome of the analysis was that, relative to false-memory procedures that do not incorporate suggestion (chapters 4 and 5), the misinformation phase of this paradigm causes additional traces to be stored that support false-memory responses. Specifically, because the meaning content of misinformation-phase material is the same as that of the earlier target material (e.g., "traffic accident"), earlier gist memories are strengthened, and because specific items of false information are presented (e.g., stop sign), verbatim traces of those gist-consistent false items are also stored. Thus, when memory probes for false-but-gist-consistent information are subsequently administered (e.g., stop sign or yield sign?), the misinformation phase may be expected both to increase subjects' baseline tendency to process the gist of experience (which elevates error rates) *and* to increase their baseline tendency to retrieve verbatim traces of those items (which also elevates error rates).

This same analysis applies to developmental studies of memory suggestibility because the misinformation paradigm has also been the centerpiece of such work. As always in developmental work, the further question of age changes in the memory abilities that support true versus false responses must be duly weighed. That matter has already been broached in chapter 5, where the issue of what is known about ontogenetic changes in verbatim and gist memory was examined. The conclusion of that discussion was that the accessibility of memory for the surface form of experience and memory for the meaning content of experience both improve as children mature, and therefore, developmental trends in semantic false-memory effects will vary as a function of the types of verbatim or gist memories that are tapped by particular false-memory tasks.

Despite such task variability, we saw that two prototypical situations can be identified. First, the most common type of developmental study has been research in which (a) children are exposed to familiar targets whose meanings are well understood (everyday words; sentences composed of everyday words; pictures or videos of well-known people, objects, and events), and (b) subsequent false-memory responses are consistent with the meanings of individual targets (e.g., false alarms or intrusions of *cow* and *chair* following a word list on which *horse* and *table* appeared). In experiments of this first type, age improvements in verbatim memory for targets, which help subjects reject false-memory responses, will be more pronounced than age improvements in gist memory, which support such responses. Therefore, opponent-processes distinctions predict that semantic false alarms and intrusions ought to decline with age, and we saw in chapter 5 that developmental findings have been consistent with that prediction. Second, the other prototypical situation is one in which the meaning of the target events is unfamiliar to children (e.g., a narrative about adult emotional relationships) or in which children must connect meaning across target events whose individual meanings are understood (e.g., a word list consisting of 10 animal names and 10 furniture names). In experiments of this second type, age improvements in gist memory will outstrip age improvements in verbatim memory. Therefore, opponent-processes distinctions make the contrasting prediction that semantic false alarms and intrusions will increase with age, a prediction that we also saw has been borne out in developmental studies.

In earlier analyses of developmental work with the misinformation paradigm, Reyna (1992, 1995) pointed out that experimentation with children conforms to the first of the preceding prototypes. In the usual design (e.g., Ceci et al., 1987; Howe, 1991; Toglia, Ross, Ceci, & Hembrooke, 1992), the target material consists of familiar objects, events, and people that are part of some everyday situation to which children are accustomed (e.g., a trip to the mall, shopping at the grocery store, going to school). Following exposure, the misinformation material usually consists of a question-and-answer "review" of the target material, during which unpresented objects, events, or people are inserted. Because the meaning content of the target material is familiar, opponent-processes distinctions specify that age changes in the memory-falsifying effects of misinformation will be chiefly dependent upon age changes in verbatim memory abilities—in particular, upon age changes in children's tendency to access verbatim traces of target material during the misinformation phase as memory suggestions are presented (supporting recollection rejection of those suggestions) and during later memory tests, when memory suggestions are presented as probes (again supporting recollection rejection of those suggestions). As both of these abilities ought to improve with age, the baseline expectation of opponent processes is that false alarms and intrusions involving material that is presented as memory suggestions ought to decline with age.

An early series of developmental misinformation experiments by Ceci et al. (1987) was among the first to provide consistent support for this prediction. In Ceci et al.'s initial experiment, preschool and elementary-school children were read a story about a girl named Loren who was attending her first day at a new school and who had a stomach ache from eating her breakfast too rapidly. The story was accompanied by a series of pictures that illustrated the main events (e.g., eating breakfast, putting on a coat and hat). The day after being read the story, the children returned for the misinformation phase. Children were asked a series of questions about the story, with children in the treatment condition receiving questions that contained false information (Do you remember the story about Loren, who had a headache because she ate her cereal too fast?) and children in the control condition receiving questions that contained true information (Do you remember the story about Loren, who had a stomach ache because she ate her eggs too fast?). Two days after the misinformation phase, the children received a Loftus-type (1975) forced-choice recognition test on which some of the probes pitted true events from the story against the corresponding misinformation that was administered in the treatment condition (e.g., eggs versus cereal, stomach ache versus headache). The results are shown in Figure 7-4, where the probability of a correct response to such items is plotted by age level and experimental condition.

The first point to note in Figure 7-4 is that misinformation elevated false-memory responses throughout the preschool and elementary-school age range (i.e., treatment subjects made more errors than did controls on memory probes that pitted true events against misinformation). This is hardly surprising, considering the adult misinformation findings in chapter 6. A second and more fundamental point

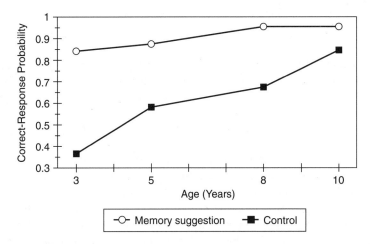

Figure 7-4. Effects of memory suggestion on children's false recognition of memory probes. Based upon Experiment 1 of Ceci, Ross, and Toglia (1987).

is that the magnitude of misinformation effects, as measured by the spread between the treatment and control conditions, decreased with age, just as one would expect on theoretical grounds. The influence of memory suggestion on preschoolers was truly dramatic: These children gave false-memory responses to 63% of the probes in the treatment condition but to only 16% of the probes in the control condition. However, the influence of memory suggestion was still quite pronounced among 5-year-olds (42% versus 13%) and 8-year-olds (33% versus 5%). Ceci et al. (1987) reported further experiments that replicated this age decline in sensitivity to memory suggestion, and they concluded that preschoolers are particularly vulnerable to suggestion. Forensically speaking, this is an especially probative conclusion because reports of suspected sexual abuse are highest for this age level.

Ceci et al.'s (1987) basic pattern of developmental declines in susceptibility to memory suggestion has been confirmed in several subsequent experiments. To illustrate, in 1993, Ceci and Bruck reviewed 18 developmental studies of memory suggestion and reported that significant age declines in the effects of memory suggestion were obtained in 15 of them, the latter studies being distributed across articles by Cassel and Bjorklund (1995), Ceci et al. (1987, 1995), Delamonthe and Taplin (1992), Goodman and Aman (1990), Goodman, Hirschman, Hepps, and Rudy (1991), Goodman and Reed (1986), Goodman, Rudy, Bottoms, and Aman (1990), Gordon, Ornstein, Clubb, Nida, and Baker-Ward (1991), Marin, Holmes, Guth, and Kovac (1979), Oates and Shrimpton (1991), Ornstein, Gordon, and Larus (1992), Rudy and Goodman (1991), and Saywitz et al. (1991). The remaining three studies merely produced null findings. The findings of the Cassel and Bjorklund (1995) and Ceci et al. (1995) studies were available at the time of Ceci and Bruck's review, though the articles in which the studies were ultimately reported had not yet been published. As further experiments have accumulated, Ceci and Bruck have written follow-up reviews in which Ceci et al.'s original conclusions about developmental variability in vulnerability to memory suggestion have been reiterated (e.g., Bruck & Ceci, 1999; Bruck, Ceci, & Melnyk, 1997).

Although developmental declines in suggestibility have been routine findings, it must be borne in mind that opponent-processes distinctions predict that it is possible to obtain the opposite pattern under certain conditions. It is therefore important to note, as an existence proof, that such reverse age trends have been reported in some experiments. The best-known examples are some studies by Pezdek and Roe (1995, 1997). Taking Pezdek and Roe's first experiment as an illustration, 4- and 10-year-old children were first exposed to one of two slide sequences—a sequence that depicted a woman returning home from grocery shopping, putting away groceries in the kitchen, and preparing to bake a cake versus a sequence that depicted a man working at a construction site, who performed activities such as hammering, sawing, and moving boards. As usual in memory-suggestion studies, these slide sequences had been previously piloted with preschoolers to ensure that the respective stories would be familiar to young children. Following presentation of the slide sequence, children in the treatment condition were read a narrative that contained misinformation about some of the objects in the slides (e.g., in the kitchen sequence, that the woman had used a bowl rather than a plate and a fork rather than a spoon when preparing the cake). In contrast, children in the control condition were read a narrative that did not mention these objects. Finally, a yes-no recognition test was administered, which consisted of a series of sentence probes that described the earlier slide sequence. The crucial items were probes for the true objects that had been subjected to misinformation (Did the woman use a plate?) and probes for false objects that had been presented as memory suggestions (Did the woman use a bowl?). To separate the effects of memory suggestion from baseline differences in response bias, probes for false objects that had not been presented as memory suggestions (Did the woman use a cup?) were also included. In Figure 7-5, the resulting levels of false-memory responses are plotted for each age level and treatment condition. Because separate probes were administered for true and false items, much like the earlier adult experiments of Belli (1989) and Tversky and Tuchin (1989), the effects of memory suggestion could be separately determined for targets (Figure 7-5a) and for distractors (Figure 7-5b).

Comparing the two graphs in Figure 7-5, note that, just as in adult experiments, memory suggestion both suppressed acceptance of targets and increased children's false recognition of distractors that were presented as memory suggestions. Also as in adult experiments, note that memory suggestion elevated children's false-memory responses more than it suppressed their true-memory responses. Thus, the within-subject patterns are very much like those in adults. Between age levels, however, the consequences of memory suggestion were more deleterious for 10-year-olds than they were for preschoolers, and this developmental trend held for suppression of true responses (Panel a) and for elevation of false responses (Panel b). Although this reversed developmental trend seems surprising from the perspective of the larger literature on children's suggestibility, remember that opponent-processes distinctions actually predict such reversals when suggestion effects (a) depend on processing meaning content that is better understood by older children, or

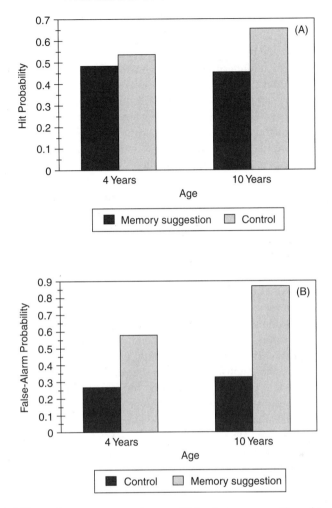

Figure 7-5. Effects of memory suggestion on children's true recognition of targets (Panel A) and false recognition of memory suggestions (Panel B) at two age levels. Based upon Pezdek and Roe (1995).

(b) depend on processing verbatim traces of misinformation, which are better retained by older children. In the case of Pezdek and Roe's findings, the second option is the probable explanation. Between the ages of 4 and 10, improvements in verbatim memory are known to be great (chapter 5), but age improvements in gist memory for these particular materials ought to be small (because their meaning content is known to be familiar to preschoolers).

Concerning the tendency of memory suggestion to suppress true-memory responses, the first point to note is that older children's verbatim memory for the specific objects in the slide sequence was apparently not much better than younger children's: According to Figure 7-5a, the target acceptance rates in the control condition were only about .10 higher in older children. Most probably, this result was due to the fact that the focal items were incidental objects to which children paid little attention. Regardless, the implication is that older children would not have been much better than younger children at performing recollection rejection of memory suggestions during the misinformation phase. However, the children were forced to pay attention to memory suggestions during the misinformation phase because they had to answer questions about them (Remember when the woman used a bowl to make the cake?). Consequently, on later memory tests, verbatim traces of these suggestions would be more likely to be accessible to older children than to younger ones. When targets were presented for test (Did the woman use a plate?), older children would therefore have been more likely to retrieve verbatim traces that conflicted with those *specific targets* (Remember when the woman used a bowl?), resulting in greater suppression of true-memory responses. Likewise, when memory suggestions were presented for test (Did the woman use a bowl?), older children would therefore have been more likely to retrieve verbatim traces that confirmed those specific distractors, resulting in greater elevation of false-memory responses.

Now that the question of developmental trends in memory suggestibility has been aired, we move on to a consideration of factors that opponent-processes distinctions predict should increase or decrease children's vulnerability to suggestion. Although the literature on children's susceptibility to suggestion is not so vast as the corresponding adult literature, it is nevertheless quite extensive, consisting of more than 100 articles published between the late 1980s and the present. Providing an exhaustive account of the empirical effects in that literature would be just as daunting and mind-numbing a task as it would be for the adult literature. Hence, as in chapter 6, we concentrate on experimental findings that bear on opponent-processes explanations of false alarms and intrusions that are congruent with erroneous suggestions that children received in misinformation experiments, with a view toward shedding theoretical light on children's suggestibility. Thus, our emphasis will be once again on findings that show how false-memory phenomena can be explained in sensible ways and how new phenomena can be predicted by those explanations.

The remaining material in this section will follow the now-familiar organizational plan of considering findings about theoretically motivated storage variables first, continuing with findings about theoretically motivated retrieval variables, and concluding with findings about theoretically motivated forgetting variables. It will be remembered from chapter 5 that developmental research adds an additional layer of complexity to corresponding adult research—namely, developmental interactions. We saw in chapter 5 that age variability in verbatim and gist abilities means that developmental interactions are important considerations in achieving predictive control of children's spontaneous false memories. Below, we shall see that the same is true for predictive control of children's implanted false memories. When a theoretically motivated variable is manipulated in developmental studies of memory suggestion, it is not automatically expected to have the consistent effects on false alarms and intrusions that it has in adult studies; instead, a variable's effects may increase, decrease, or even reverse as children mature. We learned in chapter 5 that this complication does not preclude predictive control because the nature of developmental interactions can be forecast in advance by considering whether the demands of a particular experiment are slanted toward memory for the surface content of experience or toward memory for meaning content. In fact, far from precluding predictive control, developmental interactions enhance predictive control by supplying a further arena in which opponent-processes predictions can be evaluated.

Storing Memories

We already know that opponent-processes predictions about the effects of specific storage variables turn on (a) whether verbatim or gist traces are being strengthened, and (b) whether the traces that are being strengthened are stored during the exposure phase or during the misinformation phase. Variables that chiefly strengthen memory for the surface content of experience (e.g., verbatim repetition, increasing presentation duration, surface-processing instructions, perceptual distinctiveness, "remember" consolidation instructions) ought to reduce the influence of suggestion if exposure-phase memories are strengthened (because verbatim traces of true events will be enhanced), but they ought to increase the influence of suggestion if misinformation-phase memories are strengthened (because verbatim traces of false events will be enhanced). On the other hand, variables that strengthen gist memories of experience, relative to verbatim memories (e.g., gist repetition, semantic-processing instructions), ought to increase the influence of memory suggestion if exposure-phase memories are strengthened (because subjects will be less likely to process verbatim traces of true events), but they ought to decrease the influence of suggestion if misinformation-phase memories are strengthened (because subjects will be less likely to process verbatim traces of misinformation). These basal predictions will, however, be modified by developmental interactions.

Five storage factors have been extensively investigated in developmental studies of memory suggestion and have produced consistent findings: repetition (both verbatim and gist), surface-processing instructions, storing negative suggestions, misinformation credibility and plausibility, and central versus peripheral information. Beyond their theoretical probity, each of these manipulations turns out to be relevant to some properties of child sexual abuse that routinely figure in the investigation and prosecution of such cases.

Repetition

Recall that verbatim repetition refers to multiple presentations of the same target or misinformation item (e.g., presenting a picture containing a chair four times during the course of a slide sequence), whereas gist repetition refers to presenting *different* targets or misinformation items that revolve around the *same meaning* (e.g., presenting pictures of a chair, a couch, a table, and a bookcase during the course of a slide sequence). In line with opponent-processes predictions about repetition, it turns out that the potential consequences of both forms of repetition are quite pertinent to child sexual abuse cases (e.g., Ceci & Bruck, 1995; Poole & Lamb, 1998). With respect to the repetition of target events, some cases involve low-incidence abuse (a child plaintiff is alleged to have been victimized on one occasion), whereas others involve high-incidence abuse (a child plaintiff is alleged to have been repeatedly victimized). In high-incidence prosecutions, both verbatim repetition (a specific sexual act that occurs during each abuse episode) and gist repetition (different sexual acts that occur during different abuse episodes) may be present. Likewise, with respect to the repetition of misinformation items, the child interviews that figure in abuse prosecutions may involve either lower levels of suggestive questioning or higher levels (e.g., Figure 7-3). When higher levels are present, both verbatim repetition (asking the same suggestive question multiple times) and gist repetition (asking different suggestive questions that converge on the same meaning, such as genital touching) may be used (e.g., Figures 7-2 and 7-3). Thus, the precise effects of verbatim and gist repetition on memory for target events and misinformation items, whether those effects are as predicted, and how those effects interact with children's age are all questions of great relevance to triers of fact in these types of cases, and not surprisingly, data bearing on them have been central in many cases (e.g., *State of California v. Kosher*, 1999; *State of Washington v. Highland*, 2003).

The developmental literature on memory suggestibility contains considerable evidence on the effects of verbatim repetition of both target events and misinformation items, and in both instances, the predominant empirical patterns are consistent with opponent-processes predictions. This literature contains only limited evidence on gist repetition, though again the data conform to theoretical predictions.

Verbatim Repetition   Developmental data on the effects of verbatim repetition of targets were gathered in the aforementioned experiments by Pezdek and Roe (1995) and in subsequent studies by others, including Holliday, Douglas, and Hayes (1999), Marche (1999), and Marche and Howe (1995). It will be remembered that, in Pezdek and Roe's experiment, preschoolers and 10-year-olds had been shown one of two slide sequences (kitchen or construction site). Half of the children at each age level subsequently received misinformation about some of the objects in whichever slide sequence had been administered during the presentation phase, with half of the children having seen the slide sequence once and half having seen it twice. Hence, this experiment provided data on how a single verbatim repetition contributes to the effects of suggestion on children's true and false memories. Those data are shown in Figure 7-6, with the findings for true memory appearing in Panel a and the findings for false memory appearing in Panel b. Concerning true memory, it can be seen that, as predicted on theoretical grounds, the tendency of memory suggestions to lower children's recognition of target objects was greater when the slide sequence was presented once (a .09 mean drop in hit rates between the control and misinformation conditions) than when it was presented twice (a zero mean drop in hit rates between the control and misinformation conditions). Concerning false memory, it can be seen that, also as predicted, the tendency of memory suggestions to increase children's false recognition of misinformation was greater when the slide sequence was presented once (a .43 mean increase in false-alarm rates between the control and misinformation conditions) than when it was presented twice (a .07 *drop* in false-alarm rates between the control and misinformation conditions). With respect to de-

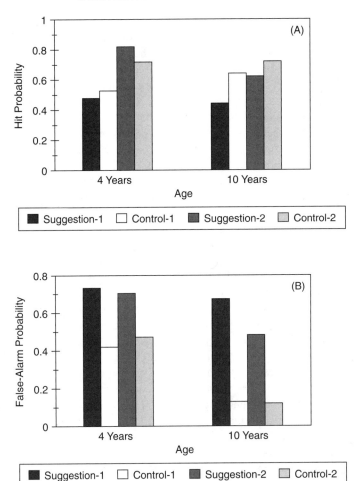

Figure 7-6. Effects of memory suggestion on children's true recognition of targets (Panel a) and false recognition of memory suggestions (Panel b) at two age levels. Prior to the misinformation phase, target material was presented either once (1-Suggestion and 1-Control) or twice (2-Suggestion and 2-Control). Based upon Pezdek and Roe (1995).

velopmental interactions, the tendency of verbatim repetition to decrease the influence of memory suggestion on target recognition did not interact with age. (The influence of memory suggestion on target recognition was small in comparison to its effects on false alarms, so this may simply be a floor effect.) However, there was a large developmental interaction in the tendency of repetition to decrease false alarms to misinformation items, an interaction that was consistent with the idea that verbatim prosthetics are more helpful to older children because they retain at least some accessible verbatim memories: The reduction in the size of the misinformation effect was greater for older children (a drop of .18) than for younger ones (a drop of .08).

316 THE APPLIED SCIENCE OF FALSE MEMORY

Similarly, the experiments by Holliday et al. (1999), Marche (1999), and Marche and Howe (1995) also revealed that target repetition tends to inoculate children against the influences of memory suggestion. The Marche and Howe experiment is particularly interesting because it was designed to ensure that children in the repetition condition had very good verbatim memory for the target materials. From the perspective of opponent-processes predictions, a limitation of designs in which a fixed number of repetitions is administered is that repeating the target material does not *guarantee* that verbatim traces of targets will be strengthened because children may not encode the repetitions if they are not paying attention or if interfering information is present during repetitions. In Pezdek and Roe's (1995) design, for example, the second presentation would only strengthen verbatim traces of targets for children who were paying attention, and because attention is more likely to wander in younger children, this may be responsible for the fact that 10-year-olds derived more benefit from repetition than did preschoolers.

Marche and Howe eliminated this problem by adopting a criterion learning procedure. Their subjects were preschool children, all of whom were exposed to a narrative and an accompanying slide show about a child who was attending a costume party. The narrative contained 20 targets for which memory was to be measured (e.g., foods that the child ate). Children in the low-repetition condition received a single exposure to the narrative plus slide show, followed by a cued-recall test for the targets (e.g., What did she eat for breakfast?). Children in the high-repetition condition received *criterion exposure*: For individual children, the narrative plus slide show plus cued-recall cycle was presented as many times as was necessary for the child to achieve perfect performance on the cued-recall test. The children in both repetition conditions were then assigned to each of three conditions: control, positive suggestion, and misinformation. One week later (i.e., 4 weeks after their original exposure to the target materials), the children in all three conditions returned to the laboratory and received a series of recall tests for the 20 targets, with the key result being that the tendency of misinformation to impair recall was smaller in children who had participated in the criterion-repetition condition.

The other form of verbatim repetition—repetition of *misinformation*—has been studied in children by Bjorklund, Bjorklund, and Brown (1998), Holliday et al. (1999), Quas and Schaaf (2002), and Zaragoza, Dahlgren, and Muench (1992), among others. The latter investigators tested a sample of preschool children and failed to find that two presentations of misinformation produced higher levels of memory falsification than did a single presentation. Again, however, this is simply a null result. The other experiments confirmed the opponent-processes prediction about verbatim misinformation repetition, and the Holliday et al. experiment detected a developmental interaction that may explain Zaragoza et al.'s null result. In Bjorklund et al.'s experiments, 5- and 7-year-old children first watched Cassel and Bjorklund's (1995) bicycle-theft video. This was followed by three sessions in which misinformation was administered, with each administration of misinformation being followed by a memory test for information in the video. False recognition of peripheral details rose from 27% after the first administration to 30% after the second administration to 37% after the third administration.

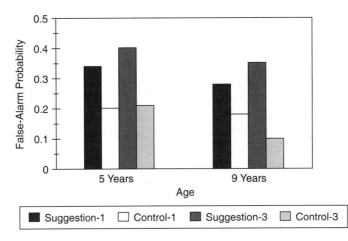

Figure 7-7. Effects of verbatim repetition of memory suggestions on children's false recognition of suggestions at two age levels. During the misinformation phase, memory suggestions were presented either once (Suggestion-1 and Control-1) or three times (Suggestion-3 and Control-3). Based upon Holliday, Douglas, and Hayes (1999).

In Holliday et al.'s (1999) experiment, 5- and 9-year-old children were exposed to a narrative and an accompanying picture sequence about going to the beach. On the following day, all of the children were read a narrative that purportedly reviewed the previous day's target materials. This review contained correct reminders about half of the target items and misinformation about the other half. The review was read once to half of the children, while the other half listened to the review three times. On the third and final day, the children were administered a Loftus-type (1975) forced-choice recognition test. The key findings are shown in Figure 7-7, where false-alarm rates for two types of memory probes are plotted: *control probes*, in which targets (e.g., a striped t-shirt) were pitted against related distractors that had *not* been presented as misinformation (e.g., a spotted t-shirt), and *suggestion probes*, in which targets were pitted against distractors that had been presented as misinformation. The first finding to note is that there was a clear misinformation effect at both age levels. Children's tendency to choose false items was greater when those items had been presented as memory suggestions. The second finding to note is that misinformation repetition had the predicted effect. Pooling across the two age levels, the size of the misinformation effect was twice as large following three presentations as following one. Third, there was a developmental interaction in the effects of misinformation repetition that parallels Pezdek and Roe's (1995) developmental interaction in the effects of target repetition. Specifically, the increase in the size of the misinformation effect that was produced by repetition was three times as large in 9-year-olds as in 5-year-olds (.15 versus .05). As before, the opponent-processes interpretation of this interaction is that the older children preserved more of the additional verbatim traces that accumulated from three presentations over the 1-day interval between the misinformation session and the memory tests. This implies a straightforward explanation of Zaragoza et al.'s failure to find lower levels of memory falsification following two presentations versus one presentation of misinformation. Their subjects were younger than Holliday et al.'s 5-year-olds and therefore would have been even less able to preserve the additional verbatim traces that accumulated from multiple administrations of misinformation.

Finally, in chapter 6, we considered a verbatim repetition manipulation for misinformation that was especially interesting because it resembles a police interrogation technique that is known to prompt false confessions from criminal suspects: forced confabulation (see Kassin, 1997). In a forced-confabulation experiment, it will be remembered, the memory suggestions that are presented during the misinformation phase are qualitatively different than the leading questions that comprise the standard misinformation manipulation. Now, subjects are required to lie about the events they have just witnessed or experienced. The specific procedure is to pose questions about the target material that assert the presence of false events (e.g., in the Zaragoza et al. [2001] experiments, that one of the characters in the film clip had cut himself in a fall) and then to require subjects to confabulate further details for these false events (e.g., to state where the character had cut himself), with the experimenter providing confirmatory feedback for the confabulations of some subjects (e.g., Yes, he was cut on the knee). With adult subjects, Zaragoza and associates found that forced confabulation by itself was a particularly powerful form of misinformation: It tripled false-alarm rates for memory suggestions on later recognition tests. Adding confirming feedback made the manipulation even more powerful: It produced an equivalent further increase in false-alarm rates to memory suggestions.

What about children? The obvious opponent-processes prediction is that forced confabulation ought to have even more devastating effects on the accuracy of children's memory reports. When subjects have been forced to confabulate details of false events, the ability to preserve verbatim traces of actual events and access those traces to reject false suggestions during misinformation sessions is even more critical than with standard misinformation manipulations. Given that such abilities are in shorter supply in children, the effects of forced confabulation on children's memories ought to be quite marked. Ackil and Zaragoza (1998) confirmed this prediction in an experiment that focused on subjects of three age levels (7 years old, 9 years old, and adult). The procedure was the same as that of Zaragoza et al. (2001; see chapter 6), except that the experimenter did not provide confirmatory feedback for the confabulations of any of the subjects in the forced-confabulation condition. The pattern of results is shown in Figure 7-8, where the false-alarm rates for probes that involved memory suggestions are plotted for treatment and control groups at each age level. As in Zaragoza et al.'s research, it can be seen that the adults' performance was impaired by forced confabulation. It can also be seen, consistent with earlier discussions of developmental trends in spontaneous false memory (chapter 5), that there was a marked developmental decrease in false alarms in the control condition. The most striking finding, however, was the developmental decrease in the effects of forced confabulation on subjects' tendency to falsely accept memory suggestions on recognition tests: The difference between the false-alarm rates in the confabulation and control conditions was three times as great when the subjects were 7-year-olds as when the subjects were adults.

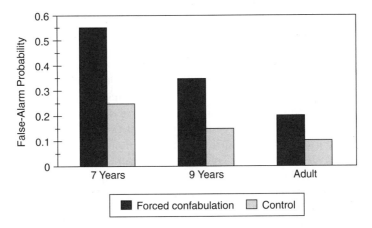

Figure 7-8. False acceptance of memory suggestions at different age levels following forced confabulation. Based upon Ackil and Zaragoza (1998).

Gist Repetition   Opponent-processes distinctions lead to a counterintuitive prediction about the effects of gist repetition on the susceptibility of children's memories to suggestion, which for the sake of clarity will be illustrated with a hypothetical word-list experiment. Suppose that a group of children is exposed to a list of 30 words that contains a single word that is the name of a familiar color (say, *green*), and suppose that another group is exposed to a list of 30 words that contains six color names (say, *blue, brown, green, orange, pink, purple*). Opponent-processes analysis says that the memories of the children in the second group will be more accurate in one respect but less accurate in another. Specifically, if, after a delay of a few hours or days, the children are asked to describe the types of words that were on the list (much as when children are asked to provide a narrative of abusive experiences in a forensic interview), children in the second group will be much more likely to recall that there were color words on the list (because the color meaning was repeatedly cued by different targets) and to be able to recall one or more of the specific color names (because the chances that a verbatim trace of at least one color word is still accessible will be greater). However, opponent-processes analysis also says that these children's memories will be more susceptible to falsification by questioning that attempts to implant information that is consistent with the gist of their experience (e.g., Remember when you heard the word *red*? Remember when you heard the word *yellow*?). The meaning of a false color word will seem much more familiar to these children (because the color meaning was repeatedly cued), and consequently, it will be difficult for them to be sure that they did not hear that particular word (because so many color names were presented).

In addition to being predicted theoretically, the notion that gist repetition makes children more susceptible to suggestions that cohere with the meaning of experience is highly pertinent to child sexual abuse prosecutions involving high-incidence abuse, though perhaps not in an obvious way. Opponent-processes distinctions predict that, at one level, the memory reports of children who are victims of high-incidence abuse will provide more reliable evidence of sexual crimes than the memory reports of children who are victims of low-incidence abuse but that, at another level, the memory reports of high-incidence victims will be *less* reliable. On the one hand, for the same memory reasons as the children who listened to a list containing multiple color words, children who are high-incidence victims will be more likely to have accessible gist memories of abuse than children who are low-incidence victims and will be more likely to have accessible verbatim traces of specific examples of abuse. Thus, high-incidence victims will be more likely to spontaneously report to other adults that they have been abused, and once official investigations are under way, such children will be more likely to confirm that they are abuse victims and to provide correct reports of specific acts, which can be used to formulate criminal charges. All of this is on the positive side of the ledger when it comes to identifying and prosecuting perpetrators. On the other hand, the fact that high-incidence victims have strong gist memories of abuse, together with the fact that they have been subjected to multiple varieties of abuse, means that if suggestive questioning methods are used, such children will be more susceptible to suggestions about false events that are consistent with the abuse theme. Theory predicts, in particular, that such children will be especially vulnerable to suggestions about types of abuse that have occurred in different ways from incident to incident (e.g., sexualized touching) and about abusive acts that have either not occurred or have only occurred once.

Why is this problematical, considering that high-incidence children have in fact been sexually abused? It is problematical because such false-memory reports can cut the ground from under valid prosecutions, allowing the guilty to go free. A criminal prosecution cannot be generic with respect to felonious behavior. Successful prosecutions require that defendants be charged with *specific* acts that the law defines as felonies and that the *particular* times and places of those acts be stated (e.g., in the preschool bathroom on the Monday before Thanksgiving). Once charges have been formulated at that level of precision, they are amenable to conclusive disproof by a variety of exculpatory evidence (e.g., medical examinations of victims, credit card or telephone records of defendants, testimony of eyewitnesses). When children describe specific acts of abuse and name specific perpetrators, it is common, in investigative interviews, to follow up with questions about other potential acts that the law defines as felonies, about other potential times and places, and about other potential perpetrators, and these questions may be especially suggestive (because the target information was not spontaneously reported). The fact that high-incidence victims are expected to be quite susceptible to abuse-consistent suggestions means that they will be prone to accept suggestions about other potential perpetrators (e.g., Did both Mr. Smith [true] and Mr. Jones [false] touch your privates?), about other potential acts of abuse (e.g., vaginal penetration [false] as well as genital fondling [true]), about other places (e.g., in the cloakroom [false] as well as in the bathroom [true]), and about other times (e.g., after Christmas [false] as well as before Thanksgiving [true]).

Although the information in such suggestions may be true, when it is not, victims' false-memory reports are, in principle, open to disproof by exculpatory evidence, which may surface during the course of police investigations or may be unearthed by defense counsel. This can have grievous consequences for the prose-cution of actual perpetrators. In our own forensic work, we have encountered some standard examples, perhaps the most common of which is medical disconfirmation of allegations of repeated vaginal penetration. When a girl spontaneously alleges re-peated acts of sexual abuse against a male perpetrator and those allegations do not include vaginal penetration, it is commonplace for forensic interviewers to ask, usu-ally repeatedly, in direct follow-up questions, whether vaginal penetration also oc-curred. If the child agrees that it did, it is also commonplace to request statements of frequency, which can result in estimates of multiple incidents of penetration. However, a subsequent medical examination may reveal an intact hymen, coupled with no evidence of trauma to vaginal tissues. Even if the child's original allega-tions were true, such medical findings raise peremptory doubts in the minds of all concerned about the veracity of the child's memory, and in our experience, cases of this sort do not usually yield convictions of the defendant on charges stemming from the original allegations. Rather, the typical results are a not-guilty verdict, if the case goes to trial, or, if the case does not go to trial, either the charges are dropped or a plea bargain involving lesser charges (e.g., criminal negligence) is negotiated.

Another standard example from our forensic work involves cases in which chil-dren who have made initial spontaneous allegations of high-incidence abuse in-volving a specific individual, later, in response to direct suggestions, name addi-tional perpetrators from the same general environment (e.g., other preschool or elementary-school teachers), who are subsequently ruled out. (Recall in this con-nection that six individuals working at the McMartin Preschool were initially charged with acts of abuse, but the charges against four of them ultimately were dropped.) Again, doubts are raised about the accuracy of children's memories, and such cases often do not result in convictions on charges stemming from the origi-nal allegations. However, according to opponent-processes distinctions, this may be a miscarriage of justice. Other things being equal, the chances are that the original, spontaneous reports of abuse were quite accurate, with the subsequent false reports merely being by-products of the heightened susceptibility of high-incidence victims to memory suggestions that revolve around the abuse theme.

Despite the relevance of gist repetition to forensic interviewing of children who are suspected victims of sexual abuse and despite the fact that opponent-processes distinctions make clear predictions about the effects of gist repetition, this variable has not been extensively studied in research on children's suggestibility. However, Powell, Roberts, Ceci, and Hembrooke (1999) have reported a carefully designed experiment with 3- to 8-year-old children that demonstrated the predicted patterns. During the target-exposure phase, all of the children participated in a staged series of events called "Aussie activities," which involved 24 events for which children's memories would eventually be tested (e.g., the child sitting on a mat, the teacher sitting on a chair, the activity leader wearing a colored cloak). This activity was re-peated four times across the course of 3 weeks, so that each child participated in the activity five times. Thus, the children were high-incidence participants in Aussie events, so that by the end of the fifth session, the children would possess highly ac-cessible gist memories of the basic situation. Across the five sessions, some items

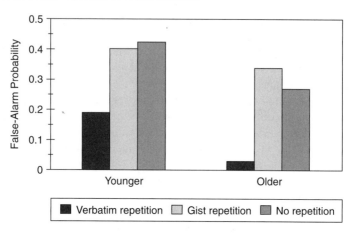

Figure 7-9. Effects of verbatim and gist repetition of target material on children's false recognition of memory suggestions. Based upon Powell, Roberts, Ceci, and Hembrooke (1999).

occurred only once; some items were subjected to verbatim repetition (e.g., the teacher sat on the same chair during all five sessions); and some items were subjected to gist repetition. As an illustration of the latter, if the child sat on a mat during Session 1, the child might sit on a board during Session 2, on bubble wrap during Session 3, on a blanket during Session 4, and on a bed sheet during Session 5. After the fifth exposure session had been completed, children participated in two interviews, which occurred on the third and fourth days following the last exposure session. The first interview was a misinformation session in which memory suggestions were provided for some of the items (e.g., Remember when the teacher sat on the floor? Remember when you sat on a bag?). The second interview was simply a delayed memory test, which consisted of cued-recall prompts for the 24 target items (What did the teacher sit on? What did you sit on?).

The findings for children's tendency to accept false-memory suggestions during the first interview are shown in Figure 7-9, where the probability that children accepted false suggestions during the misinformation interview is plotted separately by age level. To begin, note that two findings were present that confirm findings that we have previously mentioned: Young children were more susceptible to suggestion than were older children, and verbatim repetition inoculated children of both age levels against suggestion. With respect to the latter point, note that the older children were highly resistant to memory suggestions that focused on items that had received verbatim repetitions. On the other hand, note that children were quite susceptible to suggestions that focused on items that had received *gist* repetitions, so much so that the usual age difference in suggestibility all but disappeared for these items. Further, note that the suggestibility of gist-repetition items was also high in comparison to items that had only been presented once. It might be thought that because the core event that was involved in all of the gist-repetition items had occurred five times (e.g., sitting on *something* on the floor), these items would be much more resistant to suggestion than items that had only occurred once. However, the two types of items were equally susceptible to suggestion in younger children, and gist-repetition items were *more* susceptible to suggestion than were single-presentation items in older children. Finally, Figure 7-9 reveals a developmental interaction in the effects of gist repetition on suggestibility that is similar to developmental interactions that we have already mentioned: The tendency of gist repetition to elevate susceptibility to suggestion, relative to verbatim repetition, was more pronounced in older children.

Another opponent-processes prediction about repetition that is both counterintuitive and of great relevance to sexual abuse investigations is that children who have only been exposed to a series of events once are likely to be less suggestible than children who have been exposed multiple times, *if the multiple exposures involved gist repetition.* (Gist repetition is inevitably involved in high-incidence sexual abuse because there is always some variation in the details of individual criminal acts.) The reason, again, is that memory for the gist of experience will necessarily be stronger following multiple exposures to an experience, and when multiple exposures do not involve verbatim repetition, gist memories will be much more accessible than will be verbatim traces of individual events (Reyna & Lloyd, 1997).

Some clear data on this prediction were obtained by Connolly and Lindsay (2001). Children from the preschool through early elementary-school age range participated in either a single play session or in four play sessions that were conducted on separate days. During each play session, the children played three different games: a smelling game, a paper-folding game, and a magic game. For children in the multiple-exposure condition, some of the features of each game were the same during each play session (e.g., the location of the game, the colors of the props), but other features varied from session to session (e.g., the type of paper-folding activity, the type of magic trick). Following their play sessions, all of the children participated in an interview session, which was conducted on a separate day. The interview contained questions that presented false suggestions about some of the play activities and control questions that asked about true items and events. For children in the multiple-exposure condition, some of the memory suggestions focused on information that had received verbatim repetitions (e.g., the color of the magician's wand), and other memory suggestions focused on information that had received gist repetitions (e.g., the magic words that had been spoken). One day later, the children were administered a yes-no recognition test containing probes for true events, for distractors that had been presented as memory suggestions, and for distractors that had not been presented as memory suggestions. The children's levels of false acceptance of distractors are shown in Figure 7-10, with the spread between the error rates for the two types of distractors being the measure of the effects of memory suggestion.

Note that the predicted effect for gist repetition was present. Children who had participated in four play sessions were much more likely to accept false suggestions about information that had received gist repetitions than children who had encountered that information only once in a single play session. We cannot emphasize too

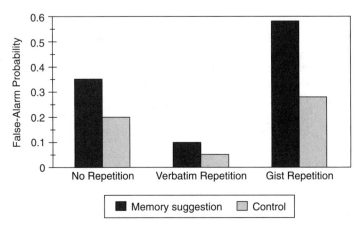

Figure 7-10. How children's susceptibility to memory suggestions is influenced by different forms of repetition of target experiences. Based upon Connolly and Lindsay (2001).

strongly that this finding is surprising from the perspective of common sense and is therefore a striking confirmation of opponent-processes predictions. Unaided common sense, unaided by opponent-processes distinctions that is, would simply view the memories of multiple-exposure children as being inherently more accurate than those of single-exposure children and therefore more resistant to memory suggestion. Opponent-processes distinctions say that the reverse is true when multiple exposures do not involve verbatim repetition, and that is the pattern in Figure 7-10. These same distinctions say that the commonsense prediction is correct, however, when multiple exposures involve verbatim repetition. A glance at the middle bars in Figure 7-10 shows that this prediction was also confirmed: Memory suggestions produced only a tiny elevation in false-alarm rates for information that was presented in the same way during all four play sessions.

Surface-Processing Instructions

As we already know, deep- versus shallow-processing instructions have been investigated in hundreds of studies of adults' true memory and in a much more modest, but still extensive, number of studies of children's true memory. Only limited information is available on how such instructions affect adults' and children's spontaneous false memories, but that information is consistent with the opponent-processes prediction that deep-processing instructions will elevate false-memory reports (by increasing the accessibility of gist traces relative to verbatim traces) but shallow-processing instructions will lower them (by increasing the accessibility of verbatim traces relative to gist traces). The predictions about how the two types of instructions should affect children's susceptibility to memory suggestion and the theoretical reasons for those predictions are the same as for spontaneous false memories. Unfortunately, there appear to be no experiments in the literature in which the size of the misinformation effect has been compared for children who received deep-processing instructions during the presentation of target materials versus children who received shallow-processing instructions. However, several experiments have been reported in which the effects of a specific type of shallow-processing instruction—source monitoring—have been compared to no instructions. The findings of these experiments, which we now sketch, are in broad agreement with theoretical predictions.

Over the years, the source-monitoring framework (Johnson et al., 1993; Lindsay & Johnson, 2000) has been one of the most influential theoretical accounts of children's memory suggestibility (Reyna, 2000a). The essential idea, as will be recalled from chapter 3, is that false-memory reports occur because subjects become confused about the origins of their memories and attribute their memories to mistaken points of origin. This can happen with spontaneous false memories (as when subjects falsely recall or recognize *red* after studying a list containing the words *blue*, *brown*, *green*, *orange*, *pink*, and *purple* because they assume that the high familiarity of *red*'s color meaning is due to having studied it) or with implanted false memories (as when subjects falsely recall or recognize "yield sign" because they assume that its familiarity is due to having seen it in the slide show rather than having heard it as a suggestion). The latter explanation of suggestion effects (e.g., Lindsay & Johnson, 1989a, 1989b) has often figured in studies with children (Ackil & Zaragoza, 1995; Ceci, Huffman, Smith, & Loftus, 1994; Poole & Lindsay, 2002; Roberts & Blades, 2000; Steward & Steward, 1996; Thierry, Spence, & Memon, 2001). Our interest here lies with the effects of a form of shallow processing that falls out of that explanation.

According to the source-monitoring framework, it should be possible to reduce the influence of memory suggestions by (a) encouraging children to pay attention to the sources of target information during the exposure phase, or (b) reminding children to think about the sources of target information during the misinformation or testing phase. From the perspective of opponent processes, the latter is a form of verbatim retrieval cuing and will therefore be postponed to the next section of this chapter. The former, however, is an encoding orientation that presumably focuses children on the surface content of target information because it is surface features that most clearly differentiate information sources from each other (Reyna, 1995; Reyna & Titcomb, 1997). For instance, in a typical source memory experiment, different sources of target information might be distinguished by such visual properties as size, color, and spatial position (e.g., Hicks & Cockman, 2003; Hicks & Hancock, 2002; Marsh & Hicks, 2001; Marsh, Hicks, & Davis, 2002). In studies of child suggestibility, of course, the key source distinction is between the target-exposure phase and the misinformation phase, which is a discrimination that depends heavily on memory for the distinguishing surface characteristics of the two phases. The source-monitoring framework predicts that children will be better able to make that discrimination, and will therefore be less susceptible to memory suggestions, if they pay close attention to the sources of target memories during the exposure phase. Similarly, opponent-processes analysis expects that this should make children more resistant to suggestion because stronger verbatim traces of targets ought to be stored, therefore making it easier to perform recollection rejection of memory suggestions (either during the misinformation phase or on memory tests).

This prediction was confirmed in a recent series of experiments by Thierry et al. (2001). These investigators exposed children of two age levels, preschoolers (3- and 4-year-olds) and younger elementary-schoolers (5- and 6-year-olds), to six science demonstrations from the Mr. Science series developed by Poole and Lindsay (1995). The demonstrations included such things as charging balloons with static electricity and determining the types of materials to which magnets are attracted. During the exposure phase, three of the science demonstrations were presented as live sequences of events, and the remaining three were presented on videotape, so that the source manipulation for target events was live versus video. At the conclusion of the demonstrations, half of the children were assigned to a source-monitoring condition, and half were assigned to a control condition. The children in the source-monitoring condition participated in an activity that was intended to cause them to review and consolidate their memories for the origins of the events in the science demonstrations. Specifically, they responded to a forced-choice recognition test on which they were required to select the source (live, video, didn't happen) of several actions that Mr. Science had or had not performed (i.e., targets and distractors). To answer such questions, the children would presumably attempt to visualize the events that they had just seen, which would involve accessing verbatim traces of those events, thereby strengthening memory for the surface content of the science demonstrations. The control children, on the other hand, simply responded to a yes-no recognition test about the same targets and distractors. Next, the children in both conditions performed a free-recall test in which they were asked to remember the events in the live demonstrations and in the video demonstrations. Finally, the free-recall test was followed by 10 misleading questions about events in the science demonstrations. The children were warned that some of the information in these questions might be erroneous and that they should feel free to inform the experimenter whenever they detected false information. The key results of the children's error rates for the 10 misleading questions are summarized in Figure 7-11.

The bars on the left side of Figure 7-11 show the preschoolers' false-alarm rates, while those in the center show the elementary-schoolers' false-alarm rates. As expected, source-monitoring questions increased preschoolers' resistance to memory suggestions. However, the elementary-schoolers did not exhibit the predicted effect; the difference in the susceptibility of children in the source-monitoring and control conditions to suggestion was not statistically significant. Thierry et al. (2001) hypothesized that their design might have unintentionally produced the latter result because the recall test that *all* of the children received following the monitoring-activity phase had required that children remember the individual sources (live versus video) of the science demonstrations. Thus, the recall test provided the same sort of encouragement to *all of the children* to visualize the earlier events as the earlier source-monitoring questions had provided to children in the source condition. For older children, whose verbatim memories are better in the first place, the source test may have added nothing to the effects of the recall test. To evaluate this possibility, the experiment was repeated with a new sample of elementary-schoolers,

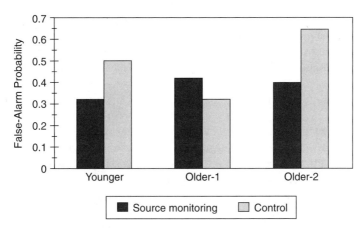

Figure 7-11. Influences of source-monitoring activity on children's susceptibility to memory suggestions. Based upon Thierry et al. (2002).

using a design in which the recall test was omitted. These follow-up results appear in the bars on the right side of Figure 7-11, where it can be seen that the source-monitoring activity substantially improved these children's resistance to memory suggestions.

There are two other approaches to measuring the effects of source storage, which are simple in conception and about which opponent-processes distinctions make straightforward predictions. The first is merely to measure, in a standard misinformation experiment without special source instructions, how well children remember source information about target materials and to relate children's performance on source memory tests (e.g., Did you see Mr. Science use magnets *on the video-tape*?) to their performance on the usual tests for susceptibility to memory suggestions. If source memory tests are slanted toward verbatim memory, the opponent-processes hypothesis would be that children's performance on such tests will predict their susceptibility to suggestion—that is, children who perform better on source tests will be less suggestible (because their verbatim memories of target events are better).

This prediction was confirmed in an experiment by Giles, Gopnik, and Heyman (2002). Preschool children were presented a story in a silent video and a story in a spoken narrative. Children who were later able to correctly distinguish video events from narrative events proved to be more resistant to memory suggestions about the stories than children who were unable to make this discrimination. The other approach to measuring the effects of source memory has not been carefully studied, but we briefly describe it in the hope of stimulating research: Provide children with source-monitoring instructions *before* they are exposed to target materials. The opponent-processes prediction is that this manipulation's effects should be analogous to those of shallow-processing instructions; that is, it ought to focus children's attention on the surface content of subsequent events, thereby yielding stronger verbatim traces and increased resistance to suggestion. It follows that presenting source-monitoring instructions before target exposure ought to enhance resistance to memory suggestions more than postexposure instructions because pre-exposure instructions will yield stronger verbatim traces, whereas postexposure instructions will simply help children to preserve previously stored (weaker) verbatim traces.

Storing Negative Suggestions

We come now to an especially interesting storage manipulation, which can be thought of as *negative* memory suggestion. In the usual suggestibility design, as we know, children receive postevent information stating that they should report events on later memory tests that were not present during the exposure phase. The complement of this manipulation would be to provide information stating that children should *not* report events that *were* present during the exposure. In memory terminology, this is a form of *output blocking*, which is reminiscent of directed forgetting (e.g., Kimball & Bjork, 2002), the chief difference being that children are not instructed to forget target information; indeed, their attention is focused on specific events, but they are merely told not to report it when their memories are queried. Thus, if such negative suggestions reduce children's tendency to report the corresponding events, it might be because (a) retrieval of the relevant memories was blocked at the time of the memory test (i.e., negative suggestions act like directed-forgetting instructions), or (b) the events were remembered quite well but children also remembered the cue to avoid reporting those particular events. The second possibility is the more likely of the two.

The fact that children's attention must be focused on the critical events in order to instruct them not to report those events means that verbatim traces of the critical events should be strengthened, relative to other events that are not foci of attention. Hence, other things being equal, negative suggestions should increase the chances that children possess vivid memories of the critical details. For example, after reading the word list *black, brown, grey, green, orange, pink, purple, red, tan, yellow*, imagine the effect of instructing children as follows: "Two of the words that you just heard were *orange* and *tan*. If someone asks you what we talked about today, you can tell them anything you remember, but please don't tell them that I read you those two words." Thus, from the perspective of memory, the effect of negative suggestions is to arbitrarily mark some items from the exposure phase with a "don't tell" flag, with children's task on a later memory test being to remember which specific items were flagged. This is a quintessential example of a verbatim-memory task, one that is very similar to source discrimination and one that ought to be difficult for young children, given their known limitations when it comes to preserving arbitrary surface features of experience. Hence, the obvious opponent-processes prediction is that the effectiveness of don't-tell instructions will improve with age because older children will be more likely to have accessible verbatim traces that discriminate flagged from nonflagged items.

The effects of don't-tell instructions have received considerable attention in the literature on children's suggestibility because they parallel a common feature of child sexual abuse cases, a feature that also crops up in some other types of cases in which children are key witnesses. Adults who abuse children often caution them not to report the abuse events to other people. The most common variants on such cautions, in cases that we have reviewed, are for a perpetrator (a) to inform a child that the adult will be harmed in a major way (e.g., arrested, fired from his job) if the child reports the abuse, or (b) to threaten harm to the child, the child's friends, or members of the child's family. When incestuous abuse is committed by a family member, the child may be warned that reporting the abuse will result in destruction of the family and the child being taken into the custody of strangers (e.g., Herman, 1981; Summit, 1983).

Other types of legal cases in which children have been given don't-tell instructions are domestic violence and other forms of domestic crime. In domestic violence, children may be the only witnesses to spousal or sibling assaults, and when they are, they may be warned that reporting what they have seen will have dire consequences for the family and themselves. They may receive similar warnings when their parents or older siblings are using the home to conduct criminal activities, such as the preparation or distribution of drugs, storage of stolen property, and prostitution. In all of these circumstances, children are pressured by trusted adults—such as parents, teachers, neighbors, or relatives—to conceal specific experiences but not to conceal others. The questions for research are: Do such instructions lower reporting, and if they do, does the effectiveness of such instructions vary with age? Data on these questions can be crucial in criminal cases in which it is alleged (or demonstrated via evidence) that child victims or witnesses have been given don't-tell instructions about the crimes that are under investigation.

The effects of don't-tell instructions have been investigated in simulated forensic situations in which children respond to memory tests following participation in a staged sequence of events, some of which involve transgressions of rules by adult confederates (e.g., Bottoms et al., 2002; Bussey, 1990; Bussey, Lee, & Grimbeek, 1993; Pipe & Wilson, 1994; Thompson, Clarke-Stewart, & LePore, 1997; Wilson & Pipe, 1989). In some studies, the confederates are strangers (e.g., Thompson et al., 1997), which simulates situations in which children are victimized by strangers, whereas the confederates are family members in other studies (e.g., Bottoms et al., 2002), which simulates situations in which children are victimized by relatives.

The most recent of these studies, by Bottoms et al., provides excellent illustrations of the principal features of such research and the key findings. Children of two age levels (3–4 years old and 5–6 years old) participated in a structured experience with their mothers that took place in a laboratory play room that contained a variety of attractive toys. Half of the mother-child pairs were assigned to a don't-tell condition, and half were assigned to a control condition. Prior to entering the play room, the mother-child pairs received instructions that were different for the two conditions. In the don't-tell condition, they were told that they could play with some of the toys in the room but that they were specifically forbidden from playing with a group of toys located on a bookshelf because those toys were reserved for someone else, after which they were left alone in the play room. However, the mothers in the don't-tell condition had been secretly told that they should violate the instructions and play with the toys on the bookshelf, that they should "accidentally" break one of the toys on the shelf, and that they should hide the broken toy behind another toy. These mothers had also been secretly told that after the play session

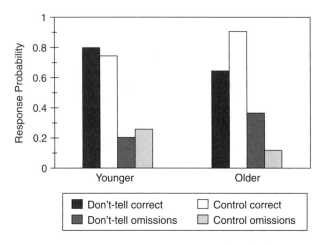

Figure 7-12. How children's reports of a play experience are influenced by instructions to conceal information. Based upon Bottoms, Goodman, Schwartz-Kenney, and Thomas (2002).

was completed, they should implore their children not to tell that they had played with the forbidden toys, stating that they would get in trouble if the experimenter knew and that the child would be denied a promised reward. The procedure in the control condition was the same, except for two changes: The mother-child pairs were told that they were free to play with any of the toys, and the mothers were not asked to implore their children to conceal any of their play activities.

Following the play session, the child and mother were taken to separate rooms. The child was then given a memory interview that focused on events that occurred during the play session. The interview resembled procedures that are commonly used in forensic interviews about suspected abuse (see the last section of this chapter) in that it began with some warm-up questions, continued with a request for a free narrative of the play session, and concluded with 25 yes-no questions that focused on specific events that might have occurred during the play session. Some of those questions were critical ones, which dealt with activities that had been forbidden in the don't-tell condition (e.g., Did your mom break the Barbie doll? Did your mom tell you to keep a secret? Did your mom tell you that something would happen to you if you told the secret?). The effects of don't-tell instructions on children of both age levels appear in Figure 7-12, where two types of data are shown: the proportions of correct responses on yes-no questions about critical events, and the proportions of incorrect responses that involved omissions of any details (i.e., if the child denied breaking the Barbie doll, an omission response would be failing to provide an alternative explanation, such as that the doll might have fallen). The four bars on the left are the data of the 3- and 4-year-olds. As can be seen, don't-tell instructions had no effect on these children. Preschoolers in the don't-tell condition did not give (statistically significant) fewer correct answers than preschoolers in the control condition, nor were their incorrect answers characterized by higher levels of omission errors. In contrast, the same instructions reduced the accuracy of 5- and

6-year-olds' reports. Children in the don't-tell condition gave fewer correct answers, and their incorrect answers were accompanied by higher levels of omission errors. Other analyses revealed that don't-tell instructions failed to suppress reporting of noncritical events, which did not involve playing with the forbidden toys. This pattern of results is consistent with the conclusion that in order for such instructions to be effective, the key memory skill is being able to remember precisely which events were singled out by the instructions, something at which older children are more adept than younger children.

Findings from other don't-tell experiments reinforce this conclusion. For example, Thompson et al. (1997) administered don't-tell instructions to 5- and 6-year-olds, who had observed an adult engage in forbidden doll play, and then administered memory interviews to these children 1 week later. Unlike Bottoms et al.'s findings for children of the same age, such instructions failed to suppress memory reports of forbidden activities, relative to control instructions, which is consistent with the notion that (labile) verbatim memories of precisely which events have been flagged are critical to this effect. If this notion is correct, the problem of being able to remember precisely which events have been flagged could be alleviated, to some degree, by flagging only a *single, highly salient event*. Wilson and Pipe (1989) confirmed this possibility in a study in which 5- and 6-year-old children participated in a magic show in which the magician accidentally destroyed his gloves during the course of performing a trick. Only this particular event was flagged as don't tell, and although children were not interviewed about their memories until 10 days after the magic show, *no* child who received such instructions mentioned the destruction of the gloves during a free narrative of the events. In another study, Pipe and Wilson (1994) replicated the finding that don't-tell instructions suppress delayed reporting of a single salient event in children of this age.

Misinformation Credibility and Plausibility

The chief benefits that are conferred by sound theories, as we have said, are that they simultaneously explain extant findings and predict new (and surprising) ones. A secondary benefit is theoretical unification, the discovery that phenomena that previously seemed to be quite distinct are the same in some fundamental sense. In the case of opponent processes, an example of such unification is provided by two social variables that have been studied in connection with the misinformation presentation. One of them, *source credibility*, was covered in chapter 6. The other, *misinformation plausibility*, refers to whether proffered memory suggestions seem "logical" or "sensible" to subjects. The assumption behind source-credibility manipulations, it will be recalled, is that memory suggestions are more likely to be accepted if the interviewer who offers them is considered to be authoritative and trustworthy by subjects. (This is why police interviewers, for example, are trained to issue repeated reminders that they are well versed in the facts of the case, that interviewees should trust interviewers' statements, and that interviewees should believe that interviewers are attempting to help them to do the right thing [see Inbau et al., 2001].) While credibility is concerned with the *people* who proffer memory suggestions, plausibility is concerned with the *content* of the "memories" that they suggest. The assumption behind plausibility manipulations is that children will be more likely to accept suggestions that seem sensible to them than suggestions that do not.

From the perspective of opponent processes, the memorial basis for credibility and plausibility effects is the same, but to see why, it is necessary to consider how each has been operationalized in misinformation experiments. In chapter 6, we saw that credibility is usually operationalized by comparing the effectiveness of memory suggestions that are delivered by someone whom the subject considers to be highly knowledgeable about the target material versus someone who is considered to be less knowledgeable. For children who viewed the film clip in Ackil and Zaragoza's (1998) experiment, for instance, an adult who portrayed himself as the director of the film would be a person of high credibility, whereas another child who watched the same film clip would be a person of lower credibility. Plausibility, on the other hand, has usually been manipulated by making memory suggestions about everyday situations that are familiar to children versus those that are unfamiliar. For instance, in the research of Pezdek and associates (e.g., Pezdek et al., 1997; Pezdek & Hodge, 1999), the effectiveness of suggestions about family trips to the mall (plausible situation) have been compared to suggestions about trips to the emergency room to receive unfamiliar medical treatments, such as an enema (implausible situation).

When credibility and plausibility are operationalized in these ways, opponent-processes logic says that they should reduce the chances that children will use verbatim traces of target events to reject memory suggestions *during misinformation sessions*. Concerning credibility, if the person who presents the suggestions is a trusted authority on the target information, children will be less likely even to attempt to access their own memories of that information, and when they do, it is less likely that they will trust their memories when they fail to access supportive information. Likewise, concerning plausibility, when memory suggestions involve typical events from everyday situations, there is less need for children even to access their memories for confirming information, and when they do, there is less reason to trust their memories when confirming information cannot be retrieved.

In studies of children's suggestibility, both credibility and plausibility have been found to have the predicted effect of increasing the power of misinformation to falsify memory. Although various investigators have produced the predicted effect for credibility (e.g., Lampinen & Smith, 1995; Welch-Ross, 1999), Toglia et al. (1992) reported the earliest evidence. They used the same materials and procedure as in the previously discussed experiments of Ceci et al. (1987), and their subjects were preschoolers. Credibility was manipulated by having memory suggestions presented to half of the children by an adult (high credibility) and to the other half of the children by another child (low credibility). On Loftus-type (1975) forced-choice tests, children falsely recognized memory suggestions 61% of the time when they had been provided by the high-credibility interviewer, whereas they falsely recognized memory suggestions only 36% of the time when they had been provided by the low-credibility interviewer. (The suggestions of the low-credibility interviewer falsified children's memories to some extent, however, because control children, who had not received suggestions, falsely recognized the same distractors only 22% of the time.)

In a subsequent experiment with 4- and 8-year-olds, Toglia et al. (1992) manipulated credibility using two adult interviewers, one who portrayed himself as being extremely familiar with Ceci et al.'s story of a child attending her first day at a new school (high credibility) and one who portrayed himself as being only slightly acquainted with the story (low credibility). Once again, false recognition of memory suggestions was higher when the suggestions had been presented by the high-credibility adult rather than by the low-credibility adult. A developmental interaction was also obtained, such that the credibility effect was more marked in 4-year-olds than in 8-year-olds. This is quite consistent with what we know about age improvements in verbatim and gist memory. Because older children's memories of target events, particularly their verbatim memories, are stronger than young children's, older children's baseline tendency to access those memories and use them to reject false suggestions is higher than younger children's, thereby reducing the effectiveness of the credibility manipulation.

Turning to plausibility, Pezdek and Hodge (1999) used a manipulation that had been previously developed by Pezdek et al. (1997). Children of two age levels (younger elementary-schoolers and older elementary-schoolers) received true reminders about an event that had happened to them and false suggestions about a frightening event that was said to have occurred when they were 4 years old: getting lost in the mall while shopping with their parents (plausible suggestion), and having been given an enema to relieve a sickness that resulted from eating excessive amounts of junk food (implausible suggestion). Two days later, children were asked to provide a free narrative of what they remembered about the events that had been discussed during the earlier sessions. Whereas 44% indicated that they remembered the plausible false experience, only 3% indicated that they remembered the implausible false experience. Moreover, in line with the standard age trend in susceptibility to suggestion, most of the children who remembered the plausible false experience were in the younger age group.

Central Versus Peripheral Information

We have previously pointed out that in any real-life or staged experience that is the object of subsequent memory suggestion, some objects and events are more central to the experience than others. Memory theories predict (and any number of experiments have confirmed) that subjects pay closer attention to central than to peripheral details, resulting in the core prediction that verbatim traces will be more likely to be accessible for central than for peripheral details and that the former will therefore be less susceptible to memory suggestions. Available data on this prediction show that, like adults, suggestions are less apt to falsify children's memories of central details than their memories of peripheral details. Although other procedures have been used (e.g., Warren & Lane, 1995), perhaps the most consistent data on this issue have been produced with the previously described paradigm of Cassel and Bjorklund (1995), which has been used in several studies with children (e.g., Bjorklund et al., 1998; Bjorklund et al., 2000; Cassel et al., 1996; Roebers, Rieber, & Schneider, 1995). In this paradigm, it will be recalled, the exposure phase consists of a video depicting a teenage boy arguing with a girl in a public park and eventually taking the girl's bicycle. (This video provides an objective method of measuring the suggestibility of central versus peripheral details because the events in the video were independently rated on a scale of centrality by a sample of psychology faculty and graduate students.) One week later, subjects are administered a mock-forensic interview following the common investigative procedure of first requesting a free narrative (Tell me everything you can about the video), followed by cued-recall questions (Tell me what the girl was wearing), followed by a series of suggestive questions, some of them containing false information (e.g., The bicycle frame was painted red, wasn't it?). This same interview is repeated approximately 3 weeks later.

Two consistent findings from studies with children have been that children are less likely to adopt memory suggestions concerning central information about the bicycle theft and that the tendency of central information to be more resistant to suggestion is greater in older than in younger children. Actually, both of these findings were obtained in the original Cassel and Bjorklund article, which included samples of 6- and 8-year-old children in addition to the adult sample that we discussed in the last chapter. In line with opponent-processes analysis, the resistance of central details to suggestion was tied to better verbatim memory for such information: In the free- and cued-recall portion of the 1-week interview, children of both age levels recalled much larger percentages of central than peripheral details from the video.

A particularly interesting extension of the heightened suggestibility of peripheral information was reported by Cassel et al. (1996). They tested samples of 5-, 7-, and 9-year-olds using Cassel and Bjorklund's procedure, except that only the 1-week follow-up interview was administered. After the memory suggestions in the third step of Cassel and Bjorklund's procedure had been posed, Cassel et al. asked a series of follow-up multiple-choice questions about the same information. In addition to central information being less susceptible to suggestion during the third step, the researchers found that when children succumbed to suggestions about central details, they often changed their responses *back to the correct information* on the follow-up items. This indicates that, for central but not for peripheral details, verbatim traces of the original information are sufficiently strong that they can remain accessible even after memory suggestions have been administered.

When it comes to forensic application, it is essential not to extrapolate too much from the fact that central information is less susceptible to memory suggestion than is peripheral information. In particular, it is important not to infer that memory suggestion is unable to induce false memories of information that is thematically central to children's experiences. The speciousness of such a conclusion has been demonstrated in studies by Bruck, Ceci, et al. (1995) and others, which focused squarely on central details. The subjects in Bruck, Ceci, et al.'s experiment were 5-year-olds who had made visits to their pediatricians to receive inoculations for diphtheria, pertussis, and tetanus. Thus, the injection that the children received was the most central of all of the events that occurred during the visit. At the end of the visit, the children were suggestively interviewed, with some children being told that the injection had been very painful, with other children being told that it had not been painful, and control children not being given any pain suggestions. One week later, the children were asked to rate how much the injection had hurt using a 5-point rating procedure, and it was found that the three groups did not differ in their average reported levels of pain. One year later, when most children's verbatim memories of their pain experiences would no longer be accessible, the children were again questioned suggestively about the pediatrician visit. The design was pared down to only two of the previous three conditions. In three interviews, spaced over several days, one group was told that the injection had *not* been painful, and a second group was not given pain suggestions. During a fourth interview, children were asked to repeat the 5-point ratings and to rate how much they cried, on the same scale. Now, suggestions about pain were found to be quite effective. The mean pain rating for the suggestion group was 1.9, compared to 2.5 for the control group, and the mean crying rating was 2.7 for the suggestion group, compared to 3.5 for the control group. Hence, notwithstanding the greater resistance of children's memories of central information to suggestion, such memories can be influenced by suggestion, even when, on analogy to sexual abuse, the central events are painful ones that evoke strong emotions.

Retrieving Memories

As in adult suggestibility research, the study of how retrieval factors contribute to children's susceptibility to suggestion has been a particularly vigorous area of experimentation, albeit for different reasons. We saw in the last chapter that the retrieval focus of adult research was prompted by a theoretical debate over whether or not memory suggestions alter the original memory traces that are stored during the target-exposure phase, which led to intensive study of the effects of different types of recognition tests (particularly so-called standard versus modified tests). With children, however, the motivation for focusing on retrieval factors, not surprisingly, is child sexual abuse and other types of crimes in which children may be victims or witnesses. When a crime is reported, the crucial events that correspond to the exposure phase of a misinformation experiment have already happened, and typically, no physical record (e.g., a video or audio recording) of the crime exists. When an investigation begins, therefore, law enforcement personnel have no control over the target events, which are already in the past, and they do not know the precise content of those events (because no physical record exists). Indeed, an investigator's job is to determine the content of events but *only to a reasonable degree of probability*, given the absence of a physical record. We saw in chapter 6 that such determinations are made primarily through victim, witness, and suspect interviews. Here, investigators have control over the crucial class of *interview* variables, which influence the accuracy of the memory reports that they obtain—namely, retrieval factors.

In the literature on children's memory suggestibility, many retrieval factors have been identified that affect children's tendency to falsely report memory suggestions. Below, we summarize findings on five factors for which considerable predictive control has been achieved: standard versus modified recognition tests; source cuing; retrieval instructions; interviewer supportiveness; and anatomically correct dolls. The first factor was extensively discussed in chapter 6; the second was just considered in connection with storage variables; and developmental findings on both are in good conformity with opponent-processes predictions. Hence, child research on standard versus modified tests and source cuing is only briefly described below. As the other three factors have not yet been examined in connection with suggestibility research, they are considered in somewhat greater depth.

Standard Versus Modified Tests

When subjects receive forced-choice recognition tests following misinformation, they may be so-called standard tests, in which the alternatives are a target and the corresponding memory suggestion (e.g., stop sign versus yield sign), or they may be so-called modified tests, in which the alternatives are a target and a nonsuggested-but-gist-consistent item (e.g., stop sign versus railroad sign). In adult research, it has been found that standard tests almost invariably detect misinformation effects (e.g., Loftus et al., 1978), that modified tests sometimes fail to detect misinformation effects (e.g., McCloskey & Zaragoza, 1985), and that when the two types of tests are compared within a single experiment, standard tests yield more pronounced misinformation effects (e.g., Titcomb & Reyna, 1995). These patterns are well predicted by opponent-processes distinctions, which posit that standard tests are better retrieval cues for verbatim traces of misinformation than are modified tests (Reyna & Brainerd, 1995a). Does the standard versus modified test manipulation have similar effects when it comes to misinformation experiments with children? It should, according to opponent processes, because the quality of retrieval cues for misinformation is just as important a consideration in children as in adults.

The first clear data on this question were reported in Ceci et al.'s (1987) studies. In two of their experiments, preschool children were assigned to three conditions: control (no misinformation), standard (misinformation followed by standard tests), and modified (misinformation followed by modified tests). The false-memory data of Experiments 3 and 4 are displayed in Figure 7-13, where it can be seen that the familiar adult pattern was present: Preschoolers in *both* misinformation conditions made more false-memory responses than preschoolers in the control condition, and the misinformation effect was larger for standard than for modified tests.

Although Ceci et al.'s (1987) findings are in good agreement with theoretical predictions and adult data, they stimulated considerable controversy in the years immediately following their publication, the reason being that some other investigators were unable to produce evidence of misinformation effects in children using modified tests (Zaragoza, 1987, 1991). Of course, the latter findings are null results that are not especially informative, absent a showing that the original Ceci et al. data were due to some artifact. However, Reyna (1995) eventually explained that the difference between the positive versus null studies was probably due to a methodological discrepancy in their respective designs, a discrepancy that opponent-processes distinctions predict should affect the size of misinformation effects. We

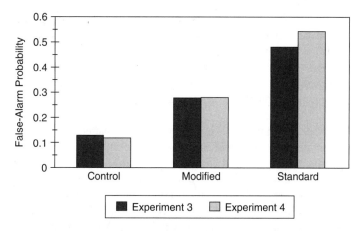

Figure 7-13. Effects of standard and modified tests on children's false reports of memory suggestions. Based upon Ceci, Ross, and Toglia (1987).

postpone discussion of this point, however, until the later section on forgetting. For the present, we will simply note that in line with this explanation, subsequent studies have confirmed Ceci et al.'s results. For instance, the standard versus modified test manipulation has been examined in a series of experiments by Holliday (Holliday et al., 1999; Holliday & Hayes, 2001). Holliday has consistently detected misinformation effects in children using modified tests, and like Ceci et al., has found larger effects in younger than in older children. Consistent with opponent-processes predictions, Holliday has also found that modified tests yield larger effects under conditions that should produce stronger verbatim memories of misinformation and weaker verbatim memories of target events.

Source Cuing

Above, we considered the manner in which source cues reduce the power of subsequent misinformation to falsify children's memory reports when those cues are administered as part of the exposure phase. However, in early adult misinformation experiments in which the effects of source monitoring were explored, source cues were administered after misinformation, as part of memory tests. Specifically, subjects' performance on recognition probes that did not contain explicit source cues, which are the usual probes that are administered in misinformation experiments, was compared to their performance on recognition probes that contain such cues. As a concrete illustration, suppose that the memory test consists of yes-no probes for targets and distractors. Examples of typical probes would be: Was there a stop sign at the corner? Was there a yield sign at the corner? When source cues are added, the corresponding probes would be: During *the slide show*, did you *see* a stop sign at the corner? During *the slide show*, did you *see* a yield sign at the corner? From an opponent-processes standpoint, the first question is a better retrieval cue for verbatim traces of target events because it contains additional surface information that matches the surface features of the exposure phase, and the second question is a poorer retrieval cue for verbatim traces of misinformation events because it contains additional surface information that *mis*matches the surface features of the misinformation phase. Consistent with this analysis, a standard finding of adult experiments is that providing source cues as part of memory tests reduces misinformation effects and sometimes completely eliminates them (Johnson et al., 1993; Reyna & Lloyd, 1997).

Developmental experiments have yielded a similar pattern. Illustrative findings can be found in an article by Poole and Lindsay (1995), as well as in later work by the same investigators. In the study reported in this article, children in the 3–6-year-old range participated in the science demonstrations that were subsequently used in the paper by Thierry et al. (2001). Three months later, the parents of some of the children received a four-page booklet entitled *A Visit to Mr. Science*, which purported to be a review of the events that the children experienced during the science demonstrations, and parents were instructed to read from this booklet to their children for 3 consecutive days. However, the booklet also contained memory suggestions about events that had not happened, some of which were intended to simulate sexual abuse experiences (e.g., that Mr. Science had wiped the child's mouth with something that "tasted yucky"). On the day following the third reading of the booklet, an experimenter arrived at the child's home to administer a memory interview about the science demonstrations. The interview included a series of yes-no questions that covered the memory suggestions and a series of follow-up questions that contained source cues. Children's performance was far more accurate on the latter questions, although misinformation elevated false alarms when explicit source cues were present, as well as when they were absent.

Retrieval Instructions

In chapter 4, we described research with adults which demonstrated that semantic false alarms and intrusions can be made more or less frequent via memory-test instructions that encourage subjects to weaken or strengthen their subjective criteria of memorability (e.g., Koriat & Goldsmith, 1994, 1996; Reyna & Kiernan, 1994). The general idea behind such research is that encouraging subjects to strengthen their subjective criteria slants retrieval toward verbatim traces, making recollection rejection easier and reducing false-memory responses, whereas encouraging subjects to weaken their subjective criteria slants retrieval toward gist traces, making recollection rejection more difficult and increasing false-memory responses. The same logic ought to apply to memory tests that are administered following misinformation (Brainerd & Reyna, 1998a).

The effects of retrieval instructions on children's susceptibility to memory suggestions have been investigated in a ground-breaking series of experiments by Holliday and associates (Holliday, 2003; Holliday & Hayes, 2000, 2001, 2002). In all of these experiments, the instructional manipulation was based upon Jacoby's (1991) process-dissociation paradigm, which was first devised to study word recognition in adults. The original procedure involves *two* target-exposure phases. For instance, subjects might listen to a list of words during Phase 1 and then view (e.g., on a computer screen) a new list of words during Phase 2. Next, subjects are assigned to two recognition-testing conditions, one in which they are instructed to implement a strong subjective criterion (called *exclusion* instructions) and the other in which they are instructed to implement a weaker subjective criterion (called *inclusion* instructions). Exclusion subjects are told to accept only probes that appeared on a specific list (say, List 2), whereas inclusion subjects are told to accept probes that appeared on either list. The opponent-processes interpretation of this manipulation is that exclusion instructions slant retrieval toward verbatim traces, because subjects must be sure that accepted items provoke remembrance of the surface properties of the correct list, and inclusion instructions slant retrieval toward gist traces, because any item whose meaning seems familiar can be accepted (regardless of whether that familiarity stems from List 1 or List 2).

Holliday and Hayes (2000) noted that the process-dissociation procedure can be extended to the misinformation paradigm in a straightforward manner. In that extension, Phase 1 = target exposure; Phase 2 = interpolated misinformation; exclusion instructions = accept only target probes; and inclusion instructions = accept both targets and material from the misinformation phase. The transparent opponent-processes prediction is that memory suggestions will be recognized at higher rates under inclusion instructions because, again, any item whose meaning is familiar can be accepted (regardless of whether the familiarity is due to the exposure phase or the misinformation phase). Developmentally, the equally transparent prediction is that this instructional effect ought to be more marked in older children, who reject misinformation at higher rates than younger children because their verbatim memories of the target material are superior.

Holliday and associates' experiments have confirmed these predictions. In her most recent experiments, for example, Holliday (2003) first exposed children of two age levels (4 and 8 years old) to a video about two children who attended a birthday party, which had been previously developed by Scullin and Ceci (2001). The video was followed, on the next day, by a neutral interview about the birthday party, which was followed by a further interview that contained misinformation about the video (e.g., that the children had arrived at the birthday party in a red car). Last, the children were administered a yes-no recognition test for information in the video. The distractor probes on the test consisted of some items that had been presented as memory suggestions during the misinformation interview and some others that had not been presented as memory suggestions. The recognition test was administered to children under both exclusion instructions and inclusion instructions.

Children's mean acceptance rates for distractors that had been presented as memory suggestions and control distractors are displayed in Figure 7-14 for one of Holliday's experiments. First, consider the data for the exclusion instructions, which is a standard "accept only targets" test. It can be seen that the usual developmental trend in susceptibility to misinformation was present: The spread between the false-alarm rates for control distractors versus memory suggestions was roughly twice as large in 4-year-olds as in 8-year-olds. More important, however, variations in retrieval instructions altered children's tendency to accept distractors that had been presented as memory suggestions, with acceptance rates being lower under exclusion instructions. The effect of retrieval instructions was *specific to memory sug-*

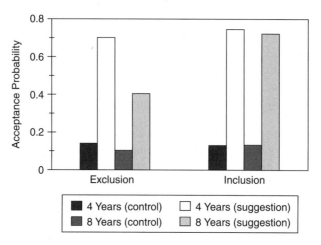

Figure 7-14. How children's acceptance of memory suggestions is influenced by strict test instructions (exclusion) versus lax instructions (inclusion). Based upon Holliday (2003).

gestions, however, because acceptance rates for distractors that were not presented as misinformation were unaffected. Taken together, the differing results for the two types of distractors indicate that exclusion instructions enhance children's ability to perform verbatim-based rejections of memory suggestions, rather than merely inducing a conservative response bias for all probes. A final critical datum is that the expected developmental interaction is present: Although memory suggestions were accepted at lower rates under exclusion instructions than under inclusion instructions, the spread between the two acceptance rates was much larger in 8-year-olds, which is again consistent with the notion that exclusion instructions enhance verbatim-based rejections (because the older children would have been more likely to have accessible verbatim traces of the events in the video).

A further feature of Holliday and associates' experiments is the identification of variables that, according to opponent processes, ought to increase or decrease the retrieval-instructions effect. The general theoretical expectations are that manipulations that strengthen verbatim traces of target events, relative to other types of memories, and manipulations that strengthen verbatim traces of memory suggestions, relative to other types of memories, should both enhance this effect. Holliday (2003) reported data that support the second prediction. During the misinformation phase, memory suggestions were presented in two ways. Some suggestions were simply read to children, whereas children were forced to confabulate information in response to other suggestions, with the latter method presumably yielding stronger verbatim traces of suggestions. The spread between the exclusion and inclusion acceptance rates was found to be greater when children were forced to confabulate memory suggestions than when they merely listened to them. There was also a developmental interaction such that the tendency of confabulation to enhance the influence of retrieval instructions was greater for 8-year-olds than for 4-year-olds.

An interesting twist on this procedure was implemented by Holliday and Hayes (2002). They presented the same two types of memory suggestions to 5- and 6-year-olds on the day *before* they watched the video. The idea here is that pre-exposure to suggestions ought to be less effective in falsifying children's memories than postexposure suggestions because, by the time that memory tests are administered, forgetting will be more pronounced for verbatim traces of misinformation than for verbatim traces of target material. Holliday and Hayes observed such a reduced misinformation effect, and they again found that inclusion instructions increased children's acceptance of memory suggestions, relative to exclusion instructions.

Interviewer Supportiveness

We know from earlier discussions—for instance, of false identification of criminal suspects in line-ups and photo spreads—that false-memory responses are apt to increase when subjects are anxious or fearful during the course of memory tests. That anxiety should impair any form of memory performance is unremarkable, but the fact that it has disproportionate effects on false memory is noteworthy and demands theoretical interpretation. According to the opponent-processes approach, the heightened sensitivity of verbatim retrieval to cognitive noise of various sorts means that anxious subjects will be more apt to process the gist of experience when responding to memory tests. Theory aside, available data leave little doubt that children are more sensitive than adults to the debilitating effects of anxiety (McGough, 1993), and therefore, a standard recommendation about interviewing child witnesses is that interviewers should be emotionally supportive and that interviews should begin with a rapport-building phase that demonstrates interviewers' supportiveness to children (e.g., Home Office, 1992; Warren & McGough, 1996). But is there any empirical support for these commonsense rules?

This question has prompted several studies aimed at evaluating whether interviewer supportiveness has mitigating effects on the tendency of suggestion to falsify children's memory reports. Among the better-known examples are studies by Carter, Bottoms, and Levine (1996), Davis and Bottoms (2002), Imhoff and Baker-Ward (1999), Ricci, Beal, and Dekle (1996), and Welch-Ross (1999). The general approach in all studies has been to manipulate interviewer effectiveness during the memory-test phase by comparing children's responses to the questions of two interviewers, who differ on features that cut along the supportiveness dimension. In the recent study by Davis and Bottoms, for instance, the manipulation consisted of a single interviewer who exhibited a planned sequence of supportive behaviors when interviewing one group of children but not when interviewing another group of children. Davis and Bottoms first exposed a sample of 6- and 7-year-olds to a play session in a "dinosaur room." Each child played with a "baby sitter" (research assistant). The baby sitter engaged the child in activities involving pictures, stories, a Barbie doll, bubbles, balloons, a camera, and a puppet. During the course of the play session, the baby sitter touched the child at various times in an innocuous manner. Following the play session, the children were assigned to either a supportive-interview condition or to a control condition. In the supportive condition, the child was escorted to an interview room and introduced to an adult interviewer, who began the session with a period of rapport building, who smiled at the child throughout the interview, who maintained supportive eye contact with the child, and who asked questions using warm and positive vocal intonations. In the control condition, on the other hand, the child was escorted to an interview room and introduced to the same adult interviewer, who asked questions straight away, without any preliminary rapport building, and who did not engage in the supportive behaviors just described during the course of the interview. The questions that were posed in the two conditions focused on the play session, and naturally, these questions included memory suggestions. Some memory suggestions focused on neutral events (e.g., What color was the robe that you put on?), but others were abuse-related (e.g., She kissed you, right? You didn't keep your pants on, did you?). Analysis of the interview data revealed that children who were interviewed by the supportive adult were significantly less likely than control children to succumb to such suggestions, and they were also significantly less likely to confabulate details to support the suggestions.

It is worth remarking that interviewer suggestiveness can be manipulated in other ways and that most of these alternative manipulations have produced similar findings. However, there is an exception to this rule that is especially pertinent to child sexual abuse cases—namely, parental interviewing. Generally speaking, children are more likely to be fearful in the presence of strangers than in the presence of familiar, trusted adults (McGough, 1993), and therefore, interviews conducted by children's parents are inherently more supportive than interviews that are conducted by strangers. Hence, it is tempting to infer that parental interviews will yield low levels of false-memory reports and that, in fact, parents might be the best of all possible interviewers when it comes to promoting resistance to memory suggestions. Because child victims and witnesses often make their first disclosures to parents, this inference encourages the dangerous view, in criminal prosecutions, that memory reports that children supply to parents are inclined to be highly accurate and that hearsay testimony from parents about such reports is therefore especially probative of guilt. This view is dangerous because the inference upon which it is founded is erroneous. In fact, this inference is a classic illustration of the perils of drawing conclusions from real-life situations, rather than controlled laboratory experiments; other factors are confounded with supportiveness when interviews are conducted by parents, the most obvious and worrisome contaminant being source credibility.

Children's parents are far and away the most credible sources of information in their lives. Thus, although, on the one hand, children are apt to regard parental interviews as highly supportive, thereby reducing their susceptibility to memory suggestion, they also regard parental interviews as the most authoritative sources of information, thereby increasing their susceptibility to memory suggestion. These considerations, in themselves, cut the ground from under the proposition that hearsay statements from parents about the memory reports of their children should be regarded as particularly reliable by triers of fact. Further, available data indicate that the high-credibility feature of parental interviews swamps the supportiveness feature, yielding heightened susceptibility to memory suggestions made in parental interviews, relative to suggestions made by interviewers who are strangers.

On this point, Ricci et al. (1996) reported an important experiment involving kindergartners who had viewed a slide show about a theft, while they listened to an accompanying narrative. Half of the children were then interviewed by one of their parents, and the other half were interviewed by a stranger. During the course of the interview, a photo spread was administered to determine whether children could identify the culprit in the slide show. Some of the interviewer's questions contained explicit suggestions about which picture was the culprit's. Children's baseline levels of accuracy were lower with parental interviews than with stranger interviews, and children changed their initial identifications more often with parental interviews. Worse, however, children were more susceptible to the interviewer's suggestions about which person was guilty when the suggestions were made by parents. In criminal investigation and prosecution, such findings argue for heightened caution, rather than heightened acceptance, when confronted with hearsay statements from parents about their children's memory reports.

Anatomically Detailed Dolls

The last retrieval variable that we shall consider—the use of anatomically detailed dolls as cues during child interviews—is one of the most controversial topics in the literature on child suggestibility, one on which there has been extensive research and scientific commentary (e.g., Bruck, Ceci, & Francoeur, 2000; Bruck, Francoeur, Ceci, & Renick, 1995; Dammeyer, 1998; Dawson, Geddie, & Wagner, 1996; De-Loache & Marzolf, 1995; Koocher, Goodman, White, Friedrich, Sivan, & Reynolds, 1995). It is also a topic that would probably not have figured in experimentation, and would certainly not have been discussed in this volume, were it not for the close connection between child suggestibility research and the prosecution of sexual abuse crimes.

Anatomically detailed dolls have a rectal cavity and, depending on the doll's gender, structures corresponding to either the male or female genitalia. Such dolls may be representations of children or adults, and in the latter case, they will usually have pubic hair. Anatomically detailed dolls were originally developed as instructional aids in sex education. However, during the period of intensified investigation of child sexual abuse that we described earlier, it became increasingly common to use such dolls to investigate sexual abuse allegations. From a memory standpoint, this use of anatomically detailed dolls is as a source of retrieval cues. Specifically, children would be provided with such dolls by investigative interviewers as a way of stimulating detailed recollections of specific acts of abuse. Children might also be asked to participate in a form of show-and-tell, in which they might be asked to point to the places on a doll's body where they had themselves been touched by a perpetrator or to demonstrate a perpetrator's actions on a doll's body (e.g., by inserting a pointer into a doll's rectum, vagina, or mouth). It is this investigative application of anatomically detailed dolls that has generated controversy because suspects may be charged on the basis of statements and physical demonstrations that are stimulated by such dolls.

The controversy boils down to a disagreement over the relative importance of false-negative versus false-positive errors in investigative interviewing. As we know, young children are not the most voluble of witnesses when it comes to recounting criminal acts that they have observed or in which they have participated. Psychometrically, this simply means that interviews of young children, as opposed to interviews of adolescents and adults, are prone to high rates of false-negative error: Children will often fail to recollect felonies that were actually committed, allowing the guilty to go free. As we also know, this same circumstance has prompted some to argue for the use of suggestive questioning techniques in investigative interviews of children.

Anatomically detailed dolls came into use as yet another device for overcoming the false-negative problem (e.g., Boat & Everson, 1988). However, this practice led others to argue that, like suggestive questioning, dolls may produce false-positive errors (i.e., dolls may stimulate descriptions or demonstrations of sexual acts that children have neither experienced nor observed, that children have experienced but that were committed by a different person than the suspect, or that children have simply observed in sexually explicit videos or magazines that are present in their homes). A further psychometric criticism of anatomically detailed dolls was also raised—namely, that the assumption that such dolls reduce false-negative errors, though plausible on its face, was an unproved assumption at the time that interviewers began using dolls to investigate sexual abuse allegations. Controlled experiments provided data that were consistent with both criticisms.

Bruck, Francoeur, et al. (1995) reported one of the earliest research projects that sought to determine whether the assumption that anatomically detailed dolls reduce false-negative errors was sound. These authors described two experiments in which 3-year-old children received a routine medical check-up that involved genital touching for half of them but not for the other half. Children were interviewed about the details of how they were examined following the check-up, with the question of principal interest being their recollections of bodily touches. Children in both conditions were either asked to demonstrate bodily touches that might have occurred using their own bodies or to demonstrate bodily touches using anatomically detailed dolls. An initial and rather troubling finding, from an investigative perspective, is that children were not accurate at recounting genital touching, *regardless of whether the check-up had included such touches.* With children whose check-ups included genital touches, the children were not more likely to report such touches when dolls were used than when dolls were absent, contrary to the hypothesis that dolls reduce false-negative errors. With children whose check-ups did not include genital touches, the use of dolls increased inaccurate reporting because some children demonstrated how the pediatrician had inserted fingers into their anus or vagina (which had not actually occurred), thereby supporting the hypothesis that anatomically detailed dolls produce false-positive errors.

A follow-up study yielding a similar pattern of findings was reported by some of these same authors (Bruck et al., 2000). Preschool children were again given routine medical check-ups, half with genital touching and half without. Rather than split the children into doll versus no-doll groups, during the memory interview, all children were asked to demonstrate touches on their own bodies and on anatomically detailed dolls. Once again, there was no evidence that dolls reduced underreporting of genital touches in children who had received such touches. Also as before, dolls stimulated some false-positive errors in which children who had not received genital touches nevertheless reported such touches; these errors were confined to girls (who falsely demonstrated anal and vaginal insertions with the dolls).

Upon first impression, Bruck and associates' (1995, 2000) finding that anatomically detailed dolls do not reduce underreporting of genital touches among children who have actually been touched seems very surprising, so surprising that one is inclined to dismiss the data and suspect the presence of design flaws. After all, experimental demonstrations that young children's memories for a target experience are aided by realistic retrieval cues, such as actual objects that were present during the index experience, are thick on the ground (e.g., Howe, 2000; Poole & Lamb, 1998), and anatomically detailed dolls are certainly realistic retrieval cues. So, how could they fail to reduce false-negative errors, regardless of whether or not they increase false-positive errors?

The explanation was given by DeLoache and Marzolf (1995), and it revolves around a prior literature that delineated young children's limited understanding of the relationship between physical reality and models of reality (DeLoache, 1989; DeLoache, Kolstad, & Anderson, 1991; DeLoache & Marzolf, 1992). According to this explanation, the difficulty with anatomically detailed dolls lies in the fact that during an investigative interview, they function as *models* of an aspect of reality (i.e., children's bodies) *rather than reality itself*. Thus, the use of such dolls is predicated on a hidden assumption: If dolls are to stimulate accurate reports of bodily touches from young children, children must understand the relation between the doll and their own bodies. As adults, it would not occur to us even to consider that comprehension of this relation would be an obstacle because we are so accustomed to relying on models to guide our behavior in the real world. Suppose that you are attending a convention in an unfamiliar hotel and wish to locate a room in which a talk is being presented, or suppose that you wish to locate a drugstore in an unfamiliar mall. In both instances, you would locate a map of the building, examine it, and proceed immediately to your destination. But imagine your confusion if you did not grasp the relation between the map and the actual building, the technical relation being one of structural isomorphism in Euclidean space. In essence, this is the predicament of young children. In an impressive series of investigations spanning 2 decades, DeLoache and her associates have repeatedly found that preschoolers' comprehension of the relation between simple models and the corresponding real objects is limited.

Forgetting Memories

Misinformation Delay

Delaying the presentation of misinformation was perhaps the earliest variable to be widely acknowledged as one that has palpable effects on children's susceptibility to suggestion. It came about in this way. The time was the late 1980s. Ceci et al.'s (1987) experiments had recently been published, which demonstrated false-memory levels above 60% in preschoolers, above 40% in 5-year-olds, and above 30% in 8-year-olds following *brief, one-time suggestions*. However, as mentioned earlier, other investigators, notably Zaragoza (1987), had been unable to replicate Ceci et al.'s results and, in fact, had failed to obtain statistically reliable suggestibility in children using procedures that were similar to Ceci et al.'s. The discrepancy between the two sets of findings, along with the question of whether one should be concerned about the suggestive questioning of child witnesses, which was lurking in the background, was the topic of intense discussion at an international conference on children and the law that was held at Cornell University in 1989 (for the proceedings of this conference, see Doris, 1991). A few years later, some additional experiments with children had been published. When Ceci and Bruck (1993b) reviewed them, they concluded that (a) most had obtained reliable suggestibility effects, and (b) most had obtained reliable age decreases in such effects. However, it remained unclear why some studies had failed to detect that suggestion falsified children's memory reports.

The answer was found 2 years later when Reyna (1995) reviewed the methodologies of these same studies. She noted that the designs of studies that had produced reliable suggestibility effects versus studies that had produced null findings differed in a factor whose importance will be obvious to readers of this volume but was far from obvious at the time. In studies that had produced statistically significant suggestibility effects, the target-exposure phase and the misinformation phase occurred during different experimental sessions, with a substantial time lag between them. (Remember that in Ceci et al.'s experiments, the target-exposure phase and the misinformation phase took place on consecutive days.) In the studies that had failed to produce reliable suggestibility effects, on the other hand, the target-exposure phase and the misinformation phase took place during the same session, with only a few minutes separating them. As we learned in chapter 6, a delay of a day or so between the two phases ought to yield larger suggestibility effects, owing to the rapid loss of verbatim traces and, because such forgetting is more pronounced in younger children, such a delay should also produce larger suggestibility effects in younger children than in older ones.

These latter predictions have been borne out in subsequent experiments in which the length of the target-exposure-to-misinformation interval has been varied. An early example is Cassel and Bjorklund's (1995) study, in which adults viewed a video of a bicycle theft and were suggestively interviewed about the video 1 week later and 1 month later. Cassel and Bjorklund also included a sample of 6-year-olds and a sample of 8-year-olds in their design. In Figure 7-15, the effects of memory suggestions administered after a 1-week delay and after a 1-month delay are shown. The probability that subjects at each age level falsely recalled suggested details is plotted for each of the testing sessions. A very instructive developmental pattern emerged. On the 1-week test, subjects at all three age levels exhibited suggestibility effects (the average false-recall probability was .45), but there were no reliable developmental differences in susceptibility to suggestion. On the 1-month test, however, the usual developmental trend in susceptibility to suggestion was observed, the reason being that suggestion had a much greater impact on 6-year-olds at 1 month than at 1 week (the false-recall probability increased to nearly 70%).

Other studies that have examined how delay affects children's susceptibility to suggestion include Bruck, Ceci, Francouer, & Barr (1995), Huffman, Crossman, and

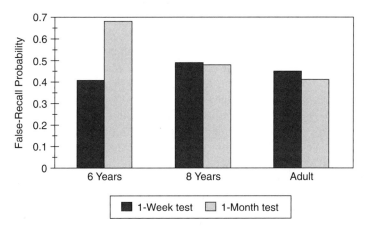

Figure 7-15. Effects of suggestive questioning at 1 week and 1 month on false recall of details of a bicycle theft by subjects of three age levels. Based upon Cassel and Bjorklund (1995).

Ceci (1997), Jones and Pipe (2002), Roberts, Lamb, and Sternberg (1999), and Sutherland and Hayne (2001). For instance, Roberts et al. reported a study that was concerned with the effects of a 1-day delay versus a 1-month delay. The presentation phase consisted of a structured play experience ("photography studio") in which 4-year-olds were dressed in a pirate costume by an experimenter who was dressed in a cowboy costume. Photographs of the child were taken during the play session. Children were assigned to three conditions: (a) 1-day review, (b) 4-week review, and (c) control. Children in Group a were interviewed 1 day later in their homes. The interview, which followed a fixed script, was portrayed to children as a review of the events that had occurred during the play session, but in fact, the review was a misinformation session containing several inaccurate statements (e.g., Some children told me that they sat on the photographer's knee for a photograph). Children in Group b were interviewed in exactly the same way, except that the misinformation session occurred 4 weeks after the play session. Finally, the children in all three groups were given a memory test, consisting of free- and cued-recall questions, 5 weeks after the presentation phase. There was a definite suggestibility effect: Control children, who were not exposed to misinformation, did not recall *any* inaccurate details about the play experience, whereas the children in the two misinformation conditions recalled some of the inaccurate details that had been suggested to them. There was also an effect of misinformation delay: The children in the 4-week group recalled roughly seven times as many inaccurate details, on average, as did children in the 1-day group.

Persistence of False Memories

When misinformation leads to false-memory reports in children, do those errors persist over time? We raised this question in chapter 5, in connection with children's *spontaneous* false memories, and noted that it is of considerable legal significance. The relevant legal principle is the *consistency rule* of testimony: that other things being equal, the law assumes that memory reports that are consistent over repeated interviews are more apt to be accurate than those that are inconsistent (Fisher & Cutler, 1992). We saw, however, that opponent processes lead to predictions that are at variance with the consistency rule—specifically, to the prediction that reports of false-but-gist-preserving information can be quite stable over time and that, under theoretically specified conditions, they can be more stable than reports of true information. We saw, further, that the data of developmental (and adult) studies were in better agreement with theoretical predictions than with the consistency rule.

What about the stability of false reports that have been produced by suggestion? According to opponent-processes analysis, this memory situation is different from spontaneous false reports, and therefore, the predictions are different. Gist traces provide the basis for spontaneous false reports and because such traces are reasonably stable over intervals of days and months, so too are spontaneous false reports. However, verbatim traces of misinformation, as well as gist traces of the meaning of target experiences and of misinformation, provide the basis for implanted false reports. Moreover, a few studies have been published in which researchers have measured the relative contributions of the two types of traces to children's *initial* false reports on memory tests that were administered shortly after misinformation sessions (Brainerd & Reyna, 1998a; Holliday & Hayes, 2000, 2001). In those studies, initial false reports have been based predominantly upon memory for the surface form of misinformation. Therefore, the opponent-processes predictions would be that children's implanted false reports will be less stable over time than spontaneous false reports, and importantly, in line with the consistency rule, they will be less stable than true-memory reports (Brainerd & Poole, 1997). To see how the latter prediction falls out, it must be remembered that in the basal

Target Presentation → Misinformation → Memory Test

procedure, verbatim traces of target events will already have undergone considerable forgetting by the time that misinformation is presented and, indeed, such forgetting is a concomitant of strong misinformation effects (e.g., Belli, 1993). By the time that memory tests are administered, verbatim traces of target events will have undergone still more forgetting, and the level of forgetting will necessarily be greater than it is for verbatim traces of misinformation (because the misinformation phase occurs after the presentation phase). What these considerations add up to, obviously, is that initial true reports are less apt to be based upon verbatim traces of target events than initial false reports are inclined to be based upon verbatim traces of misinformation. If so, the latter ought to be less stable over time because their predominant memorial basis is less stable.

This prediction was first examined in a literature review by Brainerd and Poole (1997). Although the studies that they reviewed were not explicitly designed to test the prediction, they concluded that the data supported two broad conclusions. First, false reports resulting from memory suggestion, like spontaneous ones, display significant persistence over time, and second, such false reports have sometimes been found to be less stable than true reports. For instance, the designs of the series of "mousetrap" studies by Ceci and his colleagues (Ceci, Huffman, et al., 1994; Ceci, Loftus, et al., 1994; Huffman et al., 1997), in which the children received repeated suggestions over several sessions to the effect that they had once caught their fingers in a mousetrap and had to be taken to the hospital to have it removed, allowed children's false reports of memory suggestions to be measured from one session to another. These reports displayed considerable intersession stability: The correlations between consecutive sessions ranged from .62 to .94. However, unlike findings for spontaneous false reports (chapter 5), children's false reports of memory suggestions declined over time. Huffman et al. retested a subsample of the children who had received the mousetrap suggestions 2 years earlier. These children's false-report rates had dropped from an average of 22% to an average of 13%. Over the same interval, the decline in their true-report rate was only half as large. When declines in true and false reporting were calculated as proportions of their respective levels 2 years earlier, the findings were more dramatic: The proportionate decline was 45% for false reports of memory suggestions versus 8% for true information.

Along similar lines, Salmon and Pipe (1997) retested some children who had participated 1 year earlier in a study by Salmon, Bidrose, and Pipe (1995). Approximately 38% of the true information that children had remembered in the Salmon et al. study was still present in their memory reports 1 year later. In contrast, only 14% of the false reports that children had made in the Salmon et al. study were still made 1 year later. Also, Poole and Lindsay (1996) observed differential declines in true reports and false reports of suggestions in a follow-up study that made use of the Mr. Science procedures that had been implemented in their earlier misinformation experiment (Poole & Lindsay, 1995). In the 1995 experiment, it will be remembered, 3 months after participating in a series of science demonstrations, children were read a "review" of the demonstrations, which contained memory suggestions about things that had not happened. In the follow-up study, children (aged 3 to 8) received an initial memory test during the 3-month session, and they also received a follow-up test 1 month later (i.e., 4 months after the science demonstrations). Because the first memory test took place 3 months after the science demonstrations, children's initial true reports should have been based mostly upon gist memories, which means that they should have been stable between the 3- and 4-month tests. That prediction was confirmed: Virtually all of the true information that was recalled at 4 months had also been recalled at 3 months. However, because the first memory test took place *at the same time that misinformation was presented*, children's initial false reports were more likely to be based upon verbatim traces (of misinformation) than were their initial true reports. Consistent with that notion, false reports were less stable over time: Only 66% of the false information recalled at the earlier test was recalled at 4 months.

These findings regarding the long-term persistence of children's false reports of memory suggestions illustrate just how impressive a level of predictive control over children's false memories can be achieved by relatively simple theoretical distinctions. The same opponent-processes distinctions that predicted the counterintuitive finding of higher levels of persistence for false than for true reports under certain conditions are now seen to predict the opposite pattern under conditions that are well specified theoretically. Such theoretical power can be of great assistance in court cases involving child witnesses by helping triers of fact to understand aspects of children's testimony that trouble their intuitions and by helping them to resolve inconsistencies in the testimony of different children (Brainerd et al., 2000). As an example, suppose that grand jurors who are reviewing the facts of a sexual abuse case are told that over time, a certain child has made consistent reports of specific types of abuse involving the defendant, whereas that child's sibling has made inconsistent abuse reports about the same suspect. The normal result is that jurors would doubt the truthfulness of the second child, and because the two children are siblings, they might also doubt the truthfulness of the first child. In contrast, if the jurors learned that the second child had initially been interviewed in a highly suggestive manner and the first child had not, and if the research on this point were explained to them by an expert, such doubts might not arise.

A concluding word of caution: Findings showing that implanted false reports are less stable over time than are true reports should not be interpreted to mean that time cures all ills with respect to suggestion. It does not, especially when children have been subjected to repeated misinformation (Bruck and Ceci, 1999). Recall in this connection that in the study by Huffman et al. (1997), *2 years* after children had received repeated memory suggestions, false reports of those suggestions had declined by less than 50%.

Fulfilling the Promise of Research: Scientifically Based Protocols for Child Interviewing

At a general level, research on children's suggestibility firmly establishes that the coercive and manipulative tactics that are central to police interviewing (chapter 6) are highly inappropriate for interviewing children, even when they are suspects in crimes. At a more specific level, as we have just seen, experimentation has isolated a number of variables that increase or decrease children's susceptibility to memory suggestions, variables that might be thought of as comprising a list of dos and don'ts that child interviewers should take into account (e.g., *do* take the time to ensure that children are not anxious and fearful; *don't* repeatedly suggest events to children that they have not reported themselves). However, it is possible to take this list a step further and incorporate dos and don'ts *whose effects have been established in research* into model protocols for interviewing child witnesses. From the perspective of prosecuting sexual abuse crimes (or other crimes in which children are victims or witnesses), such protocols have three important benefits, each of which redounds to the accuracy of legal decisions. First and most obviously, model protocols should maximize the yield of true information from child witnesses and minimize the yield of false information. Second, because model protocols are formalized interviewing instruments, instructional programs can be developed to train child interviewers in how to use those protocols. Ideally, such programs can be included as part of the normal training that is received by frontline investigative personnel, especially police officers and child protective services investigators. Training in model child-interviewing protocols could even be mandated by statute (and has been so mandated in California in the wake of the Mc-Martin case). Third, the adoption of model protocols as best-practice methods of child interviewing means that during the course of legal proceedings, the performance of interviewers can be evaluated by experts for their degree of adherence to the gold standard. That is, experts in the scientific literature can evaluate individual child interviews and, based upon what they find, can advise the courts as to the likely reliability of the information that was elicited. Indeed, it has already become common practice in child sexual abuse cases for prosecution and defense experts to review child interviews for the presence of factors such as those that were covered in the preceding section and in chapter 5.

Since the mid-1990s, by which time a substantial literature on children's spontaneous and implanted false memories had accumulated, we are pleased to say that the development of model interviewing protocols has been a vigorous area of research. In response to early findings on child suggestibility, professional organizations and groups of researchers had already published statements calling for the development of such protocols, spelling out the general features that they should incorporate, and in some instances, advocating for legislation to require that such protocols be followed in the investigation of certain types of crimes (particularly, sexual abuse). Examples are the Memorandum of Good Practice (Home Office, 1992) and the Guidelines for Psychosocial Evaluation of Suspected Sexual Abuse in Young Children (American Professional Society on the Abuse of Children, 1990). It is the business of the present section of this chapter to familiarize readers with some of the detailed protocols that have evolved since then, so that they can see for themselves how false-memory research has been translated into forensic practice. For the sake of historical completeness, we begin by briefly considering the earliest example of a model protocol, which was devised for adult rather than child witnesses in response to some of the problems that we discussed in chapter 6 but which has strongly influenced the construction of corresponding procedures for children. We then consider two influential model protocols for child interviewing.

The Cognitive Interview

During the 1980s, researchers Fisher and Geiselman began to develop and test a protocol, which came to be called the *cognitive interview* (CI; e.g., Fisher & Geiselman, 1992; Fisher, Geiselman, & Amador, 1989; Fisher, Geiselman, & Raymond, 1987). This protocol was designed to overcome some of the more egregious problems with police interviewing procedures by basing the instructions that witnesses receive and the questions that are posed to them on established laboratory principles of memory. Because memory research continues to accumulate, another feature of CI is that it has been regularly updated as new principles have emerged from experimentation. The specific principles that guide CI are stated in the protocol, which permits evaluation of the protocol's face validity by researchers. The protocol also states concrete principles of communication that should guide interviewers' behavior when they are questioning witnesses and provides a road map for the proper sequence of events in witness interviews.

Memory Principles

At present, CI is guided by five memory principles: (a) limited cognitive resources; (b) context recreation; (c) encoding specificity and retrieval variability; (d) multiple coding; and (e) representational-compatible questions. The first principle has been a familiar theme throughout the history of psychology (e.g., James, 1890; Miller, 1956)—namely, that the number of items to which people can simultaneously pay attention or hold in memory, or the number of simple cognitive tasks that people can perform simultaneously is sharply limited. This leads to the recommendation that witness interviews should not be conducted in noisy, distracting environments, such as a crowded nightclub with loud music, because witnesses will inevitably use some of their limited cognitive resources to process distracting information, thereby impairing their retrieval of accurate memories. The second and third principles are implementations of ideas about the relation between storage and retrieval that were introduced in chapter 3. According to those ideas (e.g., Tulving & Thomson, 1971), features of the context in which events are experienced are stored in memory traces, and consequently, the ability of retrieval cues to produce access to memory traces depends to some degree on the level of match between features that are present in cues and features that were present when the traces were stored. Thus, the second principle specifies that recreating during interviews the context in which crimes occurred (e.g., visiting the scene of the crime) ought to enhance retrieval of pertinent memories by increasing the overlap between stored features and cue features. This can be done using methods other than physical presence at crime scenes, which may be impossible or may create ancillary reliability problems (e.g., the crime scene may be a noisy and distracting one, such as a busy city intersection, which would violate the first principle). For instance, witnesses might be shown photographs or drawings of the crime scene, or they might be asked to recreate the appearance of the crime scene in their mind's eye or to recreate the sounds of the crime scene in their mind's ear. In addition, the third principle specifies that witnesses should be encouraged to search their memories in different ways, using different retrieval cues. For instance, witnesses might be asked to search their memories using sensory cues such as sights and sounds that accompanied the target events and then to re-search their memories using cues such as the temporal ordering or duration of events. Here, the assumption is that because only a limited number of contextual cues is stored in memory traces (e.g., Shiffrin, 2003), using varied cues to guide retrieval will increase the chances that witnesses will hit upon ones that were stored. The fourth principle—multiple coding—is a forensic instantiation of one of the core assumptions of the opponent-processes view of false memory: Witnesses store two distinct types of representations, traces of the surface content of target events and surrounding contextual cues and traces of the meanings and relations in which target events participate: verbatim and gist traces, in short. As we know, the latter type of representations is more open to errors, so that witnesses should be encouraged to process representations of the first sort. The last principle is concerned with the fact that people have difficulty switching from one memory representation to another during questioning, so that interviewers' questions should take account of the representations with which witnesses are currently working.

Communication Principles

Interviewers are instructed to follow three conversational rules when questioning witnesses: (a) encourage detailed responses, (b) develop rapport, and (c) transfer control to witnesses. The first principle acknowledges that witnesses may remember generic aspects of a situation without remembering many details (as when witnesses merely recall the age, gender, and build of a suspect) but that with encouragement (e.g., Please continue; is there anything specific that you recall?), they can flesh out details. The second principle is yet another embodiment of the notion that anxiety and fear impair accuracy and that an interviewer should therefore put witnesses at their ease and assure them that the interviewer is supportive and sympathetic. The third principle acknowledges a fundamental truth that is often lost in police interviews: It is witnesses, not interviewers, who are experts on target events because it is witnesses, not interviewers, who were present when those events happened. CI advises interviewers to make witnesses aware that interviewers understand this truth by encouraging them to describe events in their own way, at their own pace, and by asking open-ended questions, rather than direct questions that suggest to witnesses that interviewers already know the answers.

Sequence of CI Events

CI pioneered an idea that has become central to subsequent model interviewing protocols for children: There is an optimal sequence of events in an interview that will maximize the yield of accurate information. More specifically, CI treats witness interviews as consisting of five steps that ought to occur in the following sequence: (a) introduction, (b) request for an open-ended narrative of events, (c) follow-up probing, (d) review of responses, and (e) conclusion. The fourth and fifth phases require particular comment. The purpose of the fourth phase is not to suggest information to witnesses that interviewers want to hear, but rather, to prompt witnesses to flesh out generic recollections with specific verbatim features and generally to empty their memories of all pertinent information. Therefore, interviewers are instructed to use varied retrieval cues to triangulate on information about a crime, but to avoid leading witnesses. (Note that although, on the one hand, such a procedure seems in good agreement with the finding that subjects often require more time and effort to access verbatim memories of surface details than to access sketchy gist memories, the procedure may also encourage reconstructive processing of gist if verbatim memories are inaccessible.) For instance, the interviewer may select segments of the free-narrative report, especially ones for which some physical details were described (e.g., the appearance of the room in which a crime occurred), and ask the witness to report anything further that can be remembered about it. Interviewers are also instructed to caution witnesses that they should not rely on imagination or inference as they search their memories for additional details. Concerning the fourth step, the objective here is for the interviewer to be certain that she has correctly understood the witnesses' responses and has not recorded any information incorrectly. However, it is inherent in the process of reviewing a witness's responses that the witness is provided with further opportunities to retrieve additional crime details.

Research on CI

Although CI is based upon well-researched memory principles, whether it actually improves the yield of accurate information from witnesses is an empirical question. The effectiveness of CI has been investigated in both laboratory studies and in the field (e.g., Ascherman, Mantwill, & Kohnken, 1991; Fisher & Geiselman, 1992; Fisher, Geiselman, Raymonds, Jurkevich, & Warhaftig, 1987). *Laboratory studies* refer to designs in which witnesses are exposed to simulated crimes and are then interviewed, using either CI or standard police procedures. *Field studies* refer to designs in which witnesses to actual crimes are interviewed, again using either CI or standard police procedures. The two types of studies are complementary and provide converging evidence on the effectiveness of CI because each has an inherent weakness that the other does not: Laboratory studies allow researchers to know with certainty which memory reports are true and which are false, but they do not approximate the levels of memory interference that are present in actual crimes (e.g., high levels of fear, anxiety, and environmental distractors), whereas field studies provide the conditions under which witnesses are typically interviewed in actual crimes, but they do not allow researchers to discriminate true reports from false ones with certainty.

Initial studies of both types showed that the performance of CI was superior to standard police procedures. For instance, in an early laboratory study by Fisher et al., CI produced more than twice as much true information as a standard interview without any increase in false reports, and an early field study cited in Fisher and Geiselman showed that CI produced one third more true information than a standard interview. More recently, Kohnken, Milne, Memon, and Bull (1999) published a review of 55 empirical comparisons of CI to alternative procedures. They concluded that there was strong evidence that CI improves total recall of true information but that there was also consistent evidence that CI increases the recall of false information. Opponent-processes theories provide a straightforward explanation of the elevation in false reporting: Even though the questioning during the fourth step of CI is not suggestive, it will inevitably encourage a prototypical source of false-memory reports: the reconstructive processing of gist. Because witnesses have already completed a free narrative of events, they will have already reported most of the details for which they are able to access verbatim traces. In order to recall further details, therefore, it will be necessary to rely on the reconstructive processing of gist (Let's see. I must have seen Mr. Smith at the convenience store during the robbery because I know that he works there on Saturday nights). Even though witnesses are cautioned not to rely on their imaginations, we know that rememberers are not particularly good at distinguishing reality from constructions or suggestions (chapter 6).

The NICHD Protocol

When it comes to forensic interviewing of children, the current gold standard is a protocol that was developed by Michael Lamb and associates at the National Institute of Child Health and Human Development. This protocol was expressly devised for use in sexual abuse investigations, and it has been the subject of extensive research involving both laboratory studies and field work in multiple countries (e.g., Hershkowitz, Orbach, Lamb, Sternberg, & Horowitz, 2001; Lamb, 1998; Lamb & Garretson, 2003; Lamb, Sternberg, & Esplin, 2000; Orbach, Hershkowitz, Lamb, Sternberg, Esplin, & Horowitz, 2000; Orbach & Lamb, 2000, 2001; Sternberg et al., 2001). Thanks to the resources of Lamb's NICHD laboratory, the level of scientific substantiation for this protocol far outstrips that of any alternative procedures.

Like CI, the NICHD protocol consists of a sequence of steps that interviewers are instructed to execute in a specific order. There are 17 steps in all, which are named and explained in Table 7-1. There, it can be seen that the sequence incorporates a number of features that, based upon the research reviewed earlier in this chapter, ought to maximize the yield of true reports and minimize the yield of false ones. For example, the introduction and rapport steps would be expected to reduce fears and anxieties that children might be experiencing about what will transpire during the interview and whether it is safe to report what they have experienced. The fifth step should help focus children on verbatim retrieval rather than on reconstructive processing of gist.

Most important, the structure of the memory questions conforms to what research has shown about the nature of the questions that stimulate accurate recollections versus questions that stimulate erroneous ones. Note that whenever children are asked about their memories of the allegations that are under investigation, they are always asked, *first*, to provide a free narrative in their own words. Because young children often provide little information in response to such invitations, field interviewers usually proceed immediately to direct or suggestive questions. However, in the NICHD protocol, the invitation is accompanied by *repeated neutral prompts* (e.g., Do you remember any more? Can you tell me anything else?). The research of Lamb and associates has demonstrated that such neutral prompts stimulate an impressive amount of additional information, thereby greatly reducing the need to rely on direct or suggestive questions (Lamb, 1998; Orbach et al., 2000).

When neutral prompts fail to elicit sufficient details, interviewers may move on to cued-recall questions (Steps 7, 10, and 13), which name a reference point that children have already mentioned in their narratives (e.g., the kitchen or living room) and ask them to provide further information about it. Available data (e.g., Pipe et al., 1999) indicate that such questions produce only slightly more false reports than completely neutral prompts. When cued recall fails to elicit detailed reports, interviewers may move on to pairs of open and direct questions about crucial features of the target allegations (Steps 8, 11, and 14). Children are *first* provided with the opportunity to recall details in response to an open question (You said he took you to another room. Tell me about that), and if that does not work, children are asked direct questions (You said he took you to another room. Was it the kitchen, the living room, the bathroom, or somewhere else?). Research has shown that, for most children, the relatively unsuggestive combination of neutral prompting of free narratives, coupled with cued-recall and open-ended invitations about specific reference points can elicit a large amount of information that bears directly on the allegations, which obviates the need for leading questions.

Table 7-1. The Steps of the NICHD Protocol

Step	Explanation
1. Introduction	The parties to the interview introduce themselves and discuss their respective roles during the interview.
2. Truth and lies	The parties to the interview discuss the difference between truth and lies and the need to tell only the truth.
3. Rapport	The interviewer visits with the child to lower anxiety and answers any questions that the child has. At the same time, the interviewer monitors the child's language to determine the child's level of linguistic sophistication.
4. Recent event	As a memory warm-up, the child is asked to provide a narrative of a recent salient event (e.g., a birthday party, a visit to a zoo or museum).
5. First narrative	The child is asked to provide a free narrative of the allegations that are under investigation. Neutral prompts are used to keep the narrative going (e.g., Could you tell me some more about that? Do you remember more about what happened? Can you remember anything else?).
6. Last incident	For multiple-incident crimes, the child is asked to provide a free narrative of the last instance of the allegations that are the subject of the investigation. Neutral prompts are used to keep the narrative going.
7. Recall cues	Cued-recall prompts are used to obtain additional information about crucial features of the narrative (e.g., You said something about some things happening in the living room. Can you tell me anything else about that?).
8. Open/direct	For especially important details that are crucial to prosecution, follow-up open-ended questions are paired with direct questions (e.g., Can you tell me where that happened? versus Did that happen in the kitchen, the living room, the bathroom, or somewhere else?).
9. First incident	For multiple-incident crimes, the child is asked to provide a free narrative of the first example of the allegations that are under investigation. Neutral prompts are used to keep the narrative going.
10. Recall cues	Same as Step 7.
11. Open/direct	Same as Step 8.
12. Another incident	For multiple-incident crimes, the child is asked to provide a free narrative of any other example that the child can remember of the allegations that are under investigation. Neutral prompts are used to keep the narrative going.
13. Recall cues	Same as Steps 7 and 10.
14. Open/direct	Same as Steps 8 and 11.
15. Leading questions	Despite neutral prompting of narratives, follow-up cued-recall questions, and follow-up pairs of open versus direct questions, a child may fail to provide any specific information that squares with the allegations that the child has previously made or that others have made. The interviewer may then use leading questions that contain that information (e.g., You were at the store when he touched your pee-pee, weren't you? He rubbed your bottom in the bathroom, didn't he?).
16. Other information	The child is invited to provide any further information that the child can think of that relates to the allegations that are under investigation.
17. Neutral topic	The interviewer moves away from the substantive focus of the interview and returns to a neutral topic like those that were covered during the rapport phase. The interviewer and the child discuss that topic for a while before the interview is concluded.

Table 7-2. Components of the Step-Wise Interview

Step	Explanation
1.	Build rapport with the child by discussing neutral topics that are within the range of the child's experience.
2.	Invite the child to recount two recent events from the child's life.
3.	Explain to the child the need to tell only the truth.
4.	Begin the substantive part of the interview by introducing the topic of concern, which is normally a report of abuse that has been made by the child or by one of the child's peers.
5.	Ask the child to provide a free narrative of the events that are under investigation. This is accompanied by script-based follow-up questions (e.g., Can you tell me how he usually does it to you?) and by detailed follow-up questions about particular abuse episodes.
6.	Probe for further information using general questions (e.g., You talked about some bad touching in the bathroom. Can you tell me some more about that?).
7.	Probe for further information using more specific questions (e.g., Did he touch you on your bottom or your pee-pee or somewhere else?).
8.	If a child has disclosed sexual abuse in response to earlier questions, the interviewer is permitted to use props, such as drawings and anatomically detailed dolls, to obtain further details.
9.	The interview concludes by thanking the child for the help and informing the child that the interviewer can be contacted at any time if the child wants to talk again.

Note. From Yuille (e.g., 1988).

When all else fails, the interviewer may resort to leading questions (Step 15). The operative phrase is "when all else fails"; every attempt should have been made to secure information by nonsuggestive means. That is crucial for successful prosecution, as well as to avoid charging innocent defendants. In court, if the evidence of child witnesses has been secured entirely (or even primarily) via leading questions, that evidence will be vigorously (and correctly) challenged on the basis of scientific findings about children's susceptibility to suggestion.

The Step-Wise Interview

The earliest example of a scientifically based protocol for maximizing true reports and minimizing false reports in child sexual abuse interviews was developed in Canada by Yuille and associates (e.g., Yuille, 1988; Yuille & Farr, 1987; Yuille, Hunter, Joffee, & Zaparniuk, 1993). The research literature on this protocol, which is called the *step-wise interview* (SWI), is far less extensive than the corresponding literature on the NICHD protocol. Nevertheless, it merits attention because many of the features of the NICHD protocol that have been subjected to scientific study first appeared in the SWI. This can easily be seen by comparing Table 7-2, which jlists the nine steps of the SWI, to the corresponding NICHD steps in Table 7-1. Note that rapport building and establishing the importance of telling the truth figure in the opening phase of both protocols. More important, however, note that both protocols rely on the less-suggestive-to-more-suggestive ordering of questions, beginning with invitations for free narrative and moving on to progressively more specific questions. Thus, in both instances, the guiding strategy is to attempt to secure as much information as possible via the least suggestive types of questions and only to resort to more direct questions as the need arises.

There are notable differences between the two protocols, though, that reflect the more advanced state of scientific knowledge at the time that the NICHD protocol was developed. For instance, the NICHD protocol makes extensive use of neutral prompts during free narratives, whereas the SWI moves immediately to cued-recall questions as follow-ups during free narratives. At the time that the SWI was developed, it was widely thought that completely neutral prompts would be a waste of time because they would not elicit much additional information, but subsequent research has shown otherwise. Also, note that the SWI allows interviewers to use anatomically detailed dolls, as well as drawings, to elicit further details from children, whereas the NICHD protocol does not. Again, at the time that the SWI was developed, experiments challenging the assumption that such props reduce false-negative errors and identifying the suggestive properties of such props (e.g., Bruck, Francoeur, Ceci, & Renick, 1995; Bruck et al., 2000) had not yet been published.

Synopsis

For some years, the study of false memory in child interviewing and testimony has been closely connected to the investigation and prosecution of a special class of felonies: child sexual abuse crimes. Although there is little disagreement among scientists regarding the basic empirical patterns that have emerged from the research, the interpretation of those patterns has provoked much public controversy, owing to their legal implications for abuse cases. Criminalization of child abuse is a relatively recent advance in the law, with vigorous prosecution of sexual abuse, in particular, being a phenomenon of the last quarter of the 20th century. For students of false memory, a noteworthy feature of child sexual abuse is that it rarely leaves detectable physical traces. Thus, the evidentiary burden is usually on children's shoulders or, more precisely, on the shoulders of children's memories, which makes the consequences of false-memory reports far more serious than in other types of cases (in which memory reports can be checked against physical evidence). During the 1980s, in order to make it easier for children to provide evidence, modifications were urged in methods for interviewing alleged child abuse victims and in the law's procedures for handling child witnesses over the course of an investigation and prosecution.

With respect to child interviewing methods, the use of suggestive lines of questioning were advocated on the hypothesis that children do not, in response to such questioning, make false reports about personal events involving their own bodies. Early experiments seemed to confirm that hypothesis. Later experimentation did not, however, which raised concerns about the possibility of false allegations of sexual abuse in cases whose prosecution had been based upon disclosures that were stimulated by suggestive questioning. The McMartin Preschool case is a classic illustration of such concerns. Further, the most common way in which children provide evidence in legal proceedings is not as victims of sexual abuse but, rather, as witnesses to other types of crimes or as witnesses to domestic events that figure in custody decisions. Here, it has always been clear that, like adults, children are susceptible to suggestions about events that they have observed. It therefore appears that suggestive questioning of children is to be avoided in legal proceedings, regardless of whether children are suspected victims of abuse or are simply witnesses to events that pertain to legal decisions.

With respect to modifications in the law's procedures for handling child witnesses, the changes that were advocated included a lowering of barriers to the introduction of hearsay evidence, reducing and simplifying children's involvement in the pre-trial process, and creating environments in which children could supply testimony that are less forbidding and potentially traumatic than traditional courtrooms. Although most reforms in the last category have been uncontroversial, those in the first two categories have stimulated considerable disagreement. Concerning the admission of hearsay evidence, the argument for hearsay exemptions revolves around the fact that young children often make their initial disclosures to trusted adults, such as parents or teachers, and that they may be unable to remember what they reported during later forensic interviews. However, children's initial statements may have been produced by suggestive questioning by adults who suspect abuse for other reasons. Research has shown that children are especially susceptible to suggestions that are made by trusted adults. Concerning reductions in children's pre-trial involvement, this has often meant restrictions in defense counsel's ability to challenge children's competence, even when the statements of abuse that children have made include reports of events that are fantastic or seem to be impossible.

Studies of the suggestibility of children's memories provide the primary scientific database upon which recommendations about interviewing child victims or witnesses and recommendations about legal procedures for handling children are currently predicated. Although those studies have been largely motivated by a desire to improve the law's ability to prosecute sexual abuse crimes, it is important to remember that this is not the sole criterion by which such research should be judged. The findings of such research are essential to our theoretical understanding of memory development, and they also bear upon just about any type of legal proceeding that involves obtaining evidence from children.

Systematic developmental studies of child suggestibility have been appearing at a steady pace since the 1980s, and the results have generally been consistent with an opponent-processes analysis of the effects of suggestion (according to which memory suggestions instill false-memory reports by increasing both the baseline tendency to process the gist of experience and the baseline tendency to retrieve verbatim traces of suggestions). Although some early studies failed to find that children were susceptible to memory suggestions, using Loftus's misinformation paradigm, the great bulk of published studies have yielded two crucial results: Even brief, one-time suggestions increase children's false reports, and children's susceptibility to suggestion declines with age. Interestingly, the age decline in suggestibility can be reversed under conditions that are specified by opponent-processes distinctions.

Research has established that children's susceptibility to suggestion can be modified by storage, retrieval, and forgetting factors and that the influences of those factors interact with subjects' age. Key storage variables whose modifying effects have been found to be consistent with opponent-processes predictions are the verbatim and gist repetition of target events, verbatim repetition of misinformation, source-monitoring instructions, don't-tell instructions, misinformation credibility, misinformation plausibility, and central versus peripheral details. Key retrieval variables whose modifying effects have been found to be consistent with opponent-processes predictions are standard versus modified tests, source cuing, verbatim versus gist instructions, interviewer supportiveness, and anatomically detailed dolls. Concerning forgetting, extant studies vary considerably in the amount of delay that they impose between target presentation and misinformation presentation. Children's susceptibility to suggestion has typically been found to increase as delay increases, and indeed, variations in delay seem to explain the discrepant findings of early studies that detected child suggestibility effects versus studies that did not. Although implanted false memories exhibit significant long-term stability, they do not appear to be as persistent as spontaneous false memories, yet another result that falls out of opponent-processes distinctions.

The construction of model protocols for interviewing witnesses has been a major field of application of research on child and adult suggestibility. Historically, the CI is the earliest and best-known example of such a protocol, and it has generated an extensive research literature comparing the accuracy and completeness of witnesses' reports when interviewers use CI versus other procedures. Although CI was developed for adult witnesses, many of its core principles have been incorporated into model interviewing protocols for children. The first of these child protocols was developed in Canada by Yuille and associates. More recently, a second-generation protocol that incorporates the past 2 decades of research on child suggestibility has been developed and tested at NICHD by Lamb and associates. The NICHD protocol has been the subject of considerable research, and as a result, its use in the forensic interviewing of child witnesses is backed up by an unusually high level of scientific evidence.

8

False Memory in Psychotherapy

During the mid- to late 1990s, leading professional organizations that number counselors and psychotherapists among their members issued official statements regarding the recovery of repressed memories of sexual abuse and the therapeutic practices that stimulate such recovery experiences. A sample of those statements appears in Figure 8-1. What was going on?

In civil law, negligence and negligent supervision are time-honored liability concepts. Individuals or institutions may be sued for negligence if they fail to put procedures in place to prevent the occurrence of actions that are known to be harmful to others or whose harmfulness could reasonably be foreseen. (In the latter circumstance, the courts look with special favor upon defendants who foresaw that certain actions *might* be harmful and took steps to correct the anticipated damage before becoming defendants in litigation.) Even when appropriate procedures are in place, individuals and institutions may be sued for negligent supervision if they fail to ensure that those procedures are followed by individuals for whom they are responsible (e.g., dependent children, employees). As a case in point, the Boy Scouts of America has sometimes been sued for failures to develop personnel-screening procedures that would reduce the chances of pedophiles becoming Boy Scout leaders, and the organization has also been sued for failures to ensure that screening procedures were followed in personnel decisions about specific individuals (e.g., *Catalina Council v. Hunter*, 1998).

But, to return to the question: What was going on with statements like those in Figure 8-1? Pay particular attention to legalistic-sounding phrases such as "due diligence" (words that the law uses in reference to negligence), "subscribe to the *Principles of Medical Ethics* when treating their patients" (organizations often attempt

American Medical Association (1995)

The general issues have come to be referred to under the umbrella term "repressed memories" or "recovered memories." Both terms refer to those memories reported as new recollections, with no previous memories of the event or circumstances surrounding the event, although some "fragments" of the event *may* have existed. Considerable controversy has arisen in the therapeutic community over the issue, and experts from varied professional backgrounds can be found on all sides.

Under such circumstances, therapists should exercise care in treating their patients, maintaining an empathic and supportive posture. Due diligence for and reference to the *Principles of Medical Ethics*, or similar statements in the case of nonphysician therapists, should be given high priority. In some cases, a second opinion should be considered.

RECOMMENDATIONS

The following statements, recommended by the Council on Scientific Affairs, were adopted as AMA Policy at the 1994 AMA Annual Meeting.

The AMA:

1. Recognizes that few cases in which adults make accusations of childhood sexual abuse based on recovered memories can be proved or disproved and it is not yet known how to distinguish true memories from imagined events in these cases;

2. Encourages physicians to address the therapeutic needs of patients who report memories of childhood sexual abuse and that these needs exist quite apart from the truth or falsity of any claims; and

3. Encourages physicians treating possible adult victims of childhood abuse to subscribe to the *Principles of Medical Ethics* when treating their patients and that psychiatrists pay particular attention to the *Principles of Medical Ethics With Annotations Especially Applicable to Psychiatry.*

Figure 8-1. Excerpts from selected statements issued by professional associations of psychologists and physicians.

to fulfill their supervisory responsibilities by creating manuals of proper procedure and then requiring that individuals adhere to those manuals as a condition of employment, licensure, and so forth), and "independent corroboration" (a specific procedure that would reduce liability for negligence in psychotherapy). In this same connection, note the cautions to therapists that they should not base diagnoses of childhood sexual abuse upon criteria that have not been scientifically substantiated; they should not adopt uncritical attitudes of acceptance with respect to recovered memories of childhood abuse; they should be aware that scientific research does not generally support the notion of recovered memories of childhood abuse; they should be aware that certain therapeutic procedures can stimulate false recovered memories; they should avoid using memory-regression techniques that are predicated upon a presumed history of sexual abuse of which patients were hitherto unaware; they should recognize that a number of therapeutic techniques lack scientific support;

American Psychological Association (1995)

First, it's important to state that there is a consensus among memory researchers and clinicians that *most* people who were sexually abused as children remember all or part of what happened to them although they may not fully understand or disclose it. Concerning the issue of a recovered versus a pseudomemory, like many questions in science, the final answer is yet to be known. But most leaders in the field agree that although it is a *rare occurrence*, a memory of early childhood abuse that has been forgotten can be remembered later. However, these leaders also agree that it is possible to construct convincing pseudomemories for events that never occurred. The mechanisms by which both of these phenomena happen are not well understood and, at this point, it is impossible, without other corroborative evidence, to distinguish a true memory from a false one. . . . there is no single set of symptoms which automatically indicates that a person was a victim of childhood abuse. . . . There is no scientific evidence that supports this conclusion. . . . A therapist should not approach recovered memories with the preconceived notion that abuse must have happened or that abuse could not possibly have happened.

Australian Psychological Society (1994)

Memory is a constructive and reconstructive process. . . . Memories can be altered, deleted, and created by events that occur during and after the time of encoding, and during the period of storage, and during any attempts at retrieval. . . . Although some clinical observations support the notion of repressed memories, empirical research on memory generally does not. Moreover, scientific evidence does not allow global statements to be made about a definite relationship between trauma and memory. "Memories" that are reported either spontaneously or following the use of special procedures in therapy may be accurate, inaccurate, fabricated, or a mixture of these. The presence or absence of detail in a memory report does not necessarily mean that it is accurate or inaccurate. The level of belief in memory or the emotion associated with the memory does not necessarily relate directly to the accuracy of the memory. The available scientific and clinical evidence does not allow accurate, inaccurate, and fabricated memories to be distinguished in the absence of independent corroboration.

British Royal College of Psychiatrists (1997)

- Psychiatrists are advised to avoid engaging in any "memory recovery techniques" which are based upon the expectation of past sexual abuse of which the patient has no memory. Such "memory recovery techniques" may include drug-medicated interviews, hypnosis, regression therapies, guided imagery, "body memories," literal dream interpretation, and journaling. There is no evidence that the use of consciousness-altering techniques . . . can reveal or accurately elaborate factual information about past experiences, including childhood sexual abuse. Techniques of regression therapy including "age regression" and hypnotic regression are of unproven effectiveness.

- Forceful or persuasive interviewing techniques are not acceptable psychiatric practice. Doctors should be aware that patients are susceptible to subtle suggestions and reinforcements whether these communications are intended or unintended.

- The psychiatrist should normally explore his or her doubts with the patient about the accuracy of recovered memories of previously totally forgotten sexual abuse. . . . Memories, however emotionally intense and significant to the individual, do not necessarily reflect factual events.

Figure 8-1. *Continued.*

and they should avoid interviewing patients in a persuasive manner. All of this suggests major concerns about possible liability on the part of therapists for the use of scientifically unsubstantiated practices in patients' recovery of repressed memories of childhood sexual abuse.

Those concerns were precipitated by litigation filed during the mid-1990s against therapists across the United States for having implanted false memories of horrific childhood experiences in their patients—in most instances, false memories of having been sexually abused as children (Simpson, 1996). Although other examples could easily be given, two prominent cases that received national media coverage at the time involved the psychiatrists Bennet G. Braun (e.g., Belluck, 1997; Grinfeld, 2001) and Diane Humenansky (e.g., Loftus, 1998; Gustafson, 1995, 1997). Braun practiced in Chicago, Illinois, and Humenansky practiced in St. Paul, Minnesota.

Braun was sued for malpractice by a former patient, who alleged that he had practiced repressed-memory therapy on her (*Burgus v. Braun*, 1993). In the suit, the patient stated that she had originally sought treatment by Braun in 1986 for postpartum depression following a difficult birth experience and that she was under his care until 1992. During that time, the patient stated, she had been subjected to therapy sessions in which she was treated with high doses of medication and interviewed under hypnosis, and as a result, she was no longer able to distinguish fantasy from reality and was made to believe that she had more than 300 alternate personalities. She further alleged that her treatment made her believe that her multiple-personality disorder (MPD) was caused by an unremembered history of childhood abuse, which included having been tortured by members of her family and having participated in Satanic religious practices, including murder and cannibalism. She stated that her two sons, aged 4 and 5, had been hospitalized, at Braun's request, to determine whether they had a genetic predisposition toward multiple-personality disorder and that, while hospitalized, they had participated in therapy sessions in which they were encouraged to act out behaviors that were consistent with ostensible alternate personalities. Other complaints were that the patient's sons had been provided with suggestive props during therapy, such as guns and handcuffs, in order to stimulate memories of having been abused; the children had been subjected to suggestive therapy methods in order to stimulate memories of being part of a transgenerational cult of Satan worshipers; the patient's sons had been administered rewards during therapy that were contingent upon telling alleged secrets about abusive and Satanic experiences; the patient's treatment had destroyed her relationship with her husband and caused her to falsely believe that she had abused her own children; the treatment that the patient's sons received caused them to become mentally ill; and the total cost of the treatment exceeded $3 million. In addition to Braun, the hospital in which his clinic was housed was named as a defendant for negligent supervision—explicitly, for failure to supervise his activities and for failure to conduct regular inspections of his clinic.

This suit was scheduled for trial in November 1997, but on the day that the trial was to commence, the patient and her family agreed to an out-of-court settlement of $10.6 million, $3.5 million on behalf of the hospital and the remainder on behalf of Braun and another psychiatrist, Elva Poznanski, who had been named as his codefendant. Two years later, Braun's medical license was suspended by the state of Illinois for 2 years. In 2001, he was expelled from both the American Psychiatric Association and the Illinois Psychiatric Association after being found to have provided incompetent medical treatments and to have violated ethical standards.

In the other case, Diane Humenansky was sued for malpractice by six former patients, who made a variety of allegations (e.g., *Hamanne v. Humenansky*, 1995), including that they had received treatments, such as recovered-memory therapy, that implanted false memories of sexual abuse by family members and of Satanic cults. Other allegations of mistreatment focused on the inappropriate use of psychotropic drugs, the inappropriate use of hypnosis, false diagnosis of MPD, uncritical acceptance of repressed memories of childhood sexual abuse in patients, and failure to obtain independent verification of recovered memories. Several other, more technical allegations of malpractice also were made, which arose from the core complaints about memory implantation (e.g., Barden, 1996), such as the practitioner's failure to follow appropriate guidelines for diagnosis, breaches of standards of reasonable expected care, misapplication of psychiatric concepts, improper extension of treatment, failure to inform patients of the risks of treatments, and failure to inform patients of alternative treatments that have been proven to be safe and effective by scientific research. This was the first series of recovered-memory cases to go to trial in the United States during the 1990s.

During the initial trial, Humenansky testified that she did not believe that patients could recover false memories of sexual abuse; she did not believe in the phenomenon of false memory; and her patients' recovered memories were therefore true. However, the presiding judge ruled that the psychological theory upon which recovered-memory therapy is based—the theory of repression—does not meet an accepted standard of scientific proof and that, in consequence, expert testimony that assumes the validity of this notion could not be presented at trial. Following a 6-week trial, the jury awarded the plaintiff more than $2.6 million for medical expenses, loss of income, pain, and suffering. The plaintiff was awarded a further $461,000 for anticipated future damages, and her husband was awarded $210,000 for loss of partnership. In a second trial, the jury awarded another plaintiff, Elizabeth Carlson, $2.5 million for injuries that she had received as a result of negligent treatment aimed at recovering repressed memories. Humenansky again testified that her psychiatric treatments could not produce false memories of such appalling experiences. During both trials, memory researchers provided extensive testimony on false-memory research and on the parallels between recovered-memory therapy and procedures that have been found to induce false memories under controlled conditions. These researchers also testified that, contrary to the theory of repression, which hypothesizes that many people are unaware of past traumatic experiences because they somehow block the memories from entering consciousness, scientific studies have established that people remember traumatic experiences particularly well, sometimes to the point of pathology, which arises from fixation upon such memories (e.g., post-traumatic stress disorder [PTSD]).

After the verdict in the second trial, Humenansky's insurance carrier arranged out-of-court settlements with the remaining defendants. In November 1996, Humenansky entered a plea of no-contest to 20 malpractice complaints that had been filed with the Minnesota Board of Medical Practice. The board concluded that she had engaged in conduct that was unprofessional and that she had displayed professional incompetence. The board suspended her medical license indefinitely. As in the Braun case, Humenansky was subsequently expelled from membership in the American Psychiatric Association (and later from the Minnesota Psychiatric Association). Among the stated grounds for expulsion were the use of therapeutic techniques that induced false memories of sexual abuse in patients and the commission of substantial violations of certain sections of the *Principles of Medical Ethics With Annotations Especially Applicable to Psychiatry.*

Readers will already have noted several parallels between the statements of professional organizations in Figure 8-1 and the allegations in the Braun and Humenansky cases. It was cases such as these that created broad awareness among memory researchers and the public at large about the possibility of large-scale, interwoven collections of false memories that may arise from certain psychotherapeutic practices—a possibility that has latterly come to be known as *false-memory syndrome* (e.g., Boakes, 1999; de Rivera, 1996; Freyd, 1997; Gudjonsson, 1997; Pope, 1997, 1998; Sher, 1995).

In the present chapter, we explore the question of false memory in psychotherapy from the perspective of experimental research. To establish the dimensions of the question, we first review some case studies of alleged adult recovery of repressed memories of childhood sexual abuse. Four of them are examples of the classic form of this phenomenon: recovery of repressed memories of childhood sexual abuse committed by parents or Satanic cults. The other two are examples of a more recent variant: recovery of repressed memories of sexual abuse committed by religious clergy. Following these cases, we consider some general conditions of psychotherapy that, based upon opponent-processes distinctions and research that has been reviewed in earlier chapters, would be expected to set the stage for false-memory reports of life experiences, and we also consider parallels between specific therapeutic practices and experimental manipulations that are known to elevate false-memory reports. Last, we examine what experimental research has shown with respect to a key scientific question that is at issue: Is it possible, through procedures that are analogous to techniques that are used in psychotherapy, to instill convincing memories of traumatic experiences in people who never had those experiences?

Some Illustrative Cases

Examples of the Classic Type

Beth Rutherford

In 1992, Tom Rutherford, an ordained minister, was employed at the denominational headquarters of the Assemblies of God in Springfield, Missouri. He was living with his wife, Joyce, and their three daughters, Beth, Lynette, and Shara. The following events unfolded after Beth began working as a nurse in a local cancer clinic (e.g., see Rutherford, 1998a, 1998b).

Beth, who was 19 years old at the time, alerted her father to the fact that the stress of her nursing job was making it difficult for her to sleep. Tom recommended

Table 8-1. Illustrative Adult Behavioral Traits That Were Listed in the "Incest Survivors Aftereffects Checklist"

Trait	Additional Features
Absent memories of early years	Also includes absent memories of specific places or persons
Anger problems	Also includes imagined fears of rage and hostility toward all people of a particular gender or ethnicity
Avoidance of mirrors	Also includes shame and low self-esteem
Believing one is crazy	Also includes creation of fantasy worlds, relationships, or identities
Body alienation	Also includes poor care of the body, poor body image, and changing body size to make it sexually unappealing
Childhood hiding	Also includes security seeking and adult feelings of being watched
Denial	Also includes memory repression, dreams of memories, and inappropriate negative reactions to people or places
Depression	Also includes excessive crying
Desire to change one's name	None
Eating disorders	Also includes drug, alcohol, and other addictions
Excessive clothing	Also includes failure to remove clothing when swimming and extreme privacy requirements during urination or defecation
Fear of the dark	Also includes nightmares and fear of sleeping alone
Feeling that one has a secret	Also includes secretive behavior and feeling that one is a marked person
Gagging sensitivity	Also includes aversion to water on one's face while swimming or bathing
Gastrointestinal problems	Also includes vaginal infections, headaches, and arthritis
High risk-taking problems	Also includes high risk-avoidance
Intolerance of happiness	Also includes active withdrawal from and lack of trust in happiness
Multiple personalities	None
Noise aversion	Also includes verbal hypervigilance and speaking in muted tones
Relationship problems	Also includes ambivalence, conflicts, and intimacy concerns
Self-destructiveness	Also includes body mutilation and self-abuse
Sexual problems	Also includes aversion to being touched, feelings of being betrayed by one's body, feelings of violation, and becoming a prostitute or stripper
Stealing	Also includes setting fires and stealing as a child
Suicidal thoughts	Also includes suicide attempts and obsessiveness
Thought control	Also includes lack of a sense of humor and excessive solemnity

Note. From Blume (1991).

that she schedule an appointment with an Assemblies of God counselor, which she did. When Beth Rutherford began her counseling sessions, she believed that she had experienced a happy childhood with warm and loving parents. However, during her first session, she was nonplused when the counselor asked if she had ever been sexually abused. Rutherford replied firmly that she had not been, but she was told that her symptoms fit those of sexual abuse victims (see Table 8-1). Belief that unsuspected childhood sexual abuse could be reliably detected via behavioral profiles, such as Blume's (1991) Incest Survivors Aftereffects Checklist, was rampant in pop psychology circles at the time. As we have already commented, however, scientific evidence indicates that there is no constellation of behavioral symptoms that is uniquely diagnostic of such abuse (e.g., Kendall-Tackett et al., 1993).

During her second session, Rutherford confided that she sometimes had dreams of arguing vigorously with her father, of her father attacking her with a knife, and of her father sending bears after her. She was told that these are the sorts of strange dreams that sexually abused people experience and that she was therefore a victim of such abuse, notwithstanding that she had no memory of it. Thereafter, the counseling sessions began to focus increasingly on the sexual abuse theme and on the recovery of her supposed repressed memories of abuse. Rutherford (1998a) has described an assortment of procedures that were used by her counselor, which eventually led her to recover false memories of having been sexually abused by her father and of the complicity of her mother in such abuse, including (a) interpretation of behavioral symptoms, (b) age regression, (c) interpretation of the behavior of others, (d) dream interpretation, and (e) forced accusation and confrontation.

Concerning Procedure a, judging by the statements of professional organizations in Figure 8-1, such organizations have reason to believe that professional therapists, as well as pop psychologists, hold to the mistaken belief that there are constellations of behavioral symptoms, like those in Table 8-1, that are reliable signs of a history of sexual abuse. Rutherford was told in that regard that the fact that she was an A-student in high school was a sign that she had been abused, that she had concentrated on academic work as a way of coping with the ongoing abuse at home. When she asked why she was unable to recall this, the counselor informed her that she had repressed her memories of abuse in order to avoid the trauma but that she was now old enough to deal with the pain that would be provoked by memory recovery. With respect to Procedure b, Rutherford was assured that the counselor was an expert in sexual abuse who could help her uncover her repressed memories by regressing her back to childhood, that the counselor was qualified to help her work through the consequences, and that this process must be undertaken if she hoped to become mentally healthy. To stimulate recovery, Rutherford was instructed to relate memories of childhood experiences—such as conversations that she remembered having, events in which she recalled participating, the appearance of the homes in which her family had lived—and to provide concrete details of those experiences. The counselor then interpreted those reports in ways that were consistent with sexual abuse. When Rutherford described a storage shed in one home, for instance, this was transformed into a place in which she had been tied up and where objects had been inserted in her body. Rutherford was taught how to enter a state of self-hypnosis while concentrating on childhood experiences. As she was recovering from these trance-like states, the counselor would sometimes inform her that she had just made revelations regarding sexual abuse experiences, revelations that Rutherford could not recollect making. Concerning Procedure c, activities involving her parents were interpreted so as to support the sexual abuse story. For example, when Rutherford related a story of writing checks with her father to pay bills when she was 9 years old, her counselor characterized this as evidence that her father was treating her as a spouse, rather than as a daughter, and that he preferred Rutherford over her mother. When she related stories about her parents encouraging her to do well in school, Rutherford was told that such encouragement demonstrated that her parents were experiencing guilt about abusing her and that they felt that outstanding school achievement would demonstrate that the abuse had not harmed her.

Regarding Procedure d, as the emphasis on sexual abuse increased, Rutherford began having dreams with intense sexual content, dreaming, for instance, of occasions on which she and her friends were raped while her father watched. During each session, the counselor questioned her about the content of dreams that she had experienced since the last session. The counselor informed her that the dreams were true memories and that her mind was using the mechanism of dreams to reveal the reality of her abuse. With respect to Procedure e, the counselor instructed Rutherford to confront her parents and to openly accuse them of abusing her. Rutherford was urged to take these steps on the ground that they were essential if she wished to heal the damage that had been caused by the abuse. Ultimately, Rutherford confronted her parents, and when they denied her accusations, she told them that she firmly believed that she had been abused and would not retract her accusations. She also convinced her two sisters that she had been abused by their parents.

After 2.5 years of counseling, Rutherford had recovered highly specific "memories" of repeated sexual abuse by her father between the ages of 7 and 14, including being sodomized by him with a curling iron and being raped by him with a fork and scissors. Among other memories, she recalled being twice impregnated by her father. Upon discovering that she was pregnant for the first time, she remembered that her father had used a coat hanger to perform a painful abortion on her. Upon discovering that she was pregnant for the second time, Rutherford remembered using a coat hanger to perform a self-abortion. She also remembered her father cutting her and licking the blood from her body. In addition to recovering these memories, she was in a state of physical deterioration: Her weight had dropped below 90 pounds and she was taking mood-controlling medications.

Following Rutherford's recovery of specific memories of abuse, the counselor reported to her and her father's joint employer, the General Council of the Assemblies of God, that Mr. Rutherford had molested his daughter. Mr. Rutherford was dismissed from his job, though he was not informed of the reasons. The first inkling that Rutherford had of the grounds for the dismissal occurred in October 1994, when charges were brought against him at an ecclesiastical meeting. Rutherford was accused of molesting his daughter, and Mrs. Rutherford was accused of training her daughter to submit to her father's abuse. He was divested of his ministerial credentials and confronted with a choice: Sign a statement of guilt or the charges would be referred to the police for investigation, which might result in a prison sentence of 7 years to life. Rutherford refused to admit guilt. He knew not only that the charges were false but that they could be conclusively disproved. Rutherford had undergone a vasectomy when his daughter was 4 years old and was therefore unable to impregnate anyone. He decided not reveal this fact at the time, however, foreseeing potentially damaging consequences for his daughter, who was already in a state of deterioration, for being branded as a liar with respect to something so horrific as incestuous abuse. Also, Rutherford was thoroughly outraged at an organization that would bring such charges based upon no evidence other than hearsay statements by a counselor. He spent the next 2 years working odd jobs, such as janitor and temporary postman.

Beth Rutherford was instructed by her counselor to shatter the cycle of abuse by separating herself completely from her parents. She decided to move from Springfield to Oklahoma City. She persuaded her sister Lynette to move with her, and at the same time, she persuaded her other sister, Shara, to break contact with their parents. Shara moved to an undisclosed location in Springfield because she believed that her father intended to murder her. After arriving in Oklahoma City, Beth Rutherford maintained contact with her counselor via telephone for a few months but eventually terminated those contacts. Although she and her parents no longer communicated, her mother telephoned on April 19, 1995, following the Oklahoma City bombing incident. Mrs. Rutherford knew that her daughter worked in the area in which the bombing had occurred and wished to determine if her daughter had been injured. She left a message on Beth Rutherford's answering machine. By this time, Shara had returned home to live with their parents. Later, Beth Rutherford telephoned her mother and asked if she would meet her to do some shopping at a neutral location between Oklahoma City and Springfield. They met and discussed topics unrelated to the family, such as their mutual nursing jobs. This led to further telephone conversations and to a meeting with her father at the home of an aunt and uncle. This, in turn, led to subsequent telephone conversations and meetings with both parents and, eventually, to a protracted family discussion of Rutherford's accusations of sexual abuse. Rutherford became aware that, despite her recovered memories, some of those "memories" were unquestionably false because events such as paternal impregnation and abortion were impossible.

The Rutherfords filed suit against the Assemblies of God and Rutherford's counselor for malpractice and defamation, citing among other things the medical fact of Mr. Rutherford's vasectomy. At the request of the Rutherfords' attorney, Beth Rutherford underwent a gynecological examination to determine whether she had ever been pregnant. The examination revealed not only that she had never been pregnant but that, indeed, she was still a virgin. This invalidated not only her recovered memories of impregnation and abortion but also her recovered memories of being raped with foreign objects and of other forms of vaginal penetration. In November 1996, the Rutherfords accepted a settlement of $1 million in lieu of their claims against the Assemblies of God and the counselor.

Elizabeth Carlson

In 1989, Elizabeth Carlson, a married mother of two children with a prior history of hospitalization for mental illness, was admitted to a hospital for symptoms of depression. The events that we now summarize followed that hospitalization (e.g., Acocella, 1999; Kramer, 1999).

Carlson received a referral for psychiatric treatment and was told by her psychiatrist that her problems extended well beyond the symptoms of depression for which she had sought treatment—in particular, that she was suffering from multiple-personality disorder (MPD). Similar to the Rutherford case, she was told that although she was unaware of being taken over by alternate personalities, there were behavioral symptoms that were known to be reliable indicators of MPD. When the psychiatrist described the illustrative symptoms, Carlson reported having experienced some of them (e.g., driving to a destination but being unable to remember the route that was followed after arriving there). The psychiatrist also informed her that MPD was often a concomitant of repressed memories of childhood sexual abuse. In fact, Carlson had been molested by two men as a child; she had always remembered being molested; and she reported this information to her psychiatrist. However, she was told that she might also have experienced other, more serious instances of sexual abuse and repressed the memories. To stimulate memory recovery, Carlson was instructed to engage in a procedure known as *bibliotherapy*, wherein patients read factual or fictional accounts of people with conditions that are similar to those that the patients themselves are thought to have experienced (e.g., Poole, Lindsay, Memon, & Bull, 1995). One of the readings that she was assigned was a book that declared that one third of adult women in the United States have been victims of childhood sexual abuse and that many are unable to remember having been abused (Bass & Davis, 1988). This book also asserted, consistent with what Carlson had been told, that girls who had been victims of repeated molestation may repress their memories of abuse and develop multiple personalities in order to keep the memories under wraps. She was also assigned fictional accounts—readings and movies— of MPD and was provided with videotapes of television programs dealing with this topic. Carlson was told that if she felt symptoms of bodily irritation while viewing the movies and videos, these were body memories of having had similar experiences.

During the course of her reading and viewing, Carlson recovered memories of having been molested by several family members, including her parents, grandparents, and great-grandparents. Like Beth Rutherford, she began having disturbing dreams and, also like Rutherford, she was told that the dreams were true memories that were trying to surface. During therapy sessions, Carlson was instructed to act out episodes of molestation. She was also trained in the use of *guided imagery*, a procedure in which a patient attempts to recover memories by reporting physical details (e.g., sights, sounds, smells) of episodes that are only vaguely recollected or that are hypothetical. In one particularly disturbing example, Carlson was asked to visualize a number of events associated with Satanic ritual abuse, and the resulting images that she constructed included candles, knives, a woman giving birth on an altar, and people, herself included, eating a baby. Recovered memories of cannibalism occurred during multiple sessions, and she was given tranquilizers by her psychiatrist to calm the accompanying emotional reactions, with drugs from the benzodiazapine family being among the medications that she received.

At the same time, memories of Carlson's supposed alternate personalities began to emerge: girls named Fluff and Susarina, a teenager named Nikata, a lesbian, an old woman, two nuns, and even an animal. The number of alternate personalities ultimately exceeded 25. The recovery of alternate personalities was stimulated by a second procedure that Carlson was instructed to follow outside of therapy sessions: *journaling* (e.g., Poole et al., 1995). In this procedure, patients are instructed to keep records of recurrent thoughts and feelings, which their therapist will interpret for them (in this instance, as signs of multiple personalities or of repressed memories of sexual abuse). She was told that various behaviors that she exhibited during therapy sessions were caused by one or the other of these alternate personalities. The recovery of alternate personalities was also stimulated by attendance at group therapy sessions composed of several of her psychiatrist's MPD patients. During those sessions, Carlson observed other patients switching back and forth between alternate personalities.

As in the Rutherford case, rather than improving, Carlson's condition worsened as her therapy proceeded. She became fearful of leaving her home and was so heavily medicated that she slept most of the day. She experienced repeated nightmares followed by vomiting, and she no longer washed or groomed herself. She was unable to care for her children. She believed that her husband was attempting to murder her and repeatedly expelled him from their home, which meant that care of the household and child care fell to her eldest child, a high school student. She believed that the family members who sexually abused her were members of a transgenerational Satanic cult who were also attempting to murder her and were able to control her behavior through hypnotic suggestions that they had previously implanted. Carlson also physically mutilated herself.

After she had been under treatment for a year and a half, some of the patients in Carlson's MPD group objected to certain of the events that occurred during their group sessions, and they were informed by the psychiatrist that they could form a separate group, which they did. They began to meet without the psychiatrist being present. During the course of their meetings, they discovered two remarkable things: The details of their recovered memories of sexual abuse were quite similar and closely resembled details that were discussed in the material that they had been given as part of bibliotherapy. Also, many of the patients in the group had alternate personalities with identical names. Although the patients continued in treatment, they did not divulge this surprising information to the psychiatrist. Eventually, however, the psychiatrist suspected that the patients were in league and discontinued their treatment.

Soon thereafter, Carlson and another patient sued the psychiatrist for malpractice. Following an extended trial, which at the time was the longest trial for psychiatric malpractice in U.S. history, the jury awarded her more than $2 million in damages. At trial, Carlson's attorney characterized memory repression as a bogus theory, described MPD as junk science, and characterized recovered-memory therapy as sheer quackery.

Ms. duM and Mr. Q

The Beth Rutherford and Elizabeth Carlson cases emanate from the heyday of recovered-memory therapy for suspected childhood sexual abuse, in the 1980s to early 1990s, and from the heyday of patients litigating against practitioners of such therapy for implanting false memories, in the early to mid-1990s. Given the size of the settlements in these and other cases, the fact that the courts ruled in several instances that the theory of repressed memories of traumatic childhood experiences is not a scientifically validated hypothesis, and the fact that recovered-memory therapy has been described as a quack treatment inside and outside the courtroom, it might be supposed that therapeutically induced recovery of repressed memories of sexual abuse would have disappeared from the scene. Not so. Cases of the classic type, in which adults exhume memories of previously unsuspected familial abuse, continue to surface from time to time, and a new type of case has emerged, in which adults recover memories of previously unsuspected abuse by priests. We consider two examples of ongoing cases of the classic type here and then move on to two examples of the more recent type.

At the time of this writing, various cases are being litigated in the United States in which plaintiffs are claiming that memories of unsuspected childhood sexual abuse that were recovered during therapy are *valid* (i.e., therapists are not being charged with implanting false memories), and damages are being requested from defendants. Two examples that present instructive and rather different features are the cases of Ms. duM and Mr. Q. The defendant in the case of Ms. duM is being sued for sexual harassment, which stimulated the recovery of agonizing *true* memories of previously unknown childhood sexual abuse, whereas the defendant in the case of Mr. Q is being sued for having sexually abused Mr. Q as a child.

Our description of Ms. duM's case comes from documents that have been submitted as part of the litigation. Ms. duM and her husband are immigrants to the United States. He is a student and she is employed by a financial institution. Ms. duM's supervisor is Mr. A, who travels to various cities on behalf of their joint employer and assigns Ms. duM work to complete in his absence. Mr. A is nearing retirement, whereas Ms. duM is in her early 30s. Ms. duM characterizes Mr. A as someone who does not subscribe to modern standards for the treatment of women in the workplace, who makes gender-discriminating remarks, including sexual remarks that the law defines as harassment, who is vulgar and condescending, and who is frequently intoxicated on the job. Although Mr. A is usually satisfied by the work that she completes during his absences, when he is displeased, he expresses his displeasure in inappropriate ways that constitute gender discrimination and sexual harassment. Ms. duM states that she tolerated this behavior for many months because, for inexplicable reasons, she has never been able to respond assertively to men who make inappropriate sexual remarks or advances. She eventually filed a sexual harassment charge against Mr. A with her employer following an episode in which Mr. A made her stand in the corner of his office and spanked her. She also sought counseling for depression and stress.

During her initial counseling session, Ms. duM described her interactions with Mr. A, along with the feelings of humiliation and exploitation that resulted from those experiences. The therapist made a diagnosis of extreme depression and PTSD. During her next session, she expressed feelings of shame about the way Mr. A had treated her throughout her period of employment and indicated confusion over how she could have let things go so far. The therapist asked whether Ms. duM was intimidated by other authority figures. Following a discussion of this topic, she concluded that she was intimidated by her father, and the therapist suggested that this might account for her acquiescence in her mistreatment at work. Between the second and third sessions, Ms. duM began having dreams that caused her to believe that she had an extensive history of childhood sexual abuse. She reported her dreams in the next therapy session, but was unable to describe specific abuse experiences from her childhood.

To help Ms. duM flesh out her memories, her therapist advised bibliotherapy, recommending in particular that she read one of the same books that had been given to Carlson (Bass & Davis, 1988). This book contains assertions such as "If you are unable to remember any specific instances [of childhood sexual abuse] like the ones mentioned but still have a feeling that something happened to you, it probably did" (p. 21); "Many survivors suppress all memories of what happened to them as children" (p. 58); and "Many women don't have memories, and some never get memories. This doesn't mean they weren't abused" (p. 81). In addition, the book contains graphic discussions of the types of sexual acts in which children and teenagers may be forced to participate with adults. Those discussions include numerous first-hand reports of harrowing childhood sexual experiences, often at the hands of fathers and other male relatives. With respect to recovering memories of unsuspected abuse, although references to this phenomenon are sprinkled throughout the book, one chapter is devoted entirely to remembering specific episodes of abuse. This chapter begins with the thesis that "you may have to remember that you *were* abused at all" (p. 70), and continues with an exegesis of various methods of stimulating recovery of such memories, including memory-regression therapy ("Another way to regain memory is through regression" [p. 73]) and journaling ("If you don't remember what happened to you, write about what you *do* remember" [p. 83]).

While reading this book, Ms. duM was unable to finish certain passages because they reminded her too much of her own abusive experiences. During the next session, the therapist explained to her that talking about her memories of abusive experiences and reliving them could help her to overcome their negative effects. Ms. duM began talking about her memories during therapy and talking about them at home with her husband. By her sixth session, she had developed detailed recollections of having been molested at age 5 by a domestic employee in her parents' home, of the molestation being discovered by other members of the household, and of the employee being dismissed. She had also developed specific memories of having been molested by her uncle and by a close friend of the family. Prior to entering counseling and reading the Bass and Davis (1988) book, she had no memory of these occurrences. Ms. duM continued reading the book, attending counseling sessions, and recovering further details of her abusive experiences (e.g., of having been molested by a second domestic employee and by a close family friend). However, people who were living in the home at the time Ms. duM remembers being molested provided statements denying that the events occurred and denying that they were aware that Ms. duM was being abused (whereas she remembers them being aware of the abuse).

Ultimately, a suit was filed on Ms. duM's behalf, naming Mr. A and their employer as defendants. Interestingly, the suit claims that Mr. A and their employer are responsible for the pain and suffering caused by Ms. duM's history of sexual abuse, not because Mr. A committed the abuse itself but because his harassment of her on the job was the stimulus that caused excruciating memories to be recovered. In other words, the core thesis is that Ms. duM had successfully repressed these terrifying memories, was able to lead a normal life that was untroubled by ghosts of the past, and would have continued to do so had not Mr. A caused those memories to be exhumed. At the time of this writing, Ms. duM's case is still at the pre-trial stage.

Turning to Mr. Q, our description of the features of his case also comes from documents that have been submitted as part of the litigation. Mr. Q, who is now in his late 30s, is the son of an investment counselor, holds bachelor's and master's degrees in engineering, and works for an electronics firm. Mr. Q's mother and father were divorced many years ago, and his father has subsequently remarried. During a recent telephone conversation with his aunt, Mr. Q was told a family secret: His mother and father had divorced because the aunt had a sexual liaison with his father, and her sister had discovered the relationship. His aunt stated that she was only 18 at the time of the affair and because his father was several years older, she and her sister both blamed him for taking advantage of her. Hence, his mother and aunt had remained close, but his mother had divorced his father. While listening to this conversation, Mr. Q experienced eerie feelings that, as a child, he had been aware of other inappropriate sexual activities by his father, but he was unable to retrieve any specific episodes. Some of the sensations involved swimming in the nude, however.

Mr. Q sought counseling for his disturbing feelings about his father. Detailed records of the subsequent counseling sessions were not preserved, but after several sessions, he had recovered clear memories of two episodes of sexual abuse. According to one memory, Mr. Q and his brother had been compelled to watch their father have sex with a woman, after which Mr. Q was sexually abused by his father in his brother's presence. According to the other memory, he was sexually abused by his father in a bedroom at their vacation home, again when his brother was present. Although Mr. Q did not recover further memories of specific instances of abuse, he remembered discussing the abuse with his brother on multiple occasions. He also remembered fleeing his home on multiple occasions to avoid abuse, sleeping at a friend's home, and discussing the abuse with his friend. Mr. Q's therapist urged him to confront his father, which he did in a letter stating that he had been abused as a child. The letter also requested financial compensation.

His father vigorously denied having abused Mr. Q, but offered to assist him in obtaining qualified psychiatric treatment and to pay for that treatment. His father's denial prompted Mr. Q to consult an attorney to determine whether he could sue his father for damages. The attorney informed him that because the abuse was believed to have occurred more than 20 years earlier, the statute of limitations had long since run out. However, the attorney advised that a suit could be filed claiming that the statute of limitations had not yet expired because Mr. Q had not remembered being abused until recently. This approach took account of the fact that statutes of limitations, in addition to specifying the period of time after which a person cannot be prosecuted for a crime or sued for a tort, specify certain conditions (called *estoppel rules*) under which they do not run out. One such condition is that plaintiffs must be *aware* of a defendant's actions before the statute begins to run because, obviously, plaintiffs must know that they have been damaged and who damaged them before they can initiate legal action. (In the Rutherford case, for instance, Tom Rutherford was not immediately aware that he had been dismissed from his position for unsubstantiated allegations of sexual abuse and, hence, could not sue the Assemblies of God for that action until he was informed of it.) Thus, the approach taken by Mr. Q's attorney was to argue that the statute of limitations for child sexual abuse did not begin to run *until he recovered memories of specific acts of abuse.*

Mr. Q's litigation against his father is still in the pre-trial investigative phase. Statements have been gathered from Mr. Q's brother, from the childhood friend to whose home he remembers fleeing, and from the woman whom he remembers being forced to watch having sex with his father. None of these individuals' statements confirm Mr. Q's memories. His brother does not remember seeing him abused by their father or of talking to him about it; his childhood friend remembers him occasionally sleeping at his house but not of talking to him about abuse; and the woman denies that he watched her having sex with his father. Mr. Q continues to maintain that he has clear memories of being sexually abused by his father.

Examples of Recovered Memories of Abuse by Priests

As we write, the Roman Catholic church in the United States has been under intense scrutiny for more than 4 years owing to allegations of decades of widespread sexual abuse of minors by priests, coupled with conspiracy to cover up such crimes. The church has suffered much justified public calumny as a result. Church leaders have been accused of following policies of secrecy with respect to such allegations, of failing to investigate accused priests, and of reassigning accused priests to new parishes, thereby providing guilty individuals with opportunities to commit further offenses. Specific individuals have been identified, such as John Geoghan in Massachusetts and Robert Trupia in Arizona, who were accused of abuse by numerous individuals over many years, but who continued to serve as members of the priesthood, moving from parish to parish as new allegations surfaced. The archdiocese of Boston has admitted covering up allegations of molestation against priests and of allowing accused priests to remain in holy orders. The archdioceses of New York and Los Angeles have made similar admissions, as has the diocese of Phoenix. Large financial settlements have been paid to victims of sexual abuse by priests. The archdiocese of Boston, for example, paid $10 million to settle only a portion of the claims against Geoghan, and it reached a settlement in excess of $30 million with other victims of sexual abuse. The diocese of Tucson paid more than $10 million to settle some of the claims against Trupia. With respect to the United States as a whole, publicly disclosed settlements during this period have been in the $200- to $300-million range, though the inclusion of confidential settlements would probably put the total well above $500 million (Cooperman, 2002).

In many of the cases that have resulted in compensation, either through jury awards or out-of-court settlements, the plaintiffs were children who alleged that they had recently been abused (e.g., a child who had been serving as an altar boy may have stated that he was fondled in the vestry). Because the crime is fresh, the statute of limitations has not run out; individual priests and the church are still liable. There is another category of victims, however, for whom the statute of limitations has long since run out. Typically, these are young adults who have *always remembered* being abused by priests as children. However, they may not have reported the abuse at the time because they were told to remain silent by the perpetrators, because they did not understand that the behavior was wrong, because they feared consequences from the church, or for other reasons. Other individuals reported the abuse to their parents or guardians when it occurred, but this did not result in criminal prosecution or in church actions against the perpetrators. In some instances, the adults to whom reports were made chose not to pass the information on to church officials, fearing that the children's statements were incorrect or that such reports would do more harm than good. In other instances, reports of abuse were transmitted to church officials, but nothing was done about them. For example, documents of the diocese of Tucson reveal that in the mid-1970s, when several parishioners in Yuma, Arizona, informed church officials that their children had accused Trupia of molesting them, Trupia was transferred to Tucson, installed as head of the church's marriage council, and was eventually promoted to monsignor (Innes & Steller, 2002). A quarter of a century later, when it was learned that Trupia had not been punished by the church, 11 of his former accusers filed criminal charges. Although Trupia was arrested and booked by the Yuma police, he was released and the charges were dropped in January 2001 because prosecutors determined that the statute of limitations on all of the crimes had expired.

This brings us back to adult recovered memories of childhood sexual abuse. As mentioned, courts may rule that a statute of limitations did not run (called *tolling* the statute) when plaintiffs were unaware that crimes or torts had been committed. Similar to the case of Mr. Q, if children who were molested by priests repressed all memories of those acts afterward but subsequently recovered the memories as adults, the statute of limitations would not begin to run until they were aware that they had been abused, meaning that their abusers would still be liable. Two suits of this sort were filed in Arizona during the past few years, *Watson v. Catholic Diocese of Phoenix* (1999) and *Frei v. Catholic Diocese of Tucson* (2000). Sean Watson, a resident of Phoenix, and David Frei, a resident of Yuma, were both troubled young men with long histories of failed relationships, inability to hold jobs, alcohol and drug abuse, and in Frei's case, criminal violations. (Frei had been discharged from the Air Force for selling drugs, and his parents had filed a restraining order against him for theft of property from their residence and from a second home that they owned.) In their suits, Watson and Frei claimed that their problems as adults stemmed from childhood sexual abuse by priests, and both requested financial compensation for the damage. Both men stated that they had repressed their memories of childhood sexual abuse; they had recently recovered those memories during counseling; and the statute of limitations should therefore be tolled.

According to Watson's litigation, he had been molested more than a decade before by George Brademann, a defrocked priest who was already serving a prison sentence for having molested other children of his parishioners. Watson stated that although he previously had no memory of the abuse, he began to believe that he might have been abused in a recent conversation with a friend. He and his friend were discussing distasteful things that had happened to them, some of which were intentional fabrications, and Watson blurted out that he had been molested by a priest. Although this statement was made for effect, as a way of topping something that his friend had just said (and therefore is analogous to the forced confabulation procedure that has been discussed in prior chapters), Watson experienced a disturbing sensation that he had actually been abused by a priest, a feeling that he confided to his friend. Watson thought about this possibility repeatedly during the following few weeks, sometimes while under the influence of drugs, in an attempt to reconstruct what had happened. However, he was unable to recover any specific memories of abusive acts or of the identity of the abuser. He then sought legal advice. His attorney recommended that he enter counseling and referred him to a therapist. At this time, Watson was still using drugs.

During the therapy sessions, Watson worked on recovering specific memories of what had happened, using techniques such as guided imagery and age regression. Eventually, he recalled having been abused by Brademann on two occasions during a camping trip with Brademann and other boys. During pre-trial investigations, defense attorneys interviewed and deposed members of Watson's family to determine whether, at the time of the alleged abuse, there were any signs that Watson had been molested by Brademann. These individuals stated that, in fact, there was positive evidence to the contrary. According to their statements, the arrest of Brademann and his subsequent admission of guilt were topics of extensive discussion among parishioners at the time and that this matter had been repeatedly discussed in their home. Watson had been questioned by his parents during the course of those discussions as to whether he had been molested by Brademann, and he had firmly denied it. In addition, church investigators had interviewed parishioners other than those who accused Brademann to determine whether there were unreported incidents of abuse. Watson and his mother were among the parishioners who were interviewed, and both had denied that he had been molested by Brademann.

At trial, defense attorneys for the church argued that the Arizona statute of limitations on child sexual abuse should be not tolled in Watson's case because (a) the theory of repressed memories of trauma is not a scientifically substantiated hypothesis; (b) there was evidence from the time of the alleged abuse showing that it did not occur; and (c) Watson's recovered memories might be false memories arising from multiple, powerful sources of suggestion (e.g., repeated suggestive questioning at the time of Brademann's arrest, therapy sessions that accepted the truth of his recovered memories and that implemented suggestive procedures to help him flesh them out, and reconstructive remembering that occurred outside therapy sessions under the influence of drugs). The court found in the defense's favor, ruling that although Watson had probably been abused by Brademann, memory repression was not a sound basis for tolling the statute of limitations. This decision has twice been appealed to higher courts, including the Arizona Supreme Court, and the lower court's decision has been affirmed in both instances.

Turning to the other case, in 1995, Frei's mother persuaded him to seek counseling for his many personal problems, helped him to locate a counselor, and drove him to his first appointment. When they arrived, his mother reminded him that he should tell the therapist that he had been sexually abused by Robert Trupia in the mid-1970s, while serving as an altar boy. Frei reported being shocked by his mother's statement and of expressing disbelief. His mother assured him that it was true, and he duly informed his therapist of his mother's statement. He continued to have no memories of abuse for more than a year. In December 1997, he began recovering specific memories when he switched to a new therapist, who gave him memory exercises to perform. As time passed, he recovered specific memories of being molested on more than five occasions by Trupia. Among the procedures that the therapist used to stimulate memory recovery were bibliotherapy, journaling, encouraging Frei to write songs about abuse, encouraging Frei to write letters to Trupia accusing him of abuse, explaining the stages of memory recovery to Frei and working through them with him, and explaining the relations among abused children, molesters, and children's parents, which allegedly lead to memory repression.

As in Watson's case, the suit that Frei's attorneys filed on his behalf argued that the statute of limitations should be tolled because he had no memory of the abuse until recently. Also as in Watson's case, other evidence came to light during pretrial investigation that was inconsistent with Frei's claims. His mother stated that, to the best of her knowledge, he had remembered his abuse after it happened. She noted that at the time he was an altar boy, he had reported to her that he was being abused by Trupia; she conveyed this information to a church deacon; and the deacon had interviewed Frei in their home about the allegations. The deacon confirmed these statements and added that the abusive acts that Frei had described to him at the time were quite different and far less serious than the acts in his recovered memories. In addition, two of Frei's former partners, one of whom was the mother of his children, stated that Frei had informed them that he had been sexually abused by a priest during the late 1980s and early 1990s. Some of the descriptions of the reported acts of molestation were quite specific, and one of these individuals stated that while she and Frei were living together, his molestation was a topic of discussion and argument at family gatherings.

In pre-trial submissions, defense attorneys for the church argued that the statute of limitations should not be tolled because (a) the theory of repressed memories of trauma is not a scientifically substantiated hypothesis; (b) Frei had demonstrably remembered the abuse for nearly 2 decades following its occurrence; (c) Frei may have subsequently forgotten that he had been abused, perhaps as a consequence of drug use; (d) Frei's current memories of childhood sexual abuse were false memories that had arisen through suggestive therapeutic procedures; and (e) Frei may also have forgotten that he was able to remember the abuse on earlier occasions, again perhaps as a consequence of drug use. With respect to the last argument, defense attorneys cited studies of recovered-memory cases by Schooler and associates (e.g., Schooler, Bendiksen, & Ambadar, 1997). In that research, the authors found that some individuals who thought that they had recovered memories of previously unsuspected childhood sexual abuse had, like Frei, remembered and reported the abuse to family members some years after its occurrence, though they could no longer remember having made such reports. The question of whether to toll the statute of limitations was not decided by the court, however. In January 2002, before the trial was scheduled to begin, the Catholic diocese of Tucson announced that it had reached a settlement with Frei and the other 10 men who had instigated criminal charges against Trupia (Cooperman, 2002).

Suggestive Aspects of Psychotherapy

In earlier chapters, we have explored many variables that, based upon available research, increase the incidence of false-memory reports. In chapters 6 and 7, we commented in connection with the criminal interviews of adults, eyewitness identifications, and investigative interviews of children that these real-life retrieval situations are apt to contain a confluence of such memory-falsifying variables. This is how science explains the facts that baseline error rates are so high in eyewitness identification, that adults can recollect false details of crimes (including details that are self-incriminating), and that children can recollect false episodes of sexual abuse and other crimes.

Criminal investigation and psychotherapy are wildly different situations, of course. The former makes life more difficult, especially if it leads to prosecution and punishment, whereas the latter is supposed to make life easier; the former elevates fear and anxiety, often deliberately, whereas as the latter is intended to reduce noxious emotions. Despite their obvious differences, there is one striking parallel between the two situations. From the perspective of false memory, psychotherapy also contains a confluence of variables that, when viewed through the prism of controlled experimentation, would be expected to elevate false-memory reports in patients. For convenience of exposition, those variables can be thought of as falling into two broad categories: general properties of the psychotherapeutic context, including characteristics of patients and therapists, and specific therapeutic practices that might be used in treating some patients but not others. In the first subsection below, we discuss what we consider to be the most salient exemplars from the first category—specifically, processing gist memories, weak remembering criteria, delay, reconstructive retrieval, source credibility, confirmation bias, patient susceptibility to false memory, and repetition. In the next section, we move on to salient exemplars from the second category that have been identified in surveys of therapeutic practices.

General Properties

Processing Gist Memories

Retrieval conditions that slant remembering toward the processing of gist traces, as when subjects study materials that repeatedly cue certain meanings (e.g., DRM lists, narratives that revolve around an obvious theme) or when witnesses are asked to focus retrieval on a target crime and remember everything they can about it, are known to elevate false-memory reports for multiple reasons. If remembering is slanted toward gist, rather than verbatim traces, opponent-processes distinctions say that there is an increased likelihood of false alarms and intrusions that involve gist-consistent information—again, for multiple reasons. It is inherent in most forms of psychotherapy that patients' remembering has a gist orientation. Typically, people seek psychotherapy because they have perceived problems with which they wish to deal (e.g., depression, a failed relationship, substance abuse), but they are uncertain as to the causes of those problems, how to address them, and in many instances, even the precise nature of the problems. Consequently, patients normally enter psychotherapy in states of uncertainty about crucial aspects of their lives. They are therefore encouraged to maintain attitudes of openness and discovery, with therapists acting as partners and supporters in the discovery process (e.g., Simpson, 1996). Patients are also encouraged to explore nonspecific feelings, impressions, and sensations in the hope of improving their condition. From the narrow perspective of memory research and opponent-processes distinctions, these features converge on a gist-processing orientation.

False-memory research has established that such an orientation can lead to a range of false reports about events that are consistent with gists that people believe to be part of their experience, as when police interviewees report false details of crimes that they have witnessed or eyewitnesses confidently identify innocent suspects, and about events that are consistent with gists that are familiar but that people do *not* believe are part of their experience, as when innocent suspects who deny guilt nevertheless make false incriminating reports during interviews. Examples of both of these possibilities are present in the cases reviewed above.

Regarding the first possibility, the patients in some of these cases are known to have begun therapy with gist memories of being sexually abused as children (e.g., Frei, Mr. Q, and Watson). Indeed, in each of these instances, the individuals sought professional assistance because they were troubled by those gist memories and wished to discover what had happened. Hence, the resulting therapy focused squarely on fleshing out memories of abuse, much like police interviews that focus on fleshing out sketchy witness accounts of crimes. In other cases, there is no positive evidence that the patients began therapy with a gist memory of having been abused, but a gist memory emerged almost immediately, after which it became a focal point of treatment (Ms. duM).

Regarding the second possibility, there is no positive evidence in the remaining cases that the patients began therapy with gist memories of having been abused. Such a memory did not emerge for many sessions, and in some instances, its existence was at first vigorously denied (e.g., by Beth Rutherford), much like police suspects who make false confessions following initial denials. However, it is quite probable that the patients in all of these cases, like millions of other adults, were *familiar* with the idea that many people who have psychological problems are actually victims of unremembered childhood sexual abuse. This conjecture has been rampant in pop psychology books and articles since the 1980s (e.g., Blume, 1991; Bass & Davis, 1988), has received extensive coverage on television talk shows, and is even the theme of some well known literary works (e.g., F. Scott Fitzgerald's *Tender Is the Night*). Concerning television talk shows, interviews with people who relate gruesome details of previously unremembered abuse have figured conspicuously. The key point from the perspective of false-memory research is that baseline familiarity with the psychological-problems-caused-by-childhood-sexual-abuse gist is high among adults, as is familiarity with specific illustrations of this gist.

Weak Remembering Criteria

We know that weak remembering criteria elevate false reports of gist-consistent information (e.g., Koriat & Goldsmith, 1994, 1996). In the first place, people are more apt to falsely recognize such information when it is presented to them or to falsely generate such information during recall if strong subjective evidence is not required for something to count as a memory. Moreover, people are less likely to use recollection rejection to weed out gist-consistent false alarms and intrusions from their memory reports if strong subjective evidence is not regarded by them as a superior basis for deciding what is a memory and what is not.

In psychotherapy, weak remembering criteria are necessary adjuncts to the gist-processing orientation. It is self-evident that the exploration of experiences that are only dimly sensed, of vague impressions and feelings, cannot involve strong remembering criteria for the simple reason that the process would be stopped dead in its tracks. On the contrary, to facilitate this process, it is sometimes necessary to discourage patients from "censoring" their memory retrieval by applying stringent criteria. Some therapists even advocate that the veracity of patients' recollections should never be questioned. According to this view, the success of therapy depends upon exploring what is subjectively real for patients, not what is objectively true (Simpson, 1996), and consequently, patients' recollections, even if far-fetched, must be accepted because they represent patients' personal truths. (For instance, note in Figure 8-1 that one of the statements stipulates that, regardless of the accuracy of recovered memories of sexual abuse, physicians must "address the therapeutic needs of patients who report memories of childhood sexual abuse . . . these needs exist quite apart from the truth or falsity of any claims.") Without prejudging the validity of this position, it is clear that it is the antithesis of strong remembering criteria.

Delay

Experiments on spontaneous and implanted false memories have consistently pointed to the importance of the delay between target experiences and remembering. As time passes, spontaneous false reports increase (e.g., Pipe et al., 1999; Reyna & Kiernan, 1994), and subjects are more likely to accept false suggestions as true events (e.g., Belli et al., 1992; Cassel & Bjorklund, 1995). The opponent-processes explanation, as we know, is that memories of the exact surface form of experience become inaccessible more rapidly than memories of its meaning content, so that delay forces retrieval in the direction of the types of representations that support false alarms and intrusions. In short, the passage of time *enforces* gist-based remembering, regardless of the retrieval instructions that subjects are given, because that is the only remaining option.

With respect to psychotherapy, it is instructive to note that the delays that have been found to elevate false-memory reports in experimentation have been on the order of a few days to a week—though delays of a few months have occasionally been used (e.g., Toglia et al., 1999) and, in rare instances, delays of more than a year have been used (e.g., Poole & White, 1993). By comparison, average delays are much longer in psychotherapy. As the events in patients' lives are examined, the storage-retrieval interval for even "recent" events will be on a scale of weeks or months, far longer than the intervals that have typically been used to inflate false reports in experimentation. As a rule, however, the exploration of patients' lives will extend much further back, to include whatever time span is thought to contain events that are responsible for patients' problems—often encompassing the years of childhood and adolescence. This was true, for instance, in every one of the recovered-memory cases at the start of this chapter. From the standpoint of false-memory research, the scale of psychotherapeutic delays between storage and retrieval means that quite apart from the gist orientation of psychotherapy, remembering will necessarily be overwhelmingly gist-based.

Reconstructive Retrieval

Reconstruction is a form of retrieval that subjects are inclined to use when they are unable simply to read out surface information from verbatim traces and must fall back on sketchy gist traces (chapter 3). Reconstructive retrieval begins with general concepts (Let's see. The thief was a Hispanic youth) and attempts to generate events by constructively processing those concepts (Did he have a mustache? Was his hair dark? Did he have a tattoo? Were his eyes brown?). Subjectively, the experience is one of rummaging about in one's memory, using the starting concepts as guides, in an attempt to find events that fit with those concepts. The problem with reconstruction is that although it is an efficient method of recovering true information when verbatim traces cannot be accessed (e.g., dark hair, tattoo), it is also prone to intrusions, especially intrusions that are deemed to be characteristic of the starting concepts (e.g., mustache, brown eyes). As time passes, during the course of a single retrieval episode or across different retrieval episodes, the incidence of reconstruction has been found to increase (Brainerd, Wright, Reyna, & Payne, 2002) and, with it, the incidence of intrusions (e.g., Brainerd, Payne, Wright, & Reyna, 2003; Toglia et al., 1999).

In psychotherapy, given the low accessibility levels of verbatim traces, which are consequences of long storage-retrieval delays, it is inevitable that patients' reports about their lives will involve heavy doses of reconstructive retrieval. This is perhaps most apparent when patients are exploring beliefs or feelings about their lives that are only dimly perceived. The recovered-memory examples above are rich in examples of reconstructive retrieval during therapy. Watson, for instance, recovered an impression that he had been sexually abused by a priest, but despite thinking intensely about it, he was unable to recover specific episodes. He sought therapy, on the advice of his attorney, with the aim of determining if memories of specific episodes could be reconstructed. In contrast, Frei did not believe that he had been sexually abused by Trupia, but reconstructive retrieval exercises, such as writing songs about abuse and writing letters to Trupia accusing him of abuse, eventually led Frei to remember specific episodes of abuse. Interestingly, Loftus (1997) pointed out that reconstructive retrieval seems to be a consistent feature of cases in which patients recovered false memories of sexual abuse (see also Loftus & Ketcham, 1994). Loftus reviewed several cases in which patients had either recovered memories that were definitively disproved by other facts or that they later recanted as being false. She concluded that, in all instances, there was evidence that patients had made systematic attempts to reconstruct information that they could not clearly remember.

Source Credibility

Studies of the misinformation paradigm have demonstrated that people are more likely to remember false information as though it were true when that information has been suggested to them by individuals whom they perceive as being highly credible. For example, witnesses to crimes and suspects are more prone to remember false information that is suggested to them by highly knowledgeable police investigators than by other people (chapter 6), and children are more prone to remember false information that is suggested by trusted adults, such as teachers or parents, than by strangers or other children (chapter 7). It is in the nature of psychotherapy that patients regard therapists as trusted and authoritative individuals. After all, patients have sufficient faith in therapists' abilities to pay them substantial fees in the belief that those abilities will help them to solve various problems in their lives, problems that they may be unwilling to discuss with anyone else. Indeed, the bond of trust between patient and therapist can be so strong that it can result in a ceding of personal responsibility to the therapist, a phenomenon that is known as *transference*.

The memory implication is that, for patients, psychotherapists are highly credible sources of information about their lives, perhaps uniquely credible sources. Thus, data on source credibility in misinformation experiments lead to the expectation that suggestions by therapists are particularly likely to be accepted by patients, as long as the suggestions fall within the general domains of therapists' perceived competence (e.g., psychological problems and their causes). Although one of the statements in Figure 8-1 cautions therapists against "persuasive interviewing" of patients and another cautions them that they should not adopt "the preconceived notion that abuse must have happened," when patients recover childhood memories of abuse, there is nothing in these statements that discourages therapists from offering opinions and interpretations to patients that are grounded in their training and clinical experience. On the contrary, that is an accepted part of their job. The law also recognizes this by permitting therapists to opine on the basis of their training and clinical experience during sworn testimony. However, data on source credibility raise concerns when opinions and interpretations are erroneous (e.g., as the courts ruled in the Humenansky cases): By virtue of therapists' stature as high-credibility sources, such erroneous information is likely to be accepted as true by patients, even by patients who initially believe it to be false (e.g., Beth Rutherford).

Confirmation Bias

The phenomenon of confirmation bias was previously encountered in chapter 6 in connection with criminal investigation. When witnesses are interviewed by investigators who are steeped in the facts of a case, investigators, both by virtue of their expert knowledge of the case and their prior experience as investigators, are apt to form strong hypotheses about key elements of the case (e.g., regarding method, motive, opportunity). Further, they are apt to convey those hypotheses to witnesses and to structure their questions so as to lead witnesses in the direction of their hypotheses. When the hypotheses are incorrect, the result is elevated levels of false-memory reports from witnesses and tainted evidence if those reports are introduced at trial.

The label *confirmation bias* is intended to convey that interviewers are verifying preferred hypotheses, rather than conducting objective searches for facts, and it is one of the most well studied phenomena in social psychology (for a review, see

Rosenthal & Rubin, 1978). An early scientific demonstration appeared in an article by Rice (1929), who examined interviews of 2000 homeless men that had been conducted by 12 social services interviewers in the wake of the stock market crash. He discovered remarkable parallels between the interviewers' personal hypotheses about the reasons for destitution and the reasons that they identified during individual interviews. In two stark examples, an interviewer who was a self-styled prohibitionist was three times more likely than other interviewers to report that alcohol had caused his interviewees' difficulties, and an interviewer who was a self-styled socialist was three times more likely to report that economic forces, such as layoffs and plant closings, had caused his interviewees' difficulties. Most important for our purposes, interviewees' memories were influenced by their interviewers' preferred hypothesis: When interviewed by others, homeless men who had been questioned by the prohibitionist were more likely to make statements that were consistent with alcohol problems, whereas homeless men who had been questioned by the socialist were more likely to make statements that were consistent with economic problems. Subsequent research has shown that confirmation bias occurs automatically in expert interviewers, without conscious awareness that they are verifying hypotheses rather than gathering facts (Ceci & Bruck, 1993a). This makes confirmation bias an especially insidious source of memory falsification whose influence can only be reduced by special training and monitoring (Poole & Lamb, 1998).

Research on confirmation bias has detected its presence in many professions in which experts make evaluations on the basis of formal and informal interviews. For instance, it is known to operate in teachers (where it has been given a special name, the *Pygmalion effect*), distorting both their assessments of children's educational performance and children's memories of their performance (e.g., Rosenthal, 1985). Not surprisingly, confirmation bias also operates in psychotherapy. Therapists, by virtue of their training and experience, will generate hypotheses about the nature and causes of patients' problems. In fact, this is one of their primary professional functions; it is called *diagnosis*. However, research has established that hypothesis formation will stimulate confirmation bias. This would not be especially problematical if the hypotheses were infallible. It is well known, however, that therapists form erroneous hypotheses that grow out of their knowledge and their personal life histories *rather than out of the facts of patients' cases* (e.g., Gore-Felton, Arnow, Koopman, Thoresen, & Spiegel, 1999; Jackson & Nuttall, 1993, 1994; Peters, 2001).

As a concrete example, Jackson and Nuttall (1993) found that therapists' hypotheses about patients' sexual abuse histories were influenced by numerous extraneous variables. They presented 16 case histories of alleged sexual abuse to a sample of practicing psychiatrists and psychologists, asking them to rate the likelihood that each patient had been sexually abused. The cases were equal with respect to the levels of objective evidence for abuse that they presented, but they varied in certain extraneous characteristics of victims and perpetrators. It was found that therapists' ratings varied systematically across the case histories as a function of six extraneous variables: perpetrator race (abuse was judged to be more likely when the alleged perpetrator was Caucasian); victim-perpetrator relationship (abuse was judged to be more likely when the alleged perpetrator was a family member); victim race (abuse was judged to be more likely when the alleged victim was a minority); victim emotion (abuse was judged to be more likely when the alleged victim expressed negative emotions); victim age (abuse was judged to be more likely when alleged victims were younger than when they were older); and substance abuse (abuse was judged to be more likely when the alleged perpetrator had a history of substance abuse). It was also found that across the 16 case histories, therapists' mean ratings of abuse likelihood were influenced by four personal characteristics: age (younger therapists provided higher ratings); gender (female therapists provided higher ratings); theoretical orientation (therapists who were trained in family-systems theory provided higher ratings); and personal abuse history (therapists who had been sexually or physically abused provided higher ratings).

In sum, it is well documented that professionals, therapists included, who evaluate people through formal and informal interviews formulate hypotheses based upon factors other than the actual information provided by interviewees, which stimulates hypothesis verification rather than fact gathering. When those hypotheses are erroneous, they can yield both the production of erroneous "facts" during interviews (e.g., Ceci & Bruck, 1993a) and distortions of interviewees' memory of events (e.g., Rice, 1929). Here, it might be recalled by way of illustration that in the Braun and Humenansky litigations, the defendants were accused of diagnoses that were sheer confirmation bias. In both instances, the alleged confirmation bias was extreme inasmuch as the diagnosed condition (MPD) was one for which it was argued that there was no scientific evidence, only a belief in its existence among certain groups of therapists. Likewise, therapists have also been accused of sheer confirmation bias when diagnosing another condition, Satanic ritual abuse, for which no scientific evidence exists (e.g., Ofshe & Watters, 1994; Simpson, 1996).

Patient Susceptibility to False Memory

In chapters 4–7, we encountered a number of characteristics of individual subjects that make them more susceptible to spontaneous and implanted false memories. Adults who are sleep-deprived or intoxicated are more susceptible; adults who are in states of high emotional arousal are more susceptible; children are more susceptible; children or adults of subnormal intelligence are more susceptible; and individuals who score highly on psychological tests of suggestibility, such as the Gudjonsson (1984) scale, are more susceptible. Some of the characteristics of individuals who seek therapy would seem to increase their susceptibility to false memories that are related to reasons for seeking therapy. For example, individuals often seek therapy because they are prone to be in states of high emotional arousal. Also, emotion aside, people who understand the nature, causes, and solutions of their problems are less apt to seek therapy than people who are confused and uncertain about these matters. Confused and uncertain people are looking for information that will shed light in dark corners, and they may believe that it can be found in therapy. To find answers, however, they must adopt attitudes of openness, exploration, and discovery with respect to the events of their lives, and they must trust in the wisdom and experience of their therapists. Obviously, these latter characteristics are not commensurate with a narrow, reality-based perspective on memory. Rather, the perspective is a much broader one that searches for answers and solutions in the events of one's life, which is not precisely the same thing as searching for autobiographi-cal facts. The implication for the potential accuracy of patients' memory reports is straightforward: These characteristics would be expected to heighten vulnerability to false memories, whether they be spontaneous by-products of the search for an-swers and solutions or information that is suggested by other sources as part of that search.

Beyond such group characteristics of people who seek psychotherapy, it is con-ceivable that some patients who develop false memories of traumatic experiences may be dispositionally prone to false memories of all sorts. This possibility has been explored in an important series of studies by McNally and associates (e.g., McNally, 2003; McNally, Clancy, & Schacter, 2001; McNally, Clancy, Schacter, & Pittman, 2000a, 2000b). The core research strategy was to ascertain whether individuals who had recovered memories of childhood sexual abuse, as well as individuals who had recovered memories of more exotic and improbable events, are more prone to make spontaneous false alarms and intrusions on standard laboratory false-memory tasks (e.g., DRM lists such as those in Table 2-1). In some studies, levels of false mem-ory were compared for three groups of subjects: (a) a *repressed-memory* group, con-sisting of people who reported believing that they had been sexually abused as chil-dren but could not remember any specific episodes of abuse; (b) a *recovered-memory* group, consisting of people who reported recovering memories of specific episodes of childhood sexual abuse after having been unaware of the abuse for many years; and (c) a *continuous-memory* group, consisting of people who reported being sex-ually abused as children and of having always remembered the abuse. If false mem-ories of previously unsuspected abuse are sometimes due to individual differences in a predilection to false memories, subjects in the second group ought to exhibit higher false-alarm and intrusion rates than subjects in the other two groups on stan-dard laboratory tasks. Consistent with this prediction, McNally and associates have found that DRM false memory is higher in the second group than in the other two groups. They have reported a similar pattern for subjects whose recovered memo-ries are most probably false—namely, people who remember being abducted by space aliens (and sometimes being sexually abused by aliens). Levels of false mem-ory were again compared for three groups: people who believed that they had been abducted by aliens but could not remember any specific episodes; people who had recovered memories of specific episodes of alien abduction; and people who did not believe that they had ever been abducted by aliens. As with recovered memories of sexual abuse, subjects in the second group displayed elevated levels of false mem-ory on laboratory tasks.

Repetition

Repetition is a variable that has been consistently tied to false-memory responses, and in prior chapters, we have summarized data on three varieties: verbatim repe-tition of target events, verbatim repetition of misinformation, and repetition of the gist of target events or of misinformation. The data show that the first form of rep-etition reduces false-memory responses, presumably by strengthening verbatim traces of target events, but that the other two forms of repetition increase false-memory responses. Because patients typically participate in many therapy sessions, often spanning months or years (e.g., the Carlson, duM, and Rutherford cases), there is considerable opportunity for repetition. Normally, barring a verbatim record of target events (e.g., videotapes of important life experiences), verbatim repetition of the original experiences that are foci of discussion during therapy sessions is impossible. As we have observed, those experiences are typically in the distant past. However, gist repetition, as we have also observed, is a routine feature of psychotherapy in that the same theme (e.g., possible childhood sexual abuse) may be the focus of many sessions. Also, whenever a therapist provides invalid information to a patient (see the sections on symptom interpretation and dream interpretation, below), that information is, strictly speaking, *mis*information. Obviously, the fact that patients participate in multiple therapy sessions provides opportunities for repetition of such misinformation. Thus, in sum, an inherent feature of psychotherapy is that it is rich in opportunities for the two forms of repetition that are known to elevate false-memory responses but not in opportunities for the form of repetition that is known to suppress them.

Specific Practices

The preceding contextual characteristics of psychotherapy create fertile ground for the growth of false memories. The formation of specific false memories can then be prompted by different therapeutic procedures that provide false information to patients, stimulate the production of false information by patients, or increase their tendency to accept false information as true. Below, we review eight procedures that would be expected to have one or more of these effects, based upon available research: hypnosis, guided imagery, memory work, interpretation of the meaning of behavioral symptoms, dream interpretation, age regression, the use of family photographs to stimulate memory recovery, and giving free rein to the imagination to stimulate memory recovery. Although other procedures might also have been chosen as illustrations (e.g., bibliotherapy), these were selected on the basis of surveys of practicing therapists (Poole et al., 1995), which indicate that each is used by a substantial percentage of therapists to help patients recover memories (see Figure 8-2) and that more than 70% of therapists use a subset of these procedures for that purpose. Hence, in addition to the confluence of contextual factors, which creates fertile ground for false memories in psychotherapy, surveys of practicing therapists indicate that there is also a confluence of procedures, which sow the seeds of specific false memories on that ground.

Hypnosis

Hypnosis is a family of techniques for inducing deep relaxation and trance-like states. In the classic technique used by trained hypnotists, patients arrange themselves in a comfortable position, close their eyes, and focus on a mental image of some sort. The hypnotist then guides them into deeper states of relaxation, using a soft, monotonous voice. A key concomitant of reaching such states is reality detachment (becoming increasingly unaware of physical stimulation from the sur-

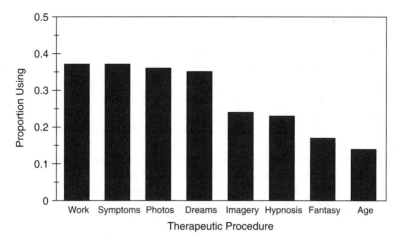

Figure 8-2. Proportions of practicing psychotherapists who use each of eight procedures that would be expected to increase false memories. *Work* = instructions to work at remembering, including journaling; *Symptoms* = interpretation of the meaning of behavioral symptoms; *Photos* = the use of family photographs to stimulate memory recovery; *Dreams* = dream interpretation; *Imagery* = guided imagery; *Hypnosis* = methods of encouraging deep relaxation and trance-like states; *Fantasy* = giving free rein to the imagination; and *Age* = age regression. From Poole, Lindsay, Memon, and Bull (1995).

rounding environment), which is aided by focusing on mental images and on the hypnotist's monotonous voice. When a trance-like state has been reached, the hypnotist may ask questions or make suggestions. This technique can also be taught to patients, and often is, in which event it is called *self-hypnosis*. Self-hypnosis allows patients to detach themselves from the surrounding environment and reach states of deep relaxation on their own, outside of therapy sessions. Certain patients are exceptionally adept at self-trancing, and some, so-called Grade 5 individuals (Spiegel, 1974), are capable of reaching trance-like states without any formal training in methods of hypnosis. These people tend to achieve high scores on psychological tests that measure hypnotic susceptibility, such as the Hypnotic Induction Profile (Spiegel, 1974) and the Responsiveness to Suggestion Scale (Spanos, Burnley, & Cross, 1993; Spanos, Liddy, Baxter, & Burgess, 1994), to be highly empathic, to spontaneously confabulate details when asked to recall distant events, and to be highly accepting of memory suggestions.

Trance-like states can also be reached via methods other than therapist-guided or self-guided relaxation. For instance, psychotropic drugs, such as sodium amytal, can be used. Recall that the use of such drugs was part of the complaints in the Braun and Humenansky litigations. In the Braun case, in particular, the defendants were accused of using such drugs to induce trance-like states in which the plaintiffs were highly susceptible to suggestions about childhood sexual abuse, Satanic cults, multiple personalities, and so forth. Other methods of reaching such states involve physical manipulation, such as body massage. While administering body massage, therapists may talk to patients in the same soft, monotonous voice that hypnotists use to help subjects detach from reality.

In addition to using hypnosis to relieve various forms of psychological distress, such as eating disorders (e.g., Yapko, 1986), it has been used for the explicit purpose of helping patients to recover deteriorated memories (Yapko, 1994). It will be recalled that the improper use of hypnosis to recover false memories was alleged in the Braun and Humenansky suits and that hypnotically induced false memories were central in the Rutherford case. Hypnotic recovery of deteriorated memories is a practice that is founded upon the widespread popular belief that hypnosis improves memory. In support of this belief, there are numerous accounts of police investigations in which hypnosis was successfully used to refresh witnesses' memory for crucial crime details that could not be recalled (e.g., the number on the license plate of a getaway car), resulting in apprehension of suspects whose identities would not otherwise have been known. The problem with such anecdotal accounts is that they provide no baseline data about other investigations in which hypnotically released memories proved to be inaccurate, and the cases went unsolved. Without baseline data, the belief that hypnosis improves memory is just a hypothesis. Moreover, when such data have been gathered under controlled conditions, they have not supported the hypothesis (e.g., Spanos, 1987) and, instead, have shown that (a) hypnotic retrieval is not more accurate than conscious retrieval; and (b) false memories are more likely to be reported during hypnotic retrieval than during conscious retrieval.

Illustrative findings of this ilk were obtained in a study described by Raveen (1987). The study was conducted by a trained hypnotist who was performing a series of television demonstrations of hypnosis. Three employees of the television station had been assigned to assist the hypnotist. Without their knowledge, the hypnotist had arranged to have a fake armed robbery committed across the street from a nearby restaurant. The hypnotist invited the employees to go to lunch with him, and upon arrival at the restaurant, the robbery was in progress in a building across the street, in full view of the employees as they exited their car. They watched as the "robbers" left the building and made a noisy escape in a car. Shortly thereafter, as part of the ensuing "investigation," the employees were hypnotized to obtain their accounts of the robbery. Each hypnotic account was rich in relevant details, such as the number and gender of the robbers and the make and color of the getaway car. The employees were quite confident of the accuracy of their memories. However, none of the three accounts agreed with the others. Each employee gave a different car color, a different number of robbers, and different numbers of robbers of each gender. Moreover, on analogy to Bartlett's (1932) studies of the retelling of folktales and to studies of repeated recall of word lists (e.g., Payne et al., 1996), the employees' hypnotic accounts became progressively less accurate when they were asked to retell their stories. Importantly, these inaccuracies were present even though the robbery had occurred shortly before the employees were hypnotized.

The general conclusions that have emerged from research on hypnotically retrieved memories is that, on the one hand, hypnotic retrieval usually yields more extensive memory reports than conscious retrieval, which encourages the view that it is helpful to memory. This view is an illusion, however. Hypnotic retrieval is not more accurate than conscious retrieval because increases in true information are balanced by increases in false information. In opponent-processes terms, the likely explanation is that although states of deep relaxation and physical detachment allow more information to come to mind by reducing various sources of interference, such states are incommensurate with screening that information using strong criteria of accuracy. Regardless of the theoretical explanation, following a review of extant research on hypnotic memory retrieval, an American Medical Association panel summarized the empirical picture as follows:

> Hypnosis can also lead to increases in false recollection and confabulation. . . . There is no data to support [the belief] that hypnosis increases remembering of only accurate information . . . recollections that are obtained during hypnosis not only fail to be more accurate but actually appear to be generally less reliable than nonhypnotic recall. Furthermore . . . hypnosis may increase the appearance of certitude without a concurrent increase of veracity. (1985, p. 1921)

The panel went on to draw some obvious conclusions about the use of hypnosis to induce memory recovery in patients (see also Figure 8-1):

> When hypnosis is used for recall . . . pseudomemories may be the result of hypnosis transforming the subject's prior beliefs into thoughts or fantasies that they come to accept as memories. Furthermore, since hypnotized subjects tend to be more suggestible, subjects become more vulnerable to incorporating any cues given during hypnosis into their recollections . . . there is no way for either the subject or the hypnotist to distinguish between those recollections that may be accurate and those that may be pseudomemories. (1985, p. 1921)

Guided Imagery

According to Poole et al.'s (1995) statistics, guided imagery is used by roughly one quarter of therapists to assist memory recovery (see also Polusny & Follette, 1996), and it was present in some of the cases reviewed at the start of this chapter (e.g., Watson). In this procedure, patients make mental excursions to locations and times for which memories are being sought. During those visits, the emphasis is on experiencing realistic sensory images under the therapist's guidance—hence, *guided imagery*. For example, patients may be asked to "view" mental scenes with the mind's eye and report the people, events, objects, buildings, and natural formations that they "see" in as much detail as possible. Patients may be asked to "listen" to scenes with the mind's ear and report what they "hear," including conversations, animal sounds, street noise, music, and so forth. Patients may even be asked to "smell" mental scenes with the mind's nose, reporting odors that they detect, or to feel the temperature.

That guided imagery, like hypnotic retrieval, can generate false memories of past experiences, including false memories of childhood experiences, has been established in a number of recent experiments (e.g., Arbuthnott, Arbuthnott, & Rossiter, 2001; Arbuthnott, Geelen, & Kealy, 2002; Clancy, McNally, & Schacter, 1999; Hyman, Husband, & Billings, 1995; Hyman & Pentland, 1996). The research of Hyman and Pentland is illustrative. The parents of 123 college students completed a questionnaire covering 10 categories of childhood experiences in which the students might have participated (e.g., vacations, birthdays, car accidents, hospitalizations). Once questionnaires had been completed and returned, the experimenter telephoned the corresponding students, asking them to participate in the experiment. The experiment consisted of three sessions. During Session 1, subjects were told that the purpose of the experiment was to investigate how well people remember childhood experiences. They were told that their parents had already provided descriptions of some of their childhood experiences, and it was these particular events that they would be asked to remember. Subjects were then asked to recall two to five true experiences, and also to recall one false experience (i.e., an event, such as a hospitalization, that their parents stated *had not happened*). Subjects were told that they might have difficulty remembering some events and that if they did, they would be given help. Subjects were assigned to two conditions for recall: guided imagery and control. In the guided-imagery condition, subjects were asked to imagine the target events and were told that this would help them to remember. They were instructed to describe the images that they generated in detail, including the visual appearance of people and objects and the ways in which particular actions occurred. This procedure was designed to ensure that the subjects actually generated mental images, but it also parallels the manner in which guided imagery is traditionally used in psychotherapy. In the control condition, guided-imagery instructions were replaced by instructions to sit and think quietly about events. Subjects were required to think quietly for 45–60 seconds before describing an event, and they were told that this would help their memory. At the end of Session 1, subjects were encouraged to continue trying to remember the target events between Sessions 1 and 2 by generating images (guided-imagery condition) or by thinking about the events (control condition). The same procedure was repeated 1 week later, during Session 2, and a week after that, during Session 3. After Session 2, subjects were again encouraged to continue trying to remember the target events between Sessions 2 and 3.

There were three key findings. First, contrary to what would be expected from the use of guided imagery to recover memories during psychotherapy, there was no difference in the amount of true information that was recalled by guided-imagery subjects and by control subjects. Second, there was a substantial between-group difference in the amount of false information that was recalled. On average, control subjects recalled about 10% of the childhood experiences that had not happened, but guided-imagery subjects recalled about 30%. Third, much like the effects of repeated recall on false memory for word lists (e.g., Brainerd, Payne, Wright, & Reyna, 2003), the tendency of guided imagery to produce false-memory reports increased across sessions: The percentage of false childhood experiences that were recalled was under 20% during Session 1 but exceeded 35% during Session 3.

Why does guided imagery elevate false memory? Two potential causes have been discussed in the memory literature (e.g., Hyman & Pentland, 1996), both of which are familiar elements of opponent-processes analysis. First, guided-imagery instructions direct subjects to focus their efforts squarely on reconstructive retrieval, which is known to generate false as well as true information under controlled conditions. The objective is to recover memories that have proved to be inaccessible by other means, and subjects are told that generating images will help them to gain access to those recalcitrant memories. Thus, subjects execute a particular reconstructive activity in connection with specific episodes in their lives, which is capable of delivering false memories about that episode. In addition, repeatedly practicing that activity, coupled with assurances that it is helpful to memory, may spill over into other areas of remembering, increasing subjects' baseline tendency to rely on this error-prone form of retrieval.

The second feature of guided imagery is the seductive phenomenology that accompanies subjects' memory constructions. As we know from earlier chapters, people rely on vivid, realistic phenomenology to suppress false-memory reports in two general ways. The first way is recollection rejection (e.g., Brainerd & Reyna, 2002a, 2002b; Reyna & Brainerd, 1995b): When comparing competing candidate memories, all of which are consistent with the gist of experience (Did I eat a hot dog or a hamburger or a slice of pizza at the baseball game?), memories that do not provoke vivid phenomenology are rejected in favor of those that do. The second way is the distinctiveness heuristic (e.g., Dodson & Schacter, 2001, 2002b; Schacter et al., 1999): There is a general inclination to avoid reporting memories that do not provoke vivid phenomenology, especially when subjects believe the relevant memories should be distinctive. Guided imagery cuts the ground from under these two editing procedures by requiring the generation of "memories" with accompanying phenomenologies of the very sort upon which we rely in everyday life to gauge the trustworthiness of memories. Thus, false memories that are generated via guided imagery are especially beguiling because their vivid qualities instill illusions of reality. We will return to this point at the end of the chapter in connection with experimentation on imagination inflation.

Memory Work

Memory work refers to the domain of memory-recovery exercises, activities that patients are given to perform outside therapy sessions (sometimes, inside as well) in the hope of exhuming memories. According to Poole et al.'s (1995) survey, this, along with the interpretation of behavioral symptoms, is the most common therapeutic procedure for stimulating memory recovery, being used by more than one third of practicing therapists. Examples of memory work from the cases that were presented at the start of this chapter include writing songs about childhood abuse and writing accusatory letters to suspected abusers. Journaling, however, is a particularly common form of memory work in which therapists can receive specialized training. The assumptions underlying journaling, which have been discussed in writings by leading practitioners of this method, such as Progoff (e.g., see Juline, 1992; Kaiser, 1981), are that there is an unconscious stream of memories that flows continuously along and that journaling allows one to tap into that stream and bring the memories to conscious awareness. Patients are instructed to begin keeping a journal in which they record thoughts, feelings, and memories that relate to the reasons they sought therapy. Patients receive instruction and encouragement in how to submerge themselves in the underground memory stream (meditation and other forms of self-hypnosis are often involved), how to enter other hidden mental worlds (e.g., the world of imagination), and how to write down what they discover. Patients are told that they may expect to encounter images and flashbacks from long-dormant memories; they should not be judgmental when those images are far-fetched; and they should simply record their experiences in a particular type of journal that is reserved for such experiences (sometimes called a *period log*). Other types of specialized journals may be used for specific categories of memory work. For example, a *life history log* may be devoted purely to autobiographical memories, and an *imagery log* may be devoted to images that come to mind. Typically, patients will discuss the contents of these logs during therapy sessions.

Although the psychotherapy literature contains numerous articles on the use of memory-work procedures such as journaling (e.g., Ullrich & Lutgendorf, 2002), there has been little systematic memory research on the effects of the procedures. However, there are obvious similarities between these procedures and manipulations that are known to increase false-memory reports. In the first place, memory work is a suggestive activity because it implies that with enough effort, it is possible to exhume faded memories. Research shows that while this assumption is true for some memories (the phenomenon of *reminiscence*), it is not true for others— some memories can never be resuscitated. However, the assumption itself encourages rememberers to regard information that is generated by memory work as true and provides rememberers with no criteria for deciding between true and false information. Because, by definition, patients lack clear recollections of information that is the focus of memory work, it follows that error-prone reconstructive retrieval will predominate. In addition, memory work necessarily consists of repeated attempts to retrieve target information, and a consistent finding of false-memory experiments is that memory errors increase as the number of retrieval attempts increases.

Finally, note the deep parallels between memory work and the highly contaminating technique of forced confabulation (Ackil & Zaragoza, 1998; Zaragoza et al., 2001). In forced confabulation, subjects are required to produce physical descriptions of false events, usually in the form of written or oral statements. Because the events for which confabulations are supplied have just occurred, subjects are well aware that the material they are generating is false. Nevertheless, the production of such confabulations elevates false reports on memory tests that are administered a few days later; statements that were previously *known* to be confabulations are now reported as memories of actual events. In memory work, patients also produce physical descriptions of events that cannot be precisely remembered (e.g., as lyrics to songs, letters to third parties, or journal entries). When those descriptions refer to false events, they are, strictly speaking, forced confabulations because patients have been instructed to engage in such activities as part of their therapy and have been trained in how to perform the activities. Thus, some of the confabulations would be expected to become part of patients' memories. A further consideration suggests that the tendency of patients to accept memory-work confabulations as true memories will be greater than the tendency of experimental subjects to accept forced confabulations as true memories. Experimental subjects *know* that they are confabulating, which provides a potential mechanism for suppressing those "memories" on later tests (No, the character in the film did not bleed after falling off the chair because I made that up). However, patients who are doing memory work do not know when they are confabulating and, instead, are led to believe that their efforts will yield true memories.

Interpretation of Behavioral Symptoms

Symptom interpretation occurs when therapists inform patients that some of their salient behavioral characteristics are signs of a history, even a previously unsuspected history, of certain forms of physical or psychological trauma, such as childhood sexual abuse. As a rule, these characteristics are undesirable (e.g., depression, eating disorders, nightmares), including serious forms of maladjustment (e.g., suicide attempts), but they need not be (e.g., Beth Rutherford's superior academic performance in high school). We have mentioned that pop psychology writings are rife with lists of behavioral signs of prior trauma, and books by Ryder (1992) and Weiss (1992) may be added to previously mentioned ones and previously mentioned references. However, as some of the statements of professional organizations in Figure 8-1 indicate, there is no scientific basis for such readings of behavioral signs. Symptom lists were not originally derived from studies showing that individuals who have confirmed histories of a certain index trauma exhibit elevated levels of the cited behaviors. Rather, such lists were constructed on the basis of anecdotes, intuition, the case histories of individual patients, and clinical experiences (see Blume, 1991). Moreover, when appropriate studies have been conducted, they have failed to support the notion that behavioral characteristics, even symptoms of serious maladjustment, are reliable signs of specific prior trauma. In the case of sexual abuse, in particular, reviews of such studies have concluded that there is no unique collection of behavioral characteristics that exhibits elevated levels either in children who have recently experienced such abuse (Kendall-Tackett et al., 1993) or in adults who experienced such abuse as children (Rind et al., 1998).

Because available data run counter to the underlying thesis of symptom interpretation, providing such interpretations to patients is a form of therapeutic misinformation, in the sense that it asserts "facts" that are known to be untrue. The data of hundreds of misinformation experiments suggest that this will tend to falsify the contents of memory, leading some patients to conclude that they experienced index traumas, even though they cannot remember having done so. The same experiments suggest that the probability of such misinformation acceptance will be heightened by the fact that the misinformation is being supplied by a highly credible source, one who has treated dozens if not hundreds of patients with similar problems, and by the fact that the misinformation is plausible. With respect to plausibility, because the interpreted symptoms are usually undesirable characteristics of which patients would just as soon be rid, it is natural to suppose that they were caused by unpleasant experiences.

Although, on the basis of scientific evidence, symptom interpretation is misinformation, surveys establish that it is quite popular among practitioners. Indeed, as noted above, Poole et al.'s (1995) results showed that symptom interpretation and memory work were the two most popular memory-recovery procedures, being regularly used by more than one third of practitioners. This is troubling, given the scientific evidence, and it is also surprising, given the statements of some professional organizations (Figure 8-1). Although it is not remarkable that therapists would use procedures that have been disconfirmed in studies of which they are unaware, particularly if those studies were conducted after they were trained, symptom interpretation has been specifically repudiated in widely disseminated statements of professional organizations.

A possible explanation for its continued popularity is that, despite statements such as the American Psychological Association's conclusion that "there is no single set of symptoms which automatically indicates that a person was a victim of childhood abuse," therapists receive mixed messages about the types of evidence upon which clinical practice should be based. Although controlled studies are acknowledged as perhaps the best basis, clinical experience and wisdom are also acknowledged as acceptable bases. In the law, for example, clinical practitioners are allowed to provide expert testimony concerning which treatments are best, or concerning the defining characteristics of patients with index problems, purely on the basis of their clinical experience *without recourse to supporting research*. (For instance, "I diagnosed Ms. Jones as a survivor of childhood sexual abuse because she was obese, obsessive, and depressed. I have treated dozens of sexually abused women, and they are almost invariably obese, obsessive, and suffering from depression" would be perfectly acceptable expert testimony in most courts.) Thus, as a form of evidence, clinical experience may be placed on a par with research data, in the law as well as in clinical practice. Therefore, it is understandable that any procedure that is believed to be strongly supported by clinical experience would continue to be used, despite nonsupportive research findings. Moreover, the history of medicine is replete with examples of procedures that were in common use long after research had demonstrated that they were harmful. It was difficult, for instance, to convince 19th-century physicians whose clinical experience was held in high esteem that their belief in the effectiveness of bleeding could be mistaken.

Dream Interpretation

In some of the earlier recovered-memory cases, patients discussed their dreams with therapists, and therapists interpreted them as being connected in various ways to unremembered traumas. Beth Rutherford was told that her strange dreams about her father (e.g., sending bears after her) were the very sorts of dreams that sexually abused people experience; Carlson was told that her disturbing dreams were real memories that were trying to resurface; Ms. duM's therapist assumed that her vague dreams of abuse represented true memories of abuse and prescribed bibliotherapeutic activity to help her recover more explicit memories. That dreams can have special significance, either as windows to the past or as harbingers of the future, has long been enshrined in folk wisdom and theology. The Bible, for instance, contains some familiar examples, such as Moses' analysis of the pharaoh's dreams as foretelling famine years. Freud thought that dreaming provided access to the unconscious, and some early psychoanalysts—notably, Jung (e.g., 1953)—placed special emphasis on this putative power of dreaming.

As it is practiced in modern psychotherapy, dream interpretation is a multifaceted procedure in which, like hypnosis or journaling, therapists can receive specialized training (indeed, there are centers devoted entirely to this purpose). The shared elements are that patients report salient dreams to therapists, dreams that have occurred before as well as after entering therapy, and possible interpretations are explored. One or more specific methods are used to ensure that the exploration is both systematic and comprehensive. Some of the more common ones are (a) dialoguing, (b) enactment, (c) free association, (d) free writing, and (e) mental imagery. *Dialoguing* involves the patient engaging in a spoken or written conversation about his or her dream, talking to the dream, posing questions to people and to objects in the dream, and reporting their answers. During *enactment*, the content of a dream is acted out by the patient, as though it were a play. The patient plays the role of some characters, with other characters being enacted by the therapist or by other patients (during group therapy). *Free association* resembles the word-association tests that are used to generate semantic norms for memory research (e.g., Table 2-2): As patients recount their dreams, they are asked to free associate to individual people, objects, and events (What's the first thing that this brings to mind?), and they are usually asked to generate as many associations as possible. *Free writing* is a written variant of free association, which can occur outside of therapy sessions in closer proximity to the actual occurrence of dreams. Patients are instructed to make lists of the people, objects, and events in their dreams and then to write down their free associations to each. Last, *mental imagery* is a variant of guided imagery, the chief difference being that imagery generation is guided by the content of dreams, rather than by therapists' questions. Specifically, patients are instructed to mentally review the contents of a dream and, as each person, object, or action comes to mind, to generate more elaborate visualizations or other sensory experiences associated with that item.

Of course, the use of such dream-exploration methods presupposes that patients can remember their dreams, something that people often lament being unable to do. Therefore, patients are usually instructed in the use of procedures that will help them to preserve or recover dreams. Common examples are to focus on the possibility of dreaming and the need to remember dreams when going to sleep, to keep a pad and pencil near the bed on which to make rough notes about the content of dreams, to keep a dream journal in which more elaborate accounts based upon the rough notes are recorded, and to enter trance-like states (e.g., through meditation or self-hypnosis) to access the content of elusive dreams.

Our interest lies with the narrow issue of dream interpretation as a false-memory mechanism. Here, a core problem with dream interpretation is that there is no scientific support for the hypothesis that dreams provide privileged access to weak or forgotten memories (e.g., Simpson, 1996). On the contrary, dreaming resembles hypnosis in the sense that we are in deep, trance-like states—indeed, sleep is a natural state of trance—in which we are detached from physical stimulation emanating from the surrounding environment. Therefore, one would expect that, like hypnosis, dreaming should be highly susceptible to suggestion and false memory. Consistent with that hypothesis, controlled studies of people who possess memories of fantastic or seemingly impossible experiences indicate that dreams are the most common origin for those "memories." For example, Spanos, Cross, Dickson, and Dubreuil (1993) compared subjects who reported having unidentified flying object (UFO) experiences with subjects who reported never having such experiences. For subjects in the first group, it was found that their initial UFO "memories" often occurred while dreaming: Of those subjects who believed that they had been abducted by aliens, 58% first "encountered" the aliens as they awoke from sleep in the middle of the night. Further, other research by Spanos and associates (e.g., Spanos, McNulty, Dubreuil, Pires, & Burgess, 1995) indicates that certain people are particularly likely to have vivid, compelling dreams of false events. In this study, nearly 2000 college students served as subjects. Approximately, 10% of these individuals, as identified by a battery of instruments, reported dreams of unlikely events that were accompanied by compelling imagery.

The problems with regarding dreams as a window on weak or forgotten memories are that, on the one hand, there is no scientific corroboration for this assumption and, on the other, there are data showing that dreaming is a suggestible state in which there is a propensity to "remember" fantastic or seemingly impossible events, often with compelling imagery. Consequently, interpreting dreams as true memories has the same status as interpreting behavioral symptoms: It is a form of therapeutic misinformation because it asserts hypotheses, which lack scientific support, as though they were facts. Also, like symptom interpretation, the chances that such misinformation will result in false memories are increased by the fact that the interpretations are being provided by highly credible sources and by the fact that dreams seem highly plausible when they revolve around the same topics as therapy sessions (e.g., Beth Rutherford's intensely sexual dreams).

That dream interpretation is an effective form of misinformation that produces false memories under controlled conditions has been demonstrated in experiments by Mazzoni and Loftus (1998) and by Mazzoni, Loftus, Seitz, and Lynn (1999). In these experiments, subjects were exposed to simulated therapy sessions in which their dreams were analyzed by a clinical psychologist. The crucial feature was that the subjects' dreams were interpreted as demonstrating the occurrence of certain childhood experiences that the subjects had previously reported had not happened to them. Such dream interpretations increased subjects' belief in the reality of the false childhood experiences, and many subjects reported memories of concrete details that accompanied the experiences.

Age Regression

Age regression sometimes occurs as an adjunct to hypnosis (e.g., Martinez-Taboas, 2002; Spanos, Burgess, Burgess, Samuels, & Blois, 1999; Vandenberg, 2002). Patients are first taken through the ordinary steps of hypnosis, until they reach the state of relaxation during which hypnotists normally pose questions and make suggestions. Next, they are instructed to focus on an image that will transport them backward in time. They may, for instance, be instructed to imagine lying comfortably on the back seat of a limousine that is traveling in reverse gear, back through time, or lying comfortably on a magic carpet that is floating back through time. As time travel progresses, the hypnotist describes, in the usual soft and monotonous voice, historical milestones that are being passed (e.g., birth of children, marriage, graduation from high school), until a specific era is reached. Questioning then centers on what patients can remember about that era.

That age regression is a procedure that is susceptible to suggestion and false memory is evident from the fact that it occurs under hypnosis. We have already seen that a standard finding about hypnotic retrieval is that it yields higher levels of false reports about life events than does conscious retrieval, including vivid confabulations that are compelling to rememberers. That age regression, in particular, is prone to false-memory reports is evident from the fact that it is a major source of an improbable class of memories—namely, recollections of previous lives. As a hypnotized subject travels backward in time, there is no requirement that the process stop at a point after birth. The subject may be regressed to a point between conception and birth—so-called womb regression. Such subjects have reported memories of hearing things that their mothers said or of hearing arguments between their parents (Simpson, 1996).

Regression can also continue to a time before conception—so-called past-life regression (Haraldsson, 2003; Plowman, 1996). When it continues in that way, subjects have reported detailed memories of one or more prior lives. The best-known illustration, the one that first focused popular attention on past-life regression, is the case of Virginia Tighe (Bernstein, 1956). Bernstein was an amateur hypnotist in Pueblo, Colorado, who practiced his craft on his neighbor Virginia Tighe. In the course of being regressed back to a time before her birth, Tighe remembered living a previous life as Bridey Murphy in County Cork, Ireland. The reported memories had great verisimilitude: While under hypnosis, Tighe spoke of her prior life with an Irish accent, told Irish stories, and sang Irish folksongs. Audio recordings were made of some of those sessions. Eventually, however, serious doubt was cast upon Tighe's recollections through newspaper investigations. Those investigations failed to turn up any records of a Bridey Murphy who lived in County Cork during the specified years. More tellingly, they located records of a Bridey Murphy Corkell, who had lived in a house across the street from the one in which Tighe had resided as a child.

Although anecdotes of womb recollections and past-life recollections raise concerns about the veracity of age-regression memories, such anecdotes are not scientific demonstrations that age regression produces high levels of false memory under controlled conditions. Such evidence is available, however. In an experiment by Spanos, Burgess, Burgess, Samuels, and Blois (1999), for example, subjects were administered a series of psychological tests, after which they were given misinformation about their test results. Subjects were told that they possessed personality profiles that result from particular activities that occur during the first few days after birth, the activities being intense practice at coordinated eye movements and visual search. They were also told that most people who have this profile are born in hospitals that affix interesting mobiles on newborns' cribs. The subjects were then hypnotized and age regressed back to the day after their birth. They were asked to look around and describe what they saw. They were also asked to change perspectives and to look at themselves lying in the hospital crib from another location in the room. Subjects were then awakened, and before leaving the laboratory, they were informed that because age regression stimulates long-dormant neural circuits, they might now experience itching sensations around their navels and that they might begin having thoughts and dreams of infancy.

One week later, the subjects returned for a second laboratory session during which they rated their level of confidence that their hypnotically recovered memories referred to real experiences, rather than to fantasies, and they rated the frequencies with which they had experienced navel itching and thoughts/dreams about infancy between the two sessions. The results showed that in the first session, during hypnotic regression, 79% of the subjects reported false memories about the day after birth. (At the risk of redundancy, adults cannot, for neurological reasons, have true memories about the day after birth.) For instance, during hypnotic regression, 46% of the subjects reported seeing a mobile attached to their cribs. During the second session, 49% of the age-regressed subjects stated that the infant memories that they had recovered were true experiences; 35% were uncertain; and only 16% correctly stated that their recovered memories were fantasies. Finally, 50% of the age-regressed subjects reported dreaming about infant experiences during the previous week, and 31% reported one or more occasions of navel itching. On the whole, then, age regression seems to be a powerful method of inducing false memories.

Family Photographs

Most patients have access to family albums or other collections of family photographs. When they are unable to retrieve memories of index childhood experiences (e.g., being taken to the hospital by one's parents for treatment of a traumatic injury), a therapist may suggest that such photographs be used as sources of additional retrieval cues. The underlying assumption is that if patients inspect the faces of other people who were part of the index experience, this may permit access to additional memories. Actually, this is a sound assumption that coheres with a familiar memory principle that we have mentioned on previous occasions—namely, retrieval variability (Tulving & Thomson, 1971). According to this principle, the retrieval of true memories is facilitated by increasing the degree of overlap between the information in retrieval cues and information that was present in the index experience (and would therefore have been stored in memory traces). Obviously, adding pictorial cues that match things that patients saw at the time increases such overlap, and as a rule, such cues stimulate recall of further memories.

The problem is that there is no guarantee that pictorial cues will only stimulate the retrieval of further *true* memories. On the contrary, other research suggests that they can stimulate a rather high proportion of false memories. The reason is that retrieval variability is not the only memory principle that is operative in this situation. We must also consider that when family photographs are used, the situation is analogous to laboratory studies of repeated recall. Patients have already attempted to recall information about index experiences but have not been successful. So, they are encouraged to make further recall attempts. A familiar finding, which has come up before in this chapter, is that repeated recall increases the yield of false as well as true information. Another familiar finding about repeated recall (e.g., see chapter 7) is that *newly recalled* information (i.e., information that shows up on a later recall test that did not show up earlier) is particularly likely to be false. Moreover, both of these results are especially apt to occur when there are long delays between repeated-recall tests and the index experience, a pattern that has been obtained with both autobiographical memory (e.g., Pipe et al., 1999; Poole & White, 1993) and laboratory tasks (e.g., Brainerd, Payne, et al., 2003). Of course, such delays are integral to psychotherapy. A recent confirmation of the ability of family photographs to induce false memories of childhood experiences was obtained in a carefully controlled study by Lindsay, Hagen, et al. (2004).

Giving Free Rein to the Imagination

This last procedure seeks to increase the flow of memories by, in effect, substituting fantasy for memory. When patients are unable to access memories of index experiences, they are asked to *imagine* people and things that might have been present or events that might have occurred. Here, the assumptions are that patients may be able to access additional memories if they shift from a narrow, perhaps effortful and stressful, focus on remembering to a more relaxed, playful process, such as imagining, and that the products of imagination can be critically evaluated at some later point to sort true memories from fantasy. Unfortunately, various lines of research that were explored in earlier chapters argue against both of these assumptions and suggest that the principal effect of this procedure will be to generate false information. Concerning the first assumption, instructions to imagine rather than remember obviously weaken a patient's subjective memorability criterion—in fact, they eliminate it—which is a well-known stimulus to false-memory reports. Also, encouraging patients to imagine things that might have happened is quite similar to the gist-oriented retrieval instructions that have been investigated in some false-memory experiments (chapters 4 and 5). It will be recalled that a standard finding about such instructions is that they greatly expand the amount of false information that is remembered, without producing much expansion in the amount of true information that is remembered (e.g., Reyna & Kiernan, 1994, 1995). Finally, concerning the second assumption, memory experiments have repeatedly shown (e.g., chapter 6) that once false memories are generated, subjects have great difficulty discriminating them from the real thing. On this point, a probative finding is that, in certain situations (e.g., eyewitness identification of suspects), subjects' expressed confidence in the accuracy of their memories is not well correlated with genuine truth or falsity.

Answering the Big Question

The big question is: Can psychotherapy actually produce extensive false memories of life experiences in adults, including false memories of traumas such as repeated sexual abuse during childhood? Could such gruesome memories literally result from the combination of the suggestive context of psychotherapy and specific suggestive practices? It might be thought that this is a settled matter, for at least three reasons. First, the courts have already ruled that this is exactly what happened to some plaintiffs (e.g., those in the Humenansky litigation) and have made large financial awards as compensation. Second, some patients have developed memories of traumatic experiences that were later proved to be false, such as Beth Rutherford's memories of being twice impregnated by her (vasectomized) father and twice aborted. Third, patients have developed extensive memories of traumatic experiences that they believed to be true at the time but that they later recanted, such as Elizabeth Carlson's recanting of her memories of being molested by several family members, of participating in Satanic rituals, and of committing cannibalism.

Although such considerations provide some grounds for believing that the answer to the above question is yes, each has inherent limitations and falls short of rigorous standards of scientific proof. Juries can make errors in interpreting scientific evidence, and judicial opinions can be based upon inferential leaps that are not warranted by available data. To take but one example, defendants are often convicted on the basis of eyewitness identifications because many judges and juries believe that confident identifications are highly reliable when, in fact, they are not (e.g., Wells et al., 1998). Also, the fact that some details of the traumatic memories that patients have recovered during therapy were shown to be false does not disprove other details, nor does it disprove the overall gist of the memories. In the Rutherford case, notwithstanding that the results of the medical examination disproved the patient's recovered memories of instances of vaginal penetration, those results did not disprove her recovered memories of being sodomized by her father or of having been abused in other ways (e.g., sexual fondling). Further, researchers who study recovered memories of abuse have often commented (e.g., McNally, 2003) that circumstances in which it is possible to disprove even a small fraction of patients' recovered memories are extremely rare owing to time lags. The remembered events are so far in the past that no physical evidence usually survives, and alleged perpetrators are often deceased. Finally, recantings, unless they are accompanied by determinative physical or medical evidence, which is usually impossible to obtain, do not disprove the prior occurrence of the traumatic experiences in recovered memories any more than the recovered memories themselves prove the occurrence of the traumatic experiences. Thus, Elizabeth Carlson—who, after all, had always remembered being sexually abused by two men as a child—might have recovered true memories of being abused by family members and then falsely recanted them for other reasons (e.g., she believed the memories had to be false merely because other patients had recovered similar memories or because she desired to sue her therapist for malpractice). Moreover, a number of studies of recanting have pointed to the fact that they sometimes occur under conditions that are just as suggestive as the therapeutic conditions that have been alleged to induce false memories of trauma (see Bradley & Wood, 1996; Gonzales, Waterman, Kelly, McCord, & Oliveri, 1993; Marx, 1996; Rieser, 1991; Sarbin, 1997).

Unless one utterly dismisses clinical experience as a sound basis for opinion, something that the courts are unwilling to do, one must add to these considerations the passionate disbelief of many practitioners in the ability of psychotherapy to induce false memories of trauma in the first place. Recall that this was a featured element of Diane Humenansky's testimony in two malpractice trials, as it has been in other malpractice suits. One former recovered-memory practitioner characterized clinical wisdom on this point as follows:

> *"You just can't make up a traumatic event."* . . . it's one thing to admit that memory loss and retrospective bias can distort details of a traumatic experience, but it's quite another matter to argue that an entirely fictional event can be created in a client's mind . . . [when] a client recovers the memory of her rape that occurred thirty years ago. Maybe she gets the colors of the curtains wrong, but certainly she can't make the whole thing up. The core of the memory is what's important. (Simpson, 1996, p. 67)

Even if false memories of prior trauma can be constructed from whole cloth during psychotherapy, it might be that this only occurs in a small set of patients who have especially severe emotional disorders or neurological damage. (For example, remember that Carlson had a history of repeated hospitalizations for mental illness and that Watson and Frei had long histories of alcohol and drug abuse.) Finally, a related and more measured criticism that has figured prominently in the writings of some critics of the false-memory syndrome (e.g., Pope, 1997) is that the hypothesis that memory research has demonstrated that psychotherapy can induce extensive false memories of prior trauma is incorrect; differences between false-memory experiments and psychotherapy run far too deep for this hypothesis to be anything more than a shaky inference.

The types of experiments that are required to answer the big question are randomized control designs in which samples of ostensibly normal adults are assigned to treatment and control conditions, with treatment subjects being exposed to simulated therapeutic procedures that are suspected of inducing false memories of prior traumatic experiences and with control subjects being exposed to equivalent amounts of procedures that do not focus on memory recovery. To achieve absolute comparability with cases such as those at the start of the chapter, the procedures in the treatment group would have to focus on false memories of interconnected experiences (rather than single events) of a horrific nature, preferably repeated childhood sexual abuse by relatives or Satanic ritual abuse. That is impossible, of course, for legal and ethical reasons. On the legal side, it would be wrong, naturally, to knowingly induce false memories that certain people have committed crimes. On the ethical side, it would be improper to knowingly induce false memories of experiences that are so traumatic that collateral damage might result.[1]

The ethical line is not as sharp as the legal one, however. Everyone experiences trauma as a matter of course, and although many traumas cause only passing discomfort (e.g., forgetting to pay last month's credit card bill, resulting in a $100 interest charge), it is not always clear which traumatic experiences are innocuous and which have long-term consequences. False memories of experiences of repeated childhood sexual abuse are obviously on the wrong side of the ethical line, but what about false memories of causing a pet bird to die when you were a child because you forgot to feed it or false memories of causing a car accident as a child through disruptive behavior that distracted the driver? To answer such questions, proposals to conduct research whose objective is to implant false memories must be thoroughly reviewed for ethical implications by independent panels. At colleges and universities in the United States, such reviews are conducted by formal units known as institutional review boards, and similar reviews are conducted by federal granting agencies from which investigators request financial support for their research. The mandate of such panels is always to err on the side of caution in protecting the

---

1. There are exceptions to this rule. As mentioned in chapter 6, Ofshe implanted false memories in Paul Ingram of Ingram having sexually molested his daughters. However, Ingram had already confessed to similar crimes and was imprisoned and awaiting trial. The purpose of Ofshe's implantation was therefore exculpation rather than false incrimination. More specifically, the purpose was to demonstrate that Ingram's confessions might be false because he was susceptible to the implantation of false memories of molestations.

interests of human subjects. Therefore, the tendency of such panels is only to approve false-memory research that focuses on negative experiences that are transparently innocuous—experiences that, if they had occurred, would have caused at most transitory discomfort rather than true trauma—and to require that researchers reverse the effects of memory implantation after subjects have completed their participation (which is usually accomplished via a debriefing procedure).

In short, although research on the big question can follow the dictum that randomized control designs should be used with normal adults and although such research can focus on any of the therapeutic practices that were discussed above, it cannot, for legal and ethical reasons, attempt to implant false memories with serious traumatic content. With that limitation in mind, we now consider some streams of experimentation that demonstrate that it is possible, using specific practices, to induce false memories of extensive, interconnected life experiences in normal adults, events that "occurred" in the distant past, including during childhood. We examine three specific lines of research: implantation of alternate identities, implantation of distressing childhood experiences, and imagination inflation.

Implanting Alternate Identities

It is perhaps arguable whether contemporary institutional review boards would still permit the type of research that we now consider. The research is already available in the literature, however, because it was conducted and published in the early 1990s by Spanos and associates (Spanos et al., 1991). During his lifetime, Spanos, who died an untimely death in an airplane crash in 1994, was one of the world's most respected investigators of therapeutically induced false memories—most especially, false memories arising from deep relaxation techniques, such as the many variants of hypnosis, and false memories associated with MPD (e.g., Spanos, 1996).

When Elizabeth Carlson's attorney characterized MPD as junk science, he was referring to the widespread belief that MPD is caused by an unsuspected history of childhood sexual abuse, the usual hypothesis being that sexual abuse is so terrifying and confusing for children that they preserve their psychological integrity by creating other identities to whom the horrible experiences happened. The more the abuse is repeated, the larger the number of alternate identities that may be created, according to the hypothesis. Consistent with this notion, in modern times, a strong correlation has been reported between the diagnosis of MPD and reports by patients of having been sexually abused as children (e.g., Boor, 1982; Gleaves, 1996; Saltman & Solomon, 1982). Correlation does not mean causation, however, and other facts suggest that this particular correlation may be artifactual. For example, because reports of multiple personalities have been with us for hundreds of years, one might ask whether they have always been accompanied by concomitant reports of childhood sexual abuse. The answer is no. For example, MPD diagnoses at the beginning of the 20th century were not accompanied by reports of sexual abuse of any sort (Putnam, 1989), nor are modern experiences of alternate identities in non-Western cultures (Spanos et al., 1991). Thus, the high MPD-abuse associations that have been reported may be spurious consequences of the fact that the two variables that are being correlated are both measured by the same people—namely, treating therapists—and those measurements may therefore be contaminated by those people's beliefs. For instance, when therapists who subscribe to the MPD-abuse correlation are confronted with patients who report alternate identities, they may be far more likely to initiate recovered-memory therapy to look for unsuspected abuse or, on the other hand, when patients report a history of abuse, such therapists may be far more likely to initiate procedures (e.g., hypnosis) that are designed to reveal unsuspected alternate identities. (This is a therapeutic example of the previously discussed phenomenon of confirmation bias in criminal investigation.) Taken together, these considerations suggest that MPD, like recovered memories of childhood sexual abuse, may sometimes be false memories that arise from suggestive therapeutic practices.

Prior to Spanos et al.'s meticulous sequence of experiments, there had been desultory reports in the literature indicating that it might be possible to create false memories of alternate identities via hypnotic regression (e.g., Kampman, 1976). The creation of such false memories would be ethically dubious if it were likely that some subjects might come to believe that their current lives were infected by personalities of which they were unaware. That possibility was avoided by focusing on false memories that involve *deceased* identities. The general research strategy was to have college-student volunteers participate in past-life hypnotic regression sessions, which would determine if large samples of ostensibly normal subjects would exhibit Bridey Murphy–type alternate identities, and if they did, to gather information from those alternate identities that would conclusively establish that the alternate identities are false memories (rather than true memories of previous lives).

In an initial experiment, 110 college students first responded to some psychological tests that measure the propensity for certain types of psychopathology, such as the Minnesota Multiphasic Personality Inventory (MMPI), a test of digressive affect, a test of magical thinking, some tests of the tendency to engage in fantasy and imagery, and a test of absorption. After the subjects responded to these tests, they were informed that belief in reincarnation was a deeply held conviction in many cultures and that scientific research was beginning to produce data confirming that belief. They were also told that past-life hypnotic regression is a standard technique for investigating reincarnation and that some people are actually able to recover memories of past lives during hypnosis. Next, the subjects received a 10-minute hypnotic induction procedure, followed by a 5-minute age-regression procedure in which they traveled back through their lives to a point preceding their birth and into an alternate dimension. They were then told that they were someone else, reliving a previous life in some earlier time and place. Following this instruction, the subjects were asked to provide their new names, to describe what they were wearing, and to state where they were. Subjects who answered these questions appropriately were considered to be responding in an alternate identity.

Roughly one third of the subjects answered the questions appropriately, with the remaining subjects stating that they were still themselves. The former subjects were administered a 40-minute interview consisting of questions that were designed to establish that they had actually adopted an alternate identity and possessed the detailed memories that would be associated with a true identity. The questions inquired about such things as time, place, government, and social conditions. For example, alternate-identity subjects were asked what year it was, their age, in what country they were living, who the leader of the country was, and whether their coun try was at war or at peace. They were also asked to state their religion, to describe their religious practices in detail, to describe the form of money that was used in their country, and they were particularly asked to describe what or who was engraved on their coins and paper currency. Finally, the subjects were asked to describe the homes in which they lived, whether they were married, whether they had children, and to outline the routine of a typical day. These questions were readily answered, indicating that the subjects were indeed experiencing the "memories" of an alternate identity.

Although these questions were readily answered, analyses of the subjects' responses indicated that, consistent with opponent-processes conceptions, the alternate-identity memories were false-but-gist-preserving constructions, rather than true memories of previous lives. That the memories were false was demonstrated by the fact that responses to questions about specific items of historical information were usually wrong, notwithstanding that those items were common information that would have been well known to anyone living at the stated time. For example, the subjects often named the wrong person as the country's political leader, described events that would have been impossible during the indicated era, described technology that did not exist during the indicated era, misstated whether the country was at war or at peace, or gave the locale a name that was different than the one that was used during the indicated era. As a rule, the subjects could not describe any of the specific features of coins or paper currency. This is an especially probative demonstration that the past-life memories were false: Such information would be familiar to anyone living in the indicated era, but it is not the sort of information that people living in later eras would be expected to acquire from other sources (e.g., high school and college classes). Another clear demonstration of falsity is that some subjects adopted identities from an era (the 1950s) in which the people's lives would be expected to overlap with their own. That the alternate-identity memories were gist-preserving constructions was demonstrated by the simple fact that the subjects did not provide exotic answers that were outside the bounds of their personal experience or education. The subjects were all Canadian undergraduates attending an English-speaking university in the nation's capital. Consistent with this background, the names that they chose for their alternate identities were usually common anglicized names; the countries that they chose were usually North American or Western European; and more than three quarters of the subjects chose an era during the 19th or 20th centuries. Indeed, only one subject chose an alternate identity from an ancient era, Julius Caesar. Although this seems to break the mold of gist-preserving constructions, it was discovered that this subject was studying Caesar's life in a history course. Also, the genders and races that the subjects chose for their alternate identities were invariably the same as their own.

For our purposes, the key findings of this experiment are that (a) a single, relatively brief hypnosis plus age-regression session induced a substantial proportion of the subjects to adopt alternate identities, and (b) the "memories" of those identities were consistent with gists with which the subjects would have been familiar, either from their own lives or by virtue of their education. In addition, the experiment produced findings that bear on the hypothesis that alternate identities are a sign of psychopathology (as in an MPD diagnosis). When the psychological test scores of subjects who did and did not adopt alternate identities were compared, there were no reliable differences between the groups. In total, Spanos et al. (1991) compared the mean scores of the two groups on five dimensions of psychopathology and four dimensions of fantasizing and found no differences on *any* of the dimensions. The lack of correlation between measures of psychopathology and whether hypnotically regressed subjects adopted an alternate identity was subsequently replicated by Ferracuti, Cannoni, De Carolis, Gonella, and Lazzari (2002). Finally, in light of the hypothesis that alternate identities are often a consequence of childhood sexual abuse, it would be expected that the subjects who adopted such identities would be more likely to describe being sexually abused, either in the alternate identity or in their current life. Spanos et al. did not report any such descriptions, however.

In a follow-up experiment, Spanos et al. (1991) investigated whether the alternate identities that are adopted by hypnotically regressed subjects can be experimentally controlled by information that they are provided just prior to hypnosis. As mentioned, the "memories" of the alternate identities in the first experiment were consistent with gists that would have been familiar to Canadian college students. In the next experiment, the treatment focused on shifting this baseline tendency. Each subject was randomly assigned to the treatment condition or the control condition, and just prior to hypnotic induction, the subjects in the former group were told that people who undergo past-life regression often discover a previous life in which they were of the opposite gender, of a different race, and lived in a remote land that is quite different from the one in which their current ancestors lived. The subjects in both groups were then administered the same hypnosis plus age-regression procedure as in the first experiment. The results showed that alternate identities could be experimentally controlled by prehypnotic information: Of the three items of prehypnotic information (opposite gender, different race, exotic locale), two thirds of the subjects in the treatment condition adopted an alternate identity with one or more of these characteristics, whereas only 27% of the control subjects did so.

To test the hypothesis that the commonly reported MPD-abuse correlation may be due to artifacts such as those described above, Spanos et al. (1991) conducted a third experiment that focused on whether false memories of sexual abuse, as well as false memories of past lives, could be induced during hypnotic regression. The same prehypnotic information procedure as in the second experiment was used. Also as before, each subject was randomly assigned to a treatment condition or a control condition, and just prior to hypnotic induction, the treatment subjects were told that research had established that people who lived in earlier eras experienced much more trauma than modern people, that people who lived in earlier eras were often abused during their childhoods by their parents and other adults, and that the treatment subjects would therefore be questioned in detail about the childhoods of any past lives that they discovered under hypnosis. Treatment and control subjects were then administered the same hypnosis plus age-regression procedure as in the first two experiments. For subjects who adopted an alternate identity, the interview now included specific questions about childhood abuse. Subjects who stated that their alternate identity had been abused as a child were asked to describe episodes of abuse in detail. As predicted, treatment subjects reported much higher levels of childhood abuse than did control subjects.

In a fourth and final experiment, Spanos et al. (1991) sought to gain further experimental control over alternate identities by focusing on subjects' levels of belief in the reality of the past lives that they discovered. This particular experiment was based upon a prior study by Baker (1982), who had explored past-life regression in subjects receiving instructions that supported reincarnation, subjects receiving neutral instructions, and subjects receiving instructions that challenged reincarnation. Baker found that subjects in the third condition were less likely than subjects in the other two conditions to adopt alternate identities during past-life regression. The aim of Spanos et al.'s experiment was somewhat different—explicitly, to determine whether such information would affect the perceived reality of alternate identities by subjects who *did* adopt such identities.

Subjects were randomly assigned to three experimental conditions, which provided different prehypnotic rationales for the alternate identities that are discovered during past-life regression: reincarnation, fantasy, or neutral. Subjects in the reincarnation group received instructions to the effect that scientific research has established the reality of reincarnation and that past-life regression has been successfully used to treat patients by enabling them to recover memories of traumas that occurred during their previous lives. In contrast, subjects in the fantasy group were told that the purpose of the experiment was to study the use of creative fantasy during hypnosis and that the past-life regression procedure would allow them to experience a fantasy of living a previous life. Subjects in the neutral condition were simply told that they would be hypnotized and given a suggestion that involved regression to a prior life. The subjects in all groups then received the hypnosis plus age-regression procedure. As in prior studies, subjects who adopted alternate identities were questioned while they were hypnotized. Following hypnosis, they responded to three psychological tests: a self-fading scale (which measured the extent to which they perceived their current self as fading into the background when they adopted the alternate identity), a subjective intensity scale (which measured the extent to which the memories of the alternate identity were vivid), and a past-life credibility scale (which measured the extent to which subjects thought their past-life experiences were real or fantasies).

As in the first experiment, subjects did not report identities that were outside the bounds of their personal experience or education, concentrating instead on identities from 19th- or 20th-century North America or Western Europe. The principal new finding was that subjects' perceptions of the reality of those identities could be controlled by prehypnotic instructions: The average level of credibility that was assigned to alternate identities was highest in subjects who received pro-reincarnation instructions, next highest in the subjects who received neutral instructions, and lowest in subjects who received pro-fantasy instructions.

On the whole, this series of experiments provides impressive support for the notion that a standard psychotherapeutic procedure—hypnosis—can induce normal subjects to create alternate identities, complete with extensive supporting collections of false memories. These subjects were also induced to create alternate identities that were accompanied by false memories of severe trauma, such as childhood sexual abuse. Both the alternate identities and the false memories that supported them were eminently consistent with opponent-processes predictions. When left to their own devices, the subjects chose identities from cultures and eras with which they were familiar. Although the details of the supporting memories were often false and although subjects were unable to "remember" details that they could not have acquired from sources other than prior lives, the supporting memories were congruent with familiar gists. Finally, there was consistent evidence that hypnotically induced alternate identities were amenable to experimental control. By varying the suggestive information that was supplied to subjects prior to hypnotic induction, Spanos et al. (1991) were able to control the gender, race, and nationality of alternate identities, to control the reported incidence of childhood trauma, and to control the perceived credibility of prior life experiences.

Implanting Distressing Childhood Memories

Although hypnotic-regression results demonstrate that whole identities can be implanted, identities that are buttressed by extensive false memories, including traumatic childhood memories, those findings may not generalize to adults' memories of their own autobiographies. Past-life memories are, after all, fantasies. Many subjects who adopt such identities under hypnosis subsequently state that they realize that the identities and memories were fantasies. Even subjects who state otherwise may nevertheless be aware that past-life identities are of dubious validity and may therefore also regard their memories as fantasies. To deal with this criticism, it is necessary to determine whether adults are susceptible to the implantation of false memories of childhood traumas that ostensibly occurred during their own lives. Now, however, the ethical obstacles become serious. Truly traumatic experiences, ones that routinely lead adults to seek professional help, cannot be considered, nor can experiences that could be expected to produce this result with some substantial probability. To avoid ethical obstacles but preserve as much similarity to trauma as possible, researchers are left with the more restricted research question of whether adults are susceptible to the implantation of childhood memories that are emotionally negative or mildly distressing. This does not instantly remove the obstacle because peremptory ethical questions can often be raised in connection with any negative experience, so that institutional review boards must answer such questions on a case-by-case basis. Those reviews have resulted in the approval of several studies, with the general rule being that memory implantation that focuses on mildly negative experiences that are part of most people's childhoods is acceptable, as long as subjects are informed that memories were implanted after they complete their participation.

The earliest evidence that false memories of whole childhood events of a negative sort could be implanted in adults were anecdotal reports about an undergraduate student named Chris (Loftus, 1993). Chris recollected that, as a young child, he had been lost in a shopping mall while on a trip with his parents and older brother, Jim. His lost-in-the-mall recollection was accompanied by several specific memories: Chris remembered that he had been quite frightened by the experience; he thought he might never see his family again; he was eventually rescued and returned to his family; and his mother told him that he should never wander off again. Chris also remembered that his rescuer was an elderly man, who was partially bald and wore glasses and a blue flannel shirt. He also rated his lost-in-the-mall memory as being very clear, giving it a score of 8 on a 10-point scale of clarity.

Actually, however, all of these memories were false. Chris's older brother, Jim, was a graduate student who had made up the lost-in-the-mall story and passed it along to Chris. Jim had simply told Chris that he had been lost in a shopping mall at the age of 5 and had been rescued by an elderly person. The detailed "memories" that supported this gist were not suggested by Jim. Those memories were recovered by Chris during the next few weeks: Like psychotherapy patients who engage in journaling, he was asked to keep a diary in which he recorded memories of this experience as they came back to him and also, for control purposes, to record memories of two actual childhood experiences that Jim had also transmitted to him. Interestingly, when Chris was asked to rate the clarity of his memories, the lost-in-the-mall experience received a higher rating than the true experiences. When his older brother at last informed him that the lost-in-the-mall experience was a hoax, Chris remarked, "Really? Well, no . . . 'cause I thought I was . . . I remember being lost and looking around for you guys. . . . I do remember that. . . . And then crying, and Mom coming up and saying, 'Where were you? Don't you ever do that again!' " (Loftus, 1997b).

Since this anecdote appeared, several experiments have been published in which researchers have attempted to implant false memories of negative or embarrassing childhood experiences in large samples of adults. We consider examples of the designs of those experiments and their findings below. Specifically, we examine two research projects, one by Hyman et al. (1995) that, along with an article by Loftus and Pickrell (1995), is the earliest example of this sort of work, and a later one by Porter, Yuille, and Lehman (1999). We then provide some general conclusions that can be drawn from these and similar experiments.

Hyman et al.'s Research

If the aim is to assess adults' susceptibility to the implantation of false memories of childhood experiences, one must first isolate experiences that the subjects in one's sample have not had. This can be done, to a fairly high level of probability, via the type of parental questionnaire that we described earlier in this chapter. The specific questionnaire used by Hyman et al. (1995) inquired about six categories of childhood events: birthday parties, deaths of pets, family vacations, getting lost, going to the hospital, and meeting famous people. The questionnaires were sent to the parents of students who were attending Hyman et al.'s university. When a questionnaire was returned, the corresponding student was contacted and asked to participate in the experiment. Based upon the responses of the students' parents, two to five true childhood experiences and two false experiences were selected. The same two false experiences—a positive one (an exciting birthday party at age 5 that included a visit by a clown and the serving of pizza) and a negative one (overnight hospitalization at age 5 for treatment of a high fever)—were used for all subjects.

The subjects who agreed to participate received two memory interviews, spaced 1 to 7 days apart. The implantation procedure was a combination of repeated recall and memory work. During the first interview, subjects were told that the aim of the experiment was to determine how well people can remember childhood experiences. Each subject was then asked to recall details of two to five true child-hood experiences and *one* of the two false experiences. Of course, they were told that all of the experiences were true and, for the sake of verisimilitude, that this information had been obtained from their parents. When subjects were unable to recall an event, whether true or false, they were asked to make further attempts and were provided with additional cues, such as the location of the event and the people who were involved. At the end of the first session, outside memory work was encouraged: Subjects were told that they should continue reflecting upon the target events and trying to remember as much as possible about them before the next session. During the second session, the interview procedure from the first session was repeated.

The results showed that subjects' memory for true childhood experiences was quite good: Roughly 84% of those experiences were recalled during the first inter-view. More important, there was also evidence of the implantation of false memo-ries. During the first session, none of the subjects falsely recalled either the birth-day party episode or the hospitalization episode. By the second session, however, following repeated recall attempts during the first session and subsequent memory work, 20% of the subjects recalled one of the false episodes. As in the story of Chris, their memories were accompanied by recollections of specific details: "I re-member from pictures a girl there that I might have known, her name was Molly" (Hyman et al., 1995, p. 187).

Hyman et al. (1995) attempted to replicate their findings in a second experiment that involved only negative childhood experiences. A new questionnaire was sent to parents that inquired about the same six experiences as before, plus four new ones: automobile travel, mischief with other children, weddings, and winning a con-test. Students were contacted about experimental participation as questionnaires were returned. The procedure was the same as in the first experiment, except for two key modifications: Only negative false experiences were used, and subjects participated in three sessions (spaced 1 week apart) rather than two. Three negative experiences were used: (a) attending a wedding reception, bumping into a table with a punch bowl, and spilling the punch on the bride's parents; (b) shopping with a parent in a grocery store when the sprinkler system was activated and the store had to be evac-uated; and (c) being left alone in a car by a parent, playing with the emergency brake, and releasing it, causing the car to roll into another object. In addition to these modifications, stronger emphasis was placed on engaging in memory work between the first and second sessions and between the second and third sessions. This emphasis, coupled with the additional interview, produced stronger evidence of implantation than did the first experiment.

As before, no subject recalled the false experience during the first session. Dur-ing the second session, 18% of the subjects recalled the false experience. By the third session, 26% of the subjects recalled the false experience. False memories were again accompanied by the recollection of specific supporting details: "The wedding was [of a relative of] my best friend in Spokane. . . . Her brother, older brother, was getting married, and it was over here . . . cause that's where her family is from and it was in the summer or spring because it was really hot outside and it was right on the water" (Hyman et al., 1995, p. 191). Moreover, the second experiment revealed a pattern of false memories that is highly consistent with opponent-processes predictions. Here, an obvious prediction is that subjects would be most likely to generate rich supporting memories of false experiences that referred to situations with which they were familiar and for which they would therefore possess strong gist memories. Consistent with this hypothesis, subjects who discussed personal knowledge during the first interview that was relevant to the false experience were more likely to remember the experience later and supply supporting details.

Porter et al.'s Research

As a historical matter, Porter et al.'s (1999) experiment was the first to demonstrate that multiple varieties of highly emotional, stressful, and potentially traumatic childhood events can be "recovered" as false memories. Like Hyman et al. (1995), Porter et al. mailed a questionnaire about childhood experiences to the parents of potential subjects. However, their instrument focused exclusively on six distressing experiences: getting lost, serious animal attacks, serious indoor accidents, serious injuries inflicted by other children, serious medical procedures, and serious outdoor accidents. Three events, a true one and two false ones, were selected for use with each subject. As in Hyman et al.'s research, the implantation procedure involved a combination of repeated recall and memory work. Subjects were interviewed three times about each experience in sessions spaced 1 week apart.

The interview for each experience was in the nature of a mock forensic interview, following the step-wise procedure of Yuille (1988), which was described in chapter 7. That is, the interview began with a free narrative of the experience, continued with a general-questions phase that elicited further details, and concluded with a specific-questions phase that went into greater detail about the experience. During the first interview, subjects were told that, according to their parents, *all* of the experiences had happened to them and that the purpose of the experiment was to determine how well different retrieval cues could help them to remember these childhood events. They were then interviewed about one true experience and one false experience. The interviewer provided four specific details about each experience, under the cover story that it would aid the subjects' memory. Subjects were told to work hard at recovering memories of each experience, to take all the time that was necessary, and to bear in mind that if they failed to recover memories of an experience, they probably were not working hard enough. At the end of the first session, subjects were urged to continue trying to remember information about the two experiences between the first and second sessions.

The procedure for the first session was repeated at the beginning of the second session. Next, the interviewer left the room, and the subjects opened a sealed envelope that had been provided by a research assistant. The envelope contained instructions asking subjects to *fabricate* memories of a false event. The cover story was that the purpose was to determine whether the interviewer could tell the difference between true and false memories, and the subjects were offered a monetary reward if they were able to deceive the interviewer. The interviewer returned 15 minutes later and interviewed subjects about this (second) false experience. At the end of the second session, subjects were urged to continue memory work between the second and third sessions. Finally, the procedure for the second session was repeated 1 week later, during the third session.

To analyze their data, Porter et al. (1999) used stringent criteria of false memory, ones that approximate the compelling false memories that patients sometimes develop during psychotherapy. More explicitly, the subjects were said to have exhibited a false memory for an untrue stressful event only if the memory met five criteria: (a) Subjects reported that they remembered the event when the interviewer suggested it; (b) subjects agreed with the four items of specific information about the event that were suggested by the interviewer; (c) subjects added further specific information beyond the information that was suggested by the interviewer; (d) subjects did not remember the event the *first* time that the interviewer suggested it to them; and (e) the subject and his parents confirmed that they had not discussed the event at any time during the course of the experiment.

Porter et al.'s (1999) results showed that, on the whole, their procedure of repeated recall, coupled with within- and between-session memory work, was quite effective at instilling false memories of stressful childhood events. More than half of their subjects (56%) experienced false memories for an untrue childhood event. Across the subject sample as a whole, false memories for each of the six stressful events in the parental questionnaire were displayed by some of the subjects. Moreover, the false memories appeared quite quickly: Of the subjects who were classified as exhibiting false memories of one or more of the stressful events, 35% were classified as exhibiting such memories during the first session, 50% during the second session, and the remaining 15% during the third session. Thus, intersession memory work was not necessary to produce false memories of stressful events; repeated recall and memory work during the initial session were sufficient for some subjects. Also, when subjects were asked to rate the vividness of their recovered childhood memories and their confidence in those memories on 1–7 scales, memories of the false events received quite high ratings. For instance, 75% of the false memories were given confidence ratings at or above the midpoint of the scale, and 20% were given "absolutely certain" (7) ratings.

Some Conclusions

The big question in recovered-memory cases such as those at the start of the chapter is whether it is possible to have false memories of complex childhood events, including highly emotional incidents. As things now stand, a number of experiments that have used the basic elements of Hyman et al.'s (1995) and Porter et al.'s (1999) research (i.e., a parental questionnaire that isolates false childhood experiences plus multiple interview sessions involving repeated recall and memory work) have succeeded in implanting false memories of complex childhood events, including stressful events (e.g., Pezdek et al., 1997; Porter, Birt, Yuille, & Lehman, 2000; Wade, Garry, Read, & Lindsay, 2002). On the basis of the accumulated data, some general conclusions can be drawn that bear informatively on the big question. A key obstacle to such research—knowing which childhood experiences subjects have *not* had—has been overcome with the simple device of parental questionnaires. Although one cannot be certain, on the basis of parents' responses, that a specific subject did not experience a specific childhood event, one can be confident to a high degree of probability. The accumulated data establish that it is indeed possible to implant false memories of distressing childhood experiences and even childhood experiences that would have involved substantial physical pain. Moreover, these false memories have been implanted using what would seem to be, on their face, some of the more innocuous of the therapeutic procedures that we mentioned earlier—repeated recall and memory work—as opposed to, say, hypnotic regression and memory recovery under the influence of psychotropic drugs.

With these "weaker" procedures, experimenters have convinced subjects that, as children, they experienced such complex and emotionally negative events as being lost in shopping malls, attending a wedding reception at which they spilled the contents of a punch bowl on the bride's parents, undergoing a serious medical procedure, and being seriously injured by other children. In all of these instances, subjects have remembered specific details to support the false experiences and expressed high confidence in the reality of their memories. In support of an implanted memory of overnight hospitalization, for instance, a subject remembered: "I woke up and mom and dad were wrapping me in one of my blankets. And I can picture the nurse's desk, or the nurse's office. And I can see the, like, the yellowish, like a fluorescent light there" (Loftus, 1997a, p. S79).

Another important finding that is highly pertinent to the aforementioned repetition properties of psychotherapy is that false memories for complex events tended to emerge across experimental sessions, rather than appearing suddenly, in finished form, during the first experimental session. Much like Beth Rutherford, who at first vigorously denied being sexually abused as a child, all of the subjects in some studies (e.g., Hyman et al., 1995) and the majority of subjects in other studies (e.g., Porter et al., 1999) failed to exhibit false-memory responses during the initial session. However, those responses emerged during follow-up sessions, after intersession memory work.

A final conclusion, which goes beyond existence proofs of implantation of complex childhood events to theoretical explanation, is that known variations in the implantability of different false experiences is consistent with opponent-processes predictions. If we assume, absent compelling evidence to the contrary, that the same theoretical rules apply here as with smaller-scale false memories, the expectation would be that complex events that instantiate childhood gists that are more familiar to adults would be more susceptible to implantation than complex events that instantiate less-familiar gists. Pezdek and associates have reported some informative data on this prediction.

In an initial experiment, Pezdek (1995) compared the susceptibility of college-student volunteers to implantation of two types of stressful childhood memories about events that allegedly occurred at age 5–6, a more-familiar and standard one (getting lost) and a less-familiar and more atypical one (receiving an enema). The interviewers who attempted to implant the memories were family members who knew the students when they were children (and were therefore highly credible sources of information about childhood experiences). The implantation procedure consisted of a paragraph that asserted the truth of a false event and provided a few details (e.g., the subject wandered away while the family was window shopping; the enema was administered because the subject had eaten large quantities of junk food), which was read aloud by subjects' relatives. Following this brief procedure, 15% of the subjects exhibited false memories of being lost as a child, but none exhibited false memories of receiving an enema. Of course, getting lost and receiving an enema differ on so many content dimensions that the difference in implantability could well be due to some of these uncontrolled factors.

A later experiment by Pezdek et al. (1997) provided more definitive evidence by factorially crossing the type of false memory that was being implanted with subjects' likely familiarity with the basic gist that was involved. The subjects in this experiment were high school students, some of whom were Catholic and some of whom were Jewish. The to-be-implanted false memories involved the high school students' participation in Catholic and Jewish religious rituals when they were 8 years old, during which an embarrassing event occurred (Catholic = returning to the wrong seat after communion; Jewish = dropping a loaf of bread during Shabbat). During Session 1, a description of the alleged childhood participation in each ritual was read to all subjects by the experimenter, along with descriptions of three true events, under the cover story that the information had been provided by their mothers. The subjects were asked to recall each event after its description was read, and they were subsequently asked to rate the clarity of their memories of each event on a 1–10 scale. After Session 1, they were instructed to continue memory work on the events until they returned for a second session, 1 week later. During the second session, subjects were tested to determine if they had any further memories of the five events. Subjects were identified as having false memories if they recalled additional details of the untrue events beyond those that were presented in the descriptions. The opponent-processes expectation, of course, is that Catholic students would be more likely to exhibit false memories of the embarrassing communion episode and that Jewish students would be more likely to exhibit false memories of the embarrassing Shabbat episode. In line with this prediction, 31% of Catholic students displayed false memories of the communion incident, with only 10% displaying false memories of the Shabbat incident. In contrast, 14% of the Jewish students displayed false memories of the Shabbat incident, with none displaying false memories of the communion incident.

Imagination Inflation

A shared feature of most of the psychotherapeutic practices that we discussed earlier is that *mental imagery* (phenomenology with sensory qualities, as in seeing with the mind's eye or hearing with the mind's ear) figures prominently. In particular, mental imagery is central in hypnosis, guided imagery, memory work, dream interpretation, family photographs, and giving free rein to the imagination. In all of these practices, patients' attempts to recover lost memories are accompanied by the construction of visual images of how things might have looked, auditory images of how things might have sounded, and so forth. Of course, it has long been understood that the use of mental imagery *at storage* has beneficial effects on true memory (e.g., Bower, 1970; Paivio, 1969, 1971). For example, if subjects are instructed to use visual imagery as they study verbal materials (e.g., word lists, sentences), this normally improves hit rates and levels of true recall. An illustration of the typical pattern of results can be found in an early experiment by Erdelyi, Finkelstein, Herrell, Miller, and Thomas (1976). A long list of words was studied once by control subjects, who were simply told that their memories would be tested later, and once by treatment subjects, who were also instructed to generate mental pictures of each word as they read it. Later, a recall test was administered. The treatment subjects recalled 53% of the words, whereas the control subjects recalled only 46%.

Because the use of mental imagery at storage is known to improve the accuracy of recognition and recall, it is not typically thought of as a false-memory manipulation. However, returning to psychotherapeutic practices, it might be that the use of mental imagery *at retrieval* stimulates false-memory reports (as well as true-memory reports, perhaps), particularly when retrieval occurs after long delays, as it does in psychotherapy, and verbatim memory is therefore poor. According to opponent-processes distinctions, the use of mental imagery at retrieval, which we will call *imagination* to distinguish it from the true imagery that accompanies storage, could inflate false reports by creating illusions of vividness, which impair the processes that people normally use to weed out false-but-gist-consistent information from memory reports. As we mentioned earlier in this chapter, people lean on vivid phenomenology to help distinguish false-but-gist-consistent memories from true ones, the operative principle being that memories of true events are far more likely to be accompanied by mental images of surface content because the events' surface forms were actually experienced. In the process of recollection rejection, for instance, we have seen that the vivid phenomenology that accompanies retrieval of verbatim traces can be used to make positive rejections of false-but-gist-consistent information, and we have also seen that experienced adult rememberers have a general expectation that true memories will be accompanied by vivid phenomenology.

It is now easy to see how imagination could, in principle, elevate false memories: If people usually rely on vivid phenomenology as an index of truth when retrieving information from memory, imagining how hypothetical events may have looked or sounded creates an illusion of veracity for false events, making them seem just as real as true events. This possibility has now been explored in several experiments via a procedure that has come to be known as the *imagination-inflation paradigm*. The earliest work on this paradigm was conducted by Garry, Manning, Loftus, and Sherman (1996) and by Goff and Roediger (1998). To provide readers with an understanding of the basic methodology and the standard pattern of findings, we first describe Goff and Roediger's work. We then summarize key results that have emerged in subsequent experiments by other investigators.

Because the problematic memories in the earlier recovered-memory cases revolved around participation in real-life actions, rather than reading words or sentences, the target materials in imagination-inflation research have usually been actions of some sort. In Goff and Roediger's research, those materials were a series of 96 common actions that almost everyone has performed, some of which involve objects (e.g., flipping a coin) and some of which do not (e.g., tugging on one's ear lobe). The experimental design involved three sessions. During Session 1, 72 of the actions were presented as the to-be-remembered target materials, with the actions being presented in three distinct ways: The subjects listened to the experimenter read statements describing 24 of the actions; the subjects were instructed to perform 24 of the actions; and the subjects were instructed to imagine themselves performing 24 of the actions. During Session 2, which took place 1 day later, the subjects

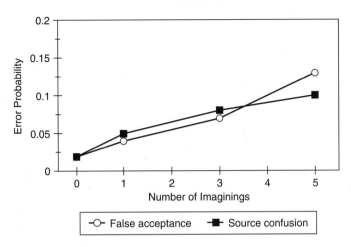

Figure 8-3. The effect of imagining the performance of actions on subjects' false memory for those actions. Based upon Goff and Roediger (1998).

imagined performing the same actions. Specifically, statements describing each of the 72 actions from Session 1 were read to subjects. Following each statement, subjects were instructed to imagine performing the target action and were given 12 seconds to generate mental images before the next statement was read. Crucially, statements describing 24 actions that had not been presented during Session 1 were also read, and subjects were instructed to imagine performing these new actions. To simulate the repetition feature of psychotherapy, the number of imaginings per action was varied. That is, the number of times that each action was described and imagined was zero, one, three, or five. During Session 3—2 weeks later—the subjects returned for memory tests. They received a recognition test that focused on the actions presented during Session 1. The test contained probes for the 72 action statements from Session 1 (targets), the 24 additional statements from Session 2 (imagined distractors), and 40 filler statements (control distractors). For each probe, subjects first made a recognition decision (i.e., whether that action had been presented during Session 1), and if that response was positive, they also made a source decision (Was the action read-only, read-plus-performance, or read-plus-imagination during Session 1?). The key results are displayed in Figure 8-3.

The crucial datum to extract from the graph is the lawful relation between false memory for prior actions and imagination, which is apparent at a glance. In Goff and Roediger's (1998) design, there were two distinct types of false-memory responses of interest: (a) false acceptance of actions that were not presented during the first session, and (b) correct recognition of actions that were presented during the first session coupled with incorrect memory for the way in which the action was presented (e.g., mistakenly remembering that an action was performed when, in fact, it was only read). The former are labeled false acceptance and the latter are labeled source confusion in Figure 8-3. Note that both types of false memory exhibit the same imagination-inflation effect: The more times that subjects imagined performing an action, the more likely they were to falsely remember it as having actually occurred, or if it occurred, the more likely they were to misremember the exact way in which it occurred. In light of these results, it appears that imagination, which is so central to psychotherapeutic remembering, has the ability, by itself, to cause subjects to remember events as having happened that did not and to cause subjects to misremember the details of how events happened.

A number of subsequent imagination-inflation experiments have been reported (e.g., Drivdahl & Zaragoza, 2001; Heaps & Nash, 1999; Paddock, Joseph, Chan, Terranova, Manning, & Loftus, 1998; Paddock, Noel, Terranova, Eber, Manning, & Loftus, 1999; Thomas, Bulevich, & Loftus, 2003; Thomas & Loftus, 2002) that go beyond replicating the basic effect and that elaborate the effect in various ways. For example, it is now known that imagination inflation occurs for more distant events of the sort that are central in psychotherapeutic remembering (e.g., childhood experiences), as well as for recent actions. As we write, there remains some theoretical controversy as to the exact reasons for imagination inflation. The two most prominently discussed explanations in the literature (see Thomas et al., 2003) rely on two theoretical distinctions that were introduced in chapter 3: reality monitoring and familiarity.

According to the first explanation, imagination inflation is a standard reality-monitoring error of the sort postulated by Johnson and Raye (1981). That is, subjects fail to realize that falsely remembered events were merely thought of, rather than directly experienced. According to the second explanation, imagination inflation is a standard familiarity illusion of the type described by Jacoby (e.g., Jacoby & Dallas, 1981; Jacoby, Kelley, Brown, & Jasechko, 1989) and others (e.g., Whittlesea, 2002; Whittlesea & Leboe, 2003). That is, imagining a certain action makes it seem more familiar when it is subsequently proposed as a recognition probe because the probe is more easily processed, leading subjects to make a memory-attribution error, wherein they wrongly ascribe the probe's familiarity to actual prior occurrence rather than to mere imagination. Although it might seem sufficient, for purposes of evaluating the potential of psychotherapeutic practices to produce false memories, simply to know that the imagination-inflation effect is real and to establish its boundary conditions via experimental manipulations, determining whether one, both, or neither of these theoretical explanations is correct could be of immense help in making best-practice recommendations about how to minimize false memories during psychotherapy (e.g., Brainerd et al., 2000).

Recently, Thomas et al. (2003) pitted the reality-monitoring and familiarity explanations against each other in two experiments and obtained data that favored reality monitoring. A key difference between the two explanations, they reasoned, is the ostensible role that is played by vivid surface information. According to reality monitoring, as we know from chapter 3, memory representations that contain vivid surface information are particularly important in distinguishing true memories of actual events from memories of mere thoughts because surface information accompanies actual events but not thoughts. According to the familiarity explanation, on the other hand, surface information does not have special status. Increased feelings of familiarity can result from greater ease of processing *any* of the features of

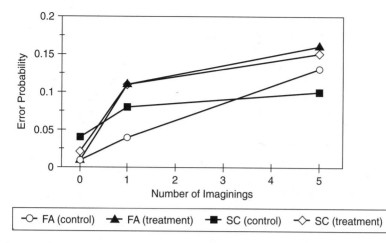

Figure 8-4. The effect of different types of imaginings of the performance of actions on subjects' false memory for those actions. *FA (control)* = false acceptance of unpresented actions by subjects who received standard imagination instructions; *FA (treatment)* = false acceptance of unpresented actions by subjects who received elaborated imagination instructions; *SC (control)* = source confusion by subjects who received standard imagination instructions; and *SC (treatment)* = source confusion by subjects who received elaborated imagination instructions. Based upon Thomas, Bulevich, and Loftus (2003).

a probe, and more explicitly, it can result from greater ease of processing its meaning content just as well as from greater ease of processing its surface content. Therefore, in Thomas et al.'s experiments, the focus was on imagination activities that varied in the extent to which subjects were specifically instructed to generate perceptual phenomenologies as part of their imaginings.

The procedure with respect to such details as target materials, presentation methods, imagination instructions, number and spacing of sessions, and memory tests resembled those of Goff and Roediger (1998). The principal new feature of the design was that subjects were randomly assigned to two conditions during the second session: a control condition in which subjects received standard imagination instructions and a treatment condition in which the standard instructions were enriched by encouraging more elaborate imaginings, which included perceptual information. The prediction of interest, which follows from the reality-monitoring explanation but not from the familiarity explanation, is that imagination inflation ought to be more marked in the treatment condition. The results, which are exhibited in Figure 8-4, are consistent with this prediction. First, note that the usual imagination-inflation effect was present in that both false acceptance of previously unpresented actions and source confusions of presented actions increased as a function of the number of imaginings during Session 2. Further, in line with the reality-monitoring explanation, the increase in both types of errors was more pronounced if subjects received instructions to include perceptual information in their imaginings.

Synopsis

During the mid-1990s, professional organizations such as the American Medical Association and the American Psychological Association began issuing statements that revolved around the potential unreliability of therapeutically stimulated recovery of memories of childhood trauma, particularly childhood sexual abuse. These statements were prompted by high-profile legal cases (e.g., *Burgus v. Braun*, 1993; *Hamanne v. Humenansky*, 1995) in which psychiatrists, clinical psychologists, and other counselors were sued for implanting false memories of childhood sexual abuse, and the plaintiffs received multimillion-dollar damage awards. In addition to sexual abuse, the patients' recovered memories encompassed bizarre related activities, such as Satanic worship and cannibalism, for which no physical evidence existed. The statements of professional organizations cautioned practitioners that some of their presuppositions about recovered memories had not been scientifically substantiated, that others were known to be false, and that some popular therapeutic procedures might be capable of inducing patients to "remember" events, even frightening and painful ones, in which they had never participated. In line with such cautions, particular patients, such as Beth Rutherford, had recovered memories of childhood abuse whose details were later shown to be false on the basis of unimpeachable physical evidence. Other patients, such as Elizabeth Carlson, had recovered memories of gruesome traumas that they later recanted for other reasons. Despite the reservations of professional societies and the scientific community, instances of therapeutically induced recovery of memories of childhood trauma continue to surface in litigation, though the plaintiffs in these more recent cases usually regard the memories as true. Some of these cases (e.g., Ms. duM and Mr. Q) are of the classic variety, wherein patients recover memories of being abused by parents or other relatives, while other cases (e.g., Watson and Frei) are of a newer variety, wherein patients recover memories of being abused by priests. The common element in both instances is that the theory of repression and the subsequent recovery of repressed childhood memories are proffered as legal grounds for tolling the statutes of limitations that apply to the alleged crimes.

Psychotherapy, like criminal investigation, presents a confluence of variables that, in light of laboratory research, have the potential to elevate patients' tendency to make erroneous reports about the events of their lives. Those variables fall into two broad categories—namely, general attributes of the psychotherapeutic context that hold more or less universally and specific therapeutic practices whose use varies considerably from patient to patient and from therapist to therapist. Variables in the first category include the facts that therapeutic remembering is heavily slanted toward the processing of gist memories; weak subjective criteria of memorability are standard; there are long delays between the storage of memories and their retrieval during psychotherapy; error-prone reconstructive retrieval dominates memory recovery during psychotherapy; therapists generate hypotheses about the nature and causes of patients' problems, which can stimulate interactions that are aimed at confirming those hypotheses rather than at neutral fact gathering; the reasons that patients seek therapy, together with the exploratory attitude that they are encouraged to adopt during therapy, make them especially vulnerable to spontaneous and implanted false memories; and multiple therapy sessions provide repeated opportunities for gist repetition and verbatim repetition of misinformation, without compensating opportunities for verbatim repetition of original experiences. Variables in the second category include detaching patients from reality by hypnotizing them, by teaching them how to hypnotize themselves, and by other forms of deep relaxation; guided-imagery sessions; requiring memory work (e.g., journaling) during and outside of therapy sessions; interpreting behavioral symptoms as being reliable signs of the causes of patients' problems; interpreting patients' dreams as being true memories or as providing important information about the nature or causes of their problems; hypnotically regressing patients back to earlier eras in their lives, to the womb, or to supposed previous lives; stimulating memory recovery by inspecting photographs of patients' relatives; and stimulating memory recovery by instructing patients to give free rein to their imaginations during and outside of therapy sessions.

Although the courts ruled in some early cases that patients' recollections of horrific childhood traumas were indeed false memories that had been induced by psychotherapy, such rulings fall short of being clear and convincing scientific demonstrations that psychotherapy can produce extensive false memories in adults of childhood traumas, such as repeated sexual abuse. Further, neither the fact that some details of the patients' recovered memories proved to be false (e.g., Beth Rutherford's recollections of pregnancy) nor the fact that some patients have recanted their recovered memories constitute convincing scientific demonstrations. Also, experienced practitioners with many years of clinical work passionately believe that psychotherapy is incapable of instilling interconnected false memories of extensive life experiences. The types of experiments that would be required to resolve definitively this big question would involve designs in which (a) samples of ostensibly normal adults are randomly assigned to treatment and control conditions; (b) treatment subjects are exposed to simulated therapeutic procedures that are suspected of inducing false memories of prior traumatic experiences; (c) control subjects are exposed to equivalent amounts of procedures that do not focus on memory recovery; (d) the procedures in the treatment group focus on interconnected false memories of extensive childhood experiences (rather than single events); and (e) the childhood experiences are of a sufficiently traumatic nature that they would be expected to cause lasting problems, with experiences of repeated sexual abuse by relatives or Satanic practices being preferable. For obvious ethical reasons, it is impossible to conduct experiments that satisfy all five criteria. However, it is possible to conduct experiments that satisfy the first four criteria and that, with respect to the fifth criterion, focus on life experiences that are at least moderately distressing (rather than deeply traumatic).

Several experiments of this sort have been conducted, and as a group, they have yielded evidence that simulated therapeutic treatments can indeed produce interconnected false memories of extensive childhood experiences. Early experiments involving one such treatment—hypnotic age regression—generated particularly clear findings. In those experiments, subjects adopted alternate identities from previous lives and created a range of false autobiographical memories to support those identities. Importantly, manipulations that were designed to prompt recovery of false memories of childhood abuse during hypnotic regression, including sexual abuse,

PART IV

FUTURE DIRECTIONS

9

Some Growing Tips

We are nearing the end of our journey through the science of false memory. For us, beginning the last chapter of this volume generates mixed emotions: exhilaration at entering the final stage of a project that was long in the planning and longer in the execution; remorse at the impending loss of a constant companion that enforced intellectual discipline and stimulated careful thought about the state of false-memory research; and uncertainty about which projects are the best ones to fill the void that will be left by the completion of this one. The work of producing this volume—alternating cycles of close reading of the research literature followed by reflection, discussion, and writing—has consumed the better part of 2 years. Now, at the close, one important task remains: to decide how best to end.

The customary coda would be a summary chapter that reprises core ideas and findings from previous chapters, and in so doing, effects at least an illusion of integration of the material in those chapters. Although such a traditional closing has much to recommend it, from the outset it seemed to us that this would not be the appropriate way to end an exegesis of false-memory research. Inevitably, such retrospection, if well reasoned and tightly argued, would foster the impression of a mature discipline with well-drawn lines of investigation, wide consensus with respect to key experimental findings, and well-tested theoretical explanations. That would be an inaccurate impression to leave in connection with a discipline that is as new as the science of false memory. It is quite apparent from the assortment of fields that it has been necessary to cover—from mainstream experimental psychology to child development to criminology to psychotherapy—that false-memory research is not yet a settled discipline with firm boundaries. On the contrary, it is very much a work in progress, one that is apt to transform itself in major respects in the next few years, one that must transform itself if it is to fulfill the promise of what has been accomplished to date. Indeed, an underlying agenda of this book has been to stimulate such evolution through various devices—for instance, by encouraging experimentation to shift in the direction of prediction-driven research that tests theoretical principles and by focusing attention on the deep parallels among such disparate fields as psychotherapy, criminal interrogation, and the laboratory study of memory. For these reasons, the best way to close this exegesis, we believe, is by exemplifying the continuing evolution of false-memory research through an examination of some emerging areas of investigation that, a decade from now, may prove to be as well mined as, say, the study of childhood memory suggestion. To permit ourselves the luxury of ending in this way, we have laced the foregoing pages with running summaries and integrative commentaries, most particularly in the synopsis sections with which the individual chapters conclude.

This leaves us with the question of precisely which topics to dress in the mantle of "emerging research areas from which important new knowledge is likely to emanate during the next few years." Our survey of the literature presented many tempting possibilities, but we decided to be conservative in our choices by selecting areas (a) whose intrinsic scientific gravity seems self-evident, (b) in which critical masses of research have already been published, and (c) to which increasing numbers of investigators are turning their attention. Eventually, there were three areas that seemed to meet these criteria: mathematical models of false memory, aging and false memory, and the cognitive neuroscience of false memory. As we shall see, research in each of these areas is designed to contribute some fundamental pieces of knowledge that are currently missing from our understanding of false memory. Moreover, enough work has accumulated in each area that the near-term chances of success look quite promising, more than promising enough to warrant inclusion in the present chapter.

Mathematical Models of False Memory

In chapter 3, we considered some of the hallmarks of good scientific theories, emphasizing the role of prediction, more especially counterintuitive prediction, in adjudicating among competing theories. It will be remembered that because theories are models of reality, rather than reality itself, vigorous research literatures are inclined to beget multiple explanations of the same core phenomena, a confusing if predictable circumstance. As a rule, competing theories will not be readily distinguishable on a priori logical grounds (e.g., parsimony) or on the basis of aesthetic criteria (e.g., prima facie plausibility), which means that new data must eventually decide among them. This is where prediction enters the picture. Other things being equal, theories that do a better job of forecasting new findings are superior to those that do a poorer job. All predictions are not equal, however. Those that violate commonsense expectations are prized above more prosaic ones inasmuch as they demonstrate that theories are leading us in directions that would not otherwise have been explored. Despite the allure of counterintuitive predictions, only those that can be verified experimentally count on the credit side of the ledger.

We have encountered various predictions of this sort that fall out of opponent-processes theory. A few familiar examples: False-memory reports can be more stable over time than true-memory reports, and they can increase over time, even as true-memory reports are declining; measured levels of true and false memory are often remarkably independent of each other, making it seem as though memory is of two minds about experience; presenting target material and memory tests in perceptually identical formats sometimes reduces false-memory reports, relative to presenting them in perceptually distinctive formats; repeated encounters with some aspects of experience elevate false-memory reports and decrease true-memory reports, but repeated encounters with other aspects have the reverse effect; instructing subjects to pay close attention to the meaning of experience, something that has long been known to enhance true memory, also increases false memory; allowing subjects more time to respond to a memory test decreases false reports on some types of tests but increases them on others; when adults are questioned about crimes, suggestive retrieval cues can cause them to falsely identify suspects, falsely report details of crimes, and even falsely confess to crimes; when children are questioned about crimes, suggestive retrieval cues can cause them to falsely remember being victims of crimes; and suggestive psychotherapeutic practices can cause patients to falsely remember participating in appalling experiences, such as childhood sexual abuse, cannibalism, and Satanic rituals. In these and other instances, the relevant predictions were derived by analyzing the basic assumptions of the opponent-processes approach with reference to some experimental paradigm or real-life situation (e.g., a recall experiment in which memory tests were administered after various delays, an eyewitness identification in which photo spreads were administered after various delays) and forecasting the most likely patterns of results (e.g., that semantic intrusions and false identifications will increase with delay). Although confirmed predictions were interpreted as providing support for opponent-processes assumptions, there are two unsatisfactory aspects of such findings and, indeed, of the results of all of the research that we have examined thus far: (a) Predicted results were only qualitative; and (b) the memory processes that are supposedly responsible for the results were never directly measured.

Concerning item a, by a *qualitative* prediction or result, we mean one that is formulated in purely categorical language and does not specify the amounts of whatever form of performance is being measured. For instance, the notions that semantic false-alarm rates will vary as inverted-U functions of the number of verbatim repetitions of targets (Figure 4-4), the presentation duration of targets (Figure 4-5), and the amount of retrieval time that is allowed on recognition tests (Figure 4-16) are all qualitative. In each case, we are merely told that initial increases in an independent variable (repetition, duration, retrieval time) will elevate false alarms, whereas subsequent increases in that same variable will suppress them. We are not told such crucial things as how much of an increase or decrease in the false-alarm rate will be produced by a unit increase in the independent variable, or how many units of the independent variable must accumulate before the inflection point of an inverted U is reached. In science, qualitative predictions and results are only first approximations to the actual numerical relations that exist between independent and dependent variables. We seek to evolve away from qualitative results toward quantitative ones, to replace predictions of the form "subjects will have higher average scores in Condition A than Condition B" with predictions of the form "the difference between subjects' average scores in Conditions A and B will be X." As long as empirical confirmation for a theory, such as the opponent-processes approach to false memory, is confined to qualitative patterns, the level of confirmation is inherently weak, and ways must be found to move toward quantitative predictions.

With respect to the other limitation that we mentioned, none of the experiments that have been considered in prior chapters was designed to measure the opponent processes that ostensibly control false memory, and hence, the results provide no direct information about those processes. All of these lines of evidence provide, at most, weak and indirect information about the controlling memory processes. The *measured* false-memory variables in all studies consisted of such things as false alarms on recognition tests, intrusions on recall tests, or concomitant features of these two types of responses (e.g., the speed with which false alarms occur, the positions of intrusions within recall protocols). Such variables do not supply any *specific* data on the levels of verbatim and gist memory that were present in the various experimental conditions. Instead, the strongest measurement assumption that researchers would be willing to entertain as a working hypothesis is what theorists of psychological measurement (e.g., Dunn & Kirsner, 1988; Howe, Rabinowitz, & Grant, 1993) call the *monotonicity conjecture*—namely, that levels of false reporting are ordinally related to underlying levels of the controlling memory mechanisms. In the case of opponent processes, an ordinal relation simply means that (a) the level of false reporting never increases when the level of verbatim memory increases (it must either decrease or remain constant); and (b) the level of false reporting never decreases when the level of gist memory increases (it must either increase or remain constant). Of course, this "more false reporting means more gist memory" or "more false reporting means less verbatim memory" conjecture is flimsy from the perspective of understanding the nature of these processes. Worse, the fact that there are two processes rather than one means that neither statement is valid in itself: If some manipulation causes false reporting to increase, changes in either or both processes could be responsible, so that the actual conjecture must be "more false reporting means more gist memory, or less verbatim memory, or both." Thus, the two memory mechanisms are completely confounded under even the weak monotonicity conjecture.

This confounding leads to still further problems, which revolve around the interpretation of null results—circumstances in which a manipulation is predicted to affect false reporting but experimentation fails to confirm that prediction. Returning to one of the above examples, according to opponent-processes distinctions, false-alarm rates for meaning-preserving distractors should vary as an inverted-U function of retrieval time on recognition tests. Although this prediction has been confirmed for some types of materials (e.g., Gronlund & Ratcliff, 1989), it has been disconfirmed for others (e.g., Rotello & Heit, 1999). What do the latter findings mean? Normally, they would count against the theoretical distinctions that generated the prediction. However, because verbatim memory and gist memory are both more strongly expressed as retrieval time increases, another legitimate interpretation is that the strengthening of verbatim memory, which suppresses false alarms, is masked by the continued strengthening of gist memory. Increases in verbatim memory never sufficiently predominate over increases in gist memory to cause the net false-alarm rate to decrease. Under this alternative interpretation, the theoretical analysis that generated the inverted-U relation is correct in all of its particulars, but the influence of the process that produces inflection points in retrieval-time/false-alarm curves is being masked by that of the process that causes false-alarm rates to increase. More generally, because the processes that are presumed to control false reporting work in opposition to each other, findings that depend primarily upon variations in the expression of one of those processes (e.g., inflection points in U-shaped functions, decreases in false reporting as a consequence of verbatim repetition) may be masked by correlated variations in the other process. Manipulations that (as predicted) enhance verbatim memory may fail to reduce false reporting because they also enhance gist memory, and manipulations that (as predicted) enhance gist memory may nevertheless fail to increase false reporting because they also enhance verbatim memory. Even when a manipulation is expected to have disproportionate effects on one process *and it does* (as would be expected for manipulations such as verbatim repetition, presentation duration, and retrieval time; see chapter 4), this does not guarantee that predicted increases or decreases in false reporting will be confirmed unless the response scales for the two processes are reasonably similar.[1] Obviously, this is an unsatisfactory state of affairs.

It turns out that the two problems that we have been discussing—qualitative predictions and the absence of direct measurement of controlling memory processes—are connected. In fact, the second is responsible for the first, so that overcoming the second also overcomes the first. To deal with the second problem, experimentation cannot be confined to weak and confounded measurement procedures. Instead, stronger procedures must be implemented that allow researchers to separate oppo-

---

1. In psychological measurement, a *response scale* is a mathematical transformation that maps *true* levels of theoretical variables (opponent memory processes, in this instance) with their *expressed* levels on experimental tasks. Readers can readily convince themselves of the importance of this distinction by generating numerical examples that involve different levels of underlying memory processes and different response scales that convert those levels to the amounts of those processes that are expressed on memory tests. For example, consider a simple verbatim-repetition experiment in which some subjects respond to a recognition test after a study list has been presented once, while other subjects respond to the same test after the study list has been presented twice. Suppose, in accordance with opponent-processes analysis, that verbatim repetition increases the underlying strength of verbatim memory more than the underlying strength of gist memory—say, increasing verbatim strength from .05 to .25 and gist strength from .2 to .3—leading to the prediction that repetition will suppress semantic false alarms. Suppose, further, that the response scale that maps underlying levels of memory strength with expressed levels on the recognition test is a simple ratio transformation of the form $Y = bX$, where Y is the expressed level; X is the true level; and b is a constant of proportionality. It is easy to see that the prediction of lower false-alarm rates following one presentation than following two will be confirmed if the constant of proportionality is equal for verbatim and gist memory or is larger for verbatim memory. However, the prediction can fail if the constant of proportionality is greater for gist memory. For instance, suppose that $b = .1$ for verbatim memory and .3 for gist memory. If so, then even though the strength of verbatim memory increases more than the strength of gist memory, the *expressed* level of gist memory will increase more than the *expressed* level of verbatim memory. Hence, the prediction would not be confirmed.

nent processes, quantify the respective amounts of the processes that are present in experimental conditions, and test predictions about how manipulations affect the *processes themselves* (rather than the raw levels of false reporting). The accomplishment of these objectives requires the development of mathematical models of false-memory paradigms. There is a growing realization that these objectives are in need of attention because, of late, mathematical models of false memory have begun to appear in the false-memory literature. There are currently two lines of model-driven research, one that focuses on a family of techniques that are known as conjoint-memory models and the other that focuses on alternative techniques that are extensions of the process-dissociation model in chapter 3. In the remainder of this section, we sketch both of these technologies, along with some of the major patterns of findings that they have produced. We begin, however, with some brief background on mathematical modeling.

What Is a Mathematical Model of Memory?

First, it is important to address a common misunderstanding about mathematical models by saying what they are *not*. Mathematical models are not free-floating architectures that provide high-altitude conceptions of memory that are divorced from actual experiments and findings. On the contrary, in mathematical modeling, the emphasis is on "modeling," not on "mathematical." First and foremost, a mathematical model of memory must be a model of *something*, and that something consists of the data that are generated by a well-defined task. It is simply impossible to have a mathematical model without first having experimental data from a specific task, which means that "mathematical model of memory" is something of a misnomer. It would be more accurate, though far too long-winded, to say that a model is (a) a set of mathematical expressions of some sort (e.g., polynomials, differential equations) that is used to (b) supply a numerical description of some index of memory performance (e.g., the probability of intrusions on a recall test, the probability of false alarms on a recognition test) by (c) assuming that the expressions' variables (parameters) measure different memory processes (e.g., direct access of verbatim traces, reconstructive processing of gist memories). All of this can be better grasped by considering a familiar example from algebra: finding the roots of polynomials.

One of the simplest types of problems that all of us confronted in our first middle or high school course in algebra involved solving simple equations to find specific numerical values of variable quantities. For instance, suppose that one is asked to do this for the expression $X - Y + Z = 10$. This equation contains a certain "known" (the number 10) and certain "unknowns" (X, Y, and Z), and the objective is to use the former to find the values of the latter. One would immediately say that this is impossible because the equation contains more unknowns than knowns, and therefore, there is an infinite number of possible values of X, Y, and Z that would be consistent with the equation. However, suppose we are provided with the additional expressions $2X - 3Y - Z = 4$ and $X + 2Y + 4Z = 16$. Now, the system is easily solved by adding, subtracting, and balancing the three expressions. For example, adding the first two equations yields the derived equation $3X - 4Y = 10$, and multiplying the second equation by 4 and adding it to the third yields the derived equation $9X - 10Y = 32$. Multiplying the first derived equation by 3 and subtracting it from the second derived equation yields $Y = -5$. Inserting the value of Y into either derived equation yields $X = -2$. Inserting the values of X and Y into the original equations yields $Z = 7$.

The parallel between this family of elementary algebraic problems and mathematical modeling is quite exact. On the one hand, like 4, 10, and 16 in the three polynomials, memory researchers have some known numerical values in hand—specifically, experimentally determined levels of performance on memory tests, such as the probability of false alarms to meaning-preserving distractors on recognition tests. These experimentally determined quantities are assumed to be the result of certain memory processes, such as the retrieval of surface and semantic representations of experience. Values of the latter are unknown because memory processes are assumed to combine to produce performance on individual tests. However, like unknown quantities in polynomials, the values of memory processes can be estimated by expressing empirically determined values as mathematical functions in which the memory processes appear as variable quantities. In fact, we have already encountered a historically important example of such an expression in chapter 3—Mandler's (1980) equation specifying how item-specific recollection of target presentations and global-familiarity evaluation of target probes combine to produce hits. Recall that in contrast to earlier dual-process theorists (e.g., Atkinson & Juola, 1974), Mandler posited that recollection and familiarity are executed in parallel, so that hit rates are additive functions of the respective probabilities of the two retrieval processes. This principle was expressed in the equation $p(H) = F + R - RF$, where $p(H)$ is the probability of a hit, F is the probability that a hit is due to familiarity evaluation, and R is the probability that a hit is due to recollection. Although unknown values of the retrieval processes have now been expressed as algebraic functions of an experimentally determined quantity, those values cannot be estimated because Mandler's equation poses the same difficulty as the polynomial $X - Y + Z = 10$. There are more unknowns (F and R) than there are knowns $p(H)$, so that multiple expressions involving these same unknowns are needed. Those expressions were provided by Jacoby (1991), as also seen in chapter 3.

Because a mathematical model must be a model of something, the only way to secure further expressions in which F and R appear as variables is to select experimentally determined quantities other than $p(H)$. Jacoby (1991) selected two quantities that are provided by a new recognition test, which he called *process dissociation*. It will be recalled from chapter 3 that in this procedure, subjects first study a list of words on which the individual targets are presented in two different formats. For example, a standard procedure is to present a list of familiar concrete nouns on a computer screen, with subjects being required to pronounce each word before the next word is presented. The formatting manipulation involves presenting half of the list in the usual way as regular printed words (e.g., *snake, tree, cloud*) and presenting the other half as printed anagrams, which subjects must unscramble before they can pronounce them (e.g., *koob, parep, ybab*). Following list presentation, a normal recognition test is administered in which half of the probes are targets that are presented as regular printed words (e.g., *snake, book*), and half of the probes are distractor words that are unrelated to any of the targets (i.e., this is not a false-memory test because semantically related distractors are omitted). Subjects are assigned to two groups, which respond to this test list under different sets of instructions, which generates two values of the quantity $p(H)$. Those who are assigned to an *inclusion* group are instructed to accept all targets that appear on the test list and to reject all distractors, but those who are assigned to an *exclusion* condition are instructed to accept only targets that were printed as anagrams and to reject both distractors and regularly presented targets.

It is the two acceptance probabilities for the latter targets that are of interest, which are denoted $p_I(H)$ and $p_E(FA)$, respectively. The inclusion condition is just a standard recognition condition for regularly presented words, so Mandler's original expression still applies, although Jacoby rearranged it to yield $p_I(H) = R + F(1 - R)$. In the exclusion condition, however, (false) acceptance of regularly presented words must be familiarity-based because those words were not presented as anagrams. That is, if subjects can recollect that, say, *snake* was not presented as an anagram, they will reject it, but if they have no specific recollection of how *snake* was presented and if familiarity evaluation produces a high value, they will accept it. Therefore, Jacoby reasoned, the expression for the exclusion condition is $p_E(FA) = (1 - R)F$. This system of two equations contains two experimentally determined quantities and two unknown quantities, and it can be solved to yield the following values of recollection and familiarity: $R = p_I(H) - p_E(FA)$ and $F = p_E(FA) \div [1 - p_I(H) + p_E(FA)]$.

Conjoint-Memory Models

The general features of model development that we have just sketched have also figured in the development of mathematical models of false memory. The first group of false-memory models was developed in our laboratories, beginning with some articles that appeared in 1998 (Brainerd & Reyna, 1998a; Brainerd et al., 1998; Reyna & Brainerd, 1998). Those models were designed to be applicable to all of the false-memory paradigms that were reviewed in chapter 2. Although those paradigms are numerous, they rely on just two behavioral measures of false memory: semantic false alarms on recognition tests and semantic intrusions on recall tests. Consequently, two families of models were developed, one for false recognition and one for false recall. Below, we first consider the recognition models, then the recall models, and conclude with a summary of the recent findings about false memory that those models have produced.

Conjoint Recognition

Conjoint-recognition models provide measurements of the opponent memory processes that are ostensibly responsible for semantic false alarms. These models also provide measurements of the response bias (nonmemorial strategies, such as guessing) that infects any recognition test. For the sake of concreteness, consider (a) a standard Underwood (1965) spontaneous false-memory experiment in which subjects study words and respond to recognition tests composed of targets (e.g., *poo-*

dle), semantically related distractors (e.g., *collie*), and unrelated distractors (e.g., *for-est*), and consider (b) a standard Loftus (1975) implanted false-memory experiment in which subjects are exposed to a simulated crime (e.g., a video of a theft), followed by an interview that contains misinformation (e.g., the suggestion that the robber was carrying a knife rather than a screwdriver), followed by a recognition test composed of target probes (e.g., the robber was wearing a mask), distractors that tap misinformation (e.g., the robber was carrying a knife), and other distractors (e.g., the cash register was brown). Conjoint-recognition models assume that in both of these familiar situations, false-memory probes can provoke one of three types of memory retrieval, which will be familiar from earlier chapters. First, subjects may access verbatim traces of the corresponding targets (e.g., *poodle*), which supports the rejection decisions to which we have referred as recollection rejection (No, I didn't read *collie*, because I distinctly remember reading *poodle*). Second, subjects may also access gist traces of the corresponding meaning content of targets (e.g., "dog," "pet"). If they do not access verbatim traces of the corresponding targets, these gist traces support false alarms. Actually, research (Lampinen, Neuschatz, & Payne, 1998; Brainerd et al., 2001; see also chapter 3) suggests that the retrieval of gist memories can provoke two different types of false alarms, which are referred to as *similarity judgment* and *phantom recollection*. Similarity judgments resemble Mandler's (1980) notion of familiarity in that a distractor is falsely accepted because its meaning content seems familiar (I'm sure I studied the word for a pet), though nothing is recollected about the presentation of specific items. Phantom recollection is a powerful form of false alarm in which gist memories provoke illusory vivid experiences of a distractor's prior presentation (e.g., visual images of the "presentation" of *collie* flash in the mind's eye, even though it did not appear on the study list).[2] As we show below, these two types of false alarms can be distinguished with some simple variations in recognition-test instructions. Third, false-memory probes might not access either verbatim memories of corresponding targets or gist memories that are strong enough to support false recognition, so that subjects must resort to various irrelevant strategies to generate responses (e.g., guessing, response perseveration, response alternation), a procedure that is usually called *response bias.*

2. It is perhaps not surprising that false alarms in Loftus-type experiments would sometimes be phantom recollections rather than similarity judgments. After all, false-memory probes are physically presented in such experiments (as suggestions during the misinformation phase), and subjects may therefore retrieve verbatim traces of those presentations and use those experiences as a basis for accepting the probes. Such experiences are not phantom recollections, strictly speaking, but are true recollections that are being misinterpreted by subjects. However, it would be surprising if false alarms were sometimes phantom recollections in Underwood-type experiments because the false-alarm memory probes appear for the first time on recognition tests. Consistent with this notion, similarity judgments, rather than phantom recollection, are the rule in most experiments of this sort (e.g., Dewhurst, 2001; Reyna & Lloyd, 1997). However, phantom recollection usually occurs at detectable levels (e.g., Lampinen et al., 2001), and in certain Underwood-type experiments, most semantic false alarms are due to phantom recollection (e.g., Brainerd et al., 2001). It has been proposed that in such experiments, high levels of phantom recollection will occur when retrieved gist memories are very strong and when false-memory probes are especially good instances of the relevant meanings (Brainerd & Reyna, 1998b). However, research on the conditions that elevate levels of phantom recollection is thin.

With these distinctions in mind, the probability of accepting a false-memory probe is expressed as

$$p_{fm} = (1 - R_{fm})P_{fm} + (1 - R_{fm})(1 - P_{fm})S_{fm} \\ + (1 - R_{fm})(1 - P_{fm})(1 - S_{fm})\beta \tag{9-1}$$

In Equation 9-1, p_{fm} is the experimentally determined probability of accepting false-memory probes; R_{fm} is the probability that such probes produce recollection rejection by accessing their corresponding verbatim traces; S_{fm} is the probability that such probes produce similarity judgments by accessing their corresponding gist traces; P_{fm} is the probability that such probes produce phantom recollection by accessing their corresponding gist traces; and β is the probability that response bias produces distractor acceptance when verbatim and gist retrieval fail to produce a response. It is obvious that this equation poses the same problem as Mandler's (1980) model of true recognition, but the problem is more severe because the gap between knowns (one) and unknowns (four) is far greater. One of the unknowns, β, can be disposed of by using the false-alarm rate for *unrelated* distractors. By definition, such distractors cannot produce retrieval of either verbatim or gist traces that support recollection rejection, similarity judgment, or phantom recollection because their surface forms and meanings are unrelated to those of any of the targets. Thus, the false-alarm probability for unrelated distractors, p_{ud}, provides a direct measure of the probability of accepting recognition probes purely on the basis of response bias, so that Equation 9-1 becomes

$$p_{fm} = (1 - R_{fm})P_{fm} + (1 - R_{fm})(1 - P_{fm})S_{fm} + (1 - R_{fm})(1 - P_{fm})(1 - S_{fm})p_{ud}$$

There are still three more unknowns to eliminate, which means that at least two more equations involving the parameters R_{fm}, P_{fm}, and S_{fm} must be found. This is done by assigning subjects to three different groups prior to administering the recognition test, with each group being instructed to respond to the probes in a different way. The three types of instructions were introduced earlier, in the discussion of retrieval variables in chapter 4. They are *verbatim* (V: accept targets and reject all distractors); *meaning* (M: accept meaning-preserving distractors, or distractors that capture misinformation, and reject targets and all other distractors); and *verbatim plus meaning* (V+M: accept targets and meaning-preserving distractors, or distractors that capture misinformation, and reject all other distractors). V instructions are merely a standard recognition test, so the equation for this condition is

$$p_{Vfm} = (1 - R_{fm})P_{fm} + (1 - R_{fm})(1 - P_{fm})S_{fm} \\ + (1 - R_{fm})(1 - P_{fm})(1 - S_{fm})p_{Vud} \tag{9-2}$$

where p_{Vud} is the false-alarm probability for unrelated distractors under such instructions. M instructions are the type of recognition test in which the basis for acceptance should be meaning only (or misinformation only); acceptance is supposed to be based upon the joint absence of verbatim memory for that distractor and the presence of gist memory for its meaning content. Hence, the equation for this condition is

$$p_{Mfm} = R_{fm} + (1 - R_{fm})(1 - P_{fm})S_{fm} \\ + (1 - R_{fm})(1 - P_{fm})(1 - S_{fm})p_{Mud} \tag{9-3}$$

where p_{Mud} is the false-alarm probability for unrelated distractors under such instructions. V+M instructions are a combination of V and M instructions; probes can be accepted on either the basis that is supposed to be used in the V condition or the basis that is supposed to be used in the M condition. Hence, the equation for this condition is

$$p_{VMfm} = R_{fm} + (1 - R_{fm})P_{fm} + (1 - R_{fm})(1 - P_{fm})S_{fm}$$
$$+ (1 - R_{fm})(1 - P_{fm})(1 - S_{fm})p_{VMud} \qquad (9\text{-}4)$$

where p_{VMud} is the false-alarm probability for unrelated distractors under such instructions.

At this point, the number of known and unknown quantities matches, and the three equations can be solved to obtain estimates of the three memory processes. The solutions are cumbersome to execute algebraically, so it is far easier (and more reliable) in research applications to estimate R_{fm}, P_{fm}, and S_{fm} using computer programs that have been written for this purpose (e.g., Hu, 1995), rather than to estimate them by solving Equations 9-2, 9-3, and 9-4.

Summing up, it is possible to conduct false-memory experiments in which the effects of opponent processes on semantic false alarms are separated and quantified. This is done by adding conditions with M and V+M instructions to a condition with standard recognition instructions. The acceptance rates for false-memory probes and unrelated distractors are then inserted in Equations 9-2, 9-3, and 9-4, which are solved to find the probability of verbatim-based rejection of false-memory probes and the probabilities of two types of gist-based acceptance of such probes.

Conjoint Recall

Conjoint-recall models, on the other hand, provide measurements of opponent memory processes that are ostensibly responsible for semantic intrusions. These models are simpler than those for recognition because it is not necessary to include bias parameters. Again, for the sake of concreteness, assume that subjects either (a) participate in a Deese-type (1959) spontaneous false-memory experiment in which they study a list that contains some semantically related targets (e.g., *oak*, *elm*, *maple*, *willow*) and perform free recall, or (b) participate in a Loftus-type (1975) implanted false-memory experiment in which they are asked to recall as many of the details of a simulated crime as possible following the presentation of misinformation. In both cases, semantic intrusions (e.g., *pine* or the robber had a knife) are the false-memory index.

Brainerd, Payne et al. (2003) developed a model of false recall that, like the model for conjoint recognition, assumes that such intrusion rates are controlled by the opposing influences of verbatim and gist processing. Specifically, the model postulates that subjects generate intrusions via the constructive processing of gist memories and that, like semantic false alarms, the intrusions are of two sorts: phantom recollections and similarity constructions. A *phantom recollection* is a memory construction that is accompanied by vivid experience of its prior "presentation," notwithstanding that it was not part of the target materials. Because this experience emulates the true recollective phenomenology that accompanies the retrieval of verbatim traces of targets, phantom recollections are read out of memory (i.e., are recalled) without further processing. *Similarity constructions*, on the other hand, are not accompanied by an illusory vivid experience of prior presentation. The meaning seems familiar, but prior presentation is not remembered. These productions are subjected to further processing in which subjects search their memories to determine whether verbatim traces of the constructions can be located. Of course, such verbatim traces will not be accessible (because the items were never presented), but verbatim traces of corresponding targets may be found, in which event the construction is suppressed (i.e., is not read out memory). The construction is not suppressed if such traces are not found.

Brainerd, Payne et al. (2003) noted that these assumptions yield the following equation for semantic intrusions on standard recall tests:

$$p_{SI} = P + (1 - P)S(1 - R) \tag{9-5}$$

where p_{SI} is the intrusion probability; P is the phantom-recollection probability; S is the similarity probability; and R is the recollection-rejection probability. As before, however, the last three variables cannot be estimated because the number of knowns (one) is smaller than the number of unknowns (three). Also as before, that problem is corrected by adding further conditions in which recall is performed under different instructions. Three instructional conditions are used, which parallel those for recognition: *verbatim* (V: recall only studied targets); *meaning* (M: recall only unpresented items that preserve the meaning of targets, or only false suggestions from the misinformation phase); and *verbatim plus meaning* (V+M: recall both targets and unpresented items that preserve the meaning of targets, or false suggestions from the misinformation phase). The expression for the V condition, which is a standard recall test, is

$$p_{VSI} = P + (1 - P)S(1 - R) \tag{9-6}$$

The expression for the M condition is

$$p_{MSI} = (1 - P)S \tag{9-7}$$

The expression for the V+M condition is

$$p_{VMSI} = P + (1 - P)S \tag{9-8}$$

These three equations are far less cumbersome than the corresponding equations for conjoint recognition, and hence, they are easily solved to obtain simple roots for P, S, and R. The respective solutions are

$$P = p_{VMSI} - p_{MSI} \tag{9-9}$$
$$S = p_{MSI} \div [1 - p_{VMSI} + p_{MSI}] \tag{9-10}$$
$$R = 1 - [p_{VSI} - p_{VMSI} + p_{MSI}] \div p_{MSI} \tag{9-11}$$

Thus, it is possible to conduct false-memory experiments in which the effects of opponent processes on semantic intrusions are separated and quantified using a procedure that is very similar to one that accomplishes the same objective with semantic false alarms. That is, recall conditions with M and V+M instructions are added to a condition with standard recall instructions. The recall rates for unpre-

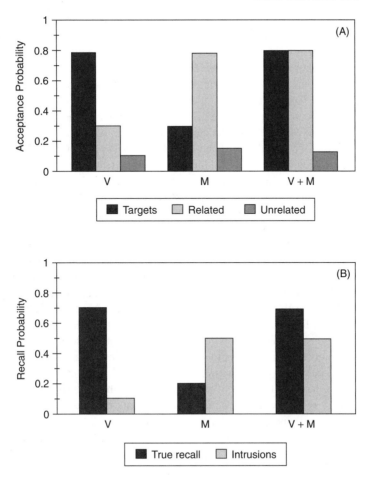

Figure 9-1. Expected variation in levels of true- and false-memory responses in recognition (Panel A) and recall (Panel B) when the accompanying phenomenology consists predominantly of generic feelings of familiarity.

sented but meaning-preserving items (or items that were presented as misinformation) are then inserted in Equations 9-9, 9-10, and 9-11, and the equations are solved to find the probability of verbatim-based rejection of unpresented items and the probabilities of two types of gist-based intrusions.

Although the principal advantage of the conjoint-recall and conjoint-recognition methodologies is that they separate and quantify opponent processes in false memory, a further advantage is that they discriminate between situations in which false responses consist overwhelmingly of similarity judgments and situations in which false responses consist overwhelmingly of phantom recollections. The first scenario is shown in Figure 9-1, with separate panels for conjoint recognition (Panel a) and conjoint recall (Panel b). If meaning-preserving distractors overwhelmingly provoke the weaker similarity phenomenology in conjoint recognition, subjects will be far more reticent about accepting them under V instructions than under M or V+M instructions. Thus, from left to right in Panel a, the acceptance rate for such distractors will increase dramatically as we move from the V condition to the M condition and will remain high as we move from the M condition to the V+M condition, whereas the acceptance rate for unrelated distractors will remain relatively constant. As also shown in Panel a, the acceptance rate for targets, which will often provoke vivid (true) recollective experience, will decrease dramatically as we move from the V condition to the M condition and increase dramatically as we move from the M condition to the V+M condition. The parallel pattern for conjoint recall appears in Panel b. The incidence of semantic intrusions jumps considerably between the V and M conditions and remains high between the M and V+M conditions, whereas true recall of targets drops precipitously between the V and M conditions and then recovers to its original level between the M and V+M conditions.

The contrasting phantom-recollection scenario is shown in Figure 9-2, with separate panels for recognition (a) and recall (b). Note in Panel a that the intercondition patterns for targets and unrelated distractors are unchanged, but the pattern for meaning-preserving distractors is different: Acceptance rates are high in the V condition, drop precipitously between the V and M conditions, and recover to their previous level between the M and V+M conditions. Likewise, in Panel b, the intercondition pattern for true recall is the same, but the pattern for semantic intrusions has changed: The intrusion rate is high under V instructions, drops precipitously when participants switch to M instructions, and recovers to its previous level when participants switch to V+M instructions. In both instances, the new pattern for false-memory items parallels the pattern for targets. Thus, the hallmark of situations in which phantom recollection predominates is that data patterns for true- and false-memory items are indistinguishable.

Evidence From Conjoint-Memory Experiments

Although the conjoint-recognition and conjoint-recall models appeared recently, a modest number of experiments has already accumulated, which provide quantitative measurements of the memory processes that figure in the opponent-processes approach. Not surprisingly, most of these experiments have focused on testing theoretical assumptions about the nature of opponent processes, which has been done primarily by studying some of the same manipulations that we discussed in earlier chapters. The general strategy has been to determine whether manipulations that have produced confirmations of qualitative predictions *actually* affect underlying memory processes in the predicted manner. For example, consider two manipulations of this sort, which were introduced in chapter 4—the storage manipulation of verbatim repetition and the retrieval manipulation of verbatim cuing.

Recall that, according to opponent-processes distinctions, when subjects study familiar targets, such as lists of everyday words, they are better able, after a single presentation, to preserve gist traces of words' meaning content than verbatim traces of their surface form. Consequently, the theoretical argument goes, further repetitions are apt to increase the accessibility of verbatim traces more than the accessibility of gist memory, yielding net reductions in semantic false alarms and intru-

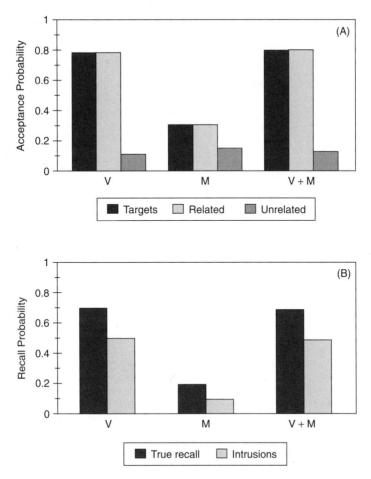

Figure 9-2. Expected variation in levels of true- and false-memory responses in recognition (Panel A) and recall (Panel B) when the accompanying phenomenology consists predominantly of illusory vivid feelings of prior presentation.

sions because it is easier for subjects to perform recollection rejection. Also, according to opponent-processes distinctions, presenting target probes on recognition tests provides excellent retrieval cues for verbatim traces, which should also decrease false recognition of meaning-preserving distractors that are presented immediately thereafter by increasing recollection rejection (e.g., recollection-rejection levels will be higher for the distractor *collie* if it is preceded by the target *poodle*) and by suppressing the tendency to access gist memories. Although predicted qualitative variations in false-memory responses have been confirmed in some studies (e.g., Brainerd, Reyna, & Kneer, 1995; Tussing & Greene, 1999), it is not known whether repetition or cuing have the predicted effects on underlying memory processes. Brainerd et al. (1999) reported three conjoint-recognition experiments that measured the effects of both manipulations on memory processes.

Table 9-1. Numerical Values of Opponent
Processes in Semantic False Recognition

	Memory Process		
Experiment/condition	R	S	P
Experiment 1			
1-study	.13	.43	0
2-study	.31	.36	0
Experiment 2			
1-study	.32	.49	0
2-study	.50	.27	0
Experiment 3			
Verbatim cuing	.49	.11	0
No cuing	.13	.50	0

Note. R is the probability of recollection rejection of meaning-preserving distractors; *S* is the probability of acceptance
of such distractors based upon similarity judgment; and *P*
is the probability of acceptance of such distractors based
upon phantom recollection.

Data from Brainerd, Reyna, and Mojardin (1999).

Brainerd et al.'s (1999) experiments were standard false-recognition designs in
which the subjects studied lists of familiar words and then responded to recognition
tests that contained distractors that preserved the meaning content of some targets
under V, M, or V+M instructions. Those distractors were synonyms in Experiment
1 (e.g., the distractor *hill* was added to the test list if the target *mountain* was studied), antonyms in Experiment 2 (e.g., the distractor *cold* was added if the target *hot*
was studied), and category labels in Experiment 3 (e.g., the distractor *tree* was added
if the target *oak* was studied). Verbatim repetition was manipulated in the first two
experiments: Half of the targets for which meaning-preserving distractors were
added had been presented once on the study list, and the other half had been presented twice. The results of primary interest are shown in the first two data columns
of Table 9-1, which contain the probabilities of recollection rejection and false acceptance based upon similarity judgment. Clearly, repetition had the predicted effect of elevating verbatim-based rejection: The value of *R* nearly tripled in the syn-
onym experiment, and it increased by roughly 60% in the antonym experiment.
Moreover, also as predicted, the effect of repetition on verbatim-based rejection was
much greater than its effect on gist-based acceptance. It had no effect at all on phantom recollection; it increased similarity judgment slightly in both experiments. Turning to cuing, in the third experiment, half of the category-label distractors were immediately preceded by their instantiating targets (e.g., *tree* was preceded by *oak*)
and half were preceded by an unrelated target (e.g., *dog* was preceded by *computer*).
Again, the relevant results are shown in the first two data columns of Table 9-1,

where it can be seen that verbatim cuing had the opposing effects on verbatim- and gist-based processes that were predicted on theoretical grounds and, further, that the two effects were of roughly equivalent magnitude. There was nearly a fivefold increase in R, coupled with nearly a fivefold reduction in S.

A final result of theoretical importance can be seen in the last column of Table 9-1. In these particular experiments, which were standard false-recognition designs in which participants studied long lists of unrelated words, there was no evidence of phantom recollection; meaning-preserving distractors did not provoke illusory vivid experiences of their "presentation" at detectable levels. This finding is consistent with the opponent-processes notion that in spontaneous false recognition, phantom recollection is an atypical phenomenon that only occurs at high levels under special conditions. Those conditions (e.g., distractors that are outstanding retrieval cues for very strong gist memories) were not present in these three experiments, and hence, the absence of phantom recollection is consistent with the theoretical expectation.

In addition to spontaneous false memories, conjoint-memory procedures have been used to separate and quantify opponent processes in Loftus-type misinformation designs. Here, two experiments have been reported that used similar procedures and that produced similar results, one by Mojardin (1999) and the other by Brainerd, Reyna, Wright, & Mojardin (2003). In Mojardin's experiment, the basic design was similar to Experiments 1 and 2 of Brainerd et al. (1999) in that subjects studied a long word list and subsequently responded to a recognition test on which the false-memory probes were synonyms and antonyms of studied targets. As these experiments were similar and produced similar findings, we consider only the initial Mojardin study.

In Mojardin's design, all subjects studied the same target list once and then studied an interpolated list before responding to a recognition test under V, M, or V+M instructions. The interpolated list was presented under the cover story that it would help subjects to consolidate their memories of the first list (which, they were also told, would be the focus of subsequent testing). Subjects were then assigned to two conditions—control and misinformation—before the interpolated list was presented. For controls, the interpolated list was a verbatim repetition of the first list. For misinformation subjects, half of the items on the interpolated list were repetitions of targets from the first list but half were misinformation items—specifically, either synonyms or antonyms of first-list targets (e.g., *hill* and *cold* appeared on the interpolated list if *mountain* and *hot* had appeared on the first list). The design included another manipulation that is particularly interesting from the standpoint of the opponent-processes assumption that verbatim traces become inaccessible more rapidly than do gist traces. All subjects responded to a recognition test immediately after the interpolated list (under V, M, or V+M instructions) and 1 week later (under the same instructions as before). During the delayed test, some of the false-memory items (synonyms and antonyms that had been presented as misinformation) were ones that had been tested 1 week earlier and others were ones that had not been previously tested. The key results of this experiment are shown in Table 9-2, where estimates of recollection rejection, similarity judgment, and phantom recollection are reported for the control and misinformation conditions.

Table 9-2. Numerical Values of Opponent
Processes in False Recognition of Misinformation

Condition	Memory Process		
	R	S	P
Immediate test			
control	.43	.12	.25
misinformed	.29	.28	.40
Delayed (tested)			
control	.30	.10	.29
misinformed	.27	.37	.28
Delayed (untested)			
control	.27	.06	.24
not repeated/misinformed	.24	.01	.46

Note. R is the probability of recollection rejection of meaning-preserving distractors; *S* is the probability of acceptance of such distractors based upon similarity judgment; and *P* is the probability of acceptance of such distractors based upon phantom recollection.

Data from Mojardin (1999).

Remember from chapter 6 that opponent-processes distinctions predict that misinformation will interfere with the retrieval of verbatim traces of targets by making alternative verbatim traces available, which should suppress recollection rejection of false-memory items and should promote gist retrieval because misinformation is gist repetition (see chapter 4). Thus, the predictions would be that on the immediate recognition test, the misinformation condition should display suppressed levels of recollection rejection, coupled with enhanced levels of similarity judgment or phantom recollection. It can be seen in the first two rows of Table 9-2 that this is exactly the pattern that was obtained: The value of R was substantially lower in the misinformation condition, but the values of S and P were substantially higher. Turning to the 1-week delayed test, opponent-processes distinctions expect different results than on the immediate test. According to those distinctions, recollection rejection is verbatim-based, while similarity judgment and phantom recollection are both gist-based, and the former memories become inaccessible more rapidly than the latter. If so, one would expect that the effect of misinformation on recollection rejection would fade rather substantially over a 1-week delay, whereas the gist effects of misinformation would be more stable. Again, Mojardin's (1999) results were consistent with expectation. As can be seen in the last four rows of Table 9-2, the large difference in R values on the immediate test for control versus misinformation had shrunk to insignificance 1 week later. In contrast, some of the gist effect was preserved: In the misinformation condition, relative to the control condition, the rate of similarity judgment remained much higher for false-memory items that had appeared on the immediate test, and the rate of phantom recollection remained slightly higher.

A final interesting feature of the results in Table 9-2 concerns the data for phantom recollection. We mentioned above that, other things being equal, this phenomenology ought to be more likely to turn up at detectable levels in misinformation experiments than in spontaneous false-memory designs because false-memory items are actually presented (as misinformation), which is a form of gist repetition. Thus, phantom recollection might occur because such repetition increases the strength of gist memories, relative to that of verbatim memories, or because verbatim traces of misinformation might be accessed by false-memory probes on recognition tests and confused with verbatim traces of earlier target presentations. Under either hypothesis, detectable levels of phantom recollection would be expected in misinformation experiments. That expectation is confirmed in Table 9-2 (the mean of the P values in the last column is .32). Closer examination of the table's values of P favors the gist hypothesis. If phantom recollection were primarily due to retrieval and misinterpretation of verbatim traces of misinformation, P would be expected to decline precipitously over the 1-week delay, but the mean immediate and delayed values of P were .25 and .27, respectively, for the control condition and .40 and .37, respectively, for the misinformation condition.

Our intention in presenting and discussing the parameter estimates in Tables 9-1 and 9-2 has not been primarily to describe findings that bear on opponent-processes assumptions. Rather, the chief objective has been to provide examples of just how much richer the information generated by conjoint-memory experiments is than the information that is generated by standard experiments. In standard experiments, there is a troubling lacuna between theoretical analysis and experimental data. Theoretical considerations predict that underlying memory processes will react in particular ways to specific manipulations (e.g., verbatim or gist repetition), which in turn leads to predictions about how semantic false alarms or intrusions will be affected by those manipulations. Because the memory processes themselves are not measured, however, data that are consistent with predictions fail to establish that those processes reacted as predicted, and data that are inconsistent with predictions fail to rule out the possibility that the processes reacted as predicted. This lacuna is filled in Tables 9-1 and 9-2. There, manipulations' effects on the *memory processes themselves* are separated and quantified, so that predictions about the nature of those effects are tested directly rather than indirectly.

Extensions of Process Dissociation to Children's Suggestibility

Beginning with a paper that appeared in 2000 (Holliday & Hayes, 2000), Holliday and her associates have reported a series of experiments in which an extended version of Jacoby's (1991) process-dissociation model has been used to measure the effects of memory suggestion on children. The basic design in all experiments involved misinformation procedures of the sort that have typically been used with children (see chapter 7 for examples), but an important modification is introduced during the test phase. Explicitly, although the familiar target-presentation-to-misinformation-to-memory-tests sequence is followed, children respond to a recognition test under two sets of instructions, inclusion and exclusion. As in most misinformation designs, three types of probes are presented on the recognition test: targets, distractors that were presented as memory suggestions, and distractors that were not presented as memory suggestions. Children in the inclusion condition are given standard recognition instructions in which they are told to accept all target probes, whereas children in the exclusion condition are given the additional instruction to avoid accepting any probe that they remember being presented during the misinformation phase. Holliday and Hayes proposed that, in this procedure, Jacoby's (1991) two equations can be applied to misinformation probes in exactly the same way as they are applied to the to-be-excluded targets in a standard process-dissociation experiment. That is,

$$p_I = R_M + (1 - R_M)F_M \qquad (9\text{-}12)$$

and

$$p_E = (1 - R_M)F_M \qquad (9\text{-}13)$$

where p_I and p_E are the probabilities of accepting *misinformation* probes in the inclusion and exclusion conditions, respectively; R_M is the probability that misinformation probes are accepted because children recollect their presentation during the misinformation phase; and F_M is the probability that misinformation probes are accepted because they seem familiar to children even though their presentation cannot be recollected.

Holliday and Hayes (2000) used this procedure to obtain preliminary findings on how recollection and familiarity (of misinformation) contribute to children's susceptibility to memory suggestions. Children of two age levels (5 years old and 8 years old) participated in misinformation experiments in which they were first exposed to a picture story and then they received misinformation about details that were not present in the story. Misinformation was presented in two ways: It was simply read to half of the children, while the other half were required to generate misinformation in response to perceptual and linguistic cues that were supplied by the experimenter. (This manipulation was included as a validity check because prior research had suggested that generation tasks elevate recollection.)

Holliday and Hayes reported two experiments of this sort. Their findings for recollection and familiarity are shown in Table 9-3. There were three key results. First, among both younger and older children, susceptibility to suggestion was overwhelmingly due to misinformation probes' familiarity rather than to explicit recollection of their presentation during misinformation. Across the eight data sets in Table 9-3, the average value of F was .48, whereas the average value of R (.08) approached zero and was zero in three of the data sets. Second, the validity check was passed in that misinformation generation elevated recollection (the mean value of R was .15 across the four generation conditions but not significantly greater than zero across the four read conditions). Third, the age-related decrease in susceptibility to suggestion that has been reported in other developmental experiments (see chapter 7) may be due to familiarity rather than recollection. While the value of F decreased from .52 to .46 overall, the overall value of R was virtually the same for the two age levels.

Table 9-3. Numerical Values of Recollection and
Familiarity Parameters in Children's False
Recognition of Misinformation

Age/condition	Memory Process	
	R	F
Experiment 1		
5-year-olds		
Read misinformation	.05	.49
Generate misinformation	.17	.54
8-year-olds		
Read misinformation	0	.43
Generate misinformation	.20	.43
Experiment 2		
5-year-olds		
Read misinformation	0	.50
Generate misinformation	.08	.55
8-year-olds		
Read misinformation	0	.48
Generate misinformation	.14	.50

Note. Parameters from Jacoby (1991). Data from Holliday and
Hayes (2000).

Holliday and associates have published further misinformation experiments with children using this modified process-dissociation model (Holliday, 2003; Holliday & Hayes, 2001, 2002). The results of those experiments have confirmed the basic conclusions that children's susceptibility to suggestion is chiefly the result of reliance upon familiarity as a basis for accepting misinformation probes and that developmental decreases in susceptibility to suggestion are chiefly due to decreases in such reliance. In addition, these experiments have separated and quantified the manner in which recollection and familiarity are affected by certain manipulations that are known to influence subjects' susceptibility to memory suggestion. Two prominent examples of such manipulations are standard versus modified recognition tests (see chapter 6) and inserting a cognitive interview between the presentation of target material and misinformation (see chapter 7).

Concerning the first manipulation, Holliday and Hayes (2001) conducted a modified process-dissociation experiment in which children of two age levels (5 years old and 9 years old) responded to both standard and modified recognition tests. Their key finding, which is illustrated in Figure 9-3, was straightforward. Modified tests reduced susceptibility to memory suggestion both by lowering children's tendency to rely upon recollection of misinformation and by lowering their tendency to rely

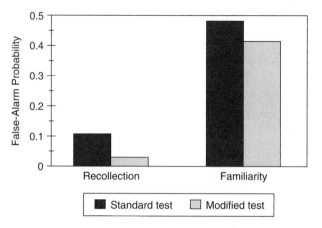

Figure 9-3. How the standard versus modified test manipulation affects recollection and familiarity in a modified process-dissociation experiment. Based upon Holliday and Hayes (2001).

on the increased familiarity of misinformation. Another, previously mentioned result is also apparent in this figure—namely, that children are far more likely to base false-memory responses upon the heightened familiarity of misinformation material than upon recollection of its presentation during the misinformation phase. Concerning the second manipulation, Holliday (2003) reported a modified process-dissociation experiment in which children of two age levels (4 years old and 8 years old) received either a cognitive interview or a more traditional interview about previously presented target material prior to the presentation of misinformation. Although the cognitive interview did not improve resistance to suggestion, Holliday again found that children were far more likely to base false-memory responses on the heightened familiarity of misinformation material than on recollection of its presentation during the misinformation phase.

On the one hand, experiments such as these represent a considerable advance over conventional qualitative studies because they separate and quantify the contributions of two important memory processes to misinformation effects and because they have yielded instructive, replicable findings about those contributions. The most important finding, from a theoretical perspective, is that childhood misinformation effects tend to be based overwhelmingly upon the increased familiarity of false-memory probes rather than on recollection of their presentation during the misinformation phase. On the other hand, the modified process-dissociation procedure has two notable limitations as a tool for increasing our understanding of how specific memory processes determine susceptibility to suggestion. The first is that the procedure does not provide a method for measuring the influence of *opponent* processes. Throughout this volume, we have seen that a large amount of data has accumulated which suggests that there are memory processes that work against each other to jointly determine levels of false alarms and intrusions in false-memory experiments, and indeed, there are several confirmed counterintuitive predictions (e.g., the reverse effects of verbatim and gist repetition; the inverted-U functions for repetition, presentation duration, and retrieval duration) that fall directly out of this principle. However, as in the original process-dissociation model of true memory, the recollection and familiarity parameters in Holliday and associates' extension of this model to misinformation both *support* acceptance of false-memory probes. Processes that actively suppress such responses are simply not included in the model, and consequently, their contribution to the overall rates of acceptance of memory suggestions cannot be determined. Moreover, we encountered several manipulations in earlier chapters whose effects should, on theoretical grounds, be entirely upon processes that suppress rather than support intrusions and false alarms, with the presentation of visually salient targets (e.g., pictures) and the administration of memory tests soon after target presentations being prime examples. Such effects cannot be measured with the extended process-dissociation model.

The other limitation concerns the interpretation of the familiarity parameter. According to Holliday and associates' findings, misinformation effects are almost entirely due to reliance upon the increased familiarity of information that is presented during the misinformation phase, so it is especially important to understand the nature of this process. We saw in the discussion of conjoint-memory models that this elevated familiarity could be of at least two general sorts, which were called similarity (the meaning content of false-memory probes seems familiar, but their presentation as part of the target material is not recollected) and phantom recollection (subjects have illusory vivid recollections of the "presentation" of false-memory probes). It is quite important to distinguish between these possibilities because the effects of memory suggestion are more insidious and more difficult to eradicate to the extent that they involve phantom recollection rather than similarity judgment. After subjects falsely report, pursuant to suggestion, that they ate a hot dog at a baseball game 2 weeks earlier, it will be harder to convince them that this is a false report if they can taste the mustard and onions than if they cannot. As we know from chapters 6 and 7, this is a matter of the first importance when it comes to the view that the courts take of evidence that is produced by suggestive questioning techniques. However, the extended process-dissociation procedure provides no direct information about the mix of "strong" and "weak" familiarity in misinformation effects.

Aging and False Memory

Memory problems are second only to physical limitations as sources of complaints about aging, and consequently, memory problems comprise one of the most extensively investigated branches of the psychology of aging. For the most part, such work has been focused upon assessing declines during late adulthood in the acquisition and retention of true memories and determining the conditions that modulate such declines (e.g., Bowles & Salthouse, 2003; Dunlosky, Kubat-Silman, & Hertzog, 2003; Dunlosky & Salthouse, 1996; Radvansky, Copeland, & Zwaan, 2003; Salthouse, 1995, 1996; Salthouse, Toth, Hancock, & Woodard, 1997; Verhaeghen, Marcoen, & Goossens, 1993; Verhaeghen & Salthouse, 1997; Wingfield, Lindfield,

& Kahana, 1998; Woodard, Dunlosky, & Salthouse, 1999). The high level of activity in this area is attributable in no small measure to the existence of a separate federal research agency for aging studies, which has made substantial funding available to support memory research. The result is an impressive and well-developed field of experimentation whose findings have major implications for the quality of life during late adulthood. Aspects of true-memory performance that exhibit substantial declines have been identified and differentiated from those that exhibit only modest declines or no declines. Powerful theories have been developed within particular domains of true-memory performance—such as short-term memory, retrieval from semantic memory, and memory for text—that attempt to explain aging effects via concepts such as working-memory capacity, executive control, speed of processing, interference sensitivity, and neurophysiological mechanisms.

Given the intense concern with how aging influences true memory, it is natural to wonder how it affects false memory. In contrast to true memory, the literature on aging and false memory is as yet sparse. For instance, the leading research journal in the psychology of aging contained only one article devoted to this topic in its 2002 volume and none in its 2001 volume. Nevertheless, interest in this topic is unquestionably growing, as illustrated by the fact that several investigators whose research figures in the earlier chapters of this book have recently reported studies of false memory and aging. At the time of this writing, a solid, if small, group of articles has accumulated that establishes some important empirical patterns, and work on aging and false memory will surely expand during the next few years. Therefore, in this subsection, we sketch some of the main things that are currently known. As in previous chapters, our underlying theme is theoretical, to discuss experiments and results not for their own sake so much as for the sake of elucidating explanatory principles that help us to understand variations in false memory during late adulthood.

An interesting feature of the aging segment of the false-memory literature is an asymmetry between experimentation on implanted versus spontaneous false memories. We saw in earlier chapters that concerns about the implantation of false memories through suggestive lines of questioning (e.g., in police interrogations of witnesses or suspects, in psychotherapy sessions) have provided the chief impetus for modern interest in false-memory research. However, the extant literature on aging and false memory has been chiefly confined to spontaneous false memories. Although some work on memory implantation has been conducted with elderly adults (Adams-Price & Perlmutter, 1992; Coxon & Valentine, 1997; Loftus, Levidow, & Duensing, 1992), comparisons of the relative suggestibility of older and younger adults are thin on the ground. The question of whether elderly adults are more susceptible to memory suggestions in the standard experimental tasks that figured in chapters 6 and 7 remains open, with some (e.g., Loftus et al., 1992) detecting increased susceptibility and others (e.g., Coxon & Valentine, 1999) failing to detect it, as does the question of which specific manipulations inoculate the elderly against the influence of memory suggestion. Of course, asymmetries of some sort are inevitable in any emerging area of research and ought not to be overinterpreted, for example, as demonstrating that implantation research is less important with elderly adults than with younger adults or children. The simple fact is that research on aging and false memory must begin somewhere, and it has begun with spontaneous false memories.

Of the basic paradigms that were introduced in chapter 2, the bulk of the accumulated experimentation relies on the following three: semantic intrusions in list recall, semantic false alarms in list recognition, and false identification of criminal suspects. Because the first two paradigms are virtually the same, differing only in the memory tests that are administered, we consider studies of aging effects in these paradigms together, in the first subsection below. In the second subsection, we consider eyewitness-identification studies that have compared the false-identification rates of elderly adults to those of younger adults.

Semantic Intrusions and False Alarms for Lists

Historically, aging research with list procedures dates to two papers, one by Smith (1975) and the other by Rankin and Kausler (1979). Both papers reported Underwood-type false-recognition studies in which the semantically related distractors were synonyms or associates of studied words. As we know from prior chapters, these are tasks on which young adults exhibit consistent but modest false-memory effects. Smith and Rankin and Kausler found that elderly adults displayed somewhat larger false-memory effects. The more interesting question, though, assuming that this pattern is replicable, is: What is responsible? Some hints as to the possible answer are provided by certain findings from studies of aging effects on *true* memory, findings that point to the hypothesis that during late adulthood, there is a shift away from reliance upon verbatim memory toward reliance upon gist memory.

One group of findings that points in that direction comes from recognition experiments that made use of Tulving's (1985) remember/know procedure. It will be recalled that in this procedure (e.g., Rajaram, 1996), subjects study target materials and then respond to a standard yes-no recognition test, with the added feature that they must make introspective reports about the phenomenologies that accompanied any items that they recognized as targets. Subjects' phenomenological reports are not extemporaneous, though, and instead, subjects are restricted to stating which of two phenomenologies was provoked by each accepted probe: *remember* (conscious recollection of physical or mental experiences that were associated with probes' prior presentation) or *know* (strong feelings that probes have been presented but without any specific recollection of their appearance on the study list). As discussed in chapter 3, remember/know experiments are one of the principal lines of empirical support for the notion that humans store and retrieve dissociated representations of the surface form of experience, on the one hand, and the meaning content of experience, on the other. The pattern that supports this idea consists of numerous findings (see Gardiner & Java, 1991) of dissociation between the effects of specific experimental manipulations on the frequency of remember phenomenology versus know phenomenology (i.e., manipulations that elevate one phenomenology without affecting the other or that elevate one while suppressing the other). Not surprisingly, manipulations that make it easier or harder to process the surface form of targets without affecting the ease of processing their meaning, such as full versus divided attention at study, tend to affect the frequency of remember phenomenology but not the frequency of know phenomenology (Gardiner & Parkin, 1990).

When such experiments are conducted with samples of young versus aged adults, there are two instructive outcomes. First, there is often no reliable age difference (and rarely more than a small one) in the level of true-memory performance; the elderly usually are just as good at recognizing previously studied lists as the young. Second, there is, nevertheless, a substantial age shift in phenomenology, with elderly subjects reporting that they were more likely than younger subjects to have accepted probes because they provoked feelings of knowing and less likely to have accepted probes because they provoked feelings of remembering.

There are many other findings in the literature that reinforce this second result, along with the conclusion that aging produces a shift away from reliance on verbatim memories and toward reliance on memory for meaning content (Brainerd & Reyna, 2001a). An example is provided by aging studies of source monitoring. As we have seen, source-monitoring experiments resemble remember/know experiments, except that the generic phenomenological judgment about accepted probes is replaced by a more focused judgment in which subjects must identify certain surface features that were associated with probes' prior presentation (Was it presented on the left or the right side of the computer screen? Was it presented in uppercase or lowercase letters? Was it presented visually or auditorially? Did you see it or think it?). In such experiments, elderly subjects have often been found to be less accurate than younger ones in making such identifications (e.g., Cohen & Faulkner, 1989; Hashtroudi, Johnson, & Chrosniak, 1989; McIntyre, 1987; Schacter, Kasniak, Kihlstrom, & Valdiserri, 1991; Spencer & Raz, 1995). Another finding in the same vein is that when target materials consist of everyday events that have been viewed in a video or a series of photographs, elderly subjects have more difficulty than younger subjects in identifying events that occurred in the video versus events that occurred in the photographs (Schacter, Koutstaal, Johnson, Gross, & Angell, 1997).

Suppose we accept as a working hypothesis that when aged subjects correctly recognize or recall presented material on memory tests, their performance is less likely than younger subjects' to be predicated upon verbatim processing and more likely to be predicated upon gist processing. If so, one would naturally expect age-related increases in semantic intrusions and false alarms on the staple list tasks that generated so much of the research that was covered in earlier chapters. Beyond this, a deeper question is: Why is there a shift away from verbatim processing and toward gist processing? And the answer will tell us how malleable aging increases in false memory should be. According to one hypothesis, which we will call the *verbatim-deficit conjecture*, when target materials are presented, elderly subjects are much poorer than younger ones at attending to their surface details and, therefore, are less apt to store the corresponding traces (Isingrini, Fontaine, Taconna, & Duportal, 1995; Rabinowitz, Craik, & Ackerman, 1982). On this hypothesis, verbatim traces would simply not be available to be retrieved on memory tests because they were not stored in the first place, owing to attentional limitations in the elderly. An obvious prediction of this hypothesis is that it will not be possible to ameliorate increased levels of false memory in aged subjects via memory-test manipulations that make it easier to access verbatim traces (see chapters 4 and 5) because such traces are not available for retrieval. According to another hypothesis, however, which we shall call the *gist-preference conjecture*, the shift from verbatim processing toward gist processing is more in the nature of a retrieval preference or tendency than a deficit in verbatim memory (Koutstaal & Schacter, 1997). That is, for some reason, as we age, we come to base our memory responses more on the meaning content of experience and less on its surface form, notwithstanding that the latter information is attended to and stored. Because there is no actual verbatim deficit, this second hypothesis predicts that it should be possible, through verbatim-slanted retrieval manipulations, to reduce and perhaps eliminate age-related increases in false memory.

Available studies, though not yet as extensive as one would wish, tell a coherent story about both the question of whether there are substantial age increases in semantic intrusions and false alarms and the question of whether such increases are verbatim deficits or gist preferences (Dodson & Schacter, 2002a; Kelley & Sahakyan, 2003; Kensinger & Schacter, 1999; LaVoie & Faulkner, 2000; Lovden, 2003; Mather & Johnson, 2003; Norman & Schacter, 1997; Prull, Light, Collett, & Kennison, 1998; Tun et al., 1998). Because the now-familiar DRM lists produce such high rates of false memory, a favorite type of design has involved administering such lists to samples of younger and older adults, followed by recall or recognition tests, with intrusions of stimulus words or false alarms to them serving as the false-memory measure.

Some early experiments of this sort were reported by Tun et al. (1998). In an initial experiment, a group of younger subjects (mean age = 20.3 years) and a group of older subjects (mean age = 70.1 years) studied DRM lists and responded to memory tests under retrieval conditions that might be expected to encourage verbatim retrieval. Explicitly, immediately after the presentation of each short list, the subjects performed a free-recall test for that list. It will be remembered from earlier chapters that recall tests are thought to be generally more dependent upon verbatim retrieval than are recognition tests and, further, that vivid traces of the presentation of the last few words on the list will still be echoing in the mind's ear or flashing in the mind's eye at the start of such a test. Immediately after the recall test, a 14-item recognition test was administered, consisting of 7 targets, the unpresented stimulus word for that list, 3 more semantically related distractors, and 3 unrelated distractors. Under the gist-preference conjecture, one would expect little or no age difference in semantic intrusions because immediate recall tests strongly encourage verbatim retrieval, but one would expect age differences in false alarms to the stimulus word because nearly one third of the probes are meaning-preserving distractors that will encourage elderly adults' baseline tendency to process gist memories. Under the verbatim-deficit conjecture, however, age differences would be expected in both false recall and false recognition of stimulus words. Tun et al.'s results, which are summarized in Figure 9-4, were consistent with the gist-preference conjecture: Intrusion rates for younger and older subjects were indistinguishable, but false-alarm rates were considerably higher in the elderly.

Under the gist-preference conjecture but not the verbatim-deficit conjecture, it should also be possible to eliminate the age increase in false alarms by more strongly encouraging verbatim retrieval on the recognition test. Tun et al. conducted another experiment using the same methodology, except for the composition of the probes

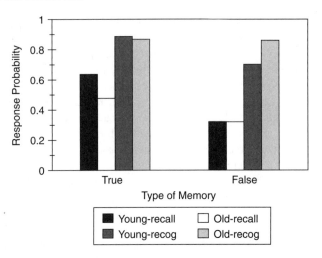

Figure 9-4. True recall, false recall, true recognition, and false recognition of DRM lists by younger and older adults. Based upon Experiment 2 of Tun, Wingfield, Rosen, and Blanchard (1998).

on the recognition test. They reasoned that if all of the related distractors except the stimulus word were eliminated from the recognition test, the tendency of probes to encourage gist retrieval would be greatly reduced because half of the probes (the targets) would definitely encourage verbatim retrieval and almost half of the probes (the unrelated distractors) would encourage neither verbatim nor gist retrieval. The results of this experiment are summarized in Figure 9-5. As before, levels of false recall were indistinguishable in younger and older subjects. The important new finding, as can be seen, is that the age difference in false recognition vanished when the recognition test's overall tendency to cue the retrieval of gist memories was reduced. These various results from Tun et al.'s research are consistent with the view that elevated levels of false memory in the elderly are more a matter of preference for processing meaning information than of an inability to process surface information.

Some other DRM data that bear informatively on the reasons for increases in false memory during late adulthood were reported by Kensinger and Schacter (1999). This research revolved around developmental interactions in how repeated presentation of DRM lists affects false recognition of stimulus words by younger versus older subjects. We have seen in earlier chapters that as long as a single presentation of target materials is sufficient to allow their meaning content to be fully processed and stored, the opponent-processes prediction is that the primary effect of verbatim repetitions of that material will be to strengthen fast-fading verbatim traces, making them more likely to survive consolidation and making them more resistant to forgetting (Reyna & Lloyd, 1997; Reyna & Titcomb, 1997). Thus, Kensinger and Schacter reasoned, repetition of DRM lists ought to encourage verbatim retrieval on recognition tests, reducing the normally high levels of false alarms

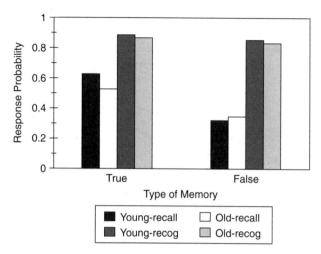

Figure 9-5. True recall, false recall, true recognition, and false recognition of DRM lists by younger and older adults. Based upon Experiment 1 of Tun, Wingfield, Rosen, and Blanchard (1998).

to stimulus words because subjects would be better able to able to reject them by accessing verbatim traces of actual targets. The question of principal interest is whether the effects of repetition on younger and older adults are comparable.

In Kensinger and Schacter's (1999) procedure, younger and older adults studied a single, long list (more than 100 words) that was composed of several DRM sublists. Within the overall list, individual DRM sublists were presented one to five times (e.g., the "window" list might appear only once, but the "doctor" list might appear five times). Following presentation of the entire list, the subjects responded to a recognition test on which the stimulus words for the DRM sublists served as the false-memory items. The gist-preference conjecture predicts that these procedures should reveal baseline differences in semantic false recognition favoring the elderly because the procedures do not encourage verbatim processing: Recall tests were not administered following individual sublists, and the recognition test was not administered until after all of the subjects had studied a long list, which allowed considerable time for verbatim forgetting of early material on the list. Consistent with this prediction, false-alarm rates for stimulus words were higher among older adults. With respect to the more interesting question—the effects of repetition— younger adults responded to this manipulation as expected in that additional presentations of DRM sublists reduced false alarms to stimulus words, from .90 in sublists that had been presented once to .50 in sublists that had been presented five times. The false alarms of aged adults, however, were resistant to repetition; sublists that had been presented more than once produced just as many errors to stimulus words as sublists that had been presented only once. This is a surprising finding from the perspective of either the verbatim-deficit conjecture or the gist-preference conjecture. However, a more detailed analysis of the data revealed

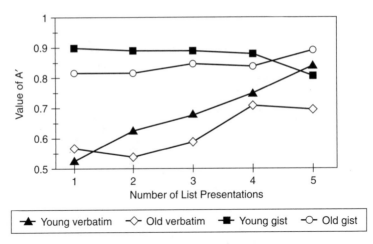

Figure 9-6. Findings for the effects of repetition on verbatim and gist memory in young and elderly subjects using the statistic A'. Data from Kensinger and Schacter (1999).

that repetition actually influenced elderly subjects in a manner that was consistent with opponent processes but that could not be detected via raw false-alarm rates for stimulus words.

Earlier in this chapter, we noted that a key motivation for developing mathematical models of false memory is the possibility that false-memory responses are controlled by the combined influences of opponent processes, which makes it difficult to detect the influence of manipulations that are supposed to affect these processes by simply analyzing intrusions and false alarms. In line with this notion, Kensinger and Schacter (1999) attempted to separate the influence of repetition on opponent processes by computing signal-detection statistics (see chapter 3) that were sensitive to verbatim memory, on the one hand, and to gist memory, on the other. The logic of the analysis runs as follows. Their recognition test consisted of the usual three types of probes: targets, semantically related distractors (stimulus words), and unrelated distractors. Targets (e.g., *nurse*) and stimulus words (e.g., *doctor*) shared gist traces, but verbatim traces could only have been stored for the former. Thus, the difference between the acceptance rates for targets (verbatim retrieval or gist retrieval) and stimulus words (gist retrieval only) is a relatively pure measure of the ease of verbatim access. Stimulus words (e.g., *doctor*) and unrelated distractors (e.g., *computer*) shared neither gist traces (because gist traces could only be stored for the former) nor verbatim traces (because verbatim traces could not have been stored for either). Thus, the difference between the acceptance rates for stimulus words (gist retrieval only) and unrelated distractors (neither verbatim nor gist retrieval) is a relatively pure measure of ease of gist access. Kensinger and Schacter computed each of these differences in acceptance rates and expressed them as the signal detection statistic A' (Snodgrass & Corwin, 1988). Their results are displayed in Figure 9-6.

It can be seen that at the level of opponent processes, repetition appeared to have exactly the effects that would be expected on theoretical grounds, in both younger and older subjects. Consider, first, the gist-retrieval index, which is represented by the two lines at the top of the figure. There are three important findings: Gist memories were highly accessible for DRM sublists that were presented only once; gist accessibility was high in both younger and older adults; and repetition did not affect gist accessibility in younger adults but it increased it in older adults. Now, consider the verbatim-retrieval index, which is represented by the two lines at the bottom of the figure. Again, there are three important findings: Verbatim memories were not highly accessible for sublists that had been presented only once (the zero level of the A' statistic is .5); verbatim accessibility was higher in younger than in older adults (after more than one repetition); and repetition increased verbatim accessibility in both younger and older adults. Thus, the reason that repetition failed to decrease semantic false alarms in elderly subjects was *not* because it failed to affect opponent memory processes. Rather, it was because repetition affected both types of processes in the elderly: Repetition-induced increases in verbatim access, which support rejection of stimulus words, were neutralized by repetition-induced increases in gist access, which support acceptance of such words. That repetition would improve gist access in the elderly is not surprising, given the difficulty of the task. Considering that the study materials consisted of a long list that was composed of several DRM sublists, it is quite reasonable to suppose that elderly subjects would be somewhat less likely than younger ones to store accessible gist memories following a single presentation of a sublist.

Kensinger and Schacter's (1999) findings underscore a key point from the earlier discussion of mathematical models of false memory—namely, that it is essential to separate the contributions of experimental manipulations on opponent processes in order to understand manipulations' actual effects. Without such separation, it is possible to conclude that a manipulation has no effect at all when, in fact, it has profound effects. Kensinger and Schacter's data suggest that this situation may be especially problematic in aging research because manipulations whose effects, at the level of memory processes, are narrow in young adults may be broader in older adults and may tend to cancel each other out at the level of intrusion or false-alarm rates. For example, the developmental conclusion about repetition that follows from considering only the raw false-alarm rates for stimulus words is that young adults are more sensitive to the effects of repetition than aged adults. Actually, however, the reverse is true: The memory processes of aged adults are more broadly affected by repetition than are those of young adults, but the fact that those processes support opposite responses to false-memory items means that they cancel each other out at the level of false alarms. This is a fundamental lesson indeed.

To conclude our sketch of aging studies of semantic intrusions and false alarms, we turn to an impressive series of experiments by Koutstaal and associates that supply probative findings on the gist-preference and verbatim-deficit conjectures (Koutstaal, 2003; Koutstaal, Reddy, Jackson, Prince, Cendan, & Schacter, 2003; Koutstaal, Schacter, & Brenner, 2001; Koutstaal, Schacter, Galluccio, & Stofer, 1999; Schacter, Koutstaal, Johnson, Gross, & Angell, 1997). These experiments compared the performance of younger and older adults on a thematic picture task that, like DRM lists, produces high levels of false memory. The basic elements of the task, as it was initially described in an article by Koutstaal and Schacter (1997), are illustrated in Figure 9-7. The study materials consist of a long list (e.g., 100–200 targets) of color photographs depicting familiar animate and inanimate objects. These targets are of two sorts: related and unrelated. Unrelated targets are pictures that are conceptually unconnected to each other (e.g., automobile, cup, mountain, lamp). Related targets are pictures with strong conceptual connections in that they are all members of a single, familiar taxonomic category. An example is shown at the top of Figure 9-7.

The study list contains several of these sublists of related targets (e.g., boats, cats, shoes, and teddy bears in Koutstaal and Schacter's experiments). When the study list is presented, subjects view the pictures one at a time at a leisurely rate (>2 seconds per target) in random order (i.e., same-meaning pictures are *not* blocked together as DRM targets sometimes are). Then, subjects respond to a long recognition test composed of targets (Figure 9-7, *bottom left*), semantically related distractors (Figure 9-7, *bottom center*), and unrelated distractors (Figure 9-7, *bottom right*). When this procedure is used with young adults, it produces false-alarm rates for semantically related pictures that are much higher than those for unrelated pictures (e.g., .30 versus .05).

Koutstaal and associates have made extensive use of this paradigm to track variations in false memory during late adulthood. In the initial experiments of Koutstaal and Schacter (1997), the performance of subjects whose mean age was below 20 was compared to that of subjects whose mean age was above 60. These experiments also included a gist-repetition manipulation that parallels manipulations that have been discussed in earlier chapters: The related targets that subjects viewed varied in the number of exemplars that were presented for different categories. In one experiment, some categories were represented by a single picture; others were represented by 9 pictures; and others were represented by 18 pictures. As in earlier chapters, the opponent-processes prediction is that gist repetition should influence false memory, with related distractors from categories for which more pictures were presented producing higher false-alarm rates than related distractors from categories for which fewer pictures were presented. However, a further prediction, also familiar from earlier chapters, is that gist repetition ought to interact with development such that subjects with poorer verbatim retrieval (elderly adults) are more affected than subjects with better verbatim retrieval (young adults). Both of these predictions were confirmed by Koutstaal and Schacter, and we display some illustrative patterns from one of their experiments in Figure 9-8. The first point to note is one that we have previously encountered: Aging did not decrease true recognition (*left*), but it elevated false recognition (*right*). With respect to the first prediction, gist repetition elevated false recognition, with the mean false-alarm rate increasing from .20 (1-picture categories) to .40 (9-picture categories) to .44 (18-picture categories). However, it can be seen on the right side of Figure 9-8 that gist repetition had more pronounced effects on older subjects than on younger ones. In the younger subjects, the presentation of 9 category exemplars increased false-alarm rates, relative to 1 exemplar, but the presentation of 18 category exemplars

STUDY MATERIALS

TARGET   RELATED   UNRELATED

TEST PROBES

Figure 9-7. Study materials and test probes of the general type used by Koutstaal and associates in their studies of false memories that arise from the formation of pictorial gist.

produced no further increase. In older subjects, on the other hand, each increase in the number of exemplars produced an increase in false alarms to related pictures. Further, the difference between the false-alarm rates for 1- versus 18-picture categories was more than twice as large in older subjects than in younger ones.

From the perspective of the gist-preference and verbatim-deficit conjectures, such data can be interpreted in two ways. Gist repetition may have more marked effects on elderly subjects because it taps into a preexisting preference for processing mean-

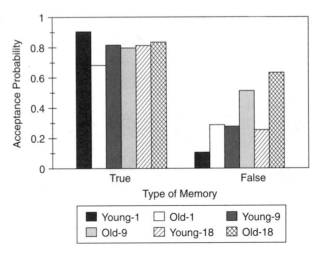

Figure 9-8. Illustrative findings from studies of aging effects in false memory for picture-gist materials. Data from Koutstaal and Schacter (1997).

ing, or because elderly subjects' deficits in verbatim memory make it more difficult for them to resist the influence of stronger gist memories, or both. Koutstaal et al. (2003) devised an ingenious procedure for obtaining differential evidence on these possibilities. Returning to Figure 9-7, note that same-category pictures resemble each other in two ways: visual composition (a form of surface information) and category membership (a form of meaning information). Both types of resemblance can contribute to the elevated false-alarm rates that are observed for related pictures, but for different reasons. Visual similarity could contribute for verbatim reasons: Because same-category pictures look alike, subjects might be likely to accept related distractors to the extent that they cannot access verbatim traces of targets that are capable of discriminating presented pictures from unpresented but visually similar ones. Category membership could contribute for gist reasons: Because same-category pictures share meaning, subjects might be increasingly likely to accept related distractors to the extent that those distractors cause them to retrieve gist memories of studied categories. Because either surface or semantic similarity can contribute to false-memory responses, elevated sensitivity to either or both among elderly adults might be responsible for age increases in such responses.

Koutstaal et al. (2003) used study and test materials like those in Figure 9-9 to decide between these possibilities. At first glance, these items appear to be nonsense shapes, some of which, like the pictures at the top of Figure 9-7, look alike, and indeed, that is what people say if they are provided no other information about them. For example, Koutstaal et al. presented such items to samples of subjects and asked them (a) to provide the names of taxonomic categories to which the shapes might belong, and (b) to sort the shapes into groups on the basis of visual appearance. While subjects readily sorted the shapes into appearance groupings (e.g., the shapes in the first row were grouped together and the shapes in the second row were grouped together), they were unable to provide names of taxonomic categories for those

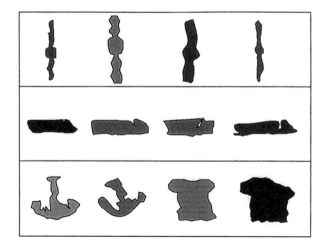

Figure 9-9. Examples of abstract pictures that were used to construct the target materials and recognition probes used in studies of aging effects in false memories that arise from the formation of pictorial gist. See color insert. From Koutstaal, Reddy, Jackson, Prince, Cendan, and Schacter (2003).

groupings. However, although the subjects were unaware of it, these "nonsense" shapes are conceptually related.

The shapes were originally generated from pictures of everyday objects belonging to the same category, like those at the top of Figure 9-7, removing enough of the visual detail so that the pictures appeared to be nonsense shapes but preserving enough detail so that the shapes looked alike. (The reader may have already guessed that the categories for the shapes in Figure 9-9 are wristwatches, trucks, anchors, and bread.) Thus, unlike the materials in Figure 9-7, if such shapes are used as study materials and recognition probes and subjects are provided with no further information about them, visual similarity (the verbatim reason) is the only basis for elevated false-alarm rates for related distractors. On the other hand, if the subjects in such an experiment are told the category of each shape, both the verbatim reasons and the gist reasons can be responsible for elevated false-alarm rates for related distractors, at least according to opponent-processes assumptions. Note that if those assumptions are correct and verbatim and gist memory are both involved, the obvious prediction is that the elevation in false-alarm rates would be greater for the second group of subjects than for the first.

Koutstaal et al. (2003) reported some experiments in which this basic procedure was used to study false recognition in samples of younger adults (mean age <20) and older adults (mean age >60). The gist-repetition manipulation was also used: Some categories were represented by one shape, others by six shapes. To illustrate the conclusions that emerged from this research, we display some of the false-memory results from one of Koutstaal et al.'s experiments in Figure 9-10, where the false-alarm rates for the related distractors (shapes) are displayed for younger versus older subjects as a function of whether or not category labels were provided

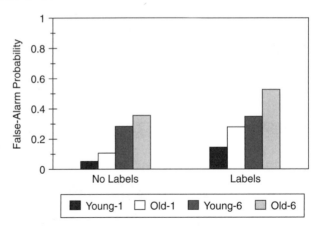

Figure 9-10. Illustrative findings from studies of aging effects in false memory for "nonsense" picture-gist materials. Data from Koutstaal, Reddy, Jackson, Prince, Cendan, and Schacter (2003).

and whether one or six exemplars of a category were presented. The first thing to notice, as a check on the validity of opponent-processes assumptions, is that false-alarm rates were much higher at both age levels and in both presentation conditions (one exemplar versus six exemplars) when category labels were provided. In fact, when labels were not provided and only one exemplar was presented, false-alarm rates for related distractors were barely above floor. The second thing to notice is that the usual aging effect was present: False-alarm rates were higher in elderly subjects. However, the third and most important thing to notice is that age increases in false alarms *depended upon whether category labels had been provided.* It can be seen that the age increases were much smaller in the no-labels condition than in the labels condition, and statistical tests showed that only the age increases in the labels condition were reliable.

Such a pattern provides clear support for the gist-preference conjecture. If the verbatim-deficit hypothesis is correct and aging increases in false memory are due to an inability to access the verbatim traces that allow related distractors to be firmly rejected, there ought to have been large age effects in the no-labels condition, in which false recognition of related shapes depends squarely upon the accuracy of verbatim memory. Further, although the verbatim-deficit hypothesis expects that the addition of category labels will increase false recognition (by providing an additional memorial basis for acceptance), such labels should not have a disproportionate effect on elderly subjects because a preference for gist processing is not the basis for aging increases in false memory. Instead, as we saw, aging increases in false memory were only reliable when category labels were supplied.

Eyewitness Identification

During the discussion of eyewitness-identification research in chapter 6, we noted in passing that aging is listed as a source of unreliability in forensic analyses of eyewitness identifications (Table 6-3). With few exceptions (Adams-Price, 1992), the data on which this claim is based grow out of a long line of research that was initiated almost 2 decades ago by Bartlett. This line of research has resulted in a steady, cumulative stream of publications on aging effects in facial memory by Bartlett and associates that is in the best traditions of experimental psychology (Bartlett & Fulton, 1991; Bartlett & Leslie, 1985, 1986; Bartlett, Leslie, & Tubbs, 1987; Bartlett, Leslie, Tubbs, & Fulton, 1989; Bartlett, Strater, & Fulton, 1991; Fulton & Bartlett, 1991; Gabbert, Memon, & Allan, 2003; Memon & Bartlett, 2002; Memon & Gabbert, 2003; Memon, Hope, Bartlett, & Bull, 2002; Memon, Hope, & Bull, 2003; Searcy, Bartlett, & Memon, 1999; Searcy, Bartlett, Memon, & Swanson, 2001). This work began with carefully controlled laboratory studies of facial recognition and then moved on, more recently, to applications of what had been learned in those studies to more naturalistic criminal identification situations.

We mentioned that aging studies of true memory that make use of recognition tests often fail to find a decrease in hit rates during late adulthood. However, faces are far more complicated stimuli than the word lists that have been the predominant target materials in aging research. For that reason, it would not be disconcerting if, in a true-memory experiment, the ability to discriminate old probes from new ones declined during adulthood for facial materials but not for word lists and, indeed, that is the finding that Bartlett and associates obtained (Bartlett et al., 1989). The type of design that figured in these early studies was one in which younger subjects (usually college students) and older subjects (usually retirees whose ages were in the 60–80-year range) viewed a moderately long (>50) list of color photographs of faces that had been sampled at random from a larger pool of facial photographs. The orientation of the faces varied (e.g., frontal view, left profile, right profile), as did the ages of the persons depicted (young adult, middle-aged adult, elderly adult) and whether the person was smiling. In some instances, an Underwood-type (1965) continuous-recognition procedure was used in which the task was to judge each presented photograph as old or new, accordingly as it had or had not been presented earlier in the list. In other instances, a study-test procedure was used in which the entire list of photographs was viewed, and this was followed by an old-new recognition test on which half of the photographs were targets and the other half were distractors that were sampled from the same pool from which the targets came. To ensure attention to the study lists, subjects sometimes made judgments about each target photograph as it appeared (e.g., they rated it for pleasantness).

Aging effects were detected with both the continuous and study-test procedures. For example, Figure 9-11A contains data from a continuous-recognition experiment reported by Bartlett and Fulton (1991). The list consisted of 84 photographs, and performance is plotted separately for each successive block of 12 photographs. The statistic that has been plotted for each block is the probability that subjects falsely identified previously unpresented photographs. Consistent with what we just said about the complexity of facial information, it can be seen that although target photographs had only just been presented (the entire procedure required slightly more than 15 minutes to complete), subjects' ability to reject unpresented faces was rarely above 80%. This was true even in the first block of photographs, when previously presented faces had been viewed only *a few seconds earlier*. With respect to the

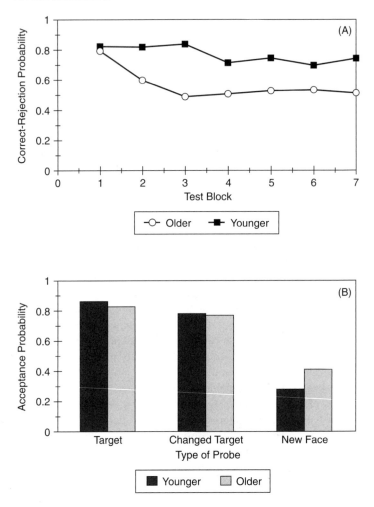

Figure 9-11. Illustrative findings from studies of aging effects in facial memory. The data in Panel A are from a continuous-recognition experiment, and the data in Panel B are from a study-test recognition experiment. From Bartlett and Fulton (1991).

question of central concern, after the first block of photographs, elderly subjects were considerably less able than younger ones to reject photographs that they had not seen: After the first block, younger subjects correctly rejected an average of 76% of the new faces, but older subjects rejected only 53%. Thus, as the experiment progressed, older subjects were just about as likely to falsely accept a new face as they were to correctly reject it.

Turning to results from the study-test method, Bartlett and Fulton also reported an experiment in which younger and older subjects responded to an old-new recognition test after viewing a sequence of facial photographs. The test probes were of three types: targets presented exactly as on the study list, targets presented in a different orientation than on the study list (e.g., tested in left profile after being viewed in right profile), and distractors that were selected from the pool from which the targets had been sampled. The task was to accept both types of targets and to reject all distractors. Key findings are summarized in Figure 9-11B. First, note that, similar to the data in Figure 9-11A, even though the target faces had been viewed only 10 minutes before, facial recognition was far from perfect. Mean recognition of target probes that were presented in exactly the same way as on the study list did not exceed 85%, and a simple change in targets' facial orientation caused mean recognition to drop below 80%. Also, subjects' ability to reject completely new faces did not exceed 70%. Concerning age effects, it is apparent that there was an asymmetry between target acceptance and distractor rejection. With respect to targets, elderly subjects were just as good at recognizing previously viewed faces as younger subjects, but elderly subjects were not as good at rejecting faces that had not been previously viewed. Note that from an opponent-processes perspective, in which verbatim and gist memory both support target acceptances but verbatim memory supports distractor rejections, these developmental patterns, like those from studies of semantic intrusions and false alarms, are consistent with increased gist reliance in late adulthood.

As we reflect upon such findings, we begin to understand why, as discussed in chapter 6, eyewitness-identification errors are so ubiquitous, even under ideal conditions (Haber & Haber, 2004). Basic research on facial memory shows that adults are far from perfect at recognizing faces that they saw just moments before and rejecting faces that they did not see. With respect to age-related increases in false facial recognition, in particular, Bartlett and associates have reported several findings that are consistent with the hypothesis of increased reliance on gist processing in later adulthood. In one experiment, for instance, younger and older subjects first participated in a continuous-recognition experiment like the one described in the preceding paragraph. Then, all of the photographs were presented again, and subjects were asked to rate each on a dimension of facial gist: *typicality* (the extent to which each face was unusual versus commonplace). Finally, older and younger subjects' typicality ratings of the photographs were correlated with their responses to distractor faces. There was a significant positive correlation in older subjects, suggesting that they relied on this dimension of facial gist when making recognition judgments, but there was no correlation in younger subjects, suggesting that they did not rely on this dimension. In another experiment, which used the study-test method, subjects viewed a series of photographs and then responded to an old-new recognition test on which all of the probes had been independently rated (by another group of subjects) on another dimension of facial gist: *facial familiarity*. Again, these ratings correlated positively with false recognition in older subjects (they were more likely to falsely recognize probes with high familiarity ratings) but not in younger subjects.

Given the similarity between this research and eyewitness identification involving photo spreads, it is natural to extend such work to the latter situation, and this has been done in recent papers. Because the observation of crimes always precedes eyewitness-identification tests in the real world, all of this work involves variations on the study-test procedure. The chief design modifications are that the study phase

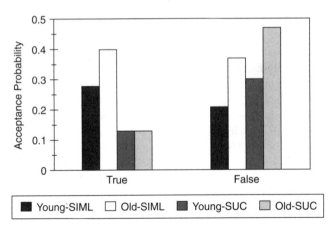

Figure 9-12. Illustrative findings from studies of aging effects in eyewitness identification. Young-SIML = younger subjects with simultaneous administration; Young-SUC = younger subjects with successive administration; Old-SIML = older subjects with simultaneous administration; Old-SUC = older subjects with successive administration. Data from Memon and Bartlett (2002).

involves the observation of a naturalistic sequence of events, rather than a series of photographs, and the test phase involves photo spreads like those that are administered in criminal investigations. For instance, a procedure that has been used in several studies (e.g., Memon & Bartlett, 2002; Memon & Gabbert, 2003; Memon, Hope, Bartlett, & Bull, 2002) involves a film clip from a television program called "Crime Stoppers," which is broadcast in regions of the United States. The film clip is a reenactment of a theft of a new car from a car showroom. Two men enter the showroom, look at the cars, and discuss them with a salesman. One of them then takes a test drive with the salesman. During the course of the test drive, the customer threatens the salesman with a pistol, stops the car, orders the salesman to leave the car, and drives away. During the film clip, the robber's face is in view for approximately half of the time. In Memon and Bartlett's experiment, younger subjects (mean age = 21) and older subjects (mean age = 70) viewed the clip and were administered a six-alternative mugshot photo spread approximately 15 minutes later. To ensure that the subjects had not previously seen the clip on television, the experiment was conducted in the United Kingdom. The simultaneous method of administration was used for half of the subjects at each age level, and the successive method of administration was used for the other half (see chapter 6).

The findings, which are summarized in Figure 9-12, were quite similar to those for the study-test facial recognition experiment in Figure 9-11b. To begin, note that in absolute terms, subjects' ability to recognize the actual culprit was poor, much poorer than their ability to recognize target photographs in facial-recognition experiments like those above: The rate of target acceptance did not exceed 50% in any of the conditions (though the nominal chance level, .17, was much lower in this experiment). Also, subjects' tendency to falsely identify an innocent person was quite high (.38 overall). With respect to aging effects, the pattern again resembles that of the previous facial-recognition studies in that the elderly subjects were not significantly worse than younger adults when it came to correctly recognizing the culprit's mug shot, but they were significantly worse than younger adults when it came to correctly rejecting the mug shots of innocent people.

Another point of similarity between the recent extensions of laboratory research on facial memory to eyewitness identification and prior studies of aging effects is that the effects of several manipulations are consistent with the view that elderly subjects are more apt to base their identifications on dimensions of facial gist. Of course, a core finding, from the opponent-processes perspective, is that aging effects are more likely to be found for correct rejection of distractors than for correct acceptance of targets. Other instructive findings show that elderly subjects are more sensitive to storage or retrieval manipulations that ought to encourage gist processing. Illustrative findings for a storage manipulation, the mugshot-bias manipulation that was discussed in chapter 6, were reported by Memon et al. (2002). Here, it will be recalled that witnesses who have reviewed mug shots of possible culprits prior to being administered a line-up or photo spread usually perform less accurately than witnesses who have not reviewed such mug shots. To determine whether the elderly are more susceptible to mugshot bias, Memon et al. exposed a sample of younger and older subjects to the car robbery clip. Before the photo spread was administered, however, half of the subjects at each age level reviewed a mug book containing 12 black-and-white photographs of individuals who *might* have been the culprit. (Actually, the culprit did not appear in the mug book.) The other half of the subjects performed an irrelevant activity for an equivalent amount of time. Finally, both groups were administered a six-alternative photo spread of mug shots, using the simultaneous method of presentation. One of the choices was the culprit in the clip; one of the choices was a distractor from the mugbook task (the critical distractor); and the remaining four choices were distractors that had not appeared in the mug book and that had been obtained from a database of police mug shots. The usual aging effect was present (i.e., the elderly adults made more false identifications than did the younger adults), as was the usual mugshot-bias effect (i.e., subjects were more likely to make false identifications, especially of the critical distractor, if they had reviewed the mug book than if they had not). Crucially, the older subjects were more susceptible to mugshot bias than were the younger subjects: The elevation in false identification of the critical distractor by subjects who had reviewed the mug book was three times as great among elderly adults as among younger adults.

Cognitive Neuroscience of False Memory

Cognitive neuroscience is a burgeoning field that seeks to pinpoint brain structures that are involved in memory, reasoning, and their development (for overviews of the field, see Gabrieli, 1998; Schacter, Norman, & Koutstaal, 1998). Research in this field has intensified in recent years. Among the factors that have stimulated this intensification, two are especially important. The first is technological—specifically, the availability of noninvasive techniques, originally invented to assist neurologists in the diagnosis and treatment of disorders of the nervous system, which allow certain aspects of brain functioning to be measured while subjects are performing ordinary memory and reasoning tasks. The other factor was stimulated by the first—namely, shifts in patterns of research funding by federal science agencies, such as the National Institutes of Health, which were designed to encourage the use of these new technologies to study the brain mechanisms that underlie specific forms of memory and reasoning. The equipment is expensive both to purchase (several million dollars per unit) and to maintain, and research with these technologies is therefore impossible without generous grant support.

Functional magnetic resonance imaging (fMRI), positron emission tomography (PET), and computed tomography (CT) imaging (or computed axial tomography [CAT] imaging) are the three most common examples of such technologies. fMRI determines which parts of the brain are most active as subjects perform particular tasks, such as studying and recalling a word list, by identifying the brain areas that exhibit increased blood flow, using an MRI scanner. Subjects lie inside a large magnet while performing experimental tasks, and numerous MRI scans of their brains are taken (e.g., one scan every 5 seconds). After a subject has completed an experiment, scans that were taken while the subject was performing the focal task are compared to scans that were taken when the task was not being performed to isolate brain regions that displayed increased blood flow during performance. The images that the scans generate are analyzed using mathematical models, such as Fourier transformations, so that the resulting pictures look like brains. Such pictures can be two-dimensional (Figure 9-13, *top*) or three-dimensional (Figure 9-13, *bottom*). Areas of increased blood flow appear as white patches in Figure 9-13, and as can be seen, the task that generated these particular images induced increases in blood flow in the left anterior region of the brain.

Turning to PET, this technique also generates brain images in the form of brilliant colored pictures that pinpoint areas of the brain where nerve cells are using more energy during the performance of focal tasks, with the red-to-purple scale of visible color indexing the level of increased energy usage from highest (red) to lowest (purple). PET measures more brain variables than fMRI, including oxygen consumption, tissue acidity, and glucose consumption, and hence, it can sometimes produce positive experimental findings with tasks for which fMRI cannot identify the loci of increased brain activity.

Finally, CAT is the oldest of the three technologies, having been developed in the early 1970s to assist in the diagnosis of tumors, lesions, cancer metastases, and various brain injuries. It is far and away the most widely accessible of the three technologies, with CAT equipment being available at tens of thousands of sites around the world. CAT also produces brain images—particularly, pictures that portray a combination of bone, soft tissue, and blood vessels. Of the three technologies, CAT is the workhorse in medical applications of brain imaging because the equipment is easier to use and maintain and also because it is more patient-friendly, requiring, for instance, far shorter intervals to generate usable brain scans than either fMRI or PET.

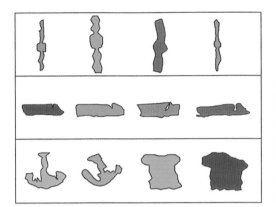

Figure 9-9. Examples of abstract pictures that were used to construct the target materials and recognition probes used in studies of aging effects in false memories that arise from the formation of pictorial gist. See text pages 459–459. From Koutstaal, Reddy, Jackson, Prince, Cendan, and Schacter (2003).

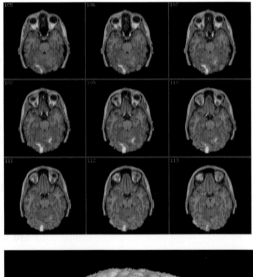

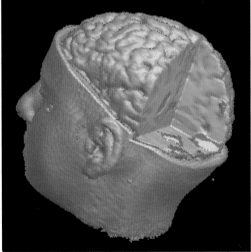

Figure 9-13. Examples of two-dimensional images *(top)* and a three-dimensional image *(bottom)* produced by functional magnetic resonance imaging. See text page 466.

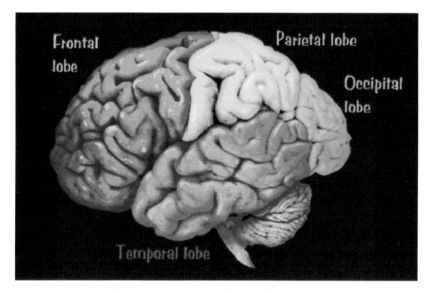

Figure 9-14. Major divisions of the human cortex. See text pages 470–471.

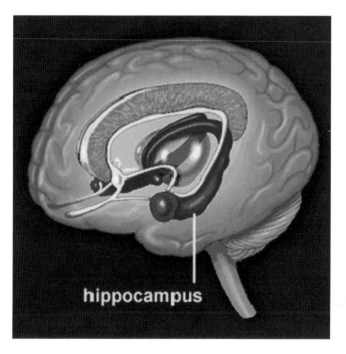

Figure 9-15. The hippocampal formation within the medial temporal lobe region of the brain. See text pages 471–472.

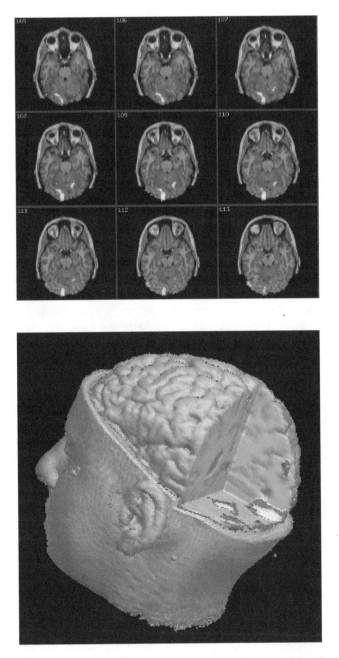

Figure 9-13. Examples of two-dimensional images (*top*) and a three-dimensional image (*bottom*) produced by functional magnetic resonance imaging. See color insert.

At present, the bulk of cognitive neuroscience research may be said to consist of five types of studies: (a) behavioral studies of normal adults (usually college students), (b) behavioral studies of normal children of varying age, (c) behavioral studies of healthy elderly adults, (d) brain-imaging studies of normal adults, and (e) neuropsychological studies of brain-damaged patients. Upon first impression, it might seem odd that the first two types of studies—which in the case of memory research are simply laboratory experiments in which subjects perform familiar memory tasks under various conditions—would be classified as neuroscience research. After all, no measurements of brain activity are taken and no brain pathology is present. However, both types of studies provide baseline data that are crucial for interpreting findings from other types of experiments. Such studies establish what performance is like when healthy adults execute target tasks under standard conditions or when children of different ages execute target tasks under standard conditions. That information can then be used to identify the performance deficits that result from distinctive types of brain pathology in adults or children. The same information can be used to answer the important methodological question of whether performing tasks in a brain-imaging apparatus substantially alters the data of normal adults or children, relative to baseline. (With respect to the latter possibility, performing memory or reasoning tasks in a brain-imaging apparatus [e.g., while lying inside an MRI scanner] is evidently a major change in procedure that may, in itself, alter the configuration of the data, and if it does, the resulting brain images cannot be interpreted as patterns of brain activity that occur under normal circumstances.)

Turning to Type c research, aging studies fall more clearly within the neuroscience sphere. There are well-known forms of neurological deterioration during late adulthood, so such studies provide data on changes in performance that may be grounded in such deterioration (e.g., Schacter, Kagan, & Leichtman, 1995). The last two types of studies are classic neuroscience research inasmuch as memory or reasoning performance is closely coupled with brain data, either in the form of noninvasive measurements that are taken during the course of an experiment or, more commonly, in the form of preexisting brain damage. The general objectives of the former studies are to isolate and catalog patterns of brain activity that are provoked by individual tasks (e.g., Johnson, Nolde, Mather, Kounios, & Schacter, 1997), whereas the objectives of studies with brain-damaged patients are to isolate and catalog deficits in (or sparing of) performance on individual tasks that are characteristic of damage to particular brain loci (e.g., Melo, Winocur, & Moscovitch, 1999).

The great preponderance of cognitive neuroscience research has focused upon true memory and accurate reasoning, rather than upon false memory or aberrant reasoning. As illustrated by our earlier discussion of aging effects, however, increasing attention is being devoted to false memory. Of the five varieties of research that were just mentioned, false-memory studies of the first two types have concerned us throughout this book, and research of the third type was considered earlier in this chapter. Therefore, the focus of the present section is on research with brain-damaged patients and, to a lesser extent, with normal subjects who perform memory tasks in a brain-imaging apparatus. We begin with a discussion of some general findings that these two methodologies have produced for *true* memory. Here, our interest lies not with true memory as a whole but with the narrow question of what research has shown about the neurophysiological basis for the two forms of remembering that are thought to work in opposite directions on false-memory tasks: recollection of precise verbatim details of experience versus familiarity with the meaning content of experience. The guiding assumption, when it comes to false memory, is that brain structures that support the first form of accurate remembering are apt to be involved in the suppression of semantic intrusions and false alarms, whereas brain structures that support the second type of accurate remembering are apt to be involved in generating those same responses. The discussion of true memory will also allow us to introduce some key brain loci that figure in false memory. We then move on, in the second subsection, to the main topic: cognitive neuroscience research on false memory.

Brain Loci of Dual-Memory Processes

We first mentioned in chapter 3 that the opponent-processes approach to false memory, as exemplified in models such as fuzzy-trace theory (Brainerd & Reyna, 2001b; Reyna & Brainerd, 1995b), is closely connected to prior work on dual-process models of true memory, particularly dual-process models of recognition memory (e.g., Atkinson & Juola, 1973, 1974; Graf & Mandler, 1984; Jacoby, 1991; Mandler, 1980; Tulving, 1985), which in turn is grounded in the early introspective findings about word recognition that Strong (1913) obtained. Strong, it will be remembered, found that when his subjects introspected upon the phenomenologies that accompanied their acceptances of certain probes, they reported two characteristic mental experiences. Some probes provoked strong feelings of familiarity that were utterly vague with respect to details of the items' presentation on the study list, but others provoked vivid reinstatement of specific events that occurred when the item was presented (e.g., a thought or emotion that the item had stimulated).

We also saw that the introduction of dual-process theories of recognition was controversial—and continues to be so—because the classic theory in this area is a one-process model (Green & Swets, 1966; Macmillan & Creelman, 1991). According to that theory, true recognition arises from a single retrieval process (called *familiarity*), which accesses a continuous memory-strength scale, with subjects making recognition decisions by setting a subjective strength threshold and accepting probes that cross that threshold. Because dual-process theories are controversial, multiple experimental procedures have been used in an attempt to secure converging evidence that recognition (and also recall) engages the separate, dissociated operations of recollection and familiarity, with recollection being conceived as a *discrete* process (a subject either does or does not recollect a probe's prior presentation) and familiarity being conceived as a *continuous* process (probes can recruit various levels of familiarity from memory), which is analogous to the idea of memory strength in the classic one-process approach (e.g., Yonelinas, 1994). The most frequently used procedures are the process-dissociation model, which was considered earlier in this chapter, and Tulving's (1985) remember/know paradigm (see chapter 3). Other procedures that have generated several studies are recognition versus recall and item recognition versus associative recognition.

As mentioned in previous chapters, some early researchers, such as Mandler (1980), treated recall tests as pure measures of recollection, so that recollection-familiarity dissociations could be demonstrated by showing that manipulations that ought to affect only familiarity change recognition performance but not recall performance (e.g., Glanzer & Adams, 1985; Gregg, Montgomery, & Castano, 1980). Concerning item versus associative recognition, we encountered associative recognition in chapter 4 in connection with studies of inverted-U relations in retrieval time (e.g., Figure 4-16). In associative-recognition experiments, subjects study lists of word pairs, such as those on the left below, and they respond to probes such as those on the right:

Month-River	Month-River
Baby-Star	Baby-Bird
Paper-Telephone	Paper-Telephone
Cake-Ball	Cake-Bottle
Store-Bird	Store-Ball
Lamp-Pump	Lamp-Pump
Tree-Bottle	Tree-Star

Notice that all of the distractor probes in this example (e.g., *baby-bird*) consist of words that were presented on the study list but not together. Thus, the argument runs, all of the words in the test probes will be equally familiar, and the ability to discriminate targets (e.g., *month-river*) from distractors (e.g., *baby-bird*) will therefore turn on being able to recollect the actual details of the target presentations (e.g., that *baby* was presented with *star*, not *bird*). If so, recollection-familiarity dissociations could be demonstrated by showing that manipulations that ought to affect only familiarity lead to changes in item-recognition performance but not to changes in associative-recognition performance (Cameron & Hockley, 2000; Westerman, 2001).

Following the same logic, cognitive neuroscience studies have attempted to demonstrate that different brain loci are involved in recollection and in familiarity—more specifically, that activity in (or damage to) certain brain areas influences performance on measures of recollection (e.g., the R parameter of process-dissociation or associative-recognition tests) but not measures of familiarity (e.g., the F parameter of process-dissociation or item-recognition tests) or that activity in (or damage to) other brain areas influences performance on measures of familiarity but not performance on measures of recollection (Mayes, 1992; Mayes, MacDonald, Donlan, Pears, & Meudell, 1992). For the most part, such research has concentrated on structures that are located within the medial temporal lobes of the brain, though important work involving the prefrontal cortex (the cortical area at the rear of the frontal lobe area in Figure 9-14) and other brain loci also figures in this literature. The temporal lobes are brain areas just above the ears (see Figure 9-14), called "temporal" because they lie under the areas of the skull known as the temples. It has long been understood that these areas are important to cognition because patients with temporal-lobe damage exhibit a range of deficits on memory and reasoning tasks. The medial (meaning "middle of") temporal lobes lie on the inner sides of the temporal lobes and are particularly important to memory because they include some struc-

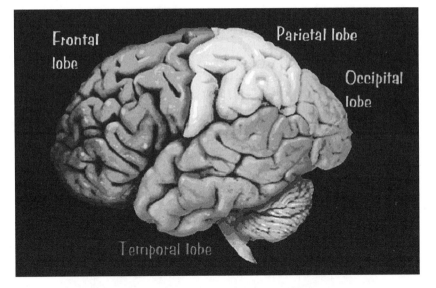

Figure 9-14. Major divisions of the human cortex. See color insert.

tures whose role in memory performance has been extensively studied, such as the hippocampus and its surrounding regions (the entorhinal cortex, the perirhinal cortex, the parahippocampal gyrus). In Figure 9-15, the hippocampus can be seen as a dark tubular structure at the bottom-center of the brain.

The hippocampus is densely packed with a type of nerve cell known as a *pyramidal* cell (e.g., Csicsvari, Hirase, Czurko, Mamiya, & Buzsaki, 1999), a key feature of which is rich interconnections to cells in other areas of the brain, including those in the surrounding cortical areas and more distant regions of the brain. This property of pyramidal cells assists in the formation of stable long-term memories via a process known as *long-term potentiation* (Eichenbaum, 2002). It is well known that the hippocampus plays a determinative role in the formation of personal autobiographical experience and fact-type (or *declarative*) memories (e.g., that Verdi composed *Don Carlos*), and the hippocampus has long been regarded as a gateway to the consolidation of such memories (Nadel & Moscovitch, 1997). For example, patients with hippocampal damage from thiamin deficiency, which can result from alcoholic Korsakoff syndrome and other varieties of malnutrition, display deficits in both types of memories. Similarly, such deficits are noted in the early stages of Alzheimer's disease, and the hippocampus is one of the first structures to be damaged by this disease. Further, deficits in autobiographical and declarative memories are often present in patients with a chronic history of epileptic seizures (e.g., Labiner, Weinand, Brainerd, Ahern, Herring, & Melgar, 2002). The hippocampus, it turns out, is a frequent site of epileptic seizures and can be damaged by chronic seizures. Finally, an adult who sustains hippocampal damage from a head injury may exhibit memories of childhood experiences and adult experiences preceding the injury that are within the normal range but display poor memory for experiences that occurred

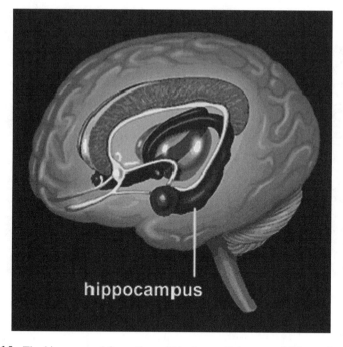

hippocampus

Figure 9-15. The hippocampal formation within the medial temporal lobe region of the brain. See color insert.

after the injury (e.g., Penfield & Milner, 1958; Scoville & Milner, 1957). The hippocampus is particularly sensitive to damage from nonfatal deprivation of oxygen, which results from events such as near-drowning, carbon-monoxide poisoning, sleep apnea, and respiratory failure.

Of central interest to us is a hypothesis about the role of the hippocampus in dual-memory processes. According to this hypothesis, recollection and familiarity are localized within different regions of the hippocampal formation; more particularly, the hippocampus is essential for recollection while the surrounding regions are essential for familiarity. The basis for this hypothesis is a parallel between patterns of neurophysiological activity in the hippocampal formation, on the one hand, and the fast-meaning-activation-versus-slow-verbatim-activation pattern that we have discussed in previous chapters, on the other. Specifically, during memory storage, the regions surrounding the hippocampus are activated first (fast familiarity?), with the activation then being passed on to the hippocampus itself for further processing (slow recollection?) (Eichenbaum, 2002). The hypothesis has received a good deal of support from studies of patients with focal brain lesions, especially patients with damage that is restricted to the hippocampus versus patients with more extensive medial temporal damage that includes some of the regions surrounding the hippocampus (Aggleton & Brown, 1999; Eichenbaum, Otto, & Cohen, 1994).

Before discussing some work of that sort, we note an interesting line of research with normal adults in which subjects are administered mild doses of the benzodiazapine family of drugs. These drugs affect a type of chemical receptor that is especially abundant in the pyramidal cells of the hippocampus (Eichenbaum, 2002). The dual-process prediction would therefore be that the administration of benzodiazapines ought to affect recollection much more than familiarity and might not affect familiarity at all. Findings of that type have been obtained in process-dissociation studies in which benzodiazepines had much larger effects on the R parameter than on the F parameter (Yonelinas, 2002). A similar pattern has emerged from studies that used the remember/know procedure (Bishop & Curran, 1995; Curran, Gardiner, Java, & Allen, 1993; Hirshman, Fisher, Henthorn, Arndt, & Passannante, 2002). In some of those studies, benzodiazepines impaired remember judgments while leaving know judgments unchanged, while in other studies, benzodiazepines impaired remember judgments more than know judgments.

Turning to studies of subjects with brain damage, a good deal of pertinent research has been reported for patients with amnesia resulting from damage to the medial temporal lobes. Such damage can vary in its extent, and an especially informative comparison is between amnesiacs whose damage is localized within the hippocampus versus amnesiacs with damage to the hippocampus and surrounding regions. Some studies that have made this comparison have used the recognition versus recall methodology. As predicted by the hypothesis that the hippocampus is crucial for recollection and the surrounding areas are crucial for familiarity, patients who have hippocampal damage that extends into the surrounding regions have been found to exhibit impairments in both recall and recognition, with some studies detecting larger impairments in recall (Hirst, Phelps, Johnson, & Volpe, 1988; Huppert & Piercy, 1976; Isaac & Mayes, 1999; Johnson & Kim, 1985) and other studies detecting equivalent impairments in recall and recognition in such patients (Haist, Shimamura, & Squire, 1992; Shimamura & Squire, 1987). In other research with the recognition versus recall methodology, the subjects have been patients whose damage is restricted to the hippocampus. As predicted by the hypothesis, such patients have consistently been found to have more severe deficits in recall than in recognition (Baddeley, Vargha-Khadem, & Mishkin, 2001; Holdstock, Mayes, Cezayirli, Isaac, Aggleton, & Roberts, 2002; Mayes, Isaac, Holdstock, Hunkin, Montaldi, Downes, MacDonald, & Cezayirli, 2001). Further, some studies of such patients have failed to detect any impairment in recognition (e.g., Aggleton & Shaw, 1996).

Other studies of amnesiac patients have produced findings that are also consistent with the hypothesis by using the associative- versus item-recognition procedure. Here, the prediction of greatest interest would be that patients with damage to the hippocampus and surrounding regions would show considerable impairment in both types of recognition, while patients with hippocampal-only damage would show much larger impairments in associative recognition and, perhaps, no impairment in item recognition. Unfortunately, studies in which this comparison was made had not been published at the time of this writing. A weaker prediction is that as long as hippocampal damage is present, regardless of whether there is also damage to the surrounding regions, amnesiacs ought to exhibit more pronounced deficits in associative recognition than in item recognition. This prediction has been confirmed in several experiments (e.g., Aggleton, McMackin, Carpenter, Hornak, Kapur, Halpin,

Wiles, Kamel, Brennan, Carton, & Gaffan, 2000; Chalfonte, Verfaellie, Johnson, & Reiss, 1996; Mayes et al., 2001; Parkin & Hunkin, 1993).

Studies of amnesiac patients have also been conducted with process-dissociation methodology and with the remember/know paradigm. In both instances, evidence on the weaker hypothesis above has been reported. Consistent with findings for associative versus item recognition, amnesiacs have displayed larger deficits in the R parameter than in the F parameter (Verfaellie & Treadwell, 1993; Yonelinas et al., 1998), and they have displayed larger deficits in remember judgments than in know judgments for accepted recognition probes (Blaxton & Theodore, 1997; Schacter, Verfaellie, & Anes, 1997; Schacter, Verfaellie, & Pradere, 1996). Also, some stronger findings are available with the remember/know procedure in which patients with hippocampal damage resulting from epileptic seizures exhibited very little disruption in know judgments (Blaxton & Theodore, 1997). Finally, one study has been reported in which the remember/know procedure was used to compare patients with selective damage to the hippocampus to patients with much more extensive medial temporal lobe damage (Lazzara, Yonelinas, Kroll, Kishiyama, Suave, Zusman, & Knight, 2001). This particular study produced a very strong result—namely, that patients with selective hippocampal damage showed deficits in remember judgments only but patients with more extensive damage showed deficits in both remember and know judgments.

At present, the consensus of opinion is that research focusing on the medial temporal lobes has provided converging evidence of distinct neurological substrata for recollection and familiarity, evidence that favors the hypothesis that the hippocampus is intimately involved in recollection of the surface form of experience and that the surrounding regions are intimately involved in nonspecific familiarity (Yonelinas, Kroll, Quamme, Lazzara, Suave, Widaman, & Knight, 2002). However, research with other forms of brain damage suggests that there are additional cortical locations that are important to recollective experience: the prefrontal cortex, in particular.

Both the recall versus recognition procedure and the associative- versus item-recognition procedure have been used to study patients with lesions in the dorsolateral regions (upper left and right sides) of the prefrontal cortex. With both procedures, substantial deficits in performance on the recollection measure have been found with little or no impairment in performance on the corresponding familiarity measures (Greshberg & Shimamura, 1995; Jetter, Poser, Freeman, & Markowitsch, 1986; Kopelman & Stanhope, 1997). In addition, there is evidence that the recollection of different surface characteristics of stimuli may be lateralized, with damage to the right dorsolateral region producing larger deficits in recollection of nonverbal materials, such as pictures, and damage to the left dorsolateral region producing larger deficits in recollection of verbal materials, such as words and sentences (Milner, Corsi, & Leonard, 1991).

Finally, in addition to research with brain-damaged patients, neuroimaging studies of possible recollection and familiarity loci have been conducted using the recall versus recognition and the associative- versus item-recognition methods. This work is newer and far less extensive than studies of recollection and familiarity in brain-damaged patients, but it provides an important refinement that yields more probative, differentiated data. It is possible to separate areas of high brain activity during the storage phase of a memory experiment, when target materials are being presented to subjects, from areas of high brain activity during the retrieval phase, when subjects are responding to memory tests, because brain scans are being taken continuously during a memory experiment. Although we have not mentioned this possibility hitherto, it is conceivable that the brain loci that are involved in recollection and familiarity may be somewhat different during these two phases, and certain neuroimaging results suggest that this may indeed be the case.

Extant neuroimaging studies provide findings about the brain loci of recollection that are quite consistent with the general patterns that we have described for studies of brain-damaged patients, but as yet, neuroimaging research has generated little information about the brain loci of familiarity. During encoding, the presentation of stimuli that subsequently produce recollective responses on memory tests (correct recall, remember judgments) often produces increased levels of activation in the prefrontal cortex and in the medial temporal lobes, as one would expect from studies of patients with lesions in these areas (Brewer, Zhao, Desmond, Glover, & Gabrieli, 1998; Henson, Rugg, Shallice, Josephs, & Dolan, 1999; Wagner, Koutstaal, & Schacter, 1999). Analogously, the presentation of targets during an associative-recognition experiment produces more activation in the hippocampus than does the presentation of targets during an item-recognition experiment, and increased hippocampal activation during the presentation of individual items is positively correlated with successful performance on later recall tests (Henke, Buck, Weber, & Wieser, 1997; Strange, Otten, Josephs, Rugg, & Dolan, 2002). During the retrieval of previously presented material, increased activation in the hippocampus and in the surrounding regions is associated with successful associative recognition but not item recognition (Yonelinas, Hopfinger, Buonocore, Kroll, & Baynes, 2001), and moreover, the same pattern of increased activation on item-recognition tests is associated with remember judgments but not with know judgments (Eldridge, Knowlton, Furmanski, Bookheimer, & Engel, 2000). Similarly, increased activation in the prefrontal cortex during retrieval is associated with successful associative recognition but not item recognition (Nolde, Johnson, & D'Esposito, 1998), and increased prefrontal activation is also associated with the recognition of items that produce remember judgments rather than know judgments (Henson et al., 1999). In addition to these results, which parallel the findings of studies with brain-damaged patients, imaging research has produced evidence of another brain locus that is important in recollection: the parietal lobes (see Figure 9-14). During retrieval, remember judgments produce greater parietal lobe activation than do know judgments (Eldridge et al., 2000; Henson et al., 1999).

In brief, the overall picture from both neuroimaging research and research with brain-damaged patients is one in which particular brain loci map with recollection of the surface details of experience and other brain loci map with familiarity of meaning content. The hippocampus and certain areas of the prefrontal cortex, in particular, seem to support recollective remembering, whereas the cortical areas surrounding the hippocampus seem to support familiarity-based remembering. These patterns have straightforward implications for research on brain structures that may be involved in false-memory responses, implications that we now explore.

Brain Loci of Opponent Processes in False Memory

In light of what is known about the brain loci of recollection and familiarity, what would opponent-processes distinctions predict about how false-memory responses ought to vary as a function of damage to different brain regions or of levels of activity in different brain regions? One obvious prediction is that brain damage (or reduced activity in particular regions) will not automatically result in increased levels of false memory; false memory can be suppressed, too, if the regions in question are involved in storing or accessing the meaning of experience. Another obvious prediction is that brain regions that seem to be implicated in storing and accessing memories of the surface content of experience ought to have different influences on false-memory responses than brain regions that seem to be implicated in storing and accessing its meaning content. Other things being equal, focused damage (or reduced activity) in areas that have been implicated in recollection-based remembering ought to increase semantic false alarms and intrusions by decreasing subjects' ability to reject false-but-meaning-preserving items on the basis of surface mismatches with actual experience, whereas damage (or reduced activity) that includes areas that have been implicated in familiarity-based remembering ought to decrease semantic false alarms and intrusions by decreasing subjects' ability to store or retrieve meaning content. More specific possibilities are that damage (or reduced activity) that is restricted to the hippocampus will increase semantic false alarms and intrusions and that damage (or reduced activity) to the dorsolateral regions of the prefrontal cortex will have similar effects (owing to reduced verbatim processing), but that damage (or reduced activity) that includes the regions surrounding the hippocampus will decrease semantic false alarms and intrusions (owing to reduced gist processing).

Although all of these predictions are straightforward when opponent-processes distinctions are combined with the research that was reviewed above, for the most part they are in advance of the present state of cognitive neuroscience research on false memory. From a theoretical standpoint, this lag is not problematical. One sign of a good theory is that it can forecast results that are a few steps ahead of current experimentation. The situation is not problematical from an empirical standpoint either; instead, it has the positive consequence of giving direction to research by supplying targets to shoot for that are guaranteed to increase theoretical understanding. So, just what is known about the brain loci of false memory?

At the time of this writing, a few brain-imaging studies of laboratory false-memory tasks have been reported, but such data are as yet too scarce to yield consistent conclusions (e.g., Curran, Schacter, Johnson, & Spinks, 2001; Schacter, Buckner, Koutstaal, Dale, & Rosen, 1997). A larger database has accumulated for patients with brain damage, particularly amnesiacs with medial temporal lobe damage (e.g., Schacter & Dodson, 2001; Schacter, Verfaellie, & Pradere, 1998) and Alzheimer's patients (e.g., Balota, Burgess, Cortese, & Adams, 2002; Balota, Cortese, Duchek, Adams, Roediger, McDermott, & Yerys, 1999; Budson, Sullivan, Daffner, & Schacter, 2003; Watson, Balota, & Sergent-Marshall, 2001). We summarize findings for amnesiac patients first, then findings for Alzheimer's patients. We end with a brief discussion of an extreme variety of false memory—pathological false recognition—

which has been identified in patients with frontal lobe damage (Parkin, 1997; Parkin, Bindschaedler, Harsent, & Metzler, 1996; Ward & Parkin, 2000).

Amnesiac Patients

Studies of amnesiac patients with damage to the medial temporal lobes have produced conflicting conclusions with respect to whether this condition is associated with increases or decreases in false-memory responses. On the one hand, Kroll, Knight, Metcalfe, Wolfe, and Tulving (1996) found that such patients exhibited increased levels of false memory on one familiar measure—false recognition of related distractors—using a paradigm known as the *illusory conjunction* task. In this paradigm (e.g., Rubin, Van Petten, Glisky, & Newberg, 1999), which resembles associative recognition, subjects study lists of two-syllable words (e.g., *barter, baseball, footstool, handstand, shotgun, valley*) and then respond to recognition tests composed of targets and related distractors that are formed by pairing syllables from different targets (e.g., *barley, football, handgun*).

In contrast, a series of studies by Schacter and associates has revealed lower levels of false recognition of related distractors in amnesiacs with medial temporal damage, relative to matched control subjects. This research relied on variants of the DRM procedure. In an initial study (Schacter et al., 1996), patients with medial temporal damage that was pursuant to alcoholic Korsakoff syndrome (half of the patients) or other causes (e.g., anoxia, encephalitis) were tested. Such damage normally includes regions surrounding the hippocampus, as well as the hippocampus itself. Although the amnesiacs exhibited normal attentional abilities, they were known to display severe deficits on a variety of true-memory tests. The subjects listened to eight DRM lists, performed free recall immediately following half of the lists, and after all eight lists had been presented, they responded to a recognition test on which the probes consisted of targets (e.g., *nurse, hospital*), stimulus words (*doctor*), and unrelated words (e.g., *cake, spider*). After the recognition test, the subjects made remember/know judgments about accepted probes. The recall results are summarized in Panel a of Figure 9-16, where it is apparent that, as would be expected, the amnesiac patients were noticeably poorer at true recall and also slightly poorer at false recall of stimulus words. The latter difference was much more marked on the recognition tests, the results of which are summarized in Panel b of Figure 9-16. There, the overall false-alarm rates for stimulus words are shown, and these false-alarm rates are broken down into the proportion that provoked remember phenomenology and the proportion that provoked know phenomenology. The former, which is a type of phantom recollection, is a particularly striking mental experience, both because it is an illusory vivid mental state that is akin to hallucination and because it seems to result from especially robust gist memories. It can be seen that amnesiacs' false-alarm rates, like their intrusion rates, were lower than controls'. However, consideration of the remember/know data reveals that the mental experiences that accompanied these responses were dramatically different in the two groups. As is usually the case when DRM lists are administered to normal adults (e.g., Roediger & McDermott, 1995; Payne et al., 1996), controls' false alarms were overwhelmingly accompanied by phantom recollection of stimulus words' prior

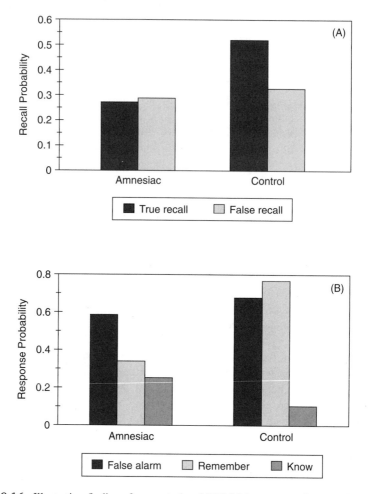

Figure 9-16. Illustrative findings from a study of DRM false memory in amnesiacs with medial temporal lobe damage versus control subjects. Panel A presents recall results, and Panel B presents recognition results. Data from Schacter, Verfaellie, and Pradere (1996).

"presentation" on the study list—indicating, again as usual with such subjects, the presence of strong gist memories. However, amnesiacs' false alarms did not show this disparity; such responses were accompanied by know phenomenology about as often as they were accompanied by remember phenomenology, suggesting that amnesiacs with this type of brain damage are deficient in the formation of gist memories of DRM lists' meaning content.

Although Kroll et al.'s (1996) finding of elevated false-alarm rates for related distractors in amnesiacs seems at odds with Schacter et al.'s finding of lowered false-alarm rates for related distractors, an opponent-processes analysis shows that, in fact, there may be no inconsistency because the false-alarm rates in the two studies are probably due to different memory processes. As we said, the illusory-conjunction task resembles associative recognition because conjunction distractors are created by pairing halves of targets. Thus, like associative recognition, all of these distractors will be familiar, and therefore, whether they are accepted will depend primarily upon whether subjects are able to access verbatim traces of the targets from which they were generated. If medial temporal lobe damage impairs verbatim access, as the aforementioned studies of true memory consistently indicate that it does, amnesiacs should have more difficulty rejecting conjunction distractors than controls have. Further, if we accept the logic of the recognition versus recall procedure, Schacter et al.'s amnesiacs also displayed impairments in verbatim access because their true recall rates were much lower than were controls' (Figure 9-16a). In addition, Schacter et al.'s amnesiacs were deficient in the ability to access gist memories of meaning content because false-alarm rates and false-remember judgments were suppressed, relative to controls. Thus, the reconciliation of the two studies is that Kroll et al.'s false-memory measures primarily tapped verbatim memory, that Schacter et al.'s measures primarily tapped gist memory, and based upon prior studies of recollection and familiarity, medial temporal damage that encompasses regions that surround the hippocampus can produce deficits in both verbatim and gist memory.

Further DRM research confirming reduced levels of DRM false memory in amnesiacs with medial temporal lobe damage was subsequently reported by Schacter, Verfaellie et al. (1998). Importantly, Schacter et al. also found that a standard manipulation that strengthens verbatim memory and suppresses false memory—verbatim repetition—was ineffective with amnesiacs. However, Melo et al. (1999) reported a DRM study that produced conflicting results. As in Schacter et al.'s original study, the performance of medial temporal lobe amnesiacs was compared to the performance of matched controls. All subjects listened to eight DRM lists, performing free recall following half of the lists and responding to a terminal-recognition test for all eight lists once the presentation phase was complete. The results are summarized in Figure 9-17, and two discrepancies with Schacter et al.'s results can be seen. First, the amnesiacs' levels of false recall were much higher than controls', roughly twice as high in fact, and second, the amnesiacs' levels of false recognition were also much higher than controls'. Concerning the recognition test, the amnesiacs' levels of false alarms to *unrelated* distractors were also higher than controls'. To correct for this and to provide an accurate representation of group differences in true and false memory, the values that have been plotted for the recognition tests are hits-minus-unrelated-false-alarms (for true memory) and stimulus-word-false-alarms-minus-unrelated-false-alarms (for false memory).

Although Melo et al.'s results provide a different picture of false memory in amnesiacs, the picture is quite coherent from an opponent-processes perspective, and opponent-processes distinctions provide a simple explanation of the differences between Melo et al.'s amnesiacs and Schacter et al.'s. A key feature of Melo et al.'s subjects, relative to Schacter et al.'s, can be seen by considering the hit rates in Figure 9-17. Note that the hit rate for amnesiacs was zero; targets and unrelated distractors were accepted at the same rate. Thus, the amnesiacs showed *no verbatim memory at all* on the recognition tests, and although they did exhibit some ability to recall targets on the earlier recall test, much of that information would have been

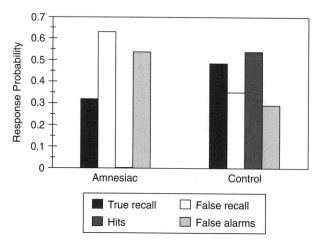

Figure 9-17. Illustrative findings from a study of DRM false memory in amnesiacs versus control subjects. Data from Melo, Winocur, and Moscovitch (1999).

read out of short-term memory rather than by retrieving consolidated verbatim traces, because the recall tests were administered immediately. On the other hand, Melo et al.'s amnesiacs, like Schacter et al.'s, were able to form stable gist memories of meaning content because they made more false alarms to stimulus words than to unrelated distractors. Importantly, those gist memories were not any stronger than in Schacter et al.'s amnesiacs because the difference between the two false-alarm rates was approximately the same in the two studies. Hence, the likely difference between Melo et al.'s and Schacter et al.'s medial temporal lobe patients, which produced the reversal in observed levels of false memory in amnesiacs versus controls, is simply that Melo et al.'s patients were seriously deficient in the ability to access verbatim traces of targets, indicating that they may have had more extensive hippocampal damage than Schacter et al.'s patients.

An important question that remains is whether medial temporal lobe amnesiacs are deficient in storage or retrieval of the gist memories that support semantic intrusions and false alarms, as Schacter et al. (1996) originally hypothesized. Koutstaal, Schacter, Galluccio, and Stofer (1999) repeated the design that had been used in other false-memory studies with such patients, but they added a meaning-oriented testing condition along the lines of the V+M condition of conjoint-memory experiments (see above). In their study, half of the subjects responded to a recognition test for previously studied lists under standard instructions (accept only targets) and half responded under V+M instructions (accept any meaning-preserving probe). This is an instructive comparison because the V+M condition tends to equalize amnesiac patients and controls for differences in verbatim-memory abilities, which Melo et al.'s (1999) results suggest can be considerable. According to opponent-processes logic, such differences are contaminants when it comes to detecting deficiencies in gist memory because verbatim and gist memory both contribute to intrusions and false alarms, albeit in opposite ways. Consistent with this logic, Koutstaal et al.

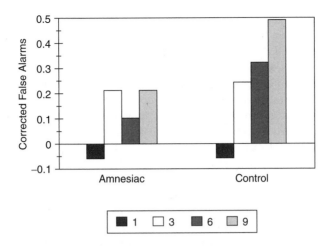

Figure 9-18. Illustrative findings from a study of false memory in amnesiacs versus controls, using the abstract picture-gist procedure. 1, 3, 6, and 9 refers to the number of pictures that were presented for each category on the study list. Data from Koutstaal, Schacter, Verfaellie, Brenner, and Jackson (1999).

found that under V+M instructions, where meaning-preserving distractors *should* be accepted, medial temporal lobe amnesiacs accepted those distractors at lower rates than did controls, which is consistent with Schacter et al.'s original hypothesis.

Additional evidence supporting this hypothesis has been generated using a different procedure: the picture-gist paradigm of Koutstaal and associates (e.g., Koutstaal & Schacter, 1997). It will be recalled that there are two versions of this procedure, one in which subjects study color photographs of familiar objects that belong to a single class (Figure 9-7) and one in which subjects study pictures that also depict objects that belong to a single class, but the pictures have been degraded to a point where subjects can only identify the class if they are told what it is (Figure 9-9). The latter procedure was used in an initial study by Koutstaal, Schacter, Verfaellie, Brenner, and Jackson (1999). In that study, amnesiac Korsakoff patients were matched to a control sample of alcoholics who were not suffering from Korsakoff syndrome. As in Koutstaal et al.'s (2003) research, subjects were exposed to a series of lists like those in Figure 9-9, and then responded to a recognition test composed of targets, related distractors, and unrelated distractors. Also as in Koutstaal et al.'s (2003) research, the strength of stored gist memories was manipulated by varying the number of same-category pictures—specifically, the number of exemplar pictures that were presented per list was either one, three, six, or nine. The data for false recognition of related distractors, which are summarized in Figure 9-18, were again consistent with the view that medial temporal lobe amnesiacs exhibit impaired gist memory. Because, as in Melo et al.'s (1999) study, false-alarm rates for unrelated distractors were much higher in amnesiacs, this false-alarm rate has been subtracted from that for related distractors in Figure 9-18. As can be seen, presentation of a single exemplar was insufficient to produce a false-memory effect in either group. With additional exemplars, both groups displayed false-memory effects, and crucially, those effects were always more marked in the controls. Moreover, the amnesiac versus control difference increased as additional exemplars were presented, the reason being that whereas controls displayed the standard tendency (see chapters 4 and 5) for false-memory effects to increase with increasing gist repetition, the amnesiacs did not (e.g., note that their corrected false-alarm rates were the same following nine exemplars as following three). Naturally, all of this is consistent with the hypothesis of gist-memory deficits in medial temporal lobe amnesiacs. Further supportive data were reported in another picture-gist study by Koutstaal, Verfaellie, and Schacter (2001). In that study, however, the target and test materials consisted of realistic color photographs like those in Figure 9-7, so that the category membership of all objects was easily identifiable. The basic pattern was the same as with abstract pictures in that amnesiacs again exhibited decreased levels of false recognition of category-related pictures.

Considering the literature as a whole, there appears to be solid evidence of impaired memory for the gist of word lists and pictures in medial temporal lobe amnesiacs. Because such damage usually includes the regions surrounding the hippocampus, the evidence is quite congruent with the research on the brain loci of recollection and familiarity that we examined earlier. However, this gist deficit may not produce reduced false-memory effects in such patients, relative to controls, because they also display impaired verbatim memory. Because verbatim and gist memory make opposite contributions to false-memory effects, sufficiently severe verbatim deficits can result in no amnesiac versus control differences or differences favoring amnesiacs (Melo et al., 1999). Although the amnesiac data argue for poorer gist memory as a consequence of medial temporal lobe damage, it should not be concluded that this is the only brain locus that supports gist memory: Other research with semantic false recognition tasks has revealed lower levels of false recognition in patients with damage to the amygdala (Beversdorf, Smith, Crucian, Anderson, Keillor, Barrett, Hughes, Felopulos, Bauman, Nadeau, & Heilman, 2000), a structure in the anterior of the brain that is involved in memory for the emotional content of experience (e.g., Eichenbaum, 2002), and in patients with frontal lobe damage (Parkin, Ward, Bindschaedler, Squires, & Powell, 1999).

Alzheimer's Patients

Alzheimer's disease is a progressive neurological disorder in which neurons deteriorate, with the key biochemical mechanism being the build-up of neuritic plaques and neurofibral tangles. The former are patches of a protein called beta amyloid, which blocks the production of an important neurotransmission molecule (acetylcholine), and the latter are coils of a protein called tau, whose presence in brain tissue interferes with the normal chemical processes of neurons. As mentioned earlier, Alzheimer's disease often begins in the hippocampus and spreads to the surrounding tissue. Hence, in light of findings about the role of the hippocampus in recollection-based true memory, Alzheimer's patients, especially in the early stages of the disease, might be expected to display substantial deficits in verbatim memory, coupled with normal or near-normal gist memory, the net effect of which should be elevated levels of false memory. An important series of studies by Balota and associates and by Budson and associates has generated evidence on this possibility.

In an early study, Balota et al. (1999) used the DRM paradigm to compare the performance of two groups of healthy elderly adults, old (mean age = 71) and very old (mean age = 86), to the performance of Alzheimer's patients with two levels of severity of the disease, very mild and mild. A further comparison sample of young adults (mean age = 20 years) was also included. All subjects listened to six DRM lists, performing oral free recall immediately following each list. After the sixth list had been presented and recalled, all subjects responded to a recognition test composed of targets, the stimulus words for the presented lists, and unrelated distractors that were taken from other DRM lists, which had not been presented. The resulting data were analyzed in two ways. The first method is summarized in Panel a of Figure 9-19, which shows the mean intrusion rates and false-alarm rates for unpresented stimulus words in all five subject groups. The salient pattern in this figure is the one that was described in the earlier section on aging and false memory—namely, that whether false memory is measured by semantic intrusions or semantic false alarms, there is a dramatic increase between young and late adulthood. With respect to the question of interest here, however, there is no sign that Alzheimer's disease elevates these false-memory responses; intrusion and false-alarm rates of both patient groups were comparable to those for healthy elderly adults.

Another way of looking at these data provides a different picture, however. The best-known characteristic of Alzheimer's disease is a deficit in true memory for autobiographical events and recently learned facts. Because such memories have a distinctly verbatim slant, it is reasonable to say that the disease produces verbatim deficits, and this notion can be used to construct a *relative measure* of false memory, by which we mean a measure that is relative to each group's baseline level of true memory. Data of this sort are summarized in Panel b of Figure 9-19, for both recall and recognition. These data were generated by subtracting each group's level of false recall (or false recognition) from its corresponding level of true recall (or true recognition). Thus, upward-pointing bars mean that true memory exceeded false memory, and downward-pointing bars mean that false memory exceeded true memory. Based upon the earlier discussion of aging, a large jump in relative false memory would be expected between early and late adulthood, and that jump is apparent from the fact that the upward-pointing bars are much taller for the young adult group than for any of the elderly groups. In addition, however, the hypothesis of interest is that Alzheimer's disease may cause elevations in relative false memory, as compared to healthy aged adults. This finding was clearly evident for semantic intrusions: The upward-pointing bars for recall are considerably shorter for very mild Alzheimer's patients than for healthy aged adults, and the bar for those with mild Alzheimer's points downward. For recognition, there was a trend in the same direction, but it can be seen that the trend was moderate in comparison to recall. Interestingly, note that for the four elderly groups, all of the bars point downward, indicating no ability to discriminate presented words from stimulus words among the elderly groups.

Further clear evidence of elevated levels of false memory in Alzheimer's patients comes from a more recent study by Budson et al. (2003). These investigators also used the DRM paradigm, administering such lists to patients with diagnoses of probable Alzheimer's disease, to healthy elderly adults, and to young adults. Budson et

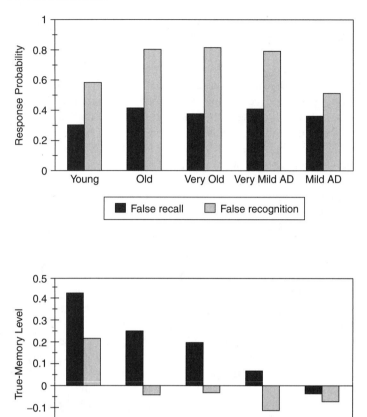

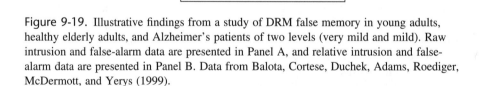

Figure 9-19. Illustrative findings from a study of DRM false memory in young adults, healthy elderly adults, and Alzheimer's patients of two levels (very mild and mild). Raw intrusion and false-alarm data are presented in Panel A, and relative intrusion and false-alarm data are presented in Panel B. Data from Balota, Cortese, Duchek, Adams, Roediger, McDermott, and Yerys (1999).

al. argued, based upon fuzzy-trace theory, that Alzheimer's patients are impaired in both the formation of gist memories of DRM lists and in the preservation of verbatim traces of targets, and they argued that the two impairments could be disentangled by measuring false memory under conditions that provide different levels of verbatim support. To evaluate this argument, the individual DRM lists that were administered to their subjects were presented one, two, three, four, or five times during the study phase. This was followed by the usual recognition test containing targets, stimulus words, and unrelated distractors. As previously discussed, in young adults, who readily extract the gist of DRM lists, and to a lesser extent in healthy

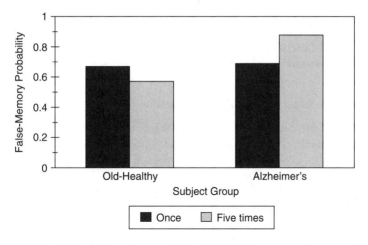

Figure 9-20. Illustrative findings from a study of DRM false memory in young adults, healthy elderly adults, and Alzheimer's patients. Subjects studied each DRM list once or five times. Data from Budson, Sullivan, Mayer, Daffner, and Black (2002).

elderly adults (Kensinger & Schacter, 1999), the overriding effect of verbatim repetition is to strengthen labile verbatim traces, relative to their more-stable gist counterparts, the net effect of which is therefore to reduce semantic intrusions and false alarms. However, if Alzheimer's disease produces major impairments in gist as well as verbatim memory, the effect of verbatim repetition might be more like that of *gist* repetition with young adults (see chapter 4)—namely, to strengthen the gist memories that support intrusions and false alarms.

Budson et al.'s findings, which are illustrated in Figure 9-20, were dramatic. The data plotted in this figure are A' values for false recognition of stimulus words, a signal-detection statistic that, like the data in Figure 9-6, adjusts for group differences in false alarms to unrelated distractors. It can be seen that when DRM lists were presented only once, the results for Alzheimer's patients versus healthy elderly adults resembled those of Balota et al. (1999): no difference in false-memory levels. When DRM lists were presented five times, however, there was a dramatic difference in the expected direction: a much higher level of false memory in Alzheimer's patients than in healthy elderly adults. The reason is that verbatim repetition had opposite effects on the two groups. For healthy elderly adults, the effect was the standard one of decreased false recognition of stimulus words. As predicted on theoretical grounds, for Alzheimer's patients, verbatim repetition acted like gist repetition and increased false recognition. In later work that, owing to the vagaries of journal publication lags, received an earlier publication date, this pattern was replicated by Budson, Sullivan, Mayer, Daffner, Black, and Schacter (2002). These researchers suggested that collateral damage to the frontal lobes may be responsible for the tendency of verbatim repetition to act like gist repetition in Alzheimer's patients.

Thus, available evidence points to the conclusion that Alzheimer's patients display elevated levels of false memory, relative to healthy elderly adults. This is consistent with the hypothesis of profound verbatim-memory deficits in such patients. However, owing to parallel, if smaller, deficits in gist memory, the detection of elevated levels of false memory in Alzheimer's patients may require special statistical analyses or experimental conditions that ensure the storage of gist memories.

Note on Pathological False Recognition

Although our chief concern in this section has been with the neuropsychology of standard false-memory effects and with how opponent-processes distinctions explain them, it should be noted that certain types of brain damage produce extreme forms of memory falsification in which patients seem to be completely unable to distinguish recently presented material from unpresented material on the basis of either its surface form or its meaning. An important example is provided by a phenomenon that is called *pathological false recognition*, which has been reported by Parkin and his associates (e.g., Parkin, 1997; Parkin et al., 1999) in connection with patients who have extensive frontal lobe damage. Parkin has conducted several studies of individual patients with this condition, and on recognition tasks, they sometimes display high false-alarm rates for *both* unrelated distractors and meaning-preserving distractors, suggesting profound impairments in the ability to access verbatim traces of targets and to perform recollection rejection. In line with this hypothesis, pathological false recognition can be markedly reduced by providing frontal lobe patients with verbatim prosthetics. Prosthetics that have been found to have this effect include perceptual distinctiveness manipulations in which the visual appearance of distractors is different than the visual appearance of studied targets.

Synopsis

Mathematical modeling, aging studies, and cognitive neuroscience studies are significant emerging domains of false-memory research. Enough data have already accumulated in these areas to discern some major trends. Each promises to be a field of vigorous investigation in future years because each contributes some important missing pieces to the puzzle of false memory: the quantification of opponent processes and the measurement of dissociation among those processes in the case of mathematical modeling, the determination of whether standard varieties of false memory increase during the final stages of life and of the theoretical reasons for those increases in the case of aging studies, and the identification of brain structures that support individual processes that have been implicated in standard varieties of false memory in the case of cognitive neuroscience studies.

When it comes to evaluating the predictions of the opponent-processes approach, a crucial limitation of extant research is that predictions have customarily been formulated as qualitative statements about variations in subjects' performance on the usual indexes of false memory: semantic intrusions and false alarms. The theoretical gain from such research is restricted because exact amounts of variation in those indexes are not specified and because changes in the underlying memory processes that are supposedly responsible for such variation are not measured. The latter problem creates serious obstacles in the interpretation of experimental findings because underlying memory processes are confounded in subjects' performance on the usual indexes of false memory. Specifically, because the underlying memory processes that are assumed to control false-memory responses work in opposition to each other, theoretically predicted changes in one process can be masked by correlated changes in another process, so that correct theoretical predictions appear to be disconfirmed at the level of experimental data. This limitation of traditional false-memory research and also the lack of quantitative predictions about subjects' performance can both be overcome with mathematical models.

A mathematical model of false memory makes two additions to traditional research designs. First, it expresses performance on focal memory tasks as a mathematical function of distinct memory processes, such as the retrieval of verbatim and gist traces of experience or recollection and familiarity. Second, it provides an expanded experimental procedure for focal tasks that delivers sufficient new empirical quantities to allow all of the memory processes that are posited in the model to be estimated from those quantities. Two families of models are currently available, each of which has generated a series of studies: conjoint-memory models and modified process-dissociation models.

Conjoint-memory models have been developed for both recognition and recall. The recognition model expresses semantic false alarms as a function of four processes (recollection rejection, similarity judgment, phantom recollection, and response bias), and the recall model expresses semantic intrusions as a function of three processes (recollection rejection, similarity construction, and phantom recollection). These models have been used to measure those memory processes in spontaneous false-memory experiments and misinformation experiments using a paradigm in which subjects respond to memory tests under three types of instructions: verbatim (accept, or recall, only targets), meaning (accept, or recall, only semantically related distractors), and verbatim plus gist (accept, or recall, both targets and semantically related distractors). In such experiments, attention has been centered upon securing direct tests of opponent-processes predictions by studying manipulations that ought to affect those processes in specific ways, and the accumulated data are generally consistent with theoretical expectations: Recollection rejection has reacted predictably to manipulations that ought to strengthen or weaken verbatim traces, and similarity judgment and phantom recollection have reacted predictably to manipulations that ought to strengthen or weaken gist traces.

Turning to the other family of models, Holliday and associates have modified Jacoby's process-dissociation paradigm for use in misinformation experiments with children. Applications of this modified paradigm in a series of studies have produced several informative results. Perhaps the most fundamental results are that children's susceptibility to suggestion is chiefly due to the familiarity of false-memory probes, rather than to recollection of their presentation during the misinformation phase, and that variations in susceptibility, whether between age levels or across experimental conditions, are chiefly due to variations in children's reliance on familiarity.

The next emerging area of research—studies of false memory in elderly adults—is an off-shoot of a quarter century of intensive research on declines in true memory during late adulthood. The bulk of the research in this new area has been focused upon spontaneous rather than implanted false memories, with the DRM paradigm (and its variants) and eyewitness-identification tasks being favored procedures. DRM-type studies have generally shown that healthy elderly adults display higher levels of semantic intrusions and false alarms than do younger adults, though levels of false memory in younger and older adults can be comparable when tasks encourage verbatim processing. If age-related increases in false memory are the baseline pattern, the deeper question is: Why? Several findings, including some from studies of true memory, converge on the conclusion that there is a shift away from verbatim processing and toward gist processing during late adulthood. Two theoretical explanations of this shift have been offered: a verbatim-deficit conjecture and a gist-preference conjecture. According to the former, elderly adults often fail to store verbatim traces of target materials, and they deposit much weaker verbatim traces when they do store them, because they are poorer than younger adults at attending to those materials. This hypothesis implies that elevated levels of gist processing among older adults are a consequence of the fact that verbatim traces are simply not available. According to the gist-preference conjecture, on the other hand, the shift toward gist processing is more in the nature of a retrieval preference or tendency than a deficit in verbatim memory, that older adults tend to base their responses predominantly on meaning content even though verbatim traces are available for retrieval. Empirically, a key difference between the verbatim-deficit and gist-preference conjectures is that the latter forecasts that manipulations that encourage verbatim retrieval will eliminate age differences in false memory, whereas this should not be possible under the former hypothesis. The current literature favors the gist-preference conjecture in that verbatim-retrieval manipulations have dramatically suppressed false-memory responses among elderly subjects. In a particularly probative series of experiments by Koutstaal and associates, using a paradigm that separated the contributions of surface and semantic similarity to false memory, aging increases in false memory were wholly attributable to semantic similarity.

Research on the false identification of criminal suspects by elderly adults evolved from a prior literature on facial recognition by such subjects. In that literature, the bulk of which consists of studies by Bartlett and associates, younger adults and older adults studied pictures of faces that varied in the usual everyday features (e.g., age, gender, spatial orientation) and then responded to recognition tests consisting of target faces and distractors that shared these same features. A consistent finding was that false recognition of distractors was higher in elderly subjects than in younger ones, a discrepancy that could be increased by manipulations that increased the difficulty of verbatim processing or decreased by manipulations that supported verbatim processing. Like aging studies using the DRM paradigm, the findings of earlier facial-recognition studies pointed to an increased preference for gist processing in elderly adults, relative to younger adults. More recent studies in this literature have dealt with age differences in facial recognition under conditions that simulate eyewitness identification (e.g., subjects respond to photo spreads after observing a sequence of events in which a crime was committed). A key finding of these newer studies, one that was also obtained in prior work on facial recognition and that is consistent with statistics showing that false identification is the leading cause of wrongful convictions, is that the tendency to falsely identity photographs of innocent people is quite high at all age levels, even though the events of a crime were observed only a few minutes before. In addition, rates of false identification of suspects are higher in elderly subjects, a tendency that appears to be due to increased reliance on specific dimensions of facial gist, such as typicality and familiarity.

The final emerging area of research—cognitive neuroscience studies of false memory—is part of an increasing emphasis upon neurophysiological mechanisms throughout the memory literature. This shift in focus has been encouraged by the availability of noninvasive brain-imaging technologies for studying brain functioning (e.g., CAT, fMRI, PET) and by increased availability of grant funds to support the use of those technologies in memory research. As in experiments on aging, the bulk of cognitive neuroscience research has focused upon true rather than false memory. One point of emphasis in such research has been the identification of brain regions that support recollection-based remembering and familiarity-based remembering, and much of that research has concentrated upon the medial temporal lobes. Findings that have been generated by five different paradigms (recall versus recognition, associative recognition versus item recognition, remember/know, process dissociation, and neuroimaging) point to the conclusion that the hippocampus, which contains cells that are richly connected to other areas of the brain, is important for recollection, whereas the cortical regions that surround the hippocampus are important for familiarity. This conclusion is consistent with data on the neurophysiological relationship between the hippocampus and its surrounding regions, data showing that incoming stimulation from target materials produces activation in the surrounding regions, which is then passed on to the hippocampus. Research suggests that, in addition to the medial temporal lobes, there are other brain regions, especially the prefrontal lobes, that are important to recollection-based remembering.

Based on such findings, some opponent-processes predictions about false memory are that (a) increased activity in (or damage to) brain regions that are associated with recollection-based remembering ought to be related to subjects' ability to reject false-memory responses; and (b) increased activity in (or damage to) brain regions that are associated with familiarity-based remembering ought to be related to subjects' tendency to make such responses. Prior studies of true memory make the hippocampal and prefrontal regions promising sites for testing such predictions. Although some research along those lines has been reported with the brain-imaging technologies that have been used to study true memory, the bulk of research on brain loci of false-memory responses consists of studies of subjects with focal brain damage, particularly amnesiac patients with medial temporal lobe damage and Alzheimer's patients. The brain damage of the amnesiac populations that have been studied has usually resulted from Korsakoff syndrome, anoxia, or encephalitis and would therefore be expected to include some of the regions surrounding the hippocampus, as well as the hippocampus itself. This leads to the prediction that such patients might show reduced levels of false memory, relative to controls, because they are deficient in extracting and storing the gist of experience. Such reductions among amnesiac samples have been detected in several studies, and lowered levels of phantom recollection of unpresented distractors have also been detected. In contrast, other studies have detected elevated levels of false memory in

References

Abrams, R. L., & Greenwald, A. G. (2000). Parts outweigh the whole (word) in unconscious analysis of meaning. *Psychological Science, 11,* 118–124.

Abrams, R. L., & Greenwald, A. G. (2002). Subliminal words activate semantic categories (not automated motor responses). *Psychonomic Bulletin & Review, 9,* 100–106.

Ackerman, B. P. (1992). The sources of children's source errors in judging causal inferences. *Journal of Experimental Child Psychology, 54,* 90–119.

Ackerman, B. P. (1994). Children's source errors in referential communication. *Journal of Experimental Child Psychology, 58,* 432–464.

Ackil, J. K., & Zaragoza, M. S. (1995). Developmental differences in eyewitness suggestibility and memory for source. *Journal of Experimental Child Psychology, 60,* 57–83.

Ackil, J. K., & Zaragoza, M. S. (1998). Memorial consequences of forced confabulation: Age differences in susceptibility to false memories. *Developmental Psychology, 34,* 1358–1372.

Acocella, J. (1999). *Creating hysteria: Women and multiple personality disorder.* San Francisco, CA: Jossey-Bass.

Adams, J. K. (1957). Laboratory studies of behavior without awareness. *Psychological Bulletin, 54,* 383–405.

Adams-Price, C. (1992). Eyewitness memory and aging: Predictors of accuracy in recall and person recognition. *Psychology and Aging, 7,* 602–608.

Adams-Price, C., & Perlmutter, M. (1992). Eyewitness memory and aging research: A case study in everyday memory. In R. L. West & J. D. Sinnott (Eds.), *Everyday memory and aging: Current research and methodology* (pp. 246–258). New York: Springer-Verlag.

Aggleton, J. P., & Brown, M. W. (1999). Episodic memory, amnesia, and the hippocampal-anterior thalamic axis. *Behavioral and Brain Sciences, 22*, 425–444.

Aggleton, J. P., McMackin, D., Carpenter, K., Hornak, J., Kapur, N., Halpin, S., Wiles, C. M., Kamel, H., Brennan, P., Carton, S., & Gaffan, D. (2000). Differential cognitive effects of colloid cysts in the third ventricle that spare or compromise the fornix. pt. 4. *Brain, 123*, 800–815.

Aggleton, J. P., & Shaw, C. (1996). Amnesia and recognition memory: A re-analysis of psychometric data. *Neuropsychology, 34*, 51–62.

Alba, J. W., & Hasher, L. (1983). Is memory schematic? *Psychological Bulletin, 93*, 203–231.

American Association for Protecting Children. (1985, 1987). *Highlights of official child abuse and neglect reporting.* Denver, CO: American Human Rights Association.

American Medical Association, Council on Scientific Affairs. (1985). Scientific status of refreshing recollection by the use of hypnosis. *Journal of the American Medical Association, 253*, 1921.

American Professional Society on the Abuse of Children. (1990). *Guidelines for psychosocial evaluation of suspected sexual abuse in young children.* Chicago, IL: Author.

Anderson, J. R. (1983). *The architecture of cognition.* Cambridge, MA: Harvard University Press.

Anderson, J. R., & Pirolli, P. L. (1984). Spread of activation. *Journal of Experimental Psychology: Learning, Memory, and Cognition, 10*, 791–798.

Anderson, N. H. (1981). *Foundations of information integration theory.* New York: Academic.

Ankrum, C., & Palmer, J. (1989, November). *The perception and memory of objects and their parts.* Paper presented at Psychonomic Society, Atlanta, GA.

Arbuthnott, K. D., Arbuthnott, D. W., & Rossiter, L. (2001). Guided imagery and memory: Implications for psychotherapists. *Journal of Counseling Psychology, 48*, 123–132.

Arbuthnott, K. D., Geelen, C. B., & Kealy, L. L. K. (2002). Phenomenal characteristics of guided imagery, natural imagery, and autobiographical memories. *Memory & Cognition, 30*, 519–528.

Arlin, M. (1986). The effects of quantity and depth of processing on children's time perception. *Journal of Experimental Child Psychology, 42*, 84–98.

Armstrong, K., Milles, S., & Possley, M. (2001, December 16). Coercive and illegal tactics torpedo scores of Cook County murder cases. *Chicago Tribune.*

Arndt, J., & Hirshman, E. (1998). True and false recognition in MINERVA 3: Explanations from a global matching perspective. *Journal of Memory and Language, 39*, 371–391.

Asch, S. E. (1950). Effects of group pressure upon the modification and distortion of judgments. In H. Guetzkow (Ed.), *Groups, leadership, and men* (pp. 177–190). Pittsburgh, PA: Carnegie.

Ascherman, E., Mantwill, M., & Kohnken, G. (1991). An independent replication of the effectiveness of the cognitive interview. *Applied Cognitive Psychology, 5*, 489–495.

Atkinson, R. C., & Juola, J. F. (1973). Factors influencing speed and accuracy in word recognition. In S. Kornblum (Ed.), *Attention and performance* (Vol. 4). New York: Academic.

Atkinson, R. C., & Juola, J. F. (1974). Search and decision processes in recognition memory. In D. H. Krantz, R. C. Atkinson, R. D. Luce, & P. Suppes (Eds.), *Contemporary developments in mathematical psychology: Vol. 1 (pp. 243–293). Learning, memory, and thinking.* San Francisco, CA: Freeman.

Atkinson, R. C., & Shiffrin, R. M. (1968). Human memory: A proposed system and its control processes. In K. W. Spence & J. T. Spence (Eds.), *Advances in the psychology of learning and motivation* (pp. 89–195). New York: Academic.

Atkinson, R. C., & Wescourt, K. T. (1975). Some remarks on a theory of memory. In P. M. A. Rabbitt & S. Dornic (Eds.), *Attention and performance* (Vol. 5). London: Academic.

Bach, M. J., & Underwood, B. J. (1971). Developmental changes in memory attributes. *Journal of Educational Psychology, 61*, 292–296.

Baddeley, A. D., Vargha-Khadem, F., & Mishkin, M. (2001). Preserved recognition in a case of developmental amnesia: Implications for the acquisition of semantic memory? *Journal of Cognitive Neuroscience, 13*, 357–369.

Baker, R. A. (1982). The effect of suggestion on past-lives regression. *American Journal of Clinical Hypnosis, 25,* 71–76.

Baker-Ward, L., Hess, T. M., & Flannagan, D. A. (1990). The effects of involvement on children's memory for events. *Cognitive Development, 5,* 55–69.

Balota, D. A., Burgess, G. C., Cortese, M. J., & Adams, D. R. (2002). The word-frequency mirror effect in young, old, and early-stage Alzheimer's disease: Evidence for two processes in episodic recognition performance. *Journal of Memory and Language, 46,* 199–226.

Balota, D. A., Cortese, M. J., Duchek, J. M., Adams, D., Roediger, H. L., McDermott, K. B., & Yerys, B. E. (1999). Veridical and false memories in healthy older adults and in dementia of the Alzheimer's type. *Cognitive Neuropsychology, 16,* 361–384.

Barclay, C. R., & Wellman, H. M. (1986). Accuracies and inaccuracies in autobiographical memories. *Journal of Memory and Language, 25,* 95–103.

Barclay, J. R. (1973). The role of comprehension in remembering sentences. *Cognitive Psychology, 4,* 229–254.

Barden, C. (1996). What do consumers expect? *False Memory Syndrome Foundation Newsletter, 5*(10).

Barnhardt, T. M., Choi, H. Gerkens, D. R., Corbisier, B., & Smith, S. M. (2004, November). *Output position of veridical and false memories for words.* Paper presented at the meetings of the Psychonomic Society, Minneapolis, MN.

Bartlett, F. C. (1932). *Remembering: A study in experimental and social psychology.* Cambridge: Cambridge University Press.

Bartlett, J. C., & Fulton, A. (1991). Familiarity and recognition of faces in old-age. *Memory & Cognition, 19,* 229–238.

Bartlett, J. C., & Leslie, J. E. (1985). Age-differences in memory for faces vs. views of faces. *Bulletin of the Psychonomic Society, 23,* 285.

Bartlett, J. C., & Leslie, J. E. (1986). Aging and memory for faces versus single views of faces. *Memory & Cognition, 14,* 371–381.

Bartlett, J. C., Leslie, J. E., & Tubbs, A. (1987). Aging and memory for pictures of faces. *Bulletin of the Psychonomic Society, 25,* 330.

Bartlett, J. C., Leslie, J. E., Tubbs, A., & Fulton, A. (1989). Aging and memory for pictures of faces. *Psychology and Aging, 4,* 276–283.

Bartlett, J. C., Strater, L., & Fulton, A. (1991). False recency and false familiarity of faces in young adulthood and old-age. *Memory & Cognition, 19,* 177–188.

Basden, B. H., Basden, D. R., & Gargano, G. J. (1993). Directed forgetting in implicit and explicit memory tests: A comparison of methods. *Journal of Experimental Psychology: Learning, Memory, and Cognition, 19,* 603–616.

Bass, E., & Davis, L. (1988). *The courage to heal.* New York: Harper & Row.

Bastin, C., & Van der Linden, M. (2003). The contribution of recollection and familiarity to recognition memory: A study of the effects of test format and aging. *Neuropsychology, 17,* 14–24.

Battig, W. F. (1965). Further evidence that strongest free-recall items are not recalled first. *Psychological Reports, 17,* 745–746.

Battig, W. F., Allen, M., & Jensen, A. R. (1965). Priority of free recall of newly learned items. *Journal of Verbal Learning and Verbal Behavior, 4,* 175–179.

Battig, W. F., & Montague, W. E. (1969). Category norms for verbal items in 56 categories: A replication and extension of the Connecticut category norms, Pt. 3. *Journal of Experimental Psychology Monograph, 80*(3).

Bedau, H. A., & Radelet, M. L. (1987). Miscarriages of justice in potentially capital cases. *Stanford Law Review, 40,* 21–179.

Bellezza, F. S. (2003). Evaluation of five multinomial models of conscious and unconscious processes in the recall-recognition paradigm. *Journal of Experimental Psychology: Learning, Memory, and Cognition, 29,* 779–796.

Belli, R. F. (1989). Influences of misleading postevent information: Misinformation interference and acceptance. *Journal of Experimental Psychology: General, 118,* 72–85.

Belli, R. F. (1993). Failure of interpolated tests in inducing memory impairment with final modified tests: Evidence unfavorable to the blocking hypothesis. *American Journal of Psychology, 106,* 407–427.

Belli, R. F., Windschitl, P. D., McCarthy, T. T., & Winfrey, S. E. (1992). Detecting memory impairment with a modified test procedure: Manipulating retention interval with centrally presented event items. *Journal of Experimental Psychology: Learning, Memory, and Cognition, 18,* 356–367.

Belluck, P. (1997, November 6). Memory therapy leads to a lawsuit and big settlement. *New York Times,* pp. A1, A10.

Benjamin, A. S. (2001). On the dual effects of repetition on false recognition. *Journal of Experimental Psychology: Learning, Memory, and Cognition, 27,* 941–947.

Bergman, E. T., & Roediger, H. L., III. (1999). Can Bartlett's repeated reproduction experiments be replicated? *Memory & Cognition, 27,* 937–947.

Bernstein, D. M., Whittlesea, B. W. A., & Loftus, E. F. (2002). Increasing confidence in remote autobiographical memory and general knowledge: Extensions of the revelation effect. *Memory & Cognition, 30,* 432–438.

Bernstein, M. (1956). *The search for Bridey Murphy.* Garden City, NY: Doubleday.

Beversdorf, D. Q., Smith, B. W., Crucian, G. P., Anderson, J. M., Keillor, J. M., Barrett, A. M., Hughes, J. D., Felopulos, G. J., Bauman, M. L., Nadeau, S. E., & Heilman, K. M. (2000). Increased discrimination of "false memories" in autism spectrum disorder. *Proceedings of the National Academy of Sciences of the United States of America, 97,* 8734–8737.

Binet, A. (1900). *La suggestibilite.* Paris: Schleicher.

Binet, A. (1903). *Etude experimentale de l'intelligence.* Paris: Schleicher.

Binet, A. (1911). Le bilan de la psychologie en 1910. *L'anne Psychologie, 17,* v–xi.

Binet, A., & Fere, C. (1887). *Animal magnetism.* New York: Appleton.

Bishop, K. I., & Curran, H. V. (1995). Psychopharmacological analysis of implicit and explicit memory: A study with lorazepam and the benzodiazepine antagonist flumazenil. *Psychopharmacology, 121,* 267–278.

Bjork, R. A. (1970). Positive forgetting: Noninterference of items intentionally forgotten. *Journal of Verbal Learning and Verbal Behavior, 9,* 255–268.

Bjorklund, D. F., Bjorklund, B. R., & Brown, R. D. (1998). Children's susceptibility to repeated questions: How misinformation changes children's answers and their minds. *Applied Developmental Science, 2,* 99–111.

Bjorklund, D. F., Cassel, W. S., Bjorklund, B. R., Brown, R. D., Park, C. L., Ernst, K., & Owen, F. A. (2000). Social demand characteristics in children's and adults' eyewitness memory and suggestibility: The effect of different interviewers on free recall and recognition. *Applied Cognitive Psychology, 14,* 421–433.

Bjorklund, D. F., & Hock, H. H. (1982). Age differences in the temporal locus of memory organization in children's recall. *Journal of Experimental Child Psychology, 33,* 347–362.

Bjorklund, D. F., & Jacobs, J. W. (1985). Associative and categorical processes in children's memory: The role of automaticity in the development of free recall. *Journal of Experimental Child Psychology, 39,* 599–617.

Bjorklund, D. F., Miller, P. H., Coyle, T. R., & Slawinski, J. L. (1997). Instructing children to use memory strategies: Evidence of utilization deficiencies in memory training studies. *Developmental Review, 17,* 411–441.

Bjorklund, D. F., & Muir, J. E. (1988). Children's development of free recall memory: Remembering on their own. *Annals of Child Development, 5,* 79–123.

Bjorklund, D. F., & Thompson, B. E. (1983). Category typicality effects in children's memory performance: Qualitative and quantitative differences in the processing of category information. *Journal of Experimental Child Psychology, 35,* 329–344.

Blair, I. V., Lenton, A. P., & Hastie, R. (2002). The reliability of the DRM paradigm as a measure of individual differences in false memories. *Psychonomic Bulletin & Review, 9,* 590–596.

Blaxton, T. A., & Theodore, W. H. (1997). The role of temporal lobes in recognizing visuospatial materials: Remembering versus knowing. *Brain and Cognition, 35,* 5–25.

Blume, E. S. (1991). *Secret survivors.* New York: Ballantine.

Boakes, J. (1999). False complaints of sexual assault: Recovered memories of childhood sexual abuse. *Medicine, Science, and the Law, 39,* 112–120.

Boat, B. W., & Everson, M. D. (1988). Use of anatomical dolls among professionals in sexual-abuse evaluations. *Child Abuse and Neglect, 12,* 171–179.

Boor, M. (1982). The multiple personality epidemic: Additional cases and inferences regarding diagnosis, etiology, dynamics, and treatment. *Journal of Nervous and Mental Disease, 170,* 302–304.

Borchard, E. M. (1932). *Convicting the innocent: Errors of criminal justice.* New Haven, CT: Yale University Press.

Bornstein, B. H., Liebel, L. M., & Scarberry, N. C. (1998). Repeated testing in eyewitness memory: A means to improve recall of a negative emotional event. *Applied Cognitive Psychology, 12,* 119–131.

Bottoms, B. L., Goodman, G. S., Schwartz-Kenney, B. M., & Thomas, S. N. (2002). Understanding children's use of secrecy in the context of eyewitness reports. *Law and Human Behavior, 26,* 285–313.

Bousefield, W. A. (1953). The occurrence of clustering in recall of randomly arranged associates. *Journal of General Psychology, 49,* 229–240.

Bower, G. H. (1970). Imagery as a relational organizer in associative learning. *Journal of Verbal Learning and Verbal Behavior, 9,* 529–533.

Bower, G. H., Black, J. B., & Turner, T. J. (1979). Scripts in memory for text. *Cognitive Psychology, 11,* 177–220.

Bower, G. H., & Karlin, M. B. (1974). Depth of processing pictures of faces and recognition memory. *Journal of Experimental Psychology, 103,* 751–757.

Bower, G. H., & Mann, T. (1992). Improving recall by recoding interfering material at the time of retrieval. *Journal of Experimental Psychology: Learning, Memory, and Cognition, 18,* 1310–1320.

Bowles, R. P., & Salthouse, T. A. (2003). Assessing the age-related effects of proactive interference on working memory tasks using the Rasch model. *Psychology and Aging, 18,* 608–615.

Bowman, L. L., & Zaragoza, M. S. (1989). Similarity of encoding context does not influence resistance to memory impairment following misinformation. *American Journal of Psychology, 102,* 249–264.

Bradley, A. R., & Wood, J. M. (1996). How do children tell? The disclosure process in child sexual abuse. *Child Abuse and Neglect, 20,* 881–891.

Brainerd, C. J. (1983). Varieties of strategy training in children's concept learning. In M. Pressley & J. R. Levin (Eds.), *Children's strategies: Psychological foundations* (pp. 3–27). New York: Springer-Verlag.

Brainerd, C. J. (1997). Development of forgetting, with implications for memory suggestibility. In N. L. Stein, P. A. Ornstein, B. Tversky, & C. J. Brainerd (Eds.), *Memory for everyday and emotional events* (pp. 209–235). Hillsdale, NJ: Erlbaum.

Brainerd, C. J., & Gordon, L. L. (1994). Development of verbatim and gist memory for numbers. *Developmental Psychology, 30,* 163–177.

Brainerd, C. J., Holliday, R. E., & Reyna, V. F. (2004). Behavioral measurement of memory phenomenology: So simple a child can do it. *Child Development, 75,* 505–522.

Brainerd, C. J., & Howe, M. L. (1982). Stages-of-learning analysis of developmental interactions in memory, with illustrations from developmental interactions in picture-word effects. *Developmental Review, 2,* 251–273.

Brainerd, C. J., & Kingma, J. (1985). On the independence of short-term memory and working memory in cognitive development. *Cognitive Psychology, 17,* 210–247.

Brainerd, C. J., & Mojardin, A. H. (1998). Children's false memories for sentences: Long-term persistence and mere testing effects. *Child Development, 69,* 1361–1377.

Brainerd, C. J., Payne, D. G., Wright, R., and Reyna, V. F. (2003). Phantom recall. *Journal of Memory and Language, 48,* 445–467.

Brainerd, C. J., & Poole, D. A. (1997). Long-term survival of children's false memories: A review. *Learning and Individual Differences, 9,* 125–152.

Brainerd, C. J., & Reyna, V. F. (1988). Generic resources, reconstructive processing, and children's mental arithmetic. *Developmental Psychology, 24,* 324–334.

Brainerd, C. J., & Reyna, V. F. (1990a). Gist is the grist: Fuzzy-trace theory and the new intuitionism. *Developmental Review, 10,* 3–47.

Brainerd, C. J., & Reyna, V. F. (1990b). Inclusion illusions: Fuzzy-trace theory and perceptual salience effects in cognitive development. *Developmental Review, 10,* 365–403.

Brainerd, C. J., & Reyna, V. F. (1993). Memory independence and memory interference in cognitive development. *Psychological Review, 100,* 42–67.

Brainerd, C. J., & Reyna, V. F. (1995). Autosuggestibility in memory development. *Cognitive Psychology, 28,* 65–101.

Brainerd, C. J., & Reyna, V. F. (1996). Mere memory testing creates false memories in children. *Developmental Psychology, 32,* 467–476.

Brainerd, C. J., & Reyna, V. F. (1998a). Fuzzy-trace theory and children's false memories. *Journal of Experimental Child Psychology, 71,* 81–129.

Brainerd, C. J., & Reyna, V. F. (1998b). When things that never happened are easier to remember than things that did. *Psychological Science, 9,* 484–489.

Brainerd, C. J., & Reyna, V. F. (2001a). Fuzzy-trace theory: Dual-processes in reasoning, memory, and cognitive neuroscience. *Advances in Child Development and Behavior, 28,* 49–100.

Brainerd, C. J., & Reyna, V. F. (2001b, April). *Recollection rejection: Can young children spontaneously suppress false-memory reports?* Paper presented at Society for Research in Child Development, Minneapolis, MN.

Brainerd, C. J., & Reyna, V. F. (2002a). Fuzzy-trace theory and false memory. *Current Directions in Psychological Science, 11,* 164–169.

Brainerd, C. J., & Reyna, V. F. (2002b). Recollection rejection: How children edit their false memories. *Developmental Psychology, 38,* 156–172.

Brainerd, C. J., Reyna, V. F., & Brandse, E. (1995). Are children's false memories more persistent than their true memories? *Psychological Science, 6,* 359–364.

Brained, C. J., Reyna, V. F., & Forrest, T. J. (2002). Are young children susceptible to the false-memory illusion? *Child Development, 73,* 1363–1377.

Brainerd, C. J., Reyna, V. F., Harnishfeger, K. K., & Howe, M. L. (1993). Is retrievability grouping good for recall? *Journal of Experimental Psychology: General, 122,* 249–268.

Brainerd, C. J., Reyna, V. F., Howe, M. L., & Kevershan, J. (1990). The last shall be first: How memory strength affects children's retrieval. *Psychological Science, 1,* 247–252.

Brainerd, C. J., Reyna, V. F., Howe, M. L., & Kevershan, J. (1991). Fuzzy-trace theory and cognitive triage in memory development. *Developmental Psychology, 27,* 351–369.

Brainerd, C. J., Reyna, V. F., & Kneer, R. (1995). False-recognition reversal: When similarity is distinctive. *Journal of Memory and Language, 34,* 157–185.

Brainerd, C. J., Reyna, V. F., & Mojardin, A. H. (1999). Conjoint recognition. *Psychological Review, 106,* 160–179.

Brainerd, C. J., Reyna, V. F., & Poole, D. A. (2000). Fuzzy-trace theory and false memory: Memory theory in the courtroom. In D. F. Bjorklund (Ed.), *False memory creation in children and adults* (pp. 93–128). Mahwah, NJ: Erlbaum.

Brainerd, C. J., Reyna, V. F., Wright, R., & Mojardin, A. H. (2003). Recollection rejection: False-memory suppression in children and adults. *Psychological Review, 110,* 762–784.

Brainerd, C. J., Stein, L. M., & Reyna, V. F. (1998). On the development of conscious and unconscious memory. *Developmental Psychology, 34,* 342–357.

Brainerd, C. J., Wright, R., Reyna, V. F., & Mojardin, A. H. (2001). Conjoint recognition and phantom recollection. *Journal of Experimental Psychology: Learning, Memory, and Cognition, 27,* 307–327.

Brainerd, C. J., Wright, R., Reyna, V. F., & Payne, D. G. (2002). Dual-retrieval processes in recall. *Journal of Memory and Language, 46,* 120–152.

Bransford, J. D., Barclay, J. R., & Franks, J. J. (1972). Sentence memory: A constructive versus interpretative approach. *Cognitive Psychology, 3,* 193–209.

Bransford, J. D., & Franks, J. J. (1971). The abstraction of linguistic ideas. *Cognitive Psychology, 2,* 331–380.

Brewer, J. B., Zhao, Z., Desmond, J. E., Glover, G. H., & Gabrieli, J. D. E. (1998). Making memories: Brain activity that predicts how well visual experience will be remembered. *Science, 281,* 1185–1187.

Brewer, W. F., & Treyens, J. C. (1981). Role of schemata in memory for places. *Cognitive Psychology, 13,* 207–230.

Brown, A. L., & Smiley, S. S. (1977). Rating the importance of structural units of prose passages: A problem of meta-cognitive development. *Child Development, 48,* 1–8.

Brown, A. L., Smiley, S. S., Day, J. D., Townsend, M. A. R., & Lawton, S. C. (1977). Intrusion of a thematic idea in children's comprehension and retention of stories. *Child Development, 48,* 1454–1466.

Bruck, M., & Ceci, S. J. (1995). Amicus brief for the case of *State of New Jersey v. Michaels* presented by committee of concerned social-scientists. *Psychology, Public Policy, and Law, 1,* 272–322.

Bruck, M., & Ceci, S. J. (1997). The nature of applied and basic research on children's suggestibility. In N. Stein, P. A. Ornstein, B. Tversky, & C. J. Brainerd (Eds.), *Memory for everyday and emotional events* (pp. 371–400). Hillsdale, NJ: Erlbaum.

Bruck, M., & Ceci, S. J. (1999). The suggestibility of children's memory. *Annual Review of Psychology, 50,* 419–439.

Bruck, M., Ceci, S. J., & Francoeur, E. (2000). Children's use of anatomically detailed dolls to report genital touching in a medical examination: Developmental and gender comparisons. *Journal of Experimental Psychology: Applied, 6,* 74–83.

Bruck, M., Ceci, S. J., Francoeur, E., & Barr, R. (1995). I hardly cried when I got my shot: Influencing children's reports about a visit to their pediatrician. *Child Development, 66,* 193–208.

Bruck, M., Ceci, S. J., & Melnyk, L. (1997). External and internal sources of variation in the creation of false reports in children. *Learning and Individual Differences, 9,* 289–316.

Bruck, M., Francoeur, E., Ceci, S. J., & Renick, A. (1995). Anatomically detailed dolls do not facilitate preschoolers' reports of a pediatric examination involving genital touching. *Journal of Experimental Psychology: Applied, 1,* 95–109.

Bruck, M., Melnyk, L., & Ceci, S. J. (2000). Draw it again Sam: The effect of drawing on children's suggestibility and source monitoring ability. *Journal of Experimental Child Psychology, 77,* 169–196.

Bryant, P., & Trabasso, T. (1971). Transitive inferences and memory in young children. *Nature, 232,* 457–459.

Buchanan, L., Brown, N., & Westbury, C. (1999, November). *Generating false memories: Conscious or nonconscious spread of activation during study?* Paper presented at the Psychonomic Society meeting, Los Angeles, CA.

Budson, A. E., Sullivan, A. L., Daffner, K. R., & Schacter, D. L. (2003). Semantic versus phonological false recognition in aging and Alzheimer's disease. *Brain and Cognition, 51,* 251–261.

Budson, A. E., Sullivan, A. L., Mayer, E., Daffner, K. R., Black, P. M., & Schacter, D. L. (2002). Suppression of false recognition in Alzheimer's disease and in patients with frontal lobe lesions. Pt. 12. *Brain, 125,* 2750–2765.

Burgus v. Braun. (1993). Circuit Court, Cook County, IL.

Bussey, K. (1990, March). *Adult influence on children's eyewitness reporting.* Paper presented at American Psychology and Law Society, Williamsburg, VA.

Bussey, K., Lee, K., & Grimbeek, E. J. (1993). Lies and secrets: Implications for children's reporting of sexual abuse. In G. S. Goodman & B. L. Bottoms (Eds.), *Child victims, child witnesses: Understanding and improving children's testimony* (pp. 147–168). New York: Guilford.

Cameron, T. E., & Hockley, W. E. (2000). The revelation effect for item and associative recognition: Familiarity versus recollection. *Memory & Cognition, 28,* 176–183.

Carrier, M., & Pashler, H. (1992). The influence of retrieval on retention. *Memory & Cognition, 20,* 633–642.

Carter, C. A., Bottoms, B. L., & Levine, M. (1996). Linguistic and socioemotional influences on the accuracy of children's reports. *Law and Human Behavior, 20,* 335–358.

Case, R., Kurland, D. M., & Goldberg, J. (1982). Operational efficiency and the growth of short-term memory span. *Journal of Experimental Child Psychology, 33,* 386–404.

Cassel, W. S., & Bjorklund, D. F. (1995). Developmental patterns of eyewitness memory and suggestibility: An ecologically-based short-term longitudinal study. *Law and Human Behavior, 19,* 507–532.

Cassel, W. S., Roebers, C. E. M., & Bjorklund, D. F. (1996). Developmental patterns of eyewitness responses to repeated and increasingly suggestive questions. *Journal of Experimental Child Psychology, 61,* 116–133.

Cassell, P. G. (1999). The guilty and the "innocent": An examination of alleged cases of wrongful conviction from false confessions. *Harvard Journal of Law and Public Policy, 22,* 523–603.

Catalina Council v. Hunter. (1998). Superior Court, Pima County, AZ.

Ceci, S. J., & Bruck, M. (1993a). Children's recollections: Translating research into policy. *SRCD Policy Reports, 7*(3).

Ceci, S. J., & Bruck, M. (1993b). The suggestibility of the child witness: A historical review and synthesis. *Psychological Bulletin, 113,* 403–439.

Ceci, S. J., & Bruck, M. (1995). *Jeopardy in the courtroom.* Washington, DC: American Psychological Association.

Ceci, S. J., & Bruck, M. (1998). The ontogeny and durability of true and false memories: A fuzzy trace account. *Journal of Experimental Child Psychology, 71,* 165–169.

Ceci, S. J., & Friedman, R. D. (2000). The suggestibility of children: Scientific research and legal implications. *Cornell Law Review, 86,* 33–108.

Ceci, S. J., Huffman, M. L. C., Smith, E., & Loftus, E. F. (1994). Repeatedly thinking about a non-event: Source misattributions among preschoolers. *Consciousness and Cognition, 3,* 388–407.

Ceci, S. J., Leichtman, M., & White, T. (1995). Interviewing preschoolers: Remembrance of things planted. In D. P. Peters (Ed.), *The child witness in context: Cognitive, social, and legal perspectives.* Netherlands: Kulwer.

Ceci, S. J., Loftus, E. F., Leichtman, M. D., & Bruck, M. (1994). The possible role of source misattributions in the creation of false beliefs among preschoolers. *International Journal of Clinical and Experimental Hypnosis, 42,* 304–320.

Ceci, S. J., Ross, D. F., & Toglia, M. P. (1987). Suggestibility in children's memory: Psycholegal implications. *Journal of Experimental Psychology: General, 116,* 38–49.

Ceci, S. J., Toglia, M. P., & Ross, D. F. (Eds.). (1987). *Children's eyewitness memory.* New York: Springer-Verlag.

Chalfonte, B. L., Verfaellie, M., Johnson, M. K., & Reiss, L. (1996). Spatial location memory in amnesia: Binding item and location information under incidental and intentional encoding conditions. *Memory, 4,* 591–614.

Chandler, C. C. (1989). Specific retroactive interference in modified recognition tests: Evidence for an unknown cause of interference. *Journal of Experimental Psychology: Learning, Memory, and Cognition, 15,* 256–265.

Chandler, C. C. (1991). How memory for an event is influenced by related events: Interference in modified recognition tests. *Journal of Experimental Psychology: Learning, Memory, and Cognition, 17,* 115–125.

Chandler, C. C., & Gargano, G. J. (1995). Item-specific interference caused by cue-dependent forgetting. *Memory & Cognition, 19,* 701–708.

Chapman, M., & Lindenberger, U. (1992). Transitivity judgments, memory for premises, and models of children's reasoning. *Developmental Review, 12,* 124–163.

Christianson, S. A. (1992). Emotional stress and eyewitness memory. *Psychological Bulletin, 112,* 284–309.

Clancy, S. A., McNally, R. J., & Schacter, D. L. (1999). Effects of guided imagery on memory distortion in women reporting recovered memories of childhood sexual abuse. *Journal of Traumatic Stress, 12,* 559–569.

Clark, S. E., & Gronlund, S. D. (1996). Global matching models of recognition memory: How the models match the data. *Psychonomic Bulletin & Review, 3,* 37–60.

Cloitre, M., Cancienne, J., Brodsky, B., Dulit, R., & Perry, S. (1996). Memory performance among women with parental abuse histories: Enhanced directed forgetting or directed remembering? *Journal of Abnormal Psychology, 105,* 204–211.

Cohen, B. H. (1963). Recall of categorized word lists. *Journal of Experimental Psychology, 66,* 227–234.

Cohen, G., & Faulkner, D. (1989). Age differences in source forgetting: Effects on reality monitoring and on eyewitness testimony. *Psychology and Aging, 4,* 10–17.

Cole, M. (1976). Probe trial procedure for the study of children's discrimination-learning and transfer. *Journal of Experimental Child Psychology, 22,* 499–510.

Collins, A. M., & Loftus, E. F. (1975). Spreading activation theory of semantic processing. *Psychological Review, 82,* 407–428.

Connolly, D. A., & Lindsay, D. S. (2001). The influence of suggestion on children's reports of a unique experience versus an instance of a repeated experience. *Applied Cognitive Psychology, 15,* 205–223.

Connors, E., Lundregan, T., Miller, N., & McEwan, T. (1996). *Convicted by juries, exonerated by science: Case studies in the use of DNA evidence to establish innocence after trial.* Alexandria, VA: National Institute of Justice.

Conway, M. A., Collins, A. F., Gathercole, S. E., & Anderson, S. J. (1996). Recollections of true and false autobiographical memories. *Journal of Experimental Psychology: General, 125,* 69–95.

Cooperman, A. (2002, January 30). For dioceses, legal toll quietly rises. *Washington Post,* pp. A1, A3.

Cornell Death Penalty Project. (2002). Ithaca, NY: Cornell Law School. http://www.lawschool.cornell.edu/library/death/.

Corsini, D. A., Jacobus, K. A., & Leonard, S. D. (1979). Recognition memory of preschool children for pictures and words. *Psychonomic Science, 16,* 192–193.

Coxon, P., & Valentine, T. (1997). The effects of the age of eyewitnesses on the accuracy and suggestibility of their testimony. *Applied Cognitive Psychology, 11,* 415–430.

Coy v. State of Iowa, 487 U.S. 1012 (1988).

Craik, F. I. M., & Lockhart, R. S. (1972). Levels of processing: A framework of memory research. *Journal of Verbal Learning and Verbal Behavior, 11,* 671–684.

Craik, F. I. M., & Tulving, E. (1975). Depth of processing and retention of words in episodic memory. *Journal of Experimental Psychology: General, 104,* 268, 294.

Cramer, P. (1972). A developmental study of errors in memory. *Developmental Psychology, 7,* 204–209.

Crowder, R. G. (1976). *Principles of memory.* Hillsdale, NJ: Erlbaum

Csicsvari, J., Hirase, H., Czurko, A., Mamiya, A., & Buzsaki, G. (1999). Oscillatory coupling of hippocampal pyramidal cells and interneurons in the behaving rat. *Journal of Neuroscience, 19,* 274–287.

Cull, W. L. (2000). Untangling the benefits of multiple study opportunities and repeated testing for cued recall. *Applied Cognitive Psychology, 14,* 215–235.

Curran, H. V., Gardiner, J. M., Java, R. I., & Allen, D. (1993). Effects of lorazepam upon recollective experience in recognition memory. *Psychopharmacology, 110,* 374–378.

Curran, T., & Hintzman, D. L. (1995). Violations of the independence assumption in process dissociation. *Journal of Experimental Psychology: Learning, Memory, and Cognition, 21,* 531–547.

Curran, T., Schacter, D. L., Johnson, M. K., & Spinks, R. (2001). Brain potentials reflect behavioral differences in true and false recognition. *Journal of Cognitive Neuroscience, 13,* 201–216.

Dammeyer, M. D. (1998). The assessment of child sexual abuse allegations: Using research to guide clinical decision making. *Behavioral Sciences & the Law, 16,* 21–34.

Davis, S. L., & Bottoms, B. L. (2002). Effects of social support on children's eyewitness reports: A test of underlying mechanism. *Law and Human Behavior, 26,* 185–215.

Dawson, B., Geddie, L., & Wagner, W. (1996). Low-income preschoolers' behavior with anatomically detailed dolls. *Journal of Family Violence, 11,* 363–378.

Deese, J. (1959). On the prediction of occurrence of certain verbal intrusions in free recall. *Journal of Experimental Psychology, 58,* 17–22.

DeFiebre, C. (1995, June 24). Ex-patient says memory of sex abuse was planted. *Minneapolis Star Tribune.*

Delamonthe, K., & Taplin, E. (1992, November). *The effects of suggestibility on children's recognition memory.* Paper presented at Psychonomic Society, St. Louis, MO.

DeLoache, J. S. (1989). Young children's understanding of the correspondence between a scale model and a larger space. *Cognitive Development, 4,* 121–139.

DeLoache, J. S., Kolstad, V., & Anderson, K. N. (1991). Physical similarity and young children's understanding of scale models. *Child Development, 62,* 111–126.

DeLoache, J. S., & Marzolf, D. P. (1992). When a picture is not worth 1000 words: Young children's understanding of pictures and models. *Cognitive Development, 7,* 317–329.

DeLoache, J. S., & Marzolf, D. P. (1995). The use of dolls to interview young children: Issues of symbolic representation. *Journal of Experimental Child Psychology, 60,* 155–173.

DeMarie-Dreblow, D. (1991). Relation between knowledge and memory: A reminder that correlation does not imply causality. *Child Development, 62,* 484–498.

Dent, H. R., & Stephenson, G. M. (1979). An experimental study of the effectiveness of different techniques of questioning child witnesses. *British Journal of Social and Clinical Psychology, 18,* 41–51.

de Rivera, J. (1997). The construction of false memory syndrome: The experience of retractors. *Psychological Inquiry, 8,* 271–292.

Dewhurst, S. A. (2001). Category repetition and false recognition: Effects of instance frequency and category size. *Journal of Memory and Language, 44,* 153–167.

Dodhia, R. M., & Metcalfe, J. (1999). False memories and source monitoring. *Cognitive Neuropsychology, 16,* 489–508.

Dodson, C. S., & Schacter, D. S. (2001). "If I said it, I would have remembered it": Reducing false memories with a distinctiveness heuristic. *Psychonomic Bulletin & Review, 8,* 155–166.

Dodson, C. S., & Schacter, D. L. (2002a). Aging and strategic retrieval processes: Reducing false memories with a distinctiveness heuristic. *Psychology and Aging, 17,* 405–415.

Dodson, C. S., & Schacter, D. L. (2002b). When false recognition meets metacognition: The distinctiveness heuristic. *Journal of Memory and Language, 46,* 782–803.

Donaldson, W. (1996). The role of decision processes in remembering and knowing. *Memory & Cognition, 24,* 523–533.

Doris, J. (Ed.). (1991). *The suggestibility of children's recollections.* Washington, DC: American Psychological Association.

Dosher, B. A. (1984a). Degree of learning and retrieval speed: Study time and multiple exposures. *Journal of Experimental Psychology: Learning, Memory, and Cognition, 10,* 541–574.

Dosher, B. A. (1984b). Discriminating preexperimental (semantic) from learned (episodic) associations: A speed-accuracy study. *Cognitive Psychology, 16,* 519–555.

Dosher, B. A., & Rosedale, G. (1991). Judgments of semantic and episodic relatedness: Common time-course and failure of segregation. *Journal of Memory and Language, 30,* 125–160.

Draine, S. C., & Greenwald, A. G. (1998). Replicable unconscious semantic priming. *Journal of Experimental Psychology: General, 127,* 286–303.

Drivdahl, S. B., & Zaragoza, M. S. (2001). The role of perceptual elaboration and individual differences in the creation of false memories for suggested events. *Applied Cognitive Psychology, 15,* 265–281.

Dunlosky, J., Kubat-Silman, A. K., & Hertzog, C. (2003). Training monitoring skills improves older adults' self-paced associative learning. *Psychology and Aging, 18,* 340–345.

Dunlosky, J., & Salthouse, T. A. (1996). A decomposition of age-related differences in multitrial free recall. *Aging, Neuropsychology, and Cognition, 3,* 2–14.

Dunn, J. C., & Kirsner, K. (1988). Discovering functionally independent mental processes: The principle of reversed association. *Psychological Review, 95,* 91–101.

Ebbinghaus, H. (1913). *Memory: A contribution to experimental psychology.* New York: Teachers College, Columbia University. (Original work published 1885)

Eichenbaum, H. (2002). *The cognitive neuroscience of memory.* New York: Oxford University Press.

Eichenbaum, H., Otto, T., & Cohen, N. J. (1994). Two functional components of the hippocampal memory system. *Behavioral and Brain Sciences, 17,* 449–517.

Eldridge, L. L., Knowlton, B. T., Furmanski, C. S., Bookheimer, S. Y., & Engel, S. A. (2000). Remembering episodes: A selective role for the hippocampus during retrieval. *Nature Neuroscience, 3,* 1149–1152.

Elkind, D. (1967). Piaget's conservation problems. *Child Development, 38,* 15–28.

Erdelyi, M. H., Finkelstein, S., Herrell, N., Miller, B., & Thomas, J. (1976). Coding modality vs. input modality in hypermnesia: Is a rose a rose a rose? *Cognition, 4,* 311–319.

Erdelyi, M. H., Finks, J., & Feigin-Pfau, M. B. (1989). The effect of response bias on recall performance: With some observations on processing bias. *Journal of Experimental Psychology: General, 118,* 245–254.

Esposito, N. J. (1975). Review of discrimination shift learning in young children. *Psychological Bulletin, 82,* 432–455.

Evans, R. C. (1980). Depth of processing and recognition memory performance in first-graders, third-graders, and eighth-graders. *Journal of Experimental Education, 48,* 217–222.

Felzen, E., & Anisfeld, M. (1971). Semantic and phonetic relations in false recognition of words by third- and sixth-grade children. *Developmental Psychology, 3,* 163–168.

Ferracuti, S., Cannoni, E., De Carolis, A., Gonella, A., & Lazzari, R. (2002). Rorschach measures during depth hypnosis and suggestion of a previous life. *Perceptual and Motor Skills, 95,* 877–885.

Fisher, R. P., & Cutler, B. L. (1992, September). *The relation between consistency and accuracy of eyewitness testimony.* Paper presented at the Third European Conference on Law and Psychology, Oxford, England.

Fisher, R. P., & Geiselman, R. E. (1992). *Memory-enhancing techniques for investigative interviewing: The cognitive interview.* Springfield, IL: Thomas.

Fisher, R. P., Geiselman, R. E., & Amador, M. (1989). Field test of the cognitive interview: Enhancing the recollection of actual victims and witnesses of crimes. *Journal of Applied Psychology, 74,* 722–727.

Fisher, R. P., Geiselman, R. E., & Raymond, D. S. (1987). Critical analysis of police interview techniques. *Journal of Police Science and Administration, 15,* 177–185.

Fisher, R. P., Geiselman, R. E., Raymond, D. S., Jurkevich, L. M., & Warhaftig, M. L. (1987). Enhancing enhanced eyewitness memory: Refining the cognitive interview. *Journal of Police Science and Administration, 15,* 291–297.

Flagg, P. W. (1976). Semantic integration in sentence memory? *Journal of Verbal Learning and Verbal Behavior, 15,* 491–504.

Flavell, J. H. (1970). Concept development. In P. H. Mussen (Ed.), *Carmichael's manual of child psychology* (Vol. 1, pp. 983–1060). New York: Wiley.

Fleet, M. L., Brigham, J. C., and Bothwell, R. K. (1987). The confidence-accuracy relationship: The effects of confidence assessment and choosing. *Journal of Applied Social Psychology, 17,* 171–187.

Forrest, T. J. (2002). *Memory errors in elementary school children.* Unpublished doctoral dissertation, University of Arizona, Tucson.

Frei v. Catholic Diocese of Tucson. (2000). Superior Court, Pima County.

Freyd, J. J., & Jones, K. T. (1994). Representational momentum for a spiral path. *Journal of Experimental Psychology: Learning, Memory, and Cognition, 20,* 968–976.

Freyd, J. J., Kelly, M. H., & DeKay, M. L. (1990). Representational momentum in memory for pitch. *Journal of Experimental Psychology: Learning, Memory, and Cognition, 16*, 1107–1117.

Freyd, P. (1996). False memory syndrome. *British Journal of Psychiatry, 169*, 794–795.

Frye v. United States, 293 F. 1013 (DC Cir. 1923).

Fulton, A., & Bartlett, J. C. (1991). Young and old faces in young and old heads: The factor of age in face recognition. *Psychology and Aging, 6*, 623–630.

Gabbert, F., Memon, A., & Allan, K. (2003). Memory conformity: Can eyewitnesses influence each other's memories for an event? *Applied Cognitive Psychology, 17*, 533–543.

Gabrieli, J. D. E. (1998). Cognitive neuroscience of human memory. *Annual Review of Psychology, 49*, 87–115.

Gallo, D. A. (2000). *Variability among word lists in eliciting false memory: The role of associative activation and decision processes.* Unpublished master's thesis, Washington University, St. Louis, MO.

Gallo, D. A., McDermott, K. B., Percer, J. M., & Roediger, H. L., III. (2001). Modality effects in false recall and false recognition. *Journal of Experimental Psychology: Learning, Memory, and Cognition, 27*, 339–353.

Gardiner, J. M., & Java, R. I. (1990). Recollective experience in word and nonword recognition. *Memory & Cognition, 18*, 23–30.

Gardiner, J. M., & Java, R. I. (1991). Forgetting in recognition memory with and without recollective experience. *Memory & Cognition, 18*, 617–623.

Gardiner, J. M., & Parkin, A. J. (1990). Attention and recollective experience in recognition memory. *Memory & Cognition, 18*, 579–583.

Garry, M., Manning, C. G., Loftus, E. F., & Sherman, S. J. (1996). Imagination inflation: Imagining a childhood event inflates confidence that it occurred. *Psychonomic Bulletin & Review, 3*, 208–214.

Gauld, A., & Stephenson, G. M. (1967). Some experiments related to Bartlett's theory of remembering. *British Journal of Psychology, 58*, 39–49.

Gaultney, J. F., Kipp, K., Weinstein, J., & McNeill, J. (1999). Inhibition and mental effort in attention deficit hyperactivity disorder. *Journal of Developmental and Physical Disabilities, 11*, 105–114.

Gee, S., & Pipe, M. E. (1999). Helping children to remember: The influence of object cues on children's accounts of a real event. *Developmental Psychology, 31*, 746–758.

Gernsbacher, M. A. (1985). Surface information loss in comprehension. *Cognitive Psychology, 17*, 324–363.

Ghetti, S., Qin, J., & Goodman, G. S. (2002). False memories in children and adults: Age, distinctiveness, and subjective experience. *Developmental Psychology, 38*, 705–718.

Giles, J. W., Gopnik, A., & Heyman, D. (2002). Source monitoring reduces the suggestibility of preschool children. *Psychological Science, 13*, 288–291.

Glanzer, M., & Adams, J. K. (1985). The mirror effect in recognition memory. *Memory & Cognition, 13*, 8–20.

Glanzer, M., & Cunitz, A. R. (1966). Two storage mechanisms in free recall. *Journal of Verbal Learning and Verbal Behavior, 5*, 351–360.

Gleaves, D. H. (1996). The sociocognitive model of dissociative identity disorder: A reexamination of the evidence. *Psychological Bulletin, 120*, 42–59.

Goff, L. M., & Roediger, H. L. (1998). Imagination inflation for action events: Repeated imaginings lead to illusory recollections. *Memory & Cognition, 26*, 20–33.

Goldberg, S., Perlmutter, M., & Myers, N. (1974). Recall of related and unrelated lists by 2-year-olds. *Journal of Experimental Child Psychology, 18*, 1–8.

Gonzales, L. S., Waterman, J., Kelly, R. J., McCord, J., & Oliveri, M. K. (1993). Children's patterns of disclosures and recantations of sexual and ritualistic abuse allegations in psychotherapy. *Child Abuse and Neglect, 17*, 281–289.

Goodman, G. S., & Aman, C. (1990). Children's use of anatomically detailed dolls to recount an event. *Child Development, 61*, 1859–1871.

Goodman, G. S., & Clarke-Stewart, A. (1991). Suggestibility in children's testimony: Implications for child sexual abuse investigations. In J. L. Doris (Ed.), *The suggestibility of children's recollections* (pp. 92–105). Washington, DC: American Psychological Association.

Goodman, G. S., Hirschman, J. E., Hepps, D., & Rudy, L. (1991). Children's memory for stressful events. *Merrill-Palmer Quarterly, 37,* 109–158.

Goodman, G. S., & Reed, R. S. (1986). Age differences in eyewitness testimony. *Law and Human Behavior, 10,* 317–332.

Goodman, G. S., Rudy, L., Bottoms, B., & Aman, C. (1990). Children's concerns and memory: Issues of ecological validity in the study of children's eyewitness testimony. In R. Fivush & J. Hudson (Eds.), *Knowing and remembering in young children* (pp. 249–284). New York: Cambridge University Press.

Gordon, B. N., Ornstein, P. A., Clubb, P. A., Nida, R. E., & Baker-Ward, L. (1991). Visiting the pediatrician: Long-term retention and forgetting. *Bulletin of the Psychonomic Society, 29,* 498.

Gore-Felton, C., Arnow, B., Koopman, C., Thoresen, C., & Spiegel, D. (1999). Psychologists' beliefs about the prevalence of childhood sexual abuse: The influence of sexual abuse history, gender, and theoretical orientation. *Child Abuse and Neglect, 23,* 803–811.

Gotlib, D. A. (1997). Psychotherapy for the alien abduction experience. *International Journal of Clinical and Experimental Hypnosis, 45,* 475–476.

Graesser, A. C., Gordon, S. E., & Sawyer, J. D. (1979). Recognition memory for typical and atypical actions in scripted activities: Tests of a script pointer + tag hypothesis. *Journal of Verbal Learning and Verbal Behavior, 18,* 319–332.

Graf, P., & Mandler, G. (1984). Activation makes words more accessible, but not necessarily more retrievable. *Journal of Verbal Learning and Verbal Behavior, 5,* 553–568.

Green, D. M., & Swets, J. A. (1966). *Signal detection theory and psychophysics.* New York: Wiley.

Greenberg, R., & Underwood, B. J. (1950). Retention as a function of stage of practice. *Journal of Experimental Psychology, 40,* 452–457.

Gregg, V. H., Montgomery, D. D., & Castano, D. (1980). Recall of common and uncommon words from pure and mixed lists. *Journal of Verbal Learning and Verbal Behavior, 19,* 240–245.

Greshberg, F. B., & Shimamura, A. P. (1995). Impaired use of organizational strategies in free-recall following frontal lobe damage. *Neuropsychologia, 33,* 1305–1333.

Gribben, J. (1995). *Schrodinger's kittens and the search for reality: Solving the quantum mysteries.* New York: Little, Brown.

Grinfeld, M. J. (2001). Lawsuit raises questions about APA liability insurance program. *Psychiatric Times, 24*(1).

Gronlund, S. D., & Ratcliff, R. (1989). Time course of item and associative information: Implications for global memory models. *Journal of Experimental Psychology: Learning, Memory, and Cognition, 20,* 1355–1369.

Gross, S. R. (1996). The risks of death: Why erroneous convictions are common in capital cases. *Buffalo Law Review, 44,* 469–500.

Gudjonsson, G. H. (1984). A new scale of interrogative suggestibility. *Personality and Individual Differences, 5,* 303–314.

Gudjonsson, G. H. (1992). *The psychology of interrogations.* London: Wiley.

Gudjonsson, G. H. (1997). False memory syndrome and the retractors: Methodological and theoretical issues. *Psychological Inquiry, 8,* 296–299.

Gudjonsson, G. H., & MacKeith, J. A. C. (1990). A proven case of false confession: Psychological aspects of the coerced-compliant type. *Medicine, Science, and the Law, 30,* 329–335.

Gustafson, P. (1995, August 1). Jury awards patient $2.6 million: Verdict finds therapist Humenansky liable in repressed-memory trial. *Minneapolis Star Tribune,* p. B1.

Gustafson, P. (1997, February 8). Board suspends license of psychiatrist Diane Humenansky. *Minneapolis Star Tribune,* p. B1.

Haber, R. N., & Haber, L. (2001, November). *A meta-analysis of research on eyewitness line-up accuracy.* Paper presented at Psychonomic Society, Orlando, FL.

Haber, R. N., & Haber, C. (2004). *A meta-analysis of research on eyewitness line-up accuracy.* Manuscript submitted for publication.

Haist, F., Shimamura, A. P., & Squire, L. R. (1992). On the relationship between recall and recognition memory. *Journal of Experimental Psychology: Learning, Memory, and Cognition, 18,* 691–702.

Haith, M. M., & Benson, J. B. (1998). Infant cognition. In D. Kuhn & R. S. Siegler (Eds.), *Handbook of child psychology: Vol. 2. Cognition, perception, and language* (pp. 199–254). New York: Wiley.

Hall, J. W., & Halperin, M. S. (1972). Development of memory-encoding processes in young children. *Developmental Psychology, 6,* 181.

Hall, J. W., & Kolzoff, E. E. (1970). False recognition as a function of number of presentations. *Journal of Experimental Psychology, 83,* 272–279.

Hamnane v. Humenansky. (1995). 2d Dist., Ramsey County, Minnesota.

Haraldsson, E. (2003). Children who speak of past-life experiences: Is there a psychological explanation? *Psychology and Psychotherapy: Theory, Research, and Practice, 76,* 55–67.

Harmon, T. R. (2001). Predictors of miscarriages of justice in capital cases. *Justice Quarterly, 18,* 949–968.

Hashtroudi, S., Johnson, M. K., & Chrosniak, L. D. (1989). Aging and source monitoring. *Psychology and Aging, 4,* 106–112.

Hasselhorn, M., & Richter, M. (2002). The development of efficient retrieval inhibition during elementary school: The role of motivation and insight. *Zeitschrift fur Entwicklungspsychologie und Padagogische Psychologie, 34,* 149–155.

Hastie, R., & Park, B. (1986). The relationship between memory and judgment depends on whether the judgment task is memory-based or on-line. *Psychological Review, 93,* 258–268.

Hay, J. F., & Jacoby, L. L. (1996). Separating habit and recollection: Memory slips, process dissociations, and probability matching. *Journal of Experimental Psychology: Learning, Memory, and Cognition, 22,* 1323–1335.

Heaps, C., & Nash, M. (1999). Individual differences in imagination inflation. *Psychonomic Bulletin & Review, 6,* 313–318.

Heaps, C. M., & Nash, M. (2001). Comparing recollective experience in true and false autobiographical memories. *Journal of Experimental Psychology: Learning, Memory, and Cognition, 27,* 920–930.

Henke, K., Buck, A., Weber, B., & Wieser, H. G. (1997). Human hippocampus establishes associations in memory. *Hippocampus, 7,* 249–256.

Henkel, L. A., Johnson, M. K., & De Leonardis, D. M. (1998). Aging and source monitoring: Cognitive processes and neuropsychological correlates. *Journal of Experimental Psychology: General, 127,* 251–268.

Henson, R. N. A., Rugg, M. D., Shallice, T., Josephs, O., & Dolan, R. J. (1999). Recollection and familiarity in recognition memory: An event-related functional magnetic resonance imaging study. *Journal of Neuroscience, 19,* 3962–3972.

Herman, J. L. (1981). *Father-daughter incest.* Cambridge, MA: Harvard University Press.

Hershkowitz, I., Orbach, Y., Lamb, M. E., Sternberg, K. J., & Horowitz, D. (2001). The effects of mental context reinstatement on children's accounts of sexual abuse. *Applied Cognitive Psychology, 15,* 235–248.

Hicks, J. L., & Cockman, D. W. (2003). The effect of general knowledge on source memory and decision processes. *Journal of Memory and Language, 48,* 489–501.

Hicks, J. L., & Hancock, T. W. (2002). Backward associative strength determines source attributions given to false memories. *Psychological Bulletin & Review, 9,* 807–815.

Hintzman, D. L., Block, R. A., & Inskeep, N. R. (1973). Memory for mode of input. *Journal of Verbal Learning and Verbal Behavior, 11,* 741–749.

Hintzman, D. L., & Curran, T. (1994). Retrieval dynamics of recognition and frequency judgments: Evidence for separate processes of familiarity and recall. *Journal of Memory and Language, 33,* 1–18.

Hirshman, E., Fisher, J., Henthorn, T., Arndt, J., & Passannante, A. (2002). Midazolam amnesia and dual-process models of the word-frequency mirror effect. *Journal of Memory and Language, 47,* 499–516.

Hirst, W., Phelps, E. A., Johnson, M. K., & Volpe, B. T. (1988). More on recognition and recall in amnesiacs. *Journal of Experimental Psychology: Learning, Memory, and Cognition, 14,* 758–762.

Holdstock, J. S., Mayes, A. R., Cezayirli, E., Isaac, C. L., Aggleton, J. P., & Roberts, N. (2002). A comparison of egocentric and allocentric spatial memory in a patient with selective hippocampal damage. *Neuropsychologia, 38,* 410–425.

Holliday, R. E. (2003). Reducing misinformation effects in children with cognitive interviews: Dissociating recollection and familiarity. *Child Development, 74,* 728–751.

Holliday, R. E., Douglas, K. M., & Hayes, B. K. (1999). Children's eyewitness suggestibility: Memory trace strength revisited. *Cognitive Development, 14,* 443–462.

Holliday, R. E., & Hayes, B. K. (2000). Dissociating automatic and intention processes in children's eyewitness memory. *Journal of Experimental Child Psychology, 75,* 1–42.

Holliday, R. E., & Hayes, B. K. (2001). Automatic and intentional processes in children's eyewitness suggestibility. *Cognitive Development, 16,* 617–636.

Holliday, R. E., & Hayes, B. K. (2002). Automatic and intentional processes in children's recognition memory: The reversed misinformation effect. *Applied Cognitive Psychology, 16,* 617–636.

Holliday, R. E., Reyna, U. F., & Hayes, B. K. (2002). Memory processes underlying misinformation in child witnesses. *Developmental Review, 22,* 37–77.

Home Office. (1992). *Memorandum of good practice on video recorded interviews with child witnesses for criminal proceedings.* London: Her Majesty's Stationery Office.

Horowitz, L. M., & Prytulak, L. S. (1969). Redintegrative memory. *Psychological Review, 76,* 519–533.

Horvath, F., & Meesig, R. (1996). The criminal investigation process and the role of forensic evidence: A review of empirical findings. *Journal of Forensic Sciences, 41,* 963–969.

Horvath, F., & Meesig, R. (1998). A content analysis of textbooks on criminal investigation: An evaluative comparison to empirical research findings on the investigative process and the role of forensic evidence. *Journal of Forensic Sciences, 43,* 133–140.

Hosch, H. M., & Bothwell, R. K. (1990). Arousal, description, and identification accuracy of victims and bystanders. *Journal of Social Behavior and Personality, 5,* 481–488.

Howe, M. L. (1991). Misleading children's story recall: Forgetting and reminiscence of the facts. *Developmental Psychology, 27,* 746–762.

Howe, M. L. (1997). Children's memory for traumatic experiences. *Learning and Individual Differences, 2,* 153–174.

Howe, M. L. (2000). *The fate of early memories: Developmental science and the retention of childhood experiences.* Washington, DC: American Psychological Association.

Howe, M. L. (2002). The role of intentional forgetting in reducing children's retroactive interference. *Developmental Psychology, 38,* 3–14.

Howe, M. L., Brainerd, C. J., & Kingma, J. (1985). Storage-retrieval processes of learning-disabled children: A stages-of-learning analysis of picture-word effects. *Child Development, 56,* 1120–1133.

Howe, M. L., Courage, M. L., & Peterson, C. (1995). Intrusions in preschoolers' recall of traumatic childhood events. *Psychonomic Bulletin & Review, 2,* 130–134.

Howe, M. L., Courage, M. L., Vernescu, R., & Hunt, M. (2000). Distinctiveness effects in children's long-term retention. *Developmental Psychology, 36,* 778–792.

Howe, M. L., O'Sullivan, J. T., Brainerd, C. J., & Kingma, J. (1989). Localized development of ability differences in organized memory. *Contemporary Educational Psychology, 14,* 336–356.

Howe, M. L., Rabinowitz, F. M., & Grant, M. J. (1993). On measuring (in)dependence of cognitive processes. *Psychological Review, 100,* 737–747.

Hu, X. (1995). *Statistical inference program for multinomial binary tree models* (Version 1.1) [Computer software]. Irvine: University of California.

Huffman, M. L., Crossman, A. M., & Ceci, S. J. (1997). "Are false memories permanent?": An investigation of the long-term effects of source misattributions. *Consciousness and Cognition, 6,* 482–490.

Hull, D. L.. (1973). *Darwin and his critics: The reception of Darwin's theory of evolution by the scientific community.* Chicago, IL: University of Chicago Press, 1973.

Humphreys, M. S., & Yuille, J. C. (1973). Errors as a function of noun concreteness. *Canadian Journal of Psychology, 27,* 83–94.

Hunt, R. R., & Lamb, C. A. (2001). What causes the isolation effect? *Journal of Experimental Psychology: Learning, Memory, and Cognition, 27,* 1359–1366.

Hunt, R. R., & McDaniel, M. A. (1993). The enigma of organization and distinctiveness. *Journal of Memory and Language, 32,* 421–445.

Huppert, F. A., & Piercy, M. (1976). Recognition memory in amnesic patients: Effect of temporal context and familiarity of material. *Cortex, 12,* 3–20.

Hyman, I. E., Husband, T. H., & Billings, F. J. (1995). False memories of childhood experiences. *Applied Cognitive Psychology, 9,* 181–197.

Hyman, I. E., & Pentland, J. (1996). The role of mental imagery in the creation of false childhood memories. *Journal of Memory and Language, 35,* 101–117.

Imhoff, M. C., & Baker-Ward, L. (1999). Preschoolers' suggestibility: Effects of developmentally appropriate language and interviewer supportiveness. *Journal of Applied Developmental Psychology, 20,* 407–409.

Inbau, F. E., Reid, J. E., Buckley, J. P., & Jayne, B. C. (2001). *Criminal interrogation and confessions* (4th ed.). Gaithersburg, MD: Aspen.

Inhelder, B., & Piaget, J. (1964). *The early growth of logic in the child.* New York: Norton.

Innes, S., & Steller, T. (2002, February 17). Diocese saw signs, didn't act. *Arizona Daily Star,* pp. A1, A9.

Irvine, W. (1955). *Apes, angels, and Victorians: The story of Darwin, Huxley, and evolution.* New York: McGraw-Hill.

Isaac, C. L., & Mayes, A. R. (1999). Rate of forgetting in amnesia: I. Recall and recognition of prose. *Journal of Experimental Psychology: Learning, Memory, and Cognition, 25,* 942–962.

Isingrini, M., Fontaine, R., Taconna, T. L., & Duportal, A. (1995). Aging and encoding in memory: False alarms and decision criteria in a word-pair recognition task. *International Journal of Aging and Human Development, 41,* 79–88.

Israel, L., & Schacter, D. L. (1997). Pictorial encoding reduces false recognition of semantic associates. *Psychonomic Bulletin & Review, 4,* 577–581.

Jackson, H., & Nuttall, R. (1993). Clinician responses to sexual abuse allegations. *Child Abuse and Neglect, 17,* 127–143.

Jackson, H., & Nuttall, R. (1994). Effects of gender, age, and history on social-workers' judgments of sexual abuse allegations. *Social Work Research, 18,* 105–113.

Jacoby, L. L. (1991). A process dissociation framework: Separating automatic from intentional uses of memory. *Journal of Memory and Language, 30,* 513–541.

Jacoby, L. L. (1996). Dissociating automatic and consciously controlled effects of study/test compatibility. *Journal of Memory and Language, 35,* 32–52.

Jacoby, L. L., & Dallas, M. (1981). On the relationship between autobiographical memory and perceptual-learning. *Journal of Experimental Psychology: General, 110,* 306–340.

Jacoby, L. L., Debner, J. A., & Hay, J. F. (2001). Proactive interference, accessibility bias, and process dissociations: Valid subjective reports of memory. *Journal of Experimental Psychology: Learning, Memory, and Cognition, 27,* 686–700.

Jacoby, L. L., Kelley, C., Brown, J., & Jasechko, J. (1989). Becoming famous overnight: Limits on the ability to avoid unconscious influences of the past. *Journal of Personality and Social Psychology, 56,* 326–338.

Jacoby, L. L., Toth, J. P., & Yonelinas, A. P. (1993). Separating conscious and unconscious influences of memory: Measuring recollection. *Journal of Experimental Psychology: General, 122,* 139–154.

James, W. (1890). *The principles of psychology.* New York: Holt.

Java, R. I. (1996). Effects of age on state of awareness following implicit and explicit word association-tasks. *Psychology and Aging, 11,* 108–111.

Jensen, G. L. (2001). Therapy-induced false memories. *Nordisk Psykologi, 53,* 133–156.

Jetter, W., Poser, U., Freeman, R. B., & Markowitsch, H. J. (1986). A verbal long-term memory deficit in frontal-lobe damaged patients. *Cortex, 22,* 229–242.

Johnson, J. W., & Scholnick, E. K. (1979). Does cognitive development predict semantic integration? *Child Development, 50,* 73–78.

Johnson, M. K. (1988). Reality monitoring: An experimental phenomenological approach. *Journal of Experimental Psychology: General, 117,* 390–394.

Johnson, M. K., Foley, M. A., Suengas, A. G., & Raye, C. L. (1988). Phenomenal characteristics of memories for perceived and imagined autobiographical events. *Journal of Experimental Psychology: General, 117,* 371–376.

Johnson, M. K., Hashtroudi, S., & Lindsay, D. S. (1993). Source monitoring. *Psychological Bulletin, 114,* 3–28.

Johnson, M. K., & Kim, J. K. (1985). Recognition of pictures by alcoholic Korsakoff patients. *Bulletin of the Psychonomic Society, 23,* 456–458.

Johnson, M. K., Nolde, S. F., Mather, M., Kounios, J., & Schacter, D. L. (1997). Test format can affect the similarity of brain activity associated with true and false recognition memory. *Psychological Science, 8,* 250–257.

Johnson, M. K., & Raye, C. L. (1981). Reality monitoring. *Psychological Review, 88,* 67–85.

Jones, C. H., & Pipe, M. E. (2002). How quickly do children forget events? A systematic study of children's event reports as a function of delay. *Applied Cognitive Psychology, 16,* 755–768.

Jones, L. W., Sinclair, R. C., & Courneya, K. S. (2003). The effects of source credibility and message framing on exercise intentions, behaviors, and attitudes: An integration of the elaboration likelihood model and prospect theory. *Journal of Applied Social Psychology, 33,* 179–196.

Juline, K. (1992, July). An interview with Ira Progoff. *Science of Mind.*

Jung, C. G. (1953). *The collected works of C. G. Jung.* New York: Pantheon.

Juola, J. F., Fischler, I., Wood, C. T., & Atkinson, R. C. (1971). Recognition time for information stored in long-term memory. *Perception & Psychophysics, 10,* 8–14.

Kaiser, K. B. (1981, March). The way of the journal. *Psychology Today.*

Kampman, R. (1976). Hypnotically induced multiple personality: An experimental study. *International Journal of Clinical and Experimental Hypnosis, 24,* 215–227.

Karpel, M. E., Hoyer, W. J., & Toglia, M. P. (2001). Accuracy and qualities of real and suggested memories: Nonspecific age differences. *Journals of Gerontology Series B: Psychological Sciences and Social Sciences, 56,* P103–P110.

Kassin, S. M. (1985). Eyewitness identification: Retrospective self-awareness and the accuracy-confidence correlation. *Journal of Personality and Social Psychology, 49,* 878–893.

Kassin, S. M. (1997). The psychology of confession evidence. *American Psychologist, 52,* 221–233.

Kassin, S. M. (1998). Eyewitness identification procedures: The fifth rule. *Law and Human Behavior, 22,* 649–654.

Kassin, S. M. (2001). On the "general acceptance" of eyewitness testimony research: A new survey of experts. *American Psychologist, 56,* 405–416.

Kassin, S. M., & Kiechel, K. L. (1996). The social psychology of false confessions: Compliance, internalization, and confabulation. *Psychological Science, 7,* 125–128.

Kassin, S. M., & Sukel, H. (1997). Coerced confessions and the jury: An experimental test of the ''harmless error'' rule. *Law and Human Behavior, 21,* 27–46.

Kassin, S. M., & Wrightsman, L. S. (1981). Coerced confessions, judicial instruction, and mock juror verdicts. *Journal of Applied Social Psychology, 11,* 489–506.

Kassin, S. M., & Wrightsman, L. S. (1985). Confession evidence. In S. M. Kassin & L. S. Wrightsman (Eds.), *The psychology of evidence and trial procedure* (pp. 67–94). Beverly Hills, CA: Sage.

Kelley, C. M., & Sahakyan, L. (2003). Memory, monitoring, and control in the attainment of memory accuracy. *Journal of Memory and Language, 48,* 704–721.

Kempe, C. H., Silver, H. K., Silverman, F. N., Droegemueller, W., & Silver, H. (1962). Battered-child syndrome. *Journal of the American Medical Association, 181,* 17–24.

Kendall-Tackett, K. A. (2000). Physiological correlates of childhood abuse: Chronic hyperarousal in PTSD, depression, and irritable bowel syndrome. *Child Abuse and Neglect, 24,* 799–810.

Kendall-Tackett, K. A., Williams, L. M., & Finkelhor, D. (1993). Impact of sexual abuse on children: A review and synthesis of recent empirical studies. *Psychological Bulletin, 113,* 164–180.

Kendler, H. H., & Kendler, T. S. (1962). Vertical and horizontal processes in problem-solving. *Psychological Review, 69,* 1–16.

Kendler, H. H., Kendler, T. S., & Wells, D. (1960). Reversal and nonreversal shifts in nursery school children. *Journal of Comparative and Physiological Psychology, 53,* 82–88.

Kensinger, E. A., & Schacter, D. L. (1999). When true memories suppress false memories: Effects of aging. *Cognitive Neuropsychology, 16,* 399–415.

Kessen, W. (1965). *The child.* New York: Wiley.

Kessen, W. (1996). American psychology just before Piaget. *Psychological Science, 7,* 196–199.

Kiernan, B. J. (1993). *Verbatim memory and gist extraction in children with impaired language skills.* Unpublished doctoral dissertation, University of Arizona, Tucson.

Kimball, D. R., & Bjork, R. A. (2002). Influences of intentional and unintentional forgetting on false memories. *Journal of Experimental Psychology: General, 131,* 116–130.

Kintsch, W. (1974). *The representation of meaning in memory.* Hillsdale, NJ: Erlbaum.

Kintsch, W., Welsch, D., Schmalhofer, F., & Zimny, S. (1990). Sentence memory: A theoretical analysis. *Journal of Memory and Language, 29,* 133–159.

Kohnken, G., and Malpass, A.. (1988). Eyewitness testimony: False alarms or biased instructions? *Journal of Applied Psychology, 73,* 363–370.

Kohnken, G., Milne, R., Memon, A., & Bull, R. (1999). The cognitive interview: A meta-analysis. *Psychology, Crime, and Law, 5,* 3–27.

Kolers, P. A. (1976). Reading a year later. *Journal of Experimental Psychology: Human Learning and Memory, 2,* 554–565.

Koocher, G. P., Goodman, G. S., White, C. S., Friedrich, W. N., Sivan, A. B., & Reynolds, C. R. (1995). Psychological science and the use of anatomically detailed dolls in the child sexual-abuse assessments. *Psychological Bulletin, 118,* 199–222.

Kopelman, M. D., & Stanhope, N. (1997). Rates of forgetting in organic amnesia following temporal lobe, diencephalic, or frontal lobe lesions. *Neuropsychology, 11,* 343–356.

Koriat, A., & Goldsmith, M. (1994). Memory in naturalistic and laboratory contexts: Distinguishing the accuracy-oriented and quantity-oriented approaches to memory assessment. *Journal of Experimental Psychology: General, 123,* 297–315.

Koriat, A., & Goldsmith, M. (1996). Monitoring and control processes in the strategic regulation of memory. *Psychological Review, 103,* 490–517.

Koriat, A., Goldsmith, M., & Pansky, A. (2000). Toward a psychology of memory accuracy. *Annual Review of Psychology, 51,* 481–538.

Koriat, A., Goldsmith, M., Schneider, W., & Nakash-Dura, M. (2001). The credibility of children's testimony: Can children control the accuracy of their memory reports? *Journal of Experimental Child Psychology, 79,* 405–437.

Koriat, A., Levy-Sadot, R., Edry, E., & de Marcas, S. (2003). What do we know about what we cannot remember? Accessing the semantic attributes of words that cannot be recalled. *Journal of Experimental Psychology: Learning, Memory, and Cognition, 29,* 1095–1105.

Koutstaal, W. (2003). Older adults encode—but do not always use—perceptual details: Intentional versus unintentional effects of detail on memory judgments. *Psychological Science, 14,* 189–193.

Koutstaal, W., Reddy, C., Jackson, E. M., Prince, S., Cendan, D. L., & Schacter, D. L. (2003). False recognition of abstract versus common objects in older and younger adults: Testing the semantic categorization account. *Journal of Experimental Psychology: Learning, Memory, and Cognition, 29,* 499–510.

Koutstaal, W., & Schacter, D. L. (1997). Gist-based false recognition of pictures in older and younger adults. *Journal of Memory and Language, 37,* 555–583.

Koutstaal, W., Schacter, D. L., & Brenner, C. (2001). Dual task demands and gist-based false recognition of pictures in younger and older adults. *Journal of Memory and Language, 44,* 399–426.

Koutstaal, W., Schacter, D. L., Galluccio, L., & Stofer, K. A. (1999). Reducing gist-based false recognition in older adults: Encoding and retrieval manipulations. *Psychology and Aging, 14,* 220–237.

Koutstaal, W., Schacter, D. L., Verfaellie, M., Brenner, C., & Jackson, E. M. (1999). Perceptually based false recognition of novel objects in amnesia: Effects of category size and similarity to category prototypes. *Cognitive Neuropsychology, 16,* 317–341.

Koutstaal, W., Verfaellie, M., & Schacter, D. L. (2001). Recognizing identical versus similar categorically related common objects: Further evidence for degraded gist representations in amnesia. *Neuropsychology, 15,* 268–289.

Kramer, P. D. (1999, November 21). I contain multitudes: Why were so many women thought to have multiple personalities. *New York Times.*

Krantz, D. H., Luce, R. D., & Tversky, A. (1971). *Foundations of measurement.* New York: Academic.

Krantz, D. H., & Tversky, A. (1971). Conjoint measurement analysis of composition rules in psychology. *Psychological Review, 78,* 151–164.

Kress, B., & Hasselhorn, M. (2000). Are young school children not able to deliberately forget? A developmental study on directed forgetting. *Zeitschrift fur Entwicklungspsychologie und Padagogische Psychologie, 32,* 186–191.

Kroll, N. E. A., Knight, R. T., Metcalfe, J., Wolfe, E. S., & Tulving, E. (1996). Cohesion failure as a source of memory illusions. *Journal of Memory and Language, 35,* 176–196.

Kuenne, M. R. (1946). Experimental investigation of the relation of language to transposition behavior in young children. *Journal of Experimental Psychology, 36,* 471–490.

Kulig, J. W., & Tighe, T. J. (1976). Subproblem analysis of discrimination-learning: Stimulus choice and response latency. *Bulletin of the Psychonomic Society, 7,* 377–380.

Kuo, T. M., & Hirshman, E. (1996). Investigations of the testing effect. *American Journal of Psychology, 109,* 451–464.

Labiner, D. M., Weinand, M. E., Brainerd, C. J., Ahern, G. L., Herring, A. M., & Melgar, M. A. (2002). Prognostic value of concordant seizure focus localizing data in the selection of temporal lobectomy candidates. *Neurological Research, 24,* 747–755.

Lamb, M. E. (1998). Assessments of children's credibility in forensic contexts. *Current Directions in Psychological Science, 7,* 43–46

Lamb, M. E., & Fauchier, A. (2001). The effects of question type on self-contradictions by children in the course of forensic interviews. *Applied Cognitive Psychology, 15,* 483–491.

Lamb, M. E., & Garretson, M. E. (2003). The effects of interviewer gender and child gender on the informativeness of alleged child sexual abuse victims in forensic interviews. *Law and Human Behavior, 27,* 157–171.

Lamb, M. E., Sternberg, K. J., & Esplin, P. W. (2000). Effects of age and delay on the amount of information provided by alleged sex abuse victims in investigative interviews. *Child Development, 71,* 1586–1596.

Lampinen, J. M., Copeland, S. M., & Neuschatz, J. S. (2001). Recollections of things schematic: Room schemas revisited. *Journal of Experimental Psychology: Learning, Memory, and Cognition, 27,* 1211–1222.

Lampinen, J. M., Neuschatz, J. S., & Payne, D. G. (1998). Memory illusions and consciousness: Examining the phenomenology of true and false memories. *Current Psychology: Development, Learning, Personality, Social, 16,* 181–224.

Lampinen, J. M., & Smith, V. L. (1995). The incredible (and sometimes incredulous) child witness: Child eyewitnesses' sensitivity to source credibility cues. *Journal of Applied Psychology, 80,* 621–627.

LaVoie, D. J., & Faulkner, K. (2000). Age differences in false recognition using a forced choice paradigm. *Experimental Aging Research, 26,* 367–381.

Lazzara, M. M., Yonelinas, A. P., Kroll, N. E. A., Kishiyama, M. M., Suave, M. J., Zusman, E., & Knight, R. T. (2001). *Conceptual priming and familiarity-based recognition in amnesia.* New York: Cognitive Neuroscience Society.

Leavitt, F., & Labott, S. M. (1998). Revision of the Word Association Test for assessing patients reporting Satanic ritual abuse in childhood. *Journal of Clinical Psychology, 54,* 933–943.

Lechner, H. A., Squire, L. R., & Byrne, J. H. (1999). 100 years of consolidation: Remembering Muller and Pilzecker. *Learning & Memory, 6,* 77–87.

Lehman, E. B., McKinley-Pace, M., Leonard, A. M., Thompson, D., & Johns, K. (2001). Item-cued directed forgetting of related words and pictures in children and adults: Selective rehearsal versus cognitive inhibition. *Journal of General Psychology, 128,* 81–97.

Liben, L. S. (1977). Memory in the context of cognitive development: The Piagetian approach. In R. V. Kail, Jr., & J. W. Hagen (Eds.), *Perspectives on the development of memory and cognition* (pp. 297–332). Hillsdale, NJ: Erlbaum.

Liben, L. S., & Posnansky, C. J. (1977). Inferences on inference: Effects of age, transitive ability, memory load, and lexical factors. *Child Development, 48,* 1490–1497.

Liebman, J. S. (2002). Rates of reversible error and the risk of wrongful execution. *Justice, 86,* 78–82.

Lim, P. L. (1993). *Meaning versus verbatim memory in language processing: Deriving inferential, morphological, and metaphorical gist.* Unpublished doctoral dissertation, University of Arizona, Tucson.

Lindsay, D. S., Hagen, L., Read, J. D., Wade, K. A., & Garry, M. (2004). True photographs and false memories. *Psychological Science, 15,* 149–154.

Lindsay, D. S., & Johnson, M. K. (1989a). The eyewitness suggestibility effect and memory for source. *Memory & Cognition, 17,* 349–358.

Lindsay, D. S., & Johnson, M. K. (1989b). The reversed eyewitness suggestibility effect. *Bulletin of the Psychonomic Society, 27,* 111–113.

Lindsay, D. S., & Johnson, M. K. (2000). False memories and the source monitoring framework: Reply to Reyna and Lloyd (1997). *Learning and Individual Differences, 12,* 145–161.

Lindsay, R. C. L., Lea, J. A., Nosworthy, G. J., Fulford, J. A., Hector, J., LeVan, V., & Seabrook, C. (1991). Biased lineups: Sequential presentation reduces the problem. *Journal of Applied Psychology, 76,* 796–802.

Lindsay, R. C. L., Smith, S. M., & Pryke, S. (1999). Measures of lineup fairness: Do they postdict identification accuracy? *Applied Cognitive Psychology, 13,* S93–S107.

Lindsay, R. C. L., & Wells, G. L. (1985). Improving eyewitness identifications from lineups: Simultaneous versus sequential lineup presentation. *Journal of Applied Psychology, 70,* 556–564.

Lindsay, R. C. L., Wells, G. L, & Rumpel, C. M. (1981). Can people detect eyewitness-identification accuracy within and across situations? *Journal of Applied Psychology, 66,* 79–89.

Loftus, E. F. (1975). Leading questions and eyewitness report. *Cognitive Psychology, 7,* 560–572.

Loftus, E. F. (1981). The effect of leading questions on eyewitness recall. *Bulletin of the British Psychological Society, 34,* 216.

Loftus, E. F. (1993). The reality of repressed memories. *American Psychologist, 48,* 518–537.

Loftus, E. F. (1995). Memory malleability: Constructivist and fuzzy-trace explanations. *Learning and Individual Differences, 7,* 133–137.

Loftus, E. F. (1997a). Creating childhood memories. *Applied Cognitive Psychology, 11,* S75–S86.

Loftus, E. F. (1997b). Creating false memories. *Scientific American, 277*(3), 70–75.

Loftus, E. F. (1998). The price of bad memories. *Skeptical Inquirer, 22,* 23–24.

Loftus, E. F., & Hoffman, H. G. (1989). Misinformation and memory: The creation of new memories. *Journal of Experimental Psychology: General, 118,* 100–104.

Loftus, E. F., & Ketcham, K. (1994). *The myth of repressed memory.* New York: St. Martin's.

Loftus, E. F., Levidow, B., & Duensing, S. (1992). Who remembers best: Individual differences in memory for events that occurred in a science museum. *Applied Cognitive Psychology, 6,* 93–107.

Loftus, E. F., & Loftus, G. R. (1980). On the permanence of stored information in the human brain. *American Psychologist, 35,* 409–420.

Loftus, E. F., Miller, D. G., & Burns, H. J. (1978). Semantic integration of verbal information into visual memory. *Journal of Experimental Psychology: Human Learning and Memory, 4,* 19–31.

Loftus, E. F., & Palmer, J. C. (1974). Reconstruction of automobile destruction: An example of the interaction between language and memory. *Journal of Verbal Learning and Verbal Behavior, 13,* 585–589.

Loftus, E. F., & Pickrell, J. E. (1995). The formation of false memories. *Psychiatric Annals, 25,* 720–725.

Lorsbach, T. C., & Mueller, J. H. (1979). Encoding tasks and free-recall in children. *Bulletin of the Psychonomic Society, 14,* 169–172.

Lovden, M. (2003). The episodic memory and inhibition accounts of age-related increases in false memories: A consistency check. *Journal of Memory and Language, 49,* 268–283.

Luus, C. A. E., & Wells, G. L. (1994). The malleability of eyewitness confidence: Co-witness and perseverance effects. *Journal of Applied Psychology, 79,* 714–723.

Lyon, T. D. (1995). False allegations and false denials in child sexual abuse. *Psychology, Public Policy, and Law, 1,* 429–437.

Macmillan, N. A., & Creelman, C. D. (1991). *Detection theory: A user's guide.* New York: Cambridge University Press.

Malpass, R. S. (1981). Effective size and defendant bias in eyewitness identification lineups. *Law and Human Behavior, 5,* 299–309.

Malpass, R. S., and Devine, P. G. (1981). Eyewitness identification: Lineup instructions and the absence of the offender. *Journal of Applied Psychology, 66,* 482–489.

Malpass, R. S., and Devine, P. G. (1983). Measuring the fairness of eyewitness identification lineups. In S. M. A. Lloyd-Bostock & D. R. Clifford (Eds.), *Evaluating witness evidence* (pp. 81–102). London: Wiley.

Mandler, G. (1980). Recognizing: The judgment of previous occurrence. *Psychological Review, 87,* 252–271.

Mandler, J. M. (1998). Representation. In D. Kuhn & R. S. Siegler (Eds.), *Handbook of child psychology: Vol. 2. Cognition, perception, and language* (pp. 255–308). New York: Wiley.

Mandler, J. M., & Johnson, N. S. (1977). Remembrance of things parsed: Story structure and recall. *Cognitive Psychology, 9,* 111–151.

Marcel, A. J. (1983). Conscious and unconscious perception: Experiments on visual masking and word recognition. *Cognitive Psychology, 15,* 197–237.

Marche, T. A. (1999). Memory strength affects reporting of misinformation. *Journal of Experimental Child Psychology, 73,* 45–71.

Marche, T. A., & Howe, M. L. (1995). Preschoolers report misinformation despite accurate memory. *Developmental Psychology, 31,* 554–567.

Marin, B. V., Holmes, D. L., Guth, M., & Kovac, P. (1979). The potential of children as eye-witnesses. *Law and Human Behavior, 3,* 295–305.

Marsh, R. L., & Hicks, J. L. (2001). Output monitoring tests reveal false memories of memories that never existed. *Memory, 9,* 39–51.

Marsh, R. L., Hicks, J. L., & Davis, T. T. (2002). Source monitoring does not alleviate (and may exacerbate) the occurrence of memory conjunction errors. *Journal of Memory and Language, 47,* 315–326.

Martinez-Taboas, A. (2002). The role of hypnosis in the detection of psychogenic seizures. *American Journal of Clinical Hypnosis, 45,* 11–20.

Marx, M. H., & Henderson, B. (1996). A fuzzy trace analysis of categorical inferences and instantial associations as a function of retention interval. *Cognitive Development, 11,* 551–569.

Marx, S. P. (1996). Victim recantation in child sexual abuse cases: The prosecutor's role in prevention. *Child Welfare, 75,* 219–233.

Mather, M., & Johnson, M. K. (2003). Affective review and schema reliance in memory in older and younger adults. *American Journal of Psychology, 116,* 169–189.

Mayes, A. R. (1992). Brain circuits and the functions of the mind: Essays in honor of Roger, W.-Trevarthan, C. Pt. 2. *British Journal of Psychology, 83,* 297–298.

Mayes, A. R., Isaac, C. L., Holdstock, J. S., Hunkin, N. M., Montaldi, D., Downes, J. J., MacDonald, C., & Cezayirli, E. (2001). Memory for single items, word pairs, and temporal order of different kinds in a patient with selective hippocampal lesions. *Cognitive Neuropsychology, 18,* 97–123.

Mayes, A. R., MacDonald, C., Donlan, L., Pears, J., & Meudell, P. R. (1992). Amnesics have a disproportionately severe memory deficit for interactive context. *Quarterly Journal of Experimental Psychology Section A: Human Experimental Psychology, 45,* 265–297.

Maylor, E. A. (1995). Remembering versus knowing television theme tunes in middle-aged and elderly adults. *British Journal of Psychology, 86,* 21–25.

Maylor, E. A., & Mo, A. (1999). Effects of study-test modality on false recognition. *British Journal of Psychology, 90,* 477–493.

Mazzoni, G. A. L., & Loftus, E. F. (1998). Dream interpretation can change beliefs about the past. *Psychotherapy, 35,* 177–187.

Mazzoni, G. A. L., Loftus, E. F., Seitz, A., & Lynn, S. J. (1999). Changing beliefs and memories through dream interpretation. *Applied Cognitive Psychology, 13,* 125–144.

McCloskey, M., & Zaragoza, M. S. (1985). Misleading postevent information and memory for events: Arguments and evidence against memory impairment hypotheses. *Journal of Experimental Psychology: General, 114,* 1–16.

McComas, K. A., & Trumbo, C. W. (2003). Source credibility in environmental health-risk controversies: Application of Meyer's credibility index. *Risk Analysis, 21,* 467–480.

McDermott, K. B. (1996). The persistence of false memories in list recall. *Journal of Memory and Language, 35,* 212–230.

McDermott, K. B., & Roediger, H. L., III. (1998). Attempting to avoid false memories: Robust false recognition of associates persists under conditions of explicit warnings and immediate testing. *Journal of Memory and Language, 39,* 508–520.

McDermott, K. B., & Watson, J. M. (2001). The rise and fall of false recall: The impact of presentation duration. *Journal of Memory and Language, 45,* 160–176.

McEvoy, C. L., Nelson, D. L., & Komatsu, T. (1999). What is the connection between true and false memories? The differential roles of interitem associations in recall and recognition. *Journal of Experimental Psychology: Learning, Memory, and Cognition, 25,* 1177–1194.

McGaugh, J. L. (1999). The perseveration-consolidation hypothesis: Mueller and Pilzecker, 1900. *Brain Research Bulletin, 50,* 445–446.

McGaugh, J. L. (2000). Neuroscience-Memory: a century of consolidation. *Science, 287,* 248–251.

McGough, L. S. (1993). *Child witnesses: Fragile voices in the American legal system.* New Haven, CT: Yale University Press.

McIntyre, J. S. (1987). Age differences in memory for item and source information. *Canadian Journal of Psychology, 41,* 175–192.

McNally, R. J. (2003). Recovering false memories of trauma: A view from the laboratory. *Current Directions in Psychological Science, 12,* 32–35.

McNally, R. J., Clancy, S. A., & Schacter, D. L. (2001). Directed forgetting of trauma cues in adults reporting repressed, recovered, or continuous memories of childhood sexual abuse. *Journal of Abnormal Psychology, 110,* 355–359.

McNally, R. J., Clancy, S. A., Schacter, D. L., & Pittman, R. K. (2000a). Cognitive processing of trauma cues in adults reporting repressed, recovered, or continuous memories of childhood sexual abuse. *Journal of Abnormal Psychology, 109*, 355–359.

McNally, R. J., Clancy, S. A., Schacter, D. L., & Pittman, R. K. (2000b). Personality profiles, dissociation, and absorption in women reporting repressed, recovered, or continuous memories of childhood sexual abuse. *Journal of Consulting and Clinical Psychology, 68*, 1033–1037.

Mellor, C. S. (1970). First rank symptoms of schizophrenia. I: The frequency of schizophrenics in admissions to hospitals. II: Differences between individual first rank symptoms. *British Journal of Psychology, 117*, 15–23.

Melo, B., Winocur, G., & Moscovitch, M. (1999). False recall and false recognition: An examination of the effects of selective and combined lesions to the medial temporal lobe/ diencephalon and frontal lobe structures. *Cognitive Neuropsychology, 16*, 343–359.

Melton, A. W., & Irwin, J. M. (1940). The influence of degree of interpolated learning to retroactive inhibition on the overt transfer of specific responses. *American Journal of Psychology, 53*, 157–173.

Memon, A., & Bartlett, J. (2002). The effects of verbalization on face recognition in younger and older adults. *Applied Cognitive Psychology, 16*, 365–650.

Memon, A., & Gabbert, F. (2003). Improving the identification accuracy of senior witnesses: Do prelineup questions and sequential testing help? *Journal of Applied Psychology, 88*, 341–347.

Memon, A., Hope, L., Bartlett, J., & Bull, R. (2002). Eyewitness recognition errors: The effects of mugshot viewing and choosing in young and old adults. *Memory & Cognition, 30*, 1219–1227.

Memon, A., Hope, L., & Bull, R. (2003). Exposure duration: Effects on eyewitness accuracy and confidence. Pt. 2. *British Journal of Psychology, 94*, 339–354.

Merikle, P. M., & Reingold, E. M. (1991). Comparing direct (explicit) and indirect (implicit) measures to study conscious and unconscious memory. *Journal of Experimental Psychology: Learning, Memory, and Cognition, 17*, 224–233.

Merikle, P. M., & Reingold, E. M. (1998). On demonstrating unconscious perception: Comment on Draine and Greenwald. *Journal of Experimental Psychology: General, 127*, 304–310.

Merriman, W. E., Azmita, M., & Perlmutter, M. (1988). Rate of forgetting in early childhood. *International Journal of Behavioral Development, 11*, 467–474.

Miller, G. A. (1956). The magical number seven plus or minus two: Some limits on our capacity to process information. *Psychological Review, 63*, 81–97.

Miller, J. G. (1942). *Unconsciousness.* New York: Wiley.

Miller, P. H., & Seier, W. L. (1994). Strategy utilization deficiencies in children: When, where, and why. In H. W. Reese (Ed.), *Advances in child development and behavior* (Vol. 25, pp. 105–156). New York: Academic.

Milner, B., Corsi, P., & Leonard, G. (1991). Frontal-lobe contribution to recency judgments. *Neuropsychologia, 29*, 601–618.

Milner, B., Squire, L. R., & Kandel, E. R. (1998). Cognitive neuroscience and the study of memory. *Neuron, 20*, 445–468.

Minsky, M. (1975). A framework for representing knowledge. In P. H. Winston (Ed.), *The psychology of computer vision.* New York: McGraw-Hill.

Mintz, S., & Albert, M. (1972). Imagery vividness, reality testing, and schizophrenic hallucinations. *Journal of Abnormal Psychology, 79*, 310–316.

Mitchell, K. J., & Zaragoza, M. S. (1996). Repeated exposure to suggestion and false memory: The role of contextual variability. *Journal of Memory and Language, 35*, 246–260.

Mojardin, A. H. (1997). *Age differences in forgetting false memories.* Unpublished master's thesis, University of Arizona, Tucson.

Mojardin, A. H. (1999). *The underlying memory processes of adults' spontaneous and implanted false memories.* Unpublished doctoral dissertation, University of Arizona, Tucson.

Moravcski, J. E., & Healy, A. F. (1995). Effect of meaning on letter detection. *Journal of Experimental Psychology: Learning, Memory, and Cognition, 21,* 82–95.

Morrison, F. W., Haith, M. M., & Kagan, J. (1980). Age trends in recognition memory for pictures: The effects of delay and testing procedure. *Bulletin of the Psychonomic Society, 16,* 480–483.

Münsterberg, H. (1908). *On the witness stand.* New York: Doubleday & Page.

Murphy, G. L., & Shapiro, A. M. (1994). Forgetting of verbatim information in discourse. *Memory & Cognition, 22,* 85–94.

Myers, J. E. B. (1995). New era of skepticism regarding children's credibility. *Psychology, Public Policy, and Law, 1,* 387–398.

Nadel, L., & Moscovitch, M. (1997). Memory consolidation, retrograde amnesia and the hippocampal complex. *Current Opinion in Neurobiology, 7,* 217–227.

Neuschatz, J. S., Lampinen, J. M., Preston, E. L., Hawkins, E. R., & Toglia, M. P. (2002). The effect of memory schemata on memory and the phenomenological experience of naturalistic situations. *Applied Cognitive Psychology, 16,* 687–708.

Newcombe, N. A., & Siegal, M. (1997). Explicitly questioning the nature of suggestibility in preschoolers' memory and retention. *Journal of Experimental Child Psychology, 67,* 185–203.

Newman, A. W., & Thompson, J. W. (2001). The rise and fall of forensic hypnosis in criminal investigation. *Journal of the American Academy of Psychiatry and the Law, 29,* 75–84.

Nickerson, R. S. (1984). Retrieval inhibition from part-set cuing: A persisting enigma in memory research. *Memory & Cognition, 12,* 531–552.

Nolde, S. F., Johnson, M. K., & D'Esposito, M. (1998). Left prefrontal activation during episodic remembering: An event-related fMRI study. *Neuroreport, 9,* 3509–3514.

Norman, K. A., & Schacter, D. L. (1997). False recognition in younger and older adults: Exploring the characteristics of illusory memories. *Memory & Cognition, 25,* 838–848.

Note. (1953). False confessions: A neglected area of criminal investigation. *Indiana Law Journal, 28,* 374–392.

Oates, K., & Shrimpton, S. (1991). Children's memories for stressful and non-stressful events. *Medicine, Science, and the Law, 31,* 4–10.

Ofshe, R., & Watters, E. (1994). *Making monsters: False memories, psychotherapy, and sexual hysteria.* New York: Scribner's.

Orbach, Y., Hershkowitz, I., Lamb, M. E., Sternberg, K. J., Esplin, P. W., & Horowitz, D. (2000). Assessing the value of structured protocols for forensic interviews of alleged child abuse victims. *Child Abuse and Neglect, 24,* 733–752.

Orbach, Y., & Lamb, M. E. (2000). Enhancing children's narratives in investigative interviews. *Child Abuse and Neglect, 24,* 1631–1648.

Orbach, Y., & Lamb, M. E. (2001). The relationship between within-interview contradictions and eliciting interviewer utterances. *Child Abuse and Neglect, 25,* 323–333.

Ornstein, P. A., Gordon, B. N., & Larus, D. (1992). Children's memory for a personally experienced event: Implications for testimony. *Applied Cognitive Psychology, 6,* 49–60.

Ornstein, P. A., Manning, E. L., & Pelphrey, K. A. (1999). Children's memory for pain. *Journal of Developmental and Behavioral Pediatrics, 20,* 262–277.

Paddock, J. R., Joseph, A. L., Chan, F. M., Terranova, S., Manning, C., & Loftus, E. F. (1998). When guided visualization procedures may backfire: Imagination inflation and predicting individual differences in suggestibility. *Applied Cognitive Psychology, 12,* S63–S75.

Paddock, J. R., Noel, M., Terranova, S., Eber, H. W., Manning, C., & Loftus, E. F. (1999). Imagination inflation and the perils of guided visualization. *Journal of Psychology, 133,* 581–595.

Paivio, A. (1969). Mental imagery in associative learning and memory. *Psychological Review, 76,* 241–263.

Paivio, A. (1970). On the functional significance of imagery. *Psychological Bulletin, 73,* 385–392.

Paivio, A. (1971). *Imagery and verbal processes.* New York: Holt, Rinehart, & Winston.

Paivio, A., Yuille, J. C., & Madigan, S. A. (1968). Concreteness, imagery, and meaningfulness values for 925 nouns. Pt. 2. *Journal of Experimental Psychology Monograph, 76*(1).

Paley, J. (1997). Satanist abuse and alien abduction: A comparative analysis theorizing temporal lobe activity as a possible connection between anomalous memories. *British Journal of Social Work, 27,* 43–70.

Paris, S. G., & Carter, A. Y. (1973). Semantic and constructive aspects of sentence memory in children. *Developmental Psychology, 9,* 109–113.

Paris, S. G., & Mahoney, G. J. (1974). Cognitive integration in children's memory for sentences and pictures. *Child Development, 45,* 633–643.

Parkin, A. J. (1997). The neuropsychology of false memory. *Learning and Individual Differences, 9,* 341–357.

Parkin, A. J., Bindschaedler, C., Harsent, L., & Metzler, C. (1996). Verification impairment in the generation of memory deficit following ruptured aneurysm of the anterior communicating artery. *Brain and Cognition, 32,* 14–27.

Parkin, A. J., & Hunkin, N. M. (1993). Impaired temporal context memory on anterograde but not retrograde tests in the absence of frontal pathology. *Cortex, 29,* 267–280.

Parkin, A. J., Ward, J., Bindschaedler, C., Squires, E. J., & Powell, G. (1999). False recognition following frontal lobe damage: The role of encoding factors. *Cognitive Neuroscience, 16,* 243–265.

Parloff, R. (1993, May). False confessions: Standard investigations by Arizona law enforcement officials led to four matching confessions to the murders of nine people at a Buddhist temple. *American Lawyer,* pp. 58–62.

Payne, D. G., Elie, C. J., Blackwell, J. M., & Neuschatz, J. S. (1996). Memory illusions: Recalling, recognizing, and recollecting events that never occurred. *Journal of Memory and Language, 35,* 261–285.

Penfield, W., & Milner, B. (1958). Memory deficit produced by bilateral lesions in the hippocampal zone. *Archives of Neurology and Psychiatry, 79,* 495–497.

Perlmutter, M., & Myers, N. A. (1979). Development of recall in 2- to 4-year-old children. *Developmental Psychology, 15,* 73–83.

Perlmutter, M., Schork, E. J., & Lewis, D. (1982). Effects of semantic and perceptual orienting tasks on preschool children's memory. *Bulletin of the Psychonomic Society, 19,* 65–68.

Peters, D. F. (2001). Examining child sexual abuse evaluations: The types of information affecting expert judgment. *Child Abuse and Neglect, 25,* 149–178.

Peterson, C., Moores, L., & White, G. (2001). Recounting the same events again and again: Children's consistency across multiple interviews. *Applied Cognitive Psychology, 15,* 353–371.

Pezdek, K. (1995, July). *Childhood memories: What types of false memories can be suggestively planted?* Paper presented at the Society for Applied Research in Memory and Cognition, Vancouver, British Columbia.

Pezdek, K., Finger, K., & Hodge, D. (1997). Planting false childhood memories: The role of event plausibility. *Psychological Science, 8,* 437–441.

Pezdek, K., & Hodge, D. (1999). Planting false childhood memories in children: The role of event plausibility. *Child Development, 70,* 887–895.

Pezdek, K., & Roe, C. (1995). The effect of memory trace strength on suggestibility. *Journal of Experimental Child Psychology, 60,* 116–128.

Pezdek, K., & Roe, C. (1997). The suggestibility of children's memory for being touched: Planting, erasing, and changing memories. *Law and Human Behavior, 21,* 95–106.

Piaget, J. (1968). *On the development of memory and identity.* Worcester, MA: Clark University Press.

Piaget, J. (1970a). *Genetic epistemology.* New York: Columbia University Press.

Piaget, J. (1970b). Piaget's theory. In P. H. Mussen (Ed.), *Carmichael's manual of child psychology* (Vol. 1, pp. 703–732). New York: Wiley.

Piaget, J., & Inhelder, B. (1973). *Memory and intelligence*. New York: Basic.

Pickel, K. L. (1999). The influence of context on the "weapon focus." *Law and Human Behavior, 23,* 299–311.

Pipe, M. E., Gee, S., Wilson, J. C., & Egerton, J. M. (1999). Children's recall 1 or 2 years after an event. *Developmental Psychology, 35,* 781–789.

Pipe, M. E., & Goodman, G. S. (1991). Elements of secrecy: Implications for children's testimony. *Behavioral Sciences and the Law, 9,* 33–41.

Pipe, M. E., & Wilson, J. C. (1994). Clues and secrets: Influences on children's event reports. *Developmental Psychology, 30,* 515–525.

Plowman, J. M. (1996). Hypnosis, hypnotherapy, past-life regression. *International Journal of Psychology, 31,* 4474.

Pollatsek, A., Lesch, M., Morris, R., & Rayner, K. (1992). Phonological codes are used in integrating information across saccades in word identification and reading. *Journal of Experimental Psychology: Human Perception and Performance, 18,* 148–162.

Polusny, M. A., & Follette, V. M. (1996). Remembering childhood sexual abuse: A national survey of psychologists' clinical practices, beliefs, and personal experiences. *Professional Psychology: Research and Practice, 27,* 41–52.

Poole, D. A. (1995). Strolling fuzzy-trace theory through eyewitness testimony (or vice-versa). *Learning and Individual Differences, 7,* 87–93.

Poole, D. A., & Lamb, M. E. (1998). *Investigative interviews of children*. Washington, DC: American Psychological Association.

Poole, D. A., & Lindsay, D. S. (1995). Interviewing preschoolers: Effects of nonsuggestive techniques, parental coaching, and leading questions on reports of nonexperienced events. *Journal of Experimental Child Psychology, 60,* 129–154.

Poole, D. A., & Lindsay, D. S. (1996, March). *Parental suggestions and children's reports of nonexperienced events*. Paper presented at American Psychology and Law Society, Hilton Head, SC.

Poole, D. A., & Lindsay, D. S. (2002) Reducing child witnesses' false reports of misinformation from parents. *Journal of Experimental Child Psychology, 81,* 117–140.

Poole, D. A., Lindsay, D. S., Memon, A., & Bull, R. (1995). Psychotherapy and the recovery of memories of childhood sexual abuse: U.S. and British practitioners' opinions, practices, and experiences. *Journal of Consulting and Clinical Psychology, 63,* 426–437.

Poole, D. A., & White, L. T. (1991). Effects of question repetition on the eyewitness testimony of children and adults. *Developmental Psychology, 27,* 975–986.

Poole, D. A., & White, L. T. (1993). Three years later: Effects of question repetition and retention interval on the eyewitness testimony of children and adults. *Developmental Psychology, 29,* 844–853.

Poole, D. A., & White, L. T. (1995). Tell me again and again: Stability and change in the repeated testimonies of children and adults. In M. Zaragoza, J. R. Graham, G. N. N. Hall, R. Hirschman, & Y. S. Ben-Porath (Eds.), *Memory, suggestibility, and eyewitness testimony in children and adults* (pp. 24–43). Thousand Oaks, CA: Sage.

Pope, K. S. (1997). Science as careful questioning: Are claims of a false memory syndrome epidemic based on empirical evidence? *American Psychologist, 52,* 997–1006.

Pope, K. S. (1998). Pseudoscience, cross-examination, and scientific evidence in the recovered memory controversy. *Psychology, Public Policy, and Law, 4,* 1160–1181.

Porter, S., Birt, A. R., Yuille, J. C., & Lehman, D. R. (2000). Negotiating false memories: Interviewer and rememberer characteristics relate to memory distortion. *Psychological Science, 11,* 507–510.

Porter, S., Yuille, J. C., & Lehman, D. R. (1999). The nature of real, implanted, and fabricated memories for emotional childhood events: Implications for the recovered memory debate. *Law and Human Behavior, 23,* 517–537.

Posner, M. I., & Keele, S. W. (1968). The genesis of abstract ideas. *Journal of Experimental Psychology, 77,* 353–363.

Postman, L., & Keppel, G. (1977). Conditions of cumulative proactive inhibition. *Journal of Experimental Psychology: General, 106,* 376–403.

Powell, M. B., Roberts, K. P., Ceci, S. J., & Hembrooke, H. (1999). The effects of repeated exposure on children's suggestibility. *Developmental Psychology, 35,* 1462–1477.

Prawat, R. S., & Cancelli, A. (1976). Constructive memory in conserving and nonconserving first graders. *Developmental Psychology, 12,* 47–50.

Price, J. L., Metzger, R. L., Williams, D., Phelps, N. Z., & Phelps, A. M. (2001, April). *Children produce as many false memories as adults (sometimes!).* Poster presented at Society for Research in Child Development, Minneapolis, MN.

Prull, M. W., Light, L. L., Collett, M. E., & Kennison, R. F. (1998). Age-related differences in memory illusions: Revelation effect. *Aging, Neuropsychology, and Cognition, 5,* 147–165.

Puff, C. R., Tyrrell, D. J., Heibeck, T. H., & VanSlyke, D. A. (1984). Encoding activities and free-recall of categorized and noncategorized pictures by young children. *Bulletin of the Psychonomic Society, 22,* 389–392.

Putnam, F. W. (1989). *Diagnosis and treatment of multiple personality disorder.* New York: Guilford.

Quas, J. A., Goodman, G. S., Bidrose, S., Pipe, M. E., Craw, S., & Ablin, D. S. (1999). Emotion and memory: Children's long-term remembering, forgetting, and suggestibility. *Journal of Experimental Child Psychology, 72,* 235–270.

Quas, J. A., & Schaaf, J. M. (2002). Children's memories of experienced and nonexperienced events following repeated interviews. *Journal of Experimental Child Psychology, 83,* 304–338.

Rabinowitz, F. M., Grant, M. J., Howe, M. L., & Walsh, C. (1994). Reasoning in middle childhood: A dynamic-model of performance on transitivity tasks. *Journal of Experimental Child Psychology, 58,* 252–288.

Rabinowitz, J. C., Craik, F. I. M., & Ackerman, B. P. (1982). A processing account of age differences in recall. *Canadian Journal of Psychology, 36,* 325–344.

Radelet, M. L., Bedau, H. A., & Putnam, C. E. (1992). *In spite of innocence: Erroneous convictions in capital cases.* Boston: Northeastern University Press.

Radvansky, G. A., Copeland, D. E., & Zwaan, R. A. (2003). Aging and functional spatial relations in comprehension and memory. *Psychology and Aging, 18,* 161–165.

Rajaram, S. (1996). Perceptual effects on remembering: Recollective processes in picture recognition. *Journal of Experimental Psychology: Learning, Memory, and Cognition, 22,* 365–377.

Ran, A., Shapiro, T., Fan, J., & Posner, M. I. (2002). Hypnotic suggestion and the modulation of Stoop interference. *Archives of General Psychiatry, 59,* 1155–1161.

Rankin, J. S., & Kausler, D. H. (1979). Adult age differences in false recognition. *Journal of Gerontology, 34,* 58–65.

Raveen, P. J. (1987). Fantasizing under hypnosis: Some experimental evidence. *Skeptical Inquirer, 12,* 182–183.

Reese, H. W. (1970). Imagery and conceptual meaning. *Psychological Bulletin, 73,* 404–414.

Reitman, J. S., & Bower, G. H. (1973). Storage and later recognition of exemplars of concepts. *Cognitive Psychology, 4,* 194–206.

Reyna, V. F. (1981). *The animated word: Modification of meaning by context.* Unpublished doctoral dissertation, Rockefeller University, New York, NY.

Reyna, V. F. (1991). Class inclusion, the conjunction fallacy, and other cognitive illusions. *Developmental Review, 11,* 317–336.

Reyna, V. F. (1992). Reasoning, remembering, and their relationship: Social, cognitive, and developmental issues. In M. L. Howe, C. J. Brainerd, & V. F. Reyna (Eds.), *Development of long-term retention* (pp. 103–127). New York: Springer-Verlag.

Reyna, V. F. (1995). Interference effects in memory and reasoning: A fuzzy-trace theory analysis. In F. N. Dempster & C. J. Brainerd (Eds.), *New perspectives on interference and inhibition in cognition* (pp. 29–61). New York: Academic.

Reyna, V. F. (1996a). Conceptions of memory development, with implications for reasoning and decision making. *Annals of Child Development, 12,* 87–118.

Reyna, V. F. (1996b). Meaning, memory and the interpretation of metaphors. In J. Mio & A. Katz (Eds.), *Metaphor: Implications and Applications* (pp. 39–57). Hillsdale, NJ: Erlbaum.

Reyna, V. F. (1998). Fuzzy-trace and false memory. In M. Intons-Peterson & D. Best (Eds.), *Memory Distortions and Their Prevention* (pp. 15–27). Makwah, NJ: Erlbaum.

Reyna, V. F. (2000a). Fuzzy-trace theory and source monitoring: An evaluation of theory and false-memory data. *Learning and Individual Differences, 12,* 163–175.

Reyna, V. F. (2000b, November). *Phantom recollection of narratives.* Paper presented at the Psychonomic Society meeting, New Orleans, LA.

Reyna, V. F. (2004). How people make decisions about risk: A dual-processes approach. *Current Directions in Psychological Science, 13,* 60–66.

Reyna, V. F., & Brainerd, C. J. (1990). Fuzzy processing in transitivity development. *Annals of Operations Research, 23,* 37–63.

Reyna, V. F., & Brainerd, C. J. (1991). Fuzzy-trace theory and framing effects in choice: Gist extraction, truncation, and conversion. *Journal of Behavioral Decision Making, 4,* 249–262.

Reyna, V. F., & Brainerd, C. J. (1992). A fuzzy-trace theory of reasoning and remembering: Patterns, paradoxes, and parallelism. In A. Healy, S. Kosslyn, & R. Shiffrin (Eds.), *From learning processes to cognitive processes: Essays in honor of William K. Estes.* (pp. 235–259). Hillsdale, NJ: Erlbaum.

Reyna, V. F., & Brainerd, C. J. (1995a). Fuzzy-trace theory: An interim synthesis. *Learning and Individual Differences, 7,* 1–75.

Reyna, V. F., & Brainerd, C. J. (1995b). Fuzzy-trace theory: Some foundational issues. *Learning and Individual Differences, 7,* 145–162.

Reyna, V. F., & Brainerd, C. J. (1997). Fuzzy-theory applied to the theory and practice of law: Commentary on law's memory by Paul C. Wolnuth. *Journal of Contemporary Legal Issues, 8,* 287–298.

Reyna, V. F., & Brainerd, C. J. (1998). Fuzzy-trace theory and false memory: New frontiers. *Journal of Experimental Child Psychology, 71,* 194–209.

Reyna, V. F., & Hamilton, A. J. (2001). The importance of memory in informed consent for surgical risk. *Medical Decision Making, 21,* 152–155.

Reyna, V. F., Holliday, R., & Marche, T. (2002). Explaining the development of false memories. *Developmental Review, 22,* 436–489.

Reyna, V. F., & Kiernan, B. (1994). The development of gist versus verbatim memory in sentence recognition: Effects of lexical familiarity, semantic content, encoding instructions, and retention interval. *Developmental Psychology, 30,* 178–191.

Reyna, V. F., & Kiernan, B. (1995). Children's memory and interpretation of psychological metaphors. *Metaphor and Symbolic Activity, 10,* 309–331.

Reyna, V. F., & Lloyd, F. (1997). Theories of false memory in children and adults. *Learning and Individual Differences, 9,* 95–123.

Reyna, V. F., Mills, B., Estrada, S., & Brainerd, C. J. (in press). False memory in children: Theory, data, and legal implications. In M. Toglia & D. Read (Eds.), *Handbook of Eyewitness Psychology* (vol. 1). T Mahury, NJ: Erlbaum.

Reyna, V. F., & Titcomb, A. L. (1997). Constraints on the suggestibility of eyewitness testimony: A fuzzy-trace theory analysis. In D. G. Payne & F. G. Conrad (Eds.), *A synthesis of basic and applied approaches to human memory.* (pp. 157–174). Hillsdale, NJ: Erlbaum.

Rhodes, M. G., & Anastasi, J. S. (2000). The effects of a levels-of-processing manipulation on false recall. *Psychonomic Bulletin & Review, 7,* 158–162.

Ricci, C. M., Beal, C. R., & Dekle, D. J. (1996). The effect of parent versus unfamiliar interviews on children's eyewitness memory and identification accuracy. *Law and Human Behavior, 20,* 483–500.

Rice, S. A. (1929). Interviewer bias as contagion. *American Journal of Sociology, 35,* 421–423.

Rieser, M. (1991). Recantation in child sexual abuse cases. *Child Welfare, 70,* 611–621.

Rind, B., Tromovitch, P., & Bauserman, R. (1998). A meta-analytic examination of assumed properties of child sexual abuse using college samples. *Psychological Bulletin, 124,* 22–53.

Roberts, K. P., & Blades, M. (1995). Children's discrimination of memories for actual and pretend actions in a hiding task. *British Journal of Developmental Psychology, 13,* 321–334.

Roberts, K. P., & Blades, M. (2000). Children's memory and source monitoring of real-life and televised events. *Journal of Applied Developmental Psychology, 20,* 575–596.

Roberts, K. P., Lamb, M. E., & Sternberg, K. J. (1999). Effects of timing of postevent information on preschoolers' memories of an event. *Applied Cognitive Psychology, 13,* 541–549.

Robinson, K. J., & Roediger, H. L., III. (1997). Associative processes in false recall and false recognition. *Psychological Science, 8,* 231–237.

Roebers, C., Rieber, R., & Schneider, W. (1995). Eyewitness testimony and suggestibility as a function of recall accuracy: A developmental study. *Zeitschrift fur entwicklungspsychologie und padagogische psychologie, 27,* 210–225.

Roediger, H. L., III. (1996). Memory illusions. *Journal of Memory and Language, 35,* 76–100.

Roediger, H. L., III, & McDermott, K. B. (1995). Creating false memories: Remembering words not presented on lists. *Journal of Experimental Psychology: Learning, Memory, and Cognition, 21,* 803–814.

Roediger, H. L., III, & McDermott, K. B. (2000). Tricks of memory. *Current Directions in Psychological Science, 9,* 123–127.

Roediger, H. L., III, & Payne, D. G. (1985). Recall criterion does not affect recall level or hypermnesia: A puzzle for generate/recognized theories. *Memory & Cognition, 13,* 1–7.

Roediger, H. L., III, Robinson, K. J., & Balota, H. L. (2001). *False recall and false recognition following fast presentation of lists: Evidence for automatic processing in evoking false memories.* Unpublished manuscript, Washington University, St. Louis, MO.

Roediger, H. L., III, Srinivas, K., & Waddill, P. (1989). How much does guessing influence recall? Comment [on] Erdelyi, Finks, & Feigin-Pfau. *Journal of Experimental Psychology: General, 118,* 255–257.

Roediger, H. L., III, Watson, J. M., McDermott, K. B., & Gallo, D. A. (2001). Factors that determine false recall: A multiple regression analysis. *Psychonomic Bulletin & Review, 8,* 385–405.

Rohwer, W. D., Jr. (1970). Images and pictures in children's learning. *Psychological Bulletin, 73,* 393–403.

Rohwer, W. D., Jr., Kee, D. W., & Guy, K. C. (1975). Developmental changes in the effects of presentation media on noun-pair learning. *Journal of Experimental Child Psychology, 19,* 137–152.

Rosenthal, R. (1985). From unconscious expectations to teacher expectancy effects. In J. B. Dusek (Ed.), *Teacher expectancies* (pp. 37–134). Hillsdale, NJ: Erlbaum.

Rosenthal, R. (1995). State of New Jersey v. Michaels, Margaret, Kelly: An overview. *Psychology, Public Policy, and Law, 1,* 246–271.

Rosenthal, R., & Rubin, D. B. (1978). Interpersonal expectancy effects: The first 345 studies. *Behavioral and Brain Sciences, 1,* 377–386.

Ross, D. F., Ceci, S. J., Dunning, D., and Toglia, M. P. (1994). Unconscious transference and mistaken identity: When a witness misidentifies a familiar but innocent person. *Journal of Applied Psychology, 79,* 918–930.

Rotello, C. M., & Heit, E. (1999). Two-process models of recognition memory: Evidence for recall-to-reject? *Journal of Memory and Language, 40,* 432–453.

Rotello, C. M., & Heit, E. (2000). Associative recognition: A case of recall-to-reject processing. *Memory & Cognition, 28,* 907–922.

Rotello, C. M., Macmillan, N. A., & Van Tassel, G. (2000). Recall-to-reject in recognition: Evidence from ROC curves. *Journal of Memory and Language, 43,* 67–88.

Rubin, S. R., Van Petten, C., Glisky, E. L., & Newberg, W. N. (1999). Memory conjunction errors in younger and older adults: Event-related potential and neuropsychological data. *Cognitive Neuropsychology, 16,* 459–488.

Rudy, L., & Goodman, G. S. (1991). Effects of participation on children's reports: Implications for children's testimony. *Developmental Psychology, 27,* 527–538.

Rundus, D. (1973). Negative effects of using list items as recall cues. *Journal of Verbal Learning and Verbal Behavior, 12,* 43–50.

Runquist, W. N. (1983). Some effects of remembering on forgetting. *Memory & Cognition, 11,* 641–650.

Russell, W. A., & Jenkins, J. J. (1954). *Minnesota norms for responses to 100 words from the Kent-Rosanoff association test.* Technical Report No. 11, Department of Psychology, University of Minnesota.

Rust, M. E. (1986). The nightmare is real. *Student Law, 14,* 12–19.

Rutherford, B. (1988a). A retracta speaks. *False Memory Syndrome Foundation Newsletter,* January/February.

Rutherford, B. (1988b). A retractor speaks—Part II. *False Memory Syndrome Foundation Newsletter,* January/February.

Ryan, N. (1989). *Affirmation in response to vacate judgment of conviction, indictment no. 4762/89.* New York: Manhattan District Attorney's Office. Available at www.ManhattanDA.org.

Ryder, D. (1992). *Breaking the cycle of Satanic ritual abuse.* Minneapolis, MN: CompCare.

Salmon, K., Bidrose, S., & Pipe, M. E. (1995). Providing props to facilitate children's reports: A comparison of toy and real items. *Journal of Experimental Child Psychology, 60,* 174–194.

Salmon. K., & Pipe, M. E. (1997). Props and children's event reports: The impact of a 1-year delay. *Journal of Experimental Child Psychology, 65,* 261–292.

Salmon, K., & Pipe, M. E. (2000). Recalling an event one year later: The impact of props, drawing and a prior interview. *Applied Cognitive Psychology, 14,* 99–120.

Salthouse, T. A. (1995). Selective influences of age and speed on associative memory. *American Journal of Psychology, 108,* 381–396.

Salthouse, T. A. (1996). General and specific speed mediation of adult age differences in memory. *Journals of Gerontology Series B: Psychological Sciences and Social Sciences, 51,* P30–P42.

Salthouse, T. A., Toth, J. P., Hancock, H. E., & Woodard, J. L. (1997). Controlled and automatic forms of memory and attention: Process purity and the uniqueness of age-related influences. *Journals of Gerontology Series B: Psychological Sciences and Social Sciences, 52,* P216–P228.

Saltman, V., & Solomon, R. S. (1982). Incest and multiple personality. *Psychology Reports, 50,* 1127–1141.

Sarbin, T. R. (1997). The power of believed-in imaginings. *Psychological Inquiry, 8,* 322–325.

Sauer, M. (2002, December 13). Confessions in the third degree: Court TV film revisits police grilling. *San Diego Union-Tribune.*

Saywitz, K. J., Nicholas, E., Goodman, G. S., & Moan, S. F. (1991). Children's memories of a physical-examination involving genital touch: Implications for reports of child sexual abuse. *Journal of Consulting and Clinical Psychology, 59,* 682–691.

Schacter, D. L., Buckner, R. L., Koutstaal, W., Dale, A. M., & Rosen, B. R. (1997). Late onset of anterior prefrontal activity during true and false recognition: An event-related fMRI study. *Neuroimage, 6,* 259–269.

Schacter, D. L., & Dodson, C. S. (2001). Misattribution, false recognition and the sins of memory. *Philosophical Transactions of the Royal Society of London Series B: Biological Sciences, 356,* 1385–1393.

Schacter, D. L., Israel, L., & Racine, C. (1999). Suppressing false recognition in younger and older adults: The distinctiveness heuristic. *Journal of Memory and Language, 40,* 1–24.

Schacter, D. L., Kagan, J., & Leichtman, M. D. (1995). True and false memories in children and adults: A cognitive neuroscience perspective. *Psychology, Public Policy, and Law, 1,* 411–428.

Schacter, D. L., Kasniak, A. W., Kihlstrom, J. F., & Valdiserri, M. (1991). The relation between source memory and aging. *Psychology and Aging, 6,* 559–568.

Schacter, D. L., Koutstaal, W., Johnson, M. K., Gross, M. S., & Angell, K. A. (1997). False recollection induced by photographs: A comparison of older and younger adults. *Psychology and Aging, 12,* 203–215.

Schacter, D. L., Norman, K. A., & Koutstaal, W. (1998). The cognitive neuroscience of constructive memory. *Annual Review of Psychology, 49,* 289–318.

Schacter, D. L., Verfaellie, M., & Anes, M. D. (1997). Illusory memories in amnesic patients: Conceptual and perceptual false recognition. *Neuropsychology, 11,* 331–342.

Schacter, D. L., Verfaellie, M., Anes, M. D., & Racine, C. (1998). When true recognition suppresses false recognition: Evidence from amnesic patients. *Journal of Cognitive Neuroscience, 10,* 668–679.

Schacter, D. L., Verfaellie, M., & Pradere, D. (1996). Neuropsychology of memory illusions: False recall and recognition in amnesic patients. *Journal of Memory and Language, 35,* 319–334.

Schank, R. C., & Abelson, R. (1977). *Scripts, plans, goals, and understanding.* Hillsdale, NJ: Erlbaum.

Schooler, J. W., Bendiksen, M., & Ambadar, Z. (1997). Toeing the middle line: Can we accommodate both fabricated and recovered memories of sexual abuse? In M. Conway (Ed.), *False and recovered memories.* New York: Oxford University Press.

Scoboria, A., Mazzoni, G., Kirsch, I., & Milling, L. S. (2002). Immediate and persisting effects of misleading questions and hypnosis on memory reports. *Journal of Experimental Psychology: Applied, 8,* 26–32.

Scoville, W. B., & Milner, B. (1957). Loss of recent memory after bilateral hippocampal lesions. *Journal of Neurology, Neurosurgery and Psychiatry, 20,* 11–21.

Scullin, M. H., & Ceci, S. J. (2001). A suggestibility scale for children. *Personality and Individual Differences, 30,* 843–856.

Seamon, J. G., Goodkind, M. S., Dumey, A. D., Dick, E., Aufseeser, M. S., Strickland, S. E., Woulfin, J. R., & Fung, N. S. (2003). "If I didn't write it, why would I remember it?": Effects of encoding, attention, and practice on accurate and false memory. *Memory & Cognition, 31,* 445–457.

Seamon, J. G., Lee, I. A., Toner, S. K., Wheeler, R. H., Goodkind, M. S., & Birch, A. D. (2002). Are false memories dependent on mental rehearsal? Thinking out loud in the DRM procedure. *Psychological Science, 13,* 526–531.

Seamon, J. G., Luo, C. R., & Gallo, D. A. (1998). Creating false memories of words with or without recognition of list items: Evidence for nonconscious processes. *Psychological Science, 9,* 20–26.

Seamon, J. G., Luo, C. R., Kopecky, J. J., Price, C. A., Rothschild, L., Fung, N. S., & Schwartz, M. A. (2002). Are false memories more difficult to forget than accurate memories? The effect of retention interval on recall and recognition. *Memory & Cognition, 30,* 1054–1064.

Seamon, J. G., Luo, C. R., Schlegel, S. E., Greene, S. E., & Goldenberg, A. B. (2000). False memory for categorized pictures and words: The category associates procedure for studying memory errors in children and adults. *Journal of Memory and Language, 42,* 120–146.

Seamon, J. G., Luo, C. R., Schwartz, M. A., Jones, K. J., Lee, D. M., & Jones, S. J. (2002). Repetition can have similar or different effects on accurate and false recognition. *Journal of Memory and Language, 46,* 323–340.

Seamon, J. G., Luo, C. R., Shulman, E. P., Toner, S. K., & Calgar S. (2002). False memories are hard to inhibit: Differential effects of directed forgetting on accurate and false recall in the DRM procedure. *Memory, 0*(4), 225–237.

Seamon, J. G., Schlegel, S. E., Hiester, P. M., Landau, S. M., & Blumenthal, B. F. (2002). Misremembering pictured objects: People of all ages demonstrate the boundary extension illusion. *American Journal of Psychology, 115,* 151–167.

Searcy, J. H., Bartlett, J. C., & Memon, A. (1999). Age differences in accuracy and choosing in eyewitness identification and face recognition. *Memory & Cognition, 27,* 538–552.

Searcy, J. H., Bartlett, J. C., Memon, A., & Swanson, L. (2001). Aging and lineup performance at long retention intervals: Effects of metamemory and context reinstatement. *Journal of Applied Psychology, 86,* 207–214.

Shaw, J. S., III. (1996). Increases in eyewitness confidence resulting from postevent questioning. *Journal of Experimental Psychology: Applied, 2,* 126–146.

Sher, L. (1995). False-memory syndrome. *Lancet, 346,* 1704–1705.

Shiffrin, R. M. (2003). Modeling memory and perception. *Cognitive Science, 27,* 341–378.

Shimamura, A. P., & Squire, L. R. (1987). A neuropsychological study of fact memory and source amnesia. *Journal of Experimental Psychology: Human Learning and Memory, 13,* 464–473.

Siegel, L. S. (1993). The development of reading. *Advances in Child Development and Behavior, 24,* 63–97.

Simpson, P. (1996). *Second thoughts: Understanding the false memory crisis and how it could affect you.* Nashville, TN: Nelson.

Skinner, L. J. (1996). Assumptions and beliefs about the role of AD dolls in child sexual abuse validation interviews: Are they supported empirically? *Behavioral Sciences & the Law, 14,* 167–185.

Slamecka, N. J. (1968). An examination of trace storage in free recall. *Journal of Experimental Psychology, 76,* 504–513.

Smedslund, J. (1969). Psychological diagnostics. *Psychological Bulletin, 71,* 237–248.

Smith, A. D. (1975). Partial learning and recognition memory in the aged. *International Journal of Aging and Human Development, 6,* 359–365.

Smith, D. A., & Graesser, A. C. (1981). Memory for actions in scripted activities as a function of typicality, retention interval, and retrieval task. *Memory & Cognition, 9,* 550–559.

Smith, R. E., & Hunt, R. R. (1998). Presentation modality affects false memory. *Psychonomic Bulletin & Review, 5,* 710–715.

Snodgrass, J. G., & Corwin, J. (1988). Pragmatics of measuring recognition memory: Applications to dementia and amnesia. *Journal of Experimental Psychology: General, 117,* 34–50.

Snodgrass, J. G., & Vanderwart, M. (1980). A standardized set of 260 pictures: Norms for name agreement, image agreement, familiarity, and visual complexity. *Journal of Experimental Psychology: Human Learning and Memory, 6,* 174–215.

Spanos, N. P. (1987). Hypnosis research: Paradigms in conflict. *Behavioral and Brain Sciences, 10,* 525–530.

Spanos, N. P. (1996). *Multiple identities & false memories: A sociocognitive perspective.* Washington, DC: American Psychological Association.

Spanos, N.P., Burgess, C.A., Burgess, M.F., Samuels, C., & Blois, W.O. (1999). Creating false memories of infancy with hypnotic and non-hypnotic procedures. *Applied Cognitive Psychology,* 13, 201–218.

Spanos, N. P., Burnley, M. C. E., & Cross, P. A. (1993). Response expectancies and interpretations as determinants of hypnotic responding. *Journal of Personality and Social Psychology, 65,* 1237–1242.

Spanos, N. P., Cross, P. A., Dickson, K., & Dubreuil, S. C. (1993). Close encounters: An examination of UFO experiences. *Journal of Abnormal Psychology, 102,* 624–632.

Spanos, N. P., Menary, E., Gabora, N. J., Dubreuil, S. C., & Dewhurst, B. (1991). Secondary identity enactments during hypnotic past-life regression: A sociocognitive perspective. *Journal of Personality and Social Psychology, 61,* 308–320.

Spanos, N. P., Liddy, S. J., Baxter, C. E., & Burgess, C. A. (1994). Long-term and short-term stability of behavioral and subjective indexes of hypnotizability. *Journal of Research in Personality, 28,* 301–313.

Spanos, N. P., McNulty, S. A., Dubreuil, S. C., Pires, M., & Burgess, M. F. (1995). The frequency and correlates of sleep paralysis in a university sample. *Journal of Research in Personality, 28,* 285–305.

Spencer, W. D., & Raz, N. (1995). Differential effects of aging on memory for content and context: A meta-analysis. *Psychology and Aging, 10,* 527–539.

Spiegel, H. (1974). The Grade 5 syndrome: The highly hypnotizable person. *International Journal of Clinical and Experimental Hypnosis, 22,* 303–319.

Sporer, S. L. (1992). Post-dicting eyewitness accuracy: Confidence, decision-times and person descriptions of choosers and non-choosers. *European Journal of Social Psychology, 22,* 157–180.

Sporer, S. L.. (1993). Eyewitness identification accuracy, confidence, and decision times in simultaneous and sequential lineups. *Journal of Applied Psychology, 78,* 22–33.

Sporer, S. L., Penrod, S., Read, D., & Cutler, B. L. (1995). Choosing confidence and accuracy: A meta-analysis of confidence-accuracy relations in eyewitness identification studies. *Psychological Bulletin, 118,* 315–327.

Sprenger-Charolles, L. (1991). Word identification strategies in a picture context: Comparisons between "good" and "poor" readers. In L. Reiben & C. L. Perfetti (Eds.), *Learning to read: Basic research and its implications* (pp. 175–188). Hillsdale, NJ: Erlbaum.

State of Arizona v. Mejia. (2002). Superior Court, Pima County, AZ.

State of Arizona v. Sagarnaga. (2001). Superior Court, Pima County, AZ.

State of Arizona v. Sweeney. (2001). Superior Court, Pima County, AZ.

State of California v. Buckey. (1990). Superior Court, Los Angeles County, CA.

State of California v. Kosher. (1999). Superior Court, San Jose County, CA.

State of Maryland v. Craig. (1990). 497 U.S. 836.

State of New Jersey v. Michaels. (1988). Superior Court, Essex County, NJ.

State of New Jersey v. Michaels, 136 N.J., 299, 642 (A2d 1372 1994).

State of Washington v. Highland. (2003). Superior Court, King County, WA.

Stern, W. (1910). Abstracts of lectures on the psychology of testimony and on the study of individuality. *American Journal of Psychology, 21,* 270–282.

Sternberg, K. J., Lamb, M. E., Esplin, P. W., Orbach, Y., & Mitchell, S. (2001) Use of a structured investigative protocol enhances young children's responses to free-recall prompts in the course of forensic interviews. *Journal of Applied Psychology, 86,* 997–1005.

Stevenson, I. (2000). The phenomenon of claimed memories of previous lives: Possible interpretations and importance. *Medical Hypotheses, 54,* 652–659.

Steward, M. S., & Steward, D. S. (1996). Interviewing young children about body touch and handling. *Monographs of the Society for Research in Child Development, 61*(4–5) (whole No. 248).

Strange, B. A., Otten, L. J., Josephs, O., Rugg, M. D., & Dolan, R. J. (2002). Dissociable human perirhinal, hippocampal, and parahippocampal roles during verbal encoding. *Journal of Neuroscience, 22,* 523–528.

Strong, E. K. (1913). The effect of time-interval upon recognition memory. *Psychological Review, 20,* 339–371.

Suengas, A. G., & Johnson, M. K. (1988). Qualitative effects of rehearsal on perceived and imagined complex events. *Journal of Experimental Psychology: General, 117,* 371–376.

Summit, R. C. (1983). The child sexual abuse accommodation syndrome. *Child Abuse and Neglect, 7,* 177–193.

Sussman, A. L. (2001). Reality monitoring of performed and imagined interactive events: Developmental and contextual effects. *Journal of Experimental Child Psychology, 79,* 115–138.

Sutherland, R., & Hayne, H. (2001). Age-related changes in the misinformation effect. *Journal of Experimental Child Psychology, 79,* 388–404.

Takhar, J. (1995). Alien abduction in PTSD. *Journal of the American Academy of Child and Adolescent Psychiatry, 34,* 974–975.

Talmadge, S. A. (2001). Possible false confession in a military court-martial: A case study. *Military Psychology, 13,* 235–241.

Tarriance, C. A., Matheson, K., Mallard, C., & Schnarr, J. A. (2000). The role of expectation and memory-retrieval techniques in the construction of beliefs about past events. *Applied Cognitive Psychology, 14,* 361–377.

Technical Working Group for Eyewitness Evidence. (1999). *Eyewitness evidence: A guide for law enforcement.* Washington, DC: U.S. Department of Justice.

Thapar, A., & McDermott, K. B. (2001). False recall and false recognition induced by presentation of associated words: Effects of retention interval and level of processing. *Memory & Cognition, 29,* 424–432.

Thierry, K. L., Spence, M. J., & Memon, A. (2001). Before misinformation is encountered: Source monitoring decreases child witness suggestibility. *Journal of Cognition and Development, 2,* 1–26.

Thomas, A. K., Bulevich, J. V., & Loftus, E. F. (2003). Exploring the role of repetition and sensory elaboration in the imagination inflation effect. *Memory & Cognition, 31,* 630–640.

Thomas, A. K., & Loftus, E. F. (2002). Creating bizarre false memories through imagination. *Memory & Cognition, 30,* 423–431.

Thompson, W. C., Clarke-Stewart, A., & LePore, S. J. (1997). What did the janitor do? Suggestive interviewing and the accuracy of children's accounts. *Law and Human Behavior, 21,* 427–438.

Tighe, T. J., Tighe, L. S., & Schechter, J. (1975). Memory for instances and categories in children and adults. *Journal of Experimental Child Psychology, 20,* 22–37.

Titcomb, A. L. (1996). *False memories and fuzzy-trace theory: Misinforming verbatim and gist memory.* Unpublished doctoral dissertation, University of Arizona, Tucson, AZ.

Titcomb, A. L., & Reyna, U. F. (1995). Memory interference and misinformation. In F. N. Dempster & C. J. Brainerd (Eds.), *New perspectives on interference and inhibition is cognition* (pp. 263–294). San Diego, CA: Academic Press.

Toglia, M. P., & Neuschatz, J. S. (1996). *False memories: Where does encoding opportunity fit into the equation?* Paper presented at Psychonomic Society, Chicago, IL.

Toglia, M. P., Neuschatz, J. S., & Goodwin, K. A. (1999). Recall accuracy and illusory memories: When more is less. *Memory, 7,* 233–256.

Toglia, M. P., Payne, D. G., & Anastasi, J. S. (1991). Recognition level and the misinformation effect: A metaanalysis and empirical investigation. *Bulletin of the Psychonomic Society, 29,* 507.

Toglia, M. P., Ross, D. F., Ceci, S. J., & Hembrooke, H. (1992). The suggestibility of children's memory: A social-psychological and cognitive interpretation. In M. L. Howe, C. J. Brainerd, & V. F. Reyna (Eds.), *Development of long-term retention* (pp. 217–244). New York: Springer-Verlag.

Trabasso, T. (1977). The role of memory as a system in making transitive inferences. In R. V. Kail, Jr., & J. W. Hagen (Eds.), *Perspectives on the development of memory and cognition.* (pp. 333–366). Hillsdale, NJ: Erlbaum.

Trabasso, T., & van de Broek, P. (1985). Causal thinking and the representation of narrative events. *Journal of Verbal Learning and Verbal Behavior, 24,* 612–630.

Tulving, E. (1981). Similarity relations in recognition. *Journal of Verbal Learning and Verbal Behavior, 20,* 479–496.

Tulving, E. (1985). Memory and consciousness. *Canadian Psychologist, 26,* 1–12.

Tulving, E., & Madigan, S. A. (1970). Memory and verbal learning. *Annual Review of Psychology, 21,* 437–462.

Tulving, E., & Thomson, D. M. (1971). Retrieval processes in recognition memory: Effects of associative context. *Journal of Experimental Psychology, 87,* 116–124.

Tun, P. A., Wingfield, A., Rosen, M. J., & Blanchard, I. (1998). Older adults show greater susceptibility to false memory than young adults: Temporal characteristics of false recognition. *Psychology and Aging, 13,* 230–241.

Tussing, A. A., & Greene, R. L. (1999). Differential effects of repetition on true and false recognition. *Journal of Memory and Language, 40,* 520–533.

Tversky, A., & Kahneman, D. (1974). Judgment under uncertainty: Heuristics and biases. *Science, 185,* 1124–1131.

Tversky, A., & Kahneman, D. (1983). Extensional versus intuitive reasoning: The conjunction fallacy in probability judgment. *Psychological Review, 90,* 293–315.

Tversky, B., & Tuchin, M. (1989). A reconciliation of evidence on eyewitness testimony. *Journal of Experimental Psychology: General, 118,* 86–91.

Ullrich, P. M., & Lutgendorf, S. K. (2002). Journaling about stressful events: Effects of cognitive processing and emotional expression. *Annals of Behavioral Medicine, 24,* 244–250.

Underwood, B. J. (1965). False recognition produced by implicit verbal responses. *Journal of Experimental Psychology, 70,* 122–129.

Vandenberg, B. (2002). Hypnotic responsivity from a developmental perspective: Insights from young children. *International Journal of Clinical and Experimental Hypnosis, 50,* 229–247.

Varendock, J. (1911). Les temoignages d'enfants dans un proces retentissant. *Archives de Psychologie, 11,* 129–171.

Verfaellie, M., Schacter, D. L., & Cook, S. P. (2002). The effect of retrieval instructions on false recognition: Exploring the nature of the gist memory impairment in amnesia. *Neuropsychologia, 40,* 2360–2368.

Verfaellie, M., & Treadwell, J. R. (1993). Status of recognition memory in amnesia. *Neuropsychology, 7,* 5–13.

Verhaeghen, P., Marcoen, A., & Goossens, L. (1993). Facts and fiction about memory aging: A quantitative integration of research findings. *Journal of Gerontology, 48,* P157–P171.

Verhaeghen, P., & Salthouse, T. A. (1997). Meta-analyses of age-cognition relations in adulthood: Estimates of linear and nonlinear age effects and structural models. *Psychological Bulletin, 122,* 231–249.

Wade, K. A., Garry, M., Read, J. D., & Lindsay, D. S. (2002). A picture is worth a thousand lies: Using false photographs to create false childhood memories. *Psychonomic Bulletin & Review, 9,* 597–603.

Wagner, A. D., Koutstaal, W., & Schacter, D. L. (1999). When encoding yields remembering: Insights from event-related neuroimaging. *Philosophical Transactions of the Royal Society Series B: Biological Sciences, 354,* 1307–1324.

Wallace, W. P., Stewart, M. T., & Malone, C. P. (1995). Recognition memory errors produced by implicit activation of word candidates during the processing of spoken words. *Journal of Memory and Language, 34,* 417–439.

Wallace, W. P., Stewart, M. T., Shaffer, T. R., & Barry, C. R. (1998). Are false recognitions influenced by prerecognition processing? *Journal of Experimental Psychology: Learning, Memory, and Cognition, 24,* 284–298.

Ward, J., & Parkin, A. J. (2000). Pathological false recognition and source memory deficits following frontal lobe damage. *Neurocase, 6,* 333–344.

Warren, A. R., & Lane, P. L. (1995). Effects of timing and type of questioning on eyewitness accuracy and suggestibility. In M. S. Zaragoza, J. R. Graham, N. N. Hall, R. Hirschman, & Y. S. Ben-Porath (Eds.), *Memory, suggestibility, and eyewitness testimony in children and adults* (pp. 44–60). Thousand Oaks, CA: Sage.

Warren, A. R., & McGough, L. S. (1996). Research on children's suggestibility: Implications for the investigative interview. *Criminal Justice and Behavior, 23,* 269–303.

Warren, A. R., & Woodall, C. E. (1999). The reliability of hearsay testimony: How well do interviewers recall their interviews with children? *Psychology, Public Policy, and Law, 5,* 355–371.

Watson, J. M., Balota, D. A., & Sergent-Marshall, S. D. (2001). Semantic, phonological, and hybrid veridical and false memories in healthy older adults and in individuals with dementia of the Alzheimer type. *Neuropsychology, 15,* 254–267.

Watson v. Catholic Diocese of Phoenix. (1999). Superior Court, Maricopa County, AZ.

Weismer, S. E. (1985). Constructive comprehension abilities exhibited by language-disordered children. *Journal of Speech and Hearing Research, 28,* 175–184.

Weiss, B. L. (1992). *Through time into healing.* New York: Simon & Schuster.

Weiss, S. L., Robinson, G., & Hastie, R. (1977). Relationship of depth of processing to free-recall in second and fourth graders. *Developmental Psychology, 13,* 525–526.

Welch-Ross, M. K. (1999). Interviewer knowledge and preschoolers' reasoning about knowledge states moderate suggestibility. *Cognitive Development, 14,* 423–442.

Wells, G. L. (1978). Applied eyewitness testimony research: System variables and estimator variables. *Journal of Personality and Social Psychology, 36,* 1546–1557.

Wells, G. L. (1984). The psychology of lineup identifications. *Journal of Applied Social Psychology, 14,* 89–103.

Wells, G. L. (1985). Verbal descriptions of faces from memory: Are they diagnostic of identification accuracy? *Journal of Applied Psychology, 70,* 619–626.

Wells, G. L. (1988). *Eyewitness identification: A system handbook.* Toronto, Canada: Carswell.

Wells, G. L. (1993). What do we know about eyewitness identification? *American Psychologist, 48,* 553–571.

Wells, G. L., & Bradfield, A. L. (1998). "Good, you identified the suspect": Feedback to eyewitnesses distorts their reports of the witnessing experience. *Journal of Applied Psychology, 83,* 360–376.

Wells, G. L., Ferguson, T. J., & Lindsay, R. C. L. (1981). The tractability of eyewitness confidence and its implications for triers of fact. *Journal of Applied Psychology, 66,* 688–696.

Wells, G. L., Leippe, M. R., & Ostrom, T. M. (1979). Guides for empirically assessing the fairness of a lineup. *Law and Human Behavior, 3,* 285–293.

Wells, G. L., & Lindsay, R. C. L. (1980). On estimating the diagnosticity of eyewitness nonidentifications. *Psychological Bulletin, 88,* 776–784.

Wells, G. L., & Lindsay, R. C. L. (1985). Methodological notes on the accuracy-confidence relation in eyewitness identifications. *Journal of Applied Psychology, 70,* 413–419.

Wells, G. L., Malpass, R. S., Lindsay, R. C. L., Fisher, R. P., Turtle, J. W., & Fulero, S. M. (2000). From the lab to the police station: A successful application of eyewitness research. *American Psychologist, 55,* 581–598.

Wells, G. L., Rydell, S. M., & Seelau, E. P. (1993). On the selection of distractors for eyewitness lineups. *Journal of Applied Psychology, 78,* 835–844.

Wells, G. L., Small, M., Penrod, S., Malpass, R. S., Fulero, S. M., & Brimacombe, C. A. E. (1998). Eyewitness identification procedures: Recommendations for lineups and photospreads. *Law and Human Behavior, 23,* 603–648.

Wells, G. L., & Turtle, J. W. (1986). Eyewitness identification: The importance of lineup models. *Psychological Bulletin, 99,* 320–329.

Westerman, D. L. (2001). The role of familiarity in item recognition, associative recognition, and plurality recognition on self-paced and speeded tests. *Journal of Experimental Psychology: Learning, Memory, and Cognition, 27,* 723–732.

Whipple, G. M. (1909). The psychology of testimony. *Psychological Bulletin, 6,* 153–170.

Whitcomb, D. (1992). *When the child is a victim* (2d ed.). Washington, DC: National Institute of Justice.

Whittlesea, B. W. A. (2002). False memory and the discrepancy-attribution hypothesis: The prototype-familiarity illusion. *Journal of Experimental Psychology: General, 131,* 96–115.

Whittlesea, B. W. A., Jacoby, L. L., & Girard, K. (1990). Illusions of immediate memory: Evidence of an attributional basis for feelings of familiarity and perceptual quality. *Journal of Memory and Language, 29,* 716–732.

Whittlesea, B. W. A., & Leboe, J. P. (2003). Two fluency heuristics (and how to tell them apart). *Journal of Memory and Language, 49,* 62–79.

Whittlesea, B. W. A., & Williams, L. D. (2000). The source of feelings of familiarity: The discrepancy-attribution hypothesis. *Journal of Experimental Psychology: Learning, Memory, and Cognition, 26,* 747–765.

Wilson, J. C., & Pipe, M. E. (1989). The effects of cues on young children's recall of real events. *New Zealand Journal of Psychology, 18,* 65–70.

Wilson, S. P., & Kipp, K. (1998). The development of efficient inhibition: Evidence from directed-forgetting tasks. *Developmental Review, 18,* 86–123.

Wingfield, A., Lindfield, K. C., & Kahana, M. J. (1998). Adult age differences in the temporal characteristics of category free recall. *Psychology and Aging, 13,* 256–266.

Wixted, J. T. (2004). The psychology and neuroscience of forgetting. *Annual Review of Psychology, 55,* 236–269.

Woodard, J. L., Dunlosky, J., & Salthouse, T. A. (1999). Task decomposition analysis of in- tertrial free recall performance on the Rey auditory verbal learning test in normal aging and Alzheimer's disease. *Journal of Clinical and Experimental Neuropsychology, 21,* 666–676.

Wrightsman, L. S., & Kassin, S. M. (1993). *Confessions in the courtroom.* Newbury Park, CA: Sage.

Wynn, V. E., & Logie, R. H. (1998). The veracity of long-term memories: Did Bartlett get it right? *Applied Cognitive Psychology, 12,* 1–12.

Yapko, M. D. (1986). Hypnotic and strategic interventions in the treatment of anorexia-ner- vosa. *American Journal of Clinical Hypnosis, 28,* 224–232.

Yapko, M. D. (1994). Suggestibility and repressed memories of abuse: A survey of psy- chotherapists' beliefs. *American Journal of Clinical Hypnosis, 36,* 163–171.

Yonelinas, A. P. (1994). Receiver-operating characteristics in recognition memory: Evidence for a dual-process model. *Journal of Experimental Psychology: Learning, Memory, and Cognition, 20,* 1341–1354.

Yonelinas, A. P. (2002). The nature of recollection and familiarity: A review of 30 years of research. *Journal of Memory and Language, 46,* 441–518.

Yonelinas, A. P., Hopfinger, J. B., Buonocore, M. H., Kroll, N. E. A., & Baynes, K. (2001). Hippocampal, parahippocampal and occipital-temporal contributions to associative and item recognition memory: An fMRI study. *Neuroreport, 12,* 359–363.

Yonelinas, A. P., Kroll, N. E. A., Dobbins, I., Lazzara, M., & Knight, R. T. (1998). Recol- lection and familiarity deficits in amnesia: Convergence of remember-know, process dis- sociation, and receiver operating characteristic data. *Neuropsychology, 12,* 323–339.

Yonelinas, A. P., Kroll, N. E. A., Quamme, J. R., Lazzara, M. M., Suave, M. J., Widaman, K. F., & Knight, R. T. (2002). Effects of extensive temporal lobe damage or mild hy- poxia on recollection and familiarity. *Nature Neuroscience, 5,* 1236–1241.

Yonelinas, A. P., Regehr, G., & Jacoby, L. L. (1995). Incorporating response bias in a dual- process theory of memory. *Journal of Memory and Language, 34,* 821–835.

Yuille, J. C. (1988). The systematic assessment of children's testimony. *Canadian Psychol- ogy, 19,* 247–261.

Yuille, J. C., & Farr, V. (1987, Fall). Statement validity analysis: A systematic approach to the assessment of children's allegations of sexual abuse. *British Columbia Psychologist* 19–27.

Yuille, J. C., Hunter, R., Joffee, R., & Zaparniuk, J. (1993). Interviewing children in sexual abuse cases. In G. S. Goodman & B. L. Bottoms (Eds.), *Child victims, child witnesses: Understanding and improving testimony* (pp. 95–115). New York: Guilford.

Yuille, J. C., & Tollestrup, P. A. (1990). Some effects of alcohol on eyewitness memory. *Journal of Applied Psychology, 75,* 268–273.

Zaragoza, M. S. (1987). Memory, suggestibility, and eyewitness testimony in children and adults. In S. J. Ceci, M. P. Toglia, & D. F. Ross (Eds.), *Children's eyewitness memory* (pp. 53–78). New York: Springer-Verlag.

Zaragoza, M. S. (1991). Preschool children's susceptibility to memory impairment. In J. Doris (Ed.), *The suggestibility of children's memory* (pp. 27–39). Washington, DC: American Psychological Association.

Zaragoza, M. S., Dahlgren, D., & Muench, J. (1992). The role of memory impairment in chil- dren's suggestibility. In M. L. Howe, C. J. Brainerd, & V. F. Reyna (Eds.), *Develop- ment of long-term retention* (pp. 184–216). New York: Springer-Verlag.

Zaragoza, M. S., & Koshmide, J. W. (1989). Misled subjects may know more than their per- formance implies. *Journal of Experimental Psychology: Learning, Memory, and Cog- nition, 15,* 246–255.

Zaragoza, M. S., Lane, S. M., Ackil, J. K., & Chambers, K. L. (1997). Combining real and suggested memories: Source monitoring and eyewitness suggestibility. In N. L. Stein, P. A. Ornstein, B. Tversky, & C. J. Brainerd (Eds.), *Memory for everyday and emo- tional events* (pp. 401–425). Hillsdale, NJ: Erlbaum.

Zaragoza, M. S., & Mitchell, K. J. (1996). Repeated exposure to suggestion and the creation of false memories. *Psychological Science, 7,* 294–300.

Zaragoza, M. S., Payment, K. E., Ackil, J. K., Drivdahl, S. B., & Beck, M. (2001). Interviewing witnesses: Forced confabulation and confirmatory feedback increase false memories. *Psychological Science, 12,* 473–477.

Zigler, E., & Hall, N. W. (1991). Physical child abuse in America: Past, present, and future. In D. Cicchetti & V. Carlson (Eds.), *Child maltreatment* (pp. 38–75). New York: Cambridge University Press.

Zimny, S. T. (1987). *Recognition memory for sentences from discourse.* Unpublished doctoral dissertation, University of Colorado, Boulder.

Author Index

Morris, R., 126
Morrison, F. W., 181
Moscovitch, M., 471, 480
Münsterberg, H., 37, 252
Mueller, J. H., 179
Muench, J., 316
Muir, J. E., 26, 67, 90, 163
Murphy, G. L., 62, 90
Myers, J. E. B., 161, 295

Nadeau, S. E., 482
Nadel, L., 471
Nakash-Dura, M., 142
Nash, M., 257, 418
Nelson, D. L., 92
Neuschatz, J. S., 26, 41, 109, 118, 132, 134, 150–151, 433
Newberg, W. N., 477
Newcombe, N. A., 202
Newman, A. W., 273
Nicholas, E., 291
Nickerson, R. S., 141
Nida, R. E., 309
Noel, M., 418
Nolde, S. F., 468, 475
Norman, K. A., 69, 94, 451, 465
Nosworthy, G. J., 272
Nuttall, R., 385

Oates, K., 309
Ofshe, R., 252, 256, 386
Oliveri, M. K., 402
Orbach, Y., 228, 355
Ornstein, P. A., 231, 309
Ostrom, T. M., 282
O'Sullivan, J. T., 181
Otten, L. J., 475
Otto, T., 472
Owen, F. A., 231

Paddock, J. R., 418
Paivio, A., 92, 181, 415
Paley, J., 53
Palmer, J., 85
Palmer, J. C., 34, 230, 241, 243
Pansky, A., 142
Paris, S. G., 60, 159, 168–169, 174, 181–182
Park, B., 84
Park, C. L., 231
Parkin, A. J., 77, 450, 474, 477, 482, 486
Parloff, R., 252
Pashler, H., 195
Passannante, A., 473
Payment, K. E., 54, 240

Payne, D. G., 26, 29, 82, 113, 133–135, 143, 145–146, 149, 205, 236, 383, 390, 392, 400, 433, 435–436, 477
Pears, J., 470
Pelphrey, K. A., 231
Penfield, W., 472
Penrod, S., 261
Pentland, J., 391–392
Percer, J. M., 71
Perlmutter, M., 161, 179–181, 448
Perry, S., 127
Peters, D. F., 385
Peterson, C., 212, 291
Pezdek, K., 168, 177, 310–311, 314–317, 332–333, 413–415
Phelps, A. M., 171
Phelps, E. A., 473
Phelps, N. Z., 171
Piaget, J., 6, 9, 11–17, 40, 46, 83, 155
Pickel, K. L., 267
Pickrell, J. E., 410
Piercy, M., 473
Pipe, M. E., 67, 146, 202, 207, 211–212, 291, 329, 331, 347, 349, 355, 382, 400
Pires, M., 398
Pirolli, P. L., 92
Pittman, R. K., 387
Plowman, J. M., 399
Pollatsek, A., 126
Polusny, M. A., 391
Poole, D. A., 54, 67, 168, 190, 195, 201–203, 207–208, 211, 293–294, 302, 305, 313, 325–326, 338, 348–349, 371, 382, 388–389, 391, 395, 400
Pope, K. S., 366, 403
Porter, S., 410, 412–414
Poser, U., 474
Posnansky, C. J., 67
Posner, M. I., 159, 273
Possley, M., 254
Postman, L., 26, 164
Powell, G., 482
Powell, M. B., 321–322
Pradere, D., 474, 476, 478
Prawat, R. S., 169
Preston, E. L., 151
Price, C. A., 149
Price, J. L., 171, 190
Prince, S., 455, 459–460
Prull, M. W., 451
Pryke, S., 272
Prytulak, L. S., 99
Puff, C. R., 179
Putnam, F. W., 252, 404

Subject Index

contrasting phantom-recollection scenario, 438, 439*f*
cued, 80
direct access, 81–82
dual-process theories, 78–82
effects of, versus recognition, 190–191
free, 79–80
misinformation, 237 238
National Institute of Child Health and Human Development (NICHHD) protocol, 355, 356*t*
pure, 79–82
recognition-like, 79
reconstruction, 82
retrieval duration, 132–135
retrieval operation, 81–82
semantic intrusions in list, 25–28
standard test, 436–437
Vincentized analysis, 132–134
word difficulty and free, 81*f*
Recognition
amnesiac patients, 477–478
Atkinson theory, 74–75
contrasting phantom-recollection scenario, 438, 439*f*
dual-process theories, 73–78
effects of recall versus, 190–191
Jacoby theory, 75–78
Mandler theory, 75
recollection, 73
recollection-familiarity dissociations, 77–78
retrieval duration, 129–132
signal-detection theory, 74
standard test, 434–435
verbatim cuing, 140–141
Recognition-like recall, theory, 79
Recollection. *See also* Recognition
brain loci, 470
children's suggestibility, 444, 445*t*
dissociations between, and familiarity, 77–78
identification, 265
phantom, 89
recognition, 73
Recollection-familiarity dissociations, 470
Recollection rejection
gist memories, 438–439
suggestibility of memory, 36
verbatim and gist traces, 88–89
Recollective retrieval, recognition, 129
Reconstruction
gist retrieval, 87–88
retrieval operation, 82
Reconstructive retrieval
guided imagery, 392–393
psychotherapy, 383

Recovered memories
abuse by priests, 376–379
eyewitness identification accuracy, 268*t*, 275–278
official statements, 362*f*, 363*f*
Recovered-memory group, psychotherapy, 387
Recovered memory therapy. *See also* Psychotherapy
theory of repression, 365
Reincarnation, alternate identities, 408
Relative suggestibility, false-memory paradigms, 53
Remembering
delay for psychotherapy, 382–383
false memory, 5
gist memory, 5
stages, 99
with advantages, 5
Remembering: A Study in Experimental and Social Psychology, Bartlett publication, 17
Remembering criteria, weak for psychotherapy, 381–382
Remember instruction, consolidation, 127–128
Remember judgments, recognition, 77, 78*t*
Remember phenomenology
aging, 449–450
identification, 265
Reminiscence, phenomenon, 278
Repeated interviewing, children, 303–304
Repeated memory testing, retrieval variable, 187
Repeated testing
experimental design, 196, 203
retrieving memories, 194–198
Repetition
child memory suggestibility, 313–324
experience, 100
false memory and, 108–109
gist, 111, 114–116, 319–324
misinformation, 236, 238–239
psychotherapy, 387–388, 414
study of memory, 111
verbatim, 111, 112–114, 314–318
Repetition of events
children, 175–179
storing memories, 111–116
Replication, output over time, 21–22
Representational momentum, paradigm, 9
Repressed memories, official statements, 362*f*, 363*f*
Repressed-memory group, psychotherapy, 387
Research, cognitive interview, 354
Researchers, background
Bartlett, Frederic C., 17–22
Binet, Alfred, 6–11
Charcot, Jean, 8–9
Piaget, Jean, 11–17